PRINTED IN GREAT BRITAIN
AT THE UNIVERSITY PRESS, OXFORD
BY VIVIAN RIDLER
PRINTER TO THE UNIVERSITY

THE SUPREME COMMAND

GENERAL OF THE ARMY DWIGHT D. EISENHOWER, *Supreme Commander, Allied Expeditionary Force. (Photograph taken in 1947.)*

UNITED STATES ARMY IN WORLD WAR II

The European Theater of Operations

THE SUPREME COMMAND

by

Forrest C. Pogue

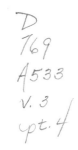

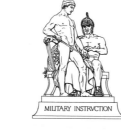

MILITARY INSTRVCTION

OFFICE OF THE CHIEF OF MILITARY HISTORY

DEPARTMENT OF THE ARMY

WASHINGTON, D. C., 1954

Library of Congress Catalog Card Number: 53–61717

Reprinted 1970

For sale by the Superintendent of Documents, U.S. Government Printing Office
Washington, D.C. 20402 - Price $8.50

UNITED STATES ARMY IN WORLD WAR II
Kent Roberts Greenfield, General Editor

Advisory Committee

(As of 1 May 1953)

James P. Baxter
President, Williams College

Brig. Gen. Verdi B. Barnes
Army War College

John D. Hicks
University of California

Brig. Gen. Leonard J. Greeley
Industrial College of the Armed Forces

William T. Hutchinson
University of Chicago

Brig. Gen. Elwyn D. Post
Army Field Forces

S. L. A. Marshall
Detroit News

Col. Thomas D. Stamps
United States Military Academy

Charles S. Sydnor
Duke University

Col. C. E. Beauchamp
Command and General Staff College

Charles H. Taylor
Harvard University

Office of the Chief of Military History

Maj. Gen. Albert C. Smith, Chief *

Chief Historian	Kent Roberts Greenfield
Chief, War Histories Division	Col. G. G. O'Connor
Chief, Editorial and Publication Division	Col. B. A. Day
Chief, Editorial Branch	Joseph R. Friedman
Chief, Cartographic Branch	Wsevolod Aglaimoff
Chief, Photographic Branch	Maj. Arthur T. Lawry

* Maj. Gen. Orlando Ward was succeeded by General Smith on 1 February 1953.

The History of

THE EUROPEAN THEATER OF OPERATIONS

prepared under the direction of Hugh M. Cole

Cross-Channel Attack
Breakout and Pursuit
The Lorraine Campaign
The Siegfried Line Campaign
Southern France and Alsace
The Ardennes
The Last Offensive: Rhineland and Central Germany
The Supreme Command
Logistical Support of the Armies (2 volumes)

This volume, one of the series UNITED STATES ARMY IN WORLD WAR II, is the fourth to be published in the subseries THE EUROPEAN THEATER OF OPERATIONS. All the volumes will be closely related, and the series will present a comprehensive account of the activities of the Military Establishment during World War II. A tentative list of subseries is appended at the end of this volume.

. . . to Those Who Served

Foreword

This is a history of coalition warfare. It is focused upon the agency in which the decisions of governments were translated into orders, and upon the decisions of General Eisenhower, the Supreme Commander, Allied Expeditionary Force. The narrative describes the plans and recounts the events, controversial or otherwise, leading up to the creation of the Supreme Command and the choice of a Supreme Commander for the cross-Channel attack. It follows the history of this great command to the surrender of Germany. It is the history not only of the decisions that led to victory, but of the discussions, debates, conferences and compromises that preceded decisions. Controversy was inevitable in an undertaking that required the subordination of national interests to the common good. The author does not gloss over the conflicts that arose between allied nations or individuals. The picture that emerges from these pages is one of discussion and argument, but nevertheless one of teamwork. Differences of opinion and the discussion incident thereto are often the price of sound decisions.

The nature of the subject, the purpose of the author, and generous contributions of information by the British make this an Anglo-American, rather than a strictly American, history. Subsequent publications based on a full exploration of British sources may be expected to round out the picture and give it deeper perspective as the history of a joint undertaking.

ORLANDO WARD
Maj. Gen., U.S.A.
Chief of Military History

Washington, D. C.
27 January 1953

ix

Note on the History of the European Theater of Operations

This volume tells the story of the Supreme Headquarters of that Allied Expeditionary Force which seized a foothold on the German-held shores of western Europe in 1944 and which, by the following year, had completed the liberation of all western Europe.

The history of the battles fought by the American armies of the Grand Alliance as they drove from the Normandy beaches into the heart of Germany is given detailed exposition in other volumes of this series, some of which already have been presented to the public. The present volume deals with the command exercised by the Supreme Allied Commander, the decisions made by the Supreme Commander and his staff, and the operations conducted under the aegis of the Supreme Headquarters.

The reader constantly will be reminded that the war in western Europe was fought by Allies and that the commands and decisions which determined the ultimate conduct of this war came from an Allied headquarters. Every effort has been made to draw on the records of all the Western Allies and the memories of their leaders, as well as the records and memories of the German High Command. But this volume is an integral part of a series dedicated to the United States Army in World War II and inevitably is written from an American point of view.

Research for the volume was completed in 1951 and an initial draft circulated to more than fifty key participants in the events therein described. The author completed a final and revised manuscript in January 1952. No effort has been made to include information or record opinions which have been published in the United States or abroad since that date.

The author, Forrest C. Pogue, has studied diplomatic history and international relations at Clark University and the University of Paris, receiving the Ph.D. degree from the former institution in 1939. Before his entry into military service, in 1942, he taught European history at Murray (Ky.) State College. Dr. Pogue made the five campaigns of the First United States Army as a combat historian, collecting information on battles from OMAHA Beach to Pilzen.

Washington, D. C.   HUGH M. COLE
15 May 1952   Chief, European Section

Preface

The purpose of this volume is to tell how the Supreme Allied Command prosecuted the war against the enemy in northwest Europe in 1944–45. A part of that story has to do with the way in which an integrated command, devoted to the Allied cause, waged one of the most effective coalition wars in history.

I have deliberately focused this account on the Supreme Commander and his staff, including for the most part only those decisions of the Prime Minister, the President, and the Combined Chiefs of Staff which affected the activities of the Supreme Commander. On the enemy side, I have included enough detail on Hitler and his commanders to provide a contrast between the Allied and enemy command organizations.

Although General Eisenhower commanded air, sea, and ground forces in the operations in northwest Europe, it has been necessary for reasons of limitations of space and time to restrict the narrative basically to his command of the ground forces. Only enough material has been retained on air and naval matters to show how they affected the SHAEF command organization and to deal with those cases where SHAEF's intervention was required. This approach has seemed doubly important in a volume comprising part of the UNITED STATES ARMY IN WORLD WAR II series.

The Allied point of view has been considered throughout, but it has not always been possible to present British and French views as fully as the American because of the lack of the same ready accessibility to British and French files.

Operations have been considered from the standpoint of their influence on the Supreme Commander's decisions and the effects of his directives on the field commanders. A corrective to this emphasis on command at the expense of tactical action may be found in the operational volumes of this series and in similar accounts now in preparation by the British and Canadian historical sections.

This volume differs from others in the European series because of the greater attention necessarily given to political or nonoperational questions. To tell the full story of SHAEF, I have had to interrupt the operational narrative on occasion in order to interject discussions of such matters as press relations, civil affairs, military government, psychological warfare, and relations with the liberated countries of Europe. As the war progressed these matters tended to occupy an ever-increasing proportion of the Supreme Commander's time.

The accounts of Allied operations in this volume rest heavily on after action reports and semiofficial histories of the army groups and armies. These in turn were based on daily situation and operational reports made during the battle. Since the latter reports were prepared under the stress of battle and may not always be wholly accurate, the narrative may repeat some of their inaccuracies as to dates, units involved, and precise achievements. Whenever it has been clear that the reports were in error, corrections have been made. The primary sources, however, represent operations much as the Supreme Commander saw them at the time when he issued his directives and are therefore more valuable for throwing light on his decisions than later amended accounts.

A word of caution is necessary for the reader who may be unduly impressed by the accounts of controversy and difference of opinion which arose between commanders of the same nationality, officers of different nationalities, and heads of governments. The debates that stemmed from divergent viewpoints were in all probability heightened by disparate national interests or by clashes of temperament and personality. When the discussions of the participants in Allied conferences are seen in cold print, without the benefit of the smile which softened a strong argument or the wry shrug which made clear that the debate was for the record, and when there is no transcript of the friendly conversation which followed the official conference, the reader may get the impression that constant argument and heated controversy marked most meetings between Allied leaders. Likewise, interoffice memorandums, written by men at planning levels, frequently give the erroneous impression that the officers concerned were engaged mainly in baiting traps and digging pitfalls for their opposite numbers. It is inevitable that a study of such discussions will emphasize the disagreements and spell out the problems in reaching accords. The numerous basic decisions which were reached with only minor debate attract less attention. No true history of the war can be written by describing merely the disputes and controversies of the Allies; even less can it be written on the assumption that even the best of Allies can achieve agreement without prolonged discussion and debate. It is important to remember that different nations, although Allies, have divergent interests, and that they are not being unfriendly if they pursue those interests.

An alliance is based on an agreement by two or more powers that they will oppose their combined forces and resources to a common enemy. They do not agree thereby to have an absolute community of interest. The success of such an alliance is to be judged, therefore, not by the amount of heat which may be engendered between the powers in their attempts to find a course of action which will most nearly preserve their individual aims while gaining a common goal, but rather by the degree to which the powers, while frankly working on a basis of self-interest, manage to achieve the one aim for which their forces were brought together. On that basis the Western Powers forged a unity seldom, if ever, achieved in the history of grand alliances. Their commanders, while striving to preserve national identity and gain individual honors for their forces, still waged a victorious war.

The Supreme Command has benefited greatly from the advice and help of a number of individuals in the United States and abroad. Only a few can be singled out for special mention. To the others, I have space only to express my deep appreciation.

For recommending me to Lt. Gen. Walter B. Smith as the person to write a history of SHAEF and for many helpful suggestions, I wish to thank Col. S. L. A. Marshall under whom I served as a combat historian in Europe. In addition to the present Chief Historian, Dr. Kent Roberts Greenfield, and other officials of the Office of the Chief of Military History whose important contributions to the volume go without saying, I should like to list the names of Maj. Gen. Harry J. Malony, Maj. Gen. Orlando Ward, Col. A. F. Clark, and Col. John Kemper, who are no longer with the Office, as persons who helped make this volume possible.

The footnotes indicate only partially the generous way in which fellow historians employed by the Army, Air Force, and Navy in this country, Great Britain, and Canada have made available information in their files. I wish to thank in particular Brigadier H. B. Latham, Chief, British Historical Section, Cabinet Office, Lt. Col. A. E. Warhurst, formerly of that section, and other members of Brigadier Latham's staff for their assistance in gathering material on British forces. I am similarly indebted to Col. C. P. Stacey, Chief, Canadian Historical Section, for aid extended to me when I was writing those portions of the volume relating to the Canadian Army. These historians, it should be noted, do not by these actions concur in the conclusions reached by me nor are they responsible for my interpretations.

Nearly one hundred British, U.S., and French officers and civilians aided me greatly by granting interviews in which they talked candidly of the work of the Supreme Commander and his headquarters. Their names have been listed in the bibliographical note. I have a special debt to Gen. Dwight D. Eisenhower, Lt. Gen. Walter B. Smith, Marshal of the Air Force Lord Tedder, Lt. Gen. Sir Frederick Morgan, and Maj. Gen. Ray W. Barker for giving generously of their time and supplying me with their private papers on the period concerned. Some fifty former participants in the activities of the Supreme Command were kind enough to read part or all of my manuscript. Of these I must make special mention of Brigadier E. T. Williams, now Warden of Rhodes Scholars at Oxford, who generously took many hours from his vacation in 1951 to check the British side of this story. It is, of course, to be understood that neither he nor the other officers who checked the manuscript necessarily agreed with my conclusions.

For assistance in exploring a number of documents in the Department of the Army files and the German sources I wish to express my especial appreciation to Mr. Royce Thompson of the European Section, and to Mr. Detmar Finke and Mrs. Magna E. Bauer of the Foreign Studies Section. I was always able to count on their willing assistance even when they were carrying on similar duties for other writers in our series. I have made specific mention elsewhere of their precise contributions to the volume. Among the employees of the Departmental Records Branch, AGO, who dealt so willingly with my requests for the files in their keeping, I wish to thank in particular Mr. Albert Whitt, Mrs. Blanche Moore, and Mrs. Ellen Smith Garrison. I have also drawn heavily on the patience and the labor of Mr. Israel Wice and members of his Reference Branch staff in the OCMH.

I have been fortunate throughout the writing of this volume in having the advice of Editor Joseph R. Friedman who has saved me from numerous errors and has made many suggestions for improving the narrative. Miss Constance Gay Morenus edited the footnotes and copy-edited the entire manuscript. Mrs. Helen McShane Bailey had the difficult job of preparing the index. Typing of the manuscript in its initial form was done by Mr. John Lee and after revision by Miss Beatrice Bierman. The excellent maps of the volume bear the imprint of Mr. Wsevolod Aglaimoff, whose skill as a cartographer has distinguished all the volumes of this series.

The Supreme Command was written under the general direction of Dr. Hugh M. Cole, Chief of the European Section, Office of the Chief of Military History. His broad knowledge of military history and wise counsel have been of great aid to me throughout the writing of this volume.

Recognition of their contributions by no means implies that the individuals who lent their assistance have approved either my English or my interpretations. For these, as well as for the general outline and the major research on this volume, I must bear the responsibility.

Washington, D. C.   FORREST C. POGUE
15 January 1952

Contents

253223 O—54——2

Tables

Charts

Maps

Illustrations

Illustrations are from the following sources

J. C. A. Redhead, FRPS, London: page 46 (Leigh-Mallory).
Bassano Ltd., London: page 46 (Ramsay).
British Information Services: page 50 (Montgomery).
Canadian Army: page 51 (Crerar).
Fayer Camera Portraits, London: page 148.
Service Cinéma des Armées, France: page 398.
Walter Stoneman, London: pages 94 (Cameron, Vulliamy, Hughes), 430.
Captured German Photographs: pages 176, 178, 195, 212.

All other photographs are from Department of Defense files

Biographical Sketches*

BRIG. GEN. FRANK A. ALLEN, JR. served as chief of the Pictorial and Radio Branch of the Bureau of Public Relations, War Department, from February to August 1941. From August 1941 to June 1943 he held various command assignments in the United States with the 1st, 5th, and 9th Armored Divisions. In June 1943 he assumed command of one of the 1st Armored Division's combat commands in North Africa. Later, in Italy, he headed Task Force Allen, which was organized by II Corps. In July 1944 he was appointed G–2 of the 6th Army Group. He came from that post in September 1944 to SHAEF as chief of the Public Relations Division.

GENERAL OF THE ARMY HENRY H. ARNOLD, one of the first Army fliers, was a pioneer in the development of airplanes and air techniques in the Army. After being selected Chief of the Air Corps in 1938, he pressed for the development of aircraft production and for a program for the civilian training of flying cadets. In 1940 he became Deputy Chief of Staff (Air) and in the following year Chief, Army Air Forces. In 1942 his title was changed to Commanding General, Army Air Forces.

GENERAL DER PANZERTRUPPEN HERMANN BALCK served as a company grade officer in World War I. At the outbreak of war in 1939 Balck was in the General Staff of the Army and was transferred to the command of a motorized rifle regiment in late October 1939. During the winter and spring of 1940–41 he commanded a Panzer regiment and later a Panzer brigade. He returned to staff duties in the Army High Command in July 1941. In May 1942, Balck went to the Eastern Front and successively commanded Panzer divisions, corps, and an army. He was transferred from command of the *Fourth Panzer Army* in Russia to the command of *Army Group G* in September 1944 and in late December was transferred back to the Eastern Front to command *Army Group Balck*. Balck was captured in Austria by Allied troops on 8 May 1945.

MAJ. GEN. RAY W. BARKER was an artillery colonel in early 1942 when he was sent to the United Kingdom. In May of that year, under orders from General Marshall, he associated himself with British planners working on plans for a cross-

---

*The rank given in each biography is the highest held by the individual concerned during the 1944–45 period. Unless otherwise noted, the last position given for each name on the list was the one held at the end of the war.

Channel operation for 1943. General Barker became head of the planning group at Headquarters, U.S. Forces in Europe, and in addition met regularly with the Combined Commanders planning group. He worked from July to September 1942 on Operation TORCH and then returned to the cross-Channel project. He served as G–5 (then head of war plans) for ETOUSA from June to October 1942, as G–3, ETOUSA, from October 1942 to April 1943, as Deputy Chief of Staff, ETOUSA, from February to April 1943, and as G–5, ETOUSA, from April to October 1943. In the spring of 1943 he became deputy to General Morgan on the COSSAC staff and remained there until the spring of 1944 when he became the SHAEF G–1.

GENERALOBERST JOHANNES BLASKOWITZ served as an infantry officer in World War I. In World War II he commanded the *Eighth Army* during the Polish campaign, and after a short term of service as Commander in Chief East in Poland he was transferred to command of the *Ninth Army* in the west. In early June 1940 he became *Military Governor of Northern France*. Blaskowitz held this position until October 1940 when he was transferred to the command of the *First Army*. He retained this post until May 1944 when he was named commander in chief of *Army Group G*. He was relieved of command of *Army Group G* in late September 1944 and reinstated on 24 December 1944. On 28 January 1945 he was appointed commander in chief of *Army Group H*. This command was redesignated in early April 1945 and Blaskowitz became *Commander in Chief Netherlands*. He was captured on 8 May 1945 at Hilversum, Holland.

GEN. OMAR N. BRADLEY in 1940 became an assistant secretary of the General Staff in the War Department. In February 1941 he was given command of the Infantry School at Fort Benning, Ga. From this post he went to the 82d Division early in 1942. In June of that year he assumed command of the 28th Division. General Marshall sent him to North Africa in February 1943 to act as an observer for General Eisenhower. A few weeks later Bradley became deputy commander of II Corps under General Patton, and in April, when Patton was given the task of planning the Sicilian campaign, he took command of II Corps. In the new command, General Bradley fought in Tunisia and Sicily. He was selected in September 1943 to head the First U.S. Army in the invasion of northwest Europe as well as a U.S. army group headquarters. General Bradley led the First Army in the Normandy campaign until 1 August 1944 when he became commander of the 12th Army Group.

LT. GEN. LEWIS H. BRERETON graduated from the U.S. Naval Academy in 1907, transferred to the Army in 1911, and in turn transferred to the flying section of the Signal Corps in 1912. He was a flier in Europe in World War I. In July 1941, General Brereton was given command of the Third Air Force. When war broke out, he was the commanding general of the Far East Air Force in the Philippine Islands. At the beginning of 1942 he became Deputy Air Commander in Chief,

Allied Air Forces, on the staff of General Wavell besides serving as commander of the Fifth Air Force. General Brereton organized and commanded the Tenth Air Force in India in March 1942. Two months later he became commander of the Middle East Air Force. In February 1943 he assumed in addition the command of U.S. Army Forces in the Middle East. In October 1943 he was transferred to the United Kingdom where he became commanding general of the Ninth Air Force. He was appointed commander in chief of the First Allied Airborne Army in August 1944.

Field Marshal Sir Alan Brooke (Now Lord Alanbrooke), a graduate of the Royal Military Academy, Woolwich, served in World War I, receiving the Distinguished Service Order with bar and other awards for his actions. By 1941 he had gained a reputation as the Army's expert on mechanization. He commanded the 2d British Corps in France in the early part of World War II and helped to make possible the successful evacuation at Dunkerque. Generals Montgomery and Alexander served under him at that time. Shortly thereafter he became commander of the British Home Forces and organized the defenses of the United Kingdom against possible attack by the Germans. He succeeded Field Marshal Dill as Chief of the Imperial General Staff in 1941.

Maj. Gen. Harold R. Bull served as Secretary, General Staff, of the War Department in 1939. He followed this duty with assignment as Professor of Military Science and Tactics at Culver Military Academy, and later as assistant division commander of the 4th Motorized Division. After the outbreak of war, he became G–3 of the War Department, and went from this post to head the Replacement School Command, Army Ground Forces. In the summer of 1943 General Marshall sent him to North Africa as a special observer. On his return, he became the commanding general of III Corps, holding this post from June to September 1943. In the latter month, he was sent to London where he became deputy G–3 of COSSAC. In February 1944 he was appointed G–3, SHAEF.

Admiral Harold M. Burrough was assistant chief of the Naval Staff, Admiralty, at the beginning of the war. From 1940 to 1942 he commanded a cruiser squadron. He was commander of Naval Forces, Algiers, in 1942, and Flag Officer Commanding Gibraltar and Mediterranean Approaches, 1943–45. In January 1945 he succeeded Admiral Ramsay as Allied Naval Commander-in-Chief, Expeditionary Force. After the dissolution of SHAEF he became British Naval Commander-in-Chief, Germany.

Lt. Gen. M. B. Burrows served in the North Russian Expeditionary Force, 1918–19. In the period 1938–40 he was military attaché at Rome, Budapest, and Tirana. He served as head of the British Military Mission to the USSR in 1943–44, and as General Officer Commanding-in-Chief of the West Africa Command in 1945–46.

GENERALFELDMARSCHALL ERNST BUSCH served as an infantry officer in World War I. He commanded the *VIII Corps* in the Polish compaign and in October 1939 was appointed commander of the *Sixteenth Army*. In November 1943 he was made acting commander in chief of *Army Group Center* on the Eastern Front. From May 1944 until August 1944 Busch was commander in chief of *Army Group Center*. He was then relieved and placed in the officers' reserve pool until March 1945 when he was made commander of *Fuehrungsstab Nordkueste* which was renamed *OB NORDWEST* in early May 1945.

MAJ. GEN. A. M. CAMERON, a member of the antiaircraft operations section of the War Office at the beginning of the war, went to Antiaircraft Command Headquarters in 1940. Later he commanded a brigade and a group in the Antiaircraft Command. He was commanding a group on the south coast of England when sent to SHAEF in May 1944.

MAJ. GEN. JOHN G. W. CLARK was commander of an infantry brigade at the start of the war and led it to France. Later he was a divisional commander in Palestine and Iraq. He served in North Africa and Sicily in 1942 and 1943 and at the end of 1943 he became Major General in Charge of Administration, Middle East. In January 1944 he was transferred to Allied Force Headquarters as chief administrative officer. One year later he became head of the SHAEF Mission (Netherlands).

LT. GEN. J. LAWTON COLLINS was chief of staff of VII Corps in January 1941. After the attack at Pearl Harbor he became chief of staff of the Hawaiian Department. In May 1942 he became commanding general of the 25th Division. He relieved the 1st Marine Division on Guadalcanal in December 1942 and later fought in the New Georgia campaign. In December 1943 he was transferred to the European Theater of Operations where he assumed command of the VII Corps and led it in the assault on northwest Europe.

AIR CHIEF MARSHAL SIR ARTHUR CONINGHAM served with the New Zealand Forces Samoa and Egypt from 1914 to 1916 and then in Europe from 1916 to 1919. In World War II he served with Bomber Command, working with the Eighth Army in North Africa and forming the First Tactical Air Force, French North Africa. He furnished air support to the Eighth Army in Sicily and Italy in 1943 and commanded the 2d Tactical Air Force in northwest Europe in 1944–45.

MAJ. GEN ROBERT W. CRAWFORD was district engineer in New Orleans in 1939 when he was called to the War Plans Division in Washington and assigned duties in connection with overseas supplies, munitions, allocations, and the like. By July 1942 he was transferred to the 8th Armored Division as head of a combat command. Near the end of 1942, he became Commanding General, Services of Supply, U.S. Army Forces in the Middle East. From this post he was sent in July

1943 to the United Kingdom where he served for a time as deputy commander and later as chief of staff of the Services of Supply organization, and as G–4, Headquarters, ETOUSA. In November 1943 he became deputy G–4 of COSSAC. On the activation of SHAEF he became G–4 of SHAEF.

REAR ADM. GEORGE E. CREASY commanded a destroyer flotilla from 1939 to May 1940. From June 1940 to August 1942, he headed the division of antisubmarine warfare at the Admiralty, and in 1942–43 commanded the *Duke of York,* taking part in the North African landings. In August 1943 he joined COSSAC as naval chief of staff, becoming chief of staff to Admiral Ramsay when the latter was named to the post of Allied Naval Commander-in-Chief, Expeditionary Force.

GEN. HENRY D. G. CRERAR was senior officer, Canadian Military Headquarters, London, in 1939–40. In 1940–41 he served as Chief of General Staff, Canada. He became commander of the 2d Canadian Division Overseas in 1941. From 1942 to 1944 he commanded the 1st Canadian Corps and for a part of the same period commanded the Canadian Corps Mediterranean Area (1943–44). He led the 1st Canadian Army in 1944–45.

ADMIRAL OF THE FLEET SIR ANDREW B. CUNNINGHAM entered the Royal Navy in 1898 and participated in World War I. As Commander-in-Chief, Mediterranean, between 1939 and 1942, he directed operations against the Italian Fleet at Taranto and Matapan and evacuated the British forces from Greece. He headed the British naval delegation in Washington briefly in 1942 before becoming Naval Commander-in-Chief, Expeditionary Force, North Africa. In October 1943 he replaced Admiral Sir Dudley Pound as First Sea Lord.

BRIG. GEN. THOMAS J. DAVIS was an aide of General MacArthur in the Philippines from 1928 to 1930 and returned with him to the U.S. to duty in the Office of the Chief of Staff in 1930. In September 1933 he returned to the Philippines, serving as assistant military adviser under MacArthur until January 1938 when he became adviser in the Philippines on adjutant general affairs. In January 1940 Davis came back to the War Department, first in The Adjutant General's Office and then as executive officer of the Special Service Branch of the War Department. In April 1942 he became executive officer in the office of the Chief of Administrative Services, Headquarters, SOS. He was appointed adjutant general of Headquarters, ETOUSA, in July 1942. From August 1942 to January 1944 he was adjutant general of Allied Force Headquarters. In February 1944 he was named adjutant general of SHAEF. In April when the SHAEF Public Relations Division was established, he became its head. In October 1944 he returned to the post of adjutant general of SHAEF.

MAJ. GEN. JOHN R. DEANE was secretary of the War Department General Staff in February 1942. He became American secretary of the Combined Chiefs of Staff in September 1942. In October 1943 he was appointed as head of the U.S. military mission to the USSR.

MAJ. GEN. FRANCIS DE GUINGAND, a graduate of the Royal Military College, Sandhurst, was Military Assistant to the Secretary of State for War in 1939–40 and later became Director Military Intelligence Middle East. In 1942–44 he served as chief of staff of the British Eighth Army, and in 1944 he took over the same post in the 21 Army Group.

GEN. SIR MILES DEMPSEY commanded the 13th Infantry Brigade in France in 1940, receiving the D.S.O. He returned to England to become Brigadier General Staff with the Canadians under Gen. A. G. L. MacNaughton. Shortly after El Alamein, he took command of the 13th Corps of the Eighth Army and led it in the Sicilian campaign and in the invasion of Italy. In January 1944 he became commander of the Second British Army, which he led through the remainder of the war in France, Belgium, the Netherlands, and Germany.

GEN. JACOB L. DEVERS became chief of the Armored Forces, Fort Knox, Ky., in the summer of 1941. From this post he went in May 1943 to the command of the European Theater of Operations. While there he helped COSSAC in its planning for the OVERLORD operation. In December 1943 he succeeded General Eisenhower as commanding general of the North African Theater of Operations. Later he was Deputy Commander in Chief, Allied Force Headquarters, and Deputy Supreme Allied Commander, Mediterranean Theater. In September 1944 he became commander of the 6th Army Group, which consisted of Seventh U.S. and First French Armies.

MAJ. GEN. RICHARD H. DEWING was a brigadier instructing at the Imperial Defence College in 1939. Shortly thereafter he was appointed Director of Military Operations at the War Office with the rank of major general. In 1940 he became Chief of Staff, Far East, and in 1942 joined the British Army staff in Washington. He spent the next two years as head of the United Kingdom Liaison Staff in Australia and in 1945 was appointed head of SHAEF Mission (Denmark).

FIELD MARSHAL SIR JOHN DILL, a veteran of the Boer War, served near the end of World War I as Field Marshal Haig's Brigadier General Staff Operations. Later he was on the general staff in India, Director of Military Operations and Intelligence in the War Office, and commander in chief at Aldershot. He served as Chief of the Imperial General Staff from May 1940 to the end of 1941. In December 1941 he was sent to Washington as head of the British Joint Staff Mission and senior British member of the Combined Chiefs of Staff organization in Washington. He was serving in this capacity at the time of his death in November 1944. He is buried in Arlington National Cemetery.

GROSSADMIRAL KARL DOENITZ served in naval air and submarine forces in World War I. He was placed in sole charge of Germany's U-Boats in 1935 when he was appointed *Fuehrer der Unterseeboote*. In early 1941 Doenitz' position was raised and he was named *Befehlshaber der Unterseeboote*. He held this position until the spring of 1943 when he was given supreme command of the German Navy and named *Grossadmiral*. In late April 1945 Hitler designated Doenitz as his successor in place of Goering. After Hitler's death Doenitz carried on the German government until his arrest by the Allied Command in May 1945.

LT. GEN. JAMES H. DOOLITTLE served in World War I as a flier. He resigned from the Army in 1930 but continued his work in aeronautics as a civilian. He was recalled to duty in 1940, and in April 1942 led the first aerial raid on the Japanese mainland. He was assigned to duty with the Eighth Air Force in the United Kingdom in July 1942 and in September of that year assumed command of the Twelfth Air Force in North Africa. In March 1943 he became commanding general of the North African Strategic Air Forces. He was named commander of the Fifteenth Air Force in November 1943. From January 1944 until the end of the war he headed the Eighth Air Force in the European Theater of Operations.

BRIG. GEN. BEVERLY C. DUNN was district engineer at Seattle, Wash., in July 1940. In March 1942 he was assigned to the North Atlantic Engineer Division, New York. He became deputy chief engineer at Headquarters, SHAEF, in February 1944. Shortly before the dissolution of SHAEF he succeeded General Hughes as chief engineer.

GENERAL OF THE ARMY DWIGHT D. EISENHOWER was graduated from West Point in 1915 and commissioned in that year. His first assignment was with the 19th Infantry Regiment. He remained with this unit, except for short periods of detached service, until 1917. In September of that year he was assigned to duty in the 57th Infantry Regiment. During World War I he served as instructor at the Officer Training Camp at Fort Oglethorpe, Ga., from September to December 1917, taught in the Army Service Schools at Fort Leavenworth, Kans., from December 1917 to February 1918, had a tour of duty with the 65th Battalion Engineers, which he organized at Fort Meade, Md., and commanded Camp Colt, Pa. After the war he commanded tank corps troops at Fort Dix, N. J., and at Fort Benning, Ga. In 1919 he returned to Fort Meade where he served in various tank battalions until January 1922. Meanwhile he graduated from the Infantry Tank School. In 1922 he went to the Panama Canal Zone where he served as executive officer at Camp Gaillard. From September to December 1924 he was recreation officer at the headquarters of Third Corps Area. This assignment was followed by a tour as recruiting officer at Fort Logan, Colo., until August 1925. He then attended Command and General Staff School at Fort Leavenworth, graduating as an honor student in June 1926. A brief tour with the

24th Division followed. From January to August 1927 he was on duty with the American Battle Monuments Commission in Washington. He graduated from the Army War College in June 1928 and then went back for a year with the Battle Monuments Commission with duty in Washington and France. From November 1929 to February 1933 he was Assistant Executive, Office of the Assistant Secretary of War. During this period he graduated from the Army Industrial College. From 1933 to September 1935 he was in the Office of the Chief of Staff (Gen. Douglas MacArthur). He served as assistant to the military adviser of the Philippine Islands from September 1935 to 1940. In 1940 he was assigned to duty with the 15th Infantry Regiment. In November of that year he became chief of staff of the 3d Division, in March 1941 chief of staff of the IX Corps, and in June 1941 chief of staff of the Third Army. He joined the War Plans Division of the War Department in December 1941 and became chief of the division in the following February. On 25 June 1942 he was named commanding general of the European Theater of Operations. In November 1942 he commanded the Allied landings in North Africa and in the same month became Commander in Chief, Allied Forces in North Africa. As commander of Allied Forces in the Mediterranean he directed operations in Tunisia, Sicily, and Italy until December 1943 when he was named Supreme Commander, Allied Expeditionary Force. In this post he directed the invasion of northwest Europe and the campaigns against Germany.

Maj. Gen. George W. E. James Erskine was a lieutenant colonel on the staff of a division in England at the outbreak of war. In June 1940 he was given command of a battalion and in January 1941 a brigade. He went with the latter to the Middle East in June 1941. In February 1942 he became Brigadier General Staff, Headquarters, 13 Corps, and in January 1943 was given command of the 7th Armoured Division. He commanded this unit in the Western Desert, Italy, and Normandy. In August 1944 he became head of the SHAEF mission to Belgium.

Generaladmiral Hans von Friedeburg, was commanding admiral of submarines in June 1944. He was appointed commander in chief of the German Navy by Doenitz in early May 1945 and as such signed the final capitulations in Reims and Berlin. He committed suicide soon thereafter.

Lt. Gen. Sir Humfrey M. Gale was deputy director of supplies and transport in the War Office at the beginning of the war. Two months later he became G-4 of 3 British Corps and went to France. In 1940, after Dunkerque, he became Major General in Charge of Administration (includes both G-1 and G-4 functions in the British Army) in the Scottish Command. He left this assignment in July 1941 to take a similar position at Home Forces under Sir Alan Brooke. In August 1942 he was appointed chief administrative officer on General Eisenhower's staff in the Mediterranean, where he remained until February 1944. At that time he was appointed one of the deputy chiefs of staff of SHAEF with the title Chief Administrative Officer.

LT. GEN. LEONARD T. GEROW was executive officer of the War Plans Division of the War Department from 1936 to 1939. He served as chief of staff of the 2d Division through 1939. In 1940 he was appointed assistant commandant of the Infantry School. In October 1940 he was transferred to the 8th Division and in December of that year he was assigned to the War Plans Division, War Department. He was chief of that division at the time of the Pearl Harbor attack. In February 1942 he was given command of the 29th Division and later was put in charge of field forces in the European theater. In July 1943 he became commander of V Corps and led that unit in the assault in northwest Europe. He became commanding general of the Fifteenth Army in January 1945.

REICHSMARSCHALL HERMANN GOERING was one of Germany's outstanding flyers in World War I. He became a member of the Nazi party in 1922 and held many party positions. In 1933 he was made Reich Minister for Air and in 1935 named Commander in Chief of the Air Force. As President of the Council of Ministers for the Defense of the Reich and as Trustee for the Four Year Plan, Goering exercised great influence on the political and economic life of the Reich. Long designated as Hitler's successor, he was removed from this position in late April 1945. Goering was captured by American forces in May 1945.

LT. GEN. SIR A. E. GRASETT, a Canadian-born officer, was stationed in China in 1938–41. He returned to the United Kingdom in 1941 to command a division, and from 1941 to 1943 a corps. He next served as chief of the Liaison Branch of the War Office, and after the organization of Supreme Headquarters he became chief of the European Allied Contact Section. In April 1944 he was appointed chief of the G–5 Division.

GENERALOBERST HEINZ GUDERIAN, a veteran of World War I, was a strong proponent of armored warfare. At the outbreak of World War II, he was given command of *XIX Panzer Corps* and in this position fought in the Polish and French campaigns. He commanded the *Second Panzer Group,* later designated *Second Panzer Army,* in the Russian campaign from June to December 1941. Guderian was then placed in an officers' reserve pool until February 1943, at which time he was assigned as *Inspector General of Panzer Troops.* In July 1944, while still on this assignment, he was designated as acting chief of the Army General Staff. He held these positions until he was relieved in March 1945. Guderian was captured near Zell am See, Tirol, 10 May 1945.

MARSHAL OF THE ROYAL AIR FORCE SIR ARTHUR T. HARRIS, who was commanding the RAF in Palestine and Transjordan in the summer of 1939, became chief of the No. 5 Group of Bomber Command at the outbreak of war. In 1940 he became deputy chief of the Air Staff under Air Chief Marshal Portal. In May 1941 he came to the United States as head of the RAF delegation and as member of the British Joint Staff Mission. He remained in Washington until February 1942 when he was named Commander-in-Chief, Bomber Command.

GENERALOBERST DER WAFFEN SS PAUL HAUSSER was a member of the General Staff
Corps and served as a divisional and corps staff officer in World War I. He was retired from the Army with the rank of *Generalleutnant* in 1932. Hausser became a
member of the Waffen SS in 1934 and by 1939 had again reached his former rank
of *Generalleutnant*. During the Polish campaign Hausser served on the staff of *Panzer Division Kempf*. From October 1939 until October 1941 he commanded the *2d
SS Panzer Division "Das Reich."* During this period he was wounded and had to be
hospitalized until June 1942, at which time he became commander of the *II SS
Panzer Corps*. He led this corps until the end of June 1944, fighting in the east, in
Italy, and finally in Normandy. At the end of June 1944 Hausser was assigned to
command the *Seventh Army*, holding this position until late August 1944, when he
was again severely wounded and hospitalized until January 1945. From the end
of January until the beginning of April 1945 Hausser commanded *Army Group G*.
Thereafter, until he was taken prisoner on 13 May 1945, Hausser served on the
staff of *OB WEST*.

REICHSFUEHRER SS UND CHEF DER DEUTSCHEN POLIZEI HEINRICH HIMMLER served as
a 2d lieutenant in a Bavarian infantry regiment in World War I. A Nazi party
member since 1925, Himmler by 1936 had brought all of the German police and
the SS under his control. After the putsch of 20 July 1944 Himmler was also appointed Chief of the Replacement Army (*Chef der Heeresruestung und Befehlshaber des
Ersatzheeres*). In late November 1944 all of the defenses on the eastern bank of the
upper Rhine were placed under him as *Oberbefehlshaber Oberrhein*. Himmler
retained this command until late January 1945 when he became commander in
chief of *Army Group Weichsel* on the Eastern Front. On 20 March 1945 Himmler
relinquished command of *Army Group Weichsel*. He was captured by Allied troops
in early May 1945 and committed suicide shortly thereafter.

GEN. COURTNEY H. HODGES, an overseas veteran of World War I, became commandant of the Infantry School, Fort Benning, Ga., in October 1940. He was named
Chief of Infantry, War Department, in May 1941, and commanding general of
the Replacement and School Command, Army Ground Forces, in March 1942.
Later he became commanding general of X Corps. From this post he went to the
command of the Third Army in February 1943. In March 1944 he was sent to
the European Theater of Operations as deputy commander of the First Army. He
succeeded General Bradley in command of that army on 1 August 1944 and led
it through France, Belgium, Germany, and to the Czechoslovakian frontier at the
war's end.

MAJ. GEN. H. B. W. HUGHES was chief engineer of the Western Command in 1939
and engineer-in-chief of General Wavell's Middle East Command from 1940 to
1943. In December 1943 he became chief engineer of COSSAC and in February
of the following year chief of the Engineer Division of SHAEF. The latter post he
held until the spring of 1945.

GENERALOBERST ALFRED JODL served as an artillery officer in World War I. In September 1939 Jodl was assigned to the *OKW/Wehrmachtfuehrungsstab,* becoming chief of this office in the following month. He held this position until the close of the war. He became a prisoner of war in May of 1945.

GENERAL ALPHONSE PIERRE JUIN was born in Algiers and spent much of his early career in North Africa. He served for a time as an aide of Marshal Lyautey and was regarded as a strong disciple of that commander. From 1938 to 1939 Juin was chief of staff to General Nogues, commander of the North African Theater of Operations. Near the close of 1939, he headed an infantry division in northern France and helped to cover the withdrawal to Dunkerque the following year. On the fall of France he became a German prisoner, but was released in 1941. In the summer of that year, he was given a command in Morocco and later in 1941 was named commander in chief of French forces in North Africa. In 1943 he was placed at the head of the French Expeditionary Corps, which performed brilliantly in Italy. In 1944 General de Gaulle appointed him to the post of Chief of Staff of the Ministry of National Defense.

GENERALFELDMARSCHALL WILHELM KEITEL served in various staff positions at corps and army headquarters in World War I. He was appointed chief of OKW in 1938, a position he held for the duration of the war. Keitel was taken into custody in mid-May 1945.

MAJ. GEN. ALBERT W. KENNER was chief surgeon of the Armored Service at Fort Knox, Ky., at the beginning of the war. He was taken by General Patton to North Africa as chief surgeon of the Western Task Force in November 1942. One month later he became Chief Surgeon, North African Forces, under General Eisenhower. In 1943 he returned to Washington as Assistant Surgeon General with the task of training and inspecting Ground Forces medical troops. He came to SHAEF in February 1944 as chief medical officer.

GENERALFELDMARSCHALL ALBERT KESSELRING, served on various divisional and corps staffs in World War I. After staff and troop assignments he was assigned as administrative chief to the Reich Air Ministry. Kesselring remained in this position until June 1936 when he was assigned as chief of the Air Force General Staff. In the Polish campaign he commanded *First Air Force* and later in 1940 *Second Air Force* in France. In December 1941 Kesselring was appointed as Commander in Chief South with command of all German Air Force units in the Mediterranean and North African theaters. In the fall of 1943 he was redesignated as Commander in Chief Southwest with nominal command of the German armed forces in Italy. Kesselring was transferred to Germany as Commander in Chief West in March 1945 and later designated as Commander in Chief South. He was taken prisoner at Saalfelden on 6 May 1945.

FLEET ADMIRAL ERNEST J. KING graduated from the Naval Academy in 1901. He served during World War I as assistant chief of staff to the Commander in Chief, U.S. Fleet. Beginning in 1937 he served in succession as member of the General Board of the Navy, commander of the U.S. Fleet Patrol Force, and commander in chief of the Atlantic Fleet. In December 1941 he became Commander in Chief, U.S. Fleet, and in 1942 also took the title of Chief of Naval Operations.

VICE ADM. ALAN G. KIRK in 1941 was naval attaché in London, where his duties included reporting on German naval organization. From March to October 1941 he served as Chief of Naval Intelligence in Washington. This assignment was followed by brief tours on convoy duty in the North Atlantic and in transporting troops to Iceland. In May 1942 he became chief of staff to Admiral Stark in London. Admiral Kirk was appointed Commander, Amphibious Force, Atlantic Fleet, in March 1943 and helped prepare the forces for the Sicilian operation. Later he was in charge of transporting some 20,000 soldiers to the Mediterranean. He served as commander of U.S. Naval Forces for the cross-Channel attack and held operational control of all U.S. naval forces under General Eisenhower except those in the south of France. Later he was head of the U.S. Naval Mission at SHAEF and was for a short time acting Allied Naval Commander after Admiral Ramsay was killed in January 1945.

GENERALFELDMARSCHALL GUENTHER VON KLUGE served as an infantry and mountain troop officer in World War I. During the Polish and French campaigns, and the early part of the Russian campaign, of World War II von Kluge commanded the *Fourth Army*. In December 1941 he was assigned as commander in chief of *Army Group Center* on the Eastern Front, a position he held until May 1944. Von Kluge relieved von Rundstedt as Commander in Chief West in early July 1944, and was relieved in turn by Model at the beginning of September 1944. On his way to Germany he committed suicide.

GEN. PIERRE JOSEPH KOENIG was serving as a captain in the French Foreign Legion at the outbreak of war. As a major he led elements of the legion at Narvik in May and June 1940. After these forces were withdrawn, he went back to France. On the fall of France he fled to the United Kingdom where he joined the Gaullist forces. Shortly thereafter he went to Africa. As the commander of a brigade, he fought at Bir Hacheim in Libya. On 1 August 1943 he became assistant chief of staff of the French ground forces in North Africa. The French Committee of National Liberation named him its delegate to SHAEF in March 1944 and also gave him the title of commander of French Forces of the Interior in Great Britain. When Allied forces entered France, he assumed command of the French Forces of the Interior in France. On the liberation of Paris in August 1944 he was named military governor of Paris and commander of the Military Region of Paris. In July 1945 he became commander in chief of French forces in Germany.

GENERAL DER INFANTERIE HANS KREBS served as an infantry officer in World War I. In 1939 he was in the *Intelligence Division* of the General Staff of the Army. Krebs was assigned as chief of staff of the *VII Corps* in December 1939 and served in this capacity until March 1941. He was then appointed as acting German military attaché in Moscow, remaining in this post until the outbreak of war between Germany and the Soviet Union. From January 1942 until September 1944 he served as chief of staff first of the *Ninth Army* and later of *Army Group Center* on the Eastern Front. Krebs was appointed chief of staff of *Army Group B* at the beginning of September 1944 and remained in this position until 1 April 1945 when he was named acting chief of the General Staff. Krebs was killed or committed suicide in Berlin in May 1945.

MAJ. GEN. FRANCIS H. LANAHAN, JR., was chief of the War Plans Division, Signal Corps, from December 1941 to June 1942. From June to December 1942 he served as assistant director of planning in charge of the Theater Section. He was director of planning of the same branch from January to June 1943. From August 1943 to February 1945 he served as deputy chief of the Signal Division at COSSAC and SHAEF. In March 1945 he succeeded General Vulliamy as chief of the Signal Division, SHAEF.

GEN. JEAN DE LATTRE DE TASSIGNY commanded the 14th Infantry Division in 1940. He withdrew his forces into the French zone in that year. He was commanding a military region in the south of France in November 1942 when he was arrested for a demonstration he made at the time of the Allied landings in North Africa. He was sentenced to ten years' imprisonment by the Vichy authorities but escaped from the Riom prison in September 1943 and went to the United Kingdom. At the end of the year he went to North Africa. On 18 April 1944 he was appointed commanding general of Armée B, which was later named the First French Army.

FLEET ADMIRAL WILLIAM D. LEAHY graduated from the Naval Academy in 1897 and served in the war against Spain. During World War I he served on ships of the line and on a transport. In 1933 he became chief of the Bureau of Navigation. Four years later he became Chief of Naval Operations. In 1939, after he had retired, President Roosevelt appointed him governor of Puerto Rico and in the following year made him Ambassador to France. He was recalled to active duty in 1942 and made chief of staff to the Commander in Chief, a post he held under Presidents Roosevelt and Truman.

AIR CHIEF MARSHAL SIR TRAFFORD LEIGH-MALLORY won the Distinguished Flying Order in the Royal Flying Corps in World War I. He commanded the 11 and 12 Fighter Groups in the Battle of Britain in World War II. From November 1942 to December 1943 he served as Air Officer Commanding-in-Chief, Fighter Command. At the close of 1943 he was appointed Commander-in-Chief, Allied Expeditionary Air Force, and as such commanded the tactical air forces in support of the Allied Expeditionary Force. He was transferred to the post of Commander-in-Chief, South-East Asia Command, in the early fall of 1944, but was killed in a plane crash en route to that headquarters in November 1944.

MAJ. GEN. JOHN T. LEWIS served in 1941 in the Office of the Secretary, General Staff, War Department. In February of the following year he was assigned to a coast artillery brigade in New York. He was named Commanding General, Military District of Washington, in May 1942. While in this post he was a member of the commission which tried the Nazi saboteurs. In September 1944 he was selected as chief of SHAEF Mission (France).

BRIG. GEN. ROBERT A. McCLURE, U.S. Millitary Attaché in London in 1941 and military attaché to the eight governments-in-exile in the United Kingdom, became G–2 of ETOUSA under General Eisenhower early in 1942. From November 1942 to November 1943 he headed the Public Relations, Psychological Warfare and Censorship Section at AFHQ. In November 1943 he was sent to COSSAC to organize a similar section. In February 1944 he became G–6 of SHAEF. When that division was divided later in the year, he was appointed chief of the Psychological Warfare Division of SHAEF.

BRIGADIER KENNETH G. McLEAN at the outbreak of war became a member of the staff of the 52d Division in Scotland. From April 1940 to June 1941 he was an Army representative on the British GHQ Planning Staff. When COSSAC was established in 1943, he became the Army member of the planning staff. On the activation of SHAEF he was named head of the Planning Section of G–3.

GENERAL OF THE ARMY GEORGE C. MARSHALL was graduated from Virginia Military Institute in 1901 and commissioned early in the following year. He served on the staffs of the First and Second Armies in World War I. In July 1938 he became Assistant Chief of Staff, War Plans Division, General Staff, and in October was appointed Deputy Chief of Staff of the Army. In September 1939 he became Chief of Staff of the Army.

GENERALFELDMARSCHALL WALTER MODEL served as an infantry officer in World War I. During the Polish and French campaigns in 1939 and 1940 he served as a corps and army chief of staff. In the Russian campaign from 1941 until 1944 he served in succession as a division, corps, and army commander. Model in January 1944 was assigned as commander in chief of *Army Group North* on the Eastern Front. In mid-August 1944 he was transferred to the west as Commander in Chief West and concurrently as commander in chief of *Army Group B*. Upon Rundstedt's return as Commander in Chief West in early September 1944, Model retained command of *Army Group B,* a post he kept until the final dissolution of *Army Group B* in April 1945. Model is said to have committed suicide at this time.

FIELD MARSHAL SIR BERNARD LAW MONTGOMERY commanded the 3d British Division in France in the winter and spring of 1939–40. He was given temporary command of the 2 Corps at Dunkerque. In the fall of 1940 he was given the 5 Corps and, in 1941, the 12 Corps. In 1942 he became head of the Southeast Command. In the summer of that year he was told that he would head the First British Army in the North African invasion, but the death of General Gott, who was slated for the command of the British Eighth Army led to Montgomery's selection for the post. As commander of this army he won the battle of El Alamein, pursued Marshal Rommel's forces to Tunisia, and helped defeat the enemy in Tunisia. Later he led the Eighth Army to Sicily and Italy. His appointment as Commander-in-Chief, 21 Army Group, was announced in December 1943. He commanded the Allied assault forces in Normandy, serving in that capacity until 1 September 1944 when General Eisenhower assumed control of field operations. Field Marshal Montgomery led the combined British and Canadian forces in France, Belgium, the Netherlands, and Germany for the remainder of the war. During much of this time the Ninth U.S. Army was also under his command. In the course of the Ardennes counteroffensive he was also given command of the First U.S. Army.

LT. GEN. SIR FREDERICK E. MORGAN served in France in 1940 as commander of a group of the 1st Armoured Division. In May 1942 he was appointed to command the 1st Corps District, which included Lincolnshire and the East Riding of Yorkshire. In October of that year he was made commander of the 1 Corps and placed under General Eisenhower. He was given the task of preparing a subsidiary landing in the western Mediterranean either to reinforce the initial landings or to deal with a German thrust through Spain. When neither operation proved necessary, he was directed to plan the invasion of Sardinia. In time this was abandoned and he was directed to plan the invasion of Sicily. This project was later given to the armies in North Africa. In the spring of 1943 he became chief of staff to the Supreme Allied Commander and as such directed planning for the invasion of northwest Europe. He served in 1944 and 1945 as Deputy Chief of Staff, SHAEF.

AMBASSADOR ROBERT D. MURPHY, a career diplomat, was counselor of the U.S. Embassy in Paris when war began in Europe. After the fall of France, he served briefly as chargé d'affaires at Vichy. In November 1940 he was detailed to Algiers. In the fall of 1942 he helped in negotiations between Allied military leaders and the French forces in North Africa. After the invasion of that area he was named political adviser to General Eisenhower. Later he became Chief Civil Affairs Adviser for Italian Affairs on General Eisenhower's staff and also served as U.S. member of the Advisory Council to the Allied Control Commission for Italy. At this time he was given the rank of Ambassador. In August 1944 Mr. Murphy was named political adviser at SHAEF and Chief of the Political Division for the U.S. Group Control Council set up to plan postwar occupation of Germany. Later he served as political adviser to Generals Eisenhower, McNarney, and Clay.

BRIG. GEN. ARTHUR S. NEVINS served in the Strategy Section of the War Plans Division of the War Department from May 1941 until after the outbreak of war with Japan. In the spring of 1942 he went to the United Kingdom as a member of the planning staff for the North African invasion. When II U.S. Corps was activated he became its deputy chief of staff. Later he became G–3 of the Fifth U.S. Army. After a month in that position he worked as an Army planner on the Sicilian invasion, and was then appointed operations officer on General Alexander's combined headquarters staff. In October 1943 he went to the United Kingdom to head the Plans and Operations Section of COSSAC, a post he was holding when he was appointed chief of the Operations Section, G–3 Division, SHAEF.

GEN. SIR BERNARD PAGET was commandant of the Staff College, Camberley, at the outbreak of war. He then took command of the 13th Division in East Anglia and in the spring of 1940 commanded British forces in the Andalsnes area during the expedition to Norway. After Dunkerque he was named Chief of Staff, Home Forces, and then served for a time as chief of the Southeast Command. When General Brooke became Chief of the Imperial General Staff in 1942, General Paget succeeded him as commander of Home Forces. As head of this command, Paget was a member of the Combined Commanders. When the 21 Army Group was established in the summer of 1943, he was named to command it. On 24 December 1943 he was assigned to the Middle East Command.

LT. GEN. ALEXANDER M. PATCH was in command of the Infantry Replacement Center at Camp Croft, N. C., at the outbreak of war. In the spring of 1942 he commanded a U.S. infantry division in New Caledonia, and on 8 December 1942 he assumed command of Army, Navy, and Marine forces operating against the enemy on Guadalcanal. He became commander of the XIV Corps in January 1943. In April of that year he returned to the United States where he took command of the IV Corps. He was designated commanding general of Seventh Army in March 1944, and in August of that year brought it into southern France. He commanded it in Alsace during that fall and winter and led it into Germany the following spring. In July 1945 he became commanding general of the Fourth Army at Fort Sam Houston, Tex., where he died in November 1945.

GEN. GEORGE S. PATTON, JR., commanded the ground elements of the Western Task Force in the landings in North Africa in November 1942. In March 1943 he assumed command of the II Corps in Tunisia. In April of that year he began the work of planning the invasion of Sicily. He commanded the U.S. forces in the assault on that island. His headquarters was renamed Seventh U.S. Army after the landings in Sicily. He was brought to the United Kingdom as commander of the Third U.S. Army in the spring of 1944. It became active on the Continent on 1 August 1944 and under his direction campaigned in France, Luxembourg, Belgium, Germany, and Czechoslovakia. After the war's end he became commanding general of the Fifteenth Army. He died as a result of an automobile accident in December 1945.

Mr. CHARLES B. P. PEAKE entered the British diplomatic service in 1922. In 1939 he was made head of the News Department of the Foreign Office and Chief Press Adviser to the Ministry of Information. In 1941 he was temporarily attached to Viscount Halifax as personal assistant in Washington and promoted to be a counsellor of embassy. From 1942 to 1943 he was the British representative to the French National Committee and in October 1943 he was appointed to General Eisenhower's staff as political liaison officer to the Supreme Commander with the rank of minister.

AMBASSADOR WILLIAM PHILLIPS began his career in the foreign service of the United States as private secretary of the U.S. Ambassador to Great Britain in 1903. Among his important appointments after that time were Ambassador to the Netherlands in 1920, Undersecretary of the Department of State, 1922–24 and 1933–36, Ambassador to Italy, 1936–41, and personal representative of the President to India, 1942–43. He was appointed political adviser to the COSSAC staff in September 1943 and held the same position at SHAEF from its activation until September 1944.

MARSHAL OF THE ROYAL AIR FORCE SIR CHARLES PORTAL served as an observer and fighter pilot in World War I. In the 1930's he commanded the British Forces in Aden and was Director of Organization, Air Ministry. Early in World War II he served on the Air Council and was Air Officer Commanding-in-Chief, Bomber Command. He was appointed Chief of the Air Staff in October 1940.

GROSSADMIRAL ERICH RAEDER served in fleet and staff service during World War I. He was commander in chief of the German Navy from 1935 until 1943, when at his own request he was replaced by Doenitz and appointed Inspector General of the German Navy *(Admiralinspekteur der Kriegsmarine)*, a nominal title.

ADMIRAL BERTRAM H. RAMSAY retired in 1938 after forty-two years in the Royal Navy, serving the last three as Chief of Staff, Home Fleet. He was recalled to duty in 1939 as Flag Officer Commanding, Dover, and in that post organized the naval forces for the evacuation of Dunkerque. Later he helped plan the TORCH operation, commanded a task force in the Sicilian invasion, and became British naval commander in the Mediterranean. He was appointed Allied Naval Commander-in-Chief, Expeditionary Force, in the fall of 1943 and served in that post until his death in a plane crash in France on 1 January 1945.

Mr. Samuel Reber entered the U.S. Foreign Service in 1926. He was stationed in Washington at the beginning of the war, but went to Martinique on a special mission in early 1942. After the landings in North Africa he was transferred to Mr. Murphy's staff in Algiers. From there he went to Italy in October 1943 as a member first of the Allied military mission and later of the Allied Control Commission. While in Italy he was attached for special duty to the Fifth Army. He left Italy in July 1944 and joined SHAEF as a political adviser.

Maj. Gen. Harold Redman was instructing at the British Staff College in 1939. He was then appointed to the War Cabinet Secretariat. In 1940 he was given command of a battalion in the United Kingdom. From June to December 1941 he commanded an infantry brigade in the Middle East. At the end of the year he was selected to be Brigadier General Staff, Headquarters Eighth Army. In March 1942 he returned again to a brigade command, which he held until 1943 when he was appointed secretary to the Combined Chiefs of Staff in Washington. In August 1944 he was promoted to major general and became deputy commander of the French Forces of the Interior. In the following month he was appointed deputy head of the SHAEF mission to France.

Air Marshal James M. Robb went to Canada at the beginning of the war to help plan the Commonwealth Air Training Plan. In 1940 he became commander of the No. 2 Bomber Group in the United Kingdom. Later, he was made chief of the No. 15 Fighter Group, commanding the Western Approaches to the United Kingdom. In 1942, he served as deputy chief of Combined Operations Headquarters and then acted for a brief period as air commander at Gibralter during the invasion of North Africa. He next served as air adviser to General Eisenhower. On the formation of the Northwest African Air Forces in 1943, he became commander of RAF North Africa and deputy to General Spaatz in the Northwest African Air Forces. He became Deputy Chief of Staff (Air), SHAEF, in March 1944. On the dissolution of AEAF in October 1944, he became Chief of the Air Staff (SHAEF).

Generalfeldmarschall Erwin Rommel served as an infantry officer in World War I. In August 1939 he was assigned as commandant of the *Fuehrerhauptquartier,* a position he held until February 1940. Rommel participated in the French campaign as commander of the *Seventh Panzer Division.* In February 1941 he was assigned to command the German troops assisting the Italians in North Africa. Rommel remained in Africa from September 1941 until March 1943 and commanded first *Panzer Army Africa* and later *Army Group Africa.* In the late summer of 1943 Rommel was assigned as commander of *Army Group B* in northern Italy. In the fall and winter of 1943 he conducted surveys of coastal defenses in the west. In January 1944 he again became commander of *Army Group B* in the west and retained this position until he was severely wounded in July 1944. Rommel, suspected of complicity in the plot of 20 July 1944, was forced to commit suicide in October 1944.

GENERALFELDMARSCHALL GERD VON RUNDSTEDT served as chief of staff of various
division and corps headquarters in World War I. He was retired in October 1938.
In June 1939 he was recalled to command *Army Group South* in the Polish campaign. After a very short term as Commander in Chief East in occupied Poland
he was redesignated as commander in chief of *Army Group A* and transferred to
the Western Front. In May 1940 his forces broke through the Ardennes and advanced to the Channel coast. In October 1940 he was designated as Commander
in Chief West, a position he held until the transfer of his headquarters to the east
in the spring of 1941. During the Russian campaign von Rundstedt commanded
Army Group South (formerly *Army Group A*) from June until December 1941, when
at his own request he was relieved of command because of ill health. In March
1942 he was assigned as Commander in Chief West. He retained this position
until he was relieved early in July 1944. Von Rundstedt was reassigned to his
former position as Commander in Chief West on 4 September 1944 and remained
as such until his final relief on 10 March 1945. He was taken prisoner in Bad
Toelz on 1 May 1945.

MAJ. GEN. LOWELL W. ROOKS was chief of the training division of Headquarters,
Army Ground Forces, in March 1942. In June of that year he became chief of
staff of II Corps. He was named G–3 of Headquarters, North African Theater of
Operations, when that headquarters was organized, and in January 1944 he was
named deputy chief of staff of Allied Force Headquarters. In March 1945 he
became Deputy G–3, SHAEF. In this position he helped to liquidate OKW at
the end of the war.

GENERALFELDMARSCHALL FERDINAND SCHOERNER served as an infantry officer in
World War I. From September 1939 until October 1943, he served with moun-
tain troops, rising from regimental to corps commander. After a short time as an
armored corps commander on the Eastern Front and then as a staff officer at
OKH, he was assigned as acting commander in chief of *Army Group A* on the
Eastern Front. Schoerner was appointed commander in chief of *Army Group A* in
May 1944 and transferred to *Army Group North* as commander in chief in July
1944. In January 1945 he became commander of *Army Group Center*.

LT. GEN. WILLIAM H. SIMPSON, veteran of overseas service in World War I, held the
command of the 9th Infantry Regiment, 2d Division, in June 1940. He was given
command of the Infantry Replacement Training Center of the Army in April
1941. Six months later he became commanding general of the 35th Division, and
he served from April to September 1942 as commander of the 30th Division. For
one month he commanded the XII Corps. In September 1943 he was placed at
the head of the Fourth Army. In the spring of 1944 an additional army headquarters (the Eighth) was formed from the Fourth Army, and General Simpson
was made commander of the new headquarters. He took it to the United Kingdom in May 1944 and remained as its head when it was renumbered the Ninth

Army. He commanded the Ninth Army in France, Belgium, the Netherlands, and Germany.

LT. GEN. WALTER BEDELL SMITH was assistant secretary of the General Staff in October 1939. He became Secretary, General Staff, in September 1941. In February 1942 he was named U.S. secretary of the Combined Chiefs of Staff and secretary of the Joint Board. General Eisenhower chose him in September 1942 to be chief of staff of the European Theater of Operations. Later he became chief of staff of the Allied forces in North Africa and of the Mediterranean theater. At the end of 1943, he became chief of staff of SHAEF.

GEN. CARL SPAATZ served with the First Aero Squadron of the Mexican Punitive Expedition in 1916. During World War I he won the Distinguished Service Cross in combat over St. Mihiel and the Meuse–Argonne. In 1940 he was sent to the United Kingdom as an official observer of the Battle of Britain. On his return to the United States he became commander of the Air Corps Materiel Division. At the beginning of 1942 he became chief of the Army Air Forces Combat Command. In May of that year he was given the command of the Eighth Air Force, which he took to the United Kingdom in the following July. Shortly thereafter he also became Commanding General, U.S. Army Air Forces in Europe. At the close of the year he was appointed commander of the Twelfth Air Force in North Africa. Two months later he was named commander of the Northwest African Air Forces. When the Mediterranean Allied Air Forces headquarters was established in 1943 under Air Chief Marshal Tedder, General Spaatz became its deputy commander. In January 1944 he went back to the United Kingdom where he assumed command of the United States Strategic Air Forces in Europe.

MAJ. GEN. KENNETH W. D. STRONG served as assistant military attaché in Berlin shortly before the outbreak of war in 1939, and in the first one and a half years of the war as head of the German Section, War Office. Later he commanded a battalion and then became chief of intelligence of Home Forces. In February 1943 he was appointed G-2 of Allied Force Headquarters in the Mediterranean. In this capacity he helped General Smith in armistice negotiations with the Italians. In the spring of 1944 he became G-2 of SHAEF.

GENERALOBERST KURT STUDENT was one of Germany's first fighter pilots—in 1913— and served in the Luftwaffe during World War I. After the outbreak of World War II, he took an active part in the paratroop attack on Rotterdam and in May 1941 commanded the paratroop attack on Crete. When the Allies invaded Europe, Student held the position of *Commander of Paratroops in OKL* in Berlin, and from 3 September until 31 October 1944 he was commander of the *First Parachute Army* under *Army Group B* in the Albert Canal–Maastricht sector. For the next three months he commanded *Army Group Student*, later renamed *Army Group H*, in Holland. During the month of April 1945 he again commanded the *First Para-*

chute Army in the Weser–Ems area. For the remaining week of the war, General Student commanded *Army Group Weichsel* on the Eastern Front. He was captured on 28 May 1945 near Flensburg.

AIR CHIEF MARSHAL SIR ARTHUR W. TEDDER served as British air commander in the Middle East in 1942, helping to stop Rommel's advance toward Egypt. His forces also contributed to the success of the El Alamein attack and the subsequent drive toward Tunisia. From February 1943 until the end of the year, he served as Commander in Chief, Mediterranean Allied Air Forces, which included RAF Middle East, RAF Malta Air Command, and the Northwest African Air Forces. In January 1944 he was appointed Deputy Supreme Commander, SHAEF.

LT. GEN. HOYT S. VANDENBERG served from June 1939 to June 1942 as assistant chief of the Plans Division in the Office of the Chief of the Air Corps. From June to August 1942 he was chief of the organization and equipment section in the A–3 Division of the same office. He went overseas in August 1942 as chief of staff of the Twelfth Air Force and served in that capacity until August of the following year. From August 1943 to March 1944 he was deputy chief of the Air Staff in Washington. He filled the post of Deputy Air Commander, Allied Expeditionary Air Force, from March to August 1944, and was then appointed to the command of the Ninth Air Force.

MAJ. GEN. C. H. H. VULLIAMY served in 1939–40 as chief signal officer of the Anti-aircraft Defence of Great Britain. In 1940 he became chief signal officer of a corps in Northern Ireland. He held a similar post in an army in 1941–42 before going to the Middle East Command as chief signal officer in 1943. In November of that year he became head of the Signals Division of COSSAC, and in February 1944 became chief of the Signal Division, SHAEF. He held this post until the spring of 1945.

MAJ. GEN. J. F. M. WHITELEY, veteran of World War I, in which he was awarded the Military Cross, served as Deputy Assistant Adjutant General India from 1932 to 1934. In the following year he became General Staff Officer, War Office, continuing as such until 1938. In World War II he served as deputy chief of staff at Allied Force Headquarters, was assigned briefly as chief of intelligence at SHAEF, and became Deputy G–3, SHAEF, in May 1944.

GENERALOBERST KURT ZEITZLER served as an infantry officer in World War I. In World War II he served as a corps chief of staff in the Polish and French campaigns and as chief of staff of *First Panzer Group*, later *First Panzer Army*, in Russia in 1941. After a short tour as chief of staff of *OB WEST* he was appointed Chief of the Army General Staff in September 1942. He was relieved of this position in July 1944 and retired from the Army in January 1945.

CHAPTER I

The Supreme Commander

Christmas Eve, 1943, found the world in its fourth year of war. The Allies, still faced with the grim spectacle of western Europe under Axis domination, gained some cheer from the knowledge that their position had improved substantially in the year just ending. Not only had they won victories in the Mediterranean, on the Eastern Front, and in the Pacific, but the Western Powers and the Soviet Union had at last agreed upon the strategy for breaking the power of Hitler. As radio audiences listened that Christmas Eve to the carols already beginning to fill the air, they heard the President of the United States announce the selection of General Dwight David Eisenhower as Supreme Commander of the Allied Expeditionary Force that was to march against Germany. The appointment meant that an important milestone in World War II had been passed. The last great phase of the war in the West was about to begin and peace seemed somehow nearer than it had before.

The Selection of the Supreme Commander

Almost a year had elapsed between the Casablanca Conference, which decided that a Supreme Commander would be named, and the announcement of 24 December.[1] The appointment had been postponed initially on the ground that more than a year would pass before the invasion of northwest Europe (Operation OVERLORD) could be launched. The conferees thought it sufficient at that stage to select a Chief of Staff to the Supreme Allied Commander (COSSAC)[2] and give him power to choose a staff and to conduct preliminary planning for the cross-Channel operation. Lt. Gen. Frederick E. Morgan was named to head the COSSAC staff. It was assumed that members of his staff would serve as a nucleus for the future Supreme Headquarters.

The final decision on a Supreme Commander was delayed further for several different reasons—some quite clear cut and others indeterminate. The first, discussed at the Casablanca Conference, had to do with the nationality of the Supreme Commander. The U.S. President, Franklin D. Roosevelt, realizing that any attack made in the near future would have to be mounted largely by the British, said that the appointment if made then should go to a British officer. Prime Minister Winston S. Churchill proposed that the decision be postponed, suggesting that the question be settled ultimately in accordance with the

---

[1] The Casablanca Conference, a meeting of the British and U.S. heads of government and the Combined Chiefs of Staff, was held in Casablanca in January 1943. This is sometimes referred to as the ANFA or SYMBOL Conference. See below, pp. 37–41, for discussion of Combined Chiefs of Staff.

[2] The title COSSAC was used to indicate both the headquarters and its head. This volume will use COSSAC to refer to the headquarters; General Morgan will be referred to as the COSSAC chief.

general rule that the command be held "by an officer of the nation which furnishes the majority of the troops." Through the spring of 1943 when plans were being discussed for small-scale operations on the Continent to be mounted in case of German weakening or at signs of Russian collapse, it seemed clear that British forces would dominate and that a British officer would command. In this period, the Prime Minister informed Field Marshal Sir Alan Brooke, Chief of the Imperial General Staff, that he would command the invasion of Europe.[3] Partly in anticipation of this appointment, General Morgan organized the early staff of COSSAC in accordance with the British staff system.[4]

By the end of April 1943, General Morgan had concluded that the command of a cross-Channel attack would have to go to an American, since the United States would have to furnish everything "to follow up the initial effort. . . ." This sentiment was echoed in the United States, where the responsible military leaders believed that the launching of the cross-Channel operation, toward which the British Chiefs of Staff were believed to be lukewarm, would be insured if it had a U.S. commander.[5] The Secretary of War, Henry L. Stimson, pressed this view on the President on the eve of the Allied conference at Quebec in August 1943, adding that the selection of Gen. George C. Marshall, the U.S. Army Chief of Staff, would be the best guarantee that the operation would be carried out. Mr. Harry L. Hopkins, unofficial adviser to the President, also strongly urged the selection of General Marshall. Mr. Roosevelt, impressed by their reasoning, reached an agreement with Prime Minister Churchill at Quebec that an American should lead the cross-Channel attack, and apparently indicated

GENERAL MORGAN

that General Marshall would be named. Roosevelt told Secretary Stimson shortly after the Quebec Conference that the first proposal had come from Churchill although it meant taking the command from General Brooke. It is clear that the President wanted Marshall to have the

[3] Winston S. Churchill, *Closing the Ring* (Boston, 1951), p. 85.

[4] CCS 169, 22 Jan 43, Notes on conf of 18 Jan 43, Casablanca Conf Min; Maj Gen Harry C. Ingles, Deputy Theater Comdr, to Maj Gen Charles H. Bonesteel, 10 May 43, photostat in AG HRB 200.3 ETOUSA Collection of Msgs; Interv with Gen Sir Hastings L. Ismay, 17 Dec 46, on selection of Brooke; Interv with Gen Morgan, 2 Apr 46. General Ingles wrote General Bonesteel on 10 May 1943 that the decision to appoint the British commander had been made in Washington, but the author has found no record of this action.

[5] The British Chiefs of Staff were officially called the Chiefs of Staff Committee just as the U.S. Chiefs were called the Joint Chiefs of Staff.

Supreme Command in Europe, and that the British interposed no objection. They expected the U.S. Chief of Staff to be appointed, and it appears that some agreement had been made whereby he would act with the British Chiefs of Staff in London on matters affecting operations in the European theater.[6]

Even after agreeing tentatively on the person to be named to the Supreme Command, the President delayed making the final selection. While he was convinced that General Marshall should be chosen in order that he might have proper credit for his work in building the American Army, Mr. Roosevelt still wished to retain the Chief of Staff's services in Washington as long as possible.[7]

Publication of statements that General Marshall was to lead the cross-Channel attack received a varied reaction in the United States. Many newspapers took the appointment as a matter of course and declared that the Chief of Staff was the logical nominee for the job. Critics of the administration in the press and Congress took a different stand. Apparently not knowing that Secretary of War Stimson was urging the appointment and saying that it was something which General Marshall wanted more than anything else, the opponents of the President attributed the selection to everything from a British plot to get rid of a U.S. Chief of Staff who opposed their schemes to a suggestion, branded by Mr. Stimson as "outrageous libel," that the proposal was prompted by an administration scheme to replace General Marshall with a political general who would manipulate the awarding of war contracts in a manner to re-elect Mr. Roosevelt in 1944. The *Army and Navy Journal* and the *Army and Navy Register*, which reflected the views of many officers

in the services, objected to the shift on military grounds. So much anxiety was evidenced by members of Congress that Secretary Stimson and General Marshall at length found it necessary to deny the charges that the President was interfering with the War Department.[8]

Part of the concern over the proposed appointment arose from reports that General Marshall's colleagues on the Joint Chiefs of Staff were opposed to the change. Their reaction was due not to the fear that politics was involved but to the feeling that it was necessary to retain General Marshall as a member of the Combined Chiefs of Staff where he could fight for U.S. con-

[6] Frederick E. Morgan, *Overture to Overlord* (New York, 1950), p. 124. General Morgan's views on the need of an American commander are cited in Ltr, Gen Ingles, Deputy Theater Cmdr, to Gen Marshall, 6 May 43, Hq ETOUSA files. For Mr. Stimson's views, see Henry L. Stimson and McGeorge Bundy, *On Active Service in Peace and War* (New York, 1948), p. 439, including quotation from his diary of August 1943. For other views, see General Ismay's interview with the author, 17 December 1946; Robert E. Sherwood, *Roosevelt and Hopkins: An Intimate History* (New York, 1948), p. 762; and Churchill, *Closing the Ring*, pp. 85, 301. Statements by various British and U.S. officials are noted in the Diary of the Office of the Commander in Chief, entries for 5, 8, and 19 October 1943, and a memorandum by General Eisenhower for 6 December 1943. The Diary of the Office of the Commander in Chief, hereafter cited as Diary Office CinC, was kept by Capt. Harry C. Butcher, USNR, for General Eisenhower. It includes summaries of the Supreme Commander's activities, memoranda written for the diary, many of the top secret letters which came to or were sent by the Supreme Commander, and copies of plans, intelligence estimates and the like. Edited portions of this diary appeared in Butcher's *My Three Years With Eisenhower* (New York, 1946).

[7] Churchill, *Closing the Ring*, pp. 303–04.

[8] Sherwood, *Roosevelt and Hopkins*, pp. 759–64, has a convenient summary of these reactions. See also *Congressional Record*, Vol. 89, Pt. 6, 7682, 7883, Pt. 11, App. 4001; *Army and Navy Journal*, September 18, 1943; *Army and Navy Register*, September 11, 18, 25, October 2, 1943; *The New York Times*, September 23–30, 1943; Stimson and Bundy, *On Active Service*, pp. 437–... Churchill, *Closing the Ring*, pp. 301–03.

GENERAL MARSHALL AND SECRETARY STIMSON

cepts of Allied strategy. Their view was shared by General of the Armies John J. Pershing who, as the elder statesman of the Army, warned the President in mid-September that the proposed transfer of the Chief of Staff would be a "fundamental and very grave error in our military policy." The President agreed on the need of keeping General Marshall in Washington, but held that the Chief of Staff deserved a chance to lead in the field the Army which he had developed.[9]

Although members of the War Department had good reason to know that there was no disposition on the part of the President to "kick General Marshall upstairs," they nonetheless feared that the shift of the Chief of Staff to a field command would result in an actual demotion and remove from the Combined Chiefs of Staff the stanchest proponent of the cross-Channel attack. They therefore backed proposals outlined by the Operations Division of the War Department giving General Marshall control of the operational forces in the cross-Channel attack but still retaining him in his position on the Combined Chiefs of Staff. Under one such plan, the Chief of Staff would command all United Nations forces and at the same time keep his vote on European matters in the Combined Chiefs of Staff organization. It was proposed that the position of Deputy Supreme Commander and the command in the Mediterranean be given to British officers, while operational command of the cross-Channel attack should go to an American.[10]

To a degree the American planners were trying to have their cake and eat it too. They wanted operational command of the OVERLORD forces, but at the same time they wanted to be sure that the OVERLORD viewpoint was fully represented in the Combined Chiefs of Staff. They were particularly anxious to place firm control of operations in the hands of an American general. This attitude was strengthened as it became increasingly clear that the United States would furnish more than half of the forces and supplies to be committed in the cross-Channel operation. The British, who in a sense had General Pershing's World War I problem of preserving their national identity in an Allied force, were equally determined to keep a large share of control over the Supreme Command and were not disposed to strengthen Washington's grip on operations and policy. They thus balked at any proposal that would place a U.S. commander, not only over the Allied forces in Europe, but over all United Nations forces fighting Germany and at the same time

---

[9] William D. Leahy, *I Was There* (New York, 1950), pp. 191–92; Interv with Admiral Leahy, 15 Jul 47; Interv with Admiral Ernest J. King, 7 Jul 47; Henry H. Arnold, *Global Mission* (New York, 1949), pp. 455–56. Texts of Pershing and Roosevelt letters, 16 and 20 September 1943, in Katherine Tupper Marshall, *Together* (New York, 1946), pp. 156–57.

[10] Air Chief Marshal Sir Charles Portal, British Chief of the Air Staff, was suggested for the Deputy Supreme Commander post, Gen. Sir Harold R. L. G. Alexander for the Mediterranean command, and General Eisenhower for the European command in this unsigned and undated memo, The System of Command in the War against Germany, apparently written near the end of September 1943 by a member of the Operations Division of the War Department. OPD Exec, Bk 12. The memorandum, while not acted on at the moment, summed up several other proposals then in the air and foreshadowed the proposal the Joint Chiefs were to make in December 1943 at Cairo. Also of interest was a suggestion made by General Eisenhower in September 1943 to Captain Butcher. The general proposed as a solution that General Marshall come to Europe to organize that theater, leaving a deputy chief of staff, possibly Lt. Gen. Brehon B. Somervell, in Washington. When the European theater was properly organized, General Marshall could then go to the Pacific and repeat the operation. Diary Office CinC, 16 Sep 43.

would leave him a voice on the Combined Chiefs of Staff. The Americans undoubtedly had few illusions that they could persuade the British to accept all of these points. It is more likely that from the beginning they were ready to settle for some expansion of General Marshall's powers beyond those of Supreme Commander in Europe.

Reports of these proposals reached the American press and allayed some fears that Marshall was to be removed from a role in determining Allied military policy. The same reports caused Mr. Churchill some uneasiness, and he wrote Mr. Hopkins that the proposals were contrary to those agreed upon at Quebec.[11]

While these plans were being discussed in Washington and London, the President and his military advisers proceeded on the assumption that General Marshall would command the cross-Channel attack. General Marshall himself began to make detailed suggestions for the command structure of Operation OVERLORD. In October he invited his prospective chief of staff for the operation, General Morgan, to Washington so that the British general could acquire information about the United States and its people which would be of value in dealing with Americans at Supreme Allied Headquarters. General Morgan, on his arrival in Washington, pressed for immediate appointment of the Supreme Commander, explaining that someone with authority was needed to secure the men and matériel for the operation. He carried his plea to the President but was told that General Marshall could not be spared at that time. Mr. Roosevelt was willing, however, for the British to name a Deputy Supreme Commander at once. The British Government repeated General Morgan's request in October, but again

the President demurred, cabling this time that the appointment of a Supreme Commander would give away Allied plans to the enemy. He added that he had made no final decision on a replacement for a Chief of Staff, since it was possible that General Eisenhower, who was being considered for Marshall's place in Washington, would be made an army group commander in the cross-Channel operation.[12]

No final decision had been taken on the Supreme Commander and his deputy on the eve of the Allied conference at Cairo and Tehran at the end of November 1943. General Eisenhower, who was regarded as the likely successor to General Marshall as Chief of Staff, had been given no official

---

[11] Stimson and Bundy, *On Active Service*, p. 441; Sherwood, *Roosevelt and Hopkins*, p. 762. War Department planners' final draft presented in Joint Chiefs of Staff (JCS) paper, Command of British and U.S. Forces Operating against Germany, CCS 408, 25 Nov 43, SEXTANT Conf Min. It is possible that Mr. Churchill's opposition to an over-all Allied command for General Marshall was responsible for the later charge that the British opposed Marshall's selection as Supreme Commander. It should be apparent that if the British desired to get rid of him as an opponent the best way to do it was to get him off the Combined Chiefs of Staff and into the Supreme Commander's position. No evidence exists that they ever opposed him for the Supreme Commander's post. Indeed, all the evidence is the other way. Both Admirals Leahy and King told the author in July 1947 that the British offered no opposition to Marshall as commander of the cross-Channel attack. This same statement had been previously made in the most categorical fashion to the author by Lords Alanbrooke, Portal, Cunningham, and Ismay. General Eisenhower said in 1943 that he had been told by Mr. Churchill that the two Americans acceptable to him for the command of the cross-Channel attack were Generals Marshall and Eisenhower. Memo, Eisenhower, Diary Office CinC, 6 Dec 43; Churchill, *Closing the Ring*, pp. 303, 305.

[12] Stimson and Bundy, *On Active Service*, p. 442; Morgan, Notes on Visit to Washington, Oct–Nov 43. A copy of these notes was given to the author by General Morgan. Morgan, *Overture To Overlord*, Ch. VIII; Interv with Morgan, 2 Apr 46; Leahy, *I Was There*, pp. 190–91. The cable to the British was drafted by Leahy and Marshall.

word, but various visitors to his headquarters from London and Washington in the fall of 1943 indicated that Marshall's appointment as Supreme Commander and Eisenhower's transfer to Washington would soon be announced. General Eisenhower had attempted to anticipate this latter move by sending word to Washington through his chief of staff, Maj. Gen. Walter Bedell Smith, that he would prefer to serve under General Marshall as army group commander rather than take the post of Army Chief of Staff.[13]

The selection of General Marshall seemed certain when British and U.S. representatives, on their way to Cairo in November 1943, stopped by at Allied Force Headquarters where General Eisenhower was in command. Mr. Hopkins said that General Marshall would definitely be Supreme Commander if the British did not "wash out" on the cross-Channel operation at Tehran. Admiral Ernest J. King, discussing the matter in the presence of General Marshall, told General Eisenhower that the President had tentatively decided to give the command to the Chief of Staff against the advice of the other members of the U.S. Chiefs of Staff. The Prime Minister somewhat later, while expressing his willingness to have either Marshall or Eisenhower, thought that the appointment would go to the Chief of Staff. Finally, in late November, the President himself explained the situation to General Eisenhower. Mr. Roosevelt was impressed by the fact that field commanders rather than chiefs of staff were remembered in history. He felt that General Marshall's contributions to American victory should be recognized by a command in the field, even at the expense of losing him as Chief of Staff. This statement seemed to clinch the matter, leaving General Eisenhower,

on the eve of his appointment as Supreme Commander, to assume that his work as a field commander would soon be ended.[14]

Shortly before the conferences at Cairo and Tehran, the U.S. Chiefs of Staff discussed plans for getting British consent to the appointment of General Marshall as commander of all western Allied operations against Germany, and to the organization of the strategic air forces in Europe and the Mediterranean under one head. General Marshall, embarrassed because the proposal that he command all Allied forces in Europe appeared over his signature, declared that he would concentrate on pushing the plan to integrate strategic air forces in Europe.[15]

In their discussions en route to Cairo, the U.S. Chiefs of Staff also considered the possibility of giving over-all command of Allied operations to a British officer if that should be necessary to get British acceptance of the OVERLORD operation. Churchill's statement early in the conference that OVERLORD "remained top of the bill" made any concession unnecessary. On 25 November, the U.S. Chiefs of Staff asked for an arrangement which, if accepted, would have placed firm strategic and tactical control in the hands of the Supreme

---

[13] See statements by Averell Harriman, Secretary of the Navy Frank Knox, Admiral Lord Louis Mountbatten, and Admiral Sir Andrew B. Cunningham in Diary Office CinC, entries for 5, 8, 15, and 28 October 1943. General Smith reported after his return from Washington on 28 October 1943 that Marshall felt that any army group command would be a step down for Eisenhower and seemed to prefer that he take the position of Chief of Staff. Eisenhower's statement possibly was responsible for Roosevelt's remark noted above. See also Butcher, *My Three Years With Eisenhower*, p. 452.

[14] Memo, Eisenhower, Diary Office CinC, 6 Dec 43; Dwight D. Eisenhower, *Crusade in Europe* (New York, 1948), pp. 197–98.

[15] JCS 123d–126th Mtgs, on shipboard, 15, 17, 18, and 19 Nov 43, ABC 334, JCS (2–14–42), Secs 5, 6.

Allied Commander.[16] With an American in the post, Washington, rather than London, would have the dominant voice in decisions on strategy. The U.S. Chiefs of Staff asked that Allied forces in the west be put at once under one commander, and that he should "exercise command over the Allied force commanders in the Mediterranean, in northwest Europe, and of the strategic air forces." They added that any delay in adopting this plan was likely to lead to confusion and indecision. Under their proposal, the Supreme Commander would be directed to carry out the agreed European strategy. He would be charged with the location and timing of operations and with the allocation of forces and matériel made available to him by the Combined Chiefs of Staff. His decisions would be subject to reversal by the Combined Chiefs.[17]

The British, impressed by the "immense political implications" of a scheme which they felt should receive the earnest consideration of the British and U.S. Governments, objected to the proposal. They pointed to political, economic, industrial, and domestic questions which a Supreme Commander would have to settle by reference to the heads of the two governments. The Supreme Commander, they concluded, would be able to settle only comparatively minor and strictly military matters. To an American argument that similar authority had been granted Marshal Ferdinand Foch in 1918, the British replied that the French commander had been given only the Western and Italian fronts, whereas the proposed arrangement would add to those two theaters the Balkan Front and the Turkish Front, if opened. They asked that the existing machinery for the high-level direction of war be retained, and that changes in it be confined to improving that machinery rather than embarking "upon an entirely novel experiment, which merely makes a cumbrous and unnecessary link in the chain of command, and which will surely lead to disillusionment and disappointment." [18]

No agreement was reached by the U.S. and British representatives at Cairo before they recessed the conference to go to Tehran for a meeting with Marshal Joseph Stalin and his advisers. They were thus unprepared to answer the Russian leader on 29 November when he asked who was to lead the cross-Channel attack. He reminded Roosevelt and Churchill that it was not enough to have a chief of staff in charge of OVERLORD planning, since a newly appointed Supreme Commander might disapprove of what had been done before his selection. If a commander was not appointed, Marshal Stalin said, nothing would come of the operation. At this, the President whispered to Admiral Leahy: "That old Bolshevik is trying to force me to give him the name of our Supreme Commander. I just can't tell him because I have not yet made up my mind."

The Prime Minister replied to Stalin that the British had already expressed their willingness to serve under a U.S. commander in the OVERLORD operation. Apparently mindful of the unsettled matter of the over-all command, Mr. Church-

[16] JCS 126th Mtg, on shipboard, 19 Nov 43, ABC 334, JCS (2–14–42), Secs 5, 6; Sherwood, *Roosevelt and Hopkins*, p. 767; 2d plenary session, CCS, 24 Nov 43, at Cairo, SEXTANT Conf Min.

[17] Memo, JCS, Command of British and U.S. Forces Operating against Germany, CCS 408, 25 Nov 43, SEXTANT Conf Min.

[18] Memo, Br COS, Command of British and U.S. Forces Operating against Germany, CCS 408/1, 26 Nov 43, SEXTANT Conf Min; Churchill, *Closing the Ring*, p. 305.

ill added that decisions at the conference might have a bearing on the choice. He said that the President could name the Supreme Commander for OVERLORD if he accepted the British offer to serve under a United States commander, and proposed that when the selection was made the Russian commander be told who it would be. Stalin hastily added that he had no desire to take part in the selection, but stressed the necessity of taking action as soon as possible. On 30 November, the President took notice of Stalin's interest in the matter by saying that the selection would be made in three or four days, certainly soon after the return of the Allied delegations to Cairo. Marshal Stalin's pressure for the immediate naming of the Supreme Commander may have hastened by a few days the announcement of the selection, but that action had already been made essential by the fact that the Allies were scheduled to launch the cross-Channel operation in May 1944, less than six months from the time of the conference.[19]

The proposal to appoint an over-all commander for the forces of the Allies in the west was apparently dropped just before the Allied leaders left Tehran or shortly after they returned to Cairo.[20] The appointment of General Marshall merely to head the OVERLORD attack would mean, as Mr. Roosevelt well realized, that he would not be available to press the U.S. case in sessions of the Combined Chiefs of Staff. Knowledge of this fact may have increased the President's reluctance to forego the services of the Chief of Staff. Furthermore, he wanted to keep General Marshall in Washington to handle the ticklish problems of relations with the Pacific theater and with members of Congress. These matters, Mr. Roosevelt believed, could be better handled by the

Chief of Staff than by General Eisenhower. On the other hand, he was convinced that Eisenhower could handle the European command successfully. Not only had he proved his ability to command Allied forces in the Mediterranean theater, but his appearance before the Combined Chiefs of Staff at Cairo had demonstrated a firm grasp of the military situation and added to the good impression he had previously made. Moreover, from the time of the first discussions of a Supreme Commander for OVERLORD his name had been coupled with that of General Marshall's as a possible choice to lead the cross-Channel operation, and it was clear that he was completely acceptable to the British for the post.[21]

Still hesitant to make the final decision, the President on 4 December sent Mr.

---

[19] 2d and 3d plenary sessions, Tehran Conf, 28, 30 Nov 43, EUREKA Conf Min; Leahy, *I Was There*, p. 208.

[20] Sherwood, *Roosevelt and Hopkins*, p. 791, quoting from a set of notes of the third plenary session at Tehran different from those available to the author, notes that Roosevelt on 30 November told Stalin that a decision had been made that morning to appoint one commander for OVERLORD, another for the Mediterranean, and a third temporarily for the southern France invasion. It is possible that the over-all commander question was settled at this time. In any event, the Combined Chiefs of Staff on 3 December at their first formal meeting after returning to Cairo omitted the over-all command question from their agenda. They did include the questions of the integration of the U.S. air command and the directive to the Supreme Commander, Mediterranean Theater. CCS 133d Mtg, 3 Dec 43, at Cairo, SEXTANT Conf Min.

[21] Captain Butcher in an entry for 10 December 1943 in Diary Office CinC records Hopkins' statement that Eisenhower's appearance before the Combined Chiefs at Cairo had made a good impression. Butcher also felt that Col. Elliott Roosevelt's outspoken belief that Eisenhower had succeeded in getting British and American forces to work together and in synchronizing Allied air, sea, and land power may have played some part in the President's decision. A somewhat contradictory statement is given in Elliott Roosevelt, *As He Saw It* (New York, 1946), p. 168.

Hopkins to the Chief of Staff to ask if he would express a preference between his present position and that of Supreme Commander. General Marshall simply replied that he would accept any decision the President might make. On Sunday, 5 December, Mr. Roosevelt personally invited the Chief of Staff to make the decision. When Marshall repeated that any action of the President would be acceptable, Mr. Roosevelt remarked that he believed he could not sleep at night with the Chief of Staff out of the country. The President then decided to name General Eisenhower Supreme Commander.[22]

The Cairo Conference adjourned without the establishment of an over-all Allied command and without the unification of British and U.S. strategic air forces in the Mediterranean and European theaters.[23]

An arrangement was made for a British officer to take charge of all Allied forces in the Mediterranean area with the title of Supreme Allied Commander, Mediterranean Theater (SACMED). The post went to Gen. Sir Henry Maitland Wilson, who was told to assume command from General Eisenhower when the latter, having regard to the progress of the operation then under way against Rome, thought it desirable.[24]

General Eisenhower's first hint of his appointment came on the morning of 7 December in a somewhat cryptic radiogram from General Marshall. Apparently assuming that General Eisenhower had been notified, Marshall said: "In view of the impending appointment of a British officer as your successor as Commander-in-Chief in the Mediterranean, please submit to me in Washington your recommendations in brief as to the best arrangement for handling the administration, discipline, training and supply of American

troops assigned to Allied Force under this new command." Later in the same day at Tunis, where General Eisenhower had gone to meet the President and his party, Mr. Roosevelt himself notified the new Supreme Commander of his appointment.[25]

General Eisenhower spent the remaining days of December in the Mediterranean theater continuing to supervise operations then in progress and preparing to hand over control of Mediterranean forces to General Wilson. The shifts in command were announced officially on

---

[22] Sherwood, *Roosevelt and Hopkins*, pp. 802–03, has General Marshall's own account. Mrs. Marshall's *Together*, pp. 168–69, has a similar account. Stimson and Bundy, *On Active Service*, pp. 441–42, gives the President's version of the decision, and Stimson's reaction to it. Compare this treatment with Roosevelt, *As He Saw It*, p. 209, in which the President's son declares that in a conversation with him (Monday, 6 December) the President said that the matter had not been finally decided, but that it seemed that Churchill would refuse to let Marshall take over. The Prime Minister's statement at Tehran and Roosevelt's offer of a choice to Marshall on Sunday, 5 December, indicate that the President was talking of opposition by the British to an over-all command for General Marshall and not to his command of OVERLORD. General Marshall on 6 December drafted for the President's signature a message to Marshal Stalin announcing, "The immediate appointment of General Eisenhower to command the OVERLORD operation has been decided upon." On the following day, at the conclusion of the Cairo Conference, the Chief of Staff sent the draft on to General Eisenhower as a memento of the appointment. Eisenhower, *Crusade in Europe*, p. 208; Stimson and Bundy, *On Active Service*, pp. 441–42.

[23] The U.S. Chiefs decided at this time to integrate their own strategic air forces in the two theaters. See below, pp. 48–49.

[24] The Combined Chiefs indicated that when Eisenhower's appointment was announced he would be given the title of Supreme Commander, Allied Expeditionary Force. CCS 138th Mtg, 7 Dec 43, SEXTANT Conf Min.

[25] Marshall's message of 6 December 1943 is quoted in Diary Office CinC, entry for 10 December 1943. For President Roosevelt's statement see Eisenhower, *Crusade in Europe*, pp. 206–07.

24 December by the President and Prime Minister. At the same time, Mr. Churchill announced that Gen. Sir Bernard Law Montgomery, commander of the Eighth British Army, would succeed Gen. Sir Bernard Paget as commander of the 21 Army Group. Near the end of December, at General Marshall's urging, General Eisenhower prepared to go to Washington to discuss with the Joint Chiefs of Staff the allocations of men and matériel for OVERLORD and to take a short rest. On 1 January 1944, after instructing Generals Montgomery and Smith to represent him in London until his return from Washington, and after a brief visit with the Prime Minister at Marrakech, Eisenhower left North Africa for the United States.

The New Commander

The newly appointed Supreme Commander had advanced rapidly since March 1941 when, as chief of staff of IX Corps at Fort Lewis, Washington, he had been promoted to the temporary rank of full colonel. At that time, with the United States still some months away from war, there was little to indicate that within three years he would be chosen for the chief Allied military role in the west. His early Army career after graduation from West Point in 1915 had included wartime tours of duty as an instructor at Fort Oglethorpe, Ga., Fort Meade, Md., and Fort Leavenworth, Kans., and as commandant of the tank training center at Camp Colt, Pa. Between the two wars he had gone through a number of Army schools, including the Infantry Tank School at Fort Meade, the Command and General Staff School at Fort Leavenworth, from which he graduated first in the class of 1926, the

Army War College, and the Army Industrial College. His Army assignments included three years in Panama with the 20th Infantry Brigade, a year in France while he was helping to revise the American Battle Monuments Commission's *Guidebook to American Battlefields in Europe,* a tour of duty at the beginning of the thirties as assistant executive officer in the office of the Assistant Secretary of War, two years in the office of Gen. Douglas MacArthur, the Chief of Staff, and four years (1935–39) as senior military assistant to General MacArthur in the Philippines. He returned to the United States in 1939 and held in rapid succession the posts of executive officer of the 15th Infantry Regiment, chief of staff of the 3d Division, and chief of staff of the IX Corps.

In the summer of 1941 Colonel Eisenhower was appointed chief of staff of Lt. Gen. Walter Krueger's Third Army, which was then preparing for the Louisiana maneuvers against Second Army. He was still inconspicuous enough to be identified in a picture taken during maneuvers as "Lt. Col. D. D. Ersenbeing," and to be dismissed by Second Army's intelligence section as a good plodding student. The results of the maneuvers, which newsmen hailed as a victory for the Third Army, brought him favorable acclaim for his performance as chief of staff.[26] In part because of this work, but undoubtedly more because of his knowledge of the Philippines, he was brought to the War Plans Division of the War Department one week after the Pearl Harbor disaster as deputy chief for the Pacific and Far East.

Once started on his way up, General Eisenhower rose rapidly. Scarcely two

---

[26] Colonel Eisenhower was promoted to the temporary rank of brigadier general after the maneuvers.

months after he arrived in Washington, he succeeded Maj. Gen. Leonard T. Gerow as chief of the War Plans Division, which shortly afterward became the Operations Division of the War Department.[27] In this post, he strongly advocated making the main Allied effort in the European theater, and helped to draw up plans for a cross-Channel attack. In May 1942 he went to London to inspect the organization of American forces in the United Kingdom. One month later General Marshall chose him to command the newly established Headquarters, European Theater of Operations (ETOUSA), in London.[28]

While holding the ETOUSA command, the future leader of the cross-Channel attack was in close contact with the officers who were planning a proposed return to the Continent. He thus became acquainted with many of the Allied political and military leaders with whom he was later associated and became familiar with the broad outlines of a plan for cross-Channel operations. His work on these projects was interrupted in July 1942 by the decision to postpone the cross-Channel attack and launch an operation against North Africa. General Eisenhower was appointed commander in chief of the Allied forces for these operations.[29] Later as Allied commander in chief, he directed the attacks of 1943 against Sicily and the south of Italy. He was engaged in planning future Italian operations when named by President Roosevelt to command the Allied Expeditionary Force in northwest Europe.[30]

General Eisenhower's career as a commander was a matter of acute interest to German intelligence agencies at the time of his assumption of command of the Allied Expeditionary Force. One estimate of the new Supreme Commander declared:

Eisenhower is an expert on operations of armored formations. He is noted for his great energy, and his hatred of routine office work. He leaves the initiative to his subordinates whom he manages to inspire to supreme efforts through kind understanding and easy discipline. His strongest point is said to be an ability for adjusting personalities to one another and smoothing over opposite viewpoints. Eisenhower enjoys the greatest popularity with Roosevelt and Churchill.[31]

This estimate hit upon that quality of the Supreme Commander's most often stressed by those who knew him in the Mediterranean theater—the ability to get people of different nationalities and viewpoints to work together. Making Allied understanding his keynote, he insisted continually that his staff officers lay aside their national differences in his command. His willingness to go an extra mile with the Allies drew from some U.S. officers the gibe that "Ike is the best commander the British have" and the view that, in all decisions settled on a 51–49 percent basis, the 51 percent was always in favor of the non-Americans.

His ability to get along with people of diverse temperaments was perhaps best exhibited in the case of Gen. Charles de Gaulle, leader of the French Committee of National Liberation. The French chief,

---

[27] General Eisenhower was promoted to the temporary rank of major general in March 1942.

[28] Roland G. Ruppenthal, *Logistical Support of the Armies*, UNITED STATES ARMY IN WORLD WAR II (Washington, 1953), discusses this organization at some length.

[29] General Eisenhower became a lieutenant general in July 1942, a four-star general in February 1943, and a general of the army at the end of 1944.

[30] Biographical details may be found in Eisenhower, *Crusade in Europe*, and Kenneth S. Davis, *Soldier of Democracy* (New York, 1945).

[31] Luftwaffe Academy Lecture, Invasion Generals, Careers and Assessments, 7 Feb 44, *Generalstab der Luftwaffe, 8. Abteilung* (hist sec), British Air Ministry files.

despite initial anger over General Eisenhower's relations with Admiral Darlan and friendliness to General Giraud in North Africa, believed that the new Supreme Commander was the one U.S. officer with whom the French Committee could do business.

General Eisenhower's conciliatory attitude was at times misleading. While genial in his approach, he could be extremely stern if the occasion demanded. His temper, as General Patton, among others, could testify, was sometimes explosive and his reprimands could be blistering. These traits were balanced by the gift of enormous patience. He showed a tendency to "make haste slowly" and to give people a chance to work out their own solutions.

Despite remarkable self-possession, the Allied commander during the North African campaign showed at times that he lacked the thick skin which public figures so often require. He was extremely sensitive to newspaper charges that he was making political mistakes by insisting on dealing with matters in his theater on a purely military basis. At one point he retorted that he would like to be allowed to fight the war and let the politicians take care of politics.

Although at times General Eisenhower and his staff showed the same impatience with some of the advice and criticism of the Combined Chiefs and the Joint Chiefs of Staff that most military commanders and staffs show toward their superiors, his relations with the high-level chiefs were cordial. He maintained a close relationship with General Marshall. In frequent personal letters, Eisenhower outlined his views on coming campaigns or discussed frankly his successes and failures. General Marshall replied with letters of encouragement and sought new ways by which he could give additional aid to his subordinate. The Chief of Staff, aware of Eisenhower's great respect for him, prefaced any proffered opinion with such statements as "don't let this worry you," "don't let me influence your judgment," "tell me exactly what you need and we will get it for you."

General Eisenhower brought to England in 1944 a reputation for dealing satisfactorily with British, French, and U.S. forces. He had established the basis for close co-operation with the heads of the Allied governments and the Combined Chiefs of Staff. After a year of working with Allied forces in the Mediterranean area, he had demonstrated his knack for making a coalition work.

CHAPTER II

The Coalition Command

Above the new Supreme Commander and his fellow commanders in the various theaters of operations of the world, there was a hierarchy of command, developed since 1942, which included the President of the United States, the Prime Minister of Great Britain, the heads of the executive departments which dealt with military matters, and an organization of British and U.S. armed services leaders known as the Combined Chiefs of Staff.[1] This hierarchy was responsible for the adoption of grand strategy and for the granting of directives to the Allied commanders in chief. Together with the Supreme Commander, Allied Expeditionary Force, and his chief subordinates they constituted the coalition command for the battle against Germany in northwest Europe.

Heads of Governments

The decisions of the Combined Chiefs of Staff reflected the views of the heads of the British and United States Governments who, with their cabinet advisers, determined major national policies and strategy. President Roosevelt and Prime Minister Churchill differed somewhat in the degree of direct control which they exercised over their chiefs of staff. The President, as Chief Executive of the United States and as Commander in Chief of its armed forces, attended the great conferences of the Allies and helped to determine

broad policy. On other occasions, as in the decision for the North African expedition in 1942, he intervened in the specific decisions of the U.S. Chiefs of Staff. He kept in touch with the members of this group through his own chief of staff, Admiral William D. Leahy, who presided over their meetings and acquainted them with the President's views. Having outlined the policy he thought the United States should follow, Mr. Roosevelt was usually content to recommend to Congress and to the Prime Minister the detailed military measures which had been worked out by the U.S. Chiefs of Staff. On political issues affecting military operations, such as the recognition of the French Committee of National Liberation[2] or the development of the formula of unconditional surrender, he often did not consult his military advisers or paid little attention to their advice. In such cases, the President had a habit of consulting individuals outside the cabinet, such as Mr. Hopkins, or heads of departments not directly concerned with military matters, such as Secretary of the Treasury Henry J. Morgenthau, Jr. This practice often left the Secretaries of War and Navy and the U.S. Chiefs of Staff without the

---

[1] Maurice Matloff and Edwin M. Snell, *Strategic Planning for Coalition Warfare, 1941–42*, UNITED STATES ARMY IN WORLD WAR II (Washington, 1953), discusses the Allied command structure at some length.

[2] See below, pp. 140–52.

information on his policy they found necessary for their own decisions.[3]

Mr. Churchill, as leader of his party in the House of Commons, as Minister of Defence, and as head of the War Cabinet, had constitutional responsibilities to the British Parliament which required a closer connection than Mr. Roosevelt's with the conduct of operations. As Minister of Defence, Churchill was linked to the British Chiefs of Staff Committee through Gen. Sir Hastings L. Ismay, his chief of staff, who regularly attended meetings of the British Chiefs. In addition, the Prime Minister himself frequently attended these sessions. It was the practice of Mr. Churchill, both because of his long-time interest in operational details and because of the British view that control must be maintained over commanders down to very low echelons, to keep much closer contact with field commanders than did President Roosevelt. In response to the Prime Minister's frequent demands for battle information, the various British commanders followed the practice of making reports direct to London. While still in the Mediterranean theater, General Eisenhower criticized this practice as "the traditional and persistent intrusion of the British Chiefs of Staff into details of our operation—frequently delving into matters which the Americans leave to their Field Commanders." He described this type of activity on another occasion as "the inevitable trend of the British mind towards 'committee' rather than 'single command.'" Efforts by the U.S. Chiefs of Staff to restrict this kind of close control brought a protest from Churchill. The Prime Minister held that, whereas such aloofness looked simple from a distance and appealed to the American sense of logic, it was not sufficient for a government

to give a General a directive to beat the enemy and wait to see what happens. The matter is much more complicated. The General may well be below the level of his task, and has often been found so. A definite measure of guidance and control is required from staffs and from the high Government authorities. It would not be in accordance with the British point of view that any such element should be ruled out.

So strong was Mr. Churchill's view on the subject of direct reports that Eisenhower on coming to the United Kingdom in January 1944 signified his willingness to permit British commanders to continue the practice if the Prime Minister so desired.[4]

Combined Chiefs of Staff

The permanent machinery through which Great Britain and the United States conducted the high-level control of the war—the Combined Chiefs of Staff—had been established in Washington in January 1942. Its task was to formulate and execute, under the direction of the heads of the countries concerned, policies and plans relating to the strategic conduct of the war, allocation of munitions, broad war requirements, and transportation requirements. *(Chart 1)* As it had developed by January 1944, the organization consisted of the U.S. Chiefs of Staff and the British Chiefs of Staff or their designated representatives in Washington (British

---

[3] Ray S. Cline, *Washington Command Post: The Operations Division*, UNITED STATES ARMY IN WORLD WAR II (Washington, 1951).

[4] Eisenhower's views on British practice are contained in a statement in Diary Office CinC, 16 Sep 43, and in Ltr, Eisenhower to Marshall, 8 Feb 43, Eisenhower personal file. Churchill to Br COS, 24 Oct 43, SHAEF SGS 322.011/1 Comd and Control for Opn OVERLORD. Speech, Eisenhower to his stf, 21 Jan 44, Min of SAC's Confs.

CHART 1—ALLIED ORGANIZATION FOR COMBINED OPERATIONS, 24 MAY 1944

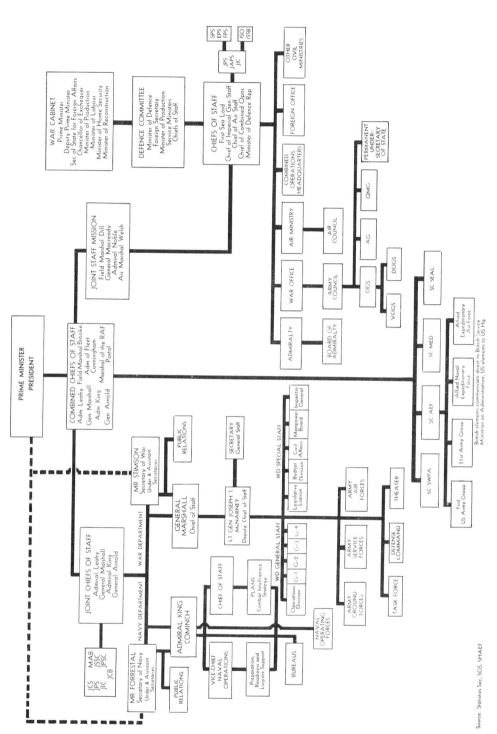

Source: Statistics Sec, SGS, SHAEF

Joint Staff Mission).[5] After mid-1942, the United States was represented by Admiral Leahy, General Marshall, Admiral Ernest J. King, Commander in Chief, U.S. Fleet, and Chief of Naval Operations,[6] and Gen. Henry H. Arnold, Commanding General, Army Air Forces. Their British opposite numbers, the Chiefs of Staff Committee, consisted of Field Marshal Sir Alan Brooke, Chief of the Imperial General Staff, Admiral of the Fleet Sir Dudley Pound (later replaced by Admiral of the Fleet Sir Andrew B. Cunningham), First Sea Lord, and Air Chief Marshal Sir Charles Portal, Chief of the Air Staff. General Ismay attended the meetings, but did not sit as a member.

In the course of the war, conferences of the Combined Chiefs of Staff were held with the President and the Prime Minister at Casablanca (SYMBOL), January 1943; Washington (TRIDENT), May 1943; Quebec (QUADRANT), August 1943; Cairo (SEXTANT)–Tehran (EUREKA), November–December 1943; Quebec (OCTAGON), September 1944; Yalta (ARGONAUT), February 1945; and Potsdam (TERMINAL), July 1945.[7]

Normally the decisions of the Combined Chiefs of Staff were made in Washington in periodic meetings of the U.S. Chiefs of Staff and the British Joint Staff Mission. Field Marshal Sir John Dill sat on the Combined Chiefs of Staff as a representative of the Minister of Defence (Mr. Churchill), and officers of the three services represented the British Chiefs of Staff.[8] The British Chiefs of Staff in London generally made their views known in cables to Field Marshal Dill, who then outlined their proposals in meetings of the Combined Chiefs of Staff. Frequently he discussed the British plans directly with General Marshall before the British views

were taken up formally in the meetings. Because of the close relationship which existed between the two men, it was often possible for Field Marshal Dill to iron out differences of opinion before the Combined Chiefs of Staff considered them formally. The ease of settling problems with Dill was probably responsible in part for Marshall's desire to centralize Combined Chiefs of Staff activities in Washington. The British, finding it much easier to settle matters with the COSSAC chief (and later with the Supreme Commander) and with other U.S. representatives in London, preferred, as the time for invasion approached, to transfer an increasing number of Combined Chiefs of Staff functions

---

[5] Gordon A. Harrison, *Cross-Channel Attack*, UNITED STATES ARMY IN WORLD WAR II (Washington, 1951), Ch. I, has an account of the development of this organization.

[6] Initially Admiral Harold R. Stark, as Chief of Naval Operations, and Admiral King, as Commander in Chief, U.S. Fleet, were both members of the U.S. Joint Chiefs of Staff. The offices held by Stark and King were combined in March 1942 and given to Admiral King. Stark went to London as Commander, U.S. Naval Forces in Europe.

[7] The official records of the conferences used the code words instead of place names for the conferences, while the press referred to place names. To avoid confusion place names are used throughout this volume except in the citation of documents or in direct quotations. ARCADIA—the conference that established the Combined Chiefs of Staff—was actually the first formal meeting of the President, Prime Minister, and the British and U.S. Chiefs of Staff. It was held December 1941–January 1942.

[8] Field Marshal Dill died in November 1944 and was replaced by Field Marshal Sir Henry Maitland Wilson. The original members of the Joint Staff Mission in Washington were Lt. Gen. Sir Colville Weymss, head of the British Army Staff; Air Chief Marshal Sir Arthur T. Harris, head of the Air Staff; and Admiral Sir Charles Little, head of the British Admiralty Delegation. Later changes were as follows: Maj. Gen. R. H. Dewing (March 1942), replaced in June 1942 by Lt. Gen. G. N. Macready; Admiral Cunningham (June 1942), replaced in December 1942 by Admiral Sir Percy Noble; Air Vice Marshal D. C. S. Evill (February 1942), replaced in June 1943 by Air Marshal Sir William Welsh.

CONFERENCE AT QUEBEC. *Present at this meeting in August 1943 were (seated, left to right) Prime Minister Mackenzie King, President Roosevelt, and Prime Minister Churchill and (standing) General Arnold, Air Chief Marshal Portal, Field Marshal Brooke, Admiral King, Field Marshal Dill, General Marshall, Admiral Pound, and Admiral Leahy.*

to the British capital. This preference and interest may have influenced their willingness to have General Marshall as Supreme Commander and may have led them to withdraw any initial opposition they had to strong powers for the Supreme Commander of Operation OVERLORD.

In issuing directives to the supreme commanders, the Combined Chiefs usually acted through the Chiefs of Staff of the country that provided the commander. The U.S. Chiefs of Staff, in turn, gave this task to the chief of the service that had supplied the commander. In the case of General Eisenhower, therefore, the wishes of the Combined Chiefs of Staff and the U.S. Chiefs of Staff were formally communicated by General Marshall. The Su-

preme Commander sent his messages to the Combined Chiefs of Staff through the same channel. There were some exceptions, however, to the use of normal channels. In initiating proposals on which it was believed that the Supreme Commander's recommendations would be required, the British Chiefs of Staff frequently sent copies of their proposals directly to Eisenhower and asked him to inform the U.S. Chiefs of Staff of his views. As a result he was sometimes able to have his recommendations in Washington by the time the British cable arrived. The U.S. Chiefs of Staff sometimes shortened the time necessary for decisions by permitting General Eisenhower to represent them in discussions with the British in London.

They did not like to resort to this device too often, however, lest the Supreme Commander be influenced unduly by the views of the British Chiefs of Staff. On several occasions Marshall warned Eisenhower against acquiring a one-sided view of Anglo-American questions, and once, at least, asked the British Chiefs of Staff not to put their views before the Supreme Commander before the matter was discussed by the Combined Chiefs of Staff in Washington.

Inasmuch as orders to General Eisenhower from the Combined Chiefs of Staff and the U.S. Chiefs of Staff were channeled through the War Department, it was possible for General Marshall to maintain a close relationship with the Supreme Commander and to keep the United States point of view constantly before him. This influence was balanced to a considerable degree by the frequent personal meetings between the Supreme Commander and the key British leaders, including General Eisenhower's attendance at some meetings of the British Chiefs of Staff. Eisenhower made it a practice to lunch weekly with the Prime Minister and often brought General Smith, Lt. Gen. Omar N. Bradley, or some other American leader with him. Even after Supreme Headquarters was moved to France, the Prime Minister and the Chief of the Imperial General Staff kept in telephonic contact with the Supreme Commander and visited him several times at his headquarters.

The Supreme Commander and His Subordinates

Principle of Unity
of Command

Two years before General Eisenhower took his new post, the British and U.S.
Chiefs of Staff had agreed that one Allied commander should have supreme command in each theater of operations. This decision had followed General Marshall's strong plea for unified command. Pointing out that problems then being settled by the U.S. and British Chiefs of Staff would recur unless settled in a broader way, Marshall asked that one officer command the air, ground, and naval forces in each theater. He added that the Allies had come to this conclusion late in World War I but only after the needless sacrifice of "much valuable time, blood and treasure. . . ." Mr. Churchill had opposed this principle for the Pacific, where the various forces would be separated by great distances, and had suggested instead individual commanders who would be responsible to the Supreme Command in Washington. After some discussion, however, Marshall's views were accepted. A few days later, the Combined Chiefs of Staff named their first supreme commander—Gen. Sir Archibald P. Wavell—to command the air, ground, and sea forces of Australia, Great Britain, the United States, and the Netherlands in the Southwest Pacific. Although the need for this particular command disappeared almost as soon as it was formed, the principle was maintained, and other supreme commanders were chosen for areas of the Pacific, Middle East, Mediterranean, and European theaters.[9]

General Eisenhower gained his first experience with the supreme commander principle as Allied commander in chief in the Mediterranean area. Here he discovered that British and United States concepts of the role of the supreme commander differed on the degree of control

---

[9] Sherwood, *Roosevelt and Hopkins*, pp. 455–57; Harrison, *Cross-Channel Attack*, p. 106.

the Allied commander in chief was to be given over troops of nationality other than his own. Later, in the European theater, he discovered that considerable differences also existed as to the operational control which a supreme commander was expected to exercise over the air, land, and sea forces under his command.

Eisenhower approached his problem in the Mediterranean theater with the intention of escaping the practice of the past in which "unity of command" had been a "pious aspiration thinly disguising the national jealousies, ambitions and recriminations of high-ranking officers, unwilling to subordinate themselves or their forces to a commander of different nationality or different service." [10] He wished to escape these problems by developing an integrated command in which British and American officers were intermingled in each section of his headquarters. Under any organization of command, however, he discovered that he had to struggle against the influence of differing national points of view and a tradition of far looser alliances.

The British, with many years of experience in coalition warfare, followed an older concept of allied command when, in 1943, they drew up their instructions placing Lt. Gen. K. A. N. Anderson, commander of the First British Army in North Africa, under General Eisenhower's command. Copying the directives given to Field Marshal Douglas Haig in World War I and to British commanders in World War II, when they were placed under commanders of a different nationality, the British Chiefs of Staff declared: "If any order given by him [the Allied Commander in Chief] appears to you to imperil any British troops in the Allied Force even

though they may not be under your direct command, it is agreed between the British and United States governments that you will be at liberty to appeal to the War Office before the order is executed." [11] Following a principle which he was to emphasize throughout his service as an Allied commander, General Eisenhower asked Prime Minister Churchill and the British Chiefs of Staff for a directive stressing the unity of the Allied forces. He contended that they were "undertaking a single, unified effort in pursuit of a common object stated by the two governments; and that for attainment of this object our sole endeavor must be to use every resource and effort for the common good." The British acceded to this request. They revised General Anderson's instructions to say that, in the unlikely event he should be given an order which would give rise to a grave and exceptional situation, he had a right to appeal to the War Office, "provided that by so doing an opportunity is not lost nor any part of the Allied Force endangered. You will, however, first inform the Allied Commander in Chief that you intend so to appeal and you will give him your reasons." This was satisfactory to Eisenhower, who sent a copy to the War Department as a useful model "in future cases of this kind." [12]

---

[10] CinC Dispatch, North African Campaign, MS, p. 1, OCMH files.

[11] Annex, Ltr, Stirling to Eisenhower, 8 Oct 42, SGS AFHQ 381–2, quoted in History of AFHQ, August–December 1942, 1945, MS, OCMH files.

[12] For exchange of correspondence, see entry for 9 October 1942 in Diary Office CinC. General Ismay informed the author on 20 December 1947 that he recalled no similar instructions being issued Montgomery in 1944. Something like the "model" instructions were later issued by the Joint Chiefs of Staff to Lt. Gen. Joseph T. McNarney when he assumed command of U.S. Forces in the Mediterranean theater.

Control by the Supreme Commander

In the course of planning for the cross-Channel operation, the British and U.S. Chiefs of Staff differed over the degree of control the Supreme Commander should exercise over operations. The British, accustomed to a committee type of joint command in which no service had over-all control, favored a plan which gave broad powers to the land, sea, and air commanders under the Supreme Commander. Under this system, the Allied commander in chief became a chairman of a board rather than a true commander. The U.S. Chiefs of Staff opposed the British suggestions as "destructive in efficiency in that none of them provide for an absolute unity of command by the Supreme Commander over all elements land, air and naval. . . ." [13]

Illustrative of the British views was a Royal Air Force suggestion that the staff of the Supreme Commander concern itself primarily with inter-Allied issues which would be largely political. Under the Supreme Commander three Allied commanders in chief would implement all broad decisions through their staffs, each of which would be organized on a combined basis. [14]

The matter of command was brought to a head in the summer and fall of 1943 when General Morgan pressed for an agreement on the ground command in the assault and for a directive to the Allied tactical air force commander. In the initial outline of the OVERLORD plan, the COSSAC chief recommended that the Allied forces in the initial assault be under a British army commander and that the Allied ground forces be under a British army group commander until the Brest peninsula had been taken or a U.S. army

group had been established on the Continent, whichever development came first. [15]

Lt. Gen. Jacob L. Devers, the U.S. theater commander, in early September took exception to the Morgan proposal. He felt that it would put units smaller than a corps under direct British command and would deprive the Supreme Commander of operational control in the early stages of the assault. [16] He suggested instead that separate U.S. and British zones of action be established with all U.S. forces, land, sea, and air, under a single U.S. commander, and that both Allied forces be directed and controlled as self-sufficient units by the Supreme Commander. His proposal for close co-ordination of the initial assault by the advanced headquarters of SHAEF was considered unsound by the COSSAC staff members who held that Supreme Headquarters was a strategic and

---

[13] Br COS Memo, CCS 75, 5 Jun 42; JCS Memo, CCS 75/1, 26 Aug 42.

[14] RAF Note on Comd Organization, 16 Apr 43, SHAEF SGS 322 Comd and Control of Allied Air Forces. It should be noted that at a time when it appeared that a British commander would lead the cross-Channel forces, U.S. military leaders had suggested proposals somewhat like those recommended by the British. For example, Eisenhower, in the Operations Division of the War Department in May 1942, had suggested something like the system discussed above. See Eisenhower proposals, 11 May 42, CofS file, BOLERO 381.

[15] Appreciation of Opn OVERLORD Plan, Sec. 40, Pt. I, SHAEF SGS 381 Opn OVERLORD, I(a). Morgan's proposals included three other principles which were to be accepted: (1) British-Canadian forces should be based on ports nearest the United Kingdom to simplify lines of communications, since it was assumed that U.S. forces would ultimately be supplied direct from the U.S. and would need to be on the western side of the attack; (2) normally no formation smaller than a corps should be placed under command of another nationality; and (3) troops of both nationalities should take part in the assault.

[16] The initial COSSAC plan for OVERLORD called for one U.S. and three British divisions in the assault under a British army commander.

not a tactical command. They felt it unorthodox to cut out army group and army headquarters, and saw no place where the Supreme Commander could go forward to direct the battle in the early phases and still be in touch with the Allied governments.[17]

The British Chiefs of Staff on 11 September 1943 gave their backing to the COSSAC command proposals and asked the U.S. Chiefs of Staff for their comments. The American answer had not been delivered when, on 12 October, the British pointed to the need of integrating U.S. and British tactical air forces under an Allied tactical air commander and submitted a draft directive for U.S. approval. A week later, the U.S. Chiefs of Staff declared that "the issuance by the Combined Chiefs of Staff of directives to subordinates of the Supreme Allied Commander is unsound." They made clear that the earlier proposal to specify the nature of the ground organization was an encroachment on the powers of the Supreme Commander.[18]

Attempting to get an early solution to the ground and air command questions,[19] General Morgan discussed the problems with General Marshall in Washington in late October and early November 1943.[20] The COSSAC chief found that the U.S. Army Chief of Staff thought that "he should in some way control the assaulting army although I am quite certain that his conception falls far short of what we understand by the term 'command.'" The deputy chief of COSSAC, Brig. Gen. Ray W. Barker, pointed out that while the initial assault had to be commanded by an army commander, who would be succeeded by an army group commander about D plus 6, the Supreme Command "could and would intervene at any time"

the situation seemed to warrant such action. This procedure, he noted, had been followed at Salerno when Generals Eisenhower and Alexander had taken a hand in the battle, the former ordering the whole weight of naval and air forces into the action. In the assault stages of the cross-Channel operation, it would again be the air and sea forces that the Supreme Command would employ to influence the course of the battle. General Barker proposed that complete telephonic, telegraphic, and radio contact be provided with forward units, so that the Supreme Commander could be in the closest touch with the battle and could intervene quickly if the necessity arose. General Morgan approved this suggestion and indicated that he would tell General Marshall that arrangements would be made for him to participate directly in the battle when it took place.[21]

Discussions of the British draft directive for the tactical air forces were expanded in November to include the strategic air forces as well. The U.S. Chiefs of Staff proposed at that time to set up an Allied Strategic Air Force that would include British and U.S. strategic forces in both

---

[17] Draft Ltr (unsigned), Devers to Morgan, 4 Sep 44; Comments of COSSAC staff on Devers' letter, undated; Memo on Devers' letter, 10 Sep 43. All in SHAEF SGS 322.011/1 Comd and Control for OVERLORD. Morgan to Devers, 16 Sep 43, ABC (22 Jan 43), Sec 1.

[18] CCS 304/2, 304/3, and 304/4, 12 and 19 Oct 43.

[19] The naval command question, which was left largely to the British, was not as difficult as the other two. This was true chiefly because of the assumption until shortly before D Day that the British would furnish nearly all the naval support for the assault.

[20] It should be remembered that at this time it was generally believed that Marshall would command the OVERLORD operation.

[21] Morgan to Barker, 28 Oct 43; Barker to Morgan, 3 Nov 43; Morgan to Barker, 6 Nov 43. All in Barker personal file.

the European and Mediterranean theaters. General Marshall, holding that a committee could not fight the war, wanted part or all of the strategic air forces, as well as the tactical air forces, put under the Supreme Commander. The British Chiefs of Staff, while willing to let the Supreme Commander control those strategic air forces in support of his operations once the cross-Channel attack began, wanted to retain full control of their RAF Bomber Command. In their opinion, this organization was so highly specialized and so firmly rooted in the United Kingdom that "effective operational control could only be exercised through Bomber Command headquarters." [22]

The Combined Chiefs of Staff ultimately decided that they would have to postpone a decision on the strategic air forces and approve a directive concerning tactical forces only. Perhaps to preserve the shadow of the Supreme Commander's right to issue directives to his subordinates, the Combined Chiefs of Staff permitted General Morgan to issue in the name of the Supreme Commander the directive to the Commander-in-Chief, Allied Expeditionary Air Force. [23]

The matter of the ground command was also settled temporarily during November. When General Morgan returned to London from Washington in that month, he carried with him Marshall's views on the organization of the ground forces for the assault. Near the end of November the COSSAC chief discussed the matter with the Allied naval and air commanders and shortly thereafter, acting in the name of the Supreme Allied Command, issued a directive to the 21 Army Group commander. This officer, then General Paget, was made jointly responsible with the Commander, Allied Naval Expeditionary Force, and the Commander, Allied Expeditionary Air Force, for planning the assault. When so ordered, he was also to be responsible for its execution "until such time as the Supreme Allied Commander allocates an area of responsibility to the Commanding General, First Army Group." The 21 Army Group commander was informed that the assault would be made by two corps under the Commanding General, First U.S. Army, who would remain in charge of land operations until such time as the British commander felt that a second army headquarters should be brought in. [24]

Later when the enlargement of the assault force and the area to be attacked required the landing of two armies instead of two corps, the 21 Army Group commander was charged with the task of commanding land operations. [25] He was thus made *de facto* commander of the ground forces in the assault but was never given the title of ground commander. Further, while his tenure in this temporary position was not made clear, it was certain that the arrangement could be changed when the Supreme Commander so decided.

The Organization of the Subordinate Commands

While the question of the Supreme Commander's control over operations was

---

[22] CCS 124th and 126th Mtgs, 22 Oct and 5 Nov 43; JSM to Br COS, 6 Nov 43. Both in SHAEF SGS 322.011/2 Dirs to Subordinate Comdrs.

[23] Marshall to Devers, R–5874, 18 Nov 43, Hq SOS file, gives text of agreement of CCS on directives to Leigh-Mallory. Morgan Dir to Leigh-Mallory, 16 Nov 43, SHAEF SGS 322.011/3 Summary of Dirs.

[24] Mtg of comdrs, 25 Nov 43, SHAEF SGS 322.011/2 Dirs to Subordinate Comdrs; COSSAC Dirs to CinC 21 A Gp, 29 Nov 43, SHAEF SGS 322.011/1 Comd and Control for Opn OVERLORD.

[25] See below, pp. 180–81.

AIR CHIEF MARSHAL LEIGH-
MALLORY

at that time instructed Admiral Stark, chief of U.S. Naval Forces in Europe, to supplement the efforts of the U.S. member of the Naval Planning Branch of COSSAC. The Combined Chiefs of Staff at the Quebec Conference in August 1943 regularized the naval arrangement by naming Admiral Little as Allied Naval Commander-in-Chief (Designate) for the OVERLORD operation. The selection was

ADMIRAL RAMSAY

being considered, the subordinate commands were being organized and their commanders were being selected. The easiest problem to solve was that of the naval command. On the assumption that the Royal Navy would furnish most of the naval forces for the OVERLORD operation, the Admiralty in May 1943, shortly after the organization of COSSAC, had directed Admiral Sir Charles Little, Commander-in-Chief, Portsmouth, to proceed with naval planning for the cross-Channel operation and instructed him to increase his staff sufficiently to aid COSSAC in its work. By the summer of 1943, it was clear that some U.S. naval forces would have to be added to the attack, but that the British effort was still paramount. Admiral King

temporary since Mr. Churchill, who had Admiral Sir Bertram H. Ramsay in mind for the post, accepted it only on condition that it be reviewed later. On 25 October 1943, Admiral Ramsay, who had organized the British naval forces for the withdrawal at Dunkerque and had later commanded task forces in the Mediterranean, was selected as Allied Naval Commander.[26]

Rear Adm. Alan G. Kirk, former Chief of Naval Intelligence in Washington and later Commander, Amphibious Force, Atlantic Fleet, in the fall of 1943 was made commander of U.S. naval forces for the cross-Channel attack. In this capacity he had operational control of all U.S. naval forces in Europe except those in the south

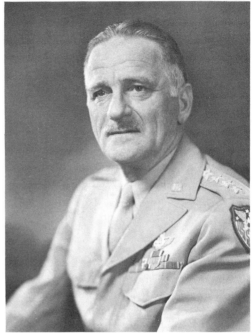

GENERAL SPAATZ. *(Photograph taken in 1946.)*

GENERAL BRERETON

of France. Administratively the elements under Kirk were controlled by Admiral Stark's headquarters in London. Operational control of the U.S. forces to be used in the cross-Channel attack was given Admiral Ramsay on 1 April 1944.[27] French naval forces taking part in the attack were attached to Admiral Kirk's force by Ad-

miral Thierry d'Argenlieu, commander of the French Navy, and were organized into a cruiser division under Rear Adm. Robert Jaujard. In January 1944, Admiral Ramsay named Admiral Kirk as commander of the Western Task Force and Rear Adm. Sir Philip L. Vian as commander of the Eastern Task Force for the D-Day assault.[28]

[26] Mr. Churchill's surprise at the British proposal of Admiral Little and his reservations are noted in Quebec Conf Min, 23 Aug 43. Ltr, H. N. Morrison to Admiral Ramsay, 4 Nov 43, SHAEF SGS 322 Organization and Personnel ANCXF.

[27] CinC U.S. Fleet and CNO to Comdr U.S. Forces, Europe, 29 Oct 43, SHAEF SGS 322.011/2 Dirs to Subordinate Comdrs.

[28] Dir, Admiral Ramsay to Naval Comdr, Western Task Force, 31 Jan 44; Dir, Admiral Ramsay to Naval Comdr, Eastern Task Force, 18 Jan 44. Both in SHAEF SGS 322.011/2 Dirs to Subordinate Comdrs.

Efforts to organize the Allied tactical air command for OVERLORD had begun in the spring of 1943 when Air Chief Marshal Portal proposed that Air Marshal Sir Trafford Leigh-Mallory, head of the RAF Fighter Command, be considered for the post of Commander, Allied Expeditionary Air Force.[29] Portal suggested that, in case the Allies were unwilling to make a final decision at the time, they direct Leigh-Mallory to give advice on tactical air planning without prejudice to the eventual appointment of someone else. On receiving a favorable reaction to this proposal from General Devers, the U.S. Chiefs of Staff agreed to Portal's plan and the British Chiefs of Staff issued appropriate orders to Leigh-Mallory in late June 1943. At Quebec the following August, the Combined Chiefs of Staff named Air Chief Marshal Leigh-Mallory as commander of the Allied Expeditionary Air Force for the cross-Channel operation.[30]

Under the terms of the directive that Leigh-Mallory received in mid-November 1943, the RAF Tactical Air Force and air units which might be allotted the Air Defence of Great Britain[31] were to pass to the Allied Expeditionary Air Force immediately, and the Ninth U.S. Air Force on 15 December 1943. The U.S. force, commanded by Maj. Gen. Lewis H. Brereton, had been brought to the United Kingdom in September 1943. It included all U.S. tactical air forces in the United Kingdom. Administrative control over Ninth Air Force training, supply, and personnel remained in the hands of the main U.S. air headquarters in the United Kingdom, United States Strategic Air Forces (USSTAF).[32]

U.S. proposals for the consolidation of U.S. and British strategic air forces in the European and Mediterranean theaters under the Supreme Commander—presented without success in Washington in the fall of 1943—were again brought forward at the Cairo Conference. The British objected to the over-all command, but reluctantly agreed to support any administrative arrangement the United States wished to make for its strategic air forces in the Mediterranean and the European theaters. The U.S. Chiefs of Staff at the close of the Cairo Conference ordered the establishment of the U.S. Strategic Air Forces in Europe. Lt. Gen. Carl Spaatz, commander of the U.S. air forces in the Mediterranean and of the Northwest African Air Forces, was named chief of the new headquarters. He was given operational control of the Eighth Air Force in the United Kingdom and the Fifteenth Air Force in the Mediterranean, and administrative control of the Eighth and Ninth Air Forces. Spaatz's control was subject to two restrictions: the Chief of the Air Staff, RAF, representing the Com-

---

[29] Before this time the U.S. strategic air forces sent to the United Kingdom for participation in the POINTBLANK operation against Germany in 1943 were placed, along with RAF Bomber Command, under the strategic direction of Air Chief Marshal Portal, who acted as agent of the Combined Chiefs of Staff.

[30] Portal to Devers, 16 Jun 43; Maj Gen Ira C. Eaker to Devers, 17 Jun 43; Devers to Portal, 19 Jun 43. All in AG Active Records Branch 312.1 Devers Correspondence (1943). Portal's proposal to Br COS, COS (43) 125th Mtg, 16 Jun 43, SHAEF SGS 322.011/2 Dirs to Subordinate Comdrs; CCS 113th Mtg, 20 Aug 43, Quebec Conf Min.

[31] Air Defence of Great Britain replaced Fighter Command in spring of 1944. (Leigh-Mallory was directly responsible to the British Chiefs of Staff for the Air Defence of Great Britain until such time as his headquarters moved overseas when separate arrangements were to be made.) In October 1944 Fighter Command was revived. *Journal of the Royal United Service Institution,* XC, February 1945.

[32] Marshall to Devers, R–5874, 18 Nov 43, Hq SOS file, gives text of agreement of CCS on directives to Leigh-Mallory. Dir, Morgan to Leigh-Mallory, 16 Nov 43, SHAEF SGS 322.011/3 Summary of Dirs.

bined Chiefs of Staff, was to co-ordinate bomber forces in Operation POINTBLANK, the Combined Bomber Offensive; the U.S. theater commanders in case of necessity could declare a state of emergency and make such use of strategic air forces as they found necessary at the time.[33]

As no agreement was reached in the summer or fall of 1943 on the selection of a ground force commander comparable in authority to the Allied naval and air force commanders, it became clear that the assignment would be likely to devolve on an Allied army group or army commander as a temporary appointment during the assault phase. The British had a claim on this post, not only because the initial assaults were to be made from Britain, but because they had both an army group and an army headquarters organized and available to start assault planning by the time the COSSAC plan was drawn up.[34] General Morgan and General Devers urged in the summer of 1943 that the United States establish similar headquarters in the United Kingdom, but not until October were the 1st U.S. Army Group and First U.S. Army activated.

General Paget was selected as the first commander of 21 Army Group. When it became apparent that this headquarters would command the Allied forces in the assault, it became necessary to place an officer recently seasoned in combat at its head. For this post the Prime Minister and the Chief of the Imperial General Staff chose General Montgomery, who had led the Eighth British Army to victory in Africa, in Sicily, and in Italy. His appointment was announced on Christmas Day, 1943. General Eisenhower was not consulted officially on this selection, inasmuch as it was one solely for the British to make. He had earlier expressed a preference for

Gen. Sir Harold R. L. G. Alexander, who had served as Allied army group commander in Italy, but was told that the officer could not be spared from the Mediterranean theater.[35]

In selecting the commander of Second British Army, General Montgomery turned to the Mediterranean theater and gave his backing to Lt. Gen. Miles C. Dempsey, who had commanded a corps in Italy in Montgomery's army. Early in 1944, Gen. Henry D. G. Crerar, who was commanding a Canadian corps in Italy, was appointed commander of the First Canadian Army.

The command of both the 1st U.S. Army Group and the First U.S. Army was given temporarily in the fall of 1943 to General Bradley. Separate headquarters were organized, the army at Clifton College, Bristol, and the army group at Bryanston Square, London.[36]

The Supreme Commander's Directive

General Eisenhower assumed command of the Allied forces in mid-January 1944, but did not receive a directive until nearly a month later. A draft had been submitted to the Combined Chiefs of Staff as early as 30 October 1943, but the failure of the U.S. and British Chiefs to agree on the exact powers of the Supreme Commander

---

[33] Wesley Frank Craven and James Lea Cate, eds., *The Army Air Forces in World War II: II, Europe— TORCH to POINTBLANK, August 1942 to December 1943* (Chicago 1949), pp. 751–56.

[34] 21 Army Group, Second British Army, and Headquarters, First Canadian Army, were all activated in the summer of 1943.

[35] Eisenhower, *Crusade in Europe*, p. 211; Ltr, Eisenhower to Marshall, 24 Aug 43, Eisenhower personal file.

[36] Omar N. Bradley, *A Soldier's Story* (New York, 1951), Ch. I. It is clear that General Bradley was the first choice of both General Marshall and General Eisenhower for this post.

GENERAL BRADLEY. *(Photograph taken in 1950.)*

or the precise objectives to be assigned resulted, as in the case of Air Chief Marshal Leigh-Mallory's directive, in a long delay.

The obstacles to agreement on these and other points lay in differences of policy which had existed between the British and U.S. leaders since 1942. On the chief point—that the main effort of the Western Allies should be exerted against Germany—there was no dispute. On the manner in which that aim was to be achieved there was less agreement. The differences had their origins in the national interests of the United States and Great Britain, in their past history, and in the political philosophy of their leaders. If these elements are taken into account, it becomes clear that the controversies which sometimes marked the meetings of the Combined Chiefs of Staff were not personal quarrels growing out of individual ambitions or bias or pique. Nor were they based on national antipathies, though the discussions were sharpened at times by clashes of temperament and personality and by differences of national interests. Rather they reflected the fact that allies, like the different armed services of a nation, can agree thoroughly on the big issue of war and yet have entirely opposite con-

GENERAL MONTGOMERY

cepts of the way in which the main object is to be reached. A failure to understand this fact could reduce the story of this great allied coalition, perhaps the most successful in history, to a study in personal and national recriminations.

In the making of Allied grand strategy, the selection of a Supreme Commander, and the writing of his directive, the Allies often disagreed as to the best way to overcome Germany. The United States, believing that only a power drive to the heart of the Continent would defeat the enemy quickly, chose the cross-Channel operation as the speediest and least costly of lives in the long run. The British, in the light of heavy commitments around the world and their doubts of the wisdom of a direct attack on enemy fortifications in northwest Europe, preferred to approach the enemy

GENERAL CRERAR

by flanking movements in the Mediterranean theater.

There was, of course, more to the matter than this. The United States in its desire to end the war in Europe quickly was motivated in large part by the fact that there were strong demands in the United States for greater pressure against Japan. The Navy in particular was reluctant to

GENERAL DEMPSEY

take additional forces from the Pacific for operations which seemed not to affect directly the war against Germany. There was also the suspicion that the British had long-range interests in the Mediterranean area which were no affair of the United States, and that U.S. resources should not be diverted from the principal operation to any enterprise which was not specifically a part of the main offensive against the enemy.

To the British, the attack in the Mediterranean was the best way of fighting the Germans, with the additional virtue of aiding British interests. It appeared, at times, that the Americans were not being completely realistic in their planning, and a note of asperity sometimes crept into the arguments of the British planners when they concluded that the Americans on the ground of eschewing politics were urging a strategy that would prove costly in men and matériel. Some British representatives also had the feeling that the United States was not thoroughly aware of all the political and strategic implications involved in a European war. As a result, particularly in the first months after the Japanese attack at Pearl Harbor, there was a tendency for the British to attempt to instruct the U.S. representatives in the proper forms of strategy. This created the impression in some quarters that the British were trying to control Allied operations. As a counteraction to this, the American representatives sought to control or have an equal share in the management of operations which involved large numbers of U.S. troops.

In describing the mission and outlining the powers of the Supreme Allied Commander, the British Chiefs of Staff were aware that the Allied commander in chief would come from the U.S. Army. Since this fact could give additional weight to U.S. views on operations, the British desired to delimit in precise terms the nature of the Supreme Commander's task, and to broaden the powers of the chief air, ground, and sea commanders, most or all of whom would be British. The U.S. Chiefs of Staff preferred to write the directive in broad terms and limit the powers of the subordinate commanders. In their proposals, they suggested grants of authority to the Allied commander in chief over British and U.S. forces which the British Chiefs of Staff would have been unwilling to give one of their own commanders.

When on 5 January 1944 the British Chiefs of Staff submitted a draft directive enumerating the duties of the subordinate commanders in chief, General Morgan, who had earlier warned General Marshall

of the plan,[37] objected in particular to a listing of the powers of the ground force commander, which he believed would later cause embarrassment to the Supreme Commander. The COSSAC chief urged that this section of the draft directive be limited to a listing of land forces to be placed at the disposal of General Eisenhower, leaving him free to issue such directives to his army group commanders as he saw fit. The U.S. Chiefs of Staff suggested that the appendixes in the British plan dealing with Allied commanders be considered only as informational guidance for the Supreme Commander. After some discussion, the British Chiefs agreed to strike out these sections.[38] The way was thus left open for the Supreme Commander to develop his control over the forces put under his command without being hampered by restrictions. The Combined Chiefs of Staff did leave one important command question unanswered, however, when they postponed for later settlement the problem of what proportion of the Allied strategic air forces in Europe should be placed under the Supreme Commander.

The demarcation of the Supreme Commander's "task" in the directive constituted still another problem for the Com-

---

[37] General Morgan had written in November that the British Chiefs of Staff would soon submit a directive for the ground force commander which "prescribes a command relationship within a component element of the forces under the command of SAC [the Supreme Allied Commander] and assigns a mission to the commander of that element. This is considered to be an exclusive function of SAC." Morgan to Marshall, 18 Nov 43, SHAEF SGS 322.011/2 Dirs to Subordinate Comdrs.

[38] Br COS to JSM, 5 Jan 44; Morgan to Marshall for Eisenhower, 7 Jan 45. Both in SHAEF SGS 322.011 CCS Dir to SCAEF. A number of charts of proposals and counterproposals submitted by the U.S. and British Chiefs of Staff in January and February 1944 and correspondence containing the arguments and final decision may also be found in the above file.

bined Chiefs of Staff. The U.S. Chiefs of Staff held that the British had not gone far enough in their initial statement, "You will enter the Continent of Europe and undertake operations to secure lodgments from which further offensive action can be aimed at the heart of Germany." Fearful that the British might be trying to limit operations to establishment of a beachhead and a holding action, while the main operations went on elsewhere, the U.S. Chiefs of Staff insisted on a more positive order: "You shall enter the Continent . . . and undertake operations striking at the heart of Germany and destroy her forces." This bold declaration seemed unrealistic to the British in view of the fact that the available Allied force of forty divisions was obviously insufficient to overwhelm the German Army. Amendments were ultimately added to the American version, which retained the aim of the U.S. statement, while associating the forces of the United Nations in the operation. This revised draft was accepted by the Combined Chiefs of Staff on 11 February, and the final directive was issued on 12 February 1944.[39]

The Combined Chiefs of Staff directive to General Eisenhower declared:

1. You are hereby designated as Supreme Allied Commander of the forces placed under your orders for operations for the liberation of Europe from the Germans. Your title will be Supreme Commander, Allied Expeditionary Force.

2. *Task.* You will enter the continent of Europe, and, in conjunction with the other United Nations, undertake operations aimed at the heart of Germany and the destruction of her armed forces. The date for entering the Continent is the month of May 1944. After adequate channel ports have been secured, exploitation will be directed to securing an area that will facilitate both ground and air operations against the enemy.

3. Notwithstanding the target date above, you will be prepared at any time to take immediate advantage of favorable circumstances, such as the withdrawal by the enemy on your front, to effect a re-entry into the Continent with such forces as you have available at the time; a general plan for this operation when approved will be furnished for your assistance.

4. *Command.* You are responsible to the Combined Chiefs of Staff and will exercise command generally in accordance with the diagram at Appendix A. Direct communication with the United States and British Chiefs of Staff is authorized in the interest of facilitating your operations and for arranging necessary logistic support.

5. *Logistics.* In the United Kingdom the responsibility for logistics organization, concentration, movement and supply of forces to meet the requirements of your plan will rest with British Service Ministries so far as British Forces are concerned. So far as United States Forces are concerned, this responsibility will rest with the United States War and Navy Departments. You will be responsible for the co-ordination of logistical arrangements on the continent. You will also be responsible for co-ordinating the requirements of British and United States Forces under your command.

6. *Co-ordination of operations of other Forces and Agencies.* In preparation for your assault on enemy occupied Europe, Sea and Air Forces, agencies of sabotage, subversion and propaganda, acting under a variety of authorities, are now in action. You may recommend any variation in these activities which may seem to you desirable.

7. *Relationship to United Nations Forces in other areas.* Responsibility will rest with the Combined Chiefs of Staff for supplying information relating to operations of the forces of the U.S.S.R. for your guidance in timing your operations. It is understood that the Soviet forces will launch an offensive at about the same time as OVERLORD with the object of preventing the German forces from transferring from the Eastern to the Western front. The Allied Commander-in-Chief, Mediter-

---

[39] See entire file SHAEF SGS 322.011 CCS Dir to SCAEF.

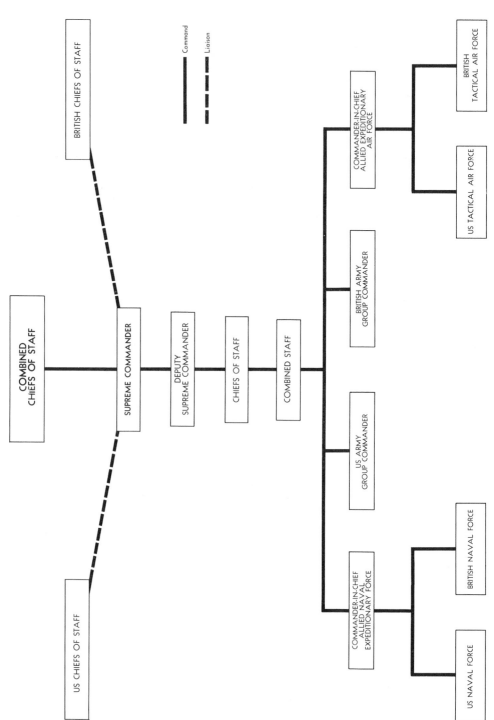

ranean Theater, will conduct operations designed to assist your operation, including the launching of an attack against the south of France at about the same time as OVERLORD. The scope and timing of his operations will be decided by the Combined Chiefs of Staff. You will establish contact with him and submit to the Combined Chiefs of Staff your views and recommendations regarding operations from the Mediterranean in support of your attack from the United Kingdom. The Combined Chiefs of Staff will place under your command the forces operating in Southern France as soon as you are in a position to assume such command. You will submit timely recommendations compatible with this regard.

8. *Relationship with Allied Governments—the re-establishment of Civil Governments and Liberated Allied Territories and the administration of Enemy Territories.* Further instructions will be issued to you on these subjects at a later date.

Under the provisions of this document, General Eisenhower, who had been functioning as Supreme Commander for nearly a month, assumed formal command of Supreme Headquarters, Allied Expeditionary Force, on 13 February, and on the following day announced the names of his principal staff officers.[40] *(Chart 2)*

The Supreme Commander had good reasons for being pleased with his directive. Stated in the most general terms, it left him great freedom in exercising command and in outlining the details of his operations against Germany. The restrictive features which might have reduced him to the position of a political chairman of allied forces or which would have narrowed the scope of his mission had been omitted. The greatest allied army in history had been placed under his control.

---

[40] The Supreme Commander's General Order 1, announcing assumption of Supreme Command effective at 1201, was dated 13 February 1944. General Order 2, listing appointments, is dated 14 February 1944.

CHAPTER III

The Nature of SHAEF

Supreme Headquarters, Allied Expeditionary Force, was formally established in London in mid-February 1944, but it had actually been in the process of development for more than two years. It drew its basic principles of organization and many of its key personnel from two headquarters which had been established many months before. One of these, Allied Force Headquarters (AFHQ), which had served as General Eisenhower's command post in the Mediterranean theater, had provided a laboratory for testing principles and procedures of the command and training of U.S. and British staffs in combined operations. The other, Headquarters, Chief of Staff to the Supreme Allied Commander (COSSAC), had been established in the spring of 1943 to plan the cross-Channel attack and to serve as the nucleus for the ultimate Supreme Headquarters.

Contributions of AFHQ

The importance of AFHQ's contribution to the SHAEF organization was expressed in General Eisenhower's postwar judgment that some of his key advisers in northwest Europe had learned "during the African campaigns, the art of dealing with large Allied forces, operating under single command." At AFHQ, General Eisenhower had developed an integrated command in which British or U.S. officers of a staff division could make decisions affecting forces of either nationality. Officers were carefully selected for their ability to fit into such a staff. Many of them, otherwise capable, were transferred when found unsuitable for such an assignment. The task, as Air Chief Marshal Sir Arthur W. Tedder, the Deputy Supreme Commander of SHAEF, later testified, involved "getting the right people and being ruthless . . . and you must be ruthless. . . . If a man does not fit he will never learn the language and you will never make a team; that is the guts of the whole thing, the team. . . ." [1] U.S. officers who were not wholly in accord with General Eisenhower's weeding-out process had a grim joke to the effect that the way to get sent back to the United States "by slow boat" was to say something insulting about a foreign officer of the headquarters. Others charged the British with using the complaint that certain officers were un-cooperative to rid the headquarters of United States officers who were aggressive in defending the American point of view. To General Eisenhower, the important thing was to establish a completely Allied headquarters. When he went to SHAEF he was able to take key advisers from AFHQ and be certain that he would have

---

[1] Address of Lt. Gen. W. B. Smith, "Problems of an Integrated Headquarters," *Journal of the Royal United Service Institution*, XC (November, 1945), 455–62, with statements by Lord Tedder; Eisenhower, *Crusade in Europe*, p. 134.

men who were thoroughly sold on Allied co-operation.

As Allied commander in chief in the Mediterranean theater, General Eisenhower learned the métier of Supreme Command and became familiar with most of the problems he later faced at SHAEF. Questions such as the recognition of a French political authority, the formulation of civil affairs and military government

GENERAL BARKER

GENERAL DEVERS. *(Photograph taken in 1946.)*

programs, the proper handling of press relations, the expansion of the psychological warfare program, and the establishment of air-ground co-operation all reappeared in the European Theater of Operations. Not only had the Supreme Commander been schooled in the techniques of approaching these problems, but

he trained a staff that was also familiar with them. Ultimately Allied Force Headquarters furnished SHAEF with the Supreme Commander, Deputy Supreme Commander, chief of staff, chief administrative officer, chief of intelligence, deputy chief of operations, deputy chief of civil affairs, chief of press relations, chief of the psychological warfare division, and adjutant general. The British Chiefs of Staff in filling key command and staff positions for the invasion of northern France also drew on the Mediterranean for a number of men acquainted with Eisenhower and his staff. This list included the chiefs of staff of the Allied Expeditionary Air Force and the Allied Naval Expeditionary Force; the commander of British land forces and his chief air commander; and the British army commander for the invasion. The

Canadian commander had also served in Italy. United States officers who had formerly served under General Eisenhower in the Mediterranean before coming to the United Kingdom included the chief of the United States Army Air Forces in Europe, the commander of the Eighth Air Force, and the commanders of the two U.S. armies listed for participation in the early phases of the attack.

Contributions of COSSAC

In many ways, Supreme Headquarters was a continuation of the COSSAC staff which had been organized in April 1943 along lines discussed by the Combined Chiefs of Staff in January 1943 at Casablanca and modified in March and April. General Morgan, as Chief of Staff to the Supreme Allied Commander (Designate), had been directed to prepare a diversionary plan with the object of pinning the enemy in the west and keeping alive the threat of a cross-Channel attack in 1943 (COCKADE), to plan a return to the Continent in the event of German disintegration (RANKIN), and to plan a full-scale assault on the Continent as early as possible in 1944 (OVERLORD).[2]

The COSSAC staff was developed throughout 1943 on the basis that it would serve ultimately as the staff of the Supreme Commander. Its chief and many of its members were taken into the SHAEF organization. It was thus possible not only to preserve but also to draw upon the ideas of early planning groups which had preceded COSSAC.

Before his appointment as COSSAC chief, General Morgan had recommended that a staff be formed immediately as "the nucleus of the eventual Allied GHQ in the field" and that it be prepared at the earliest moment to assume direction of all offensive enterprises initiated from the United Kingdom. He proposed to combine from the beginning all functions of planning and execution and to direct all future activity toward the defeat of the German Army. He desired complete amalgamation of the U.S. and British services in the machinery of the high command with the understanding that the ultimate issue would be decided by the Allied strategic reserve of land forces, "namely the American army."[3]

General Morgan set up his staff in London at Norfolk House, St. James's Square, built on the site of the birthplace of George III of England. With the aid of his U.S. deputy, Maj. Gen. Ray W. Barker, the COSSAC chief began to select the future SHAEF staff and to outline the operations which the future Supreme Commander was to carry into effect. When, in the late summer of 1943, it became clear that an American officer would become the Supreme Commander, he sought to place Americans in a number of key spots and to

---

[2] Code names mentioned above were supplied later. For background of COSSAC, see Maj Duncan Emrich and Maj F. D. Price, History of COSSAC, prep at SHAEF, 1945, MS, OCMH files; CCS 169, 22 Jan 43; 67th Mtg, 22 Jan 43, Casablanca Conf Min; COS (43) 105 (0), 8 Mar 43; COS (43) 110 (0), 9 Mar 43; COS (43) 148 (0), 23 Mar 43; COS (43) 170 (0), 1 Apr 43; COS (43) 215 (0), 26 Apr 43. These COS (43) papers are in SHAEF SGS files, Bundle D, COS (43) Papers, I, 1–299. See also COS (43) 55th Mtg (0) 25 Mar 43; COS (43) 57th Mtg (0), 26 Mar 43; COS (43) 64th Mtg (0), 2 Apr 43; COS (43) 67th Mtg (0), 6 Apr 43; COS (43) 85th Mtg (0), 23 Apr 43. These documents are in SHAEF SGS files, Bundle B, COS (43) Min, I.

[3] Memo, Gen Morgan, 23 Mar 43, Annex, Cross Channel Operations, COS (43) 148 (0); Interv with Gen Morgan, 8 Feb 47; Morgan, *Overture to Overlord*, Ch. I. General Morgan indicated in a speech of 17 April 1943 that he was following suggestions of Lt. Gen. Frank M. Andrews, Commanding General, ETOUSA. SHAEF SGS Min of COSSAC Confs.

reorganize COSSAC along American lines. Much of this work was handed over to General Barker, the ranking U.S. officer at the headquarters. As a result of this shift, two U.S. officers were brought to London as deputy chiefs of the operations and supply sections with the understanding that they would later head these two sections under the Supreme Commander. General Eisenhower's chief of publicity and psychological warfare and members of the civil affairs section of Allied Force Headquarters were also brought to COSSAC in the fall of 1943 to prepare for roles in SHAEF.[4]

General Marshall, in September 1943, at the time when it was assumed he would lead the cross-Channel operation, told General Devers, Commanding General, ETOUSA, that full support must be given General Morgan "in his difficult task of organizing an efficient, operational staff for our Supreme Commander." General Marshall suggested that the Supreme Headquarters have General Morgan as chief of staff, U.S. officers as deputy chief of staff and chief of operations, a British officer as chief of intelligence, and a British officer as chief of administration until the bulk of supplies began to come from the United States, at which time he would be replaced by a U.S. officer. Marshall proposed that the press and propaganda sections be headed by U.S. and British officers with coequal powers. He added that in each staff section the second in command was to be of the nationality opposite to that of his chief. In order that the staff should be well balanced, General Marshall recommended strong naval, air, and ground representation, with a possible reduction of naval representation after the initial assault. The Allied naval and air staffs were to be of a size necessary "to

effect the coordinated direction of the forces" under their commands.[5]

Both General Marshall and General Morgan believed that the ultimate Supreme Headquarters should be modeled on Marshal Foch's World War I staff, described by the COSSAC chief as a "really small body of selected officers who dealt with the major decisions on broad lines, the day-to-day work of the war being delegated completely to the commanders of army groups."[6] Such a headquarters would have been sufficient only for a Supreme Commander who was merely chairman of the Allied forces. Once it became clear that General Eisenhower would direct operations, the need for a larger staff became apparent.

The appointment of General Eisenhower as Supreme Commander also required other changes in the COSSAC plans. It was natural that the new commander, having developed a satisfactory staff at Allied Force Headquarters, would want to bring a number of his advisers with him. Even before he assumed his new post, General Eisenhower directed General Smith to study the personnel situation

---

[4] Emrich and Price, History of COSSAC, pp. 9–11; Morgan, *Overture to Overlord*, pp. 213–22.

[5] Marshall to Devers, 24 Sep 43, OPD Exec. Morgan, *Overture to Overlord*, Ch. IX, is valuable on the organization of the staff.

[6] Address, Morgan to stf, 17 Apr 43, SHAEF SGS Min of COSSAC Confs. The author has been unable to find a precise list of the officers on Foch's staff. Sir Frederick Maurice, *Lessons of Allied Co-Operation, 1914–1918* (London, 1942), p. 142, speaks of Foch starting with a small staff of about a dozen officers and later adding an administrative staff. Gen. Maxime Weygand, *Foch* (Paris, 1947), pp. 199–200, indicates that outside of the members of the Allied missions, who had access to the office of the General Staff, there was a group of about twenty officers with the Commander in Chief of the Allied Armies. The author is indebted to Dr. T. D. Shumate, Jr., who is working on a study of the Supreme War Council in World War I, for these references.

for SHAEF. This officer, after studying the COSSAC organization, proposed changes in it based on Allied experiences at AFHQ. He initially asked for an enlarged staff, on the ground that the existing organization was not large enough for a commander who intended to control operations in the field. Fresh from the Mediterranean headquarters, General Smith was aware that civil affairs, press relations, psychological warfare and other such activities of an Allied headquarters would require large staffs. To fill these and other posts in the new SHAEF organization he began to draw on Allied Force Headquarters for key officers whose names had already been suggested by General Eisenhower.[7]

A steady flow of personnel northward began in January 1944 and increased until the British Chief of the Imperial General Staff feared that the new Supreme Commander, Mediterranean, would not have enough experienced officers to run his headquarters. The new arrivals introduced changes in several COSSAC divisions, although an attempt was made to retain most of the COSSAC members and reassure them about the intentions of the new regime. General Eisenhower at the outset made clear that he had no purpose of sweeping clean the organization which was already functioning in London. Rather he wished "to integrate himself upon the existing staffs in SAC"[8] and develop the same unity of action which had prevailed in the Mediterranean. General Morgan was made deputy chief of staff of SHAEF, General Barker was placed at the head of one of the general staff divisions, and other key members of the COSSAC staff were retained in their positions. By selecting men from both headquarters who were faithful to the idea

of "integration," the Supreme Commander was able to make the transition without serious disturbance, although several division heads were replaced and other personnel shifted. For a time the COSSAC members, who had been planning the cross-Channel invasion for a number of months, resented the newcomers' boasts of the "sand in their boots" they had picked up in North Africa. The Allied Force Headquarters officers, for their part, often complained that the COSSAC people lacked real knowledge of combat and were inclined to be academic in their approach to operational planning. Both groups, in time, found it necessary to coalesce in the face of British and U.S. combat soldiers from the Mediterranean theater who were inclined to smile at the suggestion that members of high level headquarters knew anything about battle conditions. By the eve of the invasion, the integrated SHAEF staff was functioning as an efficient unit.[9]

The Chief Deputies

Air Chief Marshal Tedder was chosen as Deputy Supreme Commander of SHAEF in January 1944. General Eisenhower did not have a hand in his selection, but he was highly pleased that the British made this choice. The two men had been closely associated in the Mediterranean

---

[7] Interv with Gen Smith, 13 May 47; Interv with Brig Gen Thomas J. Betts, former deputy G–2 of SHAEF, 19 May 50.

[8] In this case SAC is used to mean Supreme Headquarters. Normally it was used as an abbreviation for Supreme Allied Commander. General Eisenhower was also frequently referred to as SCAEF (Supreme Commander, Allied Expeditionary Force).

[9] Address, Eisenhower to members of his stf, 24 Jan 44, summarized in Min of SAC's Confs. Statements as to integration of SHAEF based on interviews by author with many members of the SHAEF staff.

theater and shared the same views on the integration of Allied staffs. General Eisenhower had proposed Tedder for the post of chief airman at SHAEF before he knew that the British officer was being considered for the post of deputy. Tedder had served as British air commander in the Middle East in 1942, helping to stop Generalfeldmarschall Erwin Rommel's advance toward Egypt. The air marshal's forces had also contributed significantly to the success of General Montgomery's El Alamein attack and the subsequent drive toward Tunisia. From 17 February 1943 until his appointment as Deputy Supreme Commander, Tedder had served as Commander in Chief, Mediterranean Allied Air Forces, which included RAF Middle East, RAF Malta Air Command, and the Northwest African Air Forces. The Northwest African command included British and U.S. air forces in support of General Eisenhower. In the Mediterranean post, Tedder came to be held in high esteem by many of the U.S. and British airmen who were later brought to the United Kingdom to command various air units in support of the cross-Channel attack. German intelligence agencies showed a wholesome respect for the new deputy. Shortly after his selection, one of them reported:

> Tedder is on good terms with Eisenhower to whom he is superior in both intelligence and energy. The coming operations will be conducted by him to a great extent. He regards the Air Force as a "spearhead artillery" rendering the enemy vulnerable to an attack. His tactics in North Africa, Sicily and Italy, based on this theory, provided for air support for the advance of even the smallest Army units. . . . Under Tedder's influence the co-operation between the Air Force and Army has become excellent.
>
> Tedder does not take unnecessary risks. Unless other factors play a part, he will undertake the invasion only after achieving

AIR CHIEF MARSHAL TEDDER

> complete air supremacy and after large-scale bombing of the Reich.
>
> Tedder is said to be taciturn especially since he lost his eldest son in an air battle over London. He is very popular with the troops on account of his consideration and unassuming appearance.
>
> Obviously we are dealing here with one of the most eminent personalities amongst the invasion leaders.[10]

Air Chief Marshal Tedder became the chief co-ordinator of Allied air efforts in support of the cross-Channel operation. The Deputy Supreme Commander made no effort to form a special staff through which to deal with air activities, restricting his function in many cases to that of a

---

[10] Luftwaffe Academy Lecture, Invasion Generals, Careers and Assessments, 7 Feb 44, *Generalstab der Luftwaffe, 8. Abteilung* (hist sec), British Air Ministry files.

chairman or moderator of daily air conferences at which the chief strategic and tactical air commanders were represented.
He also worked with the Air Staff
(SHAEF) which was set up under a separate deputy chief of staff for air.

Tedder participated in General Eisenhower's morning conferences, giving advice both as Deputy Supreme Commander
and as chief airman. The demands of air
activities on his time and the fact that
Tedder was not a ground force officer led
many members of the SHAEF staff to consult him only on air matters. General
Eisenhower used his deputy frequently to
explain SHAEF policy to the British
Chiefs of Staff and occasionally sent him
on highly important missions, such as that
to Moscow in January 1945. In the early
months of the OVERLORD operation, the
Supreme Commander charged his deputy
with the task of insuring that ground commanders asked for and got the air support
necessary for their operations. Tedder also
intervened directly when he felt it necessary to bar projects that he considered
wasteful of planes or contrary to existing
doctrines of proper employment of air
forces in combat. In all these assignments,
he worked quietly and effectively, taking
many problems, particularly those relating to the air forces, off the Supreme Commander's shoulders.[11]

General Eisenhower had chosen as his
chief of staff at SHAEF the officer who
had held a similar post in the Mediterranean theater.[12] Prime Minister Churchill suggested that General Smith stay at
Allied Force Headquarters as deputy commander but, in the face of General
Eisenhower's insistence, gave way. Smith
had served before the war as Secretary of
the General Staff in the War Department
and later as secretary to the Combined

Chiefs of Staff in Washington. He was
thoroughly acquainted with high-level
staff work and with the individuals who
made up the Supreme Allied Command.
Capable of being extremely tough and
brusque in manner, he also knew the
value of the smooth approach. He was
thus useful as a hatchet man for the Supreme Commander, and also qualified to
represent him in missions which required
diplomatic skill. General Eisenhower considered him a perfect chief of staff.

General Smith guarded the approaches
to General Eisenhower somewhat more
jealously than the British staff members of
SHAEF would have liked. He directed the
flow of correspondence into his office and
cut down the number of direct contacts
between the Supreme Commander and
the SHAEF deputies and staff members.
Shortly after his arrival Smith made a
major change in that direction by reorganizing the Central Secretariat of COSSAC,
headed by Maj. Martin McLaren, along
lines of the American Secretary of the
General Staff system. He attempted to run
the new staff for a time with Major
McLaren and Col. Dan Gilmer, who had
been secretary of the general staff in the
Mediterranean, but the experiment
proved unsuccessful. Colonel Gilmer went
to the War Department as chief of the
European theater section of the Operations Division, and Major McLaren to the
G–3 Division of SHAEF. Lt. Col. Ford
Trimble, onetime aide of Gen. Douglas

---

[11] Interviews with many members of the SHAEF
staff, including General Smith, Air Chief Marshal Sir
James M. Robb, and General Morgan in 1946 and
1947, and especially with Wing Commander Leslie
Scarman, wartime personal assistant to Air Chief
Marshal Tedder, 25 February 1947.

[12] General Smith was also the chief of staff of Headquarters, European Theater of Operations.

GENERAL SMITH

MacArthur, became secretary of the general staff.[13]

In accord with American practice all staff studies originating in the SHAEF divisions came to the chief of staff before being passed on to the Supreme Commander. In this way papers that did not need General Eisenhower's approval were handled by General Smith. Many items of correspondence prepared for the Supreme Commander's signature were issued by the chief of staff for his chief without being passed on to him. To make certain that General Eisenhower was kept informed of all action, the secretary of the general staff prepared a special log of incoming and outgoing messages which was shown to him each day. Careful lists of all decisions by the chief of staff were kept for the inspection of the Supreme Commander. The chief of staff held his own daily morning

conference just before that of the Supreme Commander. In the latter conference it was possible for key U.S. and British members of the staff to present matters directly to the Supreme Commander.

The office of the chief of staff was tightly organized and its head gained the reputation of a driver. His ruthless cutting of verbiage from papers and his demand for clearly stated proposals were a great aid to efficiency. At the risk of exercising some of the functions that belonged to the Deputy Supreme Commander, he also saved General Eisenhower from many details of administration which could have become overwhelming. While in London, General Smith saw the Prime Minister and members of the British Chiefs of Staff frequently and proved helpful to Eisenhower in working out numerous details with them. He was even more valuable in dealing with the French after SHAEF moved to the Continent, consulting with Gen. Alphonse-Pierre Juin and Maj. Gen. Pierre Joseph Koenig on matters pertaining to the liberation of France.

The selection of General Smith as chief of staff filled the place which had previously been intended for General Morgan. Since it was felt that the COSSAC chief might not want to serve in a lesser post at Supreme Headquarters, arrangements were made to offer him command of a British corps. Instead Morgan asked to serve in some capacity in SHAEF. Thereupon, General Eisenhower accepted General Smith's recommendation that the former COSSAC head become deputy chief of staff. In this post, General Morgan acted from time to time as chief of staff.

---

[13] Colonel Trimble, who succeeded Colonel Gilmer in March 1944, gave way to Col. Carter Burgess in November 1944. The latter in turn was succeeded by Col. J. B. Moore, III, at the end of March 1945.

AIR VICE MARSHAL ROBB

He was also given numerous special assignments to co-ordinate the work of various SHAEF divisions. General Smith after the war described the COSSAC chief as his British alter ego, "a man I wouldn't willingly have dispensed with." [14]

A second deputy chief of staff (chief administrative officer), Lt. Gen. Sir Humfrey M. Gale, came to SHAEF from a similar position at AFHQ at the strong insistence of General Eisenhower. When Field Marshal Brooke demurred at the shift, Smith pointed out that Eisenhower had always felt "he would be unwilling to undertake another large Allied Command without Gale's administrative assistance. . . . He has that irreplaceable quality of being able to handle British-American supply problems with tact and judgment and he is almost as familiar with the American sys-

tem of supply as with the British." General Gale found his position at SHAEF to be somewhat different from that at Allied Force Headquarters. In the Mediterranean he had also had responsibility for British troops behind the front. In the European theater, 21 Army Group controlled its own supply and the American units had their Headquarters, Communications Zone. At SHAEF, therefore, he

GENERAL GALE

had less real control over supply and administration than at Allied Force Headquarters. His duties consisted of co-ordinating the activities of G–1, G–4, and the supply elements of G–5. He also served as chairman of various high-level committees that dealt with matters of sup-

---

[14] Interv with Gen Smith, 13 May 47.

ply. One of his chief tasks was to anticipate future bottlenecks and to study ways in which they might be avoided.[15]

The third deputy, Air Vice Marshal James M. Robb, who became Deputy Chief of Staff (Air), had served at one time in the Mediterranean as General Eisenhower's air adviser. Later he became commander of RAF North Africa and deputy to General Spaatz, commander of the Northwest African Air Forces.[16] At SHAEF the air marshal co-ordinated all correspondence and planning of the various SHAEF divisions in regard to air activities.

The selection of the chief deputies was followed in turn by the naming of the heads of the various divisions—a story which will be told in some detail elsewhere in this volume.[17] By mid-January most of the key positions of the headquarters had been filled and Supreme Headquarters was functioning. By mid-February General Eisenhower had his formal directive and his command was officially under way. It is important now to examine what had already been done by SHAEF's predecessors and what yet remained to be achieved before the offensive against northwest Europe could be launched.

---

[15] Interv with Gen Gale, 27 Jan 47.
[16] Interv with Air Chief Marshal Sir James M. Robb, 3 Feb 47.
[17] Ch. IV, below, The Machinery of SHAEF.

CHAPTER IV

The Machinery of SHAEF

Even before SHAEF had been formed, COSSAC had handed over the tactical planning of the cross-Channel attack to the Commander-in-Chief, 21 Army Group, the Allied Naval Commander-in-Chief, Expeditionary Force (ANCXF), and the Commander-in-Chief, Allied Expeditionary Air Force (AEAF). Later, the detailed planning of the ground force assault was given to the armies involved in the attack. Headquarters, ANCXF, and AEAF drew up detailed plans of their own. As a result SHAEF did not play a prominent role in the operational planning for the initial stages of OVERLORD and may appear to the casual observer to have been almost completely divorced from control of the assault. An examination of the machinery of SHAEF will help to correct this misconception.

The Powers Reserved to SHAEF

General Eisenhower, in appointing General Montgomery to command U.S. and British ground forces in the assault, gave him operational control of the forces to be used in the early days of the attack. The temporary nature of the arrangement was understood. The Supreme Commander, while delegating for an interval operational control of Allied ground forces, did not lay aside his responsibility for making tactical decisions that involved major changes in the OVERLORD plan or the calling forward of additional troops. His intervention was also necessary to get increased air or naval support for the ground forces.

In the administrative sphere, where supply and personnel were concerned, the Supreme Commander retained a large number of duties. As the chief Allied headquarters, SHAEF co-ordinated interservice and inter-Allied administrative policy. This co-ordination extended to such matters as policy on the hiring of labor, the purchase of supplies, welfare, health, discipline and awards, prisoners of war, movement, and the construction of airfields. It was the task of SHAEF to prepare outline administrative plans for future Allied operations, allocate scarce resources until shipped overseas, deal on national policy matters with non-U.S. and British powers, determine policy on POL (petrol, oil, and lubricants) matters, and make representations to the U.S. and British ministries and departments concerning policy and matériel requirements when they influenced the theater as a whole.[1] (*Chart 3*)

In the so-called political sphere the Supreme Commander and his staff were particularly busy. Few if any of these responsibilities had been delegated to subordinate commanders. Representing Great

---

[1] SHAEF Dir to Ramsay, Leigh-Mallory, and Montgomery, 10 Mar 44; see also SHAEF Dir to FUSAG, 10 Mar 44, SHAEF SGS 322.011/2 Dirs to Subordinate Comdrs.

CHART 3—SUPREME HEADQUARTERS, ALLIED EXPEDITIONARY FORCE, 6 JUNE 1944

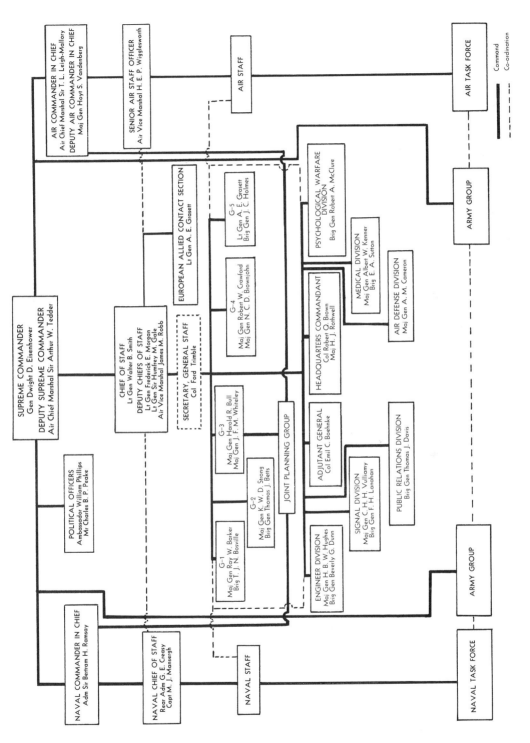

SUPREME COMMANDER
Gen Dwight D. Eisenhower
DEPUTY SUPREME COMMANDER
Air Chief Marshal Sir Arthur W. Tedder

AIR COMMANDER IN CHIEF
Air Chief Marshal Sir T. L. Leigh-Mallory
DEPUTY AIR COMMANDER IN CHIEF
Maj Gen Hoyt S. Vandenberg

SENIOR AIR STAFF OFFICER
Air Vice Marshal H. E. P. Wigglesworth

AIR STAFF

AIR TASK FORCE

ARMY GROUP

CHIEF OF STAFF
Lt Gen Walter B. Smith
DEPUTY CHIEFS OF STAFF
Lt Gen Frederick E. Morgan
Lt Gen Sir Humfrey M. Gale
Air Vice Marshal James M. Robb

EUROPEAN ALLIED CONTACT SECTION
Lt Gen A. E. Grasett

SECRETARY, GENERAL STAFF
Col Ford Trimble

G-5
Lt Gen A. E. Grasett
Brig Gen J. C. Holmes

G-4
Maj Gen Robert W. Crawford
Maj Gen N. C. D. Brownjohn

PSYCHOLOGICAL WARFARE DIVISION
Brig Gen Robert A. McClure

HEADQUARTERS COMMANDANT
Col Robert Q. Brown
Maj H. J. Rothwell

MEDICAL DIVISION
Maj Gen Albert W. Kenner
Brig Gen E. A. Sutton

AIR DEFENSE DIVISION
Maj Gen A. M. Cameron

POLITICAL OFFICERS
Ambassador William Phillips
Mr Charles B. P. Peake

G-3
Maj Gen Harold R. Bull
Maj Gen J. F. M. Whiteley

G-2
Maj Gen K. W. D. Strong
Brig Gen Thomas J. Betts

JOINT PLANNING GROUP

ADJUTANT GENERAL
Col Emil C. Boehnke

PUBLIC RELATIONS DIVISION
Brig Gen Thomas J. Davis

G-1
Maj Gen Ray W. Barker
Brig Gen T. J. N. Bosville

ENGINEER DIVISION
Maj Gen H. B. W. Hughes
Brig Gen Beverly G. Dunn

SIGNAL DIVISION
Maj Gen C. H. H. Vulliamy
Brig Gen F. H. Lanahan

NAVAL COMMANDER IN CHIEF
Adm Sir Bertram H. Ramsay

NAVAL CHIEF OF STAFF
Rear Adm G. E. Creasy
Capt M. J. Mansergh

NAVAL STAFF

NAVAL TASK FORCE

ARMY GROUP

Command
Co-ordination

Britain and the United States in relations with representatives of France, preparing for civil affairs administration after the liberation of occupied countries, and planning for military government for conquered Germany were all tasks which the Supreme Commander retained. Somewhat allied to these activities were those relating to press relations, censorship, and psychological warfare—all matters which had to be carefully co-ordinated at the highest Allied headquarters.

SHAEF also retained active control of long-range planning for the period after the establishment of the bridgehead and the drive into Germany. Before D Day, its staff had outlined plans and amassed considerable data relating to the advance into Germany and the crossing of the Rhine.

The Operations Division

The nerve center of SHAEF was the G–3 Division. Here planning and operations were combined. The chief of this division, Maj. Gen. Harold R. Bull, had been assigned to the operations branch of COSSAC in the fall of 1943 in preparation for his appointment to the SHAEF post. He had previously served as G–3 of the War Department, acted as special observer for the War Department in the Mediterranean theater in the summer of 1943, and then commanded the III U.S. Corps. On 14 February he succeeded Maj. Gen. Charles A. West (Br.) as G–3 of SHAEF. West remained as deputy until May 1944 when he was replaced by Maj. Gen. J. F. M. Whiteley (Br.), deputy chief of staff at Allied Force Headquarters and briefly chief of intelligence of SHAEF. The two most important sections of G–3, plans and operations, had initially been united under Brig. Gen. Arthur S. Nevins, for-

merly a member of the TORCH planning staff, later briefly G–3 of Fifth Army, and subsequently General Alexander's operations officer in the Sicilian campaign. Near the end of May 1944 the two sections were separated, but General Nevins continued to co-ordinate their work. Brigadier Kenneth G. McLean, who had been chief Army planner at COSSAC from the beginning, headed the plans section. In March 1945, Maj. Gen. Lowell W. Rooks (U.S.) was added as deputy to General Bull.

The planning section, designated Planning Staff, SHAEF,[2] was set up in mid-March 1944 to co-ordinate planning for SHAEF operations. Members of the staff included representatives of the Allied Expeditionary Air Force, the Allied Naval Expeditionary Force, and the general and special staffs of SHAEF. They made estimates of the current situation, outlined plans for all future operations, and made detailed plans for the posthostilities period. Before D Day, this staff worked on plans for taking the Channel Islands, for operations in northwest Europe in case Germany suddenly surrendered, for forcing the Seine and capturing the Seine ports including Paris, for action to be taken in Norway in case of a German surrender, and for a course of action to be followed after the capture of the lodgment area.[3]

The operations section prepared and issued operational directives and orders based on plans drawn up by the planning staff and approved by the chief of operations and the chief of staff. It drew up and issued detailed standing operating procedures essential to the proper co-ordination

---

[2] Known briefly in early March as the Combined Planning Staff.

[3] Minutes of eight Planning Staff meetings held prior to D Day, Gen Nevins personal papers.

GENERAL BULL *(1950 portrait)*.

GENERAL WHITELEY

GENERAL NEVINS

BRIGADIER McLEAN

of the various arms and services. It also planned projects to mislead the enemy as to Allied intentions. Special subsections dealt with the co-ordination of airborne operations, defense against chemical warfare, and the arrangements for gathering meteorological information.

The operations section also directed Resistance activities in France outside the 21 Army Group sphere, co-operated with the Psychological Warfare Division in formation of propaganda policy and co-ordinated its action with operations, provided G–3 operational contact with Allied missions, and co-ordinated the preparation of communiqués. It was also the duty of this section to aid in preparing combined situation and intelligence reports, daily and weekly summaries, reports of progress on current studies, and liaison reports.

An important activity of the operations section was that of maintaining the SHAEF War Room where information was drawn from the Allied Naval Expeditionary Force headquarters, the Allied Expeditionary Air Force, 21 Army Group, the U.S. strategical and tactical air forces, Bomber Command, the meteorological section, Special Force Headquarters, and the G–1, G–2, and G–4 Divisions. Daily and weekly reports summarized this information. In the SHAEF War Room operations officers posted information on future air, ground, and naval plans, the Allied order of battle, including location and numbers of aircraft, the situation of current operations on the eastern and western fronts, meteorological forecasts, the enemy order of battle (including ground divisional strength, the enemy coastal defense system, and the location of major enemy air forces), and G–4 movements and plans.[4]

SHAEF G–3 maintained liaison with 21

GENERAL STRONG. *(Photograph taken in 1945.)*

Army Group, the Allied Expeditionary Air Force, the Allied Naval Expeditionary Force, and the Strategic Air Forces. Part of this task was handled by regular liaison staffs which remained at the headquarters in question. The greater part was carried on by personal visits, frequent telephone conversations, and participation in combined conferences. Officers of the G–3 Division made a special effort to visit forward headquarters as frequently as possible. General Bull, who had served for a time in North Africa as an observer for the War Department and, later, for General Eisenhower, took a special interest in this phase

[4] SOP of Ops 'A' Sub-Section, 11 May 44, and Ltr, Morgan to Under Secy of State, WO, relating to Ops 'B' Sub-Section, 3 Jun 44, SHAEF G–3 322.01 Organization and Personnel G–3.

of SHAEF's work. As the forces under General Eisenhower increased in the winter of 1944 and the spring of 1945, General Bull assumed increasingly the responsibility for maintaining contact with army group commanders. The deputy G–3, General Whiteley, kept in close touch with Maj. Gen. Francis de Guingand, the 21 Army Group chief of staff, and worked out with him personally many operational questions concerning General Montgomery's forces.

Because of the command situation that existed before D Day, the Supreme Commander found himself relying on two sources of operational advice and information. When, as often occurred during the assault, he was called upon merely to give a nod of approval to a plan proposed by General Montgomery or General Bradley, he was dependent largely upon planning done by someone else's staff. In such matters as directing Resistance operations, increasing airborne forces for the assault, planning for railway bombing, and other problems involving forces of different services and more than one nationality, he turned more frequently to his own staff.

The Intelligence Division

Before leaving the Mediterranean in December 1943, General Eisenhower indicated that he wanted Maj. Gen. Kenneth W. D. Strong (Br.), G–2 of Allied Force Headquarters, as his chief of intelligence at SHAEF. This officer had served as assistant military attaché in Berlin shortly before the beginning of the war and later for more than a year as head of the German section of the War Office. Eisenhower's request, coming on the heels of numerous other shifts from the Mediterranean theater, met opposition from the

War Office. When initial appeals proved ineffective, General Whiteley was appointed to the post. In May 1944 after further requests by Generals Eisenhower and Smith, the British agreed to the transfer of General Strong, and he became chief of intelligence on 25 May 1944.[5] His deputy, Brig. Gen. Thomas J. Betts (U.S.), had come to SHAEF some weeks earlier from the Mediterranean theater.

SHAEF, of course, did not attempt to collect intelligence by interrogating prisoners, nor did it send out air and ground reconnaissance patrols. For this type of information it depended, like the army groups, on the armies and subordinate units. For spot information, it was assumed, the lower headquarters would have to depend on their own resources. Such information was collated at army headquarters and sent back to the army groups and to SHAEF.

SHAEF G–2 received estimates and information from the armies and the army groups, from Resistance groups, either directly or indirectly, from reports of the Office of Strategic Services and the Political Warfare Executive, from the estimates of the War and Navy Departments in Washington, and from the Joint Intelligence Committee (London).[6]

Shortly after its establishment, SHAEF took over much of the personnel and files of the Theater Intelligence Section (TIS) which had been set up by the British in 1940. Initially British in make-up, this organization added U.S. personnel in 1943.

---

[5] General Whiteley, as already noted, became deputy chief of operations.

[6] JIC (London) consisted of representatives of the Foreign Office, Air Ministry, Admiralty, War Office, and Ministry of Economic Warfare. It farmed out various questions to the Theater Intelligence Section, the Interservice Intelligence Section, and other intelligence groups. The joint staff then undertook to determine the significance of the information.

As a part of British Home Forces and later of COSSAC, the section conducted considerable research on Germany and enemy-occupied territory and collated reports on enemy movements and dispositions. It furnished a mass of topographical information, and detailed reports on enemy order of battle and the location of enemy guns and fortifications. Lt. Col. John Austin, a Magdalen don who had headed the order of battle section under the Theater Intelligence Section, set up a similar section under SHAEF.

General Strong at the end of June 1944 proposed that SHAEF establish a Joint Intelligence Committee (SHAEF) which would consist of one U.S. and one British representative from each service, a British or U.S. member to deal with economic questions, and, when necessary, a British and U.S. member to represent the Political Advisers of the Supreme Commander. Headed by the SHAEF chief of intelligence, this committee was to keep under constant review the military and political situation in the area for which the Supreme Commander was responsible. It was to be the sole producer of intelligence appreciations for the Planning Staff, SHAEF, and to be the final authority on all intelligence matters for SHAEF. As long as SHAEF remained in the United Kingdom, the committee was required to keep in close touch with the Joint Intelligence Committee (London) to maintain a full exchange of information. The system was adopted in July 1944 with General Smith's reluctant approval. The SHAEF chief of staff indicated that he felt it tended to recognize the "command by committee" system which the Supreme Commander was trying to avoid.[7]

The varied intelligence which came to Supreme Headquarters was collected, as-

sessed, and passed on to subordinate headquarters in weekly intelligence summaries and periodic estimates. Part of the information sifted down to the lower headquarters either in the form of news summaries or often in the form of annexes appended to the regular reports. These summaries suffered somewhat from a time lag and by no means represented the information available at SHAEF at any given time.[8] Certain intelligence that could not be issued generally for fear of endangering the sources naturally had to be omitted from the summaries. Thus, the Supreme Commander and the army groups depended for their most current and most complete information on personal briefings by their chiefs of intelligence or members of the intelligence staffs. The army groups kept the SHAEF staff abreast of developments in their areas with nightly reports direct to Supreme Headquarters.

Much of the work of SHAEF G–2, like that of the Operations Division, was carried on by personal contact between members of the SHAEF and army group staffs. The relationships between members of the G–2 staffs of SHAEF and the army groups were cordial. Unfortunately, the same thing could not always be said of relations between the army groups and the armies.

General Strong organized his group along British lines. His chief deputy, General Betts, had served for some years on the War Department G–2 staff and had attended the Combined Chiefs of Staff conferences at Washington, Quebec, and Cairo in 1943 as a G–2 representative.

---

[7] Smith to Strong, 4 Jul 44, and Dir to JIC (SHAEF), 8 Jul 44, SHAEF SGS 322.01 G–2, Organization and Personnel G–2 Div, SHAEF.

[8] In a few cases, when an important change in the military situation occurred just after a report was issued, one or more additional pages were sent out with new information.

The operational intelligence chief, Brigadier E. J. Foord (Br.) had served in the intelligence section of the War Office and then as chief of the operational intelligence subsection of Allied Force Headquarters in the Mediterranean.

Administration

COSSAC had intended initially to follow the British system of putting both personnel and supply activities under an administrative division with subsections devoted to these matters. When a decision was made near the end of 1943 to extend the U.S. system of organization throughout the headquarters, separate G–1 and G–4 Divisions were established. That neither division ever had as much operational control as the G–2 and G–3 Divisions was due chiefly to differences in personnel and supply organizations in the British and U.S. armies which required entirely separate logistic arrangements for the two forces. Control of British troops and supplies for OVERLORD was vested in 21 Army Group. Control of U.S. troops and supplies was given to Headquarters, ETOUSA, which General Eisenhower commanded as the senior U.S. commander in Europe. The actual task of supply in the battle zone was handed over to a U.S. supply headquarters. Administrative control of British tactical air forces was placed under Air Chief Marshal Leigh-Mallory as long as his Headquarters, Allied Expeditionary Air Force, existed. Headquarters, USSTAF, retained administrative control of U.S. units assigned to AEAF.

General Barker, who had been deputy chief of COSSAC, became the chief of the G–1 (Personnel) Division of SHAEF. His original deputy, Brigadier R. F. R. Becher

GENERAL CRAWFORD

(Br.), was replaced in May 1944 by Brigadier T. J. N. Bosville. The G–4 (Supply) chief of SHAEF was Maj. Gen. Robert W. Crawford, who had served as Commanding General, Services of Supply, U.S. Army Forces in the Middle East, and later as chief of staff of the Services of Supply organization in the United Kingdom. He was appointed deputy G–4 of COSSAC in November 1943 with the understanding that he would later exchange places with Maj. Gen. N. C. D. Brownjohn (Br.) then the G–4 of that headquarters. This shift took place in February 1944. General Brownjohn remained as deputy G–4 until August 1944 when he was succeeded by Maj. Gen. C. M. Smith (Br.). In March 1944 three special deputies were added to the G–4 Division to help determine priorities, allocate supplies, and assign space at railways, ports, airfields, and other facilities to the various services.[9]

Because of General Eisenhower's dual role as Supreme Commander and as U.S. theater commander, the organization of the supply services in the U.S. zone is significant to this study. To simplify U.S. administration, General Eisenhower in mid-January 1944 ordered the consolidation of Headquarters, ETOUSA, and Headquarters, Services of Supply. This enlarged headquarters inherited the name of ETOUSA, and was commanded by General Eisenhower with General Smith as its chief of staff. It was actually controlled by Lt. Gen. John C. H. Lee, deputy theater commander for supply and administration, formerly the commanding general of the Services of Supply. General Lee was also slated to command Headquarters, Communications Zone, which was to be established on the Continent after the invasion to control supply of U.S. troops. General Eisenhower tended to rely on U.S. members of his SHAEF staff for advice concerning most operational matters, and he used Headquarters, ETOUSA, for communication with the War Department on administrative matters and as an authorizing agency for all U.S. commands that operated under Supreme Headquarters. The exact responsibility of the G–1 and G–4 at SHAEF and their counterparts at U.S. supply headquarters was never thoroughly defined. While it was natural for the Supreme Commander to turn to the U.S. staff officers nearest at hand for advice on purely U.S. questions, the G–1 and G–4 at theater headquarters were more closely in touch with the War Department and had closer control of U.S. men and supplies coming to the United Kingdom and the Continent. Staff officers

GENERAL LEE

at SHAEF were never completely successful in their efforts to control supply and personnel policy relating solely to U.S. forces. On matters involving allocation of supplies and men among the Allied forces and on certain problems pertaining to the entire British, French, and U.S. force, they played a more important role.[10]

---

[9] These officers were: Maj. Gen. Charles S. Napier (Br.) and Col. Howard A. Malin (U.S.) for movement and transportation, and Brigadier Douglas H. Bond (Br.) for petroleum and fuel. In late May Col. Walter C. Pew (U.S.) was added as deputy G–4 for petroleum and fuel, and Col. Wilbur S. Elliott (U.S.) replaced Colonel Malin. In December 1944, Brig. Gen. John A. Appleton (U.S.) became Director General, Military Railways. Col. (later Brig. Gen.) E. K. Clark (U.S.) was added as deputy G–4 in January 1945, and Brig. Gen. Theron D. Weaver (U.S.) became chief of the Petroleum Branch in February 1945.

[10] The author has relied principally for these details on [Robert W. Coakley] Organization and Command in the European Theater of Operations, Pt. II

Civil Affairs

The organization of SHAEF's Civil Affairs Division (G–5) requires more detailed study than that of the other general staff divisions. Since it was of fairly recent origin, the COSSAC and SHAEF planners had to work out new procedures and systems of operating. Unlike the other general staff divisions, G–5 could not be set up simply by copying long-established U.S. or British practices. Instead, it was necessary to draw on fairly recent experiences of the Allies in the Mediterranean, and these did not conform exactly to the needs of a Supreme Headquarters in the European theater. A second factor making for difficulty arose from differences of opinion between the British and U.S. Chiefs of Staff, between the U.S. Chiefs of Staff and the State Department, between COSSAC and the AFHQ elements of SHAEF, and between individuals, as to theory of civil affairs and methods of control. Again, because of the political angles involved, SHAEF from the beginning exercised closer control of civil affairs operations than of other operations. Finally, the Supreme Commander and his chief of staff had to intervene more directly in the final settlement of the civil affairs organization than they did in the case of the other divisions.

Differences Between Military Government and Civil Affairs

At the beginning of World War II, there was no clear-cut distinction between military government and the administration of civil affairs, both of which the G–5

---

of The Administrative and Logistical History of the ETO, Hist Div USFET, 1946, MS, OCMH files. See also Ruppenthal, *Logistical Support of the Armies.*

253223 O—54——7

division of SHAEF had to deal with. It was known that military government referred to the authority established in occupied territory of the enemy and that it was intended largely to preserve order in zones in enemy areas through which the victorious armies were passing. The term was applied more often, of course, to the authority that was established in a defeated country after the conclusion of an armistice. In World War I, the practice had been to continue existing local governments in power with military supervision and with some safeguards against disobedience of the orders issued by the occupying power. Attempts were made to restore the previous economic and social framework as soon as possible in order to reduce the responsibilities of military units for feeding the population and running the government.

In World War II an entirely different situation existed. In Italian-held territory in the Mediterranean, and in German territory on the Continent, the Allies undertook to eliminate the former Fascist and Nazi officeholders, to root out the political theories which Mussolini and Hitler had put into the legal systems of the two countries, to change Fascist- and Nazi-inspired economic regulations—in short, to effect a political revolution under Allied auspices. Part of this task was handed over to the military commanders who first set foot on enemy territory. They soon discovered that former views on the subject were not suited to the new concept of military government, and they found, in the early days at least, that they lacked officers with the technical knowledge to assume the tasks of mayors, directors of railways, directors of waterworks, directors of power plants, and dozens of other key jobs which were formerly performed by the party faithful who now under Allied policy had to be ruthlessly weeded out. Under World War I conditions, it was possible for a commander to restore the former officials, under proper military supervision, and let them govern as before. The new system required the conquering armies to establish new city and district administrations.

Civil affairs had also changed since World War I. It had become clear in that earlier conflict that "total war," which choked essential highways with great masses of dispossessed people, required commanders to restore some semblance of civil authority if military operations were to be continued. In the 1914–18 period, the British and U.S. armies had been able to leave this problem largely to the French Government and Army, which at most needed only some supplies and transport to restore civil administration. In preparing for the invasion of Europe through France in the spring of 1944, SHAEF realized that the French civil administration that would be found had been either under the control of German military authority or under Vichy. In either case, it seemed likely that the existing government would have to undergo considerable change. Further, the greater damage caused by the bombardments of World War II meant that the liberating armies would have to support the local populations or furnish transport to a far greater degree than they had before. Worse still, they could not expect the French forces, which were themselves being supplied from Allied sources, to take on this responsibility. Inasmuch as hungry civilians, however sympathetic to the Allies, were likely to become dangerous if left unfed, the Allied commanders, as a matter of necessity, had to engage in widespread activities in the realm of civil affairs. Military commanders were not always pleased at having to turn their attention from the task of winning battles to the business of feeding people and of making electric plants and waterworks function again. They were frequently even less willing to have groups of officers from higher headquarters carry out civil affairs activities in the forward zone. As a result, command channels and command responsibility for civil affairs became points of contention among the various headquarters.

Developing a System of Allied Control

General Morgan, who has described the task of setting up a civil affairs organization for SHAEF as "the most vexatious and least satisfactory" of COSSAC's many tasks, attempted as early as July 1943 to establish a civil affairs branch and to draw up a set of guiding principles for civil affairs planning. Almost immediately he was caught in a debate between the British and U.S. Chiefs of Staff over whether the control of civil affairs should be centered in London or Washington, and in a COSSAC-versus-AFHQ argument over the nature of civil affairs command in the field. There is little wonder that in his description of these discussions, General Morgan recalls the remark of a member of his staff that "there were plenty of affairs, but the difficulty was to keep them civil." [11]

The British had a variety of reasons for attempting to centralize civil affairs control in London. Not only had they had considerable experience with governing occupied countries throughout modern history, but they had taken up the responsibility of military government in Italian and African possessions as early as 1940–

---

[11] Morgan, *Overture to Overlord*, pp. 227–28.

41. Before the United States entered the war, the British had established procedures and policy for military government. In June 1942, they formed an Administration of Territories (Europe) Committee under Sir Frederick Bovenschen, Permanent Under Secretary of State for War, to co-ordinate planning for military government. The commander of United States Forces in Europe was invited to send observers to meetings of the committee, apparently in the hope of making it the combined agency for determining Allied civil affairs policy.

The British were in a position to say that they had a going concern in London and were prepared to lay down military government policy. It is possible that they desired to keep this control in London, not only because they felt themselves in a better position to handle these matters, but because they believed that a London committee could act more quickly on European matters and that decisions affecting British interests would be more satisfactorily settled. Parliament and Congress had expressed some dissatisfaction over U.S. dealings with Darlan in North Africa, and there were indications that Roosevelt and Churchill did not see eye to eye on the question of colonies. The British naturally desired to have firm control over any of their former colonies which might be recovered by Allied forces.

The President wanted to make sure that U.S. forces were not used merely to restore colonies or to carry out a policy in military government laid down by another power. The U.S. Chiefs of Staff were also of the opinion that over-all control of military government could best be handled from Washington. In July 1943, they and the British Chiefs of Staff agreed to establish a Combined Civil Affairs Committee (CCAC) in Washington to control civil affairs and military government policy for all theaters. The charter of the committee gave assurances that, if British or Dominion territory were recovered from the enemy, the nations concerned could submit to the Combined Chiefs of Staff an outline of policies for use in the civil affairs administration of such possessions. The Combined Chiefs of Staff, in turn, were to consult the force commander charged with taking and holding such territory and, on his recommendation, to accept those proposals which would not interfere with the military purpose of the operation.[12]

Establishment of the committee in Washington did not settle the problem of control. The reasons for continued debate have been well stated by General Morgan:

If territory was to be liberated or conquered by combined forces, then obviously the reinstatement of the life of those territories must similarly be undertaken by combined means. But the British had been at this liberation and conquest business already for some years, and they had set up for themselves an organization to see to this thing. To them it seemed a possibly unnecessary complication to duplicate the British effort in this respect over in the United States of America. It appeared to them that there were two alternatives: one could either reinforce the British setup to give it combined status, or one could regard the British setup as it stood as the British contribution towards the combined effect desired with an equivalent United States outfit in Washington.[13]

The British attempted to pursue the first of these alternatives by holding that attendance of U.S. observers at meetings of the Administration of Territories (Europe)

---

[12] Details on early developments of the British organization are given in Historical Notes, SHAEF G–5 file. Charter CCAC, CCS 190/6/D, 15 Jul 43, ABC 014 (11–27–42), Sec 1.

[13] Morgan, *Overture to Overlord*, pp. 231–32.

Committee constituted combined action on civil affairs and military government matters. When the U.S. representatives rejected this view, the British declined for a number of weeks to deal with the Combined Civil Affairs Committee in Washington. The net effect of this impasse, according to Maj. Gen. John H. Hilldring, chief of the Civil Affairs Division of the War Department, was to deprive the Supreme Commander for three months of any guidance on military government and civil affairs.[14]

The Combined Chiefs of Staff resolved the problem at the end of January 1944 by establishing the London Sub-Committee of the Combined Civil Affairs Committee. This body was empowered to advise the Supreme Commanders of Europe and the Mediterranean, solve the civil affairs problems which did not justify reference to the Combined Chiefs of Staff, make recommendations on problems referred to it by the CCAC in Washington, and receive from the British Government its views in regard to British or Dominion territory outside the Pacific which might be recovered from the enemy. The Administration of Territories (Europe) Committee was abolished.[15] Even after this action, the War Department remained watchful lest the British try to enlarge the powers of the European Advisory Commission, organized by Britain, the United States, and the USSR in London in late 1943 to draw up surrender terms for Germany and Axis satellites and to consider such other questions on liberation of Allied countries as might be submitted by the three governments.[16]

An illustration of the delays which followed these debates over jurisdiction may be found in the efforts of the United States

and Great Britain to conclude a civil affairs agreement with the Norwegian Government-in-exile. Allied negotiations to get an agreement with Norway covering such matters as the restoration of civil authority, the requisitioning of supplies, and the hiring of labor were begun as early as May 1943 by the Administration of Territories (Europe) Committee. The Foreign Office aided in preparing the necessary documents, but negotiations were kept on a strictly military level. The British authorities, wishing to avoid delays which they feared would follow submission of the agreement to the Combined Chiefs of Staff and the Combined Civil Affairs Committee, in July 1943 sent it to General Devers on the chance that he could get direct approval from the U.S. Chiefs of Staff. Their hope proved unfounded, although General Devers promptly gave his assent to the document and proposed that with some modifications it become a model for similar agreements in the future. The U.S. Chiefs of Staff, in order to avoid any precedent which would recognize the authority of the Administration of Territories (Europe) Committee to act on civil affairs matters

---

[14] General Hilldring's opposite number in the British War Office was Maj. Gen. S. W. Kirby, head of the Civil Affairs Directorate in Great Britain.

[15] Ltr, Barker to Hilldring, 23 Nov 43; Bendetsen to Hilldring, 15 Nov 43; James C. Dunn to William Phillips, 4 Dec 43. All in CAD 370.21 COSSAC. McCloy to Winant, 3580, 4 Jan 44; Hilldring to McSherry, 53, 29 Jan 44. Both in CAD 334 CCAC. Secy War to Commanding Gens, 8 Feb 44, (text of revised charter of CCAC, 29 Jan 44), SHAEF G–5 23–27.02; Memo for Record, 19 Jan 44, COS (44), 142d Mtg (O), 28 Jan 44, ABC 014, Sec 2; Morgan, *Overture to Overlord*, pp. 231–32.

[16] This action had been decided on at the Moscow Conference in October 1943, but formal action was not taken until near the end of the war.

for the Allies, asked that both the Combined Chiefs of Staff and the Combined Civil Affairs Committee deal with the matter. An attempt was also made to get reactions of the State Deparment, but a request for its opinion brought merely the reply of "no comment." Accepting this as a negative form of approval, the Combined Chiefs of Staff proceeded with a discussion of the final draft. After some delay, which Ambassador William Phillips blamed more on questions of prestige than on details of the document, the British and U.S. Chiefs of Staff also agreed near the end of January 1944 to proceed with Belgium and the Netherlands on the basis of the Norwegian draft.[17]

Once the Combined Chiefs of Staff had agreed on the general form of the documents, the British and U.S. Governments proceeded to conclude separate accords with the occupied countries. The U.S. Chiefs of Staff in January 1944 maintained that the State Department would have to conclude agreements with these countries in order to make them binding. The State Department, as a matter of fact, already had under consideration draft agreements with Norway and the Netherlands. Secretary of State Cordell Hull held that since these were for military purposes they should be entered into directly between the Commander in Chief, U.S. Forces in Europe, and the countries concerned. At the end of February, the U.S. Chiefs of Staff instructed General Eisenhower to conclude a civil affairs agreement on behalf of the United States with Norway. After a delay to permit the USSR to conclude a similar agreement with Norway, separate accords were signed with Norway on 16 May 1944 by representatives of the United States, Great Britain, and the USSR. Later, similar documents were drawn up for the other occupied countries.[18]

Development of Civil Affairs Machinery at COSSAC and SHAEF

The development of civil affairs machinery for COSSAC and SHAEF was as complicated as the efforts, mentioned earlier, to establish Allied control of civil affairs. Initially, there had been little difficulty. The Prime Minister and the President had answered General Morgan's request for guidance on civil affairs and military government by declaring at Quebec on 22 August 1943 that their governments would assume responsibility for the administration of territory conquered by their forces. In liberated territories, the British and U.S. forces were to exercise military authority until the enemy's defeat, but would agree to the maintenance

---

[17] Memo, Col John C. Blizzard for Maj Gen Thomas T. Handy, 1 Jul 43; Notes on JCS, 95th Mtg, 6 Jul 43; JCS 96th Mtg, 13 Jul 43; CCS 102d Mtg, 16 Jul 43; Memo for record, 26 Aug 43; Draft agreement, CCS 274/4, 4 Oct 43; CCS 122d Mtg, 8 Oct 43; Memo, Col Frank N. Roberts for Gen Handy, 5 Oct 43; CCS 122d and 123d Mtgs, 8 and 15 Oct 43; Forrest B. Royal to Comdr Coleridge, 19 Oct 43; Memo, Representatives of Br COS, CCS 445, 22 Dec 43; CCS 142d Mtg, 21 Jan 44. All in ABC 014 Norway (4 Jul 43), Sec 1. Barker to Phillips, 22 Dec 43, with note by Phillips on 23 Dec 43; Cbl 21, CCS to Eisenhower, 23 Jan 44. Both in SHAEF SGS 014.1 Norway, Civil Affairs Dir for Norway.

[18] Handy to CAD, 5 Jan 44; Hilldring to Handy, 10 Jan 44; Handy to CAD, 16 Jan 44; Leahy to Secy State, JCS 398/2, 21 Jan 44; Hull to Leahy, JCS 398/3, 25 Jan 44; Rpt, Hilldring to JCS, 12 Jan 44. All in ABC 014 Norway. JCS to Eisenhower, 10 Feb 44; State Dept Rad Bull 118, 16 May 44. Both in SHAEF SGS 014.1 Norway, Civil Affairs Dir for Norway. JCS to Eisenhower, 24 Feb 44; SHAEF to AGWAR, S–50493, 19 Apr 44; AGWAR to SHAEF, W–30279, 30 Apr 44. All in SHAEF SGS 014.1 Netherlands, Civil Affairs Dir for Netherlands.

of law and order by the liberated peoples with necessary aid from the United States and Great Britain.[19]

Meanwhile, the Combined Civil Affairs Committee on 18 August 1943 had decided that the Allied commanders in chief should plan and handle civil affairs on the military level under a directive of the Combined Chiefs of Staff. General Morgan, therefore, proceeded in early September to select a civil affairs staff. Maj. Gen. Sir Roger Lumley, former governor of Bombay, was appointed senior British civil affairs officer for COSSAC, with Brig. Gen. Cornelius E. Ryan, chief of the ETOUSA civil affairs section, as his U.S. opposite number. Shortly afterward, General Ryan was chosen to organize the civil affairs section of 1st U.S. Army Group and was replaced on the COSSAC staff by Col. Karl R. Bendetsen. With the shift of General Ryan, the civil affairs section of ETOUSA was abolished and its planning functions were given to COSSAC and 1st U.S. Army Group.[20]

In developing the civil affairs branch at COSSAC, General Morgan proceeded on the theory that the civil affairs organization in the field should insure that refugees not interfere with Allied operations, that it should relieve the Supreme Commander of anxiety over events behind his lines, and that it should guarantee that liberated or captured resources of military value would be placed at the disposal of the Allied forces. This was sound doctrine on which to build, but unfortunately, when it came to establishing machinery for carrying it out, the COSSAC chief found himself at a loss. The problem has been succinctly described by General Morgan as follows:

Starting from a basis of complete ignorance and confronted with this agglomeration of confusing evidence, it is little wonder that COSSAC set off entirely on the wrong foot as regards its Civil Affairs planning. Round a small central section to study the question generally were formed "country sections" to study the problems of France, Belgium, Holland, and Norway on the broad assumption that for each of these countries would be needed something of the nature of the AMG [Allied Military Government] organisation for Italy. . . .[21]

COSSAC planners in the fall of 1943 soon disagreed over the question of how far the system of civil affairs and military government used in Sicily and Italy should be copied. Broadly speaking, the Allies had set up a system of military government which was to a great extent independent of the normal military structure. A chief civil affairs officer maintained a direct line of command through his regional civil affairs officers to provincial and local administrators. When a similar system was proposed by COSSAC planners, it was attacked by a group of civil affairs officers, led by Colonel Bendetsen, who opposed a system so largely independent of the military chain of command, and held that the principles designed to apply to conquered territory were unsuitable for liberated countries.[22] What might be called anti-

---

[19] Morgan to Under Secretary of State for War, 21 Jul 43, SHAEF G–5 Gen File 3510 Civil Agencies—Voluntary Association; CCS 320, 20 Aug 43, QUADRANT Conf Min; Copy of Roosevelt-Churchill agreement at Quebec, 22 Aug 43, SHAEF G–5 plng file 27.01.

[20] Hilldring to Hammond, 19 Aug 43; Mtg at Norfolk House, 1 Sep 43; Memo, Ryan to Hilldring, 5 Sep 43; Morgan to Hilldring, 21 Oct 43; Bendetsen to Barker, 20 Oct 43. All in CAD 370.21 COSSAC. ETOUSA GO 88, 26 Nov 43; ETOUSA Memo 90, 2 Dec 43. Both in ETOUSA files.

[21] Morgan, *Overture to Overlord*, pp. 227–29.

[22] Details of the military government system in North Africa, Sicily, and Italy are contained in Lt. Robert W. Komer, Civil Affairs in the Mediterranean

Mediterranean views were contained in the COSSAC handbook on civil affairs which was issued on 13 December 1943. By it military commanders were made responsible for civil affairs operations, which were to be handled through regular channels of command.[23]

The handbook was criticized almost immediately by Brig. Gen. Frank J. McSherry, formerly deputy civil affairs officer in Sicily and chief of Headquarters, Allied Military Government for Italy outside Naples and the Army Zone. McSherry had been assigned to the COSSAC Civil Affairs Branch in mid-December 1943. With the aid of Lt. Col. William Chanler of the Civil Affairs Division, War Department, he argued in early January 1944 for a return to a system more like that used in the Mediterranean theater. The COSSAC Civil Affairs Branch brushed these efforts aside with the statement that it had "abandoned with finality the concept applied elsewhere which undertakes to execute civil affairs operations through a separate channel either parallel to or divergent from the chain of command." General Smith, who had now arrived on the scene from the Mediterranean, countered this statement with a reminder that since he came from an area where the concept was applied, and was in large measure responsible for it, he would have to have further evidence before abandoning it.[24]

In the next two months, a fight was waged over the concept of civil affairs to be adopted and the real control of the program. The G–5 Division of SHAEF underwent two major changes in that time. On 15 February General Lumley, who had been a supporter of Colonel Bendetsen, became sole head of the division, and Brig. Gen. Julius C. Holmes, who had recently been brought up from the Civil Affairs Branch at Allied Force Headquarters, was appointed deputy. Colonel Bendetsen was transferred to another headquarters. The country sections, which had been eliminated in the shifts of the fall of 1943, were replaced, and General McSherry, Deputy Civil Affairs Officer, was made responsible for reorganizing these sections, preparing detailed civil affairs plans, and training personnel.[25] In April the G–5 Division underwent its second reorganization in fulfillment of a decision reached in early January 1944. General Smith had indicated to the War Department at that time that someone with more experience and rank than General Lumley's or Colonel Bendetsen's should be appointed. He had proposed a U.S. officer for the position, suggesting among others Maj. Gen. Lucius D. Clay, but withdrew the proposal when General Eisenhower decided that it was preferable to have a British officer in charge of civil affairs in order to avoid

[23] Handbook, Standard Policy and Procedure for Combined Civil Affairs Operations in Northwest Europe, COSSAC, 13 Dec 43, SHAEF SGS 014.1 Civil Affairs in Northwest Europe. (It should be noted that there is also a two-volume file with virtually the same designation: SHAEF SGS 014.1 Civil Affairs in Northwest Europe, Vols. I and II.)

[24] Memo, McSherry for Lumley, 30 Jan 44, SHAEF G–5 Plng File 27.01. Memo, Chanler for CofS, SHAEF, 5 Feb 44; Memo, McSherry for CofS, SHAEF, 7 Feb 44; Memo, Smith for Lumley, 8 Feb 44. All in SHAEF SGS 014.1 Civil Affairs in Northwest Europe. Unsigned, undated memo, apparently in answer to McSherry memo of 30 Jan 44, SHAEF G–5 Plng File 15.01.

[25] SHAEF Stf Memo 2, 15 Feb 44, SHAEF AG files; McSherry to Hilldring, 11 Mar 44, CAD 370.21 COSSAC.

Theater, Hist Sec, MTOUSA, 1946, MS, OCMH files. Barker to Hilldring, 23 Nov 43; Ltrs, Bendetsen to Hilldring, 20, 21, 27, 31 Oct and 6, 10, and 15 Nov 43. All in CAD 370.21 COSSAC, Sec 1. See also Albert K. Weinberg, Soldiers Become Governors, a volume in preparation for this series.

criticism of SHAEF policy in areas where the British had long-established interests.[26] The Supreme Commander, after consultation with British authorities, on 22 April appointed Lt. Gen. A. E. Grasett, the chief of SHAEF's European Allied Contact Section, to head the G–5 Division.[27] General Holmes became his deputy. In December 1944 he was succeeded by General McSherry.

These changes in organization by no means indicated that the Mediterranean concepts of civil affairs were to prevail entirely in SHAEF. Generals Holmes and McSherry asked in March 1944 that the fundamental concept of the COSSAC handbook, which placed the full civil affairs burden on tactical commanders, be abandoned and the handbook revised accordingly. General Holmes went further and asked that the deputy civil affairs officer, in addition to carrying on his duties for planning and training, be directed to supervise and direct civil affairs activities under SHAEF and issue technical instructions to civil affairs staffs at lower echelons. These suggestions were strongly opposed by General Lumley and by Brigadier T. Robbins, Chief of Civil Affairs, 21 Army Group. After some debate SHAEF decided to amend but not drop the handbook. It was also accepted that the civil affairs staffs should be more closely integrated with existing staffs throughout the command system, and that SHAEF should avoid establishment of a civil affairs headquarters which was unrelated to military headquarters.[28]

General Grasett had indicated before the formal announcement of his appointment that he accepted some of the views of his predecessor on the organization of civil affairs. He believed that field commanders should be directly responsible for civil affairs operations, and that their policy

GENERAL GRASETT

should be guided by an amended Handbook on Standard Policy and Procedure for Civil Affairs. On 30 April, he reorganized part of the G–5 Division, abolishing the post of deputy civil affairs officer and transferring General McSherry to the post of chief of operations. The country sections were now placed directly under the chief

[26] It is possible that a desire to respect similar British interests may have prompted General Smith to tell General Holmes when the revision of the handbook was proposed that "there were substantial political reasons why the document cannot be scrapped. . . ." Ltr, Holmes to Hilldring, 16 Mar 44, CAD 370.21 COSSAC.

[27] Smith to Hilldring, W–9500, 7 Jan 44, CAD COSSAC 370.21. Memo, Hilldring for Marshall, 1 Apr 44, CAD 210.31. SHAEF GO 9, 22 Apr 44, SHAEF SGS G–5 Plng File 15.01.

[28] Holmes to CofS, SHAEF, 9 Mar 44; Gale to CofS, SHAEF, 13 Mar 44; Smith to Lumley, 14 Mar 44. All in SHAEF SGS 322.01 Organization and Personnel G–5 Div, I. Robbins to CofS, SHAEF, 11 Mar 44, SHAEF SGS 014.1 Civil Affairs in Northwest Europe; McSherry to Hilldring, 11 Mar 44, CAD 370.21 COSSAC.

of the G–5 Division, and any hint of a possible echelon between SHAEF and the army groups in the field was ended. General Grasett announced that the sections for France, Norway, Denmark, and Belgium–Luxembourg would ultimately become the civil affairs sections of SHAEF missions sent to those countries, and that the German section would provide the nucleus of military government in enemy territory. He also indicated that in the first phase of operations 21 Army Group, working through its civil affairs staff, would be responsible for all civil affairs activities in France. On the activation of a U.S. army group on the Continent, the SHAEF G–5 was to assume direct responsibility for co-ordinating civil affairs operations in the field. While all branches of SHAEF would have normal staff responsibility for such operations, the small French section of the operations branch of G–5 was charged with general supervision and co-ordination of activities pertaining to France.[29]

Some of the views of the former Mediterranean civil affairs officers were incorporated in the revised handbook issued by SHAEF on 1 May 1944. The principal amendments were those specifying SHAEF's control over civil affairs activities in the field. To the declaration in the original version that tactical commanders were responsible for civil affairs operations in their area, there was added the phrase, "in accordance with the policies laid down by the Supreme Commander." To the initial statement that normal command channels would be followed was added: "with direct communications between Civil Affairs staffs of Commands on matters peculiar to Civil Affairs." The scope of such activities was broadened to apply "to the areas affected by military operations." Thus it was possible, if necessary, to apply civil affairs jurisdiction to the whole of a country even though Allied forces might be in only a part of it. The objective of civil affairs operations was restated as an effort to insure "that conditions exist among the civilian population which will not interfere with operations against the enemy, but will promote these operations." Stricken out was the statement that the commander's responsibility did not embrace the rehabilitation of a country or its industries. Both handbooks agreed that relief, except as otherwise directed, would be limited to that required by military necessity, and that civil affairs operations in liberated areas would continue only until the situation permitted the Allied national authority concerned to assume control. Finally, the revised handbook provided for consistency of interpretation and application of policies in each of the countries by requiring that country manuals be issued for the use of tactical commanders.[30]

SHAEF G–5 spent the remaining days before the invasion on improving the civil affairs organization. The training of civil affairs officers sent from the United States was emphasized. All new arrivals were interviewed at the European Civil Affairs Training Center, which had been established in December 1943 at Shrivenham under Col. Cuthbert P. Stearns, and an effort was made to train them in handling specific problems in the cities to which they were to be assigned.

General Eisenhower expressed his views as to the importance of the civil affairs officers in an address shortly before D Day. Saying that they were "as modern as

---

[29] Memo, Grasett for CofS, SHAEF, 19 Apr 44; SHAEF Stf Memo 43, 30 Apr 44. Both in SHAEF G–5 plng file 15.01.

[30] SHAEF handbook, Standard Policy and Procedure for Combined Civil Affairs Operations in Northwest Europe, 13 Dec 43, and as revised, 1 May 44. Original handbook in SHAEF SGS Civil Affairs in Northwest Europe 014.1; revision in OCMH.

GENERAL DAVIS

radar and just as important to the command," he declared that the army would fail if they did not do their job of organizing the rear areas as quickly as possible. Repeating his often-stated view that the task of soldiers was to defeat the enemy, he rejected the idea that the purpose of civil affairs was to serve any nationalistic aim and asked them to remember that "you are not politicians or anything else but soldiers." Their organization, he added, had been gradually developed as a result of experience, and had been accepted because of military necessity. Their task, therefore, although humanitarian in results, was "to help us win the war." [31]

Publicity and Psychological Warfare

A Publicity and Psychological Warfare Division (G–6) under Brig. Gen. Robert

A. McClure, who headed a similar division at Allied Force Headquarters, was formally activated by SHAEF on 14 February 1944 to co-ordinate all Allied press and psychological warfare agencies operating in northwest Europe. This general staff division proved to be short lived, since it was divided on 13 April into two special staff divisions: Psychological Warfare under General McClure, and Public Relations under Brig. Gen. Thomas J. Davis, the former adjutant general at SHAEF. Inasmuch as the two were to continue separately along lines laid down previously for the combined division, it is necessary to consider their background together and then to examine their development as they went their separate ways.

The British had begun as early as September 1939 to beam broadcasts at the enemy and to direct the dropping of propaganda leaflets through such agencies as the Ministry of Information, the Political Intelligence Department of the Foreign Office, and the British Broadcasting Corporation. The United States, after its entry into the war, reinforced British efforts with the activities of the Office of War Information and the Office of Strategic Services. Both the British and U.S. civilian organizations had their own special appropriations, personnel, and equipment. Their activities included preparation for the cross-Channel attack.[32]

Political policies affecting the work of these agencies were set then, as during the period of SHAEF's operations, by the President, the Prime Minister, the Foreign

---

[31] Remarks, Eisenhower before ECAD and SHAEF Officer Personnel at Civil Affairs Center, 9 May 44, SHAEF G–5 Hist File 10, Histories and Monograph.

[32] Psychological Warfare Division (SHAEF), *An Account of Its Operations in the Western European Operation, 1944–45* (Bad Homburg, 1945), pp. 13–20. This study was prepared by the division shortly after the end of the war and is its official after action report.

Office, and the State Department. The Ministry of Information was responsible to Parliament for British propaganda. The degree of control exercised by the Office of War Information and the Office of Strategic Services was not always so clear cut, inasmuch as President Roosevelt in giving the former the chief responsibility for foreign propaganda activities, did not bar the latter's use of propaganda weapons for breaking enemy morale.[33]

The Allies initially gave the task of issuing broad directives for Allied propaganda efforts in northwest Europe to the Political Warfare Executive[34] and the Office of War Information. Such directives naturally required agreement in Washington and London. This arrangement was modified in the late summer of 1943, after the Allies had found themselves unprepared for the task of getting maximum psychological results from the fall of Mussolini. A new organization, known as the London Coordinating Committee for Political Warfare, and consisting of the representatives of the Foreign Office, the Political Warfare Executive, British Chiefs of Staff, State Department, Office of War Information, and U.S. Chiefs of Staff, was established to issue directives for emergency propaganda activities.[35] The U.S. members of the group soon complained that the British were attempting to use it to decide routine as well as emergency propaganda policy. The U.S. Chiefs of Staff prepared a protest but reconsidered when the State Department praised the work of the London Committee. Control of propaganda was centered in London much more fully than were civil affairs and similar matters. While the Combined Chiefs of Staff passed on propaganda plans relating to military operations, they tended to restrict their activities to approval of broad plans. Indicative of the difference in War Department

GENERAL McCLURE

control over civil affairs and propaganda was the fact that civil affairs was handled by a special division, whereas propaganda was restricted to a branch of the intelligence division.[36]

[33] App. B to Note by Secy JPS, Exec Order 9312, 9 Mar 43; Incl B to note by Secys PWPS, 13 Jan 44. Both in ABC Propaganda Com (15 Aug 43) 334.

[34] Made up of representatives of War Office, Admiralty, Foreign Office, and the Ministry of Information.

[35] This committee was known also by such names as the London Political Warfare Coordinating Committee, London Emergency Propaganda Committee, and London Propaganda Coordinating Committee. Its members were Sir Orme Sargent (Foreign Office), Chairman, Sir Robert Bruce Lockhart (Political Warfare Executive), Deputy Chairman, General Ismay (representative of the British Chiefs of Staff), Howard Bucknell (State Department), Wallace Carroll (Office of War Information), and Admiral Harold R. Stark (representative of the U.S. Chiefs of Staff).

[36] Memo for Info 171, 23 Dec 43, ABC 334 Propaganda Com (15 Aug 43) 334; Paul M. A. Linebarger, *Psychological Warfare* (Washington, 1948), Chs. 10–13; PWD (SHAEF), *An Account of Its Operations*, pp. 13–20.

Development of the press and propaganda division of SHAEF was influenced to a degree by the Information and Censorship Section (INC), established at Allied Force Headquarters in January 1943 under General McClure. After studying the North African organization, General Morgan in April 1943 proposed a similar branch for COSSAC and appointed a small staff to plan such a branch for SHAEF. In September 1943 he formally proposed the establishment of a Publicity and Psychological Warfare Section for SHAEF, and "a single channel to coordinate press and radio comment guidance in the U.S. with similar guidance to the UK. . . ."[37]

COSSAC's proposal, approved promptly by the British Chiefs of Staff, was countered by a U.S. suggestion that it await the appointment of the Supreme Commander. Contrary to the views of both British and U.S. advisers in London, the U.S. Chiefs of Staff desired joint heads for the organization. General Marshall, agreeing that the proposal violated sound principles of organization, justified it on the ground that the people of the United States and Great Britain would have more confidence in the operation if they knew their interests were being looked after by their own representatives. Asked by the British to reconsider this stand, the Combined Chiefs of Staff agreed to leave the matter to the Supreme Commander. He settled it early in 1944 when he expressed a preference for a single U.S. head of the division and a British deputy, and General McClure, who had been brought from the Allied Force Headquarters in November 1943 to head the COSSAC Publicity and Psychological Branch, was selected as chief of the new G–6 Division.[38]

The new organization was criticized on the ground that one of its functions might be cultivated at the expense of the other, depending on the major interest of the chief of the division. Inasmuch as psychological warfare activities required close co-ordination between the G–6 Division and the British and U.S. civilian agencies for propaganda, the press representatives feared that their problems might be neglected. General McClure recognized the difficulty in April 1944 when he disclosed that "these fundamentally different organizations could be directed more effectively if separated and reestablished directly in contact with appropriate operational and command channels." This initial suggestion for the abolition of the G–6 Division was approved, but his later proposal of 10 April to make the Psychological Warfare Division a general staff division was disregarded. The separation, as already noted, was completed on 13 April.[39]

Psychological Warfare Division

The task of Psychological Warfare in the first phase of its activities—the period before and after D Day until German morale began to crumble—consisted of long-term efforts to create in the German soldier's mind a belief in the reliability of Allied statements, in Allied unity, and in the certainty of German defeat. The short-term objective for phase one comprised the spreading of defeatism by showing Allied supremacy in men and weapons,

[37] Morgan to Br COS, 7 Sep 43, SHAEF SGS 322.01 Publicity and Psychological Warfare Div.

[38] Ltr, Morgan to Devers, 20 Sep 43; CCS 124th Mtg, 22 Oct 43; JSM 1277, 23 Oct 43; Br COS to JSM, COS (W) 923, 2 Nov 43; Memo, Barker for CCS, 31 Dec 43. All in SHAEF SGS Publicity and Psychological Warfare 322.01. SHAEF GO 2, 14 Feb 44.

[39] Memo, McClure for CofS, SHAEF, 5 Apr 44; Memo, McClure for CofS, SHAEF, 10 Apr 44; SHAEF GO 8, 13 Apr 44. All in SHAEF SGS 322.01 Organization and Personnel Public Relations Div, I.

emphasizing kind treatment of prisoners by the Allies, stimulating German anxiety about the danger of a two-front war and of sabotage and resistance by occupied peoples, and sowing distrust between the German Air Force and Army. After D Day greater effort was to be placed on spreading distrust of foreigners in the German Army.[40]

Plans to achieve these ends, prepared by the representatives of the Political Warfare Executive and the Office of War Information at SHAEF and approved by the Supreme Commander, had been sent to the Combined Chiefs of Staff before the abolition of the G–6 Division. In order to save time, General Eisenhower directed his staff to proceed on the assumption that the plan would be accepted. The State Department, which had not been asked for its opinion in advance, concluded that it was faced by a *fait accompli* and did little more than propose a few minor changes which were incorporated by the Combined Chiefs of Staff in their statement of general agreement with the Publicity and Psychological Warfare plans on 11 May 1944. By the time final changes were approved, the plan was already being carried out in many of its essential features.[41]

Allied operations were supported by three types of propaganda: strategic, combat, and consolidation. With the first type, strategic, SHAEF had little to do. Undermining the enemy's will to resist and sustaining the morale of Allied sympathizers were missions carried on by the Office of War Information, the Political Warfare Executive, the Ministry of Information, and the Office of Strategic Services under Office of War Information–Political Warfare Executive directives. The means included radio broadcasts, dropping of leaflets, and the use of agents. Combat propaganda was carried out in accordance

with SHAEF directives by army groups and, when necessary, by Allied naval and air forces. Activities of this type included the collection of psychological warfare information, use of tactical leaflets, and operation of mobile broadcasting units, mobile public address systems, monitoring service, and field printing. Consolidation propaganda operations, reserved specifically to SHAEF, included the collection of psychological warfare information; the operation or control and servicing of local newspapers, radio stations, and motion picture houses; distribution of propaganda literature and displays; and liaison with various headquarters on psychological warfare matters. In an effort to unify psychological warfare efforts, representatives of the chief civilian agencies engaged in propaganda activities—C. D. Jackson (OWI), R. H. S. Crossman (PWE), Dennis Routh (MOI), and Fred Oechsner (OSS)—were appointed as deputies to General McClure.[42]

General McClure met difficulties in persuading the 1st and 21 Army Groups to establish a general staff section in each headquarters to handle psychological warfare matters. The 1st Army Group, while not convinced of the need of establishing such a section, agreed after a short delay, but the 21 Army Group did not comply

---

[40] Early drafts and final text of SHAEF's "Standard Directive for Psychological Warfare against Members of the German Armed Forces," 16 Jun 44, SHAEF SGS 091/412/3 Psychological Warfare against Germany, I.

[41] Eisenhower to CCS, SCAF 12, 3 Apr 44, SHAEF SGS 381/1 P and PW Outline Plan OVERLORD, I; SHAEF to Air CinC, AEAF, 11 Apr 44, SHAEF SGS 091.412 Propaganda, I; CCS 545, 13 Apr 44; Memo, State Dept to Col Frank McCarthy, 22 Apr 44; CCS 545/2, 11 May 44. Both in ABC 385 Europe (23 Sep 43), Sec 3.

[42] SHAEF Opns Memo 8, 11 Mar 44, SHAEF SGS 322.01 Publicity and Psychological Warfare Div; PWD (SHAEF), *An Account of Its Operations*, p. 15.

until March. To guide the army groups, SHAEF drew up before D Day a directive for psychological warfare against the Germans. Its principles were generally followed in the early days of the invasion, but it was not formally issued until mid-June.

The Allied propaganda program was intended to aid the Supreme Commander to fulfill his mission with the most economical use of troops and equipment possible. At the same time, nothing was to be done to prejudice Allied policy toward Germany after the war ended. There was to be no suggestion that the German Army would be absolved from guilt of aggression or that German militarism would be allowed to continue in any form after the war. It was assumed that the Germans, having heard such propaganda in 1918, would be immune to this type of appeal and would fight against it. Instead the Allies were to stress the enemy's lack of manpower and equipment, the weakness of the Luftwaffe, and the superiority of the Allies, and to play up the ineffectiveness of Hitler's leadership, the impossibility of dealing successfully with two fronts, and the unlikelihood of German victory. The German soldier was to be convinced that he had done his full duty as a fighting man and could surrender with honor.[43]

Public Relations Division

The Public Relations Division was charged with responsibility for control of press, photographic, and radio censorship in the Supreme Commander's zone of operations, for general control over all communications which might be available in the military zone for the press, for information to press and radio correspondents for communiqués, and for policy for news correspondents in the European Theater of Operations.[44]

In carrying out its various duties, the Public Relations Division was caught between the necessity of maintaining strict operational security and the attempt to give the people of Great Britain and the United States the maximum number of details about their forces. Many delicate problems faced the SHAEF officials in struggling with this dilemma. The information given correspondents before D Day, the movement of correspondents in the preinvasion period, and the briefing of correspondents from neutral countries might all be helpful to the enemy. Allied commanders found, for example, that the dating of a dispatch from a zone of concentration or a statement by a well-known correspondent like Ernie Pyle or Alan Moorehead that he had been in a specific part of the United Kingdom might draw attention to Allied preparations. The Prime Minister was alarmed when a British military writer showed him privately the main outlines of the invasion plan which he had put together from fragments of information given him unwittingly by a number of officers. Even more disconcerting were the rather accurate surmises as to Allied plans which correspondents made in the absence of official statements.[45]

The situation in the United Kingdom became worse as the number of correspondents rapidly increased in anticipa-

---

[43] SHAEF directive on psychological warfare, 16 Jun 44, SHAEF SGS 091/412/3 Psychological Warfare against Germany, I.

[44] SHAEF Opns Memo 24, Press Policy, 24 Apr 44, SHAEF SGS Policy re Release of Info to Press 000.7; History of U.S. and Supreme Headquarters, AEF, Press Censorship in the European Theater of Operations, 1942–45, MS, mimeo, Chs. 2–3, OCMH files.

[45] See Ltr, Churchill to Eisenhower, 28 Jan 44, and other correspondence on subject in SHAEF SGS 000.7 Policy re Release of Info to Press.

tion of D Day. There was no rigid control over newsmen and photographers like that enforced by censors in the field. In concern over these developments in the opening days of 1944, the British Chiefs of Staff had asked that General Eisenhower be informed of the situation as soon as he arrived in London. General McClure recommended that a carefully selected and limited number of correspondents be accredited to SHAEF and that their dispatches be subjected to military censorship. The need for some form of control was accentuated near the end of January by a British security report which showed that secrecy of invasion preparations had been compromised by continued accounts of General Montgomery's visits to invasion ports and by a statement from ENSA, the British equivalent of the United Services Organization (USO), that it was ready to proceed overseas after the end of January. The Prime Minister reminded the Supreme Commander that efforts were being made to persuade editors in the United States and Great Britain not to make forecasts as to the possible date of the cross-Channel attack or the size of forces to be employed. Churchill suggested that "a very stringent attitude should be adopted in regard to communication to Press Correspondents in this country of any background information about OVERLORD operations, either before they start, or while they proceed."[46]

General Eisenhower, preferring to proceed slowly with the accrediting of correspondents to his headquarters, said that Mr. Brendan Bracken, director of the Ministry of Information, had agreed to talk with General McClure concerning "the best means of keeping the Press securely in the dark" without appearing to treat them as outsiders. The Supreme Commander insisted on the necessity of assuring the correspondents that the SHAEF press relations staff was friendly to them. Among steps which General Eisenhower took to preserve secrecy were the reissuance of a British circular of the preceding April forbidding senior commanders to hold press conferences on operational matters without special permission, and a directive to General McClure to co-ordinate all U.S. public relations policy for the theater.[47]

As the date for the invasion approached, Mr. William Phillips, the United States political officer for SHAEF, proposed that General Eisenhower brief the press on the combined effort of the Allies in order that they might have something "exciting and imaginative" to think about before D Day. General Eisenhower agreed to the suggestion, and gave an "off the record" interview on 16 May. He had prepared the way by issuing an order to his unit commanders two weeks before the conference reminding them that correspondents once they had been accredited to SHAEF were considered as "quasi-staff officers." Therefore, they were to be given all reasonable assistance. They were to be allowed to talk freely with officers and enlisted men and to "see the machinery of war in operation in order to visualize and transmit to the public the conditions under which the men from their countries are waging war against the enemy." He read this order to the correspondents at the beginning of his

---

[46] Ismay to COSSAC, 14 Jan 44; McClure to CofS, SHAEF, 22 Jan 44; McClure to CofS, SHAEF, 23 Jan 44; Ltr, Churchill to Eisenhower, 28 Jan 44. All in SHAEF SGS 000.7 Policy re Release of Info to Press, I.

[47] Ltr, Eisenhower to Churchill, 6 Feb 44; Incl to Ltr, Brig Ian C. Jacob to Smith, 31 Jan 44; Memo, Brig Jacob for Smith, 7 Feb 44; Memo, Smith for Lee, Bradley, and others, 11 Feb 44. All in SHAEF SGS 000.7 Policy re Release of Info to Press.

mid-May conference, reiterating his belief that public opinion wins wars. "Without public opinion back of us," he added, "we would be nothing but mercenaries." The people should be informed if the tide of battle was going against them, and if the fault lay with the leadership. He promised that there would be no censorship of any criticism the correspondents might make of him, because he did not believe that "a military man in high places should use his extraordinary power to protect himself." [48]

On 1 May 1944, SHAEF issued its plans for control of the press during the OVERLORD operations. It was to accredit correspondents, radiomen, photographers, and newsreel men and assign them to lower units in accordance with a block system by which a specified number was to be accepted by each unit. Correspondents from the various Allied countries were to be treated on a basis of equality in regard to communications, transportation, and the like. During the next month, the Public Relations Division worked at the task of compiling a list of accredited photographers, press correspondents, and radiomen. The list on 7 June 1944 numbered 530. [49]

Press Censorship

In carrying out its task of censoring news and photographs, SHAEF followed British and U.S. practices developed in the United Kingdom after the outbreak of war. U.S. censors had been appointed in 1942 shortly after U.S. troops arrived in the United Kingdom, and worked in close contact with the British censors. In late April 1944, a Joint Press Censorship Group, headed by Lt. Col. Richard H. Merrick (U.S.) and including officers

from the Allied ground, sea, and air forces was organized. Its purpose was to advise the British Ministry of Information on censorship of press and radio material originating in the United Kingdom which dealt with contemplated operations, and to censor material returned to the United Kingdom from the Continent. The chief of the Public Relations Division was made responsible for the censorship of press material originating in the United Kingdom which dealt with U.S. forces. [50]

SHAEF gave responsibility for field press censorship to the army group commanders. These were to consult, if necessary, with Allied air and naval commanders. In censoring news, they were to be guided by the principle that "the minimum of information would be withheld from the public consistent with security." In general they were not to release military information that might prove helpful to the enemy, unauthenticated, inaccurate, or false reports, or reports likely to injure the morale of the Allied forces. The following items were among those which could

---

[48] Phillips to CofS, SHAEF, 10 Apr 44; Davis to CofS, SHAEF, 16 May 44; Memo, Eisenhower for all unit comdrs, AEF, 8 May 44, and draft of 3 May 44 with major changes in Eisenhower's handwriting; Eisenhower interview with correspondents, 22 May 44. All in SHAEF SGS 000.74 Press Correspondents.

[49] Public Relations plans and annexes, 1 May 44, SHAEF SGS 381/9 Public Relations Plan for OVERLORD: list of correspondents accredited by SHAEF, 7 Jun 44, SHAEF SGS 000.74 Press Correspondents. The 530 photographers, reporters, and radiomen were distributed as follows: U.S.: press associations 72, radio 25, individual newspapers 79, magazines 35, photographers (including newsreel cameramen) 25, Army correspondents 19—total 255; British: press associations 30, individual newspapers 118, radio 48, magazines 7, photographers 12—total 215; Canadian: press associations 7, newspapers 13, radio 5, magazines 1—total 26; Australian: press associations 10, newspapers 15, total—25; Allied (French, Dutch, and Norwegian)—9.

[50] SHAEF Opns Memo 27, 25 Apr 44, SHAEF SGS 000.73 Policy and Infraction of Press Censorship.

be cleared only by SHAEF censors: (1) all matters of high policy involving SHAEF or the Supreme Commander; (2) the release of information on troops of various nationalities taking part in actions; (3) casualties and troop strength; (4) cipher work and code words; (5) civil affairs; (6) confirmation of enemy allegations, atrocities, and the like; (7) escapes; (8) gas and chemical warfare; (9) military equipment; (10) strength and morale of troops; (11) high-ranking officers at SHAEF; (12) changes in command and movement of high-ranking officers; (13) stories concerning prisoners of war involving harsh treatment; (14) psychological warfare; (15) resistance and underground movements; (16) sabotage and spies; and (17) naval ships and commanders.[51]

Censors were guided by a press censorship bible, a 200-page mimeographed document containing the censorship policy of British, Canadian, and U.S. forces in the European theater. This was supplemented by daily directives, known as Press Relations Censorship Guidances and Press Censors' Guidances, which listed items to be stopped or passed by the censors; by the Secret List, issued monthly by the War Office, containing the security classification of Allied equipment; by "Trend of Copy," a summary of the type of newspaper copy which had been passed or stopped by the censors; and by pertinent Ministry of Information statements.[52]

The Special Staff Divisions

With the exception of the Adjutant General's Division, which confined its activities chiefly to Supreme Headquarters, the special staff divisions of SHAEF were supervisory rather than operational in nature. The chiefs of most of these divi-

sions spoke of their functions as being mainly those of inspectors general. The divisions strengthened the unity of Allied operations by co-ordinating the work of the army groups and the supply organizations. They estimated future needs of the various field forces, checked plans made at lower levels, helped smooth out difficulties between lower headquarters, and used the authority of the Supreme Commander to get men or equipment needed for carrying out various operations.

Adjutant General's Division

The Adjutant General's Division was established on U.S. principles of organization and staffed largely by U.S. officers and men.[53] It performed the usual adjutant general functions, handling incoming and outgoing mail, preparing and editing orders, preparing circulars and directives, and filing records. It shared some of these functions with the Office of the Secretary, General Staff. General Davis, the original adjutant general, had held the same post at Allied Force Headquarters until brought by General Eisenhower to SHAEF. At the end of March 1944 General Davis received his assignment as head of the Public Relations Division. He was succeeded as head of the Adjutant Gen-

[51] Public relations plan issued 1 May 44 with annexes, SHAEF SGS 381/9 OVERLORD Public Relations Plan; SHAEF Opns Memo 27, 25 Apr 44, SHAEF SGS 000.73 Policy and Infraction of Press Censorship, I; PRD, History of Press Censorship, pp. 102–03.
[52] PRD, History of Press Censorship, pp. 85–87. For press relations activities from June 1944 to May 1945 see below, Appendix A.
[53] Unlike other SHAEF divisions, the AG Division had no British deputy. At peak strength, the division had 23 British officers and men (1 officer, 2 warrant officers, and 20 enlisted men) as compared to 102 U.S. members (18 officers, 10 warrant officers, and 74 enlisted men).

eral's Division by his deputy, Col. Emil C. Boehnke. In October 1944, General Davis returned to his original position as adjutant general.

Signal Division

The Signal Division, like most SHAEF staff divisions, was engaged primarily in high-level planning. It also co-ordinated all Allied signal activities. The division examined the requirements of British and U.S. forces for signal personnel and equipment, and helped work out policy and priorities relative to the issuance of equipment. It prepared frequency allotments for radios and co-ordinated radar plans and operations, codes and cipher systems to be used by forces under SHAEF, all operating procedures, and all wire and cable systems in the United Kingdom and the projected areas of operations. Much of this work was done through a Combined Signal Committee of which the SHAEF chief signal officer was chairman. This committee consisted of representatives of SHAEF, the Allied Naval Expeditionary Force, the Allied Expeditionary Air Force, Headquarters, European Theater of Operations, and the army groups.

The original intention had been to select a U.S. officer as head of the division, but in view of the dependence of the Allied forces on the British communications system during the preinvasion and early invasion periods the post went to a British officer, Maj. Gen. C. H. H. Vulliamy, who was brought from the Middle East Command. Maj. Gen. Francis H. Lanahan, Jr. (U.S.), was selected as his deputy. The U.S. officer was given a free hand in dealing with U.S. signal personnel and equipment. General Lanahan succeeded General Vulliamy when the latter was trans-

ferred to the India Command in April 1945. Maj. Gen. L. B. Nicholls (Br.) then became Deputy Signal Officer.

British and U.S. signal units commanded by a U.S. colonel handled SHAEF communications. SHAEF also undertook to control the maintenance of lines up to points some twenty miles from the front lines. The actual work, however, was carried on in this SHAEF zone by Headquarters, Communications Zone. The SHAEF signal division put in lines for correspondents working for Supreme Headquarters, but had no control of psychological warfare or intelligence signal communications.[54]

Engineer Division

The work of the SHAEF Engineer Division was limited mainly to co-ordinating the work of the army groups. An important function was to anticipate army group needs for engineer supplies and help procure engineer matériel from the Allied supply organizations. These tasks were complicated because there was no clear demarcation of responsibilities between the G–4 and the Engineer Division. By planning ahead, the division was able to furnish the army groups with terrain studies, engineer intelligence studies, recommendations on new techniques, equipment, and tactics, and outline engineer estimates of the situation.

The Engineer Division's responsibilities for allocating engineer materials between the army groups were limited in northwest Europe because in most things the national forces were already well enough supplied from their own engineer stocks. One exception was timber, which tended

---

[54] Interv with Gen Vulliamy, 22 Jan 47.

to be largely in one army's area. SHAEF was required to intervene and make more equitable division of this scarce commodity.[55]

The Engineer Division was headed throughout 1944 by a British officer, Maj. Gen. H. B. W. Hughes, who held a similar position in the Middle East Command. He was succeeded by his U.S. deputy, Brig. Gen. Beverly C. Dunn in February 1945. Brigadier R. Briggs then became deputy. The four chief branches of the division—general administration, operations, transportation, and aerodrome construction—were all headed by U.S. officers. During his tenure, General Hughes usually worked with the British military groups and the Ministry of Transport and Supply, while General Dunn dealt with the U.S. units.

Medical Division

SHAEF's smallest division, the medical, which during most of the war consisted of thirteen officers and men, was responsible for the medical services of the Allied Expeditionary Force. In the words of Maj. Gen. Albert W. Kenner, the chief of the Medical Division, his job "was more that of a medical Inspector General than anything else." His task was to integrate and coordinate British and U.S. medical planning and later that of the French forces. General Kenner was directed to correct any medical practices which were not up to standard.[56]

The Medical Division performed its functions by maintaining liaison with British and U.S. army groups, Headquarters, ETOUSA, the War Office, Admiralty, Air Ministry, and Ministry of Health, giving advice and reports to the Supreme Commander and staff on all matters relating to the British and U.S.

medical service within the Command, collecting and collating all available medical data, visiting medical installations, demonstrations, exercises, experiments, and trials in the European and other theaters and making reports on them.

General Kenner, who had served as Chief Surgeon, North African Forces, remained as head of the Medical Division throughout the life of SHAEF. Three British officers, Brigadier E. A. Sutton, Brigadier R. W. Galloway, and Brigadier H. L. Garson, served in succession as his deputies.

Air Defense Division

The Air Defense Division was based on a similar organization which had been established in the Mediterranean theater in 1943 in order to prevent Allied antiaircraft units from shooting down their own planes as they had at Bari. The Mediterranean practice of having a major general at Allied Force Headquarters to command the antiaircraft group directly was made unfeasible in the European command by the presence of three, and later of four, widely separated groups. Maj. Gen. A. M. Cameron was told, therefore, on his appointment that he was to be more an inspector general than a staff chief. He was to make sure that there were no gaps in port defenses between the three services and to act in the Supreme Commander's name to make changes if they were needed.[57]

Other tasks of the Air Defense Division included the adjustment of antiaircraft units between the army groups and the Ninth Air Force. At Cherbourg, for exam-

[55] Interv with Gen Hughes, 12 Feb 47.
[56] Interv with Gen Kenner, 27 May 48.
[57] Interv with Gen Cameron, 22 Jan 47.

GENERAL CAMERON

GENERAL VULLIAMY

GENERAL KENNER

GENERAL HUGHES

ple, SHAEF added British elements to aid the U.S. antiaircraft elements; at Antwerp it did the reverse. These allocations were normally made by the deputy, initially a British officer, Col. W. S. J. Carter. He was replaced in February 1945 by Brig. Gen. Samuel L. McCroskey (U.S.).

Political Officers

The political officers at SHAEF were diplomats selected by the Department of State and the Foreign Office to represent them at Supreme Headquarters. Both the United States and Great Britain continued a practice which they had started at General Eisenhower's headquarters shortly after the landings in North Africa. The advisers thus named remained as civilian officials under the control of their superiors in Washington and London. Their purpose was to make available to the Supreme Commander political information which might help him in planning and to acquaint him with the political implications of proposed actions.[58]

The political officers were called on in particular in regard to civil affairs, military government, psychological warfare, intelligence, and posthostilities planning. The Foreign Office appointed Mr. Charles B. P. Peake as political adviser to the COSSAC organization in September 1943. About the middle of that month, the Secretary of State appointed William Phillips as his representative to the Chief of Staff to the Supreme Allied Commander with the rank of Ambassador. Early in 1944 both Mr. Peake and Mr. Phillips were appointed to the SHAEF staff with the title of Political Officers.[59] In this capacity they made suggestions relative to the civil affairs organization for France, giving their support to SHAEF's efforts to find a French political authority with which the Supreme Commander could deal. They also helped the psychological warfare division of SHAEF draw up a proposed statement on unconditional surrender which might soften that formula. They were also included among the members of the Joint Intelligence Committee (SHAEF). The SHAEF officials gave the political officers full opportunities to follow planning and to question any plans that might have a political bearing. The two advisers reported to the SHAEF chief of staff contents of political dispatches which they thought might be of interest to Generals Eisenhower and Smith.

At the beginning of September 1944 Mr. Phillips was assigned other duties and Mr. Samuel Reber, who had been counsellor of mission on Mr. Phillips' staff, was designated by the President as Political Officer at SHAEF for France and other liberated countries.[60] Shortly afterward, Ambassador Robert D. Murphy was appointed as Political Officer for German Affairs. He was well acquainted with General Eisenhower and many members of

[58] This section has drawn on information furnished by Ambassador Robert D. Murphy, former Ambassador Phillips, and Mr. Samuel Reber to the author in letters of 6 September 1951, 23 October 1951, and 30 October 1951. Mr. Murphy says of his appointment in North Africa: ". . . as far as I know, my assignment to AFHQ as Political Adviser and Chief Civil Affairs Officer was the first instance in our history of such an arrangement under which a civilian was attached to a military headquarters and permitted to participate in regular staff meetings with access to classified communications, both military and political. As there was apparently no precedent for it, General Eisenhower was guided largely by his own good judgment and conception of the needs of the situation. These usually were concurred in by the British element of his headquarters."

[59] SHAEF GO 2, 14 Feb 44. (The title Political Adviser was used from time to time in SHAEF correspondence, but Political Officer was the title which normally appeared in SHAEF organization charts).

[60] SHAEF GO 18, 2 Sep 44.

the SHAEF staff, having served as Political Adviser in North Africa, as Chief Civil Affairs Adviser on Italian Affairs at Allied Force Headquarters, and as U.S. member on the Advisory Council of the Allied Control Commission for Italy. Mr. Charles Peake remained as the British Political Officer until February 1945 when he was replaced by Mr. Christopher Steel.

In the period between the liberation of Paris and the re-establishment of the U.S. and British Embassies there, the SHAEF political officers were responsible for non-military relations with national authorities that might be functioning in France. They were also charged with co-ordinating the work of the special SHAEF missions to continental governments. As normal diplomatic channels were re-established, the functions of these officers decreased. Mr. Peake's successor devoted himself primarily to German affairs after his appointment in February 1945. Mr. Reber was transferred to another post in April 1945.

Mr. Murphy's position was somewhat complicated in that he served as a representative of the State Department with the rank of Ambassador on the SHAEF staff and also as director of the Political Division in the U.S. Group Control Council, set up under Brig. Gen. Cornelius W. Wickersham to formulate policy and create the nucleus of the organization of U.S. military government in Germany.[61] It was his responsibility to reflect the views of the Department of State in the preparation of the papers drawn up by this group. He also kept abreast of the activities of the European Advisory Commission which was engaged in drawing up surrender terms for Germany and policy for the occupation of that country.

The various political officers had their own staffs, including both military and State Department personnel. They had direct access to the Supreme Commander but usually conducted their business through the chief of staff. They also attended staff conferences of the Supreme Commander and of the chief of staff when matters pertaining to the liberated countries and Germany were discussed.

Committees

Inter-Allied committees handled much of SHAEF's work of co-ordination. In many cases, these groups were headed by SHAEF deputy chiefs of staff or chiefs of division. Their multifold activities extended to such questions as fuel, transportation, equipment of troops in liberated countries, combined civil affairs activities, censorship, intelligence, psychological warfare, displaced persons, counterintelligence, forestry and timber supply, communications, prisoners of war, and radio broadcasting. After the liberation of the various occupied countries, SHAEF was represented through its missions on a Four Party Committee, which dealt with all problems relating to imports for the civilian economy, a subcommittee on coal, a coal working party, a port working party, an inter-Allied railroad commission, an inter-Allied waterways commission, a military Rhine agency, a merchant marine commission, a POL working party, and an informal committee on food supplies. Still later, SHAEF was also represented on CCS committees dealing with military government for Germany.

Locations of SHAEF

SHAEF opened formally in the old COSSAC headquarters at Norfolk House,

---

[61] See below, p. 351.

but moved in March 1944 to Bushy Park, near Kingston-on-Thames, on the outskirts of London. WIDEWING, as it was known in military code, was built in a part of the park used by the Eighth Air Force, and opened in March 1944. It had been selected after some search to meet General Eisenhower's insistence that his headquarters not be set up in a large city. A hutted camp was built between 10 January and 1 March 1944 to fill the SHAEF request for 130,000 square feet of floor space and for billets to accommodate 688 officers and 2,156 enlisted men. New units continued to be attached to or located near Supreme Headquarters, so that at the time of invasion, accommodations had been built for 750 officers and 6,000 enlisted men.[62]

Shortly after the movement of SHAEF from London to Bushy Park, additional planning was started for the establishment of advanced echelons of Supreme Headquarters. An advance command post known as SHARPENER was opened for the Supreme Commander in early May at Portsmouth near the advance headquarters of 21 Army Group and the Allied Naval Expeditionary Force. Another advanced post of SHAEF was set up at Stanmore, adjacent to the Headquarters, Allied Expeditionary Air Force.[63]

One of the chief considerations in the establishment of these and later command posts was the availability of adequate signal communications needed to connect the Supreme Commander with London, Washington, Algiers (and later Caserta), and the army group commanders. In the United Kingdom this task was simplified by the Defence Telecommunications Network of Great Britain, consisting of circuits transferred from the civil trunk system and of circuits newly constructed. The British

naval, air, and army headquarters also had their own wire systems in addition to the regular civil telephone system. For a time after the move to Bushy Park, SHAEF used the lines of the Eighth Air Force. Later new construction improved and greatly extended these communications. Remote control lines connected SHAEF with its bombproof signal center at the north end of the underground shelter at Goodge Street Station in London, where telephone, radio, and telegraph facilities were opened on 11 March 1944. This signal center served SHAEF as an outlet until the end of the war. SHAEF communications throughout the war were handled by the U.S. 3118th Signal Service Battalion and the British 5 Headquarters Signals, both of which were frequently enlarged.[64]

By the time of the invasion, the basic framework of Supreme Headquarters had been built. Later developments were confined to minor changes to make it conform to operational demands or to prepare it for posthostilities occupation duties. Earlier concepts of a small "Foch type" headquarters suitable for a commander whose task was to be restricted to over-all coordination had been forgotten. Instead there had been organized a headquarters large enough to permit General Eisenhower to exercise, in many cases directly, the great variety of functions assigned to the Supreme Commander, including, after 1 September 1944, the direction of ground operations in the field.

---

[62] Interv with Brig Gen Robert Q. Brown (Commandant of SHAEF), Dec 45.

[63] Col Kutz's Memo dtd "April 1944" in answer to Gen Bull's Memo of 26 Apr 44, SHAEF G–3 (Movement, Composition, etc.), GCT, 370.5–41 Ops A.

[64] Rpt of Signal Div, SHAEF, I, 1–48.

CHAPTER V

Planning Before SHAEF

SHAEF drew heavily on its predecessor commands for principles of organization and key personnel. In planning, it depended even more heavily on the British and U.S. staffs which since early in the war had been making strategic decisions and tactical and logistical preparations for a cross-Channel attack. Without these preliminary efforts, the Supreme Commander and his subordinates could not have hoped to launch Operation OVERLORD in June 1944.

Early Background

Prime Minister Churchill had considered the idea of an early return to the Continent even as the final British elements were being evacuated from the ports of Normandy and Brittany in June 1940, and as he was having to improvise defensive measures against a German attack. He ordered the organization of raiding forces to hit the coasts of countries occupied by the enemy and in July 1940 set up a Combined Operations Headquarters to handle these activities. Thinking in terms of ultimate tank attacks along the Channel coast, he asked his planners to develop special landing craft which could carry armored vehicles to the far shore. These armored elements, he hoped, could make deep raids inland, cut vital communication lines, and then make their escape. Larger forces he predicted, might surprise Calais or Boulogne, kill or capture the enemy garrison, and hold the area until preparation had been made to reduce it. Mr. Churchill's orders turned the minds of the British planners toward offensive operations and launched a program of landing craft production that was essential to the ultimate cross-Channel attack.[1]

In September 1941, Gen. Sir John Dill, Chief of the Imperial General Staff, directed the British military planners to formulate a plan for a return to the Continent. He added significantly that it should take into consideration the capabilities of U.S. construction. Members of the Future Operational Planning Section, GHQ, were gathering data on such an operation before the end of that year. The British Chiefs of Staff Committee gave further impetus to this planning on 2 January 1942 by directing General Paget, then Commander-in-Chief, Home Forces, "to prepare an outline for operations on the Continent in the final phases and to review the plan periodically with a view to being able to put it into effect if a sudden change in the situation should appear to warrant such a course."[2]

---

[1] Winston S. Churchill, *Their Finest Hour* (Boston, 1949), Ch. 12; Lt Col Paddy Corbett, The Evolution and Development of Amphibious Technique and Material, 1945, MS, OCMH files; Brig A. H. Head, The Evolution and Development of Amphibious Technique and Material, 1945, MS, OCMH files; Rear Adm Viscount Mountbatten of Burma to author, 18 Feb 47.

[2] Brigadier A. H. Head, "Amphibious Operations," *Journal of the Royal United Service Institution*, XCI (No-

After a brief study of the problems involved in a cross-Channel attack, the British Joint Planners agreed that the greatest contribution to the Allied cause in 1942 would be to divert enemy forces from the Eastern Front. An examination of German fortifications on the Channel coast of Europe led them to conclude, however, that no sustained land operation could be made in that area in 1942. Their proposal that chief emphasis be placed on forcing the German Air Force to fight in the west was accepted by the British Chiefs of Staff. The latter directed the Combined Commanders—an informal planning staff consisting of General Paget, Home Forces, Air Chief Marshal Sir Sholto Douglas, Fighter Command, and Vice Adm. Lord Louis Mountbatten, Combined Operations—to make plans for this purpose.[3]

In the United States, the War Department was also turning its attention to plans for attacking the enemy in northwest Europe. Committed to the policy of defeating Germany first, the United States started moving troops to the United Kingdom in the early months of 1942. Headquarters, U.S. Army Forces in the British Isles (USAFBI), was established in London on 8 January 1942 under Maj. Gen. James E. Chaney, and Headquarters, V Corps, was sent to Northern Ireland in the same month. Brig. Gen. Ira C. Eaker and the staff of his bomber command, constituting the advance elements of the U.S. Army Air Forces in Great Britain, arrived in January; forward detachments of the VIII Bomber Command began to appear in February.[4]

The views of General Marshall and his staff were well illustrated in a War Plans Division memorandum of 28 February 1942 presented by General Eisenhower, then the WPD chief. Emphasizing the importance of keeping the USSR in the war, Eisenhower proposed that the United States immediately extend lend-lease aid to the Red forces and initiate operations to draw sizable portions of the German Army from the Russian front. In particular, he urged the development of a definite plan for operations against northwest Europe in conjunction with the British on a scale sufficiently great "to engage from the middle of May onward, an increasing portion of the German Air Force, and by late summer an increasing amount of his ground forces." On 16 March the U.S. Joint Staff Planners, made up of representatives from the planning staffs of the Army, Navy, and Air Force, reported on alternative plans for U.S. Forces. They held that the United States should restrict its Pacific theater activities to existing commitments and concentrate on building up forces in the United Kingdom. This suggestion reached the U.S. Chiefs of Staff on the same day the British presented a tentative plan for invading the Le Havre area of France during the summer of 1942 in case of severe

---

[3] The Combined Commanders contributed heavily to the fund of knowledge on which COSSAC was later to draw. This staff was later enlarged to include the British Commander-in-Chief, Portsmouth (Admiral Sir Charles Little), and the Commander, U.S. Forces in Europe, also attended some meetings. Air Chief Marshal Douglas was later replaced on the committee by Air Chief Marshal Leigh-Mallory. See Harrison, *Cross-Channel Attack*, Ch. 1, for details of the important work done by this group.

[4] The author has drawn mainly in these early sections on Harrison, *Cross-Channel Attack*, Chs. I–VII; and Cline, *Washington Command Post: OPD*. See also Sherwood, *Roosevelt and Hopkins*, Chs. XXIV, XXV, and Matloff and Snell, *Strategic Planning for Coalition Warfare, 1941-42.*

---

vember, 1946), 485–94; Br COS 2d Mtg, 2 Jan 42, quoted in Capt. Martin McLaren, The Story of SLEDGEHAMMER, MS, OCMH files. (Captain McLaren was a member of General Paget's staff and later secretary of the COSSAC staff.)

deterioration of the enemy's position. At the suggestion of General Marshall, the Combined Chiefs of Staff now ordered a study made of the possibilities of (1) landing and maintaining forces on the Continent in 1942 and (2) an invasion early in 1943.

Meanwhile, in London, the Combined Commanders continued their investigations of invasion possibilities. After a somewhat gloomy forecast in March, they reported in April that if one did not have to consider the dangerous weakening of the defenses of the United Kingdom, and if they could find means of supplying an attacking force, an operation against the Continent was practicable. They warned, however, that if the enemy made a major diversion of his forces to the west the Allies would face the loss of equipment and most of their troops. The British Chiefs of Staff now asked for a study of possible landings which could be made should Russia be dangerously hard pressed in 1942. To this query the Commanders replied on 13 April that, other than air action, raiding was the only means of achieving this objective.[5]

Shortly before the final April report by the Combined Commanders, General Marshall and Mr. Hopkins went to London to discuss Allied strategy for 1942 and 1943. In the first definite plan for a large-scale cross-Channel operation presented to the British Chiefs of Staff, General Marshall proposed to build up the U.S. force to one million men for an invasion of the Continent on 1 April 1943. The British were to contribute an additional eighteen divisions. In case of an emergency created by a serious weakening of Russia or the probable collapse of Germany, a force was to be put in readiness to enter the Continent in the fall of 1942. The British on 14

April accepted the Marshall proposals. The name BOLERO was given to the build-up preparation, and names of plans already in existence for the return to the Continent were assigned to the other phases of the Marshall proposal. The emergency return to the Continent was named SLEDGEHAMMER, and the assault in northwest Europe for 1943 was called ROUNDUP.

Almost before the Americans returned to the United States, there were indications that Mr. Churchill was uncertain that a cross-Channel operation could be put into effect in the near future. Churchill and General Brooke reopened the whole question during a trip to Washington in late June. While agreeing with the U.S. Chiefs of Staff that the Allies should be prepared to act offensively in 1942, they proposed that alternative operations be made ready in case no sound and successful plan for the cross-Channel attack could be contrived. They asked particularly that the possibilities of an attack in North Africa be explored.[6]

The Prime Minister's revival of the proposal for a North African operation and his reluctance to undertake the cross-Channel attack in 1942 upset the plans of the U.S. Chiefs of Staff, who were proceeding with the build-up in the United Kingdom. General Marshall felt that if the Allies did not divert enemy forces from the Russian front in 1942 a full-scale attack on northwest Europe might be ineffective in 1943. He feared also that if they turned to the North African operation they would make a build-up in the United Kingdom impossible in 1942 and would curtail, if

---

[5] McLaren, The Story of SLEDGEHAMMER.

[6] Such an operation had already been considered under the name of Operation GYMNAST.

not make impossible, the full-scale attack in 1943. He and Admiral King held that, if they were not to have complete adherence to the build-up plan for 1942, they should turn to the Pacific theater and strike decisively against Japan with full strength and ample reserves.[7]

The U.S. Chiefs of Staff on 25 June strengthened their build-up efforts in the United Kingdom by establishing a Headquarters, European Theater of Operations. General Eisenhower was appointed theater commander. Three weeks later the President sent General Marshall, Admiral King, and Mr. Hopkins to London to get an agreement from the British on operations for 1942 and 1943. Mr. Roosevelt stressed the importance of bringing U.S. ground troops into action against the enemy in order to aid the Russians in 1942. Believing that SLEDGEHAMMER might be the operation that would "save Russia this year," he instructed his representatives to abandon it only if they were sure it was impossible. In that event, they were to consider other plans to use U.S. troops in 1942. Unlike General Marshall and Admiral King, Roosevelt refused to consider the alternative of an all-out effort in the Pacific, insisting that the defeat of Japan would not mean the defeat of Germany, whereas the surrender of Germany would mean the downfall of Japan, perhaps without the firing of a shot or the loss of a life.[8]

The British Chiefs of Staff had taken a firm position on the cross-Channel operation before the Americans arrived. They had decided that British commitments in Africa, the Middle East, and India, their efforts in keeping the sea lanes open, and their air activities were such that it would be impossible to undertake a cross-Channel attack seriously in 1942. Further, they feared that the mounting of SLEDGEHAM-

MER would ruin prospects for ROUNDUP in 1943. Soon after General Marshall reached London he realized that an alternative plan would have to be accepted for 1942. Mr. Churchill and President Roosevelt then decided that the Allies would invade North Africa. General Eisenhower was appointed to lead the operation.[9]

The North African invasion, known as TORCH, strongly influenced preparations for the cross-Channel attack. By diverting Allied resources to the Mediterranean, it interfered seriously with the BOLERO build-up in the United Kingdom and, as General Marshall had feared, rendered ROUNDUP impracticable in 1943. So much of the air strength of the Eighth U.S. Air Force was sent to the Mediterranean that its efforts against Germany, begun in the summer of 1942, were virtually abandoned. The British, however, continued their bombing activities against the Reich. The campaign in the Mediterranean was extended in 1943 to Sicily and to Italy.

Despite the failure to get a cross-Channel attack under way, preparations for such an operation continued and many developments in the United Kingdom and the United States strengthened the Allied position for an ultimate assault on northwest Europe. Until the spring of 1943, the Combined Commanders, with representatives of Headquarters, ETOUSA, sitting in on their meetings, worked on cross-

---

[7] Sherwood, *Roosevelt and Hopkins*, pp. 590–91, has an excellent summary of possible reasons why Mr. Churchill opposed a cross-Channel attack in 1942. See also Harrison, *Cross-Channel Attack*. For General Marshall's view, see his letter to General Eisenhower, 16 Jul 42, OPD Misc File.

[8] Presidential dir to Marshall, Hopkins, and King, 16 Jul 42, copy in Diary Office CinC, 18 Jul 42.

[9] Churchill, *The Hinge of Fate* (Boston, 1950), pp. 381, 433–51; Eisenhower, *Crusade in Europe*, p. 70.

Channel plans.[10] Although planning during this period was frequently on an academic level, the various staffs gathered information on amphibious operations, assault training centers developed new techniques, and movements and transportation directors put ports and railroad centers in condition to handle the invasion forces when the proper time came. At the same time bombing raids against the enemy were increasing, and U.S. production was hitting its stride.

The period was marked by efforts in the United Kingdom to organize and aid Resistance forces in the occupied countries. Propaganda campaigns were launched against the Axis in the hope of softening enemy opposition before the invasion of northwest Europe began. In North Africa, the Allies moved toward an understanding with the French and took steps to arm French units. Some of these were to perform brilliantly against the enemy in Italy. Others, raised and equipped in 1943, were to fight later in southern France and northwest Europe.

In August 1942, while TORCH preparations were under way, a force of 5,000 troops, mostly Canadian, attacked Dieppe. Despite heavy casualties suffered by these units, the raid was of great importance to the Allies in the development of amphibious tactics. It made clear the necessity of overwhelming naval and air support for a successful assault on coastal fortifications.[11]

Perhaps most important to the future commanders of the cross-Channel attack was the time they gained during Mediterranean operations in 1942 and 1943 to develop new doctrines and to train leaders in the lessons learned in battle. New ideas acquired in fighting were passed on to units then being activated.

In the United Kingdom, the training of troops who were to fight in northwest Europe became constantly more realistic as General Paget, commander of Home Forces, prepared British soldiers for coming operations. In the United States, Lt. Gen. Lesley J. McNair, equally wedded to principles of toughness, thoroughness, and realism in training, put through a similar program for his Ground Forces. More important was the direct training in combat acquired in North Africa. To Mr. Hanson Baldwin, New York *Times* military commentator, North Africa was "a training and testing ground, a college on the conduct of war by the Allies, a dress rehearsal for the far larger and more difficult operations . . . that are still to come." [12]

Allied Planning and Preparation in 1943

In January 1943, after the first phases of the North African operations had proved successful, the Combined Chiefs of Staff met with President Roosevelt and Mr. Churchill at Casablanca to map plans for the future. The U.S. Chiefs of Staff held that the main operation in 1943 must be made in northwest Europe. The British, still uncertain that the Allies were capable of mounting a successful cross-Channel assault before 1944, maintained that the Mediterranean offered the best immediate prospects for success. General Marshall argued that the United Kingdom was a better base from which to attack since more effective air support could be given from there, and operations from there could be more easily supplied from the

---

[10] In the absence of General Eisenhower, his deputy theater commander, Maj. Gen. Russell P. Hartle, acted as chief American representative in the United Kingdom.

[11] Col C. P. Stacey, *The Canadian Army, 1939-45* (Ottawa, 1948), pp. 83–86.

[12] New York *Times,* May 12, 1943.

United States.[13] The British countered effectively that the Allies could not afford to leave their forces in the Mediterranean idle while preparations were being made in the United Kingdom for a cross-Channel operation. In the face of this fact and the British disinclination to undertake ROUNDUP in 1943, the Combined Chiefs of Staff decided to make the invasion of Sicily (Operation HUSKY) the next major operation for 1943.[14]

The Allies agreed at Casablanca to start preparations for an eventual cross-Channel attack. They decided that a combined staff should be established to plan for such an operation, and they ordered further that a combined bomber offensive be launched against Germany to undermine the enemy's capacity for armed resistance. The former decision resulted, as already indicated, in the naming of General Morgan to head the COSSAC staff. The decision on an air offensive resulted in the directive of 10 June 1943 officially opening the bombing offensive known as POINTBLANK.

In a second conference, held in Washington in May 1943, the Combined Chiefs of Staff issued a supplementary directive to General Morgan, ordering him to plan an operation with a target date of 1 May 1944 to secure a lodgment area on the Continent from which further operations could be launched. The plan was to be based on the presence in the United Kingdom of twenty-nine divisions, of which nine were available for the assault period. COSSAC was ordered to start an immediate expansion of logistical facilities in the United Kingdom and to prepare an outline plan for submission to the Combined Chiefs of Staff on 1 August 1943.[15]

After working on the plan throughout June and the first half of July, General Morgan and his staff presented it to the British Chiefs of Staff on 15 July 1943. The COSSAC planners set forth the conditions under which the attack (OVERLORD) could be made, the area where a landing would be feasible, and the steps whereby the assault would be developed.[16] As a means of aiding the assault, General Morgan asked that the most effective threat possible be made on the south coast of France in order to pin down German forces in that area. He also suggested that plans be made for the occupation of the ports of southern France in case of German withdrawal from that region.[17]

Before leaving London for the Quebec Conference in August 1943 the British Chiefs of Staff examined the OVERLORD plan and instructed General Morgan to continue his planning, paying particular attention to the enemy's power to delay the Allied advance. After examining alternative plans, the Combined Chiefs of Staff approved the COSSAC outline plan for the cross-Channel operation and endorsed the action of the British Chiefs of Staff in authorizing General Morgan to continue detailed planning and preparations. They also directed Allied Force Headquarters to plan a diversionary attack in southern France. Prime Minister Churchill accepted the OVERLORD plan subject to the warning that a review of the decision would be asked if later intelligence reports indicated that German ground or air strength was greater than that anticipated

---

[13] CCS 55th Mtg, 14 Jan 43, Casablanca Conf Min.
[14] CCS 2d Mtg with President and Prime Minister, 18 Jan 43, Casablanca Conf Min.
[15] Draft Supplementary Dir to COSSAC, 25 May 43, Washington Conf Min.
[16] See below, pp. 105–06, for more complete details.
[17] Opn OVERLORD, Rpt and Appreciation, COS (43) 416 (0), SHAEF SGS Opn OVERLORD 381 I (a).

by the planners in estimating the possible success of the operation.[18]

The Combined Bomber Offensive began almost simultaneously with COSSAC planning. The outline plan for it was endorsed by the Combined Chiefs of Staff, who directed the Eighth U.S. Air Force and the RAF Bomber Command to initiate the bomber attack against the enemy.

British bomber forces since 1940 had made an increasing number of raids over Germany, and the Eighth U.S. Air Force had joined them in these activities in the summer of 1942. Before the Casablanca Conference, however, the raids had been carried on without a definite statement as to the priorities of targets, the mission to be accomplished, or the timing of the combined activities. The Combined Bomber Offensive was an attempt to integrate and expand the British and U.S. bombing efforts against Germany. At Casablanca the Combined Chiefs of Staff specified that the purpose of the operation would be "the progressive destruction and dislocation of the German military, industrial and economic systems, and the undermining of the morale of the German people to a point where their capacity for armed resistance is fatally weakened." At the same meeting and in later conferences, Allied planners had agreed that the target priorities should include the following as primary objectives: enemy submarine yards and bases, the German aircraft industry, ball bearings, and oil. Secondary objectives included synthetic rubber and tires and military motor transport vehicles. German fighter strength was listed "as an intermediate objective second to none in priority." [19]

The late summer and early fall of 1943 saw increasing interest of the COSSAC staff in one of its initial tasks—planning

for a return to the Continent in case of German collapse or withdrawal from the occupied countries. A plan to meet this situation had been presented to the Combined Chiefs of Staff at the Quebec Conference. The march of events in August and early September, indicating growing Axis weakness, gave rise to the hope that such a plan rather than one for an all-out cross-Channel assault might be the one used by the Allies. The fall of Mussolini near the end of July, the rapid conquest of Sicily in August, and Italy's unconditional surrender at the beginning of September seemed to indicate that the Axis was disintegrating under Allied blows. On the Eastern Front there was even greater encouragement as the Russian attack, which began in the Orel salient in July, spread along the entire front. A powerful drive in the vicinity of Kharkov brought the fall of that city in mid-August and threw the Germans back toward the Dnieper. The air battle increased in intensity with August witnessing Allied attacks on the Messerschmitt factories near Vienna and the raid on the Ploesti oilfields in România. The month of September was to see the greatest air fights in Europe since the Battle of Britain. On 9 September, the day of the Allied invasion of the Italian mainland at Salerno, the Joint Intelligence Sub-Committee of the War Cabinet, impressed by the parallels between the condition of Germany in August 1918 and August 1943, concluded that "a study of the picture as a whole leads us inevitably to the conclusion that Germany is, if anything, in a worse condition today than she

---

[18] 1st and 2d Mtgs of President and Prime Minister, 19, 23 Aug 43, Quebec Conf Min.

[19] Craven and Cate, *The Army Air Forces*, Vol. II, Ch. 11; Harrison, *Cross-Channel Attack*, Ch. VI. Useful background on British bombing operations can be found in Sir Arthur Harris, *Bomber Offensive* (New York, 1947), Chs. I–VII.

was at the same period in 1918." They believed that if the Allies could take advantage of Germany's declining strength to press home attacks by land and sea; maintain and even intensify their air offensives; exploit the instability of southeast Europe; and pursue a vigorous political and propaganda campaign, we may see the defection of the rest of Germany's European Allies and, even before the end of this year, convince the German people and military leaders that a continuation of the war is more to be feared than the consequences of inevitable defeat. With the German people no longer willing to endure useless bloodshed and destruction, and the military leaders convinced of the futility of resistance there might be, as in Italy, some sudden change of regime to prepare the way for a request for an Armistice.[20]

Although this prediction proved to be nothing more than what one British officer described as "our annual collapse of Germany prediction,"[21] it required the COSSAC staff to rush planning for measures to be taken in the case of enemy collapse. A report in October that a meeting of the German high command had been called gave rise to hopeful speculation in London, leading General Barker to cable General Morgan in Washington, "We here are of the opinion that RANKIN 'C' [a plan to be put into effect in case of Germany's surrender] becomes more and more of a probability."[22]

As winter approached, the Allies became less hopeful about an early collapse of the enemy. It became clear that the enemy, despite increasingly heavy raids, was able to continue his production of aircraft by moving factories farther inside Germany. Near the year's end, the enemy's fighter force in the west was actually increasing in strength. There was also some doubt that the Combined Bomber Offensive could complete its work before the target day set for the cross-Channel attack, particularly in the light of Air Chief Marshal Portal's statement in early December 1943 that POINTBLANK was three months behind schedule. The airmen believed, nonetheless, that given sufficient bomber resources they could rapidly reduce the enemy's air force to impotence and achieve air superiority for the Allies.[23]

At the Cairo Conference in December 1943, the Combined Chiefs of Staff reached a firm conclusion as to operations for 1944. They declared that the cross-Channel attack and the landings in southern France were to be the supreme operations for 1944 and that nothing should be undertaken in any other part of the world which might prevent their success. The Allies thus made OVERLORD the chief order of business for the coming year. The appointment of General Eisenhower as Supreme Commander opened the final phase of preparations for the cross-Channel assault.[24]

The COSSAC Plans

On their arrival in London in 1944, the new members of SHAEF were briefed on the plans outlined by COSSAC in 1943. In one case, that of diversion plans, COSSAC had actually carried out a specific operation. Under the general name of COCKADE, British and United States forces had built up threats against the Continent to give the impression that an attack might be launched in 1943. U.S. forces had made feints in the direction of the

---

[20] Probabilities of a German Collapse, 9 Sep 43, JIC (43) 367 Final, OPD Exec 9, Bk 12.

[21] Intervs with Commodore John Hughes-Hallett, 11, 12 Feb 47.

[22] Barker to Morgan, 20 Oct 43, Barker personal file. See below, p. 106, for description of the RANKIN plan.

[23] Craven and Cate, *The Army Air Forces*, Vol. II, Ch. 21; Harrison, *Cross-Channel Attack*, Ch. VI.

[24] Report to the President and Prime Minister, CCS 426/1, 6 Dec 43, Cairo Conf Min.

Brest peninsula (WADHAM), British forces in Scotland had simulated preparations for attack against Norway (TINDALL), and Allied forces had directed threats toward the Pas-de-Calais (STARKEY). It was not clear to what extent these efforts had been successful in worrying the enemy, but General Morgan felt that they might have been responsible to some degree for German activity in the Pas-de-Calais and the Cotentin area. It is possible that these efforts raised fears about landings in the Pas-de-Calais which lasted until well into the following year.[25]

COSSAC had also prepared three plans, all phases of Operation RANKIN (Cases A, B, and C), designed to be put into effect in the event of a sudden change in Germany's position. The plans provided for Allied action in case of (A) "substantial weakening of the strength and morale of the German armed forces" to the extent that a successful assault could be made by Anglo-American forces before OVERLORD, (B) German withdrawal from occupied countries, and (C) German unconditional surrender and cessation of organized resistance.[26]

The newcomers from AFHQ were interested at the moment mainly in COSSAC's proposals for the invasion of northwest Europe. The OVERLORD plan related in somewhat broad terms the steps necessary for making a successful assault, for building up supply and personnel in the lodgment area, and for carrying on operations during the first ninety days of battle. Although it was quite general in nature, the plan afforded much valuable information in a series of appendixes dealing with such topics as port capacities, naval requirements, availability of ships and landing craft, availability of ground forces, attainment of the necessary air superiority for a successful landing, planning data for landing craft and shipping,

rate of build-up, Resistance groups, enemy naval forces, enemy defense system, beaches, meteorological conditions, topography of the assault area, administrative considerations, and methods of improving discharge facilities on the French coast.[27]

The OVERLORD plan had as its object the mounting and executing of "an operation with forces and equipment established in the United Kingdom, and with target date 1st May 1944, to secure a lodgment on the Continent from which further offensive operations can be developed." In the opening phases of the attack COSSAC proposed to land two British and one U.S. divisions with one U.S. and one British in the immediate follow-up to seize the Caen area, lying between the Orne River and the base of the Cotentin peninsula. They were then to seek the early capture of the port of Cherbourg and the area suitable for airfields near Caen. Before the assault, a combined offensive consisting of air and sea action, propaganda, political and economic pressure, and sabotage was to be launched to soften German resistance.[28]

Much remained to be done by the new Supreme Headquarters, but COSSAC and its predecessors had contributed mightily to the final plan by fixing in general the area of the coming attack and by providing considerable groundwork and organization on which the new Supreme Commander and his subordinates could build.

---

[25] Maj Duncan Emrich and Maj F. D. Price, History of COSSAC, prep at SHAEF, 1945, MS. For German fears of an attack in the Pas-de-Calais in 1944 see below, p. 180.

[26] Final Rpt to President and Prime Minister, CCS 319/5, 24 Aug 43, Quebec Conf Min.

[27] Details of the COSSAC plan and amendments made by later planners will be found in Harrison, Cross-Channel Attack, Chs. II, V.

[28] Opn OVERLORD, Rpt and Appreciation with appendixes, and covering letter, SHAEF SGS Opn OVERLORD 381 I (a).

CHAPTER VI

SHAEF Revises Plans for the Attack

In the months between the Quebec Conference and General Eisenhower's formal assumption of the Supreme Command, COSSAC handed over to the commanders of the 21 Army Group, the Allied Naval Expeditionary Force, and the Allied Expeditionary Air Force many of the detailed planning tasks for Operation OVERLORD. General Morgan retained for SHAEF, however, numerous administrative duties in addition to specific responsibilities for problems of a political or strategic nature. Most important, SHAEF advice was required on those broad questions of policy which had to be decided by the Combined Chiefs of Staff.

General Eisenhower, after relinquishing command of the Mediterranean theater in December 1943, went to Washington for conferences relative to the cross-Channel operation. To represent him in the United Kingdom until his arrival, the Supreme Commander sent his chief of staff, General Smith, and the newly appointed commander of 21 Army Group, General Montgomery. Before the British commander arrived in London on 2 January, his chief of staff, Maj. Gen. Francis de Guingand, and General Smith had examined the COSSAC plan for OVERLORD and were prepared to present their views to the 21 Army Group commander. Their reactions, which General de Guingand thought similar to those "of any trained soldier," favored a greater weight of assault forces, a quicker build-up, a larger airlift, and a less restricted area of landing. General Eisenhower was informed of these views by General Smith and General Montgomery before he left Washington. Montgomery was particularly insistent that General Eisenhower take personal action, saying that no final decision would be made until the Supreme Commander expressed his wishes, and asking, "Will you hurl yourself into the contest and what we want, get for us?" [1]

SHAEF now concentrated on means of strengthening the cross-Channel attack. All planning groups that had considered the OVERLORD operation were impressed by the fact that the Allies in the assault faced a potential enemy opposition far superior to the number of troops that could be landed in a few hours or days. Despite the great force located in the United Kingdom, the success of the operation depended on the number of men who could be landed in the assault waves and on the speed with which follow-up forces could be brought ashore and supplied. To gain the margin of victory, the Allies would have to limit the

---

[1] Maj. Gen. Sir Francis de Guingand, *Operation Victory* (New York, 1947), pp. 340–44; Montgomery to Eisenhower, W–4918, 10 Jan 44, SHAEF SGS 560 [Vessels].

movement of enemy reinforcements into the beachhead, capture ports rapidly, and prepare artificial harbors that would serve until natural ones could be seized. The earlier planners had foreseen these needs and had done what they could to prepare for them. But not until the commanders responsible for the actual battle were appointed was a completely realistic appraisal of the situation possible. A number of problems confronted the Supreme Commander in preparing for the cross-Channel attack: broadening the assault front, procuring additional landing craft, making better use of available landing craft, dropping or landing more airborne units, increasing naval fire support, and insuring the isolation of the beachhead by increased air operations.

Strengthening and Widening the Assault and the Postponement of ANVIL

As soon as the outline plan for OVER-LORD was presented, the need for a wider invasion front and a stronger force than recommended by COSSAC in July 1943 was widely recognized. While suggesting a landing by three divisions in the assault and two divisions in the follow-up in the Caen area, the COSSAC planners had added that additional forces would be valuable in the cross-Channel attack. (*Map I*) Churchill, Marshall, and Hopkins on seeing the COSSAC proposals at the Quebec Conference all declared that the assault should be strengthened. Similar statements were made by General Smith in October 1943 when General Morgan told him in Washington of the plan, and by General Eisenhower about the same time in Algiers when he was informed by Brig. Gen. William E. Chambers, a COSSAC staff member, of the essential

provisions of the plan. Although Eisenhower and Smith did not realize the roles they were later to play in the OVERLORD operation, they expressed surprise at the weakness of the attacking force, inasmuch as they had used greater strength in the Sicilian landings. At the end of October, General Eisenhower, then being talked of as a possible commander of the cross-Channel attack, stated his doubts about the plan because it did not have "enough wallop in the initial attack." [2]

Mr. Churchill showed General Montgomery a copy of the COSSAC plan at Marrakech on 1 January 1944. The 21 Army Group commander also found the invasion front too narrow and the assault force too small. He was told to examine the COSSAC plan in detail when he went to the United Kingdom and to recommend changes necessary to the success of the operation.[3]

Before General Montgomery arrived in London on 2 January 1944, his chief of staff and the SHAEF chief of staff had examined the OVERLORD plan and were prepared to recommend a widening of the assault area. When the 21 Army Group commander was briefed in London on 3 January, he took strong exception to the narrowness of the proposed assault area. Pointing vigorously at various points of the

---

[2] Interv with Smith, 9 May 47. Eisenhower Memo for Diary, 8 Feb 44; Eisenhower to Marshall, 8 Feb 44. Both in Diary Office CinC. General Eisenhower's statement as to the lack of "wallop" was made to Captain Butcher on 28 October 1943, Diary Office CinC. For earlier views on the size of the invasion forces by General Eisenhower, see CCS, 58th Mtg, 16 Jan 43, Casablanca Conf Min; Mtg of JCS with President, 16 Jan 43; Algiers Conf Min, 29, 31 May 43.

[3] Field Marshal Viscount Montgomery, *Normandy to the Baltic* (New York, 1948), pp. 5–6. Cf. de Guingand, *Operation Victory*, p. 338; Eisenhower, *Crusade in Europe*, p. 217. See also Diary Office CinC, 16 Jan 44, 8 Feb 44.

map on both sides of the Cotentin, in the areas of Dieppe, Le Havre, and Brest, he said, "We should land here and here." He also raised for the first time the proposal that Operation ANVIL, the landing in southern France, be dropped except as a threat in order that landing craft earmarked for ANVIL could be diverted to OVERLORD. General Smith, while privately of the opinion that a threat in the south of France would be as effective in the early stages of the cross-Channel attack as the proposed full-scale assault, declined to accede to the proposal until General Eisenhower could examine it.[4]

General Montgomery again stressed the need of broadening the assault front in his meeting with the British and U.S. army commanders on 7 January 1944. Speaking as a representative of the Supreme Commander, he insisted on changes in the COSSAC plan to strengthen the landing and follow-up forces. He no longer recommended landings around Le Havre or Brittany, but suggested an area from "Varreville on the east coast of the Cotentin to Cabourg west of the Orne"—approximately the same sector recommended by the Combined Commanders in March 1943. In order to permit the armies and corps to go in on their own fronts, he proposed a change in command arrangements by which a British army and a U.S. army would control the assault corps, thus requiring 21 Army Group instead of First U.S. Army to exercise command on D Day. The U.S. army on the right would capture Cherbourg and the Cotentin peninsula and subsequently develop operations to the south and west, while the British army would operate "to the south to prevent any interference with the American army from the East."[5]

Generals Montgomery and Smith in-formed General Eisenhower and Mr. Churchill that there must be a stronger OVERLORD even at the expense of ANVIL. The Prime Minister reminded President Roosevelt that he had always hoped "the initial assault at OVERLORD could be with heavier forces than we have hitherto maintained." The case for strengthening OVERLORD at the expense of ANVIL was also supported by General Morgan who held that landings in the south of France could do little more than pin down three or four divisions of German mobile reserves, an effect which could be achieved as well by a threat. He believed the existing strategic conception involved "an unsound diversion of forces from the main 'OVERLORD' [assault] area to a subsidiary assault area, where they [were] unlikely to pay the same dividend." His views were reinforced two days later by a request from Air Chief Marshal Leigh-Mallory, Admiral Ramsay, and General Montgomery for half of ANVIL's two-divisional lift.

The British Chiefs of Staff were not convinced at the moment of the wisdom of weakening or dropping the ANVIL operation. Admiral Cunningham believed that a landing in southern France would almost certainly force the diversion of enemy forces to that area, and Air Chief Marshal Portal declared that possession of the ports in southern France would increase the rate of build-up of U.S. forces on the Continent. When, however, on 12

---

[4] De Guingand, *Operation Victory*, pp. 340–44, tells of the work done by General Smith and himself. Brigadier McLean, who briefed Montgomery on the COSSAC plan, gave the author on 11 March 1947 a summary of the discussion. For Smith's view, see Smith to Eisenhower, W–9389, 5 Jan 44, Eisenhower personal file.

[5] 21 Army Group Memo, "Notes taken on meeting of army commanders and their chiefs of staff at Headquarters, 21 Army Group, 7 Jan 44," OCMH files.

HIGH-LEVEL CONFERENCE *in London. Seated, left to right: Air Chief Marshal Tedder, General Eisenhower, and General Montgomery. Standing: General Bradley, Admiral Ramsay, Air Chief Marshal Leigh-Mallory, General Smith.*

January the Joint Planning Staff reported the feasibility of reducing the ANVIL assault to a diversionary attack, Field Marshal Brooke and Air Chief Marshal Portal agreed that the operation should not be permitted to stand in the way of OVERLORD's success. Admiral Cunningham, on the other hand, was reluctant to accept this view, pointing out in addition to other arguments that grave difficulties would be raised with the French who had intended that the bulk of their forces should participate in the southern landing.[6] The British Chiefs of Staff on 14 January informed the Prime Minister that the ideal arrangement would be a stronger OVERLORD and a two- or three-division ANVIL.[7]

General Eisenhower on his arrival in

London was thus faced with the necessity of changing the plan for the assault and of securing the reallocation of resources intended for an operation in a theater other than his own. He promptly apprised General Marshall of his problems, assuring the U.S. Chief of Staff that he considered a serious reduction in the southern France operation justified only as a last resort. Since General Eisenhower's headquarters

---

[6] Memo, Morgan for Br COS, 6 Jan 44, Reply to JPS Questionnaire on Implications of Proposed Modification of Operation OVERLORD, 8 Jan 44; Br COS 5th Mtg, 7 Jan 44; Rpt of JPS on ANVIL–OVERLORD, 12 Jan 44; Br COS 10th Mtg, 13 Jan 44. All in SHAEF SGS 370.2/2 Opn From Mediterranean in Support of OVERLORD, I.

[7] Br COS to Prime Minister, 14 Jan 44, Eisenhower personal file.

in the Mediterranean had prepared both a diversionary plan for southern France in the fall of 1943 and the ANVIL outline plan as directed by the Cairo Conference at the end of the year, the Supreme Commander was aware of the importance of the ANVIL operation to the cross-Channel attack. He not only desired the southern France operation to draw away Germans from the OVERLORD area, but held that the landings should be made in order to keep the promise given the Russians at Tehran, to utilize French forces scheduled for commitment in ANVIL, and to make the best possible use of Allied forces in the Mediterranean.[8]

While stressing the value of preserving ANVIL, the Supreme Commander emphasized the critical importance of a stronger OVERLORD attack. On 23 January, he formally proposed that the number of divisions in the initial assault be increased from three to five. This meant that to the two British divisions and one U.S. division which COSSAC planned to land in the Caen area, there would be added a British division west of Ouistreham and a U.S. division on the east coast of the Cotentin. Besides an airborne landing in the Caen area, General Eisenhower wanted an airborne division to seize the exit from the Cotentin beaches, with a second airborne division to follow within twenty-four hours. This revised plan naturally required additional landing craft, naval fire support, and aircraft, with particular emphasis on LST's, LCT's,[9] and troop carrier aircraft. Believing that OVERLORD and ANVIL should be viewed as "one whole," the Supreme Commander said that an ideal plan would include a five-division OVERLORD and a three-division ANVIL. He agreed, however, that if forces were not available for both assaults priority should

go to OVERLORD. As the date for the attack he preferred 1 May, but he was willing to accept a postponement if that would secure additional strength for the operation.[10]

The British Chiefs of Staff, who together with the Prime Minister had become increasingly dubious over the prospects of launching ANVIL simultaneously with OVERLORD,[11] promptly agreed that the cross-Channel attack should be given overriding priority. They also asked for postponement of the invasion until the end of May or the beginning of June in order to increase the chance that the Russian attack would have begun on the Eastern Front, and to gain an extra month's production of landing craft. The U.S. Chiefs of Staff, still insistent on a two-division ANVIL, accepted the postponement of the target date to a time not later than 31 May.[12]

While the Allied planners were seeking means to mount the OVERLORD and ANVIL operations simultaneously, military events in Italy were working against their efforts. The Allies had launched an operation on 22 January 1944 at Anzio in the hope that their forces could shortly take Rome and drive northward to put additional pressure on the enemy. The Combined Chiefs of Staff had thought that

---

[8] Montgomery to Eisenhower, W–4918, 10 Jan 44, SHAEF SGS 560 [Vessels], II; Eisenhower to Marshall, 17 Jan 44, Eisenhower personal file.

[9] Landing Ship, Tank, and Landing Craft, Tank.

[10] Eisenhower to Marshall, W–9856, 22 Jan 44; Eisenhower to CCS, B–33, 23 Jan 44, Eisenhower personal file.

[11] Admiral Cunningham still held that his colleagues perhaps underestimated the value of even a weak ANVIL on the enemy. Br COS 21st Mtg, 24 Jan 44, COS (44) Min.

[12] Br COS to JSM, COS (W) 1094, 26 Jan 44; JSM to Br COS, JSM 1478, 1 Feb 44, SHAEF SGS 560 [Vessels], II.

landing craft allocated to the attack at Anzio would be needed for only a short time and would then be available for the OVERLORD and ANVIL operations. After a hopeful beginning, the Allied forces met stiffened German resistance and determined counterattacks which forced them to use units intended for ANVIL. Continuance of the beachhead battle prevented release of precious landing craft. The British, lukewarm toward ANVIL, argued that the enemy decision to fight in Italy tied up divisions which would otherwise have been available for use against OVERLORD and thus served the diversionary purpose for which ANVIL was intended. They held that the strategic situation in the Mediterranean had changed since the Cairo Conference and should be re-examined.[13]

Thus far in the discussion of plans for widening the assault area, the ANVIL operation had been mentioned merely as an attack which must be weakened or postponed in order to get additional support for OVERLORD. About 1 February, debate over the landings in southern France entered a new phase. Apparently encouraged by the fact that the Italian fighting was creating a diversion of German units from the area of the cross-Channel attack, Mr. Churchill on 4 February opened a strong onslaught against ANVIL as a desirable operation. He declared that as a result of the distance between the areas in which OVERLORD and ANVIL were to be launched, the ruggedness of the terrain which Allied forces from the south of France would have to cover in a move northward, and the defensive strength of modern weapons which would oppose them, the ANVIL operation was not "strategically interwoven with OVERLORD." At his suggestion, the British Chiefs of Staff proposed that ANVIL "as at present

planned" be canceled and that the Mediterranean commander be directed to submit plans for the use of his forces to contain the maximum number of enemy troops in his theater. They believed that a shift of landing craft intended for ANVIL to OVERLORD would meet the full requirements of the cross-Channel attack, which would then be made ready by the first week in June.[14] General Eisenhower, who still wanted the ANVIL operation, now concluded that developments in Italy created the possibility that forces there could not be disentangled in time to put on a strong operation in southern France. Privately, he expressed the doubt that ANVIL and OVERLORD could be launched simultaneously.[15]

Although the unfavorable progress of the Anzio operation gave some basis for the British proposal to cancel ANVIL, the U.S. Chiefs of Staff viewed the suggestion with suspicion. They saw in the proposed cancellation the continuation of what they described as the British policy of pushing operations in the Mediterranean at the expense of the cross-Channel attack. At the Washington Conference in May 1943, General Marshall had warned that operations in the Mediterranean would swallow the men and landing craft intended for the main operation in northwest Europe. He had agreed to the operation in Sicily because it seemed that no other use could be made of the forces in the Mediterranean at the moment. Salerno had followed, and

---

[13] Minute, Ismay for Churchill, 2 Feb 44, SHAEF SGS 370.2/2 Opn From Mediterranean in Support of OVERLORD, I.

[14] 35th Mtg, 4 Feb 44, COS (44), SHAEF SGS 370.2/2 Opn From Mediterranean in Support of OVERLORD, I; Br COS to JSM, 4 Feb 44, COS (W) 1126, COS (44) Min.

[15] Eisenhower to Marshall, W–10786, 6 Feb 44, Eisenhower personal file; Diary Office CinC, 7 Feb 44.

then Anzio, and now it appeared that more demands would be made on resources earmarked for OVERLORD. The Chief of Staff felt so strongly about the matter that, while agreeing to the cancellation of ANVIL if the Supreme Commander thought it essential to strengthen OVERLORD, he expressed fear that the British Chiefs of Staff might be influencing General Eisenhower's views. "I merely wish," he added, "to be certain that localitis is not developing and that pressure on you has not warped your judgment." [16]

The imputation of "localitis" to the Supreme Commander's views emphasized the difficulty of General Eisenhower's position throughout the ANVIL controversy. As a tactical commander desiring to strengthen the OVERLORD operation, he was sometimes receptive to proposals which the U.S. Chiefs of Staff opposed. He defended himself vigorously in this case against the suggestion of British influence, pointing out that he had advocated a broader front since the OVERLORD plan was first explained to him in October 1943 and insisting that he always fought for the preservation of the ANVIL operation.[17]

American skepticism regarding the British stand was due in part to the conviction that sufficient resources were present in Europe to provide a seven-division lift of personnel and an eight-division lift of vehicles. This the U.S. Chiefs of Staff believed to be adequate for both the OVERLORD and ANVIL operations. Neither the British nor the SHAEF planners agreed with the estimate, which they believed to be based on a faulty analysis of the number of men and vehicles that could be carried under combat conditions. In an effort to settle this disagreement and the whole problem of ANVIL, the Prime Minister invited the U.S. Chiefs of Staff to London to discuss the matter. They suggested instead that General Eisenhower act as their direct representative with the British, and they sent as his technical advisers Rear Adm. Charles M. Cooke, Jr., and Maj. Gen. John E. Hull.

Throughout February General Eisenhower attempted to find enough landing craft for both operations. The British and SHAEF planners stuck to their view that under combat conditions the landing craft available would not carry the number of soldiers and vehicles which the U.S. representatives showed mathematically the craft could hold. The technical observers from the United States were not impressed, one of them reporting that the British had no interest in ANVIL, since they believed that OVERLORD was "the only one that will pay us dividends." [18]

In an effort to meet General Eisenhower's wishes to save ANVIL, the SHAEF planners in mid-February came up with a plan to increase the size of loads and make more efficient use of the landing craft already available. General Montgomery, who believed that the landing craft allotment for OVERLORD was already too scanty, initially objected to the proposal on the ground that it would "compromise tactical flexibility, introduce added complications, bring additional hazards into the operations, and thus generally endanger success." After discussing

---

[16] JSM to Br COS, JSM 1494, 6 Feb 44; Marshall to Eisenhower, 78, 7 Feb 44. Both in SHAEF SGS 370.2/2 Opn From Mediterranean in Support of OVERLORD, I. At one point during this period, the U.S. Chiefs of Staff asked the British not to discuss certain points with General Eisenhower before he had a chance to give Washington his opinion.

[17] Eisenhower to Marshall, W–10786, 8 Feb 44, Eisenhower personal file.

[18] Gen Hull to Gen Handy, 15 Feb 44, SHAEF SGS 560 [Vessels], II.

the matter with General Eisenhower, and with Air Chief Marshal Leigh-Mallory and Admiral Ramsay, who agreed with some reluctance to accept the SHAEF proposal, General Montgomery withdrew his opposition. General Eisenhower now reported to the British Chiefs of Staff that by making sacrifices and accepting every possible risk it would be possible to launch the strengthened OVERLORD and at the same time save the two-division ANVIL operation. He admitted, however, that in the light of developments in Italy it might no longer be practicable to undertake the landings in southern France. Encouraged by this admission the British Chiefs of Staff called attention to the opportunity of "bleeding and burning German divisions" as a result of Hitler's decision to fight south of Rome, and argued that it would be "wholly unjustifiable to keep any formation out of Italy on the ground that it was going to be required for ANVIL." They proposed to the U.S. Chiefs of Staff, therefore, that the existing state of uncertainty be ended and ANVIL canceled immediately.[19]

The U.S. Chiefs of Staff, informed by their technical advisers in London that the ANVIL operation was possible if the British would attempt it, held to the view that the landings in southern France should be made. They were willing, however, if the situation had not improved in Italy by 1 April, to review the situation in the Mediterranean and then decide if ANVIL should be postponed. Arrangements made by General Eisenhower were to be supported by the U.S. Chiefs of Staff, subject to the approval of the President. That there should be no doubt of his reaction, the President directed Admiral Leahy to remind the Supreme Commander that the United States was committed to a third power (Russia) and that he did not feel the

Western Allies had any right to abandon the commitment for ANVIL without taking the matter up with that third power.[20]

The Supreme Commander's position thus became increasingly difficult as he attempted to decide what was best for him as the commander of OVERLORD and also tried to present as strongly as possible the U.S. arguments. His embarrassment was shown particularly in the discussions with the British Chiefs of Staff on 22 February. Speaking officially for the U.S. Chiefs of Staff, he opposed cancellation of ANVIL until the last possible moment for decision. He added that the U.S. Chiefs of Staff did not necessarily regard ANVIL as an operation involving an eventual use of two divisions in the assault and ten divisions in the build-up, although they did want a two-division assault force in the Mediterranean. He felt they would accept as fulfillment of the commitment at Tehran a diversionary operation on the largest scale possible after the Mediterranean theater had met the requirements of the campaign in Italy.[21]

The British Chiefs of Staff agreed to continue ANVIL planning under the interpretations given by General Eisenhower provided the Italian campaign received "overriding priority over all existing and future operations in the Mediterranean to contain the maximum number of the enemy." They asked that the situation be

---

[19] For the detailed debate over loadings and the efforts to increase the use of the available craft, see Harrison, *Cross-Channel Attack*, Ch. V. Montgomery to Eisenhower, 16 Feb 44, SHAEF SGS 560 [Vessels], II; 5th Mtg, 18 Feb 44, Min SAC's Conf. Memo, Eisenhower for Br COS, 19 Feb 44; COS (44) 52d Mtg, 19 Feb 44; Br COS to JSM, COS (W) 1156, 19 Feb 44. All in SHAEF SGS 381 OVERLORD–ANVIL, I.

[20] JCS to Eisenhower, 153, 21 Feb 44; JCS to Eisenhower, 151, 21 Feb 44; Leahy to Eisenhower, 154, 21 Feb 44, Eisenhower personal file.

[21] 54th Mtg, 22 Feb 44, COS (44).

reviewed on 20 March and that if ANVIL was found to be impracticable all craft in excess of the lift for one division should be moved from the Mediterranean. This proposal was accepted by the Combined Chiefs of Staff and approved by the President and Prime Minister.[22]

The decision of 26 February marked a retreat by the U.S. Chiefs of Staff from their positive stand for a strong ANVIL to a tentative agreement that a decision would be suspended. The operation was left at the mercy of developments in Italy which, at the time of the agreement, were becoming increasingly unfavorable to the mounting of ANVIL. Gen. Sir Henry Maitland Wilson, Supreme Commander in the Mediterranean, had reported on 22 February that continuous attacks by the enemy since the 16th of the month had inflicted heavy casualties and contributed to the exhaustion of his troops. He found it difficult to withdraw forces needed for ANVIL, and recommended cancellation of the landings in southern France. This suggestion seemed to make more likely the dropping of the ANVIL operation, but nearly a month's delay ensued before a decision was reached. Pressed by his commanders for a prompt decision, General Eisenhower suggested that he might get action by cabling General Marshall that ANVIL was impossible. General Smith, although favoring the postponement of ANVIL, felt this action was not necessary and would give the impression that they were changing their minds too quickly. The Supreme Commander agreed that Admiral Ramsay should inform the Mediterranean commander which ships he intended to withdraw from that area if ANVIL was canceled on 21 March. Nearly a month before the final review, the SHAEF planners clearly had little doubt that plans for landings in

southern France simultaneously with OVERLORD would have to be canceled.[23]

A new element was introduced into planning for Mediterranean operations at the end of February when General Alexander requested additional craft for his troop movements, thus upsetting the timetable for the transfer from the Mediterranean of certain craft earmarked for OVERLORD. The British had now gone beyond suggesting that ANVIL be canceled as a means of aiding OVERLORD to proposing that landing craft be withheld from OVERLORD in order to insure the success of operations in Italy. To get immediate aid for operations there, they requested that LST's in the Mediterranean be left there, and be replaced in the OVERLORD buildup with landing craft dispatched directly from the United States. The U.S. Chiefs of Staff agreed to delay the movement of craft from the Mediterranean, but opposed sending additional craft to that area until a decision was made on ANVIL. This compromise afforded the means of saving the southern France operation, but it created a new problem for General Eisenhower. The effort to keep ANVIL alive, he stated flatly, had created a situation which was "actually militating strongly against the plans and preparations for OVERLORD." He saw nothing in the Italian situation which indicated "an increase in the likelihood of ANVIL on the two division–ten division basis." On the contrary, he believed it would be necessary to draw on

---

[22] COS to JSM, 23 Feb 44, reproduced as CCS 465/11, 24 Feb 44, CCS files; CCS to Eisenhower, FACS 13, 26 Feb 44, Eisenhower personal file; JSM to Br COS, JSM 1538, 25 Feb 44, SHAEF SGS 381 OVERLORD–ANVIL, I.
[23] Wilson to Br COS, MEDCOS 41, 22 Feb 44, SHAEF SGS 381 OVERLORD-ANVIL, I; 6th Mtg, 26 Feb 44, Min of SAC's Conf.

landing craft intended for ANVIL for the minimum lift for OVERLORD.[24]

By the time set for reviewing the situation in the Mediterranean, Generals Eisenhower and Wilson had agreed that landing craft in that area should be reduced to a one-division lift. General Wilson wanted these craft to support intensive operations up the mainland of Italy, while General Eisenhower asked merely that everything possible be done by threat, feint, and actual operations to keep enemy troops in the Mediterranean area. Yielding to the logic of the situation in Italy, and to General Eisenhower's view that "ANVIL as we originally visualized it is no longer a possibility either from the standpoint of time in which to make all necessary preparations or in probable availability of fresh and effective troops at the appointed time," the U.S. Chiefs of Staff agreed that ANVIL must be delayed. The British Chiefs of Staff gained only a part of their wish. Instead of the cancellation of ANVIL which they recommended, they received a counterproposal that a two-division invasion of southern France be made on 10 July 1944. The Americans were willing to underwrite this operation by diverting LST's and LCT's earmarked for the Pacific on the hard and fast condition that the British agree "that preparation for the delayed ANVIL will be vigorously pressed and that it is the firm intention to mount this operation in support of OVERLORD with the target date indicated." [25]

The strong U.S. demand for a positive guarantee of an ANVIL operation in July as a price for more landing craft in the Mediterranean was compared by Field Marshal Brooke to the "pointing of a pistol," as he indicated his unwillingness to give assurances for operations four or five months in the future. General Eisenhower

reminded the British Chief of the Imperial General Staff that, in view of the pressure of U.S. opinion and Congress for greater activity in the Pacific, General Marshall had made substantial concessions by agreeing to divert craft intended for the Pacific to the Mediterranean. Aware that General Marshall had softened his demands for ANVIL to "some sizable operation of the nature of ANVIL," General Eisenhower suggested that the U.S. Chiefs of Staff might be persuaded to accept a British reservation to postpone until July a decision as to the place of attack. Thus reassured, the British suggested that General Wilson be instructed to prepare not only a plan for ANVIL, but also alternative plans for containing the maximum number of Germans in Italy if the enemy continued to fight there.[26]

Dissatisfied with the British reluctance to name a definite target date, the U.S. Chiefs of Staff asked for a decision. The British then submitted a revised directive for General Wilson which was acceptable save for a provision giving priority to Italian operations over ANVIL. The Americans declared themselves "shocked" to see "how gaily" the British "proposed to accept their legacy while disregarding the terms of the will," and they refused to divert craft to the Mediterranean on the basis of the new proposal. Mr. Churchill

[24] Wilson to WO, 28 Feb 44; Wilson to Br COS, 29 Feb 44, SHAEF SGS 381 OVERLORD–ANVIL, I; Br COS to JSM, COS (W) 1184, 1 Mar 44; JSM to Br COS, JSM 1558, 4 Mar 44, SHAEF SGS 560 [Vessels], III; Eisenhower to Marshall, B–245, 9 Mar 44, Eisenhower personal file.

[25] Eisenhower to Marshall, 21 Mar 44; JSM to Br COS, JSM 1594, 24 Mar 44. Both in SHAEF SGS 381 OVERLORD–ANVIL, I.

[26] 12th Mtg, 27 Mar 44, Min of SAC's Confs; Marshall to Eisenhower, W–14078, 25 Mar 44, Eisenhower personal file; Br COS to JSM, COS (W) 1241, 28 Mar 44, SHAEF SGS 381 OVERLORD–ANVIL, I.

now joined the discussion. He urged the continuance of operations then under way in Italy to join the Anzio bridgehead with the main forces and asked postponement of the decision on whether to go all out for ANVIL or exploit the victory in Italy. Such an option would not exist unless the LST's intended for the Pacific were diverted to the Mediterranean. General Marshall declared that the choice depended on starting ANVIL preparations immediately. The United States, he explained, could not stop the momentum it had started in the Pacific "unless there was assurance that we are to have an operation in the effectiveness of which we have complete faith." This development distressed General Eisenhower. While agreeing that the U.S. Chiefs of Staff must take a firm stand, he regarded the decision not to divert craft intended for the Pacific to the Mediterranean as a "sad blow" for OVERLORD.[27]

The British met the situation with a directive that neither fixed a target date nor mentioned additional landing craft. This tentative solution was accepted by Washington on 18 April, and on the following day the Combined Chiefs of Staff directed General Wilson to: (a) launch as early as possible an all-out offensive in Italy, (b) develop the most effective threat possible to contain German forces in southern France; and (c) make plans for the "best possible use of the amphibious lift remaining to you, either in support of operations in Italy, or in order to take advantage of opportunities arising in the south of France or elsewhere for the furtherance of your objects and to press forward vigorously and whole-heartedly with all preparations which do not prejudice the achievement of the fullest success in (a) above."[28]

The directive to General Wilson was

at best a temporary solution which settled nothing definitely in the Mediterranean. The chief effect of the three-month discussion, so far as it concerned OVERLORD, was in the gain of additional lift for the initial assault at the expense of postponing ANVIL, which had been designed to aid the Normandy landings. In the opinion of the U.S. Chiefs of Staff, the loss of the effect of ANVIL on D Day was compensated for only slightly by operations which might be carried out on the Italian mainland. They hoped, therefore, to get a positive agreement that ANVIL would be launched early enough in the summer of 1944 to aid the OVERLORD operations. The British on their side had succeeded in postponing an operation which they feared would interfere with Allied activities in Italy, and had left the way open for further advance on the Italian mainland. The failure to settle Mediterranean strategy before the OVERLORD D Day presaged further controversy between the British and U.S. Chiefs of Staff, added further complications to the OVERLORD operation, and increased the perplexities of the Supreme Commander. For the moment, however, he was able to breathe more easily in the assurance that landing craft essential to the five-division assault which had been accepted in early February would actually be diverted from the Mediterranean in time.

---

[27] Handy to Eisenhower, W–16455, 31 Mar 44, Handy to Eisenhower, W–18619, 5 Apr 44, SHAEF SGS 381 OVERLORD-ANVIL, I; JSM to Chiefs of Staff, FMD 183, 1 Apr 44, OPD Misc File; Prime Minister to Dill for Marshall, 1895, 12 Apr 44, SHAEF SGS 370.2/2 Opn From Mediterranean in Support of OVERLORD, I; Marshall to Eisenhower, W–22810, 14 Apr 44, Eisenhower personal file; Diary Office CinC, 18 Apr 44.

[28] Dir, CCS to Gen Wilson, COSMED 90, 19 Apr 44, SHAEF SGS 370.2/2 Opn From Mediterranean in Support of OVERLORD, I.

Increase of Airborne Units in the Assault

General Montgomery's proposals for increasing the width of the assault area included a landing by U.S. forces on the Cotentin peninsula. Both he and General Bradley agreed that this action was necessary to the early capture of the vital port of Cherbourg. The landing was made hazardous, however, by the nature of the terrain at the neck of the Cotentin. Marshy lands on either side of the Carentan estuary separated the areas in which the two main bodies of U.S. forces were to land. Worse still, the exits from the beaches of the eastern Cotentin were restricted to causeways along a flooded area. The Allied planners decided, therefore, that airborne drops in the Cotentin peninsula were essential in order to seize the causeways and prevent the enemy from destroying them, to prevent the enemy from sending reinforcements to Cherbourg, and to aid in the link-up with U.S. forces to the east. To carry out these plans, General Montgomery asked for two airborne divisions, in addition to the airborne division already earmarked for action east of Caen in the British sector.[29]

After considering these proposals for a time, Air Chief Marshal Leigh-Mallory, the Allied Expeditionary Air Force commander, announced his opposition. With the aircraft then allotted, he said, a second division could not be dropped until twenty-four hours after the initial landing. He was especially concerned over losses which glider forces would take both because of the unsatisfactory landing fields in the area and because of the heavy antiaircraft fire he thought they would face.[30]

Backing for a greater use of airborne forces promptly came from both London and Washington. Mr. Churchill, "not at all satisfied" at the report that a lift existed for only one airborne division, asked General Eisenhower for a statement of the maximum number of these divisions he wished to launch simultaneously in the D-Day attack. The Supreme Commander at once requested two airborne divisions in the initial attack with a third to follow twenty-four hours later. In the face of a cautious report from the chief of the air staff that the lack of trained crews made it impossible to furnish simultaneous lift for two airborne divisions, General Eisenhower reduced his demands. He asked for not less than *"one airborne division and one regimental combat team (brigade) of a second airborne division,* with sufficient depth to enable a second division to be dropped complete 24 hours later."[31]

The Prime Minister, concerned because the Supreme Commander's request for two airborne divisions was not being met, pressed the question at a War Cabinet meeting on 8 February. Portal warned that further increases in the lift would lower the quality of the forces. Leigh-Mallory added that, in view of the bottleneck which existed in the training of troop carrier crews, he thought it impossible to "increase the initial force by one more pilot." Disappointed at the list of difficulties and objections, Mr. Churchill asked that further studies be made on increasing the production of additional airlift. The discussion encouraged General Eisenhower

---

[29] Montgomery, *Normandy to the Baltic*, p. 8; Bradley, *A Soldier's Story*, pp. 232–34.

[30] 3d Mtg, 24 Jan 44, Min of SAC's Confs, SHAEF SGS 387/11; Bradley, *A Soldier's Story*, p. 234.

[31] SHAEF file COS (44) 96 (O), 29 Jan 44; COS (44) 135 (O), 6 Feb 44; Memo, Smith for Br COS, 7 Feb 44, sub: Airborne Forces for OVERLORD, SHAEF SGS 373/2 Employment of Airborne Forces in Opn OVERLORD, I. Quotation with italics from Smith memo.

to hope that he would get at least his minimum demand.[32]

While the Allied airmen struggled with the problem of increasing the airborne lift to one and two-thirds divisions, Generals Marshall and Arnold proposed an even greater use of airborne troops than that asked by General Eisenhower and his commanders. Arnold was disturbed because Eisenhower's staff spoke only of assigning airborne forces tactical missions in the rear of the enemy lines. He felt that this would put them down in the midst of enemy reserve units. He proposed instead the use of airborne forces in mass (four to six divisions) some distance beyond the enemy lines where they could strike at German reinforcements and supplies.[33]

General Marshall shared many of General Arnold's beliefs. During the period when he had been thought of for the post of Supreme Commander, he had considered ways of properly exploiting air power in combination with ground troops and had determined to make better use of airborne forces even if, in the event of British opposition to his ideas, he had to carry them out exclusively with U.S. troops. During this period General Arnold had directed airborne specialists to prepare plans for General Marshall's use. In February 1944 Marshall sent members of his staff to London to explain these projects to the SHAEF planners. Of three proposals, he preferred one for the establishment of an airhead in Normandy generally south of Evreux which would require an initial drop of two airborne divisions by D plus 2, and the landing by glider of an infantry division by D plus 6.[34] He believed this scheme, designed to divert the enemy from the bridgehead and pose an alternative strategic thrust, constituted a true vertical envelopment and would

create a strategic threat strong enough to make the enemy revise his defense plans considerably.[35]

General Eisenhower said that he could not accept the Air Force proposal. He desired to commit the initial airborne forces in a manner that would permit their regrouping for other tactical purposes and would give them ground mobility in their early operations. While approving the conception of a mass vertical envelopment, he believed that it could come only after the beachhead had been gained and a striking force built up. He insisted that the Allies first had to get firmly established on the Continent and then seize a good sheltered harbor. Next, he wanted to make certain that no significant part of the Allied forces was in a position where it could be isolated and defeated in detail. Airborne troops that landed too far from other forces would be immobile until they could be reached by ground forces. The Supreme Commander recalled in this connection that the landings at Anzio had run into difficulties when the enemy, seeing that the Allied thrust "could not be immediately translated into *mobile tactical action*," had attacked instead of withdrawing.[36]

[32] SHAEF file COS (44) 40th Mtg (O), 8 Feb 44; Ltr, Eisenhower to Marshall, 9 Feb 44, Eisenhower personal file.

[33] Arnold, *Global Mission*, pp. 520–21.

[34] The other two included: (1) the use of airborne troops in three groups to block the movement of hostile reserves as then located, which he rejected as placing too few men at critical points, and (2) the establishment of an airhead near Argentan to seize airfields and restrict hostile movements, which he opposed as failing to constitute a major strategic threat to the enemy.

[35] Marshall to Eisenhower, 10 Feb 44, Eisenhower personal file; Arnold, *Global Mission*, pp. 520–21; Mtg at Hq 21 A Gp to discuss revised airborne plan for Opn NEPTUNE, 18 Feb 44, SHAEF SGS 373/2 Employment of Airborne Forces in Opn OVERLORD, I.

[36] Eisenhower to Marshall, 19 Feb 44, Eisenhower personal file.

General Eisenhower continued with an exposition of the factors on which the existing airborne plan was based and which, he believed, compelled the Allies to visualize airborne operations "as an immediate tactical rather than a long-range adjunct of landing operations." Noting that General Marshall had complained that the only trouble with the plan for the strategic use of airborne force "is that we have never done anything like this before, and frankly, that reaction makes me tired," the Supreme Commander proclaimed that he himself was loath "ever to uphold the conservative as opposed to the bold." He promised to study the War Department ideas carefully "because on one point of your letter I am in almost fanatical agreement—I believe we can lick the Hun only by being ahead of him in ideas as well as in material resources." [37]

Generals Montgomery and Bradley agreed with General Eisenhower's views on the airborne proposals. The First Army commander argued that nothing should be allowed to deflect the Allies from the early capture of Cherbourg, and the 21 Army Group commander proposed that any additional airborne resources be used to hold the enemy away from Caen. [38] General Marshall in sending the delegation to SHAEF to explain the plans for the use of airborne troops had concluded, "Please believe that, as usual, I do not want to embarrass you with undue pressure." General Eisenhower thus felt free to disregard the strategic employment of airborne forces for the moment and to press for their tactical use in the initial assault. [39]

The problem of getting additional airlift for the attack was linked, like the question of finding more landing craft, to the Allied decision on ANVIL. If the invasion of southern France was undertaken simul-

taneously with OVERLORD, it would require all available airlift in the Mediterranean theater. The decision to postpone ANVIL helped to ease the situation. The planners in April set up a drop of the parachutists of the U.S. 82d and 101st Airborne Divisions in the Cotentin, and all but one battalion of the British 6th Airborne Division in the Caen area.

Provisions for an augmented airborne attack met increased pessimism from Leigh-Mallory. Because of the great importance attached to dropping three parachute regiments in the Ste. Mère-Eglise–Carentan area, he accepted the plan for dropping parachutists, but with reluctance. Losses to troop-carrier aircraft and gliders, he warned General Montgomery, were likely to be so high and the chance of success was so slight that glider operations could not be justified. The Allied Expeditionary Air Force commander advised General Eisenhower that the operation in its existing form violated official airborne doctrine on several counts and repeated many of the mistakes of the Sicilian campaign. In view of General Bradley's conviction, backed by General Montgomery, that the Cotentin landings should not be attempted without airborne operations, General Eisenhower decided to continue plans for both parachute and glider attacks. [40]

The airborne plans were further complicated in late May when the enemy was

[37] Eisenhower to Marshall, 19 Feb 44, Eisenhower personal file.

[38] Mtg at 21 A Gp, 18 Feb 44, SHAEF SGS 373/2 Employment of Airborne Forces in Opn OVERLORD, I.

[39] Marshall to Eisenhower, 10 Feb 44, Eisenhower personal file.

[40] Ltr, Leigh-Mallory to Montgomery, 23 Apr 44; Ltr, Leigh-Mallory to Eisenhower, 23 Apr 44. Both in SHAEF SGS 373/2 Employment of Airborne Forces in Opn OVERLORD, I. Eisenhower Memo dtd 22 May 44, Diary Office CinC, 23 May 44.

discovered to be reinforcing the area where the 82d Airborne Division planned to drop. This intelligence required a change in the drop zones, which increased the difficulties for the glider units. Air Chief Marshal Leigh-Mallory, gravely concerned over this development, warned the Supreme Commander that it was probable that "at the most 30 per cent of the glider loads will become effective for use against the enemy." He concluded that the operation was likely "to yield results so far short of what the Army C-in-C expects and requires that if the success of the seaborne assault in this area depends on the airborne, it will be seriously prejudiced." [41]

General Eisenhower was aware of the dangers faced by the airborne forces and agreed with Leigh-Mallory as to the nature of the risks involved. He found it necessary nonetheless to heed the requests of his ground force commanders. The airborne operation, he decided, was essential to the whole operation and "must go on." "Consequently," he concluded, "there is nothing for it but for you, the Army Commander and the Troop Carrier Commander to work out to the last detail every single thing that may diminish these hazards." [42]

The Revised Plan

The initial OVERLORD plan which SHAEF and the other Allied headquarters examined at the beginning of 1944 underwent many changes in the five months that followed. While the high-level questions of widening the assault area and strengthening the attack force came directly to the Supreme Commander and required his intervention with the Combined Chiefs of Staff, other Allied commanders were working out the exact details by which the operation was to be made effective. As early as 1 February 1944, the Allied naval commander, the Allied Expeditionary Air Force commander, and the Commander-in-Chief, 21 Army Group, had issued an Initial Joint Plan as the basis of planning by subordinate commanders. Detailed planning for ground forces was handed over to Second British Army and First U.S. Army, while naval and air plans were to be worked out by Headquarters, Allied Expeditionary Air Force, and Allied naval headquarters. [43]

At every level the emphasis was on strengthening the assault. Plans to this end included increased air operations to destroy rail and highway communications into the beachhead area, heavier naval fire support to destroy the beach fortifications that would oppose the invading force, and augmented ground and airborne assault and follow-up forces to achieve the initial objectives quickly and establish a firm beachhead capable of resisting the most desperate enemy counterattacks. In many of these efforts, the planners at army, corps, or divisional level were able to work out their problems without calling on the Supreme Commander. When they did ask for help, they received it without stint. Less than a month after his arrival in London, General Eisenhower had written General Marshall that from D Day until D plus 60 the operation

---

[41] Ltr, Leigh-Mallory to SAC, 29 May 44, SHAEF SGS 393/2 Employment of Airborne Forces in Opn OVERLORD, I.

[42] Ltr, Eisenhower to Leigh-Mallory, 30 May 44, SHAEF SGS 373/2 Employment of Airborne Forces in Opn OVERLORD, I.

[43] Neptune Initial Joint Plan by ANCXF, AEAF, and 21 A Gp, 1 Feb 44, as revised 2 Mar 44, SHAEF files.

would absorb everything the Allies could possibly pour into it.[44] It was a warning he let neither the British nor the U.S. Government forget.

By the end of May 1944, the initial COSSAC plan had been changed from an attack by three infantry divisions and part of an airborne division in the assault, plus two in the follow-up in the area between the Orne and the base of the Cotentin, to an attack by five infantry divisions and elements of three airborne divisions in the assault, plus two follow-up forces—already afloat—in an area some fifty miles wide between the east coast of the Cotentin and the Orne. To put these forces ashore, the number of landing craft and naval ships had been heavily reinforced both from the Mediterranean and from the United States. To make certain that the enemy could not readily reinforce the assault area with men and supplies, a strengthened tactical and strategic air program was being developed to wreck the railway and highway communications leading into northwest France.

---

[44] Eisenhower to Marshall, W-10786, 8 Feb 44, Eisenhower personal file.

CHAPTER VII

SHAEF's Air Problems, January–June 1944

Before General Eisenhower could put into effect the preparatory air plans for the OVERLORD attack, he found it necessary to deal with a number of problems relating to air command, the employment of strategic air forces, and measures to be used against enemy long-range rockets and pilotless aircraft. COSSAC had tried to settle some of these matters earlier, but had found, as in the case of landing craft and additional divisions for the assault, that it was necessary to wait until the Supreme Commander was appointed to get action.

Problems of Command

The Combined Chiefs of Staff in November 1943 had postponed a decision on the command of the strategic air forces in OVERLORD. The delay had arisen in part because the British were unwilling to hand over control of their bombers for OVERLORD until a time nearer the assault. They feared that measures might be taken which would diminish the effect of the combined bombing offensive against Germany. They were also anxious that nothing be done to affect the program of bombing rocket-launching sites or to remove forces of the Coastal Command from British control. There appeared to be even stronger feeling—shared by U.S. bomber

commanders—against entrusting the bombers to Air Chief Marshal Leigh-Mallory, whose war experience had been in the Fighter Command.[1]

This last point of opposition stressed a problem which had confronted General Eisenhower since his arrival in the United Kingdom. He personally would have preferred Air Chief Marshal Tedder as chief Allied air commander for OVERLORD, and he had made such a recommendation before Tedder was chosen Deputy Supreme Commander. Eisenhower was influenced by the fact that Tedder, as his air deputy in the Mediterranean, was aware of the problems involved in the air support of ground troops. Near the end of December the Supreme Commander had noted the importance of having a few senior officers with such experience. "Otherwise," he warned, "a commander is forever fighting with those airmen who, regardless of the ground situation, want to send big bombers on missions that have nothing to do with the critical effort." While admitting that "a fighter commander of the very highest caliber" like Leigh-Mallory would be badly needed in the battle, he deplored the tendency "to freeze organization so that the commander may not use trusted

---

[1] Diary Office CinC, 29 Feb, 22 Mar 44.

and superior subordinates in their proper spheres. . . ." [2]

General Eisenhower initially approached the British with "long and patient explaining" to show that he had no great interest in controlling the Coastal Command, no possible desire to diminish the bombing offensive against Germany, and no intention of permitting the big bombers to be misused on targets for which they were not suited. Toward the end of February he became more insistent in his requests that RAF Bomber Command be placed under his control. The Prime Minister, however, desired to keep this command independent of SHAEF or at least to limit the number of bombers under the Supreme Commander. General Eisenhower at length declared that, inasmuch as the U.S. air force in the United Kingdom, which was larger than that of the British, had been given to the Supreme Commander, he could not face the U.S. Chiefs of Staff if the British withheld their bomber force. During the period of discussion General Eisenhower declared that if the British were for anything less than an all-out effort for the cross-Channel attack he would "simply have to go home." The Prime Minister near the end of February agreed to accept any agreement that Portal and Eisenhower found satisfactory. [3]

Apparently in an effort to overcome what he believed to be the Prime Minister's reluctance to place strategic air forces under Leigh-Mallory, General Eisenhower said on 29 February that he was prepared to exert direct supervision of all air forces through Tedder. Under this arrangement Air Chief Marshal Tedder would be the directing head of all OVERLORD air forces with Leigh-Mallory, Spaatz, and Air Chief Marshal Sir Arthur T. Harris, Commander, RAF Bomber

Command, operating on a co-ordinate plane. Air Chief Marshal Leigh-Mallory's position would be unchanged so far as assigned forces were concerned, but those attached for definite periods or tasks would not be placed under his command. [4]

On 9 March Chief of the Air Staff Portal, in consultation with Air Chief Marshal Tedder, produced a draft agreement on the use of the strategic air forces which General Eisenhower described as "exactly what we want." To still any lingering fears, the Supreme Commander formally accepted intervention by the Combined Chiefs of Staff if they wished to impose additional tasks on the bomber forces, or by the British Chiefs of Staff if the requirements for the security of the British Isles were not fully met. Tedder was to co-ordinate operations in execution of the OVERLORD strategic air plan, and Leigh-Mallory to co-ordinate the tactical air plan under the supervision of Tedder. It was understood that, once the assault forces had been established on the Continent, the directive for the employment of strategic bombing forces was to be revised. [5]

The draft agreement was passed on to the Combined Chiefs of Staff in mid-March. In presenting it, the British Chiefs of Staff declared that when the air pro-

---

[2] Eisenhower to Marshall, 17 Dec 43; Eisenhower to Marshall, W-8550, 25 Dec 43. Both in Eisenhower personal file. Diary Office CinC, 29 Feb, 3 Mar 44. The latter entry contains a memorandum by the Supreme Commander explaining the problems which faced him on his arrival in London.

[3] Diary Office CinC, 3, 11, 22 Mar 44.

[4] Memo, Eisenhower for Tedder, 29 Feb 44, Diary Office CinC.

[5] Diary Office CinC, 29 Feb, 3 and 11 Mar 44. Ltr, Portal to Eisenhower, 9 Mar 44; Br COS to JSM, 13 Mar 44; CCS Memo, Control of Strategic Bombing for OVERLORD, 27 Mar 44. All in SHAEF SGS 373/1 Policy re: Control and Employment of USSTAF and Bomber Command.

gram developed by the Supreme Commander for the support of the cross-Channel operation had been approved jointly by Eisenhower, as the agent of the Combined Chiefs of Staff in executing the cross-Channel attack, and by the Chief of the Air Staff, as executive of the Combined Chiefs of Staff for the execution of the Combined Bomber Offensive against Germany, "the responsibility for supervision of air operations out of England of all the forces engaged in the program, including the United States Strategic Air Force and the British Bomber Command, together with any other air forces that might be made available, should pass to the Supreme Commander." Those strategic forces which would not be used in support of the cross-Channel attack, the British Chiefs of Staff declared, would be committed in accordance with arrangements made by Air Chief Marshal Portal and General Eisenhower, with supervision of the effort being shared by both of them. The explanatory statements added that the British were unlikely to use the proposed reservation over the control of strategic air forces unless they were needed for attacks on rocket launching sites or for a similar emergency, in which case they would inform the U.S. Chiefs of Staff immediately.[6]

The U.S. Chiefs at once protested that the new proposals did not give General Eisenhower "command" of the strategic air forces. The British, reminding the Americans that the Supreme Commander had approved their draft and had even written parts of it, explained their desire to leave in the control of the strategic air commanders those air forces not assigned to the cross-Channel attack. Despite General Eisenhower's original acceptance of the British draft, he became disturbed by

the question raised over the matter of "command" and insisted that no doubt be left that he had authority and responsibility "for controlling air operations of all three of these forces during the critical period of OVERLORD."[7] He had now reached the point where he was ready "to take drastic action and inform the Combined Chiefs of Staff that unless the matter is settled at once I will request relief from this command."[8]

The point at issue was settled ultimately on 7 April by the Combined Chiefs' statement that "the USA Strategic Air Force and British Bomber Command will operate under the *direction* of the Supreme Commander, in conformity with agreements between him and the Chief of the Air Staff as approved by the Combined Chiefs of Staff."[9] With this arrangement made, the Chief of the Air Staff notified the commanders of the British and U.S. bomber forces that he and General Eisenhower had approved, with the exception of certain targets in enemy-occupied territory, the air plan developed to support the cross-Channel attack. The direction of RAF Bomber Command and USSTAF forces assigned to the Combined Bomber Offensive and the cross-Channel attack

---

[6] Br COS to CCS, CCS 520, 17 Mar 44, SHAEF SGS 373/1 Policy re: Control and Employment of USSTAF and Bomber Command.

[7] JSM to War Cabinet Office, JSM 1581, 17 Mar 44; Br COS to JSM, COS(W) 1220, 7 Mar 44. Both in SHAEF SGS 373/1 Policy re: Control and Employment of USSTAF and Bomber Command.

[8] Eisenhower Memo, Diary Office CinC, 22 Mar 44. This memo seems not to have been passed on to anyone.

[9] CCS to Eisenhower, W–19763, 7 Apr 44, SHAEF SGS 373/1 Policy re: Control and Employment of USSTAF and Bomber Command. (This CCS message contains a reference to the CCS 520 series, which includes the statement presented to the CCS by the representatives of the British Chiefs of Staff on 17 March 44; see above, n. 6.)

was to pass to the Supreme Commander on 14 April.[10]

Tedder on 15 April defined the over-all mission of the strategic air forces as the same as that for POINTBLANK: to prepare for the cross-Channel attack by destroying and dislocating the German military, industrial, and economic system. USSTAF's primary job was described as the destruction of the German Air Force, with the secondary aim of bombing the enemy transportation system, an objective which had been accepted only a short time before after weeks of discussion.[11] The RAF Bomber Command was to continue its main mission of disorganizing German industry, with its operations complementing the operations of USSTAF as far as possible. Responsibility for dealing with the threats of long-range rockets and pilotless aircraft was placed on the commander of the Allied Expeditionary Air Force, who was authorized to ask for strategic bomber aid through the Deputy Supreme Commander.[12]

Once control of strategic and tactical air forces was settled, Air Chief Marshal Leigh-Mallory sought to unify the control of tactical air forces for the assault period. On 1 May, over the protests of General Brereton, the Ninth Air Force commander, Leigh-Mallory set up an Advanced Headquarters, Allied Expeditionary Air Force, under Air Marshal Sir Arthur Coningham, commander of the 2d Tactical Air Force, to plan and co-ordinate the operations of those British and U.S. tactical air forces allotted to him. In late May, the Supreme Commander directed the 21 Army Group commander to deal with only one air chief during the assault period. Ground force requests for air support were now to go directly to the Commander, Advanced Headquarters, AEAF,

at Uxbridge, where advanced headquarters of the 2d Tactical Air Force and the Ninth Air Force were also located. Information on targets of special importance not directly connected with the battle area was to be sent by the 21 Army Group to the Commander-in-Chief, Allied Expeditionary Air Force.[13]

At the beginning of the cross-Channel attack, therefore, General Eisenhower had under his control those portions of the strategic air forces of RAF Bomber Command and USSTAF allotted him for the POINTBLANK and OVERLORD operations. His tactical support—under the control of the Allied Expeditionary Air Force—consisted of the Ninth U.S. Air Force, the 2d Tactical Air Force, and such forces as should be allocated from the Air Defence of Great Britain. The Allied air forces were co-ordinated after 1 May through the Air Operations Planning Staff of SHAEF located at Stanmore, main headquarters of AEAF. At Stanmore daily conferences were held by the Deputy Supreme Commander, the commander of AEAF, and the Allied strategic and tactical air force commanders. The Allied tactical air force

---

[10] Ltr, Portal to Spaatz, 13 Apr 44; Air Marshal Sir Norman H. Bottomley to Comdr, Bomber Comd, 13 Apr 44. Both in SHAEF SGS 373/1 Policy re: Control and Employment of USSTAF and Bomber Command.

[11] See below, pp. 127–31.

[12] Directive by SHAEF (prepared by Deputy SAC and issued by the Supreme Commander) to USSTAF and Bomber Command for the support of OVERLORD during the preparatory period, 17 Apr 44, SHAEF SGS 373/1 Policy re: Control and Employment of USSTAF and Bomber Command.

[13] AEAF to 2d Tactical Air Force and Ninth Air Force, 9 May 44, sub: Establishment of Advanced AEAF, with atchd dir of 1 May 44; SAC Dir to 21 A Gp and C-in-C AEAF, Control of air forces during the initial phase of NEPTUNE—general principles [date uncertain—may be 18, 19, or 20 May 44], SHAEF SGS 373/1 Policy re: Control and Employment of USSTAF and Bomber Command.

commanders held similar daily meetings at Advanced Headquarters, AEAF, Uxbridge, to co-ordinate operations of the 2d Tactical and Ninth Air Forces. A Combined Operations Room, consisting of representatives of the two tactical air forces, and a Combined Control Center, including representatives of the fighter units and commands in support of operations were also established at Uxbridge. The control center "planned, co-ordinated and controlled all fighter operations in the initial phases of the operations; it was also responsible for issuing executive instructions for the fighter bombers." The Combined Reconnaissance Center at Uxbridge co-ordinated photographic and visual reconnaissance.[14]

Railway Bombing Plan

SHAEF's chief contribution to air support for the assault came from its strong insistence on the adoption of a railway bombing plan.[15] In getting the proposal adopted, Eisenhower, Tedder, and Leigh-Mallory were vigorously opposed, on both strategic and political grounds, by most of the bomber commanders, by members of the 21 Army Group staff, and by the Prime Minister and most of the War Cabinet.

Air Chief Marshal Leigh-Mallory's staff in January 1944 presented SHAEF with a plan for destroying railway marshaling yards and repair facilities in the invasion area. Based on an analysis by Professor S. Zuckerman, scientific adviser to the Allied Expeditionary Air Force on railway bombing in Italy, the proposal provided for a ninety-day attack against thirty-nine targets in Germany and thirty-three in Belgium and France for the purpose of dislocating railway systems supplying the

enemy forces in the west.[16]

As soon as it was presented, the railway bombing plan was attacked by U.S. and British bomber commanders who feared that their bombing forces would be diverted from the Combined Bomber Offensive and used on targets which did not give a satisfactory return. General Spaatz, commander of the U.S. Strategic Air Forces, had previously expressed the belief that if the Allies could use their full bombing forces against the enemy they might be able to conquer Germany without an amphibious invasion.[17] Air Chief Marshal Harris feared that if there was any major shift of strategic bomber forces to purely "army cooperation work" the Allies would soon lose the combined bombing offensive's effect for the past year. The AEAF planners, on the other hand, believed that the strategic bombing forces had already

[14] Air Chief Marshal Sir Trafford Leigh-Mallory, Despatch to the Supreme Commander, AEF, November 1944, *Supplement to The London Gazette*, December 31, 1946, pp. 1–3.

[15] The plan was known by several names: "the transportation bombing plan," "the Zuckerman plan," "the AEAF plan," "the Tedder plan," and "the railway bombing plan."

[16] Rpt of Conf at Norfolk House, 13 Jan 44, dtd 14 Jan 44, USSTAF files. (The author is indebted to Col. Charles Warner, USAF, and Dr. Gordon Harrison for these and other notes taken from the USSTAF files.) For the U.S. Air Force account of the railway bombing plan, see Wesley Frank Craven and James Lea Cate, *The Army Air Forces in World War II: III, Europe: ARGUMENT to V-E Day* (Chicago, 1951), pp. 77–79, 149–62.

[17] Butcher, *My Three Years with Eisenhower*, p. 447, quotes General Spaatz as saying in 1943 that, after the weather cleared in the spring so that bombing could be persistent and continuous from both the United Kingdom and the Mediterranean, he was confident that Germany would give up in three months. As a result he did not think OVERLORD necessary or desirable. Apparently Air Chief Marshal Harris shared this view although, once it was decided that an invasion was to be made, he "did not quarrel with the decision to place the bomber force at the disposal of the invading armies. . . ." Harris, *Bomber Offensive*, p. 192.

completed enough of their programs to spare planes that would help the ground forces insure the success of their assault operations.

There were two specific objections to the railway bombing plan: the proposed offensive would have no effect on the OVERLORD battle during the first twenty days when it was most needed; peoples of the occupied countries might react unfavorably to the attacks over their territory. The first objection was countered by eliminating targets in Germany and by increasing the number of objectives in France, including fourteen in southern France to be attacked from the Mediterranean theater. The Allied Air Bombing Committee, to which the plan was submitted for study, on 24 January accepted Leigh-Mallory's conclusion that the proposed plan was the "only practicable method of dealing with the enemy's rail communications and that it satisfied army requirements." Because of possible War Cabinet opposition to bombing targets in enemy-occupied territory, Air Chief Marshal Leigh-Mallory agreed that there were political implications which the British Chiefs of Staff would have to consider. He proposed to start the bombing program as soon as their sanction could be received.[18]

The Allied Expeditionary Air Force on 12 February 1944 formally presented its plan for destroying enemy rail transportation by striking at the "traffic flow potential" (main repair centers, servicing centers, and signaling systems). Opposition from the United States Strategic Air Forces, and the hint of disapproval from the British Chief of the Air Staff, brought Air Chief Marshal Tedder into the picture as the leading proponent of the plan. Acting with the full support of the Supreme Commander, Tedder made the proposal

his own, and in late February and early March was probably chiefly responsible for saving it.[19]

In March and early April, the opposition to the railway bombing plan mounted until it seemed to be doomed. Field Marshal Brooke doubted the effectiveness of the proposed attack, pointing to experience in Italy which left serious doubt that it would be possible to reduce the capacity of railroads decisively. Far more telling against the plan was the political objection. Air Chief Marshal Portal reminded the planners of a War Cabinet ruling of 3 June 1940 which forbade attacks in occupied countries if any doubt existed as to the accuracy of bombing and if any large error involved the risk of serious damage to a populated area. In the light of an estimate by the Ministry of Home Security that the proposed plan would cause 80,000–160,000 casualties, of which one fourth might be deaths, political approval of the plan seemed unlikely.[20]

Air Chief Tedder brought matters to a head on 24 March. He cut through many of the objections with the reminder that the Allies had to destroy the enemy's air forces before D Day and delay his movements toward the lodgment area. POINTBLANK, already contributing to this end, had to be adjusted to "prepare the way for the assault and subsequent land cam-

---

[18] Allied Air Force Bombing Com, Norfolk House, 6th Mtg, 24 Jan 44, USSTAF file. Morgan to Leigh-Mallory, 10 Jan 44; Leigh-Mallory to Morgan 31 Jan 44; Maj Gen P. G. Whiteford to Morgan, 25 Jan 44. All in SHAEF SGS 373.24 Military Objectives for Aerial Bombardment, I.

[19] The importance of the work of Tedder is confirmed by entries in Diary Office CinC, Sir Arthur Harris' *Bomber Offensive*, and statements to the author by Sir James M. Robb, Lord Portal, and others.

[20] Note by Maj Gen Hollis on mtg of Br COS, 19 Mar 44, COS(44) 273 (0), 19 Mar 44, SHAEF SGS 373.24 Military Objectives for Aerial Bombardment, I.

paign." To do the job effectively a target system was required against which all available forces could be directed, on which the maximum number of effective hits could be made, and from which the widest possible choice of targets would be provided. Tedder thus questioned the view of the strategic bombing commanders that there was no need of OVERLORD if the strategic bombing program against industry in Germany could be carried on actively for several more months. Tedder next examined General Spaatz's proposal for increased concentration on targets in Germany, with particular emphasis on the petroleum industry. This "oil plan," which became the chief alternative to the railway bombing plan in the discussions that followed, aimed not so much at immediate aid to an amphibious landing on the Continent as at an offensive which might in itself destroy the German war potential. On that issue Air Chief Marshal Tedder decided to make his fight. He held that the worth of any plan at the moment lay in the aid it would bring to OVERLORD before D Day. After considering alternate plans, he concluded that the scheme to bomb railway marshaling yards and repair centers offered a reasonable prospect of disorganizing enemy movement and supply and made it easier to block traffic with tactical air strikes after D Day. In reaching these conclusions he swept aside U.S. proposals, submitted on the basis of information that the tonnage of bombs required for the purpose would be prohibitive, for attacks that would be confined to railway and road bridges.[21]

In presenting these arguments before the Bombing Policy Conference on 25 March, Air Chief Marshal Tedder asked for continuance of the highest priority for POINTBLANK attacks deep into Germany which would weaken the German Air Force. After these requirements were fulfilled, however, he wanted the remaining air effort used to "delay and disorganize enemy ground movement both during and after the 'NEPTUNE' assault so as to help the army get ashore and stay ashore." To achieve this objective, he urged second priority for the railway bombing plan, although he admitted it would not prevent all enemy traffic from reaching the beachhead. These arguments impressed General Eisenhower who, as the commander responsible for getting troops firmly established ashore, was interested in short-range as well as long-range bombing results. The Supreme Commander insisted that, since the first five or six weeks of OVERLORD were likely to be most critical, it was essential to take every possible step to insure that the assault forces landed and held their ground. The air forces' greatest contribution in this period was hindrance of enemy movement. In the absence of a more productive alternative, Eisenhower asked for the adoption of the AEAF plan. He agreed to a War Office suggestion that a study be made to determine whether bombing of a smaller area would be more effective, but held that it was "only necessary to show that there would be some reduction of German transportation, however small, to justfy adopting this plan, provided there was no alternative available."[22]

General Spaatz now strongly urged the attack on the oil resources of the enemy as an effective alternative plan. He maintained that the strategic bomber attacks

---

[21] Memo by Tedder, 24 Mar 44, SHAEF SGS 373/1 Policy re: Control and Employment of USSTAF and Bomber Command.

[22] Bombing Policy Conf Mtg, 25 Mar 44, CAS Misc/61/Final, U.S. Air Force files.

on the railways, in the time and with the forces available, would neither affect the course of the initial battle nor prevent the movement of German reserves from other fronts. The oil plan would weaken enemy resistance on all fronts, hastening the success of OVERLORD after D Day. Furthermore, it would force the German Air Force to fight, thus giving the Allies an opportunity to reduce the remaining air strength of the enemy. General Eisenhower now intervened to say that it was clear the railway bombing plan "meant very little change in the present Bomber Command Program," and that the main question was whether the U.S. forces could carry out their part in it. In the light of Air Chief Marshal Harris' and General Spaatz's doubts that the Tedder plan could be completed before D Day, the Supreme Commander asked General Spaatz to consider information which Air Chief Marshal Tedder would supply regarding the contribution of the U.S. bomber forces and to report whether the requirements could be met. The Deputy Supreme Commander was then to prepare a draft directive based on the Spaatz study, and the Supreme Commander and the British Chief of the Air Staff would make their final decisions.[23]

In preparing his report to Air Chief Marshal Tedder, General Spaatz revealed one of his major worries over the railway bombing plan. He was willing to see it adopted for France where the bombing effort could be shared with Bomber Command and the tactical bomber forces of AEAF, but he wished to keep a free hand for the use of his surplus forces in Germany. On 31 March he accepted the attack on the German Air Force and on the railroads in France as prerequisites to the success of OVERLORD, but held that no

conclusive answer had been given to the question of whether attacks on railroads or oil in Germany would have more effect on OVERLORD. Although he agreed that the oil attack might have been a less definite impact in the time allotted, he believed it certain to be more far-reaching in the long run. He asked, therefore, that the priority for attacks by USSTAF be given to: (1) German Air Force and ball bearings, (2) rail transportation in occupied countries, and (3) synthetic oil plants.[24]

The railway bombing plan next came under fire from British quarters. The Joint Intelligence Sub-Committee, already doubtful about the proposal, reported in early April that despite bombings which had already taken place on enemy railroads there was no sign of any serious failure on their part to move vital military and economic traffic. Admitting that the shortage of railway cars was critical, the subcommittee nevertheless held it was not so severe as to prevent the system from handling the enemy's minimum rail requirements in France and the Low Countries after D Day. This report led Field Marshal Brooke to question whether the Allies were justified in taking bombers off German Air Force targets and placing them on railroads.[25]

A more serious threat to the execution of the AEAF plan was the political objection to it which became increasingly pronounced in April and May. The War Cabinet on 3 April took "a grave and on the whole an adverse view of the proposal . . ." because of possible injuries and

---

[23] *Ibid.*

[24] Memo, Spaatz for Eisenhower, 31 Mar 44, Diary Office CinC.

[25] JIC Report, 3 Apr 44, COS (44) 112th Mtg, 6 Apr 44, SHAEF SGS 373.24 Military Objectives for Aerial Bombardment, I.

deaths to thousands of French civilians. Pressed by the War Cabinet to refer the matter to the Defence Committee, President Roosevelt, and the Department of State, Mr. Churchill expressed his fear concerning the wisdom of the plan to General Eisenhower. The latter, aware of the serious implications of the railway bombing scheme, reminded the Prime Minister that one of the chief factors leading to the acceptance of the OVERLORD plan was the belief that "our overpowering air force would make feasible an operation which might otherwise be considered extremely hazardous, if not foolhardy." He asked that they proceed with the plan. While sympathetic with the views of the French, he noted that, since they were "now slaves," no one should have a greater interest than they in the measures leading to the success of the invasion.[26]

Although targets in France were still subject to War Cabinet control, the Supreme Commander and his staff moved steadily toward the implementation of the plan. The decision on 27 March by the Combined Chiefs of Staff that the strategic air forces would pass to the Supreme Commander in mid-April made the situation easier. When Air Chief Marshal Tedder objected to further delay in starting attacks on rail centers, General Eisenhower decided to use the occasion of his assumption of the strategic bombing forces to announce that the plan had been approved with the exception of certain listed targets. He made clear that the political effects of the plan would be kept under continuous review. An advisory committee consisting of the Deputy Chief of the Air Staff, a scientific adviser, and representatives of the Air Ministry, USSTAF, Bomber Command, AEAF, Railway Research Service, SHAEF G–2, and SHAEF G–3 was ap-

pointed to aid the Deputy Supreme Commander supervise the railway bombing plan.[27] The issue, however, was not yet settled.

Hopes for speedy approval of all proposed targets in occupied countries were not realized. Less than two months before D Day, Air Chief Marshal Leigh-Mallory reported that of twenty-seven targets on which clearance was requested only fourteen had been approved for attacks, and of this number only five had been listed for unrestricted bombing. SHAEF announced an enlarged list of selected targets on the following day but withdrew it on 29 April, apparently in the face of War Cabinet opposition. With the exception of the Secretaries of State for War and Air, the entire Cabinet held the plan to be of doubtful military value and likely political disadvantage. The members suggested instead that the United States Air Forces prepare a plan for the strategic air forces which would not cost more than 100 lives per target. Mr. Churchill forwarded this recommendation to the President and the Supreme Commander, sending the latter in addition a report by Sir Robert Bruce Lockhart's Political Committee that recent Allied air raids in France had been "catastrophic" for French morale. General Eisenhower and Air Chief Marshal Tedder stood firm in the face of these objections, the Supreme Commander declaring, "I have stuck by my guns because there is no other way in which this tremendous air force can help us, during the preparatory period, to get ashore and stay there." He

[26] Churchill to Eisenhower, 3 Apr 44; Eisenhower to Churchill, 5 Apr 44. Both in Diary Office CinC.

[27] Dir, 15 Apr 44, SHAEF SGS 373/1 Policy re: Control and Employment of USSTAF and Bomber Command; Mtg of air comdrs, 15 Apr 44, SHAEF SGS 373.24 Military Objectives for Aerial Bombardment, I.

pointed out that suggested alternatives for bombing troop concentrations and supply dumps would probably kill four Frenchmen for every German.[28]

To the warnings of Mr. Churchill and the War Cabinet were next added the request of the French Committee of National Liberation that the French command be consulted on targets, and the suggestion that it take control of the bombing. The latter proposal was not taken seriously, but General Smith in early May arranged for Maj. Gen. Pierre Joseph Koenig, head of the French forces in the United Kingdom, to consult with Air Chief Marshal Tedder on bombings which might involve the loss of French lives. General Smith reported that, to his surprise, General Koenig took a "much more cold-blooded view than we do." The French commander had remarked, "This is war and it must be expected that people will be killed. . . . We would take twice the anticipated loss to be rid of the Germans."[29]

General Eisenhower and Air Chief Marshal Leigh-Mallory at the end of April pressed once more for a final decision on all their targets. With the aid of Air Chief Marshal Portal, they were able to get the Prime Minister's reluctant approval for the bombings, provided the casualty list in occupied countries did not rise above 10,000. Mr. Churchill was disturbed, however, and continued to watch the operations closely, demanding only a week before D Day why the Deputy Supreme Commander had not examined the Political Committee's report on French reactions to the bombings, and adding, "I am afraid you are piling up an awful load of hate."[30]

Opinions of airmen and students of the railway bombing plan differ greatly as to its effect on German movement. The strategic air forces hold that it was the attack on the bridges and not the railway bombings which wrecked the German supply plan. Even the German commanders, while strong in their belief that the various air attacks were ruinous to their counteroffensive plans, disagreed as to which were the most successful. As to the general effectiveness of the bombings, both tactical and strategic, there can be do doubt.

By D Day some 76,200 tons of bombs had been dropped on rail centers (71,000), bridges (4,400), and open lines (800). The bridges were down the length of the Seine from Rouen to Mantes-Gassicourt before D Day, and on 26 May all routes over the Seine north of Paris were closed to rail traffic and remained closed for the following month. Railway traffic dropped sharply between 19 May and 9 June, the index (based on 100 for January and February 1944) falling from 69 to 38, and by mid-July dropping further to 23. Although French collaborationists roused some feeling against the Allies as a result of losses from bombings, there is no evidence that pro-German sentiment increased sharply because of the transportation attacks. The fears of USSTAF that it would have to bear the burden of transportation attacks did not prove correct: Bomber Command struck at a greater number of targets and

---

[28] Ltr, AEAF to SHAEF, 19 Apr 44; Dir, Eisenhower to AEAF, 20 Apr 44; Memo, SGS to CofS, 20 Apr 44; Dir, Eisenhower to Leigh-Mallory, Spaatz, and Harris, 29 Apr 44; Ltr Churchill to Eisenhower with incls, 28 Apr 44. All in SHAEF SGS 373.24 Military Objectives for Aerial Bombardment, I. Eisenhower to Marshall, 29 Apr 44, Eisenhower personal file.

[29] Memo, French Com of National Liberation, 5 May 44, File of Air Chief Marshal Robb; Interv with Sir James Robb, 3 Feb 47; Smith to Marshall, S–51984, 17 May 44, Eisenhower personal file.

[30] Copy of note, Churchill to Tedder, OCMH files.

AIR ATTACK *on the railway yards at Domfront, France (above). Shattered railway bridge over the Seine at Port du Gravier (below).*

dropped a larger tonnage of bombs on the occupied areas in the pre-D-Day period than did the United States Eighth Air Force. General Eisenhower, writing later, had no doubt that it had been wise to press for the plan. In his postwar report he declared:

The fate of the Continent depended upon the ability of our forces to seize a foothold and to maintain that foothold against everything we expected the enemy to throw against us. No single factor contributing to the success of our efforts in Normandy could be overlooked or disregarded. Military events, I believe, justified the decision taken, and the French people, far from being alienated, accepted the hardships and suffering with a realism worthy of a far-sighted nation.[31]

CROSSBOW

Prominent among the enemy weapons against which General Eisenhower found it necessary to turn the Allied air effort before D Day were the long-range rockets and pilotless aircraft known by the Germans as vengeance weapons (*Vergeltungswaffen*). General Eisenhower, fearful of attacks by these weapons on Allied marshaling areas during the critical period of concentration of assault forces, urged strong bombing attacks on their launching sites to prevent enemy forces from disrupting his invasion plans.[32]

In the spring of 1943, Allied intelligence discovered a German research station at Peenemuende on the Baltic Sea engaged in experiments with guided missiles. General Morgan was informed of these activities, but the responsibility for dealing with them was apparently given to the British Bomber Command. An effective raid on Peenemuende on the night of 17–18 August 1943 forced the enemy to disperse his experimental activities and set

up underground sites.[33]

Allied apprehension was increased in the late fall of 1943 when sixty-nine "ski sites" apparently intended as launching platforms for pilotless aircraft were photographed within a 150-mile radius of London, chiefly in the Pas-de-Calais and Cherbourg area.[34] At the rate of construction which had been observed, it appeared

[31] Harrison, *Cross-Channel Attack*, Ch. 6, has drawn heavily on German sources in addition to the other information used in other reports. His account gives strong backing to the effectiveness of the railway bombing plan. Craven and Cate, *The Army Air Forces in World War II*, Vol. III, Ch. 6, are inclined to the strategic air forces view, but they have not made use of some of the enemy records used by Harrison. The author has used statistical information from the two books. Other material on the subject may be found in "The Effects of the OVERLORD Air Plan to Disrupt the Enemy Rail Connections," 4 Nov 44, BAU Report I, SHAEF SGS BAU 334; Leigh-Mallory Despatch, p. 44; 12 A Gp Air Effects Com, Effect of Airpower on Military Operations, 15 Jul 45; Minutes of the THUNDERBOLT Conference held in London summer of 1947 to examine the effectiveness of air operations in Overlord; *Report by the Supreme Commander to the Combined Chiefs of Staff on the Operations in Europe of the AEF, 6 June 1944 to 8 May 1945* (Washington, 1946), p. 16; Army Air Forces Evaluation Board in ETO, Summary Report on Effectiveness of Air Attack Against Rail Transportation in the Battle of France, 1 Jun 45, p. 3, Air University, Maxwell Field, Ala. Leigh-Mallory Despatch, p. 14, says that in the period of the operation of the transportation plan, 9 February–6 June 44, AEAF dropped 10,125, Bomber Command 44,744, and U.S. Eighth Air Force, 11,648 tons. From the Mediterranean, the Fifteenth Air Force dropped 3,074 tons of bombs on targets in southern France. The SHAEF Bombing Analysis Unit, reporting on the period 6 March–6 June 1944, shows that AEAF dropped 10,486, Bomber Command 40,921, U.S. Eighth Air Force 7,886, and U.S. Fifteenth Air Force 3,074 tons of bombs.

[32] These weapons and the German operation employing them were referred to initially by the Allies as BODYLINE. Later the name was changed to CROSS-BOW, a general term that was applied as well to Allied countermeasures against the German long-range weapons program. The air forces in referring to target sites in their attacks spoke of NOBALL targets.

[33] For a convenient summary of early developments of the V weapons and Allied operations against them, see War Office, MI 4/14, The German Long-Range Rocket Programme, 1930–45, 30 Oct 45, G–2 Docu-

that the enemy would have twenty of the sites completed by early January 1944, and the remainder by February with the possibility of a full-scale attack by that time. Attempting to counter these new menaces, the British Chiefs of Staff ordered bombing raids against them as early as 5 December 1943. These were not completely successful, as a result of unfavorable weather.[35]

General Morgan was asked in December 1943 to study the probable effect of the enemy's vengeance weapon, which might be equal to the force of a 2000-ton bombing raid every twenty-four hours, on the launching of OVERLORD. He was to examine the steps that could be taken to mount the cross-Channel attack from British bases outside the range of the pilotless aircraft. The COSSAC staff members, after considering the probable effects of the V-weapon attacks, concluded that they might prejudice, but not preclude, the launching of the assault from the south coast of England. Although they recommended maximum dispersion before and during embarkation, a movement of assault forces outside the range of the enemy weapons, they believed, would have serious effects on training and efficiency. General Morgan declared that it was not possible to launch OVERLORD in its existing form unless the forces assembled and sailed from the south coast.[36]

British air attacks begun on 5 December 1943 were strengthened after the middle of the month by the Eighth Air Force, which was ordered to hit the NOBALL targets when weather conditions were not suitable for deep penetration of Germany. Attacks on the approximately one hundred ski sites reported between St. Omer and Neufchâtel and a small area south of Cherbourg were intensified and top priority was given the attack on five active larger sites apparently designed for the launching of rockets. Reports of successful results in January 1944, and a decline in German claims of a new weapon of reprisal, led Allied intelligence agencies to conclude near the close of the month that there was no likelihood of an attack by the new weapons for at least four weeks.[37]

The Supreme Commander was asked in early February to submit a revised report on the possible effect of CROSSBOW on OVERLORD. Impressed, perhaps, by satisfactory reports of recent Allied raids, SHAEF reported in late March that the direct effects of enemy V weapons were among the "smaller hazards of war to which OVERLORD is liable" and that the probable casualties did not make it necessary to move the assault forces west of Southampton. The Allies received additional encouragement in mid-April when the air forces reported that of the ninety-six ski sites attacked, sixty-five were in damage category A, which was believed sufficient to prevent the enemy from launching weapons before making extensive repairs. Despite this assurance, the

ment Library; Harris, *Bomber Offensive*, pp. 182–85; United States Strategic Bombing Survey (USSBS), Report on the CROSSBOW Campaign: The Air Offensive Against the V Weapons, 24 Sep 45. Also see detailed story of the operation prior to D Day in Craven and Cate, *The Army Air Forces in World War II*, Vol. III, Ch. IV; Harrison, *Cross-Channel Attack*, p. 140n.

[34] The sites were so called because "of a big store room construction which from the air looked very like a ski. . . ." Leigh-Mallory Despatch, p. 53.

[35] COS (43) 760 (0), 14 Dec 43, SHAEF files; Leigh-Mallory Despatch, p. 53.

[36] Ltr, Price to Morgan, 16 Dec 43; Interim rpt by COSSAC on effect of CROSSBOW on OVERLORD, 20 Dec 43. Both in SHAEF SGS 381 CROSSBOW.

[37] USSBS, Report on the CROSSBOW Campaign, pp. 6, 19; Leigh-Mallory Despatch, p. 53; Rpt, Asst Chief of Air Staff (Intelligence) to Br COS, War Cabinet, 28 Jan 44, SHAEF SGS 381 CROSSBOW.

British Chiefs of Staffs were apprehensive over a reduction in the scale of Allied attacks on these targets in March and April. They estimated that repair and construction of launching sites were gaining on the damage made by the bomber forces. Availing themselves of a provision in the Supreme Commander's directive permitting them to intervene in matters affecting the security of the British Isles, they asked that attacks on these sites be given priority over all other operations except POINTBLANK until the threat was overcome.[38]

Shortly before D Day, the British Chiefs of Staff reviewed the V-weapon situation and made the following recommendations: that the percentage of tactical air force efforts (10 percent of the total) then being expended against ski sites be continued until about D Day unless some unforeseen development arose; that a decision be made about 1 June concerning the attack on supply sites or "modified" sites, of which approximately fifty had been located. The Deputy Supreme Commander asked that visual attacks be carried out at the first favorable opportunity against some of the larger sites.[39]

Between August 1943 and 6 June 1944, more than 32,000 sorties were flown and 31,000 tons of bombs were dropped in the attack on launching sites. In March and April 1944, the tactical air forces expended 22 percent and the Eighth Air Force 13 percent of their total efforts in operations against these targets. However, Air Chief Marshal Leigh-Mallory noted that this activity had not interfered with his preparatory operations for OVERLORD, and the Eighth Air Force reported that on only two days between 1 December 1943 and 1 September 1944 was there any substantial diversion from its attacks on German targets. The AEAF commander concluded

that by D Day eighty-six out of ninety-seven pilotless aircraft sites and two of the seven identified rocket sites had been neutralized. At least seventy-four modified sites were not revealed by photographic reconnaissance until after D Day, and these remained as targets for future air and ground attacks. The combined efforts of the tactical and strategic air forces succeeded in delaying enemy attacks with pilotless aircraft until one week after D Day and were a strong factor in reducing the effectiveness of the ultimate assault.[40]

Effect of the Air Program

While the Supreme Commander was attempting to get full approval of the railway bombing program, the POINTBLANK operation continued in full force against its primary objectives in Germany. The USSTAF oil plan went into effect in April and was beginning to yield some results before D Day. Experiments in the bombing of bridges in occupied countries showed that these operations were much less costly than had been predicted, and the program was pressed with great success by the air forces. This, and the railway bombing operations, which at length got into full swing, effectively damaged enemy communications and interfered with

---

[38] Memo, SHAEF for Br COS, 23 Mar 44, sub: Effects of CROSSBOW on OVERLORD; USSTAF to Arnold, U–61015, 16 Apr 44; Ismay to Eisenhower, 18 Apr 44; Tedder to Spaatz, 19 Apr 44. All in SHAEF SGS 381 CROSSBOW. USSBS, Report on the CROSSbow Campaign, p. 19.

[39] COS (44) 460 (0), 26 May 44; Ltr, Hollis to CofS SHAEF, 30 May 44, SHAEF SGS 381 CROSSBOW.

[40] COS (44) 460 (0), 26 May 44; Note by Air Staff, CROSSBOW Effect of Diversion of Air Effort on OVERLORD; Leigh-Mallory Despatch, p. 54; USSBS, Report on the CROSSBOW Campaign, pp. 2–3. Cf. Craven and Cate, *The Army Air Forces in World War II*, III, 104–06.

the Germans' freedom of movement to threatened areas. The bombings of launching sites for pilotless aircraft aided the invasion forces at least negatively by postponing bombardment of the marshaling areas by these weapons. The ground forces were also helped greatly in their planning by the information on enemy movements and defenses gathered by photographic reconnaissance units. All air activities were supplemented immediately before and after D Day by the raids of thousands of tactical aircraft over the lodgment area. These combined efforts reduced almost to zero the enemy's ability to conduct aerial reconnaissance over the marshaling area or to launch any effective aerial countermeasures against the invasion forces. By D Day the Allied air forces had established their superiority over the enemy in western Europe, and the effects of months of pounding German industry and wearing away the German Air Force were to be seen at last when the invasion was launched.

CHAPTER VIII

Relations With the Occupied Countries

General Eisenhower made great efforts to strengthen the OVERLORD attack by seeking continually to get for his crusade the maximum support of the leaders and peoples of occupied Europe. In the spring of 1944 SHAEF intensified efforts, started long before D Day, to organize and direct Resistance activities. The Allied governments and SHAEF also attempted to lay the basis for smooth relationships after D Day by drawing up a series of civil affairs agreements with the governments-in-exile and by organizing SHAEF missions which would deal with these governments once they were re-established in their countries. General Eisenhower tried in particular to get the support of the French leaders-in-exile, not only because much of the early fighting would be in France, but because that country was expected ultimately to furnish some ten divisions for the coming campaigns.

Allied Liaison Machinery

In establishing liaison with the governments-in-exile, SHAEF started with machinery which had been developed in the United Kingdom as early as 1939. The governments-in-exile of Belgium, Czechoslovakia, the Netherlands, Norway,

Poland, Greece, and Yugoslavia had been established in London, and of Luxembourg in Canada in the period between 1939 and 1941. The French National Committee, organized by Gen. Charles de Gaulle in London in 1940, undertook to speak for the French government. Diplomatic relations were carried on with the various governments-in-exile by the British through representatives of the Foreign Office, and by the United States through Ambassador Anthony J. Drexel Biddle, Jr., former Ambassador to Poland. The British services also maintained special military liaison with the governments-in-exile, inasmuch as most of them had land, sea, or air contingents under British command. By August 1943 Belgian, Dutch, Polish, and Czech units had military liaison with 21 Army Group, Norwegian units with the 52d Division (Br.), and the French forces with the War Office. Once SHAEF appeared on the scene some change was required in the military and political liaison system.

In October 1943, at General Morgan's insistence, the British Chiefs of Staff agreed to the establishment of liaison missions by the governments-in-exile at COSSAC. Relations between such groups and Supreme Headquarters were co-ordinated in January 1944 by a European Contact Section, SHAEF, under Lt. Gen. A. E. Grasett and former Ambassador Biddle, now a lieutenant colonel, his chief deputy. General Grasett proposed in March 1944 that missions from these governments be appointed to SHAEF, to 21 Army Group, and, where necessary, to 1st U.S. Army Group. Members of these missions were to give advice on all matters concerning their countries to the commanders to whom they were accredited. They were to control their own administrative personnel.[1]

At the time of the invasion, Norway had a liaison mission with the Allied Land Forces (Norway) commander, General Sir Andrew Thorne. The head of this mission was assigned to SHAEF. The governments of Belgium, Czechoslovakia, and the Netherlands each had a liaison mission attached to SHAEF or to the army group to which they had assigned troops, and Poland had liaison groups with SHAEF and the U.S. and British army groups. No arrangements had been concluded with the French. In order to aid the Allied forces in France, however, approximately 150 French officers had been in training in London since November 1943 for liaison duties with tactical units. Shortly before D Day General Eisenhower asked the French Committee to supply additional officers for this purpose, indicating that some 550 would be needed.[2]

Also in process of development were SHAEF missions that were to be sent to France, Belgium and Luxembourg, the Netherlands, Denmark, and Norway after their governments had been restored to power. Toward the end of April 1944 General Grasett asked the Combined Chiefs of Staff to decide on the nationality of the heads of the missions, suggesting that the nation which occupied a given country during its liberation should furnish the chief of the mission there. The proposal was premature since the Prime Minister and the President had not yet come to a conclusion regarding the zones which their countries were to occupy. General Smith proposed as a temporary expedient that mission "cadres" be organized under acting chiefs and that the final selection be left until an agreement had been reached on British and U.S. zones. This agreement had not been made before D Day.[3]

Civil Affairs Agreements

Even before liaison arrangements had been concluded, the United States and Great Britain were negotiating civil affairs agreements with some of the governments-in-exile. These agreements were intended to govern relations between the restored governments and the Allied Expeditionary Force during the period of military control. Negotiations with Norway, Belgium, and the Netherlands were prolonged for a number of months because of questions of procedure which arose between the United States and Britain. On 16 May

---

[1] Recommendation of Gen Morgan noted in 191st Mtg, 18 Aug 43, COS Min (43); Morgan Memo, 24 Sep 43, COS Min (43) 575 (0); Conf, 2 Mar 44, SHAEF G–5, European Allied Contact Sec (General).

[2] Memo, Grasett, 14 Apr 44, SHAEF SGS 322.01 Liaison Agreement with Allied Govts. SHAEF Memo, Policy for Future Liaison Arrangements between SHAEF and the European Allies, 25 Apr 44; Lt. Col. McFie to COSSAC, 25 Nov 43; G–3 to AFHQ, S–52398, 23 May 44. All in SHAEF European Allied Contact Sec.

[3] Memo, Grasett for CofS SHAEF, 27 Apr 44; Morgan to Smith, 1 May 44; Smith handwritten memo for Morgan, undated; Morgan to Grasett, 2 May 44. All in SHAEF SGS 322.01 Liaison Agreements with Allied Govts.

1944, separate agreements were signed with Norway by representatives of the United States, Great Britain, and the USSR, and with Belgium and the Netherlands by the United States and Great Britain. The conclusion of an accord with France was delayed until after the cross-Channel attack, and the agreement with Denmark could not be signed until that country and its government were liberated.

Norway, Belgium, and the Netherlands gave the Supreme Commander control in those portions of their countries which should be liberated by him until such time as he felt the military situation would permit him to turn over administrative responsibility to the national governments. Among the salient provisions of the civil affairs agreements were those which re-established national courts, granted the Allies exclusive legal jurisdiction over members of their forces except in case of offenses against local laws, confirmed the power of the Allied commander in chief to requisition billets and supplies and make use of lands, buildings, transportation, and other services needed for military purposes, and established claims commissions. Questions not covered in these agreements were left for further negotiations; some of these were not settled until the end of the war.[4]

The military missions of Belgium, the Netherlands, and Norway were asked on 25 May 1944 to provide officers to advise the Allied military authorities on administration, intelligence, plans and operations, civil affairs, public relations, and psychological warfare in relation to the three countries. The way was thus open to simple and direct dealing with three of the five countries whose liberation SHAEF was shortly to undertake.

Troubled Relations with the French Committee

Factors Creating Difficulties

The difficulties that arose between the French Committee and the United States and Great Britain created one of the "most acutely annoying" problems faced by General Eisenhower before D Day and during the first weeks of the invasion.[5] They grew out of General de Gaulle's desire to restore France to the position of a great power with himself as the sole responsible authority. His proclamation in the summer of 1940 that the war was not lost and his prompt organization of the French National Committee in London created a rallying point for those Frenchmen who were willing to resist the Germans and the Vichy regime. Unfortunately, he and his followers alienated a number of Frenchmen both inside and outside France who felt that their efforts at resistance were being overlooked by de Gaulle. Among these were former Regular Army officers who, although they were in the area controlled by Vichy, were engaged in schemes to aid the Allies in the liberation of France. Some of the Frenchmen outside France preferred to follow the lead of Gen. Henri Honoré Giraud in his program of restoring French independence. At times these groups became so intense in their rivalry for control of the

---

[4] AGWAR to SHAEF, W–32575, 5 May 44, SHAEF SGS 014.1 Belgium, Civil Affairs Dir for Belgium, I. ETOUSA to AGWAR, S–51681, 11 May 44; State Dept Rad Bull 118, 16 May 44. Both in SHAEF SGS 014.1 Norway, Civil Affairs Dir for Norway. Details of the agreements may also be found in the directives of the three governments, which are in the above SHAEF SGS Norway and Belgium files and in SHAEF SGS 014.1 Netherlands, Civil Affairs Dir for Netherlands.

[5] The quoted phrase is General Eisenhower's.

French forces outside France that it was difficult for the Allies to know what course to follow.

The Allies' decision to make use of Admiral Jean François Darlan during the North African operations offended Frenchmen in both Giraudist and Gaullist circles and made them somewhat suspicious of Allied intentions. The de Gaulle group was further alienated by favor shown to the Giraudist group. President Roosevelt and Secretary of State Hull, while strongly in favor of restoring freedom to France, were not convinced that General de Gaulle or his followers represented the majority of the French people. They felt that any recognition of the French Committee of National Liberation, which Generals de Gaulle and Giraud had sponsored in June 1943 as a successor of the French National Committee, might force an unwanted regime on France. The President feared in particular that de Gaulle's desire was aimed more at gaining political control of France than at defeating the Germans. De Gaulle's threats of punishment for adherents of Marshal Henri Philippe Pétain left many Allied leaders with the impression that his program in a liberated France might produce civil war.

The British and U.S. Governments frequently differed in their attitudes toward de Gaulle. The British had given their backing to the first de Gaulle committee in 1940. The Prime Minister, while often stern with the French general and inclined to resent some of his views, tended to seek some understanding between the general and Mr. Roosevelt. It is probable that but for the strong opposition of the President to the French Committee the British would have recognized it as the provisional government of France before D Day—a move which would have simpli-

fied SHAEF's task in dealing with French civil affairs.

The United States in July 1942 had selected representatives to consult with General de Gaulle and the French Committee in London on all matters relative to the conduct of war which concerned the French.[6] Because the President had not been attracted to de Gaulle, however, he was prepared to deal with other representatives of the French people. Mr. Roosevelt had accepted the French Committee of National Liberation with strong reservations. In August 1943 he said that he welcomed its formation, but expected it to function on the principle of collective responsibility of all its members for the active prosecution of the war and to be subject to the military requirements of the Allied commanders. The committee was recognized as a political body functioning within specific limitations during the period of the war, but not as a government. "Later on," the President said, "the people of France, in a free and untrammeled manner, will proceed in due course to select their own government and their own officials to administer it." He directed General Eisenhower to deal with the French military authorities and not with the French Committee on matters involving French forces.[7] This instruction had the effect not only of reducing the governmental authority of the French Commit-

_____

[6] Admiral Stark, commander of U.S. Naval Forces in Europe, represented the Navy, and Brig. Gen. Charles L. Bolté, chief of staff of Headquarters, ETOUSA, represented the Army. Through his chief of staff, General Eisenhower was made aware of French problems from the time he became the ETOUSA commander. Inasmuch as there were several changes in the Army representative, Admiral Stark and his staff provided the continuity for U.S. relations with French representatives in London.

[7] Statement by Roosevelt, 26 Aug 43, ABC 334.08 French Com of National Liberation.

tee but of increasing the power of General Giraud, commander in chief of the French forces. The inevitable result was to increase division among the French factions. There continued to appear in London and other capitals committees and liaison officers representing the Giraudists, Gaullists, and various splinter groups. The task of Supreme Headquarters, which needed some specific authority with which to deal on matters of French Resistance, the command of French troops, and agreements for the administration of civil affairs in liberated France, was thus made more difficult.

Civil Affairs Agreements With France

The desire of General de Gaulle to establish the authority of the French Committee of National Liberation was responsible for many difficulties which arose between the Allies and the French in 1943 and 1944. In no case was the clash over authority more evident than in the discussions of an arrangement for the administration of civil affairs in the liberated areas of France.

Early in its preparations for civil affairs administration, COSSAC stressed the need for an agreement with the French during the operations in northwest Europe. General Barker, deputy chief of COSSAC, discussed the matter in August 1943 with Secretary Hull and Mr. James C. Dunn of the State Department. They agreed that a formula should be worked out for dealing with the French. A draft agreement to this end was presented by the United States and Great Britain at the Moscow Conference in the fall of 1943. The Western Allies declared that, subject to the primary purpose of defeating Germany, the landing in France was to have the purpose of liberating the French at the earliest moment from their oppressors and of creating conditions in which a democratically constituted government might be able to take responsibility for civil administration. Until the people could make a free choice of the government which they desired, they were to be given "the largest measure of personal and political liberty compatible with military security. . . ." The civil administration under the Supreme Commander was to be restored as far as possible to the French, and a director of civil affairs was to be appointed by the Supreme Commander from the French contingent or liaison mission connected with military operations in France. A French Military Mission for Civil Affairs was to be invited to Supreme Headquarters and associated in the direction of civil affairs once operations started. To make certain that the French would have a free choice in establishing their government, the Supreme Commander was to hold the scales even between all French groups sympathetic to the Allied cause. The Allies stated categorically that the Supreme Commander would have no dealings with the Vichy regime "except for the purpose of liquidating it," and would keep no person in office who had willfully collaborated with the enemy or deliberately acted in a hostile manner toward the Allied cause.[8]

This proposal displeased the French Committee of National Liberation. Its members felt that they had played the major part in French Resistance and were the persons best prepared to take over the

---

[8] Barker to Morgan, 23 and 30 Aug 43, Barker personal file; Annex 5 to Moscow Conf Min (U.S. title "Civil Affairs for France"; British title, "Basic Scheme for Administration of Liberated France"), 1 Nov 43, OPD 337. General Hilldring and General Devers had discussed phases of this paper in cables of 11 and 23 October 1943, and General Hilldring circulated an undated and unsigned copy of the document in question. These papers may be found in SHAEF SGS 014.1 France, Civil Affairs Dir for France, I.

reins of government in France once it was liberated. At the end of September 1943 they had placed all political authority of the French Committee as the future government of France in the hands of General de Gaulle. General de Gaulle, in turn, had specifically charged M. André Philip, as Commissioner of Interior, with the duty of setting up civil administration in liberated France. In October M. Philip informed Allied leaders in London of the intentions of his group. He also explained that, when a military liaison mission was appointed to SHAEF, it would represent the French Committee and not the military commander in chief. General Giraud would control French forces engaged in continental operations and any zone of the armies which might be established. As soon as possible after liberation, however, the liberated areas were to pass over to the zone of interior and would be administered by M. Philip. The Resistance groups then under the Council of Resistance would be expected to come under French political authority rather than under the French commander in chief. M. Philip indicated that one of the main duties of French Resistance forces at the time of the invasion would be to protect power stations and industrial property. He felt that, since the Germans would probably evacuate France soon after the landings, it was more important for the French Committee to concentrate on administering liberated areas rather than on taking measures against the enemy.[9]

This stress on political rather than military preparations strengthened Mr. Roosevelt's suspicion of General de Gaulle and the French Committee. On his way to the Cairo Conference, the President pointed out that de Gaulle would be just behind the armies when they penetrated into France and that his faction would take over as rapidly as the armies advanced. These views of French intentions were apparently responsible for President Roosevelt's insistence in November on changing the existing military plan for an emergency invasion (RANKIN), so that the United States would have no responsibility for occupying France in case of German collapse or sudden withdrawal from that country.[10]

The British, friendlier to the claims of the French Committee of National Liberation than the United States and seemingly more realistic about the extent to which that group represented the French people, proposed in December that the committee be placed on a governmental level with the United States and Great Britain. The State Department was willing to accept only an alternative British suggestion that the Allies draw up with the French necessary plans for civil affairs in metropolitan liberated areas. At the end of April the President reiterated his strong opposition to dealing with the French Committee on any save a military basis. "It is my desire at the present time," he told General Marshall, "that the military questions which involve the French forces be handled directly between the Allied Commander in Chief and French military authorities and not as one sovereign government in full possession of its sovereignty and another government which has no de facto sovereignty."[11]

The French Committee had presented a

---

[9] "Summary of views expressed by M. André Philip in London, Oct 43," with comments by Gen Barker to Ambassador Phillips, 27 Oct 43, Barker papers.

[10] Memo by T. T. H. (Handy), 19 Nov 43, sub: RANKIN; Memo by Col G. A. Lincoln, 23 Nov 43 Both in OPD Exec 9, Bks 11, 13. Mtg, President and JCS, at sea, 19 Nov 43; JCS 547/2.

[11] Dunn to Phillips, 4 Dec 43, with Incl, British proposals, Barker papers; Roosevelt to Marshall, 28 Apr 44, ABC 090.771 France (6 Oct 43), Sec 1–A.

draft agreement on civil administration to the U.S. and British representatives in Algiers on 7 September 1943. When no action had been taken by the Allies by early January 1944, the French Commissioner of Foreign Affairs, Mr. René Massigli, warned that if no agreement was made before D Day the Allies would face the alternatives of dealing with the Vichy government or establishing a regime of direct administration. Either of these, he added, would cause profound confusion among the French people.[12]

The Supreme Commander and his staff were thoroughly aware of the dangers involved in allowing this and other questions to drag on after the cross-Channel attack. They had been told by French sources in late December 1943 that the youth of France favored de Gaulle because they felt that he was "the reincarnation of the spirit of resistance to Germany and not because of any allegiance to him, of whose shortcomings they are fully aware." General Smith, who disavowed any pro-Gaullist sentiments, felt in early January 1944 that there was no better vehicle to use in dealing with liberated France than the French Committee. He hoped, if no agreement could be reached with it, that at least a French official would be selected who could handle civil affairs in France pending an election in that country.[13]

General Eisenhower, while in Washington in early January, gained the impression that the President and War and State Department officials were willing for him to deal with the French Committee of National Liberation. On his arrival in London, he urged the Combined Chiefs of Staff to take prompt action for the crystallization of civil affairs administration in France, and requested that General de Gaulle be asked to designate individuals

with whom SHAEF could enter into immediate negotiations in London. Mr. Churchill suggested caution, not only because he doubted that President Roosevelt would accept the committee as the dominant French authority, but because of his personal objection to "the crude appeal to General de Gaulle to designate individuals or groups of individuals" for negotiations in London. If the French Committee of National Liberation was to be taken into immediate partnership, the Allies should be careful about individuals selected for negotiations, and make certain they were acceptable to both sides.[14]

The Civil Affairs Division of the War Department in late January leaned toward the use of the French Committee of National Liberation in civil affairs matters, but in March it directed SHAEF to drop any planning based on this suggestion. In mid-March President Roosevelt sent a directive representing his views and approved by the State and War Departments to Secretary Stimson for transmittal to the Supreme Commander. The directive resembled in many respects the views on civil affairs submitted by the United States and Great Britain at the Moscow Conference. The initial proposal to appoint a French director for civil affairs was eliminated, and the Supreme Commander was empowered to decide "where, when and how the civil administration of France" should be exercised by French citizens. He

---

[12] Ltr, Massigli to Wilson, 6 Jan 44, SHAEF SGS 092 France, French Relations, I.

[13] Rpt from French sources, 20 Dec 43, McClure jnl, 20 Dec 43; Smith to Hilldring, W–9500, 7 Jan 44, Eisenhower personal file.

[14] Eisenhower to CCS, B–15, 19 Jan 44, SHAEF SGS 014.1 France, Civil Affairs Dir for France, I; JSM to Br COS, DON 145, 22 Jan 44, COS (44) 21st Mtg, 24 Jan 44; Minute by Prime Minister for Br COS, COS (44) 73 (0), 25 Jan 44, SHAEF SGS 092 France, French Relations, I.

was permitted to consult with the French Committee of National Liberation and at his discretion to allow it to select and install officials needed for civil administration, subject to the distinct understanding that this action did not constitute recognition of the committee as the government of France. The Supreme Commander was to require from the French Committee of National Liberation, or from any other group with which he might negotiate, guarantees that (1) it had no intention of exercising the powers of government indefinitely, (2) it favored the re-establishment of all French liberties, and (3) it would take no action to entrench itself pending the selection of a constitutional government by free choice of the French people. The Vichy government was specifically excluded from the groups with which General Eisenhower might deal. The Supreme Commander was to be guided in all his actions by three paramount aims: (1) the prompt and complete defeat of Germany, (2) the earliest possible liberation of France, and (3) "the fostering of democratic methods and conditions under which a French government may ultimately be established according to the free choice of the French people as the government under which they wish to live." [15]

In late March 1944, the President authorized Ambassador Edwin C. Wilson, who was returning from Washington to Algiers, to give General de Gaulle the following message: if General Eisenhower decided to deal with the French Committee of National Liberation, it was likely that he would continue that relationship provided the committee did a good job, refrained from extreme measures, kept good order, and co-operated with the military authorities. Both this statement and

the earlier draft directive were unilateral actions by the President without specific British sanction. Mr. Roosevelt held, however, that the matter had been settled and was later nettled by the insistence of General Smith, General Holmes, and other SHAEF officials that a positive agreement still had to be made between the Allies and the French Committee of National Liberation. [16]

The French Committee of National Liberation continued to press its claims to act as the government of liberated France. On 14 March it provided for the appointment of a delegate to exercise all regulatory and administrative powers of the French Committee in liberated French territory until the committee could handle these functions directly. Four days later General de Gaulle informed the Consultative Assembly in Algiers of the efforts to reach agreements on civil affairs with the British and U.S. Governments and added that the committee did not have a voice in foreign affairs commensurate with its obligations. Apparently weary of Allied delay, he declared on 27 March, "France, who brought freedom to the world and who has been, and still remains, its champion, does not need to consult outside opinions to reach a decision on how she will reconstitute liberty at home." A week later, he said: "Wherever they may be and whatever may happen, Frenchmen must accept

---

[15] Ltr, Smith to Ismay, 23 Jan 44; Note, Ismay to Br COS, 24 Jan 44; JSM to Br COS, DON 145, 23 Jan 44; Prime Minister to Br COS, COS (44) 73 (0), 25 Jan 44; Hilldring to Eisenhower, 233, 5 Mar 44; Marshall to Eisenhower, 324, 17 Mar 44 (original letter from Roosevelt to Secy War, 15 Mar 44, CofS 091 France). All in SHAEF SGS 092 France, French Relations, I.

[16] Memo of conversation with President by Ambassador Wilson, 24 Mar 44, SHAEF SGS 092 France, French Relations, I. Interv with Gen Holmes, 13 May 47.

orders only from this Government from the moment they are no longer personally subjected to enemy coercion. No authority is valid unless it acts in the name of this Government." The general restated this view on 21 April when he said in an interview that the establishment of the administration of France could be assured only by the French people. "The only point open for discussion is that of the collaboration to be assured between the French Administration and the inter-Allied military authorities."[17]

Apparently with an eye to allaying Allied fears as to the future intentions of the French Committee, the Consultative Assembly on 30 March adopted an ordinance providing for the election of a Constituent Assembly by universal suffrage within one year after the complete liberation of France. After elections were held in two thirds of the metropolitan departments, including the Seine, the Provisional Consultative Assembly was to become the Provisional Representative Assembly, to which the French Committee would surrender its power. These proposals were accepted by the French Committee on 21 April 1944.[18] Some of the reassuring effects of this action were lost a few days later when the French Committee of National Liberation in early April gave de Gaulle final authority in matters relating to French armed forces. General Giraud, who felt that he had been reduced to the position of a figurehead, announced his intention of resigning as head of the French forces, although General Devers and Ambassador Duff Cooper tried to dissuade him. He refused the committee's proffer of the post of Inspector General of the French Armies and announced that he would go into retirement.[19]

Still seeking a formal agreement with the French, SHAEF was encouraged on 9 April when Secretary of State Hull declared that it was "of the utmost importance that civil authority in France should be exercised by Frenchmen, should be swiftly established, and should operate in accordance with advanced planning as fully as military operations will permit." Although the United States could not recognize the French Committee of National Liberation as the government of France, Mr. Hull added, the President was disposed "to see the French Committee for National Liberation exercise leadership to establish law and order under the supervision of the Allied Commander-in-Chief." The Prime Minister, assuming that this declaration changed previous U.S. policy, promptly approved it.[20]

General Koenig, who had become senior French commander in the United Kingdom in April, and General Eisen-

[17] Ordinance Concerning the Exercise of Military and Civil Powers on the Territory of France as It Becomes Liberated, French Com of National Liberation, 14 Mar 44; Translations of speeches by Political Info Sec, U.S. Naval Hq, French Series 17, Plans for Future Administration of Liberated French Territory, 9 May 44. French texts approved by General de Gaulle may be seen in Charles de Gaulle, *Discours et Messages, 1940–46* (Paris, 1946).
[18] Draft Ordinance on Return to Republican Government in France After Liberation, SHAEF SGS 092 France, French Relations, I. The draft included comments by Mr. Charles Peake, British political officer at SHAEF, who feared that the Resistance organizations might be trying to organize a dictatorship in France.
[19] Wilson to CCS, NAF 661, 4 Apr 44; Wilson to CCS, NAF 662, 5 Apr 44; Wilson to CCS, NAF 669, 8 Apr 44. All in SHAEF SGS 092 France, French Relations, I.
[20] Memo, William Phillips for CofS SHAEF, 4 Apr 44, sub: Presidential Paper on France; Memo, Gen McClure for CofS SHAEF, 5 Apr 44, sub: Draft Dir (French); Memo, Gen McClure for CofS SHAEF, 11 Apr 44, sub: Planning With the French. All in SHAEF SGS 092 France, French Relations, 1. Churchill to Roosevelt, 643, 12 Apr 44, OPD misc file. London *Times,* April 10, 1944.

hower saw in Hull's statement a formula that could be translated into a workable agreement. The Supreme Commander asked the Combined Chiefs of Staff for authority to initiate conversations with Koenig on such matters as civilian labor, banks and security exchanges, transfer of property, custody of enemy property, public safety, public health, civilian supply, and displaced persons. He declared that he would not go beyond the limitations set by the President, as interpreted by Secretary Hull. While waiting for action by the Combined Chiefs of Staff, which he was not to get before D Day, the Supreme Commander permitted Generals Grasett and Morgan to begin informal discussions with General Koenig and his staff. At the first meeting on 25 April, General Koenig asked that questions involving the sovereignty of France be put aside until later.[21] Representatives from SHAEF, 21 Army Group, 1st U.S. Army Group, AFHQ, the European Contact Section, and the French Military Mission then agreed to establish special committees to consider the numerous civil affairs problems.[22]

Unfortunately, the French Committee suspended these informal meetings shortly after they started. Its action was in protest against a British announcement, made for security reasons at the insistence of the British Chiefs of Staff and the Supreme Commander, that from 17 April all foreign diplomatic representatives save those from the United States and Russia would be barred from sending or receiving uncensored communications.[23] The French Committee of National Liberation refused to submit to this censorship. The resultant lack of communications between the French Committee in Algiers and its mission in London made virtually impossible any formal agreement before D Day. Dur-

ing this period, however, General de Gaulle told an American correspondent that, although he was concerned over French relations with President Roosevelt, he believed negotiations between Generals Koenig and Eisenhower would "go well because of Eisenhower's friendly disposition toward France." The French general took a conciliatory line in confining his requests for lifting the censorship to cables concerning operational preparations of interest to the French. Reassured by this attitude, President Roosevelt agreed to leave the matter to Mr. Churchill's discretion. Arrangements were made whereby British and U.S. authorities examined French cables before they were dispatched from London and then permitted them to be sent in French code on General Koenig's assurance that no change would be made in the original text.[24]

Even before an agreement was worked out which might permit the reopening of discussions between SHAEF and the French representatives, Mr. Hull and the President had made clear that the Hull formula of 9 April could not be interpreted as a basic change in Mr. Roosevelt's view toward de Gaulle and the French Committee. Mr. Hull defined his position on 11

---

[21] The original minutes translated his proposal as an agreement that the question of French sovereignty would be dealt with later on. The minutes were corrected at General Koenig's request.

[22] Eisenhower to CCS, SCAF 15, 20 Apr 44; SHAEF SGS to AFHQ, S–50937, 29 Apr 44; Min of Mtg at Norfolk House, 25 Apr 44, dtd 26 Apr 44, and correction of min, 9 May 44. All in SHAEF SGS 092 France, French Relations, I.

[23] Brooke to Eisenhower, 17 Apr 44, SHAEF SGS 311.7/1 Stoppage of Diplomatic Communications.

[24] De Gaulle interv with unnamed American reporter, cited in State Dept cbl to Eisenhower, 20 May 44, Diary Office CinC, 20 and 22 May 44. Koenig to Grasett, 16 May 44; Roosevelt to Churchill, 542, 20 May 44; Churchill note to Foreign Secy, 23 May 44. All in SHAEF SGS 092 France, French Relations, I.

GENERAL DE GAULLE

May with a statement to the British Ambassador in Washington that there seemed to be a tendency of the British Government to use his speech of 9 April "exclusively as their formula for dealing with French civil affairs even though the President had declined to modify the suggested directive to General Eisenhower which was stronger than my speech in some respects. The danger of such a tendency and of employing words as a substitute formula was pointed out by me from the point of view of working relations between the Prime Minister and the President." Two days later the President reiterated to General Eisenhower his views on dealing with de Gaulle. Agreeing that the Supreme Commander had full authority to discuss matters with the French Committee on a military level, the President emphasized his

personal opposition to any action at a political level, since he was unable to recognize any government of France until the French people had an opportunity to make a free choice. Alluding again to his familiar figure of speech that the French were still shell-shocked from their war experience, the President insisted, "We have no right to color their views or to give any group the sole right to impose one side of a case on them." [25]

The President's message of mid-May had been prompted by General Eisenhower's request that he be allowed to inform General Koenig of the date and place of the OVERLORD attack and that General de Gaulle be brought to London for a D-Day broadcast to the French people in behalf of the Allies. The British Chiefs of Staff had objected to the first proposal as a violation of the Combined Chiefs of Staff instructions of 1 April forbidding the release of information to the French which might compromise the OVERLORD operation. General Eisenhower, describing his position as embarrassing and "potentially dangerous," suggested that the difficulty be met by inviting General de Gaulle to London where he could be briefed on OVERLORD. President Roosevelt agreed that General de Gaulle could be briefed provided he did not return to Algiers until after the invasion had been launched. Mr. Roosevelt had then added his warning against discussions with the French chief on a political level.[26]

---

[25] Hull to U.S. Ambassador, London, 11 May 44, SHAEF SGS 092 France, French Relations, I. Roosevelt to Eisenhower, W–36054, 13 May 44; Marshall to Eisenhower, W–36189, 13 May 44. Both in Eisenhower personal file.
[26] Eisenhower to CCS, SCAF 24, 11 May 44; Roosevelt to Eisenhower, W–36054, 13 May 44; Marshall to Eisenhower, W–36189; 13 May 44; Smith to Marshall, 14 May 44. All in Eisenhower personal file.

The proposal to bring General de Gaulle to London for a briefing on OVERLORD continued to hang fire until near the end of May. After the President's statement that the French general could be briefed only if he agreed to come to London and stayed until after the invasion, the Prime Minister indicated that to invite de Gaulle under conditions he would probably regard as insulting would be unwise. Late in May, SHAEF stressed the importance of having the French general appeal to the French to support Allied Forces under the Supreme Commander, and Mr. Churchill agreed that de Gaulle should be invited to London.[27]

On his arrival in the United Kingdom on 4 June, General de Gaulle was shown a message the SHAEF Psychological Warfare Division had prepared for him to deliver on D Day. He agreed to speak along the lines SHAEF outlined but refused to use the prepared speech, on the grounds that it stressed too strongly French obedience to the Allied Command and made no mention of the Algiers committee. This reaction was responsible for a comic opera prelude to the invasion which saw General Smith, Sir Robert Bruce Lockhart, General McClure, Foreign Secretary Anthony Eden, and Mr. Churchill arguing the question with the recalcitrant general. A series of cables to Washington charted the progress of the discussion with bulletins to the effect that "General de Gaulle will speak," "General de Gaulle will not speak," and "the General has changed his mind." The Allied leaders sought to convince de Gaulle that his standing in France would be damaged if it became known that he was in London and had refused to add his voice to those of the heads of the governments-in-exile who were also scheduled to speak to their peoples on the

GENERAL KOENIG

day of the attack. General de Gaulle's request that the Supreme Commander change his D-Day appeal to mention the French Committee could not be satisfied, since the text had been approved in London and Washington, and recordings had been made for broadcasting. The Allies finally agreed that General de Gaulle could make such an allusion in his speech. Despite this concession it was not until the early morning of 6 June that the French general at last agreed to speak. The final text represented a victory by General de Gaulle in that it stated that the first condition for the French was to follow the in-

<hr />

[27] Roosevelt to Churchill, 542, 20 May 44; Churchill to Foreign Secy, 23 May 44; Churchill to Foreign Secy, 26 May 44. All in SHAEF SGS 092 France, French Relations, I. London *Times*, May 27, 1944.

structions of their government and their chiefs in the battle that lay ahead and made no special effort to emphasize the authority of the Allied Command.[28]

Fortunately for the success of the civil affairs program in France, SHAEF and the subordinate commands had proceeded to establish working arrangements with French representatives at nonpolitical levels. A number of the officials General de Gaulle planned to use in Normandy as soon as the area was liberated were in the United Kingdom, and many of them were in contact with British and U.S. civil affairs representatives. The French liaison officers that were in training in the United Kingdom for their future assignments with the British and U.S. civil affairs detachments were concerned at the moment less with the question of political sovereignty than with their task of getting the civilian organization of the liberated areas back into operation as soon as possible after the Allies were ashore. Thus the lack of close relationship between the French Committee and the British and U.S. Governments was less serious than it might at first appear. It was perhaps especially helpful that 21 Army Group, which could be expected to reflect the British Government's willingness to make some concessions to the French Committee, was charged with responsibility for civil affairs activities during the first phase of operations in France.

The Command and Use of French Troops

Among the subjects which the French and the Allies did not settle during the pre-D-Day period was the command of French troops. Fortunately for the Supreme Commander, agreements made in early 1943 laid the basis for raising and arming French units to support Allied operations. President Roosevelt had agreed, in principle, at the Casablanca Conference to arm eight infantry and three armored divisions for the French. The eleven divisions, to be employed under the Allied commander in chief against the common enemy, were to be equipped by the United States and organized according to U.S. Tables of Organization and Equipment. The existing Gaullist forces, roughly 15,000 strong, had been equipped and supplied by the British since 1940. The British continued to maintain them until all French forces were fused in 1943. The total number of divisions to be equipped by the United States was reduced to five infantry and three armored divisions on the recommendation of General Eisenhower, who felt that the French could not provide sufficient supply units for eleven divisions organized according to U.S. models. As the divisions were equipped they were committed in the Mediterranean, five of them being employed before the summer of 1944. All plans for the invasion of southern France in 1944 relied heavily on the use of French forces, and, as a result, the Allies laid little emphasis on committing anything more than a token French force in the cross-Channel attack.[29]

Difficulties arose between the Allies and the French Committee of National Liberation in the winter of 1943, when the committee refused to send the 9th Colonial Infantry Division to Italy, despite orders of General Giraud, commander of French

---

[28] Intervs with Gen de Gaulle, 14 Jan 47, Sir Robert Bruce Lockhart, 18 Feb 47, Gen McClure, 29 Mar 47, and Gen Smith, 12 May 47; Gen McClure's jnl for May 44; de Gaulle, *Discours et Messages,* pp. 442–44 (text of speech).

[29] This introductory section has been based largely on Dr. Marcel Vigneras' monograph on Rearmament of the French Forces in World War II, now in preparation in the Office of the Chief of Military History.

Forces. This refusal, resulting from friction between the committee and General Giraud and not between the committee and the Allied commander in chief, still threatened to interfere with Allied operations. General Eisenhower warned General Giraud at this point that the United States would not continue to arm French units unless the committee gave assurances that its actions would be governed in the future by military rather than political considerations.[30]

A conference on the use of French troops was held in Algiers at the end of December by British and U.S. diplomatic and military representatives and French officers in General de Gaulle's office. The way to a firm agreement was paved by General Smith's assurance that French units would play a key role in the landings in southern France and that a token French force, preferably a division, would be used in northern France, particularly in the area near Paris. On 30 December M. Massigli informed U.S. Ambassador Wilson and British representative Harold MacMillan that General Smith's statements had satisfied the chief "anxieties" of the French Committee, and that it had now decided "to put the French Forces mentioned above at the disposition of the Combined Chiefs of Staff, to be used by the Allied commander in chief, in consultation with the French Command, for the execution of the operations of which the broad outlines have been given." He urged the Allied representatives to forward to their governments for speedy approval the draft directive for over-all command of French forces which he had presented three days earlier.[31]

The U.S. and British diplomatic representatives accepted M. Massigli's statement as settling the question of command

of French forces to be used from the Mediterranean. They found it more difficult to agree to the French Committee's reservation of the right to intervene with the British and U.S. Governments and the Allied commander in chief in order to insure that the allotment of French forces should take French interests "into account as completely as possible." The Combined Chiefs of Staff refused to consider relations on a governmental level between the French Committee of National Liberation and the United States and Great Britain.[32]

Members of the British Government were inclined to give some backing to the French Committee's claim. President Roosevelt, who considered the tone of the French replies dictatorial, in late April instructed General Marshall to see that questions involving French forces were handled between the Allied commanders in chief and the French military authorities. In mid-May, the Combined Chiefs of Staff ordered General Wilson to present the draft, as amended by the Allies, to the French Committee of National Liberation for signature.[33]

The French, already offended by the suspension of the right to use their diplomatic cipher in sending messages from the

---

[30] Eisenhower to Giraud, 14 Dec 43, text sent to CCS on following day, SHAEF SGS 475 France, Rearmament and Employment of French Forces, Policies and Agreements, I.

[31] Algiers to War Dept, NAF 578, 4 Jan 44, cites Massigli to Wilson message, 30 Dec 43, ABC 091.711 France (6 Oct 43), Sec I–A.

[32] Eisenhower to CCS, NAF 578, 4 Jan 44; Wilson to CCS, NAF 625, 22 Feb 44; CCS to Wilson, FAN 343, 12 Mar 44. All in SHAEF SGS 475 France, Rearmament, Command and Employment of French Forces, Policies and Agreements, I.

[33] JCS 804/2, 22 Apr 44; copy of French message, 3 Apr 44; Roosevelt to Prime Minister (paraphrase), 8 Apr 44; JCS 804/4, 29 Apr 44, with Incl, Note, Roosevelt to Marshall, 28 Apr 44; CCS to Wilson, FAN 343 (12 Mar 44), 18 May 44. All in ABC 091.711 France (6 Oct 43), Sec I–A.

United Kingdom, were in no mood to yield on the directive. As a result no agreement for over-all command of French forces was concluded before the invasion of northwest Europe. Inasmuch as no French forces were to be committed in the assault, the lack of a formal agreement was not of immediate importance. Further, General Eisenhower had declared in North Africa that unless his orders were obeyed, the supply of French units would cease.[34]

French Resistance

In his efforts to guarantee the success of the D-Day landings, General Eisenhower drew on the support of the Resistance organizations which had been developed in France since 1940. Organized spontaneously inside France these groups gave their allegiance to various leaders. By D Day they were divided into five movements: *L'Armée Secrète,* which consisted of four groups in the northern and three in the southern zone; the *Maquis,* made up of young men who had fled to the mountains of the Haute-Savoie to avoid German forced labor drafts; the *Francs Tireurs et Partisans,* a Communist-controlled paramilitary section of the Communist *Front National,* which had affiliated with *L'Armée Secrète;* and *Groupe de l'Armée,* which was Giraudist in sympathy and made up largely of members of the demobilized Vichy army. *L'Armée Secrète* was the largest of the movements. It was governed by the *Conseil National de la Résistance* in Paris, under the guidance of the *Bureau Central de Renseignements et d'Action (Militaire)* (BCRA), which had branches in London and Algiers. The *Bureau* acted on orders from the French Committee in Algiers.[35]

The whole Resistance movement was initially encouraged and co-ordinated by the Special Operations Executive (SOE) set up by the British early in the war to encourage patriot movements in occupied countries throughout the world. The organization, headed by Maj. Gen. Colin Gubbins, was a responsibility of the Ministry of Economic Warfare. The British Government furnished men, transport, and material for Resistance groups, and the Special Operations Executive, the War Office, and the Admiralty controlled special operations relating to the Resistance forces.[36] They dealt with *L'Armée Secrète* through a Gaullist-controlled bureau in London. The other units acted either directly or through missions or committees appointed by the Giraudists and other special groups.

The Special Operations Executive had initiated small-scale operations in France in the spring of 1941, but its plans for extensive use of Resistance forces in 1942

---

[34] Note, Gen Eisenhower, 11 Jun 51, OCMH files.

[35] Mtg at Norfolk House, 9 Mar 44, dtd 28 Mar 44; Jt Int Sub-Com Rpt on French Resistance, 19 Apr 44. Both in SHAEF SGS 370.64 France, French Resistance (Guerilla Warfare), I. The various branches of the *Bureau* were abbreviated as BCRA, BCRAL, BCRAA. Apparently the London group at one time was also abbreviated BRAL. Since the London branch was the more important as far as SHAEF was concerned, it is that branch to which this volume will refer and the abbreviation BCRAL will be used hereafter.

[36] For a discussion of SOE and its work, see Maj. Gen. Sir Colin Gubbins, "Resistance Movements in the War," *Journal of the Royal United Service Institution,* XCIII (May, 1948), 210–23. For a detailed study of the Resistance movement see The French Forces of the Interior, prep in French Resistance Unit, Hist Sec, ETOUSA, 1944, MS, OCMH files. The author is also indebted for comments on these and other matters dealing with the French to a special memorandum by Capt. Tracy B. Kittredge, USNR, who read the initial draft section on French Resistance. Captain Kittredge, who as a member of Admiral Stark's staff in London served as interpreter in many interviews with the French leaders, emphasized the important role played by those Resistance units which were not controlled by the French Committee.

had been postponed when the projected invasion was shifted from northern France to the Mediterranean. Early in 1943, planning for the use of French Resistance forces was again emphasized. In the summer of that year, the United States established a Special Operations Branch of the Office of Strategic Services in London to aid in Resistance planning.[37]

COSSAC, seeing no immediate need for Resistance plans in the spring and summer of 1943, gave little supervision to the activities of the British and U.S. special operations sections before the fall of that year although these groups maintained liaison with COSSAC. After the outline plans for OVERLORD and RANKIN had been completed, General Morgan extended COSSAC's control over the work of the special operations sections. In October 1943 the British Chiefs of Staff placed under the Supreme Commander (designate) the Special Operations Executive activities in his sphere of operations, and in November the U.S. Chiefs of Staff gave him similar authority over the Special Operations Branch of the Office of Strategic Services. In the following March, the two organizations, headed by Brigadier E. F. Mockler-Ferryman (SOE), and Col. Joseph F. Haskell (SO), took the title of Special Force Headquarters (SFHQ).[38]

Steps were also taken in the spring of 1944 to co-ordinate Allied Resistance operations with the French Committee of National Liberation and French Regular Army forces. Gen. François d'Astier de la Vigerie, who had been representing the French Committee in the United Kingdom since 1943, was directed to (1) participate in the planning of Resistance operations, (2) maintain liaison with the French Military Mission in London and with the Supreme Commander, (3) super-

vise special operations carried out in France from bases in Great Britain, (4) act as representative of the French Committee of National Liberation to the Supreme Commander in all matters concerning military administration in the northern theater of operations, and (5) act as military representative of the French Committee of National Liberation in London.[39]

General Koenig replaced General d'Astier de la Vigerie in March 1944. Near the end of April, Koenig announced the organization of the Supreme Command of French Forces in Great Britain and the European Theater of Operations. He created a general staff of the French Forces of the Interior and of Administrative Liaison (FILA). The staff included two executive branches, one, BCRAL, for Resistance work, and the other, *Mission Militaire Liaison Administrative* (MMLA), for liberated territories.

Meanwhile, the Supreme Commander on 23 March 1944 had assumed control over all special operations in his sphere of activity. A special section of SHAEF G–3 was directed to take responsibility for these operations. SHAEF's control included general direction and planning, instructions as to target priorities, reduction or increase of activities to conform to the Supreme Commander's plans, and directions

---

[37] First draft of operational dir in SOE/SO, Jan 44, SHAEF G–3 Ops C 322–7, gives background information.

[38] The period of 1942–44 is covered by Organization and Terms of Reference, SHAEF G–3 Ops C 322–7 (1st, 2d, and 3d covers). See, in particular, SOE/OSS Outline Plan for Supporting Operation OVERLORD, 30 Aug 43; Gen Morgan, Proposal for Control by COSSAC of SOE/SO Activities in Northwest Europe, 2 Oct 43; COS (43) 237th mtg, 15 Oct 43; Hq ETOUSA SC file 370.2/Gen, 11 Nov 43.

[39] Extract of memorandum signed by General Giraud, laying down the duties of the senior French general officer in Great Britain, 24 January 1944, SHAEF SGS 092 France, French Relations, I.

as to the effort to be expended on various activities. SHAEF's sphere of operations included Norway, Denmark, the Netherlands, Belgium, Luxembourg, France, northwest and southern Germany, and possibly Austria. An area in southern France was suballotted to the Mediterranean commander for operations in support of the invasion of southern France.[40] SHAEF-controlled operations were to be carried on mostly in France, both because they could be more effective there and because the Allies preferred passive rather than active resistance in the occupied countries outside France during the invasion period.[41]

SHAEF required the special operations agencies to co-ordinate their activities with 21 and 12th Army Groups and their associated air and naval commanders. The activities included sabotage, measures to undermine the enemy's morale, and interference with enemy military preparations. Special stress was to be placed on measures designed to aid the assault and on plans to be put into effect in case of a German withdrawal. SHAEF settled a jurisdictional dispute between the special operations and the psychological warfare agencies with its decision that the special operations groups could continue to distribute propaganda if such work did not affect adversely their other activities. Both the special operations and psychological warfare agencies were instructed to conform to basic plans prepared in accordance with SHAEF directives.[42]

In late May, SHAEF found it necessary to issue still another directive on the co-ordination of Resistance activities when a controversy developed between Special Force Headquarters and the commander of the Special Air Service. The latter group had been established under the control of Lt. Gen. F. A. M. Browning, commander of Airborne Troops, 21 Army Group, to furnish trained troops to stiffen Resistance organizations in France. General Browning, opposed to control of these forces by Special Force Headquarters, proposed in mid-May 1944 that a new headquarters be formed under SHAEF to co-ordinate the actions of Special Operations Executive, Office of Strategic Services, Political Warfare Executive, and the Special Air Service. General Eisenhower refused, saying that Resistance was a strategic weapon which would be controlled by SHAEF through Special Force Headquarters.[43]

SHAEF, having accepted Resistance activities as a means of aiding the cross-Channel attack, set about early in 1944 finding the means of supplying the Resistance forces with arms and sabotage material. Such a program had been outlined back in 1941 and the British special operations groups had already worked out the pattern for getting such aid to France. Initial operations had consisted of little more than the parachuting of small arms and ammunition to isolated French groups, but they gradually became more ambitious. In the fall of 1943, the Allies began to develop special units of Allied

---

[40] On 20 May 1944 control of Resistance groups in southern France reverted to SHAEF by mutual agreement of the two commanders. SHAEF then issued general directives to the Mediterranean commander for action by him in support of the Normandy invasion and the proposed assault in southern France.

[41] Appendix to rpt of 29 Apr 44, Resistance in Belgium, Holland, Denmark, and Norway, SHAEF SGS 370.64 France, French Resistance Groups (Guerilla Warfare), I.

[42] SHAEF dir to SOE/SO, 23 Mar 44, SHAEF G-3 Ops C 322-7.

[43] Ltr, Browning to Bull, 15 May 44; Lt Col J. H. Alms to Bull, 19 May 44; Bull to Browning, 22 May 44; SAC to 21 A Gp, Dir on jt opns by Resistance forces and SAS troops, 24 May 44. All in SHAEF G-3 Ops C 322-7.

officers and men to drop behind the enemy lines to aid in Resistance work. One type, called the "Jedburgh team," consisted of three commissioned or noncommissioned officers, one of whom was usually French. One member of each team was a radio operator and each team had its own means of communications. Another type, called an "operational group" and made up of four officers and thirty enlisted men, was set up to attack military targets and public works and to aid Resistance elements. Five of these groups from England and six from North Africa were ultimately sent. Still a third type, Special Air Service, consisted of two British regiments, two French parachute battalions, and a Belgian Independent Company, some 2,000 men in all. Troops of this service were trained either to operate unassisted by Resistance forces, to augment Resistance forces, to provide headquarters elements and junior leadership for a command organization in Resistance localities, or to provide trained specialists for Resistance forces.

In early February 1944, SHAEF became concerned over the lack of adequate airlift for the Resistance program. U.S. officers at SHAEF and in the Special Operations Branch of the Office of Strategic Services were worried in particular by the great difference in the number of British and U.S. planes assigned to supporting Resistance operations. The disparity between the eighty-five British and fourteen U.S. aircraft used for this purpose in February 1944 was increased toward the end of the month when the British assigned additional aircraft to the special operations units. Colonel Haskell, head of the Special Operations Branch, reported that, in terms of supplies and aircraft, aid to French Resistance was preponderantly British and would "quite rightly be recognized by the French as such." He contrasted delays and difficulties in getting the promised U.S. planes with British action in making available their supplementary number of thirty-two Stirlings one week after they had been allocated.[44]

U.S. tardiness in furnishing aircraft, which Colonel Haskell, Ambassador William Phillips, and others feared would be interpreted by the French as due to American indifference, stemmed from the difficulty of fulfilling all of the U.S. strategic bombing commitments. In mid-January, it had been found that a priority system and a careful scheduling of operations were required if the heavy demands of the Special Intelligence Services, Special Operations, Psychological Warfare, and the proposed railway bombing program were to be filled. A special committee under Lord Selborne, Minister of Economic Warfare, undertook to regularize the use of aircraft for these various activities.[45]

Both General Spaatz and Air Chief Marshal Leigh-Mallory reminded SHAEF in mid-March that the POINTBLANK commitments left no additional aircraft for Resistance activities. Air Chief Marshal Tedder expressed strong doubts concerning "the merits of the SOE/SO request and the efficacy of the organization."[46] Un-

---

[44] Ltr, Haskell to Hq OSS, Washington, 22 Feb 44, SHAEF G–3 SOE/SO Ops C 322–7 Organization and Terms of Reference, 2d cover.

[45] For view of Ambassador Phillips, see note of 17 Feb 44 in Memo, Bull for CofS, 18 Feb 44, SHAEF G–3 Ops C 322–7 SOE/SO Organization and Terms of Reference, 2d cover. Memo by Bull on mtg of 13 Jan 44; Marshall to Eisenhower, 8 Mar 44; Eisenhower to Marshall, B–270, 14 Mar 44. All in SHAEF SGS 370.64 France, French Resistance Groups (Guerilla Warfare), I.

[46] Bull to Chief, Plans and Opns Sec, SHAEF G–3, 9 Mar 44; Paper by Mockler-Ferryman and Haskell, 27 Mar 44. Both in SHAEF SGS 370.64 France, French Resistance Groups (Guerilla Warfare), I.

fortunately, General de Gaulle did not realize the factors involved in the U.S. failure to provide more aircraft. The State Department became sufficiently alarmed at his pointed references to British aid to warn General Eisenhower that the impression was being spread that the United States was opposed on political grounds to arming French Resistance forces. The Supreme Commander, at General Marshall's request, examined the situation on 1 May. He admitted that recent supplementary allotments of aircraft by the British had considerably changed the initial permanent allotment of thirty-two U.S. and twenty-two British aircraft. More British than U.S. supplies were being sent, he explained, because British stockpiles were more easily available and because British articles of issue, having been furnished Resistance forces earlier, were more acceptable to the French who were now accustomed to their use. General Eisenhower asked for more personnel and means to equalize the contributions, and added that he would try to explain the U.S. position to General Koenig.[47]

Despite shortages in aircraft, the special operations agencies were successful in getting considerable quantities of supplies to the Resistance groups in France. By mid-April, an estimated 100,000 men had arms and ammunition. In the face of vigorous German countermeasures in 1943, and the efforts of a strong Vichy police system, estimated at 250,000, headed by Joseph Darnand, the Resistance movement continued to be active. Besides supplying information on the movement of German units, the Resistance forces conducted small-scale acts of sabotage. Their major effort was directed against the railways. Pre-D-Day intelligence reports pointed to the destruction or damage of 730 locomo-

tives in a three-and-one-half month period.[48] To deal with this problem the Germans had been forced to increase their own railway employees in France from 10,000 in January 1944 to 50,000 and to install rigid supervision of rail lines and personnel. SHAEF estimated that even with these difficulties, the enemy could carry on efforts against the Allied landings if he could maintain 100 trains per day. Since the capacity of German-controlled strategic lines was about 200 per day, the margin was still large. The Joint Intelligence Sub-Committee concluded cautiously, therefore, that the effort of the Resistance would be in the nature of a bonus which could not be determined with certainty and could not be taken into account in operational planning. The SHAEF planners asked only for a measure of delay to enemy reinforcements, pointing out that, while this might seem too small a result for such a great expenditure of lives and effort, the delay would come at "the critical period of OVERLORD when every hour is vital."[49]

The French drew up a series of plans in London under the general direction of the Allied special operations agencies. These plans, approved by SHAEF in the spring of 1944, included a number of specific operations against strategic railroads and highways, the electrical distribution sys-

---

[47] JCS to Eisenhower, 17 Mar 44; Eisenhower to JCS, 1 May 44. Both in SHAEF G–3 Ops C 322–7 Organization and Terms of Reference, 2d cover. Marshall to Eisenhower, W–30283, 30 Apr 44, SHAEF SGS 370.64 France, French Resistance Groups (Guerilla Warfare), I.

[48] JIC (44) 159, War Cabinet, Jt Intel Sub-Com Rpt, 19 Apr 44, SHAEF SGS 370.64 France, French Resistance Groups (Guerilla Warfare), I.

[49] JIC (44), 159 (0), Jt Intel Sub-Com Rpt, 19 Apr 44; SHAEF G–3 Memo, 29 Apr 44, sub: Resistance by General Public in France, SHAEF SGS 370.64 France, French Resistance Groups (Guerilla Warfare), I.

tem, telephone and telegraph lines, munitions and gasoline dumps, and enemy headquarters.

Some weeks before D Day, special operations agencies instructed Resistance units to listen to British Broadcasting Corporation announcements at the beginning and middle of each month in order to get an alert for the commencement of operations. As soon as they received the first message, they were to remain on the alert for a second message which would give the signal. SHAEF's Message A was broadcast by BBC on 1 June and repeated the following day. On the night of 5 June all B messages were sent. On the following morning, the Resistance forces began to send detailed information on current enemy movements and started a series of attacks to forestall enemy reinforcement of the assault area.[50]

---

[50] The French Forces of the Interior, Ch. II, pp. 387–88, OCMH.

CHAPTER IX

Final Preparations
for the Invasion

In the final weeks before D Day, General Eisenhower spent much of his time visiting Allied units and observing maneuvers and exercises. A firm believer that a commander should show himself to the troops, he, in common with General Montgomery and General Bradley, made numerous trips to military units. In spite of conferences, staff meetings, and the reception of prominent visitors, he found time in the period between 1 February and 1 June to visit twenty-six divisions, twenty-four airfields, five ships of war, and a number of depots, shops, hospitals, and other installations.[1]

He attempted to see as many men as possible, to examine their weapons and equipment, to speak informally to them about the value of their specific tasks and the importance of the larger mission of which they were a part. He was anxious not only to inspire the troops under his command to do their best, but to develop a feeling on the part of both the British and U.S. troops that they were brothers-in-arms.

While these visits were in progress, the Allies were intensifying the air attacks on the invasion coast, strengthening the propaganda campaign against the enemy, and making plans for effective use of the French Resistance forces. The Supreme Commander himself was called on to recommend and take action on security measures, to discipline some of his commanders because of their breaches of security or issuance of unapproved statements, and to give the final order for the assault. *(Chart 4)*

Intensified Air Efforts Against the Enemy

Air preparations for OVERLORD were intensified in April 1944 and continued with increased force until the assault. Aside from the POINTBLANK operations, which aided OVERLORD by attacks on the German economy and air force, Allied air activities consisted of a number of different campaigns designed especially to expose and soften up the enemy in the invasion area. One of these, photographic reconnaissance, begun more than a year before, furnished the assault commanders with photo coverage of the European coast from the Netherlands to the Spanish frontier. It was thus possible to plot coastal defenses, bridges, prospective airfields, airborne drop zones, flooded areas, and enemy dumps and depots. From 1 April to

---

[1] A list of visits has been included in Eisenhower, *Crusade in Europe*, p. 238. Butcher, *My Three Years With Eisenhower*, contains a number of references to General Eisenhower's visits to troops in the period mentioned.

CHART 4—OPERATIONAL CHAIN OF COMMAND, AEF, 1 APRIL 1944

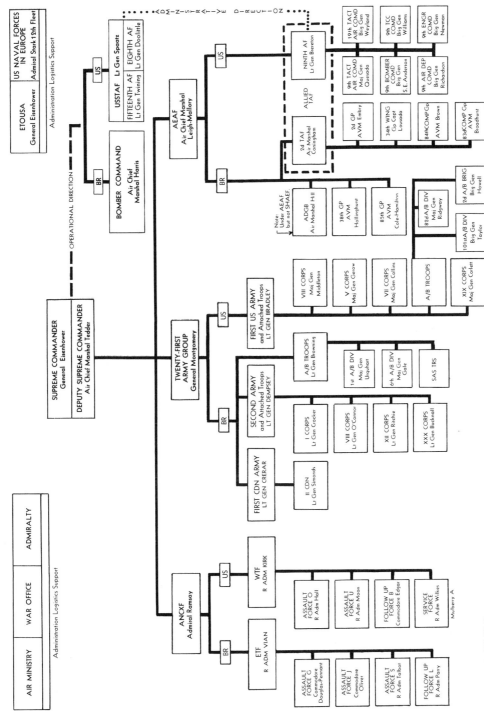

Source: Statistics Sec, SGS, SHAEF

AERIAL RECONNAISSANCE *photograph of beach defenses.*

5 June 1944, the Allied Expeditionary Air Force flew more than 3,000 photographic reconnaissance sorties and the other air commands flew an additional 1,500.[2]

In March 1944 the Allied air forces started their bombing operations against enemy lines of communications in France and Belgium with attacks against railway marshaling yards and repair stations. In the last weeks of May they began bombing locomotives and bridges. Mid-April 1944 had already seen the opening of a special campaign to neutralize coastal defenses, and early May the start of an offensive on enemy radar installations and wireless telegraph facilities, ammunition and fuel dumps, military camps and headquarters, and airfields. The attack on V-weapon launching sites, which had been inaugurated earlier in the year, was stepped up

as the invasion period approached. Air forces were also busy protecting the Allied naval and ground forces against enemy bombers and reconnaissance planes during the assembly of the assault forces. Air Chief Marshal Leigh-Mallory estimated that in the six weeks before D Day the enemy flew only 125 reconnaissance sorties in the Channel area and four over the Thames Estuary and the east coast. Very few of these approached land. Thus the

[2] The information for this section has been taken from Air Chief Marshal Sir Trafford Leigh-Mallory, Despatch to the Supreme Commander, AEF, November 1944, *Supplement to The London Gazette,* December 31, 1946, pp. 42–54. Statistical information has been included to give some idea of the forces employed and the tonnages of bombs dropped. All statistics, as the dispatch notes, are subject to correction. See also Craven and Cate, *The Army Air Forces in World War II: III, ARGUMENT to V-E Day, January 1944 to May 1945* (Chicago, 1951), pp. 138–81.

presence of the great concentrations of men and craft did not become known to the enemy. Those occasional bombers which ventured over the British Isles were usually dealt with effectively and were responsible for only incidental damage.

Propaganda Efforts Against the Enemy

Long-range strategic propaganda campaigns were continued in 1944, being changed only to focus attention on the cross-Channel attack. The British Broadcasting Corporation, which had been active since 1939 in attacking German morale and encouraging the people of occupied countries to resist, was joined before D Day by the Office of War Information short-wave transmitters operating under the name of the American Broadcasting Station in Europe (ABSIE). A leaflet campaign, carried on since 1939 with the effective aid of the Royal Air Force and augmented after August 1943 by the Eighth Air Force, was intensified in the three months before D Day. During the period between 1939 and D Day some two and three-quarter billion leaflets were distributed of which more than two billion were dropped by the Royal Air Force.[3] In addition, propaganda agencies supporting SHAEF operations produced and dropped a daily leaflet newspaper to the German troops. Beginning on 25 April 1944 and continuing until the end of the war, Allied planes dropped between a half million and a million copies of each edition of *Nachrichten fuer die Truppe.* This publication contained timely and accurate military information and news from the German home front designed to gain the German soldier's confidence in the truthfulness of the source and to keep him fully informed of the defeats suffered by the Germans and their allies.[4]

Besides carrying on pre-D-Day efforts to undermine German morale, the Allies appealed to peoples in occupied countries to resist the enemy and to prepare to support the Allied cause actively when liberating forces landed on the Continent. Allied planes dropped weekly newspapers carrying news of interest and encouragement to occupied areas. Beginning with the British *Courrier de l'Air* for the French, and adding the American *L'Amérique en Guerre,* the propaganda agencies extended their activities to other occupied countries and to Germany. The work of disseminating leaflets and newspapers, initially borne in large part by the Royal Air Force, was assumed more and more by the Eighth Air Force, which assigned a special squadron of B–17's for the purpose.[5]

On 20 May 1944 the British Broadcasting Corporation and the American Broadcasting Station in Europe began a series of "Voice of SHAEF" broadcasts beamed at France, Belgium, the Netherlands, Norway, and Denmark. Seven broadcasts made before D Day instructed the peoples of those occupied countries to gather information which the Allied forces would need on their arrival, but to refrain from premature uprisings.[6]

---

[3] Memo, SHAEF for Br COS, 14 Mar 44, SHAEF SGS 091.412 Propaganda, I. Psychological Warfare Division (SHAEF), *An Account of Its Operations in the Western European Operation, 1944–45* (Bad Homburg, 1945) pp. 17, 159.

[4] PWD (SHAEF), *An Account of Its Operations,* p. 46, says *Nachrichten* appeared in two editions which ran from 750,000 to a million copies each. The same volume speaks of "up to a half million copies daily— sometimes more . . ." (p. 163) and again "quantities per issue ranged as high as 1,700,000 copies" (Exhibit 21).

[5] PWD (SHAEF), *An Account of Its Operations,* p. 159.

[6] Texts of Voice of SHAEF broadcasts are in PWD (SHAEF), *An Account of Its Operations,* pp. 106–11.

Security for the Operation

One of the important requirements for the commander of any great military offensive is the gaining of surprise. Because of the hazards involved in assaulting a heavily fortified coast, this element was vital to the success of OVERLORD. But the extensive movements and concentrations of men, supplies, and ships made the task of preserving the necessary secrecy especially difficult. The most rigid precautions became necessary. COSSAC in August 1943 established the OVERLORD Security Sub-Committee of the Inter-Services Security Board to draft special regulations for guarding secrets of the cross-Channel operation. At the recommendation of the subcommittee, COSSAC in September 1943 adopted a special procedure, known as BIGOT, by which all papers relating to the OVERLORD operations which disclosed the target area or the precise dates of the assault were limited in circulation to a small group of officers and men and subjected to stringent safeguards. The code word NEPTUNE was applied to these papers to distinguish them from OVERLORD documents that did not have to be handled with the same extreme degree of caution.[7]

The most crucial period for secrecy was that from mid-March until after D Day when the heaviest concentrations of troops and landing craft in the coastal areas were being made. To deal with the problem, SHAEF asked for regulations during the critical weeks of preparation which would bar the entry of civilians into coastal areas, stop members of the armed forces from taking leave outside the United Kingdom, and forbid foreign diplomats from sending messages in code from the United Kingdom. A special committee headed by Sir Findlater Stewart and consisting of repre-

sentatives of the British service ministries, COSSAC (SHAEF), the Home Office, the Ministry of Home Security, and the Ministry of Health undertook to formulate such regulations.[8]

The civil ministries promptly objected to some of the proposals. General Morgan protested strongly against their stand and stressed the grave military need for security inasmuch as even a forty-eight-hour warning to the Germans of Allied dispositions or intentions would seriously diminish the chances of a successful landing. Intimating that the civil ministries were holding back in fear of offending the civilian population, he warned, "If we fail, there won't be any more politics—and certainly no more Lend-Lease!" In view of the Prime Minister's and War Office's opposition to outright bans on visits of civilians to restricted coastal areas, which Mr. Churchill thought could be handled more effectively by a ban on all communications from the United Kingdom in the final critical weeks, no action was taken in the first two months of 1944.[9]

While broad security policy was being considered by the ministries, General Eisenhower ordered all units under his command to maintain the highest standard of individual security discipline and to mete out severe disciplinary action in case of violation of security. He required that the greatest care be used, except in case of

---

[7] Memo, Maj Gen P. G. Whitefoord, 14 Aug 43; Security Instruction 1, Communications, 17 Sep 43. Both in SHAEF SGS 380.01/4 Security for Opns.

[8] Memo with appendices by Gen Whitefoord, 9 Sep 43; Barker to VCIGS, 18 Oct 43; COS (44) 7th mtg, 10 Jan 44; COS (44) 10th mtg, 13 Jan 44; Memo, Smith for Br COS, 20 Jan 44. All in SHAEF SGS 380.01/4 Security for Opns.

[9] COS (44) 7th mtg, 10 Jan 44; Memo by Gilmer for Smith concerning Morgan's ltr, 4 Feb 44; Morgan to G–2 and G–3, 9 Feb 44. All in SHAEF SGS 380.01/4 Security for Opns.

operational necessity, to guard persons familiar with the chief details of impending operations from unnecessary exposure to capture by the enemy as a result of participation in preliminary landing operations, reconnaissance, or flights over the battle area.[10]

General Montgomery in early March urged the Supreme Commander to request a ban on visits by civilians to restricted areas. General Eisenhower now insisted that the War Cabinet impose the ban. He warned that it "would go hard with our consciences if we were to feel, in later years, that by neglecting any security precaution we had compromised the success of these vital operations or needlessly squandered men's lives." Four days later the War Cabinet declared that from April a visitor's ban would be imposed "throughout the coastal region from the Wash to Cornwall, with the addition of an area in Scotland adjacent to the Firth of Forth."[11]

Despite the ban on visits to coastal areas, censorship of outgoing mail and news dispatched from the United Kingdom, and restrictions on travel, there were still possible sources of leaks. The most feared of these were diplomatic communications not subject to censorship. The Foreign Office and War Cabinet were understandably reluctant to apply so drastic a measure as censorship to the correspondence of Allied representatives. But General Eisenhower, regarding this source of leakage as "the gravest risk to the security of our operations and to lives of our sailors, soldiers, and airmen," on 9 April asked that such a ban be put into effect as soon as possible after mid-April. On 17 April, the War Cabinet ruled that from that date foreign diplomatic representatives would not be permitted to receive or send uncensored communications and that couriers of such

staffs would not be allowed to leave the United Kingdom. The restrictions were applied to all foreign countries save the United States and the USSR. Strong protests were immediately forthcoming, particularly in the case of the French Committee of National Liberation which ordered General Koenig to break off negotiations with SHAEF. A modification of the ban was later made in favor of the French, but the basic rule stood until after D Day.[12]

Despite many precautions, leaks in security occurred. A scare developed in late March when secret documents dealing with phases of the OVERLORD operation were discovered in the Chicago post office. Improperly wrapped, the envelope containing them had come open and its contents noted casually by a dozen postal employees. A flurry ensued in Washington and London until it was found that a sergeant in Headquarters, ETOUSA, had addressed the envelope to his sister in Chicago through an error. Investigation showed that carelessness and not espionage was involved.[13] Far more serious and spectacular was the case of the commander of the IX Air Force Service Command in the United Kingdom. The general, in the presence of a number of guests in a public dining room at Claridge's Hotel on 18 April, declared that the invasion would begin before 15 June 1944. When details

[10] Eisenhower to 21 A Gp, FUSAG, AEAF, and ANCXF, 23 Feb 44; Morgan to ANCXF and AEAF, 28 Feb 44. Both in SHAEF SGS 380.01/4 Security for Opns.
[11] Montgomery to Eisenhower, 3 Mar 44; Eisenhower to Br COS, 6 Mar 44; Hollis to Eisenhower, 11 Mar 44. All in SHAEF SGS 380.01/4 Security for Opns.
[12] Eisenhower to Brooke, 9 Apr 44; Brooke to Eisenhower, 17 Aug 44. Both in SHAEF SGS 311.7/1 Stoppage of Diplomatic Communication.
[13] Diary Office CinC, 23 Mar and 4 Apr 44.

of the incident were confirmed, General Eisenhower, a West Point classmate of the officer, ordered him removed from his post, reduced to his permanent rank of colonel, and sent back to the United States.[14]

After the war, German files in Berlin revealed that the enemy by the opening weeks of 1944 had discovered the meaning of OVERLORD and was certain that the main attack for 1944 would be in western Europe and not the eastern Mediterranean. This information, which reached the Germans from sources in the British Embassy, Ankara, initially identified the main attack as OVERLOCK. Later reports, rated by the Germans as accurate since their disclosure was contrary to English interest, were regarded as *"conclusive evidence that the Anglo-Saxons are determined to force a show-down by opening the second front in 1944. However, this second front will not be in the Balkans."* The analysis of 8 February 1944 by the Chief of the Western Branch of the Intelligence Division of the German Army (*OKH/Fremde Heere West*) stated:

1. For 1944 an operation is planned *outside the Mediterranean* that will seek to force a decision and, therefore, will be carried out with all available forces. This operation is probably being prepared under the code name of OVERLORD. The intention of committing large forces becomes clear from the fact that the operation is expected to produce the final military decision within a comparatively short period of time. . . . *On 18 Jan 44, therefore, the Anglo-Saxon command was committed to a large-scale operation which would seek a final decision (second front).*

The documents lack any indication of the exact area of this major attack. However, the distribution of enemy forces and troop movements clearly point to England as a point of departure.

Two weeks later, an intelligence report added:

The frequently expressed determination *to bring the war to an end in 1944* is to be considered *the keynote of the enemy's operational planning*. It is also repeatedly mentioned as a definite fact that the decision will be sought by a *large-scale attack in western Europe*. In this connection Turkey's entry into the war is considered of value only within a limited period of time. From the foregoing facts it must be concluded that a showdown is to be attempted during the first—or at latest during the second—third of 1944. The early start of operations in Italy (fighting at Cassino and Anzio) which must be considered only with the framework of the over-all operational planning of the enemy (holding attack) points in the same direction.[15]

The possibility that the name of the operation would leak out had always been considered by the OVERLORD planners. They would have been relieved to know that their most carefully guarded secret—the exact area of the main blow and the approximate date—were not included in the German intelligence estimates. Later, they would have reflected that by the end of May everything which appeared in the January and February estimates, except the code name OVERLORD, could have been easily surmised from the accounts in the Allied press.

The Patton Episode

Scarcely had General Eisenhower punished the Air Force general for a breach of security when he was faced with the prospect of removing an Army commander, Lt. Gen. George S. Patton, Jr., from command

---

[14] Diary Office CinC, 12 May 44; New York *Times*, June 7, 10, 1944; Eisenhower to Marshall, 3 May 44, Eisenhower personal file.

[15] German Foreign Office political report *IM 51 gRs*, 8 Jan 44 (copy dtd 12 Jan 44), Intelligence analysis, *Militaerische Auswertung der Sonderunterlagen WFSt ueber Tuerkei aus dem Zeitabschnitt Sept. 43–Jan. 44*, 8 and 21 Feb 44, *Oberkommando des Heeres/Fremde Heere West Handakte Chef.* [Italics in original.]

of the Third U.S. Army. In an effort to avoid any incident in the United Kingdom which might reawaken the public's memory of the Sicilian episode in which General Patton had slapped a patient in an Army hospital, General Eisenhower had warned the Third Army commander shortly after his arrival not to make public speeches without permission, and to guard all his statements so that there would be no chance of misinterpretation. Shortly afterward, as the result of a flurry over a speech he had made before a U.S. group in England, General Patton promised to refrain from public utterances. Near the end of April, however, in speaking before what he believed to be a private gathering, the Third Army commander declared that the United States and Great Britain would run the world of the future. This apparent affront to other Allied powers led to angry outcries in the U.S. Congress and press. General Marshall, who was trying to win Congressional approval for an Army permanent promotion list including General Patton's name, was dismayed by the incident which brought into question the Third Army commander's fitness for command and threatened to kill all Army promotions.[16]

General Eisenhower asked General Marshall if retention of General Patton would diminish the confidence of the public and the government in the War Department, indicating that in such a case stern disciplinary action would be required. He then sent a blistering letter to General Patton asking for a complete explanation and warning him of the "serious potentialities" of his speech. Reflecting on the fact that the Third Army commander seemed incapable of holding his tongue, General Eisenhower informed General Marshall that "on all the evi-

dence now available I will relieve him from command and send him home unless some new and unforeseen information should be developed in the case." He was reluctant to take this action in view of General Patton's proved ability to conduct "a ruthless drive," and added that there was always the possibility that the war might yet develop a situation where Patton, despite his lack of balance, "should be rushed into the breach."[17]

Before receiving the second message suggesting relief of the Third Army commander, General Marshall assured General Eisenhower that confidence of the public in the War Department had to be measured against the success of the OVERLORD operation. He declared: "If you feel that the operation can be carried on with the same assurance of success with [Lt. Gen. Courtney H.] Hodges in command, for example, instead of Patton, all well and good. If you doubt it, then between us we can bear the burden of the already unfortunate reaction. I fear the harm has already been fatal to the confirmation of the permanent list." On 1 May General Marshall gave General Eisenhower exclusive responsibility for deciding whether or not to keep Patton in command. He insisted that the position of the War Department was not to be considered in the decision, but "only OVERLORD and your own heavy responsibility for its success."[18]

The Supreme Commander, aware "that the relief of Patton would lose to us his ex-

[16] Marshall to Eisenhower (apparently 26 Apr 44), Diary Office CinC, 11 Dec 44.

[17] Smith to Marshall, 27 Apr 44; Eisenhower to Marshall, 29 Apr 44; Eisenhower to Patton, 29 Apr 44; Eisenhower to Marshall, 30 Apr 44. These messages in Diary Office CinC and Eisenhower personal file.

[18] Marshall to Eisenhower, 29 Apr 44; McNarney for Marshall to Eisenhower, 1 May 44. Both in Eisenhower personal file.

perience as commander of an Army in battle and his demonstrated ability of getting the utmost out of soldiers in offensive operations," decided on the basis of the effects upon OVERLORD to retain his subordinate in command. He informed the Third Army commander that he was being kept despite damaging repercussions resulting from his personal indiscretions. "I do this," he added, "solely because of my faith in you as a battle leader and for no other motives." The decision was applauded in Washington by Secretary Stimson who praised General Eisenhower's judicial poise and good judgment "as well as the great courage which you have shown in making this decision." [19]

Exercises and Maneuvers

The numerous exercises held before the invasion gave the Supreme Commander an excellent opportunity to see his troops in action and to find errors which would need elimination before D Day. Beginning in late December 1943, a series of exercises was held at brigade, divisional, and corps level. Final rehearsals were held in late April and early May in the south of England. Activities included the concentration, marshaling, and embarkation of troops, a short movement by water, disembarkation with naval and air support, a beach assault using service ammunition, the securing of a beachhead, and a rapid advance inland. The rehearsals were planned to resemble the OVERLORD operation, except for differences in the sequences of landings and timing made to deceive the enemy if he was observing the maneuvers. The Allies were perturbed when, during one of the last exercises, a German E-boat attacked seven LST's, sinking two of the craft with more than 700 casualties.

The enemy concluded that the craft were engaged in exercises, but seemed to draw no conclusions from them relative to the cross-Channel operation.

The rehearsals were followed by the final and major briefing of the key commanders. This conference was held under the supervision of SHAEF on 15 May in St. Paul's School, General Montgomery's headquarters in London, in the presence of the King, the Prime Minister, Field Marshal Smuts, the British Chiefs of Staff, members of the War Cabinet, and the chief Allied commanders—one of the great military gatherings of the war. General Eisenhower opened the meeting and was followed by General Montgomery, Admiral Ramsay, Air Chief Marshal Leigh-Mallory, and General Bradley who gave broad outlines of the revised plans for OVERLORD as well as a statement of the support the various commanders were to receive in their operations. The King and the Prime Minister also made short speeches. Of this dramatic meeting, General Eisenhower later wrote that it "not only marked the virtual completion of all preliminary planning and preparation but seemed to impart additional confidence as each of the scores of commanders and staff officers present learned in detail the extent of the assistance he would receive for his own particular part of the vast undertaking." [20]

The Decision To Go

With final preparations under way, the Supreme Commander considered the all-important question of the date for OVER-

---

[19] Eisenhower to Marshall, 3 May 44; Eisenhower to Patton, 3 May 44. Both in Eisenhower personal file. Stimson to Eisenhower, 5 May 44, Diary Office CinC.

[20] Butcher, *My Three Years With Eisenhower*, pp. 539–40; Eisenhower, *Crusade in Europe*, p. 245.

LORD. In the discussions at Tehran, 1 May 1944 had been provisionally accepted. When it became necessary to enlarge the assault area and seek more landing craft, the date was changed to the end of May. Ultimately the target date—Y Day—the date on which all preparations had to be complete, was set for 1 June. It was understood that D Day, the day of attack, would come as soon thereafter as the tides, phases of the moon, hours of daylight, and weather would permit. A study of these factors revealed that only three days in early June—5, 6, and 7—filled all requirements of the invasion force. On 8 May, the Supreme Commander after a discussion with his commanders selected the date of Y plus 4 (5 June). General Eisenhower informed the Combined Chiefs of Staff of this decision on 17 May, saying that 6 and 7 June were acceptable in case bad weather interfered but that any further postponement required major changes in the operation or a delay until 19 June when tidal conditions would again be favorable. He asked them to notify the Russians, who had promised to start their attack shortly after the cross-Channel assault, of the change in date.[21]

On the assumption that the attack would be made on 5 June, the Supreme Commander gave orders in mid-May for the concentration of the assault force near the invasion port areas of southern England. The enormous heaps of munitions, supplies, and equipment which had been stored throughout the United Kingdom were now moved by unending convoys to the south. As warehouses overflowed, the matériel was placed in carefully camouflaged positions along the roadways preparatory to final loading. Thousands of men next moved into tented areas in the fields of Cornwall, Devon, Sussex, and the

other southern counties, whence they could be taken to landing craft waiting in near-by coves and inlets and then transported to the great concentrations of ships at Portland, Plymouth, Portsmouth, Southampton, and the Isle of Wight.

Meanwhile, special efforts were made to get the men keyed to the proper psychological pitch for the attack. General Eisenhower urged his commanders to overcome any lack of a will to fight on the part of their troops by explaining the critical importance of defeating the Germans. Articles in Army publications stressed the vicious policies and beliefs of the enemy and the necessity of dealing ruthlessly with him. To combat the fears of those who anticipated heavy losses in the invasion and dreaded the shock and pain of battle, the Supreme Commander urged troop leaders to discuss candidly with their men the D-Day prospects. Service newspapers, like *Stars and Stripes,* ran special articles which described the miracles of modern combat medicine and gave optimistic predictions on the chance of survival.

The best psychological preparations for the cross-Channel landings lay, however, in the personal briefings which unit commanders gave their men. Gathered together in units as small as platoons and squads, the men carefully studied their particular assignment for D Day. Foam-rubber models of the beaches, detailed maps and charts of the landing area, photographs of fortifications and obstacles were analyzed for enemy strength and weakness. An attempt was made to orient each man, showing him his place in rela-

[21] Diary, Office CinC, 9 May 44; Eisenhower to CCS, SCAF 30, 17 May 44. Maj. Gen. John Russell Deane, in *The Strange Alliance: The Story of Our Efforts at Wartime Co-Operation With Russia* (New York, 1947), p. 150, tells of various changes in date which he gave the Russians in Moscow.

tion to other men in his platoon and the units on his flanks. He became familiar with the landmarks which were supposed to greet him when he got ashore, the exits by which he could leave the beach, and the likely locations of minefields and machine gun nests. More important to his peace of mind was the assurance of powerful naval and air support which was supposed to neutralize enemy opposition. At last, after the marshaling areas were carefully sealed off from the rest of England by wire and armed guards, the men were given the exact place of landing, the target date of the attack, and the broad outline of what the Allies expected to do once they got ashore. Before the end of May, it was clear that this concentration was not merely another exercise.

With the final briefings went the waterproofing of vehicles, the checking of weapons, adjustments of personal gear, and last-minute inspections. Invasion money was issued, family allotments made, and precautions given on the proper behavior of soldiers in liberated countries. Spurred by a last-minute warning that the enemy might use gas to stop the invasion, the Allied commanders reiterated their standing instructions concerning the means of detecting and combating such attacks. Nor were the perils of the sea forgotten as seasick pills and vomit bags were handed out, and lifebelts issued and tested. Now that the men knew where they were going, French phrase books were distributed and enterprising linguists held occasional classes for soldiers who looked forward to social interludes on the Continent. At length, cigarettes, toothbrushes, extra socks, K and D rations, and rounds of ammunition were passed out to each soldier. Little remained then but to get a crew cut, write a last letter home, and make a final

inspection of equipment. By 1 June, as the units farthest from the invasion area began their move, few details had been overlooked. The first days of June brought an almost unbearable tension as the men, aware that their return home depended on the speed and effectiveness with which they completed their task, waited impatiently for the word to go.

But that word depended on one factor that could not be arranged by the planners—the weather. In the last days of May, the Supreme Commander began to watch the weather forecasts very closely. He got in the habit of talking over the reports with the Chief Meteorological Officer, SHAEF, Group Captain J. M. Stagg, so that he understood fully the value of the reports and the basis on which they were made. On 1 June, General Eisenhower arranged for the Allied commanders to meet him daily to consider the final decision for the attack. He realized that it was unlikely that so great an operation could be started and then stopped again without complete loss of secrecy. Loadings of ships had begun by 1 June, and it was clear that putting back to harbor and unloading ships would give rise to mishaps. Worse still, a delay meant an additional chance for the enemy's pilotless aircraft to begin their operations, or the possibility that the next favorable period for tides in mid-June would have even less satisfactory weather than that which would prevail on 5 June. Even more important was the effect of postponement on morale. The men who composed the assault forces had been brought to a pitch of readiness which would be hard to reach again. All these factors had to be weighed by the Supreme Commander as he studied the reports of the weatherman and debated whether or not to give the signal for the attack.

Weather information was furnished the Supreme Commander by a Meteorological Committee presided over by the Chief Meteorological Officer, SHAEF, and including meteorological officers from the Allied Expeditionary Air Force, the Allied Naval Expeditionary Force, the Admiralty, U.S. Weather Services (U.S. Army Air Forces in Europe), and the Air Ministry. In most cases, the officers submitted their opinions by telephone to the chairman, their reports were opened to general discussion, and a final forecast was drawn up which was in turn presented for the approval or disapproval of the various weather officers.[22]

Forecasts which were somewhat optimistic on 29 May were less hopeful by 2 June, but since there was some lack of certainty the Supreme Commander decided to order part of the assault forces to sail toward rendezvous points the following morning. The weather experts on 3 June again reported unpromising weather which would probably rule out 5 June as D Day, but General Eisenhower confirmed orders for one of the U.S. task forces to sail subject to a possible last-minute change. In the early morning of 4 June, the meteorological officers revealed that conditions on the following day would not permit the air forces to carry out their part of the assault program. Neither the air nor the naval commanders felt they should start the attack under the circumstances, although General Montgomery indicated his forces were ready to go. General Eisenhower, recalling that the operation had been accepted as feasible only if Allied air superiority could be brought to bear, ordered a twenty-four-hour postponement and called for a meeting at 2130 that evening to decide whether the attack could begin on 6 June. Convoys already at sea were ordered to turn back.

The decisive meeting was held, as the others had been, near Portsmouth in the Allied Naval Expeditionary Force mess room at Southwick House, Admiral Ramsay's headquarters. The meeting place was a large room, lined on three sides by bookcases which were mostly empty, and containing a table and a number of easy chairs. Present in addition to General Eisenhower were Tedder, Leigh-Mallory, Robb, Wigglesworth, Smith, Montgomery, Strong, Bull, de Guingand, Gale, Ramsay, and Creasy. Once the group was seated informally in the easy chairs, the weatherman, Group Captain Stagg, accompanied as usual by Instructor Commander John Fleming of the Royal Navy and Lt. Col. Donald D. Yates of the U.S. Army Air Forces, presented the agreed-on forecast. A new weather front had recently been observed which gave some hope of improvement throughout 5 June and until the morning of Tuesday the 6th. The skies were expected to clear sufficiently for heavy bombers to operate during the night of the 5th and at H Hour the following morning, although it was possible that later changes might interfere with fighter-bombers and with spotting for naval bombardment. Some hope was thus given, but there was a chance that the reports were wrong and the fleet would be forced to turn back. Any possibility of postponing the decision for several hours until a new forecast could be made was dashed, however, by Admiral Ramsay's declaration that "Admiral Kirk must be told within

---

[22] Report by Allied Naval CinC Expeditionary Force on Operation NEPTUNE, App. 16, I, 156–65. (This appendix contains detailed forecasts during the period in question, showing the opinions of the various meteorological officers.) Memo, SHAEF, 26 May 44, sub: Weather Forecasts, SHAEF G–3 Ops A 000.91 Meteorological Matters.

the next half hour if OVERLORD is to take place on Tuesday. If he is told it is on and his forces sail and are then recalled, they will not be ready again for Wednesday morning; therefore a further postponement would be for 48 hours." General Eisenhower polled his advisers. Air Chief Marshal Leigh-Mallory was pessimistic and believed that the operation would be "chancey," a conclusion in which Air Chief Marshal Tedder concurred. General Montgomery, reiterating his advice of the previous day, voted "Go!" The question was now up to the Supreme Commander. He could take the gamble and launch the attack with the possibility he would lack air support, or he could turn back the task forces and await the fortunes of a later date. The fatefulness of his decision strongly impressed the assembled commanders, several of whom wrote accounts of the moment. General Smith was struck by "the loneliness and isolation of a commander at a time when such a momentous decision was to be taken by him, with full knowledge that failure or success rests on his individual decision." The Supreme Commander calmly weighed the alternatives, pointing out that it was the danger of not going which was "too chancey." The question, as he saw it, was "just how long can you hang this operation at the end of a limb and let it hang there." To this question there could be only one answer: "Go." [23]

The orders went out to the fleet that the attack was on, but a final meeting of the Supreme Commander and his aides was set for the early morning of 5 June. At 0330 as the Allied commanders started for their meeting place, they found little in the weather to make them hopeful. The rain and wind and mud that greeted them as they made their way to the naval headquarters gave no promise of fair weather for the 6th. However, the experts, who had made a final forecast at 0200, offered some hope that the 6th might see a break in the weather which might last thirty-six hours. They were unwilling to predict what might happen after that time. On the basis of this advice, General Eisenhower held to his decision of the previous evening. Using the code which he had already sent the War Department, he notified the Combined Chiefs of Staff: "Halcyon plus 5 finally and definitely confirmed." [24]

---

[23] Accounts of the two final meetings have been written by Air Vice Marshal James M. Robb (a signed carbon copy of his original report, written on the morning of 5 June 1944, was given by him to the author); Gen Bull, Memo for Record, 5 June 44, SHAEF G–3 file; Gen. Walter Bedell Smith, "Eisenhower's Six Great Decisions," *Saturday Evening Post*, June 8, 1946, p. 218; Eisenhower, *Crusade in Europe*, pp. 249–50; de Guingand, *Operation Victory*, pp. 372–74; and Leigh-Mallory Despatch, *Supplement to The London Gazette*, December 31, 1946, p. 55. The author has also received statements by Eisenhower, Tedder, Creasy, and Strong. There are some differences as to the exact phrasing of General Eisenhower's final statements in making the decision and for that reason the accounts of Robb and Bull have been omitted. Both General Bull and Air Marshal Robb have given lists of the persons present, although General Bull omits General Gale from the list. Both accounts indicate that Air Marshal Coningham was present at the earlier meetings.

[24] Diary Office CinC, 5 Jan 44, contains details on the decision apparently given Butcher by General Eisenhower shortly after the decision was made.

CHAPTER X

D Day to the Breakout

Unfolding of the Grand Design

The long months of planning by SHAEF, its predecessors, and the subordinate commands culminated on 6 June in the great assault. Shortly before midnight, 5 June, elements of a British and two U.S. airborne divisions took to the air from various fields in southern England and headed for the Cotentin peninsula and for points east of the Orne River. (*Map 1*) Already mine sweepers of the Eastern and Western Task Forces were clearing ship lanes to the selected beaches—UTAH and OMAHA for the U.S. forces, and GOLD, JUNO, and SWORD for the British. On their way to a rendezvous point south of the Isle of Wight were five naval forces; two additional follow-up forces were loaded and at sea. Aboard the craft of Admiral Ramsay's task force of more than 5,000 vessels were elements of three U.S., two British, and one Canadian divisions. Overhead the bombers and fighters were starting a day's offensive which was to see nearly 11,000 sorties and the dropping of nearly 12,000 tons of bombs. Meanwhile, the Supreme Commander and General Montgomery waited in their advance headquarters at Portsmouth for the first news of the landings. General Eisenhower, having stayed with elements of the 101st Airborne Division at their camp near Newbury until near midnight, returned to his camp to await news of the landings. For the moment, control

of the battle had passed from his hands.

Like most battles, that on D Day did not go exactly as planned. But in its main objective of getting ashore against a determined enemy it was completely successful and at a cost lower than anyone had hoped. The naval and air forces had prepared the way for the seaborne landings. In the Cotentin, the two U.S. airborne divisions, despite scattered drops, cleared enough of their objectives and diverted the enemy sufficiently to allow seaborne elements of the VII Corps virtually to walk ashore. All other assault troops had a hard fight on the beaches and beyond. In the center of the attack, the V Corps met a strong, determined German division, the *352d*, which had been placed in line as early as March but had not been definitely located there by Allied intelligence.[1] Suffering heavy casualties and splintered by obstinate German opposition in a series of resistance nests, the V Corps with the effective aid of naval fire struggled inland to gain by the end of the day a precarious toehold not more than a mile deep.[2] On

[1] Brigadier E. T. Williams, former chief of intelligence of 21 Army Group, says (letter to author, 1 August 1951) that there was some conjecture as to the probability of its being there, but no definite proof.

[2] V Corps lost some 2,000 dead, wounded, and missing, as opposed to VII Corps' 200. The 82d and 101st Airborne Divisions lost approximately 2,500. Harrison, *Cross-Channel Attack*, pp. 284, 300, 331; [Roland G. Ruppenthal] *Utah Beach to Cherbourg*, AMERICAN FORCES IN ACTION (Washington, 1947), p. 55.

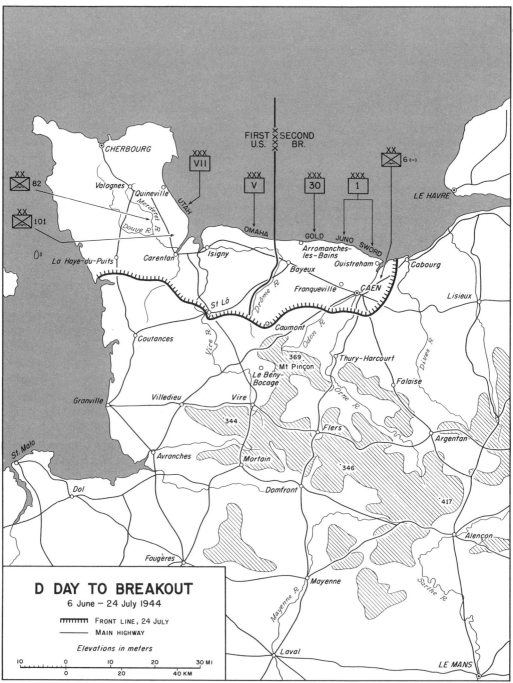

CHERBOURG

82

101

Valognes

Quineville

Merderet R.

Douve R.

UTAH

La Haye-du-Puits

Carentan

Isigny

FIRST
U.S.

SECOND
BR.

VII

V

30

1

6 (~)

OMAHA

GOLD

JUNO

SWORD

LE HAVRE

Arromanches-
les-Bains

Bayeux

Ouistreham

Cabourg

St Lô

Drôme R.

Franqueville

CAEN

Lisieux

Caumont

Odon R.

Coutances

Vire R.

369
Mt Pinçon

Thury-Harcourt

Dives R.

Le Bény-
Bocage

Falaise

Granville

Villedieu

Vire

344

Flers

Orne R.

Argentan

St. Malo

Avranches

Mortain

346

417

Dol

Domfront

Alençon

Fougères

Mayenne

Mayenne R.

Sarthe R.

Laval

LE MANS

D DAY TO BREAKOUT

6 June – 24 July 1944

Front line, 24 July

Main highway

Elevations in meters

10   0   10   20   30 MI

0   20   40 KM

H. Damon

MAP 1

the left, British airborne units had successfully secured their target areas east of the Orne. Infantry of the 1 and 30 British Corps, meeting uneven resistance, had engaged in costly fighting but were able to smash through in the direction of Bayeux. Neither Bayeux nor Caen, listed as possible D-Day objectives, was seized.[3]

Despite all the difficulties, the troops had got ashore, mostly in good condition. Only fragmentary reports of the landing drifted back to SHAEF advance headquarters at Portsmouth, where the Supreme Commander fretted for lack of news. Indications that both airborne and infantry losses along the fifty-mile front were lighter than expected were encouraging, but this bright aspect did not make up for the fact that the forces in the center had gone only 1,500 to 2,000 yards inland and were in no position to meet the enemy armored counterattack which the OVER-LORD planners anticipated by D plus 3. The marshy land at the eastern neck of the Cherbourg peninsula and hard-fighting enemy elements still lay between the Allied center and right.

In view of the difficulties in the Allied center, Eisenhower became particularly concerned with speeding up the junction of the two U.S. beachheads. On 7 June, accompanied by Admiral Ramsay and members of the SHAEF staff, he viewed the invasion front from the mine layer *Apollo* and conferred on board at various times during the day with Generals Montgomery and Bradley, and Rear Admirals Alan G. Kirk, John L. Hall, and Sir Philip L. Vian. A decision was made in the course of the day to give special attention at once to closing the Carentan–Isigny gap between VII and V Corps. Eisenhower ordered the tactical plan changed to give

priority to that task,[4] and the entire 101st Airborne Division was directed against Carentan while the V Corps continued its planned expansion east, west, and south.

Carentan fell on 12 June and the corps link-up was solidified during the next two days. The VII Corps at the same time pushed north to Quinéville and across the Merderet River. On the central front concentric drives by U.S. and British forces by 8 June had closed the initial gap at the Drôme River between the V and 30 British Corps. The V Corps then pushed through the *bocage* country to within a few miles of St. Lô before grinding to a halt in the face of stiffening enemy defense and increasing terrain obstacles. The 1 British Corps in the meantime was struggling slowly toward Caen. The Germans, considering Caen the gateway to Paris, massed their reserves to defend it and stopped the British short of the city. By the end of the first week of the invasion, Eisenhower's forces had consolidated a bridgehead eight to twelve miles deep extending in a rough arc from points just east of the Orne on the east to Quinéville in the north.

Behind the front, supply groups labored to build up a backlog of fuel, food, and ammunition which would make possible the next phase of the attack to break out of the beachheads. Considered of paramount importance in this program was the creation of breakwaters and floating piers known as MULBERRY A and MULBERRY B, which were to be built at OMAHA Beach

---

[3] Detailed accounts of the D-Day story are given in Harrison, *Cross-Channel Attack*, Ch. VIII; Ruppenthal, *Utah Beach to Cherbourg;* [Charles H. Taylor] *Omaha Beachhead*, AMERICAN FORCES IN ACTION (Washington, 1945); Montgomery, *Normandy to the Baltic*, Ch. VIII; Stacey, *The Canadian Army*, Ch. XI.

[4] Eisenhower to Marshall, SCAF 48, 8 Jun 44, Eisenhower personal file.

U.S. MULBERRY *before and after the storm of 19–22 June.*

and Arromanches-les-Bains. The task of putting these harbors into operation was fraught with great difficulties: craft and matériel had to be towed across the Channel, the ships that were to act as breakwaters had to be sunk so as to provide maximum protection for shipping, and the piers had to be anchored so as to withstand wind and tides. The British proved to be more successful with their breakwater at Arromanches than did the U.S. forces on OMAHA Beach. Although the British moved more slowly, they had their harbor more securely placed when a heavy gale struck the Channel in the period of 19–22 June and destroyed much of the U.S. MULBERRY. Virtually no unloading took place for forty-eight hours. So complete was the destruction that a decision was made to discontinue the building of the U.S. MULBERRY. Some parts were salvaged for the artificial harbor at Arromanches.

Before the gale, the Allies were approaching target figures for unloading on their beaches. They had varied the initial priorities shortly after mid-June, however, in response to General Montgomery's request for a quicker build-up of combat troops ashore. In both British and U.S. sectors combat forces were brought in a few days to a week earlier than planned, while the build-up of service and supporting troops was reduced proportionately. Some shortages occurred in supplies, but with the exception of artillery ammunition these were not serious because casualties and matériel consumption were less than had been anticipated. By the day the gale began, the British had landed 314,547 men, 54,000 vehicles, and 102,000 tons of supplies, while the Americans put ashore 314,504 men, 41,000 vehicles, and 116,000 tons of supplies.[5]

The Enemy

The combined Allied command had worked smoothly to bring the full force of naval, air, and ground power to bear on the enemy. The Germans from almost the first blow had been off balance, despite years of preparation to meet just such an attack as struck on 6 June. For this failure there are many explanations. Most striking perhaps was the German lack of the sort of unified command which the Allies had in SHAEF. At the head of the German state was Adolf Hitler, bearing the resounding title of *Fuehrer und Reichskanzler des Grossdeutschen Reiches und Oberster Befehlshaber der Deutschen Wehrmacht,* a dictator who controlled the Army, not only as the political head of the Reich, but also from 1941 on as actual Commander in Chief of the Army *(Oberbefehlshaber des Heeres— Ob. d. H.).* His Armed Forces High Command *(Oberkommando der Wehrmacht— OKW),* headed by Generalfeldmarschall Wilhelm Keitel, theoretically was used by Hitler in controlling the Army *(Oberkommando des Heeres—OKH),* the Navy *(Oberkommando der Kriegsmarine—OKM),* and the Air Force *(Oberkommando der Luftwaffe— OKL)* High Commands. But this was so in name only. OKW's control was nullified by the fact that the head of the Air Force, Reichsmarschall Hermann Goer-

---

[5] British statistics are from COSINTREP 36 (statistics for 18 June 44), 20 Jun 44, SHAEF AG 370, 2/11; U.S. statistics from [Clifford L. Jones] NEPTUNE: Training for and Mounting the Operation, and the Artificial Ports (The Administrative and Logistical History of the ETO, Pt. VI), MS, II, 175n, OCMH. COSINTREP 36 shows a figure of 307,439 men for U.S. forces as opposed to the Jones figure. Jones's figures were based on daily reports of unloadings submitted by the engineer special brigades on OMAHA and UTAH Beaches. The nature and validity of the various reports are discussed in Ruppenthal. *Logistical Support of the Armies.*

ADOLF HITLER

FIELD MARSHAL KEITEL

duct of operations was handled by the Armed Forces Operations Staff (*Wehrmachtfuehrungsstab—WFSt*) under General der Artillerie Alfred Jodl.[6]

The confusion which existed in the German high command in Berlin extended to the west as well. Until 6 June when the Allied forces stormed ashore, there existed no unified control of the

ing, and the head of the Navy, first Grossadmiral Erich Raeder and later Grossadmiral Karl Doenitz, had personal relationships with Hitler stronger than those of OKW, and by the opposition of the Army to any unification of the services. As the war in the east occupied more and more of Hitler's and the Army's attention, OKH was turned into the main headquarters for the war in the east, while OKW became the chief headquarters for dealing with the war in other theaters. Within OKH the conduct of operations was in the hands of the Army General Staff (*Generalstab des Heeres—Gen. St. d. H.*), initially under Generaloberst Franz Halder and later successively under Generaloberst Kurt Zeitzler, Generaloberst Heinz Guderian, and General der Infanterie Hans Krebs. Within OKW the con-

enemy forces in France nor any clear-cut policy on how to deal with the attack. Hitler's absorption with the problems of the Eastern Front, his lack of a consistent

[6] The organizational structure and evolution of OKW and OKH have been described in great detail by committees of German officers working under the auspices of the Historical Division between 1946 and 1948. See MSS # T-101, The German Armed Forces High Command (Winter *et al.*) and # T-111, The German Army High Command (Halder *et al.*). See also Harrison, *Cross-Channel Attack*, Ch. IV.

policy for the west, and his unwillingness to mark out clearly the authority of commanders in the field were among the factors responsible for this situation. Generalfeldmarschall Gerd von Rundstedt had been reappointed Commander in Chief West *(Oberbefehlshaber West)* in March 1942, but he had never been given control of the air and naval forces of the area. Rather their authority extended in some cases to units essential to his activities. The *Third Air Force* (Generalfeldmarschall Hugo Sperrle), whose planes were to support the ground troops in the west, had administrative control over paratroopers under Rundstedt's command, as well as control over antiaircraft units. *Navy Group West* (Admiral Theodor Krancke) controlled most of the coast artillery of the area, although an arrangement existed whereby in the event of a landing this artillery was to be placed at the disposal of the ground commanders. Security forces, used in the occupation of France, were under two military governors *(Militaerbefehlshaber)* of France and Northern France (including Belgium), who were subordinated directly to OKH. For tactical purposes against invasion forces they could be placed under Rundstedt. While the intention was to make all forces in the west available to the Commander in Chief West in case of a landing, the command organization which would make effective use of them possible was never clearly established.[7]

More damaging still to German unified command was the ground force situation. The German theater headquarters in the west (Netherlands, Belgium, and France) since late 1940 was *OB WEST*. The Commander in Chief West was concurrently the commander in chief of *Army Group D* and as such exercised command over the ground forces in the theater: *Armed Forces Commander Netherlands; Fifteenth, Seventh, First,* and, since August 1943, *Nineteenth Armies.* Rundstedt's control had been encroached upon at the end of 1943 when the energetic and able Generalfeldmarschall Erwin Rommel, commanding the *Army Group for Special Employment* and directly subordinate to OKW, came to the west. Rommel had been made responsible for the inspection of all coastal defenses in the west and ordered to prepare specific plans to repel Allied landings in this area. His headquarters was also earmarked as a reserve command to conduct the principal battle in case of an invasion. His direct subordination to OKW was terminated by mutual agreement between Rundstedt and Rommel in early January 1944. Rommel's headquarters was redesignated as *Army Group B,* and he was, in his capacity as the anti-invasion commander, given tactical command over the German forces in northwestern France, Belgium, and the Netherlands. However, Rommel retained his former inspection functions for the coastal defenses and so remained in a position to influence over-all policy.

Differences of opinion existed between *OB WEST* and *Army Group B* as to the exact role Rommel would play and the extent of his powers in case of an invasion. Rommel as a field marshal had the right of direct appeal to Hitler as Commander in Chief of the Army, and he made use of it to gain support for his views. Thus in the spring of 1944 for a short period Rommel won broader powers for his command, control of all armored and motorized units and all

---

[7] Harrison, *Cross-Channel Attack*, Chs. IV and VII, has detailed information on the enemy. As in that volume, the term Commander in Chief West will be used here to refer to the person holding the title *Oberbefehlshaber West*, while the abbreviated form *OB WEST* will refer to his headquarters.

FIELD MARSHAL VON RUND-
STEDT

GHQ artillery in the west, and some control over the German armies in southwestern France and on the Mediterranean coast. However, after further study of the effect of these powers upon the command in the west, Hitler reversed his opinion and canceled the extra powers given Rommel. In May of 1944, Rundstedt, in an effort to make clear his status as theater commander and to counterbalance Rommel's position, established *Army Group G* under Generaloberst Johannes Blaskowitz to command the German forces in southwestern France and on the Mediterranean coast. In spite of this move and in spite of his nominally subordinate position, Rommel retained a disproportionate influence in the west until after the invasion.

The lack of unity manifested itself most strikingly in the disagreement on defense policies to be followed against an Allied landing. Rommel, who had learned in Africa of the effect air superiority could have on the movement of armored forces, felt that the Germans would lack mobility to deal with an Allied invasion backed by strong air support. He held, therefore, that the British and U.S. assault must be met with mines, barricades, and heavy fortifi-

GENERAL BLASKOWITZ

cations. Ground reserves must be brought forward near the coast so that they could crush the attack in forty-eight hours. Rundstedt believed that some reserves must be held back from the coast in position to be sent against the main point of Allied strength. The period from Rommel's appointment to D Day was marked by his attempts to get control of the reserves, and by Rundstedt's efforts to hold something back. Rundstedt in November 1943 set up *Panzer Group West* (General der Panzertruppen Leo Freiherr Geyr von Schweppenburg) to control armored units in any large-scale counterattack against Allied landings. Geyr's stanch support of Rundstedt's views on defense made impossible co-operation with Rommel on the employment of armored forces against a landing. While Rommel in the spring of 1944 was unsuccessful in gaining complete control of all armored and motorized units in the west, he nonetheless achieved a partial victory when three panzer divisions were assigned to him as *Army Group B* reserves. Like many other arrangements of the period, this assignment was somewhat complicated, since Geyr retained the responsibility for the training and organization of the units, while Rommel had tactical control. The latter's position was further confused when four panzer-type divisions were set aside as a central mobile reserve under the direct command of OKW. Thus D Day found an uneasy arrangement between Rundstedt and Rommel in which neither had real control and in which the policy of defense against Allied landings was undetermined.

The forces available to the enemy commanders for use on D Day left much to be desired. Rundstedt's command at that time consisted of fifty-eight divisions. Of these, thirty-three were static or reserve and fit only for limited employment.[8] The forces available were divided into army groups: *Army Group B* under Rommel and *Army Group G* under Blaskowitz. Rommel's forces held the Brittany, Normandy, and Channel coasts, while Blaskowitz's units held southern France and the French Atlantic coast.[9] *(Map II)*

In the assault area proper, which was almost in its entirety under *Seventh Army's* jurisdiction, the enemy had seven infantry divisions.[10] One panzer division had been brought forward to Caen and some elements were on the coast in that area. In Brittany, besides the three static divisions, there were three infantry and one parachute divisions. An additional parachute division was in process of being organized. The nearest armor reserves were all south or east of the British left flank. One panzer division was in the area of Evreux, another south of Chartres, and a third was astride the Seine between Paris and Rouen. Other reinforcements had to come from south of the Loire or from the Pas-de-Calais area.

The enemy forces in the west, while considerably strengthened since February and March 1944 by new units and equipment, still showed the effects of being spread too thin, of having served as a replacement pool for the Eastern Front, and of having their ranks filled with worn-out troops from campaigns in the east. So-called mobile units frequently had little more than horse-drawn vehicles and bicycles to give them mobility. Many of the panzer units,

---

[8] Static divisions were immobile defense divisions. They were designed as permanent garrison troops for the west.

[9] Rommel's forces included: *Seventh Army* (Generaloberst Friedrich Dollmann), which held Brittany and a substantial part of Normandy; *Fifteenth Army* (Generaloberst Hans von Salmuth), which held the *Kanalkueste* (the coastal area from Dunkerque to the Seine estuary); and, for tactical purposes, *Armed Forces Commander Netherlands* (General der Luftwaffe Friedrich Christiansen). Blaskowitz' command included *First Army* (General der Infanterie Kurt von der Chevallerie), which held the Atlantic coast of France south of Brittany, and *Nineteenth Army* (General der Infanterie Georg von Sodenstern), which held the French Mediterranean coast.

[10] The *319th Division* stationed on the Channel Islands never figured in any of the fighting. Because of Hitler's orders, the Germans could not even consider it as a reserve. It will therefore not be included in any calculations of *Seventh Army's* strength.

despite a speed-up in the delivery of tanks in the spring of 1944, lacked half of their heavier armored weapons.

The area struck by the Allies was by no means the best defended. Since the main British and U.S. attack was expected in the Pas-de-Calais, the earlier emphasis had been placed on building defenses there.[11] The result was that, even though defense construction efforts between the Orne and Cherbourg had been greatly accelerated in 1944, the assault area was much less protected than Rommel had planned. Even after the D-Day attack, OKW and the field commanders held to the view that the main Allied offensive would be directed east of the Seine on the *Kanalkueste.* While Hitler, almost alone among his advisers, had concluded that the Cotentin and Caen areas were logical places for an attack and had ordered them reinforced, he shared the general delusion that the main landings would come in the Pas-de-Calais. As a result, there was no attempt in the early weeks of the invasion to order *Fifteenth Army* troops to Normandy. The Allies had worked hard to create the impression that they were massing forces on the east coast of England for an attack on the *Kanalkueste,* and German intelligence made the error of estimating the Allied force before D Day at more than double its actual strength.[12]

With confusion of authority in the German command, lack of an agreed policy for dealing with the Allies, a mistaken notion that the attack of 6 June was perhaps not the main one, lack of air support, supply difficulties, and troops who showed either the strain of too many campaigns on many fronts or the softness and carelessness promoted by four years of static duty on the Atlantic coast, the enemy was ill prepared to meet the massive blow

which the Allies unleashed by land, sea, and air. On the side of the enemy lay the advantage of fixed positions, however incomplete, against forces landing from small craft, interior supply lines, knowledge of the terrain, hedgerows which were of enormous value to the defender, and years of experience. Time would show that the advantages favored the invading forces, but there were enough factors on the side of the enemy to enable him to make a tough fight in the beachhead.

Allied Command

The command of Allied ground forces in the assault had been given to General Montgomery several months before the invasion of Europe. On 1 June 1944 General Eisenhower announced that until several armies were deployed on a secure beachhead and until developing operations indicated the desirability of a command reorganization, "all Ground Forces on the Continent [would be] under the Commander in Chief, 21st Army Group."[13] During this period, General Eisenhower retained direct responsibility only for approving major operational policies and the principal phases of operational plans. As long as the area of operations remained constricted and as long as it was necessary to keep Supreme Headquarters physically in the United Kingdom, the Supreme

---

[11] The term, "Pas-de-Calais," as used in this volume, applies to the coast line washed by the Strait of Dover between Dunkerque and the Somme.

[12] The estimate was approximately 80 divisions, 10 of which were believed to be airborne. The United States had 20 divisions in the United Kingdom on D Day; British and Canadian forces numbered 18. Not until near the end of the war did the Allied force surpass the German estimate.

[13] Memo, Command and Organization after D Day OVERLORD, 1 Jun 44, SHAEF G–3 322.011–1. Command and Control of U.S./British Forces.

Commander felt he had to place control of day-to-day actions in the hands of one man. Under plans of campaigns approved by General Eisenhower, General Montgomery held responsibility for the co-ordination of ground operations, including such matters as timing the attacks, fixing local objectives, and establishing boundaries. Until the lodgment area could be firmly held, the Allied armies were to operate under the OVERLORD plan which had been outlined before D Day.

General Eisenhower began during the first week of the operation to visit his ground commanders and early in July established a small advance command post in Normandy near the British commander. He was kept informed of operational developments and future plans were outlined to him for approval. In many cases, his intervention took the form of a mere nod of assent; in others he personally directed air or supply agencies to provide prompt and adequate support to the Allied forces. Until the 12th Army Group was established at the beginning of August,[14] however, the actual command of Allied ground forces in the field was General Montgomery's and his actions are a vital part of the story of the Supreme Command.[15]

Though the initial lodgment gained during the first week was smaller than the Allies had planned, they had grounds for optimism in that their casualties had been unexpectedly light and the anticipated enemy counterattack had failed to materialize. On 13 June General Montgomery, pleased over developments on his front, expressed his intention of capturing Caen, establishing a strong eastern flank astride the Orne River from the Channel as far south as Thury-Harcourt, some fifteen miles south of Caen, and setting up

the 8 British Corps in the area about Mont Pinçon, west of Thury-Harcourt, and Flers, some thirty-five miles south of Caen. (See Map 1.) First Army was to hold firmly at Caumont and Carentan, thrust southwest from Caumont toward Villedieu and Avranches while sending other forces in a northwesterly direction toward La Haye-du-Puits and Valognes, and capture Cherbourg. In the course of the day, the arrival of German armored elements on General Montgomery's front led him to revise his plans and limit the advance in the British zone. Emphasis was placed on pulling the enemy on to the Second British Army while U.S. forces pushed toward Cherbourg.[16]

Despite Montgomery's second thought, both Caen and Cherbourg remained the primary objectives for Allied forces in mid-June. The former opened the way to nearby airfields and small neighboring ports. Cherbourg was vitally important if the Allies were to get a major port into full operation before the end of the summer when it was feared that open beaches could no longer be used for unloading supplies and troops. General Montgomery, believing that Caen "was really the key to Cherbourg," in that capture of the former would release forces then required to insure the security of the left flank, on 18 June set the Second British Army's immediate task as the seizure of Caen. Operations were to begin on the 18th and reach their peak on the 22d. He directed the First U.S. Army to isolate the Cotentin

---

[14] See below, pages 203–04, for some changes during the month of August.

[15] An excellent summary of the command arrangements during the weeks of the assault and the reasons for the setup are given in Msg, Eisenhower to Marshall, CPA 9-0230, 19 Aug 44, Eisenhower personal file.

[16] Montgomery, *Normandy to the Baltic*, pp. 85–91.

peninsula and then thrust northward through Valognes to Cherbourg. As a second priority, the First Army was to send other units from their positions east of Carentan southward toward St. Lô to secure the high ground east of the Vire which dominated the town. Montgomery hoped that Caen and Cherbourg would be taken by 24 June.[17] The order of 18 June was changed the following day, and the strong attack planned on the left wing against Caen was shifted to the right, southeast of Caen. The operations were postponed from 18 to 22 June. The great gale forced another postponement to the 25th.

In the west better progress was reported. The VII Corps cut the Cotentin peninsula on 18 June and then, driving north with three divisions, forced the surrender of Cherbourg on 26 and 27 June. The entire peninsula was cleared by 1 July. In the operation, the corps sustained some 22,000 casualties, while the enemy lost 39,000 prisoners and an undetermined number of dead and wounded.[18]

The enemy at Caen stood firm. Montgomery's renewed attack of 25–26 June, hit hard by German armored counterattacks, could not get moving. When two new enemy panzer divisions (the *9th* and *10th SS*), brought from the Eastern Front, were identified, Montgomery ordered a halt and began regrouping his forces with the intention of withdrawing his armor into a reserve prepared for renewed thrusts.[19]

At the end of June, the Second British Army with a force equivalent to some sixteen divisions was holding a front approximately thirty-three miles long running northeastward from Caumont to the Channel.[20] Along the twenty miles of that front between Caumont and Caen, the enemy had concentrated seven armored divisions and elements of an eighth, or two thirds of the German armor in France, while two infantry divisions faced the extreme left flank of the British forces. The First U.S. Army with thirteen divisions, including two armored and two airborne, was holding a front some fifty to fifty-five miles long extending from Caumont westward to Barneville and the sea. Opposed to this force were seven German divisions.[21]

The German armored divisions, although superior to British and U.S. armored units in numbers, had been badly battered in the June fighting. Suffering from the shortage of fuel and the breakdown of tank maintenance service brought about by Allied air and artillery operations, they were unable to bring their whole strength to bear. Nevertheless, the enemy forces waged a savage fight.

The Allies were fortunate that even at the end of June the enemy still feared a main attack on the Pas-de-Calais. At Hitler's orders the *Fifteenth Army*, which could have sent additional reinforcements

---

[17] Montgomery dir to comdrs, M–502, 18 Jun 44, FUSA files 21 A Gp dirs.

[18] Ruppenthal, *Utah Beach to Cherbourg*, p. 199.

[19] Montgomery, *Normandy to the Baltic*, pp. 100–101.

[20] There were twelve and one-half divisions (including three armored and one airborne) plus seven independent armored brigades and three independent infantry brigades, or approximately sixteen divisions according to British Historical Section estimates.

[21] Actually nine divisions were listed, but of three of these there were only remnants. First U.S. Army estimated that their combined strength was "probably . . . only one full strength infantry division." At the end of June, moreover, First Army declared that only a "battle group" each from the *265th* and *275th* Divisions (included in the total) had reached its front. Some forces of the *2d Panzer Division* were active in late June on the extreme left flank of the U.S. line. Montgomery, *Normandy to the Baltic*, pp. 102–06; FUSA Rpt of Opns, pp. 91–92. Throughout this and the following chapter the author has relied heavily on a study of German units made by Mrs. Magna E. Bauer of the Foreign Studies Branch, OCMH.

against the Allies, was holding most of its divisions in place. The Allies had continued since D Day to play on German fears of another landing. A special effort had been made to persuade the Germans that General Patton was waiting with a group of armies in eastern England ready for an attack. Various ruses were used to heighten German apprehensions concerning the *Kanalkueste.* When General Patton went to the Continent as commander of the Third U.S. Army and it became necessary to commit the 1st U.S. Army Group to action, the unit was renamed 12th Army Group, and a paper unit was left in the United Kingdom. Lt. Gen. Lesley J. McNair was appointed commander of the 1st Army Group in July.

The Battle for Caen

The successful culmination of the Cherbourg campaign found neither the battle for Caen nor the attack toward St. Lô progressing well. Heavy concentrations of German armor helped slow British forces to the east; hedgerows of the *bocage* country slowed the advance of the British right wing and the entire U.S. army. Tanks were confined for the most part to narrow roads bordered by hedges which afforded excellent cover to the German guns, and the infantry had to dig out an enemy entrenched in the hedgerows of hundreds of tiny orchards in the Calvados countryside. Heavy rains interfered with air reconnaissance and virtually stopped tactical air attacks. As the struggle for St. Lô bogged down in a slow and costly fight, the danger developed that an attritional battle such as the Allies had fought in Flanders in World War I might be imminent.

With the diminution of the battle's tempo, the satisfaction which the Allies

had felt over gaining a foothold on the Continent gave way to disappointment and criticism. As early as mid-June General Montgomery was blamed not only by many U.S., but by some British, commanders for his slowness in taking Caen. Among the British, the chief critics were airmen who felt that the 21 Army Group commander had let them down by his failure to take terrain in the airfield country southeast of Caen.[22] Although General Montgomery and his chief of staff, General de Guingand, were able to argue effectively that they had made no final commitment as to the date of capturing the airfields, the critics cited the 21 Army Group commander's speech to army chiefs on 7 April 1944 in which he had said that the task of the Second British Army was "to assault to the West of the R. Orne and to develop operations to the south-east, in order to secure airfield sites and to protect the eastern flank of First U.S. Army while the latter is capturing Cherbourg." Further, they felt he had not lived up to his analysis of the situation on 15 May 1944 when he stressed the need of deep armored penetrations and the pegging out of claims well inland to hold the ground dominating road axes in the *bocage* country.[23]

These criticisms appear to rest on a fundamental misunderstanding of Montgomery's intentions in Normandy. His plan, as interpreted by him, by his staff, and, more recently, by General Bradley,

---

[22] Air Chief Marshal Leigh-Mallory was a notable exception.

[23] Brief Summary of Operation OVERLORD as Affecting the Army, address to officers in the four field armies in London, 7 April 1944; Address by General Montgomery to the General Officers of the Four Field Armies on 15 May 1944 (notes). Photostatic reproduction of the originals, including General Montgomery's penciled alterations, furnished the author by the Historical Section, Cabinet Office.

was to draw enemy forces on to the British front in the Caen area, while U.S. forces were making the main Allied drive on the right. General Bradley has appraised the situation in his statement:

For another four weeks it fell to the British to pin down superior enemy forces in that sector [Caen] while we maneuvered into position for the U.S. breakout. With the Allied world crying for blitzkrieg the first week after we landed, the British endured their passive role with patience and forbearing. . . . In setting the stage for our breakout the British were forced to endure the barbs of critics who shamed them for failing to push out vigorously as the Americans did. The intense rivalry that afterward strained relations between the British and American commands might be said to have sunk its psychological roots into that passive mission of the British on the beachhead.[24]

While General Montgomery had initially planned to take Caen and the airfields beyond in the first days of the assault, he concluded that he was achieving the main objective of pulling armor on to that front by a continued drive in the direction of Caen. There was no ruin of his main plan in the failure to take that city. The Supreme Commander, while staking great importance on the U.S. breakout west of St. Lô, was eager to see a more spirited offensive in the east. It was perhaps for this reason that the two commanders did not always see eye to eye in Normandy. Eisenhower desired to hit the enemy hard wherever he could be attacked. Montgomery held that it was enough to keep the enemy occupied in the east while the main drive went forward in the west. Some members of his staff believed that the Eisenhower policy might secure immediate gains but endanger the chance to get the enemy into a position where he could be hit decisively.[25]

Criticism was moderated for a short time during the closing days of June as U.S. forces took Cherbourg and cleared the northern Cotentin. When U.S. and British drives in the first week of July fell short of the objectives of St. Lô and Caen, charges that Montgomery was too cautious increased. General Eisenhower's closest U.S. and British advisers now proposed that he tactfully tell the 21 Army Group commander to push the fight for Caen. Clearly worried about the delay, the Supreme Commander had instructed Air Chief Marshal Tedder only a short time before "to keep the closest touch with General Montgomery or his representatives in 21st Army Group, not merely to see that their requests are satisfied but to see that they have asked for every kind of support that is practicable and in maximum volume that can be delivered." On 7 July, he sent the British commander a statement of desired objectives, rather than a firm order to fight a more aggressive battle. General Eisenhower spoke of the arrival of German reinforcements on the U.S. front which had stalled the advance toward St. Lô and permitted the enemy to withdraw armor for a reserve force. Noting that "a major full-dress attack on the left flank" had not yet been attempted, he offered to phase forward any unit General Montgomery wanted, and to make a U.S. armored division available for an attack on the left flank if needed. He assured the 21 Army Group commander that everything humanly pos-

[24] Bradley, *A Soldier's Story*, p. 326.
[25] For General Montgomery's intentions, see Montgomery, *Normandy to the Baltic*, pp. 118–24, and de Guingand, *Operation Victory*, pp. 392–400. British views were obtained in interviews with Montgomery's G–2 and G–3 and with the commander of the Second British Army. For General Bradley's views, see his *A Soldier's Story*, pp. 316–18 and 325–26.

sible would be done "to assist you in any plan that promises to give us the elbow room we need. The air and everything else will be available.[26]

General Montgomery, whose staff was already considering plans for breaking out of the lodgment area and for seizing the Brittany peninsula, responded to this friendly nudge with the confident assurance that there would be no stalemate. He stressed the difficulties of keeping the initiative, and at the same time of avoiding reverses. He reminded the Supreme Commander that the British had taken advantage of the enemy's willingness to resist at Caen to draw enemy armor to that flank while the First Army captured Cherbourg. The 21 Army Group commander indicated that a new attack to take Caen was under way, and added: "I shall always ensure that I am well balanced; at present I have no fears of any offensive move the enemy might make; I am concentrating on making the battle swing our way."[27]

An all-out attack to seize Caen was launched by the Second British Army on 8 July with three infantry divisions and two armored brigades. As a means of preparing the way, General Montgomery had requested a heavy bombardment on the northern outskirts of the city. In accordance with his request, Bomber Command dropped 2,300 tons of bombs between 2150 and 2230, 7 July. At 0420 the following morning, 1 British Corps attacked west and north of Caen. Canadian forces took Franqueville to the west, while British forces cleared two small towns just north of the city and closed into its northeast corner at the end of the day. On the following day elements of British and Canadian forces pushed into the city; mopping up was completed on the 10th. The Second British Army had thus finished the task of capturing that part of Caen which lay west of the Orne, but the large suburban areas (Faubourg de Vaucelles and Colombelles) east of the river remained in enemy hands.[28] Air Chief Marshal Harris, chief of Bomber Command, declared after the war that, while the effect of the bombing attack at Caen was such that the enemy temporarily lost all power of offensive action, the British Army had not exploited its opportunities. This was due, he said, partly to its delay in starting the attack after the bombing, and to its failure to continue the offensive after the initial successes of 8–9 July. General Montgomery, in his account of the battle, has stated that it was obviously desirable to carry out the bombing immediately before the attack, but that owing to the weather forecast it was decided to carry out the bombing on the evening before the attack. He adds that the advance was slowed by cratering and obstruction from masses of debris caused by the force of the bombing.[29]

Criticism of the Second British Army's alleged failure to follow up its opportu-

[26] Eisenhower to Montgomery, 7 Jul 44, SHAEF SGS 381 OVERLORD, I(a).

[27] Montgomery to Eisenhower, M–508, 8 Jul 44, SHAEF SGS 381 OVERLORD, I(a).

[28] Montgomery, *Normandy to the Baltic,* pp. 114–18; Stacey, *The Canadian Army,* pp. 188–90.

[29] Harris, *Bomber Offensive,* p. 211; Montgomery, *Normandy to the Baltic,* pp. 117–18. It is not clear what the forecast was which led to the decision to bomb on the evening of 7 July instead of on the morning of 8 July. The weather forecast for the night of 7–8 July was: " . . . good clear areas in France. Much cumulus and nimbocumulus at Nantes, little cloud at Paris." Operation Record Book, Appendices Bomber Command Operations, Vol. 4, 4 Jul 44, 11M/A1/5A, AHB—Night Raid Report Book 654. As early as 6 July, the air forces had been told that an appreciable air effort would probably be required on the evening of 7 July. Extract from Advanced Operational Book of Allied Expeditionary Air Force, 6 July 1944, p. 9. This extract and extracts from the report cited above are in OCMH.

nities at Caen was intensified ten days later when an attack, described by the press as a major attempt to break out toward the east, was stopped after gains of some ten thousand yards. Coming just at the time that the U.S. forces, after weeks of delays, had finally taken St. Lô, the Caen offensive was represented as having failed. This criticism rested basically on the continued misunderstanding by the general public of General Montgomery's intentions. It is well, therefore, to study them as he outlined them on 8 July to General Eisenhower. The following extracts from his letter summarized his position:

3. Initially, my main pre-occupations were:
   (a) To ensure that we kept the initiative, and,
   (b) To have no setbacks or reverses.
It was not always too easy to comply with these two fundamental principles, especially during the period when we were not too strong ourselves and were trying to build up our strength.
But that period is now over, and we can now set about the enemy—and are doing so.
4. I think we must be quite clear as to what is vital, and what is not; if we get our sense of values wrong we may go astray. There are three things which stand out very clearly in my mind:
   (a) *First.*
We must get the Brittany Peninsula. . . .
   (b) *Second.*
We do not want to get hemmed in to a relatively small area; we must have space—for manoeuvre, for administration, and for airfields.
   (c) *Third.*
We want to engage the enemy in battle, to write-off his troops, and generally to kill Germans. Exactly where we do this does not matter, so long as (a) and (b) are complied with.
5. The first thing we had to do was to capture Cherbourg.
I wanted Caen too, but we could not man-

age both at the same time and it was clear to me that the enemy would resist fiercely in the Caen sector.
So I laid plans to develop operations towards the R. Odon on the Second Army front, designed to draw the enemy reserves on to the British sector so that the First U.S. Army could get to do its business in the west all the easier. We were greatly hampered by very bad weather. . . .
But this offensive *did* draw a great deal on it; and I then gave instructions to the First Army to get on quickly with its offensive southwards on the western flank. . . .
6. The First Army advance on the right has been slower than I thought would be the case; the country is terribly close, the weather has been atrocious, and certain enemy reserves have been brought in against it.
So I then decided to set my eastern flank alight, and to put the wind up the enemy by seizing Caen and getting bridgeheads over the Orne; this action would, indirectly, help the business going on over on the western flank.
These operations by Second Army on the eastern flank began today; they are going very well; they aim at securing Caen and at getting our eastern flank on the Orne River—with bridgeheads over it.
7. Having got our eastern flank on the Orne, I shall then organize the operations on the eastern flank so that our affairs on the western flank can be got on with the quicker.
It may be the best proposition is for the Second Army to continue its effort, and to drive southwards with its left flank on the Orne; or it may be a good proposition for it to cross the Orne and establish itself on the Falaise road.
Alternatively, having got Caen and established the eastern flank on the Orne, it may be best for Second Army to take over all the Caumont area—and to the west of it—and thus release some of Bradley's divisions for the southward "drive" on the western flank.
8. Day to day events in the next few days will show which is best.
The attack of Second Army towards Caen, which is going on now, is a big show; so far only 1 Corps is engaged; 8 Corps takes up the running on Monday morning (10 July).
I shall put everything into it.

It is all part of the bigger tactical plan, and it is all in accordance with para 4 above.

.   .   .   .

11. I do not need an American armoured division for use on my eastern flank; we really have all the armour we need. The great thing now is to get First and Third Armies up to a good strength, and to get them cracking on the southward thrust on the western flank, and then to turn Patton westwards into the Brittany peninsula.[30]

On 10 July, the 21 Army Group commander issued orders for the coming Allied offensive. He directed the First Army to push its right wing strongly southward, to pivot on its left, and to swing south and east on the general line Le Bény-Bocage–Vire–Mortain–Fougères. Once it reached the base of the Cotentin peninsula, it was to send a corps into Brittany, directed on Rennes and St. Malo. Meanwhile, plans were to be made for the second phase of the drive in which First Army's strong right wing was to make a wide sweep of the *bocage* country toward Laval–Mayenne and Le Mans–Alençon.

General Montgomery reminded his commanders that his broad policy remained unchanged: "It is to draw the main enemy forces in to the battle on our eastern flank, and to fight them there, so that our affairs on the western flank may proceed the easier." He then added that since the enemy had been able to bring up reinforcements to oppose the First Army's advance, and since it was important to speed up the attack on the western flank, the operations of the Second British Army "must . . . be so staged that they will have a direct influence on the operations of the First Army, as well as holding enemy forces on the eastern flank." A degree of caution marked his statement that, while he hoped to take the Faubourg de Vaucelles, east of the Orne, in the forth-

coming attack, he was not prepared "to have *heavy* casualties to obtain this bridgehead . . . as we shall have plenty elsewhere." He assigned to his units operating south of Caen the general line Thury-Harcourt–Mont Pinçon–Le Bény-Bocage as their objective. A reserve of three armored divisions was organized for possible operations east of the Orne in the general area Caen–Falaise.[31] This directive, therefore, contained provisions for a limited-objective attack east and south of Caen (GOODWOOD) with the major aim of aiding the First Army's advance in the west (COBRA), while providing a strong reserve armored force for exploitation toward Falaise.[32]

The press did not know of these orders. Newsmen in the week preceding the attack stressed the fact that the crucial blow for the breakout from the lodgment area was to be struck near Caen. Some of General Montgomery's chief advisers have suggested that misconceptions as to the 21 Army Group commander's objectives perhaps arose from the overemphasis he placed on the decisiveness of the operation in order to insure full air support for the operation. Strategic bomber commanders did not like to take their planes off strategic targets for limited offensives. The tendency, therefore, was for the ground commander to stress heavily the importance of the attack he wanted supported. This emphasis may be seen in Montgomery's request to Eisenhower of 12 July.

---

[30] Montgomery to Eisenhower, M–508, 8 Jul 44, SHAEF SGS 381 OVERLORD, I(a).

[31] Montgomery's statement and the assignment of three armored divisions to the GOODWOOD attack led even some members of the 21 Army Group staff to believe that a deep and rapid penetration on the eastern flank was intended.

[32] Montgomery to army comdrs, M–510, 10 Jul 44, First U.S. Army files (21 A Gp dirs).

Referring specifically to his operations between Caen and Falaise, he declared: "This operation will take place on Monday 17th July. Grateful if you will issue orders that the whole weight of the air power is to be available on that day to support my land battle. . . . My whole eastern flank will burst into flames on Saturday. The operation on Monday may have far-reaching results. . . ."[33]

General Eisenhower responded enthusiastically, saying that all senior airmen were in full accord with the plan because it would be "a brilliant stroke which will knock loose our present shackles." He passed on these views to Air Chief Marshal Tedder who assured General Montgomery, "All the Air Forces will be full out to support your far-reaching and decisive plan to the utmost of their ability." The 21 Army Group commander in expressing his thanks for these promises of support explained that the plan "if successful promises to be decisive and therefore necessary that the air forces bring full weight to bear." General Eisenhower, perhaps misunderstanding the full import of Montgomery's plans, replied:

With respect to the plan, I am confident that it will reap a harvest from all the sowing you have been doing during the past weeks. With our whole front acting aggressively against the enemy so that he is pinned to the ground, O'Connor's [Lt. Gen. Sir Richard O'Connor, 8 British Corps commander] plunge into his vitals will be decisive. I am not discounting the difficulties, nor the initial losses, but in this case I am viewing the prospects with the most tremendous optimism and enthusiasm. I would not be at all surprised to see you gaining a victory that will make some of the "old classics" look like a skirmish between patrols.

As an added indication that the Supreme Commander thought the drive to the east was likely to be something spectacular,

there is the final statement that 21 Army Group could count on Bradley "to keep his troops fighting like the very devil, twenty-four hours a day, to provide the opportunity your armored corps will need, and to make the victory complete."[34]

Allied airmen were particularly impressed by the scale of air power requested to support the Caen attack. General Montgomery's request came at a time when plans were being made for the First Army's breakout west of St. Lô. Although the latter offensive was listed as the main operation in the lodgment area, the attack near Caen was supported by 7,700 tons of bombs as opposed to 4,790 tons near St. Lô.[35] While the restricted area of the St. Lô bombing meant that the small tonnage of bombs gave greater saturation of the area, Air Chief Marshal Leigh-Mallory in his survey of the six major air attacks in Normandy declared that the bombing offensive at Caen was "the heaviest and most concentrated air attack in support of ground troops ever attempted."[36]

---

[33] Dempsey to author, 12 Mar 47; Williams to author, 1 Aug 51; de Guingand, *Operation Victory*, pp. 401–03; Montgomery to Eisenhower, M–49, 12 Jul 44, Eisenhower personal file.

[34] Eisenhower to Montgomery, S–55476, 13 Jul 44; Montgomery to Tedder, M–53, 14 Jul 44; Eisenhower to Montgomery, 14 Jul 44. All in Eisenhower personal file. Tedder to Montgomery, 13 Jul 44, SHAEF SGS 381 OVERLORD, I(a).

[35] A British reviewer of this chapter has noted that General Bradley would not accept cratering and "torn-down buildings" but would have liked to have the support of Bomber Command. British heavy bombers, he adds, were excluded from the support program because for some technical reason they could not carry the necessary small bombs. The author's purpose in contrasting the tonnages dropped is not to imply lack of British air support for COBRA, but rather to note the importance attached to air support for GOODWOOD.

[36] Leigh-Mallory *Despatch*, p. 64. Harris, *Bomber Offensive*, p. 212, cites the tonnage at Caen as 6,800. Stacey, *The Canadian Army*, p. 189, uses Leigh-Mallory's figure.

Heavy bombers opened the attack south and east of Caen at 0545, 18 July, with a forty-five minute pounding. After an interval of thirty minutes, medium bombers attacked for another three quarters of an hour. In all some 1,676 heavy bombers and 343 medium and light bombers of the Bomber Command and the Eighth and Ninth Air Forces hit the German positions, dropping more than three times the tonnage loosed on Caen ten days earlier. Ground attacks began at 0745. Three armored divisions operating in the center of the line progressed well in the morning, but were brought to a standstill in the afternoon by heavy antitank fire and armored counterattacks. To the right and left of the armored units, the infantry made limited advances in heavy rain on the 19th and 20th. By evening of the 20th, the British forces had come to a halt. The infantry relieved the armored units, which were drawn back into reserve, and plans were made for a later advance to push the left flank eastward to the Dives and gain additional ground between the Odon and the Orne. Of the 18–20 July attack, General Montgomery said: "We had, however, largely attained our purpose; in the centre 8 Corps, had advanced ten thousand yards, fought and destroyed many enemy tanks, and taken two thousand prisoners. The eastern suburbs of Caen had been cleared and the Orne bridgehead had been more than doubled in size." [37]

Although the 21 Army Group attack had achieved its objective of attracting German armor to the eastern front and thus aiding the U.S. breakout to the west, now scheduled for 24 July, it was difficult to convince newsmen that so much ground and air strength had been expended with the idea of gaining such modest results. The skepticism was the more pronounced because of an interview which General Montgomery gave the press after the offensive opened. Apparently in an effort to dispel the unjust assumption that British troops were doing little fighting, and to disguise the big U.S. drive, he stressed the decisiveness of the attack then under way south of Caen. When the offensive had halted, General Montgomery's statements were contrasted with General Dempsey's pronouncement at the conclusion of the battle that there had been no intention of doing anything more than establishing a bridgehead over the Orne. The reaction of many newsmen was perhaps best expressed by Drew Middleton, a New York *Times* correspondent whose columns had been friendly to General Montgomery, but who now wrote: "In view of this statement [Second British Army's] the preliminary ballyhoo attending the offensive by Twenty-First Army Group and the use of the words 'broke through' in the first statement from that headquarters were all the more regrettable." [38]

Allied airmen were angry because their powerful air strike was followed by such limited ground gains—"seven thousand tons of bombs for seven miles" as one air marshal put it. In heated discussions at SHAEF, critics of General Montgomery condemned his slowness in advancing. Some British and U.S. staff members, who appeared unaware of Montgomery's main objectives, speculated on the possibility of relieving the 21 Army Group commander in order to speed up the advance south of Caen. The Supreme Commander was cool to these suggestions and to proposals that he speedily assume com-

---

[37] Montgomery, *Normandy to the Baltic*, pp. 127–34; Stacey, *The Canadian Army*, pp. 188–90. See also Craven and Cate, *The Army Air Forces in World War II*, III, 207–09.

[38] New York *Times* dispatches, July 17–25, 1944.

mand of the field forces. Even when a British member of his staff warned him that the U.S. forces would think he had sold them out to the British if he continued to support Montgomery, General Eisenhower showed considerable reluctance to intervene in the battle beyond making a firm request for more rapid advances on the British front. [39]

Although refraining from any positive action relative to shifts in the Allied command, General Eisenhower apparently shared the view held by others at SHAEF that Montgomery should have pushed faster and harder at Caen. In his letter of 21 July to the British commander, the strongest he had yet written to him, the Supreme Commander indicated that, after the Second British Army had been unable in late June and early July to provide favorable conditions for the First Army's drive to the south, he had pinned his hopes on a major drive in the Caen area. That he did not regard a strong, limited action around Caen as the same thing was shown rather strikingly in his next statement: "A few days ago, when armored divisions of Second Army, assisted by a tremendous air attack, broke through the enemy's forward lines, I was extremely hopeful and optimistic. I thought that at last we had him and were going to roll him up. That did not come about." Now, his immediate hopes were pinned on Bradley's attack west of St. Lô, which would require Allied aggressiveness all along the line. General Eisenhower specified a continuous strong attack and the gaining of terrain for airfields and space on the eastern flank as contributions expected of General Dempsey's forces. The Supreme Commander added that he was aware of the serious reinforcement problem which faced the British, but felt that this was another rea-

son why they should get their attack under way. "Eventually," he pointed out, "the American ground strength will necessarily be much greater than the British. But while we have equality in size we must go forward shoulder to shoulder, with honors and sacrifices equally shared." [40]

At the time this letter was being written, General Montgomery was issuing a new directive ordering intensive operations along the Second British Army front. This was sent to Eisenhower with a request that the 21 Army Group commander be informed if they did not now see eye to eye on operations. The Supreme Commander replied that they were apparently in complete agreement that a vigorous and persistent offensive should be sustained by both First and Second Armies. [41]

Even as the plans were being made for the renewed offensive which was to lead to the breakout, criticism of General Montgomery continued to mount in the press. When informed by the War Department near the end of July that some newspapers in the United States were still attacking General Montgomery, the Supreme Commander emphasized his personal responsibility for the policy which had been followed in Normandy since the invasion. He declared that such critics apparently forgot that "I am not only inescapably re-

---

[39] Butcher, *My Three Years With Eisenhower*, pp. 617–24, makes clear the strong feeling which existed at SHAEF during this period on the matter of Caen. The information has been checked by interviews with nearly every key member of SHAEF and by examination of private papers and diaries. See *Crusade in Europe*, pp. 266–68, for General Eisenhower's postwar reaction.

[40] Eisenhower to Montgomery, 21 Jul 44, Eisenhower personal file.

[41] Montgomery to Bradley, Dempsey, and others, M–512, 21 Jul 44, 12 A Gp files 371.3 Military Objectives. Montgomery to Eisenhower, M–65, 22 Jul 44; Eisenhower to Montgomery, 23 Jul 44. Both in Eisenhower personal file.

sponsible for strategy and general missions in this operation but seemingly also ignore the fact that it is my responsibility to determine the efficiency of my various subordinates and make appropriate report to the Combined Chiefs of Staff if I become dissatisfied." [42]

General Eisenhower's assurances, which might have been essential had the impasse in Normandy continued, were proved to be unnecessary by the turn of events. As his words were written, the Allied forces were on the move—toward Falaise in the east and toward Brittany in the west. The frustrations and irritations, born of inaction and stalemate, which had stirred the Allied press to criticism, were to evaporate, at least for a time, as the Allied forces burst through the German lines and swept toward Paris.

[42] Eisenhower to Surles, FWD 12498, 30 Jul 44, Eisenhower personal file.

CHAPTER XI

The Breakout and Pursuit to the Seine

Beginning on 25 July, General Eisenhower's forces unleashed a heavy air and ground attack west of St. Lô and smashed the enemy opposition blocking the Allied advance. In four weeks the battle of stalemate in the *bocage* had changed to one of great mobility as the Allied forces searched out the enemy along the Loire and toward Brest, encircled and destroyed thousands of German troops in a great enveloping movement at Falaise, and dashed to the Seine to cut off the Germans and threaten Paris. All this was in accord with the broad outlines of earlier plans, but the speed with which the drives were executed and with which the enemy opposition collapsed west of the Seine followed from the unexpected opportunities which Allied commanders had turned to their advantage. (*Map III*)

The Allied Situation in Late July

On 18 July as the British opened an offensive south of Caen, the U.S. forces ended their fight for St. Lô which had been carried on sporadically since June. The battle had been unusually bitter, costing elements of five U.S. divisions nearly 11,000 casualties in two weeks. In gaining St. Lô the First U.S. Army opened an important road center to the south and

east from the OMAHA and UTAH beaches and provided maneuver area for a drive to the south then being planned.[1] To the east, the British were poised for further advances in the direction of Falaise.

Despite these victories, the Allied gains still did not appear impressive when measured on a map of France. After nearly seven weeks of fighting, the deepest penetrations were some twenty-five to thirty miles deep on an eighty-mile front. The British and Canadians had suffered some 49,000 casualties, and the U.S. forces some 73,000. These losses had been almost completely replaced before the attack, and at the time of the breakout units were practically up to strength. At that time the British and Canadians had an equivalent of sixteen and the U.S. forces seventeen divisions in the field. By 23 July, a cumulative total of 591,000 British and Canadian and 770,000 U.S. troops had been landed in Normandy.[2] The U.S. forces had, in addition to the two airborne divi-

[1] [2d Lt. David Garth] *St. Lô,* AMERICAN FORCES IN ACTION (Washington, 1947).

[2] Cumulative strength includes only the number landed and does not reflect evacuated wounded, dead, or those units taken back to the United Kingdom for refitting. Statistics for British and U.S. casualties and strength were seldom reported for the same time of the day and often not on the same day. In the present case 22 July at 2400 is taken for U.S. casualties (SHAEF G–3 Summary 51, 27 Jul 44) and

sions then being re-equipped after their work in the assault, three divisions in the process of moving from the United Kingdom to the Continent, two more ready to move from the United Kingdom, and other divisions in the Mediterranean and the United States ready to move at the rate of three to five a month.[3]

The supply situation was for the most part favorable. Allied naval and air forces had virtually eliminated any threat to shipping in the Channel. Landing of cargo over the beaches continued to increase, and on 19 July the first supplies were brought in through Cherbourg. The ammunition shortage, which had been apparent in the first days of the invasion, had not been solved but had been improved. Supply detachments were being strengthened to handle augmented demands, although they were cramped for space as a result of the restricted area held by the Allied forces.

Notwithstanding the favorable situation, the Allies had not forgotten the gale of mid-June and the fact that the bulk of their supplies and personnel still had to come over open beaches which were at the mercy of Channel storms. The opening of both the Brittany and the Seine ports was necessary, the Allies believed, if they were to be sure of their logistical support during the fall and winter months. Their previous experience in rehabilitating ports destroyed by retreating Germans demonstrated the necessity of capturing the ports within a few weeks if they were to be put back in working order before bad weather closed in. Early planning after the invasion, therefore, emphasized operations to seize Brest, Le Havre, Quiberon Bay, Morlaix, and other French ports. While General Eisenhower looked toward the German border and beyond to the Rhine and to Berlin, he was interested immediately in the vital French ports.

The German Situation

The difficulties under which the enemy labored before D Day became greater as the battle in Normandy continued. The old problems of divided authority, low state of troops in France, lack of mobility and armament, and almost total absence of air support still remained. Allied naval fire power had been unexpectedly heavy in the beachhead during the early days of the invasion. Allied air superiority made movements of German reinforcements and supplies almost impossible while permitting the Allied forces to land their matériel and move it forward with impunity. Hitler's continual interference in tactical decisions caused confusion among the field commanders. Misjudging Allied intentions, the Fuehrer and OKW held the main forces of *Fifteenth Army* in the Pas-de-Calais until nearly the end of July. Throughout all of June and two thirds of July the enemy assumed that a second landing would be made north of the Seine, and it was not until the 19th that the first armored division was released from

---

23 July at 0600 is taken for British casualties (SHAEF G–3 Summary 30, 26 Jul 44). The nearest date to these on which both British and U.S. cumulative strengths are listed is 21 July (SHAEF G–3 Summary 47, 23 Jul 44). Statistics for 1 August 1944 show a greater disproportion both of strength and casualties. Cumulative strength for that date shows 934,000 U.S. and 682,000 British and Canadian, with casualties of 86,000 U.S. as opposed to approximately 56,000 British and Canadian (SHAEF G–3 Summary 58, 3 Aug 44).

[3] Twenty U.S. divisions were actually on the Continent by the time the drive for the Seine began. The Polish Armored Division and the 4th Canadian Armored Division were committed by 5 August. Three additional U.S. divisions came in as part of the invasion forces in southern France in mid-August.

Fifteenth Army for the Normandy front.

Widespread differences existed between *OB WEST* and OKW as to the nature of the battle to be waged in Normandy. The Germans had been forced into a defensive battle, their reserves were being committed piecemeal, and lack of replacements brought a thinning of the front which, without speedy reinforcement, meant the German line must ultimately collapse. Hitler's orders to stand and fight required units to be kept in untenable positions until there was no chance for them to withdraw without heavy losses. Von Rundstedt and Rommel discussed the situation with Hitler at the end of June, and on 1 July Rundstedt proposed that the Germans abandon the Caen bridgehead and establish a defense line running roughly from Caen to Caumont. Jodl, chief of the operations staff of OKW, opposed this move on the ground that it foreshadowed a German evacuation of France. When Hitler backed Jodl, Rundstedt replied that, unless his line was shortened in a few days, several of his armored divisions would soon be too battle weary for further action. Rundstedt was replaced a short time later as Commander in Chief West by Generalfeldmarschall Guenther von Kluge. Geyr von Schweppenburg, commander of *Panzer Group West* and a supporter of Rundstedt's views, was replaced by General der Panzertruppen Heinrich Eberbach.[4]

On 20 July an unsuccessful attempt on Hitler's life uncovered evidence of a conspiracy in which a number of generals and members of the General Staff were implicated. This effort, intended to open the way to a negotiated peace which would save Germany from total defeat, proved to be premature. Some of the bolder officers were court-martialed and executed and others were removed from posts of responsibility. Reichsfuehrer SS Heinrich Himmler's power over internal security was increased. Commanders who recommended evacuation of territory or who spoke of possible defeat were often looked upon with suspicion.

Among the commanders suspected of complicity in the plot was Field Marshal Rommel, although he had been incapable of participating in the attempted assassination because of injuries he had received on 17 July when an Allied plane strafed the staff car in which he was riding in Normandy. Suffering from an injured eye, a fractured skull, and a brain concussion, he was out of combat throughout the summer and early fall of 1944. He died in the middle of October from poison which he took in preference to standing trial. His reward was a state funeral ordered by the Fuehrer.[5] Rommel's command of *Army Group B* was assumed in mid-July by von Kluge in addition to his other duties.

Enemy losses for the period 6 June–23 July were approximately the same as those suffered by the Allies. German sources estimated casualties for that period at 116,863. While the Allies had replaced nearly all their losses by the end of July, enemy reinforcements numbered only some 10,000. The effect appeared in the number of understrength divisions which

---

[4] *Panzer Group West* was assigned to *Seventh Army* on 7 June 1944. On 10 June 1944 the headquarters of *Panzer Group West* was bombed out and the remnants were subordinated directly to *OB WEST* for rehabilitation. On 28 June 1944 *Panzer Group West* was assigned to *Army Group B* and took command of the Seine–Drôme sector.

[5] Official Notes by Martin Bormann Reference to Field Marshal Rommel, 28 Sep 44; Statement on Rommel's death by Heinrich Doose (who drove the car in which Rommel died), 30 May 45. Both in Officer's Personnel Files, *OKH/Heeres-Personalamt, Personalakten.*

the enemy had for use against the Allies. On the 25th, the *Seventh Army* had at most thirteen weak divisions to oppose fifteen full-strength U.S. divisions. *Panzer Group West,* facing a British equivalent strength of seventeen divisions, had nominally nine infantry divisions and six or seven panzer divisions, of which two or three infantry divisions and one panzer division were only then in the process of being trans-

FIELD MARSHAL VON KLUGE

FIELD MARSHAL ROMMEL

ferred to that front. It was assumed that an additional thirteen or fourteen divisions could be brought into the battle area. Of these, two had been rehabilitated in southern France, two divisions were being sent to Normandy from other theaters, five divisions were due to arrive by mid-August from northern France and Belgium,

and five additional units could be raised by stripping the coasts of the Netherlands, Belgium, and northern France.[6]

Despite obvious weakness, the enemy's position was not hopeless, as his stout resistance to Allied action demonstrated. The hedgerows of Normandy were favorable to the defender, and the Germans,

[6] *OB WEST, KTB 1.-31.VII.44,* 24 Jul 44; SHAEF G–3 Daily Summary, 25 Jul 44; Situation map (1:200,000) of the *WFSt Operations Abteilung (H)* (referred to hereafter as *WFSt/Op. [H]),* dated 26 Jul 44, showing situation on 25 Jul 44; 12th A Gp situation map for 25 Jul 44; 12th A Gp Final Rpt G–2, Vol. 3, Annex B; MS # B–722, The Situation, 24 July 1944 (Gersdorff). The last-named document is the first of a series of reports, MSS # B–722 to 729, The Campaign in Northern France 25 Jul 44–14 Sep 44, written in part by von Gersdorff, chief of staff of *Seventh Army* in Normandy, and in part by field commanders participating in that campaign.

expert at digging in, still made good use of the terrain to compensate for their inferiority in manpower and matériel. Also in their favor was the fact that the Allies still lacked room in which they could maneuver and bring the full force of their mobile units to bear. As long as they could be kept locked in the Cotentin peninsula and hemmed in at the Orne, there was a hope that Normandy could be held.

Plans for the Breakout

As early as 1942, planners of the Combined Commanders in London had visualized a landing in the Caen area and a swing southward into Brittany and then eastward to Paris. The COSSAC planners in their outline plan of 1943 had done the same. Both terrain features and military considerations favored such a campaign. An attack due south from St. Lô toward the Loire and a turning movement to the east at the base of the Cotentin peninsula would have several advantages. Such an attack would cut off the Brittany peninsula, give the formations advancing on Paris a secure right flank on the Loire, and permit the Allies to force the enemy back against the Seine. The enemy would be compelled to withdraw through hilly country lying between the British forces in the north and the U.S. forces in the south instead of using the better escape route lying through the Orléans Gap—a level area located roughly between Chartres and Orléans. A retreat southward through this area would give the Germans an opportunity to join up with their forces in southern France or to gain contact with units in Alsace. This could be forestalled by the Allies with an armored thrust that would put them in a position to outflank such a movement and force the enemy

into a narrow area north of Paris. Meanwhile, it was possible that the swing to the south would cut off enemy units in the Brittany peninsula from those in the rest of northern France and permit them to be defeated in detail. The Allies hoped that the opening of the Brittany ports would follow rapidly.

Less than two weeks after the invasion of Normandy, as the Allied forces strained to edge forward a few hundred yards each day, 21 Army Group planners outlined a plan for exploiting a deterioration in the German capacity to resist. They forecast a much more rapid sweep to the east than SHAEF planners had envisaged in their pre-D-Day plans which were based on the assumptions that the enemy would resist to the Seine and that the Brittany ports would be captured and furnishing some supplies for the U.S. forces before any major drive began to the east. This original concept of a deliberate advance to the Seine, followed by a three-week build-up, was abandoned by the 21 Army Group planners in favor of a British crossing of the Seine with the mission of enveloping Paris on the north, while the First U.S. Army followed through the Orléans Gap and south of Paris as fast as maintenance would permit. It was hoped that a pause to regroup would not be necessary until the forces were east of the Seine.[7]

---

[7] Development of Operations From the Bridgehead to Secure Lodgment Area and Advance Beyond, 21 A Gp plans. Opn LUCKY STRIKE, examination by planning staff, 20 Jun 44, and app., 21 A Gp, Appreciation of Possible Development of Operation LUCKY STRIKE, 18 Jun 44; 21 A Gp, Opn LUCKY STRIKE, Appreciation of Possible Development of Operations From the Bridgehead, 27 Jun 44. All in SHAEF AEAF 928. SHAEF planners paper, Post-NEPTUNE Courses of Action After Capture of the Lodgment Area, Sec. II, 30 May 44, and G–3's covering letter, 31 May 44, SHAEF SGS 381 Post-OVERLORD Planning, I.

Seeing no chance of any sudden deterioration of the German capacity to resist, SHAEF Planning Staff members reacted unfavorably to several features of the 21 Army Group plan. They believed that the early capture of Seine ports would not compensate for the lack of ports in Brittany, and took the position that the proposed plan would be acceptable only if it did not greatly delay the capture of the latter ports. Without a greater build-up of U.S. supplies, they saw no chance of supporting any but the smallest U.S. force east of the Seine or south and southeast of Paris. They believed, therefore, that the proposed pursuit must be limited in scope,[8] suggesting that it might be possible for British and Canadian forces to cross the Seine, while U.S. units guarded the 21 Army Group right flank west of the river.[9]

Before the Allies could rush their forces to the Seine, they first had to break out of the confines of the *bocage* country. It was to this problem that General Eisenhower and his commanders turned their attention in the early days of July. The direction of such an attack had been discussed even earlier. A broad plan indicating that the main offensive was to be on the U.S. front and would consist of a turning movement at the base of the Cotentin peninsula had been made by 21 Army Group before D Day and approved by General Eisenhower. At the end of June General Montgomery had directed First Army to swing southward and eastward to the general line Caumont–Vire–Mortain–Fougères, to send one corps westward into Brittany, and to plan for a wide sweep eastward toward the objectives Laval–Mayenne and Le Mans–Alençon.[10] Eisenhower, Montgomery, and Bradley had discussed future plans on 1 July. By 10 July, General Bradley and his First Army staff had drawn up

Operation COBRA, designed as a limited attack for the purpose of penetrating "the enemy's defenses west of St. Lô by VII Corps and exploiting this penetration with a strong armored and motorized thrust deep into the enemy's rear towards Coutances."[11] Montgomery approved the plan shortly after the middle of the month, and the field commanders then took up with Tedder, Leigh-Mallory, Spaatz, and other tactical and strategic air commanders the co-ordination of the air efforts for the attack.

---

[8] SHAEF Operations LUCKY STRIKE, BENEFICIARY, and HANDS UP, examination by Planning Staff, 29 Jun 44; SHAEF Operation LUCKY STRIKE, BENEFICIARY, and HANDS UP, examination by Planning Staff, 3 Jul 44. Both in SHAEF AEAF 928. The initial 21 Army Group draft, recognizing the difficulties that might face U.S. forces inasmuch as they might have to move 150 miles in ten to fifteen days, had indicated the possibility of stopping the advance on the line Cabourg–Sées to re-form U.S. forces and construct airfields.

[9] The air members of the SHAEF Planning Staff held that the group was too cautious and unimaginative in giving this unfavorable report. Memo by Gp Capt Peter Broad, 28 Jun 44; SHAEF Operation LUCKY STRIKE, BENEFICIARY, and HANDS UP, examination by Planning Staff, 3 Jul 44. Both in SHAEF AEAF 928.

[10] Montgomery dir to army comdrs, M–505, 30 Jun 44, FUSA files L–348 21 A Gp dirs.

[11] Operation COBRA, 13 Jul 44, FUSA files L–348 (18 B); Bradley, *A Soldier's Story*, pp. 316–32. The COBRA operation is frequently misnamed the St. Lô operation apparently because the attack on that city was so recently in the news and possibly because the short name was helpful to headline writers. COBRA is also used incorrectly to refer to the entire breakout and pursuit period. LUCKY STRIKE, the name for the earlier 21 Army Group plan to exploit a deterioration in the German will to resist, is also incorrectly used to refer to the breakout and pursuit period. No single code name covers the entire operation from 25 July to 25 August. COBRA is properly applicable only to the period 25 July–1 August 1944. The British attack made at the same time was called GOODWOOD and that of the Canadians SPRING. Later British and Canadian attacks were known as TOTALIZE and TRACTABLE.

At this crucial period between stale-mate and breakout, the Allied command arrangement of D Day was still in effect. General Eisenhower made frequent visits by plane to his field commanders while maintaining his forward command post at Portsmouth and his main headquarters at WIDEWING. Often he was called on to do little more than to give a nod of approval to the plans made by the field com-manders. He and his staff influenced the operations in this period by phasing forward additional units, by speeding up deliveries of ammunition and equipment, and by co-ordinating the Allied air effort. In some cases, General Eisenhower, by virtue of his control of U.S. forces as theater commander, dealt more directly with General Bradley than with General Montgomery.

Actual control of all ground operations was still in the hands of General Mont-gomery. He, in turn, allowed General Bradley considerable freedom relative to plans for First Army. General Bradley has said of this relationship:

He [Montgomery] exercised his Allied authority with wisdom, forbearance, and restraint. While coordinating our movements with those of Dempsey's, Monty carefully avoided getting mixed up in U. S. command decisions, but instead granted us the latitude to operate as freely and as independently as we chose. At no time did he probe into First Army with the indulgent manner he some-times displayed among those subordinates who were also his countrymen. I could not have wanted a more tolerant or judicious commander. Not once did he confront us with an arbitrary directive and not once did he reject any plan that we had devised.[12]

General Montgomery's attacks for Caen were to gain additional maneuver room and to aid the U.S. drive toward the south. His offensive of 18 July was de-signed to draw enemy forces from General Bradley's front west of St. Lô, so that U.S. forces could get into position for a large-scale advance. When General Bradley's attack, initially set for 18 July, was post-poned because of bad weather, General Montgomery set the 24th for the second try and restated his over-all plans for the breakout. The First Army was to cut off the enemy in the Périers–Lessay area in the southern Cotentin; the Third Army was then to swing south and east on the western flank into Brittany. Meanwhile, the Second British Army, fighting hard on the eastern flank, was to keep the enemy pinned down in the Caen sector and maintain a continuous threat of an ad-vance toward Falaise and Argentan. Not sure of what might happen, General Montgomery said he "intended to 'crack about' and try to bring about a major withdrawal in front of Brad."[13]

To encourage General Bradley in "the largest ground assault yet staged in this war by American troops exclusively," General Eisenhower sent the First Army commander a message accepting full per-sonal responsibility for the "necessary price of victory." Pointing out that the British forces were to carry on a vigorous attack, the Supreme Commander said that this aid would enable Bradley "to push every advantage with an ardor verging on recklessness." General Eisen-hower looked ahead to the possible results which might be attained and prophesied that, if the Second Army should break through simultaneously with the U.S. forces, the results would be "incalcu-lable."[14]

---

[12] Bradley, *A Soldier's Story*, pp. 319–20.
[13] Montgomery to Eisenhower, M–514, 24 Jul 44, Eisenhower personal file.
[14] Eisenhower to Montgomery for Bradley, FWD–12438, 24 Jul 44, Eisenhower personal file.

The COBRA Operation

General Bradley's operation got off to a false start on 24 July. The attack was postponed because of bad weather after some of the heavy bombers had actually started their preparation in the break-through area. On the following day, better weather made possible the launching of the saturation bombing plan worked out by IX Tactical Air Command (Maj. Gen. Elwood R. Quesada) and First Army. At 0940 approximately 350 fighter bombers made a twenty-minute attack on a 250-yard strip along the Périers–St. Lô road, west of St. Lô. This action was followed by an hour's bombing of an area 2,500 by 6,000 yards in which 1,887 heavy and medium bombers and 559 fighter bombers of the Eighth and Ninth Air Forces dropped more than 4,000 tons of explosives. The ground forces, despite casualties suffered by forward elements from bombs that fell short, moved forward at 1100. It was found that the air attack had stunned the enemy, destroying his communications and rendering many of his weapons ineffective. The VII Corps commander, Maj. Gen. J. Lawton Collins later concluded that "the bombing was the decisive factor in the initial success of the breakthrough." One tragic feature of the air assault was the death of General McNair, who had gone forward to view the attack and was struck by one of the U.S. bombs which fell short. To replace General McNair as head of the fictitious 1st U.S. Army Group, the War Department sent Lt. Gen. John L DeWitt, former commander of the Western Defense Command.[15]

The VII Corps followed the bombing with armored and infantry attacks. In the next three days its two armored and four infantry divisions overran enemy positions. At the same time, General Bradley's other three corps were making steady advances. News of the initial successes was slow in reaching General Eisenhower, but he maintained that the men were fighting for all their worth and that the enemy would soon crack under the pressure. Impressed by the reported effects of bombing on enemy morale, he felt that a concerted intensive drive could break through the whole defense system of the enemy on a selected front, and that the Allies were going "to get a great victory, very soon."[16]

The COBRA operation was completed in its basic details on 28 July with the First

---

[15] Unpublished draft account of VII Corps actions in Hq ETOUSA Hist Sec narrative on Opn COBRA; Eighth Air Force, Special Report on Operations, 24–25 Jul 44, dtd 11 Sep 44; USSTAF, Report of Investigation, 14 Aug 44; 12th A Gp, Effect of Air Power on Military Operations. All in OCMH files. Craven and Cate, *The Army Air Forces in World War II,* III, 231–43. Statistics on the number of airplanes and tons of bombs dropped vary in different accounts. The author has used those given in the Craven and Cate volume, p. 232.

The bombing at St. Lô, although heavy, was actually only the third largest in Normandy in number of tons dropped according to the report of Air Chief Marshal Leigh-Mallory. The largest was that at Caen on 18 July when 1,676 heavies and 343 mediums dropped 7,700 tons. The second largest was in support of the Canadian Army along the Caen-Falaise road on the night of 7–8 August and the succeeding day. More than 5,200 tons of bombs were dropped by 1,450 bombers of the Eighth Air Force and Bomber Command. There were three other important preparations in Normandy: in support of British at Caen, 8 July—2,662 tons by 467 bombers of Bomber Command; in support of British south of Caumont, 30 July—2,227 tons by 693 heavies of Bomber Command and over 500 light and medium bombers of AEAF; in support of Canadians near Falaise, 14 August—3,723 tons by 811 bombers of Bomber Command. FUSA Rpt of Opns, 20 Oct 43–1 Aug 44, Bk. I; Air Chief Marshal Sir Trafford Leigh-Mallory, Despatch to the Supreme Commander, AEF, November 1944, *Supplement to The London Gazette,* December 31, 1946, pp. 64–65.

[16] Eisenhower to Montgomery, 26 Jul 44, Eisenhower personal file.

Army's capture of Coutances. The four U.S. corps were then ordered to press their attack southward General Bradley reported that he and his men were feeling "pretty cocky" and refused to have their enthusiasm dampened by reports that the enemy was sending reinforcements. "I can assure you," he told General Eisenhower, "that we are taking every calculated risk and we believe we have the Germans out of the ditches and in complete demoralization and expect to take full advantage of them." He paid special tribute for his success to the tactical air forces, pointing to the close liaison between planes and tank formations and the "picnic" the air forces had enjoyed in dealing with enemy daylight movements. "I cannot say too much," he added, "for the fine cooperation Quesada and his command have given us in the last few days." [17]

The enemy commanders in their own way paid tribute to the effectiveness of air-ground co-operation. They complained that low-flying planes subjected traffic to long delays or stopped it entirely, with the result that reinforcements could not be brought up readily. Composite experiences of German commanders were described after the war in the following statement:

Covered by their air force, the [Allied] troops who had penetrated into the line affected the rear of the German units to such an extent that the unity of the defense deteriorated and the battle finally turned into separate fights for hills, localities, and individual farms. The command was almost entirely dependent on radio-communication, since all wire-lines had been destroyed and messengers were shot in the enemy-saturated terrain. The separate units fought—on their own—as small combat teams, and had hardly any contact with neighboring troops.[18]

While the U.S. forces advanced in the west, General Montgomery moved his British and Canadian forces forward on the eastern flank. Early on 25 July, before the heavy bombardment west of St. Lô, Canadian forces had started southward toward Falaise. In a day of desperate fighting, troops of Lt. Gen. G. G. Simonds' 2d Canadian Corps struck at an area heavily held by enemy armor. They suffered more than 1,000 casualties in an attack that took little territory but helped to conceal the direction of the main offensive and to delay the enemy's shift of reserves to the U.S. front.[19] General Montgomery now directed the Second British Army to strike in the Caumont area and ordered all British and Canadian forces to attack to the greatest degree possible with the resources available. He declared that the enemy "must be worried, and shot up, and attacked, and raided, whenever and wherever possible; the object of such activity will be to improve our own positions, to gain ground, to keep the enemy from transferring forces across to the western flank to oppose the American advance, and generally to 'Write off' German personnel and equipment." [20]

Shortly before this directive was issued, the First Canadian Army had become active on the Continent. Its commander, General Crerar, had been in Normandy since mid-June, but because maneuver space for another army was lacking his headquarters did not become operational

---

[17] Bradley to Eisenhower, 28 Jul 44, Eisenhower personal file. See also Craven and Cate, *The Army Air Forces in World War II*, III, 235–43.

[18] MS # B–723, The American Breakthrough in the Direction of Avranches (Gersdorff).

[19] Stacey, *The Canadian Army*, pp. 190–94.

[20] Montgomery to army comdrs, M–515, 27 Jul 44, 12 A Gp 371.3 Military Objectives, I; Montgomery, *Normandy to the Baltic*, pp. 139–41.

until 23 July. On that date he took over 1 British Corps and the extreme eastern sector of the Allied front; on 31 July 2d Canadian Corps came under his command. The Canadian Army now held the front south of Caen.[21]

As the U.S. attack gained momentum, General Eisenhower pressed General Montgomery to speed up his advance in the Caumont area. "Never was time more vital to us, and we should not wait on weather or on perfection of detail of preparation." In the same spirit of urgency, General Montgomery ordered General Dempsey to throw all caution overboard, to take risks, "to accept any casualties and to step on the gas for Vire."[22]

On 28 July, Generals Montgomery, Bradley, and Dempsey discussed plans for the "complete dislocation" of the enemy, and General Montgomery informed the Supreme Commander of the prospects for a great victory.[23] Highly pleased, Eisenhower replied: "From all reports your plan continues to develop beautifully. I learn you have a column in Avranches. This is great news and Bradley must quickly make our position there impregnable. . . . With Canadian Army fighting intensively to prevent enemy movement away from the Caen area Dempsey's attack coupled with Bradley's will clean up the area west of Orne once and for all. Good luck."[24]

Hitler Outlines His Plan

Severely shaken by the bombardments of 25 July and hard hit by the advancing ground forces, Field Marshal von Kluge on 27 July obtained OKW's permission to transfer a panzer corps from the British front to the western side of the line.[25] On the same day, he also requested the trans-

fer to the combat area of two divisions from the Pas-de-Calais, a third from the Atlantic coast of France, and a fourth from southern France. In support of his request for shifting forces from the Pas-de-Calais, *OB WEST* reported that there was a possibility that an alleged newly organized 12th Army Group containing the Third U.S. Army and three corps was shortly to be sent to Normandy, and that it seemed probable that no second landing would be made. Hitler approved the release of units from the Pas-de-Calais and the Atlantic coast, but refused to weaken the defenses of southern France. At the end of the month, *OB WEST* again pressed OKW to strip all quiet sectors in order to prevent an Allied breakout.[26]

On 31 July, Hitler held a particularly significant conference in his East Prussian headquarters with Jodl and other military advisers. In the course of the meeting he revealed his deep distrust of the high-level commanders of the Army, his reasons for pressing the battle in the west, and the plan of campaign he had for the coming months. Hitler's bitter reactions to the attempt on his life of 20 July bared the gulf between him and the Regular Army commanders. He described it as the symptom of blood poisoning which permeated the highest command. Condemning many of

[21] Stacey, *The Canadian Army*, p. 194.

[22] Eisenhower to Montgomery, 28 Jul 44; Montgomery to Eisenhower, M–68, 28 Jul 44. Both in Eisenhower personal file.

[23] Montgomery to Eisenhower, M–70, 29 Jul 44, Eisenhower personal file.

[24] Eisenhower to Montgomery, SHAEF FWD 12505, 31 Jul 44, Eisenhower personal file.

[25] MS # B–723 (Gersdorff).

[26] *OKW/WFSt, KTB Ausarbeitung, der Westen 1.IV.-16.XII.44* (referred to hereafter as Der Westen [Maj. Percy Schramm]); *OB WEST, KTB 1.-31.VII.44*, 25, 26, 27, 31 Jul 44; *Panzer-Armeeoberkommando 5* (referred to hereafter as *Fifth Panzer Army*), *KTB 10.VI.-8.VIII.44*, 26, 27 Jul 44.

the field marshals and generals as "destroyers" and traitors, he asked how he could keep up morale among ordinary soldiers when once-trusted leaders dealt with the enemy. He declared that the signal and supply systems were filled with traitors and insisted that he could not inform his field commanders in the west of the broad strategic plans of the Reich, since they would be known to the Allied powers almost as soon as the details reached Paris. He decided, therefore, to tell von Kluge only enough of future plans for the Commander in Chief West to carry on immediate operations. Concluding that the imminent development in the west would decide Germany's destiny, and that von Kluge could not assume such an immense responsibility, Hitler ordered a small operations headquarters established which could serve him later when he expected to go to Alsace-Lorraine or western Germany to assume the direction of operations in the west.[27]

Throughout the talk, which was little more than a monologue, the Fuehrer stressed the problem of leadership, demanding that in the future his commanders be picked on the basis of loyalty and willingness to fight rather than in accordance with seniority. He asked that brave men, regardless of rank, be selected to hold the Channel and Atlantic ports and not "big mouths" like the commander at Cherbourg who had issued bold declarations and then had surrendered at the first Allied blow. He caustically condemned commanders, particularly those of noble birth, who felt they would do well by surrendering to the Allies. He paid tribute to Marshal Tito, saying that here was a man without military background who deserved the title of marshal because he had the will to fight.

Hitler's strategy of holding tenaciously

to ports and ground in the west, a policy much attacked after the war by his commanders, can be better understood in the light of the arguments he advanced to Jodl. He insisted that Germany's problem was a moral and not a material one. So far as the Eastern Front was concerned, he believed that Germany would be able, with some effort, to stabilize the existing grave situation. He lashed out at those who felt that it was possible to come to some sort of arrangement with the Reich's enemies, saying that this was not a struggle which would be settled by negotiation or some clever tactical maneuver, but rather a Hunnish war in which one or the other of the antagonists had to perish. Speaking of his worries over the Balkans, Hitler made clear that continual losses might lead to defection by Hungary and Bulgaria or to a change in the attitude of the countries which were then neutral. A decisive action or a successful large-scale battle was essential to strengthen Germany's position.

Hitler explained that he did not wish to keep his armies tied up in Italy, but he felt that a withdrawal would free Allied forces in that area for fighting elsewhere. He added that it was better to fight in another country than to bring the battle to the Reich.

For France, the Fuehrer was quite specific. He knew that he had to make long-range plans for a withdrawal, but insisted on keeping them secret. He repeated that he intended to withhold knowledge of his broad plans from the Commander in Chief West, but did agree that certain definite points would be outlined. His orders to von Kluge included the following: (1) if

---

[27] Minutes of conference of 31 July 1944: *Besprechung des Fuehrers mit Generaloberst Jodl am 31.7.1944 in der Wolfsschanze* (near Rastenburg, East Prussia); *Der Westen* (Schramm).

German forces had to withdraw from the French coast, all major ports were to be held by garrisons under carefully picked commanders who would hold their positions to the last; (2) all railroad equipment and installations and all bridges were to be destroyed in territory that was abandoned; (3) the Commander in Chief West was to provide certain specific units with organic means of transportation and with mobile weapons; (4) no withdrawing from the line then occupied could be tolerated—the ground had to be held with fanatical determination. It was better to stand than to withdraw, Hitler pointed out, since any retreat confronted the Germans with the disadvantages of mobile warfare in an area where the Allies had air superiority. Further, the Germans lacked prepared positions to which they could pull back. Any surrender of ports increased the opportunities for the Allied forces to build up a crushing superiority in men and matériel.

Despite his fear of a retreat that would give the Allies more room for maneuver, Hitler did issue orders for the construction of new defense positions along the Somme and the Marne. He indicated his displeasure with previous efforts, saying that there was a tendency to build a "show place" in the fortifications and to display these to inspectors, while hiding the weakness of the defensive lines. Delays in constructing positions, he maintained, were due to the demands of army groups to retain control of their rear areas. Now, he insisted that the work be done by the Organization Todt with the assistance of local labor.

At the close of the conference a further meeting was held between Hitler, Jodl, and Jodl's deputy, General der Artillerie Walter Warlimont, who was to go to France to acquaint von Kluge with such

parts of the new plans as it was thought proper for him to know. Warlimont vainly endeavored to obtain from Hitler or Jodl a clear statement of what he was to tell von Kluge. Under his persistent questioning, he finally succeeded in obtaining from a thoroughly vexed Hitler an abrupt answer: "Tell Field Marshal von Kluge that he should keep his eyes riveted to the front and on the enemy without ever looking backward. If and when precautionary measures have to be taken in the rear of the theater of operations in the West, everything necessary will be done by OKW and OKW alone." [28]

Shortly after Warlimont's departure, a special staff was formed to execute measures which had been discussed at the conference, the military governor of France was charged with the responsibility for constructing the Somme–Marne position, and the commander of the Replacement Army was ordered to refit the West Wall.

Eisenhower Prepares for Action

Meanwhile, the command of U.S. forces was being reorganized in preparation for the next phase of their offensive. On 19 July General Bradley stated that as soon as Operation COBRA was completed the U.S. forces on the Continent would number eighteen divisions and would soon afterward be increased by three more. In accordance with a SHAEF memorandum of 1 June 1944, he recommended that they be organized into two armies and a U.S. army group be brought in to command them. [29] General Montgomery, who was aware that such a change would be made when the U.S. build-up on the Continent required two American armies and that

---

[28] MS # C–099 a, OKW Activities—*"Der Westen"* (1 Apr–31 Dec 1944), Pt. II (Warlimont).

[29] See below, pp. 261–63.

this would be followed in due course by General Eisenhower's assumption of personal control of operations, agreed to the proposal.

On 25 July, General Eisenhower directed that the U.S. ground forces on the Continent be regrouped into the First and Third Armies under the control of 12th Army Group which General Bradley was to command. The regrouping was to take place on a date set by Bradley, who was to give three days' prior notice to SHAEF and 21 Army Group. The new army group was to remain under the command of the commander in chief of the 21 Army Group until the Supreme Commander allocated a specific "area of responsibility" to the commanding general of the 12th Army Group. It was understood that Lt. Gen. Courtney H. Hodges, assistant commander of the First Army, was to succeed General Bradley in command of that army, and that General Patton, the Third Army commander, was to take over some of the divisions then on the Continent. To prepare them for their task, General Bradley on 28 July directed Hodges to keep touch with the three left corps, and told Patton to form the six divisions on First Army's right into two corps while they were on the move. The Third Army commander was instructed to keep track of these corps so that he would be familiar with the tactical situation when his army became operational. General Bradley set 1 August as the date for the new arrangement to go into effect. For the next month General Montgomery retained over-all control of ground forces on the Continent, but channeled all orders to U.S. forces through the 12th Army Group.[30]

General Eisenhower, encouraged by the reports of late July to hope for a complete break-through, again reminded General Montgomery of the need for bold action by Allied armored and mobile columns against the enemy flanks. He indicated that supplies could be dropped by aircraft to such units in case of an emergency, and recalled that the tremendous assets in the Troop Carrier Command and in the mastery of the air should not be neglected. "I know," the Supreme Commander added, "that you will keep hammering as long as you have a single shot in the locker."[31]

In his optimism, General Eisenhower foresaw a chance for the Allies to win a tactical victory and create virtually an open flank. If this happened he proposed to send only a small part of his forces into Brittany while using the bulk of the Allied units to destroy the enemy west of the Rhine, and exploit as far to the east as possible. As an alternative, in case the enemy stripped the area south of Caen and tried to set up a line from Caen to Avranches south of Vire, Montgomery was to thrust forward in the lower Seine valley. Operation SWORDHILT, a combined amphibious-airborne operation to seize the area east of Brest, was also to be launched. The Supreme Commander did not believe that the enemy could interfere with his plans and predicted that if the Allies could have a period of ten days to two weeks of really good weather they could secure "a most significant success."[32]

The 21 Army Group commander, it will be recalled, had already ordered the

[30] Bradley to Montgomery, 19 Jul 44, and Montgomery's concurrence; Memo, Eisenhower for Bradley, 25 Jul 44, sub: Comd and Organization, U.S. Ground Forces, SHAEF G–3 322.011–1 Command and Control of U.S./British Forces; Bradley to Eisenhower, 28 Jul 44, Eisenhower personal file.

[31] Eisenhower to Montgomery, 2 Aug 44, SHAEF SGS 381 Post OVERLORD Planning, I (a).

[32] Eisenhower to Marshall, S–56667, 2 Aug 44, Eisenhower personal file.

British forces to continue their drive southward in an effort to keep enemy armor
away from the west, while First Army
forces turned southeastward toward Vire
and Third Army began the task of clearing the enemy from Brittany. Now that
the First Army had opened the corridor at
the bottom of the Cotentin peninsula, the
spotlight was to be shifted to the Third
Army. Patton's forces were ordered to ad-

GENERAL HODGES

GENERAL PATTON. *(Photograph
taken in 1945.)*

vance south from the vicinity of Avranches
to Rennes, then to turn west and capture
the Brittany peninsula and open the Brittany ports.[33]

So far as his reserves in Brittany were
concerned the enemy was ill prepared to
meet the armored onslaught being prepared by the Third Army. Piecemeal

commitment of enemy forces from Brittany during June and July had resulted in
the serious weakening of the German position there. French Resistance forces had
harassed the enemy and interfered with
his movements. On 1 August, German
forces in Brittany amounted to fewer than
ten battalions of German infantry, four
Ost battalions, and some 50,000 naval and
service troops.[34] These troops were scattered among the various ports and so disposed that miles of front were left entirely

[33] Montgomery dir to army comdrs, M–515, 27 Jul
44, FUSA files L–345; FUSA Rpt of Opns, 1 Aug
44–22 Feb 45, Bk. I, p. 1; FO 1, 4 Aug 44 (confirmation of verbal orders issued 1Aug 44), TUSA AAR, I.
[34] *Ost* battalions had been formed on the eastern
front from anti-Bolshevik Russian peoples, frequently
prisoners of war. They had been transferred to the
west at the rate of two *Ost* battalions for one German
battalion.

open to the Third Army's advance. General Patton explained this situation to his staff, although he jokingly warned them not to let the newsmen know how weak the enemy was.[35]

Despite their weakness in Brittany, it was clear that the Germans could cause the Third Army some difficulty. Col. Oscar Koch, General Patton's chief of intelligence, warned on 2 August that the reported movement of enemy armor westward created the possibility of a major counterattack to drive a wedge to the Channel between the northern and southern columns of the Third Army, rendering the southern columns logistically inoperative. General Patton's characteristic reaction was that, while his units might be cut off for a short time, he would not find it difficult to re-establish his position.[36]

General Montgomery by 30 July had pushed two corps forward from the Caumont front toward Vire and Mont Pinçon, pinning down *II SS Panzer Corps* so that it was not available for an enemy counterattack at Avranches. On 1 August the Third Army sent one corps due west into Brittany, but launched two others southward and southeastward, holding a fourth in reserve. By 4 August Rennes had fallen and armored spearheads had bypassed St. Malo and Dinan and were headed for Brest. First Army units at the same time swung toward Vire. These rapid drives were aided not only by the weakness of enemy opposition, particularly in Brittany, but by air cover furnished the armored columns by the tactical air commands, whose scale of support increased daily.[37]

General Montgomery answered the Supreme Commander's request for continued exploitation of the enemy's weakened position on 4 August by ordering General Crerar, whose forces held the eastern flank of the British line, to drive for Falaise not later than 8 August and cut off the withdrawal of German forces then facing General Dempsey west of Thury-Harcourt. Dempsey was to continue his move south and east toward Argentan. Meanwhile, Montgomery noted, General Hodges was to maintain his swing eastward with his left flank on the Domfront–Alençon axis. General Patton's army, save for one corps needed to clear up Brittany, was to attack due east from Rennes toward Laval and Angers. The British commander, saying that the Allied forces had "unloosed the shackles that were holding us down and have knocked away the 'key rivets,' " swung the Allied right flank toward Paris with the intention of forcing the enemy back against the Seine, whose bridges had been destroyed between Paris and the sea. Minor counterthrusts that von Kluge had been making at the base of the Cotentin were discounted, since his delaying actions seemed likely to provide an opportunity for the Allies to swing around quickly and cut off the German routes of escape.[38]

The Mortain Counterattack

The Germans, meanwhile, were planning a counterthrust by the *Seventh Army* to pierce the U.S. line between Mortain

---

[35] Entry in diary of historical officer with the Third Army, OCMH files; G–2 Periodic Rpt, 2 Aug 44, TUSA AAR, II.

[36] G–2 Periodic Rpt, 2 Aug 44, TUSA AAR, II; entry in diary of historical officer with Third Army, 2 Aug 44, OCMH files.

[37] TUSA Rpt of Opns, I; FUSA Rpt of Opns, 1 Aug 44–22 Feb 45, Bk. I, p. 4; MS # B–725, The German Counterattack Against Avranches (Gersdorff); Craven and Cate, *The Army Air Forces in World War II*, III, 243–53.

[38] Montgomery, dir to army comdrs, M–516, 4 Aug 44; Montgomery, dir to army comdrs, M–517, 6 Aug 44. Both in SHAEF SGS 381 Post OVERLORD Planning, I (a).

and Avranches in the southern Cotentin and cut off and destroy U.S. forces in Brittany. Hitler's order for this counterattack reached *OB WEST* on 2 August and was passed on to von Kluge at *Army Group B* headquarters. The Commander in Chief West later declared that he believed the plan to be grandiose and impossible of fulfillment, but at the moment he appears to have expressed agreement with the directive.[39]

Hitler authorized von Kluge to shorten his line slightly east and west of Vire and move forces from there and from the Caen front to the area of Sourdeval for the counterattack. Units were also sent from the Pas-de-Calais area, inasmuch as the Germans now thought a landing in that area unlikely. A gap which had been opened between *Panzer Group West* and *Seventh Army* was closed by German forces on 3 August.[40] They succeeded in consolidating their lines on their northwestern and western front and in forming a security line to the south. Fully accepting the threat to Brittany, von Kluge pushed preparations for his operation, deciding to attack at the end of the first week of August even if the assembly of troops was not complete. Hitler, for once somewhat cautious, held that the attack could succeed only if it was postponed until all available troops were concentrated. Moreover, he ordered General Eberbach to lead the attack, but the Commander in Chief West, deciding that it was impossible to delay any longer and too late to change commanders, retained Generaloberst der Waffen SS Paul Hausser in charge of the operation.[41]

After Hitler had given his last-minute permission to execute the attack as planned, provided the two army commanders would trade places immediately after the attack, he decided to send Generalmajor Walter Buhle from his own

headquarters to see that his wishes were carried out.[42]

In the late evening of 6 August, von Kluge launched the Mortain counterattack. Hitler described it as "a unique, never recurring opportunity for a complete reversal of the situation." Elements, many very small and scattered, of six armored divisions struck by way of Mortain to assault the area between the Sée and the Sélune Rivers. The force of the leading armored units hit the First Army, dealing a heavy blow to the 30th Division. Elements of the unit were encircled but continued to fight. The Germans made some progress in the early hours of 7 Au-

---

[39] *OB WEST, KTB 1.–31.VIII.44*, 2 Aug 44; *Der Westen* (Schramm); OI Special Interrogation Report 39, Rittmeister Wilhelm Scheidt, 30 April 1947, The War in the West, 6 Jun 44–Mar 45, Headquarters, 7707 Military Intelligence Service Center, APO 757, U.S. Army (referred to hereafter as OI–SIR/39 [Scheidt]). The author of this report was the assistant to Generalmajor Walter Scherff, Hitler's Plenipotentiary for Military History. Scheidt relied heavily for his information on *Der Westen* (Schramm), which was made available to him after his capture. Consequently this report gives a good over-all picture as well as interesting details, but lays no claim to complete accuracy of fact and dates. No copy of Hitler's order of 2 August has been found so far. Its general content is reflected in the teletype from von Kluge to his army commanders ordering the preparations of the attack toward Avranches, 3 August 1944. *Heeresgruppe B* (referred to hereafter as *Army Group B*), *Ia Operations Befehle 9. VI.–31.VIII.44.*

[40] *Panzer Group West* was renamed *Fifth Panzer Army*, effective 5 August 1944.

[41] Actually Hitler was not so much concerned with relieving General Hausser as with eliminating the *XLVII Panzer Corps* commander, General der Panzertruppen Hans Freiherr von Funck. The attack proper was led by General Funck as the corps commander under General Hausser as the *Seventh Army* commander.

[42] *OB WEST, KTB 1.–31.VIII.44*, 3 to 6 Aug 44; *Der Westen* (Schramm); OI–SIR/39 (Scheidt; *Army Group B, KTB 16.VII.–4.X.44*, 3 and 6 Aug 44; Situation maps (1:200,000) of *WFSt/Op.(H)*, 3 to 5 Aug 44; *Armeeoberkommando 7* (referred to hereafter as *Seventh Army*), *KTB Anlagen* (Reports and Orders) *31.VII.–19.VIII.44*, 4 Aug 44.

gust, but the Allied air forces blasted them near noon. The enemy credited these attacks with stopping his initial thrust, mentioning especially the work of British Typhoons. German air support was almost nonexistent.[43]

General Bradley quickly countered the German thrust with two additional divisions. In the meantime, Third Army units filled the area between Laval and Le Mans, threatening the south flank of the enemy. To the northeast, General Crerar's army struck on 7 August with tanks, artillery, and air east of the Orne on the Caen–Falaise road, menacing the rear of the attackers. To meet this new situation, the Germans were forced to draw on newly arrived armored and infantry elements intended for the attack on Avranches. Toward midnight on 8 August, von Kluge found it necessary to discontinue his attack. Nonetheless, he ordered preparations for its later renewal.[44]

Hitler was not immediately convinced that his drive toward Avranches had failed. Still hoping to cut off Allied forces in Brittany and then turn north to retake important harbors and parts of the sea coast essential to Allied supply, he insisted on resuming the counterattack. On 9 August he blamed von Kluge for making his first attack too early and at a time especially suited for Allied air operations. He ordered the Commander in Chief West to renew the action, this time from the area of Domfront, southeast of Mortain. To free additional units for the operation, the *Seventh Army* was permitted to withdraw to new positions. Hitler declared that he alone would give the date for the new attack. At the same time, the *First Army* was supposed to assemble an attack force in the Paris area.[45]

Closing the Falaise Gap

While Hitler in East Prussia indulged himself in the illusion that he could roll up the U.S. forces in the Cotentin, the Allies moved boldly to encircle his troops. The enemy in sending the mass of his armored forces into the area southwest of Falaise had given the British and U.S. armies an opportunity to trap them between Falaise and Argentan. But the adoption of such a plan of action was not without its dangers for the Allies. Twelve U.S. divisions had been pushed through the corridor at Avranches and were still open to the menace of an enemy break-through to the sea which would cut the lines of communications. The question was whether to use General Bradley's remaining four divisions to hold the front at Mortain or to send them around the enemy's left flank. After some consideration, the Allied commanders decided on the bolder course. Noting that the enemy was trying to hold both Avranches and in front of Caen, General Eisenhower on 8 August concluded

[43] OI–SIR/39 (Scheidt); *OB WEST, KTB 1.-31.VIII.44*, 6, 7 Aug 44; Teletype *Army Group B to OB WEST*, 6 Aug 44. *Army Group B, Ia Operations Befehle 9.VI.-31.VIII.44.* Craven and Cate, *The Army Air Forces in World War II*, III, 249, gives statistics of British and U.S. air forces. A British Operations Research Group with the 21 Army Group which examined the knocked-out and abandoned tanks in this area shortly after the attack concluded that more of the tanks were knocked out by U.S. artillery and bazookas than by British or U.S. planes. The group did agree that the air forces were responsible for a number of indirect losses that resulted when crews fled leaving their tanks intact or when they destroyed them with special charges. (The report was shown to the author by a member of the team that made the report.)

[44] *Seventh Army, KTB* (Draft) *6.VI.-16.VIII.44*, 8 Aug 44.

[45] *Der Westen* (Schramm); Hitler's order of 2300 hours, 9 Aug 44 *(WFSt/Op.Nr.772801/44)*. *Army Group B, Ia Fuehrerbefehle 17.VI.-25.IX.44*, 10 Aug 44; Warlimont statement, 12 Aug 44. *Der Westen* (Schramm).

that the U.S. right wing, then driving due eastward, should turn to the north and attack the enemy in the rear. "On a visit to Bradley today," he wrote, "I found that he had already acted on this idea and had secured Montgomery's agreement to a sharp change in direction toward the Northeast instead of continuing toward the East, as envisaged in M–517 [Montgomery's directive of 6 August]." [46]

On the following day, the Supreme Commander reported to General Marshall: "Under my urgent directions all possible strength is turned to the destruction of the forces facing us." Seeing the chance to clear the enemy from France, he was unwilling to detach forces merely to speed capture of the Brittany ports.

Patton, Bradley, and Montgomery [he added] are all imbued with the necessity of acting and alive to the opportunity. Patton has the marching wing which will turn in rather sharply to the northeast from the general vicinity of Le Mans and just to the west thereof marching toward Alençon and Falaise. The enemy's bitter resistance and counterattacks in the area between Mortain and south of Caen makes it appear that we have a good chance to encircle and destroy a lot of his forces. You can well imagine how badly I want additional ports and the second that the issue of this battle is determined I will turn into Brittany enough forces to accomplish the quick downfall of the ports.[47]

General Montgomery confirmed the new plan in a directive of 11 August. Preparing now to deal with the Germans between the Loire and the Seine, the 21 Army Group commander called for the U.S. forces to swing their left flank from the Le Mans area almost due north to Alençon. The First Canadian Army was to seize Falaise and move on Argentan, while the Second British Army on its right moved to the west and south. General Bradley directed the Third Army to shift

its left wing toward the northeast, seize a bridgehead over the Sarthe at Le Mans, and prepare to strike the enemy flank and rear in the direction of Argentan. To its left, the First Army was to smash the enemy in the area Vire–Mortain–Domfront. General Hodges' drive, while not as sweeping as General Patton's, was more complicated. The First Army advance "consisted of a thrust toward the southeast and a ninety-degree turn toward the northeast at the enemy flank and rear. It was a left wheel against the inter-army boundary and the effort of the First Army was to be directly at and perpendicular to the boundary between our army and that of the British." All Allied forces were to be prepared to put into effect a wide envelopment at the Seine should the enemy escape the trap near Falaise.[48]

The airborne planners at SHAEF now proposed operations to bar the escape of the enemy by way of the Paris–Orléans Gap and across the lower Seine. They worked up a plan to capture and control important road nets during the period 16–27 August (Operation TRANSFIGURE). Variants on the plan called for airborne forces to block attempts at escape across the upper or lower Seine and to expedite pursuit across that river. General Bradley on 13 August even discussed the possibility of cutting off the German retreat by drawing airborne forces across the roads leading northeast from Falaise and Argentan, although he agreed with General Brereton's view that they should not be used "in

---

[46] Eisenhower Memo, Diary Office CinC, 8 Aug 44.
[47] Eisenhower to Marshall, S–57189, 9 Aug 44, Eisenhower personal file.
[48] Montgomery dir to army comdrs, M–518, 11 Aug 44, SHAEF SGS 381 Post OVERLORD Planning; 12th A Gp Ltr of Instructions 4, 8 Aug 44, 12th A Gp Rpt of Opns, V; FUSA Rpt of Opns, 1 Aug 44–22 Feb 45, Bk. I, pp. 9–10.

small harassing operations such as requested by General Montgomery." He
felt there was a possibility of using them
two weeks later in making the "Long
Hook" at the Seine, but saw no value in
tightening the noose in the "Short Hook"
near Falaise unless the drop could be
made within five days.[49]

General Eisenhower tentatively decided
on 15 August to cancel TRANSFIGURE and
utilize the airlift needed for the operation
to carry gasoline to the ground forces in
the Le Mans area. His decision virtually
brought to an end planning for that drop.
When General Patton's forces soon overran the drop area, General Whiteley,
SHAEF deputy chief of operations, suggested that available airborne forces be
used to seize Boulogne or Calais. Air Chief
Marshal Tedder and General Eisenhower,
though still uncertain whether an air drop
might be needed at the river itself, authorized the necessary plans. General Bradley
on 19 August informed XVIII Corps (Airborne) that no assistance would be needed
for a crossing in his zone of action, and
representatives of 21 Army Group indicated that, if by 21 August ground troops
were able to cross the Seine without delay,
no call would be made on the airborne
force for aid in that area.[50]

With the Allied turning movement
under way, the enemy's only chance for
escape lay in an immediate withdrawal
to the east. Instead Hitler was regrouping
his forces for another attack toward
Avranches. On 10 and 11 August, von
Kluge sent repeated messages to OKW on
the dangerous situation in which he found
himself. Late on the 10th, he announced
that the Allies were advancing from Le
Mans toward Alençon and that it was
clear the U.S. forces were trying to join
British forces in the north to pinch off the

Seventh Army and *Fifth Panzer Army*. Pointing out that a major German attack could
not be made for at least ten days, he asked
permission to make a short, sharp armored
thrust at the U.S. spearheads pushing to
the north. Before giving his approval, Hitler asked for more specific justification for
the ten-day delay. Von Kluge consulted
with his chief subordinates and declared
at midday of 11 August that another
strike at Avranches was no longer feasible.
Instead, wholehearted measures would
have to be taken against the impending
envelopment by the Third Army forces.
He proposed to regroup the armored
forces for an attack near Alençon and to
withdraw *Seventh Army's* western salient,
and he asked for additional forces to protect his flanks against the Allies. Without
waiting for Hitler's permission, he took the
responsibility of giving preliminary orders
for such action.

Hitler took von Kluge's proposal as a
personal affront, particularly when von
Kluge insisted that the Fuehrer make a
final decision. He held that the Commander in Chief West wanted an order to
retreat—a possibility that Hitler was unwilling to consider. Telephone conversations between Jodl and von Kluge may
have convinced Hitler of the need for a
temporary reversal of attack direction. On
the afternoon of the 11th, Hitler suspended his order of 9 August for a renewed attack on Avranches and declared
that the primary aim was to eliminate the

---

[49] Outline Plans 1, 2, and 3, dtd 17 and 19 Aug 44,
included in SHAEF G–3 Crossing of the Seine
GCT/24562/A. B; Lewis H. Brereton, *The Brereton
Diaries* (New York, 1946), pp. 323–24, 329–30,
332–33.
[50] Whiteley to Chief Plans Sec G–3 SHAEF, 17 Aug
44, SHAEF G–3 24533/Ops Future Opns; Tedder to
Eisenhower and latter's reply, Diary Office CinC, 19
Aug 44.

threat to the south flank of the German army group by launching a concentric armored attack under General Eberbach against the flank of American XV Corps. In addition he directed *First Army* to assemble the forces at its disposal around Chartres to meet threats in that area. He ordered troops concentrated on both wings of the northern front for defensive action in the areas of Falaise and Mortain, agreeing that von Kluge could shorten his line near Sourdeval and Mortain in order to free forces.[51]

Hitler's change of plans came too late to meet von Kluge's immediate needs. The German situation on the north had worsened steadily since 7 August when British and Canadian forces had attacked on both sides of the Orne. German units had been forced to withdraw southward on both the 8th and 9th. To the south, elements of the Third Army were near Chartres. The *Seventh Army* lost its rear installations during the period, and the task of supplying it had to be assumed by the *Fifth Panzer Army*. Shortly afterward an Allied thrust to the north cut off all but one of the enemy's supply roads.[52]

As German armor withdrew to new lines in mid-August, the First Army pressed to the northeast. Meanwhile, the Third Army, with all its corps active for the first time, threw its full weight into the battle. One corps hammered away at fortresses in Brittany, while the others pushed to the north and the east. By 14 August, elements of Patton's forces were north of Argentan; Dreux, Chartres, and Orléans were set as goals for the rest. The Third Army's northern swing sharply compressed General Hodges' zone, pinching out two corps on 15 and 16 August.

As early as 14 August many signs pointed to the enemy's collapse west of the

Seine. Not only were spectacular gains being made in northern France, but a landing in southern France scheduled for 15 August was expected to shake enemy morale.[53] General Eisenhower, sensing the possibilities of the situation, called on the Allied forces to seize the fleeting but definite opportunity to gain a major victory in France. He sent the following appeal to the troops under his command:

I request every airman to make it his direct responsibility that the enemy is blasted unceasingly by day and by night, and is denied safety either in fight or flight.

I request every sailor to make sure that no part of the hostile forces can either escape or be reinforced by sea, and that our comrades on the land want for nothing that guns and ships and ships' companies can bring to them.

I request every soldier to go forward to his assigned objective with the determination that the enemy can survive only through surrender; let no foot of ground once gained be relinquished nor a single German escape through a line once established.[54]

The deterioration of the German position was marked at this point by a com-

---

[51] General Eberbach on 9 August 1944 took command of a provisional *Panzer Group Eberbach* temporarily turning command of the *Fifth Panzer Army* over to SS Oberstgruppenfuehrer und Generaloberst der Waffen SS Sepp Dietrich. *First Army* was transferred from *Army Group G* to *Army Group B* on 11 August 1944.

[52] *OB WEST, KTB 1.-31.VIII.44*, 7 to 11 Aug 44; *Army Group B, Ia Lagebeurteilungen 20.V.-11.X.44* and *Ia Tagesmeldungen 6.VI.-31.VIII.44*, 7 to 11 Aug 44; *Der Westen* (Schramm); *Seventh Army, KTB* (Draft) *6.VI.-16.VIII.44*, 11 Aug 44; MS # B-725 (Gersdorff); OI-SIR/39 (Scheidt); Hitler's order of 11 Aug 44 (*WFSt/Op Nr. 772830/44*). *Army Group B, Ia Fuehrerbefehle, 17.VI.-25.IX.44*, 12 Aug 44; Warlimont statements, 12 and 18 Aug 44. *Der Westen* (Schramm).

[53] See below, Ch. XII, for account of landing in southern France.

[54] Messages to Troops of the AEF, 14 Aug 44, SHAEF AG 335.18. This message was not included in SGS file of the Supreme Commander's messages to AEF, but it was broadcast by General Eisenhower. It was mimeographed and distributed to the troops.

FIELD MARSHAL KESSELRING

FIELD MARSHAL MODEL

highly critical period when the subordinate commanders were clamoring for instructions led Hitler to order first that General Hausser temporarily take command of *Army Group B* and then that Generalfeldmarschall Albert Kesselring and Generalfeldmarschall Walter Model come to OKW. One or the other was to be chosen as successor to von Kluge in case

mand crisis in the west. On 14 August, Hitler, still angered by von Kluge's request for a final decision on Normandy, blamed the Commander in Chief West for the situation which had developed, saying that the difficulties had followed from improper handling of the attack on Avranches. On the morning of the following day von Kluge left the headquarters of the *Fifth Panzer Army* with the intention of meeting the commander of the *Seventh Army* and General Eberbach for a conference at the latter's command post at the front. An Allied strafing attack, which wounded members of his staff and destroyed his radio, prevented von Kluge from reaching Eberbach's headquarters until late in the day. News of his arrival did not reach *OB WEST* or OKW until early the next morning. This absence of the Commander in Chief West during a

he did not return. His absence had another and more sinister effect in that Hitler gave credence to the rumor relayed to him that von Kluge had been on his way to meet Allied representatives to arrange for a surrender of his forces. Confessions that heavily implicated von Kluge had been forcibly obtained from some of the members of the 20 July conspiracy and given to Hitler by Ernst Kaltenbrunner, Chief of the Security Police and Security

Service. The result was that Hitler on 16 August decided to remove von Kluge and appoint Model to the command of *OB WEST*.[55]

Hitler gave orders on 16 August to fight the battle of Falaise to the end. The forces in the pocket astride and west of the Falaise–Argentan road were to be moved first east of the Orne and then east of the Dives. *Army Group B* was to hold the "corner post" of Falaise and widen the escape corridor by mobile action in the area of Argentan. On the 16th General Jodl gave Model some verbal directives on the future conduct of operations in the west, supplementing them with instructions from the Fuehrer for the establishment of a new position as far west as possible in front of the Seine–Yonne line. German forces withdrawing from southwestern and southern France were to be integrated in this new position.[56] The big problem at the moment was to prevent the Allies from crossing the Seine and getting beyond Paris. Shortly before his relief von Kluge discussed this problem with Generalleutnant Dietrich von Choltitz, *Armed Forces Commander Greater Paris,* and directed him to hold the city as long as possible.

On 17 August von Kluge was formally relieved of his command. Two days later, while en route to Germany by car, he took cyanide and died. Suicide, he said in a last letter to Hitler, appeared to be the only honorable course left open to him. While he felt no guilt for the defeat of his forces, he saw little prospect of a sympathetic hearing in Germany. He called upon the Fuehrer to recognize the hopelessness of the German situation and to conclude a peace.[57]

Despite the problems of the enemy, the task of closing in for the final kill in Normandy was not easy. Not only did the *Fifth Panzer* and *Seventh Armies* fight fiercely

to hold open the jaws of the trap that was slowly closing, but the difficulty of readjusting Allied army group boundaries in the battle area interfered with the optimum use of Allied forces committed in the Falaise area. As early as 6 August, the 21 Army Group commander had set a boundary between the British and U.S. forces some sixteen miles south of Falaise and a few miles south of Argentan. On 11 August, in disregard of this arrangement, General Patton directed Maj. Gen. Wade H. Haislip, commander of the XV Corps, to "push on slowly direction of Falaise allowing your rear elements to close. Road: Argentan–Falaise your boundary inclusive. Upon arrival Falaise continue to push on slowly until you contact our Allies."[58]

By the 13th, the XV Corps had reached the vicinity of Argentan and other ele-

---

[55] This shift in command was followed at the beginning of September by the relief and arrest of Generalleutnant Han Speidel, *Army Group B* chief of staff, for suspected complicity in the 20 July plot. *OB WEST, KTB 1.-31.VIII.44; Der Westen* (Schramm); Minutes of conference between Hitler and Generalleutnant Siegfried Westphal and Generalleutnant Hans Krebs on 31 Aug 44, part of the collection known as Minutes of Conferences between Hitler and Members of the German Armed Forces High Command, December 1942–March 1945 (referred to hereafter as Minutes of Hitler Conferences); Jodl Diary, 31 Jul 44; Hans Speidel, *We Defended Normandy* (London, 1951).

[56] *OB WEST, KTB 1.-31.VIII.44,* 16 Aug 44; Warlimont statement, 18 Aug 44. *Der Westen* (Schramm); Lt Col Karl Kleyser statement, 25 Aug 44. *Der Westen* (Schramm).

[57] Von Kluge's suicide was interpreted by the Nazis, particularly by Bormann, as a means of escaping trial and almost certain execution. Minutes of Hitler Conferences, 31 Jul 44; Kluge file, 20 Jul 44 trial collection; Ltr, von Kluge to Hitler, 18 Aug 44, in Dietrich v. Choltitz, *Soldat unter Soldaten* (Zuerich, 1951).

[58] Montgomery dir to army comdrs, M–517, 6 Aug 44, SHAEF SGS 381 Post OVERLORD Planning, I (a); 12th A Gp, Ltr of Instructions 3, 6 Aug 44, 12th A Gp Rpt of Opns, V; CofS Third Army to CG XV Corps, 12 Aug 44, TUSA Rpt of Opns, I.

ments of the Third Army were pushing east and northeast of that city. General Bradley, to avoid colliding with the British forces coming from the north, firmly ordered General Patton to halt at Argentan and build up his forces on that shoulder.[59]

In the next two or three days, between the time that forward elements of General Patton's forces were barred from proceeding north of the army group boundary and the time that a readjustment in the line was made, the enemy withdrew some of his divisions while carrying on counterattacks around the eastern edges of the trap. General Patton felt that the order to halt had deprived him of a chance to take Falaise and close the gap, thus permitting a number of the enemy to escape. How many of the thousands that ultimately got out of the trap could have been held in the Falaise Pocket on 13 or 14 August if forward elements of the Third Army had been pushed across the army group boundary cannot be firmly established. Some of the enemy commanders who were in Normandy at the time were inclined to believe after the war that the rigid boundary had interfered with an envelopment of the *Seventh* and *Fifth Panzer Armies*.[60]

General Eisenhower later explained that the rapidity of U.S. movements during August made it impossible for General Montgomery "to achieve the hour-by-hour coordination that might have won us a complete battle of annihilation." Mix-ups had occurred along the front which could be straightened out only by stopping units in place, even at the expense of permitting some Germans to escape. When U.S. commanders had protested to General Bradley against restrictions on their movements across the interarmy boundary, the Supreme Commander had backed the 12th Army Group command-

er's decision to adhere to the boundary established.[61]

On 15 August, General Montgomery decided to change the boundary to permit U.S. troops to come further north. On the same day, the First Army troops pushed their way to the boundary west of Argentan, and General Hodges asked permission to continue his advance north of the line to Putanges. The 21 Army Group commander, some of whose advisers had previously favored a shift in the line, readily agreed, and the U.S. forces pushed their way across the army group boundary, advancing north of the Flers–Argentan road. Later, he approved U.S. thrusts north of the line toward Chambois and Trun.[62]

From the 15th on, the enemy attempted

---

[59] Bradley, *A Soldier's Story*, pp. 375–77. See George S. Patton, Jr., *War as I Knew It*, p. 105, for suggestion that he may have been stopped because British forces had sowed time bombs in the area. Stacey, *The Canadian Army*, p. 204 (footnote), notes that 12th Army Group informed the British that time bombs had been dropped in the Argentan–Falaise area. Craven and Cate, *The Army Air Forces in World War II*, III, 257–58, says that U.S. air forces did plant time bombs in the area to prevent the enemy's escape but concludes that "the halt order of 13 August could not reasonably have been occasioned by fear that delayed-action bombs would take American lives."

General Bradley in his memoirs notes that General Montgomery had never prohibited nor had he (Bradley) ever proposed that U.S. forces close the gap from Argentan to Falaise. He adds: "To have driven pell-mell into Montgomery's line of advance could easily have resulted in a disastrous error of recognition. In halting Patton at Argentan, however, I did not consult with Montgomery. The decision to stop Patton was mine alone; it never went beyond my CP." (p. 377.)

[60] MS # B-727, The Battle of the Falaise–Argentan Pocket (Gersdorff); MS # B-726, Defensive Fighting of the *Fifth Panzer Army* from 25 July to 25 August 1944 (Gersdorff).

[61] Eisenhower, *Crusade in Europe*, pp. 278–79; Diary Office CinC, 17 Aug 44.

[62] Ltr, Bradley to Eisenhower, 10 Sep 44, Eisenhower personal file; Ltr, Brig Williams to author, 10 Aug 51.

to pull his forces out of the trap near Falaise. Some frantic efforts were made to cut off Allied armored spearheads and thus keep open an escape route to the east. Supply difficulties increased constantly and efforts were made to fly in fuel for the German armored elements covering the retreat. Meanwhile, the 2d Canadian Corps was racing southward to close the gap. General Simonds' two armored divisions, one Canadian and one Polish, were given this task. Canadian forces took Trun on the 18th, while Polish and Canadian forces sped toward Chambois. Here on the evening of 19 August, elements of General Hodges' V Corps met Polish tankers to complete the encirclement of *Seventh Army* and parts of *Fifth Panzer Army,* an estimated 125,000 men.

Withdrawal to the Seine

Just before the trap was closed, Hitler had given Field Marshal Model a number of heavy tasks. The new Commander in Chief West was ordered to withdraw *Seventh Army* across the Seine in order to avoid being cut off, to use armored forces to connect elements forming the ring around Paris, to defend the area southeast of Paris so that *Nineteenth Army* troops from the south of France would be able to withdraw, to prevent an Allied crossing of the Seine south of Paris, and to bar Allied advances in a northerly direction along the lower Seine. These orders came too late to aid many of the forces in the trap. For three days, fighter-bombers and massed artillery had been punishing them as they sought desperately to escape. *Seventh Army,* its position now virtually hopeless, decided to move its headquarters out of the threatened area. Most of the staff escaped, but General Hausser, the army commander, was wounded. Once the pocket was completely closed, the *Fifth Panzer Army,* which Eberbach again commanded, regrouped for a counterattack to free elements of *Seventh Army.* The units still in the trap forced open a small corridor while simultaneously armored elements smashing from east of the encircled area hit the Allies near Trun and St. Lambert-sur-Dives and helped to extricate the escaping units. In the course of heavy fighting during the next three days, some 30,000 to 35,000 soldiers escaped, leaving the bulk of their tanks, vehicles, and artillery behind. The *Fifth Panzer Army,* placed in charge of the entire area from the Channel to just west of Paris, was ordered to collect fleeing units of the entrapped divisions at points west of the Seine. Few of the units were in any condition to continue the fight.[63]

On 19 August, General Eisenhower had discussed with his army group commanders plans for the pursuit of the fleeing enemy. They defined their immediate objective as the destruction of the enemy forces west of the Seine. To gain this end, General Montgomery the following day directed elements of the First Canadian Army and of 12th Army Group to hold

---

[63] Stacey, *The Canadian Army,* pp. 204–06; Craven and Cate, *The Army Air Forces in World War II,* III, 256–75. *Der Westen* (Schramm); *OB WEST, KTB 1.-31.VIII.44,* 15, 16, 17, 19, 20 Aug 44; MS # B-727 (Gersdorff); *Army Group B, Ia Tagesmeldungen 6.VI.-31.VIII.44,* 19, 20 Aug 44; *Fifth Panzer Army, KTB 9.VIII.-9.IX.44,* 20 Aug 44. Rad, *Army Group B to Seventh Army,* 18 Aug 44; Rad, *Army Group B to II SS Panzer Corps* and *Fifth Panzer Army,* 18 Aug 44. Both in *Army Group B, Ia Operations Befehle 9.VI.-31.VIII.44.* Teletype, Army Group B (Ia Nr. 6078/44) to *Fifth Panzer Army,* 16 Aug 44; Order by Model *(Ia Nr. 6376/44)* to *Fifth Panzer Army,* 21 Aug 44. Both in *Fifth Panzer Army, KTB Anlagen 9.VIII.-9.IX.44.* For the information on units that escaped from the Falaise Gap, the author has relied on a special study of German units conducted by Mrs. Magna Bauer of OCMH.

firmly the northern and southern sides of the "bottle" in which the enemy was trapped, keeping the "cork" in position in the eastern end. Other elements of the 12th Army Group were to drive northward to the lower Seine to block the enemy's withdrawal. The 21 Army Group was to give first priority to mopping up the Falaise Pocket before pushing to the Seine. When it was ready for this latter drive, the U.S. forces pushing to the north were to withdraw from the British front.[64]

These widespread shifts of Allied units created great confusion in Allied lines of communications. Already on 19 August, General Eisenhower had reported that U.S. and British units were entangled as a result of "rapid advances and consequent overlapping in attacks on a converging and fluent front." These problems were magnified when U.S. forces made a wide envelopment northward along the left bank of the Seine directly across the Second British Army's front. Generals Montgomery and Dempsey, occupied in mopping up enemy forces in the Falaise Pocket, had accepted the American maneuver as a means of destroying the enemy west of the Seine in that area and of cutting off the German retreat across the Seine.[65]

Elements of both the First and Third Armies wheeled northeast along the left bank of the Seine after 20 August. The Third Army, whose widely separated units had announced the capture of St. Malo on 17 August and the establishment of a bridgehead across the Seine at Mantes-Gassicourt on 20 August, now sent its left wing marching in the direction of Vernon. To its left, the First Army pushed a corps almost due north of Dreux on 20 August. Elements of this unit were in Evreux on the 23d and by the 25th had carried directly across the front of the Second British Army to Elbeuf some eleven miles southwest of Rouen.[66]

The Second British Army started its drive for the Seine on 20 August. Grounding one corps, whose transport was taken for the advance, General Dempsey sent forward the two other corps under his command. One corps passed through U.S. forces northeast of Argentan on the 20th and pushed forward to the Verneuil–Breteuil area where it stopped on the 23d as elements of the First Army drove across its front toward the north. The other corps, moving forward rapidly from Chambois, on the 26th sent elements across the axis of the First Army's advance in preparation for a crossing of the Seine at Louviers. The First Canadian Army, with a Canadian and a British corps under its command, sped eastward on 23 August leaving two divisions to complete mopping up activities in the pocket. The 2d Canadian Corps reached the Seine and made contact with U.S. forces near Elbeuf on the 26th. Meanwhile, General Crerar had sent the British corps under his command along his seaward flank toward the Seine. Despite heavy opposition in the Pont-l'Evêque and Lisieux areas, elements of this unit reached the Seine on 27 August.[67]

---

[64] Notes of a conference between Bradley and Patton, 19 August 1944, in which the former outlined plans agreed on at a previous meeting the same day between Eisenhower, Montgomery, and Bradley; Memo for record, 19 Aug 44. Both in 12th A Gp 371.3 Military Objectives, I. Montgomery dir to army comdrs, M–519, 20 Aug 44, SHAEF SGS 381 Post OVERLORD Planning, I(a).

[65] Bradley to Eisenhower, 10 Sep 44, Eisenhower personal file, discusses the conference with Montgomery and Dempsey in which this envelopment was approved. See also Bradley dir to army comdrs, addenda to Ltr of Instructions 5 (17 Aug 44), 19 Aug 44, 12 A Gp Rpt of Opns, V; Montgomery dir to army comdrs, M–519, 20 Aug 44, SHAEF SGS 381 Post OVERLORD Planning, I(a).

[66] Montgomery, *Normandy to the Baltic*, p. 172.

[67] *Ibid.*, pp. 176–78; Stacey, *The Canadian Army*, pp. 207–08.

The Allies by 26 August had driven the retreating Germans into new pockets near the loops in the lower Seine between El-beuf and Le Havre. No bridges existed across the Seine below Paris, and the fer-ries were insufficient to accommodate the troops hurrying to cross the river. Allied airplanes destroyed the few military bridges that were erected almost as soon as they were set up. Panic increased as troops and vehicles piled up and fighter-bombers blasted massed columns waiting to cross. Allied tanks added to the confu-sion when they reached the river and began firing on the ferries. In view of these difficulties, some German generals later expressed surprise that they were able to bring anything across at all.[68]

Some confusion resulted from the north-ward thrust of U.S. forces across the Brit-ish front. General Montgomery, in author-izing the move, had been aware of this possibility and had authorized direct con-tact between army, corps, and division commanders to settle difficulties. A mis-understanding arose, nevertheless, when General Dempsey was quoted in early September as saying that he had been de-layed forty-eight hours when required to hold back his units while the U.S. forces withdrew. General Bradley, feeling that this statement was a reflection on his com-mand, pointed out that the drive north-ward had been approved by General Montgomery after the 21 Army Group commander had said British forces were not in the position at the moment to carry out the maneuver. The U.S. commander argued that the First Army's push to Elbeuf had speeded the advance of the Second British Army by removing the enemy from its path. General Montgom-ery, informed of the complaint, immedi-ately sent his "profound apologies" to the 12th Army Group commander. General

Dempsey later declared that, while he still believed his troops could have reached the Seine earlier but for the delay caused by the withdrawal of U.S. forces across his front, he would be glad to be held up again if he could have the type of support he received from General Bradley's forces on that occasion.[69]

Although the Allies had not destroyed all of the enemy forces in Normandy, they had won a resounding victory. German troops that escaped to the right bank of the Seine arrived there with little more than their rifles. Five decimated divisions had to be sent to Germany. The broken remnants of the remaining eleven infantry divisions yielded personnel barely suffi-cient for four reconstituted units, each with only a handful of artillery pieces and little other matériel. What remained of five Army and six SS panzer divisions, when bolstered by newly arrived person-nel and matériel replacements, amounted to eleven regimental combat teams, each with five to ten operationally fit tanks and a few batteries of artillery.[70]

---

[68] *OB WEST, KTB 1.-31.VIII.44,* 26 Aug 44; MS # B-729, Report on the Fighting of the Fifth Panzer Army from 24 August to 4 September 44 (Col. Paul Frank); MSS # T-121, 122, and 123, *Geschichte des "Oberbefehlshaber West,"* edited by Generalleutnant Bodo Zimmermann (Ia [G-3] of *OB WEST*), Pt. I, B, IV (referred to hereafter as MS # T-121, MS # T-122, or MS # T-123 [Zimmermann *et al.*]). This is a million-word manuscript prepared in part by Zimmermann, in part by generals and general·staff officers associated with *OB WEST*, OKW, OKL, OKH, OKM, and various subordinate commands. It was written under the auspices of the Historical Division, U. S. War Department, between 1946 and 1948.

[69] Clipping from London *Daily Telegraph and Morning Post,* September 5, 1944, Diary Office CinC; Ltr, Bradley to Eisenhower, 10 Sep 44, Eisenhower per-sonal file; Interv with Dempsey, 12 Mar 47.

[70] Rpt. *Army Group B (Ia Nr. 6704/44)* by Model to Chief *OKW/WFSt,* 29 Aug 44. *Army Group B, Ia Lagebeurteilungen 20.V.-11.X.44.*

CHAPTER XII

The Campaign in Southern France

In mid-August as General Eisenhower's forces closed in on the enemy in the Falaise Pocket and prepared to cross the Seine, a second Allied force landed in southern France with the objects of aiding the battle in Normandy and of opening major ports through which troops could be landed for the impending battle for Germany. This operation, ANVIL, envisaged by the Combined Chiefs of Staff early in 1943 and agreed upon at Tehran in December of that year, had been laid aside temporarily in the spring of 1944. At that time OVERLORD's demands for landing craft required the shifting of resources earmarked for southern France. Some of the British appear to have hoped that they had heard the last of ANVIL, but the U.S. Chiefs of Staff and General Eisenhower continued to insist that it be launched as soon as possible. Because of his confirmed belief that the operation was important to OVERLORD's success, the Supreme Commander became deeply involved in the ANVIL controversy during the late spring and early summer of 1944.

The Second Phase of the ANVIL Controversy

The U.S. Chiefs of Staff and General Eisenhower never relinquished their view that ANVIL was essential to OVERLORD

both to divert enemy forces from the lodgment area in the north and to gain additional ports in the south. While the second factor became the more important as the time approached for the operation, it was the need for diversion which General Eisenhower stressed in June 1944. The British, however, preferred to use available resources in the Mediterranean for a thrust into northern Italy and an advance through the Trieste area and the Ljubljana Gap into central Europe to join forces with Russian troops, who had resumed their advance westward in June. Mr. Churchill made no effort to conceal his pronounced distaste for the landings in southern France and brought pressure on the Supreme Commander and the U.S. Chiefs of Staff to shake the ANVIL concept. On this issue, Mr. Churchill and General Eisenhower differed fundamentally, and the latter was deeply disturbed at the strong feeling evinced by the Prime Minister on the subject.

The Joint Chiefs of Staff before the OVERLORD D Day pressed their British colleagues to name a date for the ANVIL operation. The British Chiefs for their part asked General Wilson, Supreme Allied Commander in the Mediterranean, to suggest alternative plans for operations in his area during the summer and fall of

1944. In mid-May he suggested that the largest amphibious operation likely to be practicable was one launched against southern France in the area of Toulon or Sète, more than one hundred miles due west of Toulon. This would open the way for an advance up the Rhône valley or westward through the Toulouse Gap. Wilson warned, however, that such an operation would leave only limited offensive power for a campaign in Italy.[1]

The entry of the Allies into Rome two days before the Normandy invasion enabled General Wilson on 7 June to declare his readiness to launch an amphibious operation about 15 August on the largest scale permitted by his available resources. The statement found ready listeners at SHAEF where planners were at work on the best means of using strategic reserves to support OVERLORD. To them, an assault in the south of France would help OVERLORD either by diverting enemy forces from the bridgehead or by bringing more Allied troops into France for an all-out attack. In the case of a stalemate, an assault from the Mediterranean seemed essential as a means of drawing enemy forces from Normandy. If, on the other hand, the battle went according to plan, there were more divisions available for the European theater than could be maintained, according to current estimates, through the ports of the lodgment area up to D plus 180. Therefore, the best chance for use of maximum Allied resources against the enemy seemed to lie in ANVIL or some similar operation from the Mediterranean.[2]

Future operations in the Mediterranean theater were discussed by the Combined Chiefs of Staff in London on 11 June. While they expressed a willingness to explore various possibilities, the basic differences which had existed in the early spring between U.S. and British points of view again came to light. Field Marshal Brooke was interested in the possibilities of further advances in Italy in view of General Alexander's belief that he could reach the Pisa–Rimini line by 15 July; Air Chief Marshal Portal noted opportunities for a move northeast by way of Istria if Russian advances from the east made the project feasible. The U.S. Chiefs of Staff, though willing to discuss other plans of action, held firmly to an operation in the western Mediterranean. As a means of initiating planning, the Combined Chiefs of Staff agreed that a three-division assault should be mounted from the Mediterranean about 25 July. General Wilson was made responsible for submitting plans for operations at Sète and Istria, and General Eisenhower for the Bay of Biscay. At the moment the British Chiefs of Staff believed that landings at Sète or on the west coast of France would be the ones most likely to aid the OVERLORD operation.[3] They did not favor a landing in the Marseille area.

General Eisenhower, charged with planning an operation in southwestern France, described Bordeaux as the only worthwhile objective in that area but believed that it was impractical to attack it. In southeastern France, he preferred a landing at Sète to one at Marseille, since the former would make it easier to open

---

[1] AFHQ to JSM and JCS, MEDCOS 110, 17 May 44; AFHQ to Br COS, MEDCOS 111, 18 May 44; AMSSO to SACEA, COSSEA 105, 24 May 44. All in SHAEF SGS 370.2/2 Operation from the Mediterranean in Support of OVERLORD, II.

[2] Wilson to Br COS, MEDCOS 125, 7 Jun 44; SHAEF G-3 Plng Sec Study, Use of the Mediterranean Strategic Reserves, 10 Jan 44. SHAEF SGS 370.2/2 Operation from the Mediterranean in Support of OVERLORD, II.

[3] CCS Conf, 163d Mtg, London, 11 Jun 44; CCS to Wilson, OZ-3116, 14 Jun 44. Both in SHAEF SGS 370.2/2 Operation from the Mediterranean in Support of OVERLORD, II.

Bordeaux. As to a choice between the Adriatic and southern France, he favored the latter since a landing there would keep more Germans away from the lodgment area in the north. In addition, it would "reap the benefit of French resistance," which he said was yielding results beyond his expectations and was particularly strong in the south of France.[4]

The Mediterranean Supreme Commander on 17 June discussed the problem with his commanders in chief and with Generals Marshall and Arnold. While preferring an operation which would give complete support to a thrust from the Po valley into central Europe, he was impressed by General Marshall's argument which

brought out clearly for the first time a point which seems to be of paramount importance . . . namely that there are between 40 and 50 divisions in the United States which cannot be introduced into France as rapidly as desired or maintained there through the ports of Northwest France or by staging through the United Kingdom; and, therefore, if the weight of these divisions is to be brought to bear upon the enemy in France, we must seize another major port at an early date.[5]

General Wilson next turned to the British thesis that OVERLORD could be aided elsewhere than in the south of France. Since by 19 June there no longer seemed to be any fear about the security of the beachhead, he emphasized a strategy that would divert German units from France and face the enemy with prospects of defeat in 1944. He conceded that, if the main consideration was seizure of another major port, the ANVIL operation should be carried out as planned. In this case, he preferred an assault against Toulon rather than the Sète area inasmuch as the former would make the most effective use of

French Resistance forces, make available the huge port capacity of Marseille, and virtually end the submarine menace in the Mediterranean.

Set over against these advantages, which seemed to be sufficient to prove the case of the U.S. Chiefs of Staff, was the fact that ANVIL could not be launched until 15 August at the earliest without danger of prejudicing the fight in Italy south of the Pisa–Rimini line. Stopping the Allied forces in front of the Pisa–Rimini line, he said, meant breaking up a first-class fighting force after months of co-operation, and switching forces from Italy to southern France would impose a six-week pause on the Mediterranean operation which would permit the enemy to rest and regroup his forces. General Wilson proposed, instead, that the Allies exploit "the present success in Italy through the Pisa–Rimini line across the Po and then . . . advance toward southern Hungary through the Ljubljana Gap," the latter advance being taken in conjunction with amphibious and airborne attacks against the enemy to divert at least ten divisions from the Balkans and France into northern Italy.

General Eisenhower presented a different view of the ANVIL operation to the Combined Chiefs of Staff four days later. He stressed the fact that OVERLORD was the decisive campaign of 1944 and that a stalemate would be regarded by the world as a defeat, with possible far-reaching effects on the war effort of the Russians. With the Bordeaux expedition precluded, he found that the ANVIL operation pro-

---

[4] Eisenhower to Wilson, S–53967, 16 Jun 44, SHAEF SGS 370.2/2 Operation from the Mediterranean in Support of OVERLORD, II.

[5] This and the two succeeding paragraphs are based on General Wilson's letter to General Eisenhower, 19 June 1944, SHAEF SGS 370.2/2 Operation from the Mediterranean in Support of OVERLORD, II.

vided the most direct route to northern France, "where the battles for the Ruhr will be fought." Such an operation would not only divert enemy divisions from the OVERLORD area, but also provide a port through which reinforcements from the United States could be deployed and a route over which they could advance for battle in northern France. While agreeing that the port of Marseille was less desirable than Bordeaux from the standpoint of distance from the United States and of proximity to the OVERLORD area, the time factor was so important that he thought the Bordeaux operation could be rejected in favor of the ANVIL operation. "France," he insisted, "is the decisive theater. This decision was taken long ago by the Combined Chiefs of Staff. In my view, the resources of Great Britain and the U.S. will not permit us to maintain two major theaters in the European War, each with decisive missions." He recommended, therefore, that the Mediterranean resources be used to launch the ANVIL operation not later than 30 August and preferably fifteen days earlier. Anticipating a renewed proposal for an advance in the Adriatic area, he asked that if ANVIL was not launched by 30 August all French divisions and one or two U.S. divisions allocated for ANVIL be made available for OVERLORD operations as soon as they could be brought into the latter area.[6]

The U.S. Chiefs of Staff immediately gave their blessing to General Eisenhower's arguments, suggesting only that 1 August was a better date for the operation and ruling unacceptable any proposals to commit Mediterranean resources in large-scale operations in either northern Italy or the Balkans. To General Eisenhower's reasons for preferring the ANVIL operation, they added that it would put

French troops into the fight for their homeland, employ a number of battle-trained U.S. troops from the Mediterranean, make the best possible use of the air build-up in Corsica, and concentrate the Allied forces and put them into battle in the decisive theater.[7]

Prime Minister Churchill, whether he was disturbed by the tone of this communication, which he described as "arbitrary," or whether he saw in the American stand an end to any hope of further major advances in the Mediterranean, now opened a strong campaign with the President and the Supreme Commander to break the "deadlock" which he found existing between the British and U.S. Chiefs of Staff. On receipt of the U.S. note, he cabled Mr. Roosevelt asking that the latter "consent to hear both sides" before making up his mind. He expressed his willingness to help General Eisenhower, but not at the expense of the complete ruin "of our great affairs in the Mediterranean and we take it hard that this should be demanded of us." In a lengthy survey of the question, he held that a landing place must be chosen in relation to both the main effort of Eisenhower and the strain on Germany. Political considerations such as revolts or surrender of satellites he also believed to be valid and important factors. He found the taking of Le Havre and St. Nazaire to have a far closer relation to the battle than the seizure of ports in the Mediterranean, and believed that an action from Bayonne or some smaller port on the Bay of Biscay to take Bordeaux was to be preferred to a "heavy footed" ap-

---

[6] Eisenhower to CCS, SCAF 53, 23 Jun 44, SHAEF SGS 370.2/2 Operation from the Mediterranean in Support of OVERLORD, II.

[7] JSM to AMSSO, JSM 112, 24 Jun 44, SHAEF SGS 370.2/2 Operation from the Mediterranean in Support of OVERLORD, II.

proach from Sète. Pointing to the 400 miles from Marseille to Paris, and the additional 200 miles to Cherbourg, he called an attack in the Marseille area "bleak and sterile" and found it difficult to believe that an operation there or at Toulon or Sète could have any influence on OVERLORD in the coming summer and fall. He agreed that the proposed operation for the Adriatic was equally unrelated to OVERLORD, but cited General Wilson's belief that he could have Trieste by September. In the light of these arguments, he declared:

Whether we should ruin all hopes of a major victory in Italy and all its fronts and condemn ourselves to a passive role in that theatre, after having broken up the fine Allied army which is advancing so rapidly through that Peninsula, for the sake of ANVIL with all its limitations, is indeed a grave question for His Majesty's Government and the President, with the Combined Chiefs of Staff, to decide.[8]

Before he received the last cables of the Prime Minister, President Roosevelt had concurred completely with the stand of the U.S. Chiefs of Staff and had declared unacceptable General Wilson's proposal to use nearly all Mediterranean resources for an advance into northern Italy and thence to the northeast. He agreed that nothing could be worse than a deadlock of the Combined Chiefs of Staff as to a future course, adding: "You and I must prevent this and I think we should support the views of the Supreme Allied Commander. He is definitely for ANVIL and wants action in the field by August 30th preferably earlier."[9]

This answer did not deter the British Chiefs of Staff and the Prime Minister from making other attempts to change the U.S. stand. General Eisenhower encouraged the Washington Chiefs to hold their

ground with a statement on 29 June that while he believed the British were honestly convinced that a drive toward Trieste would aid OVERLORD more than an assault in southern France, and would make one more attempt to persuade the U.S. Chiefs of Staff of the value of the Trieste move, they would not permit "an impasse to arrive" and would "consequently agree to ANVIL." He thought that in such an event they would propose to strengthen that operation, with General Alexander taking over responsibility for ANVIL as the principal offensive in the Mediterranean theater. "I would personally be glad to see him in charge. . . . Since in the long run France is to be more the business of Britain than of ours, I would be delighted to see more British divisions in that country."[10]

General Eisenhower's prediction as to the approaching British decision on ANVIL proved correct. The Prime Minister on 1 July in the course of a telephone conversation with the Supreme Commander, during which the latter stressed the need of an additional port through which to pour U.S. divisions waiting in the United States, indicated that he would approve the operation. On the following day the Combined Chiefs of Staff issued a directive to General Wilson along the lines of the earlier U.S. proposals. The Mediter-

[8] Churchill to Roosevelt, 714, 25 Jun 44; Prime Minister to President, 718, 28 Jun 44; Prime Minister to President, 717, 28 Jun 44. All in OPD Exec 10, 63c.

[9] President to Prime Minister, 575, 28 Jun 44, OPD Exec 10, 63b. A note on the message indicated that this was in answer to 714. It would appear to have been sent before messages 717 and 718 were received. The entire correspondence is summarized in the following messages from Marshall to Eisenhower: W-58039, W-58040, W-58041, 29 Jun 44, Eisenhower personal file.

[10] Eisenhower to Marshall, S-54760, 29 Jun 44, Eisenhower personal file.

ranean commander was instructed to make every possible effort to launch ANVIL on a basis of a three-division assault by 14 August. The SHAEF commander was directed to release as early as possible the additional resources required for ANVIL—in accordance with agreements already concluded with the Mediterranean commander.[11]

During late June, while the broader strategy in the Mediterranean was being discussed, representatives of SHAEF and AFHQ had worked out details on the release of naval support and landing craft as well as air strength needed from northwest Europe for the ANVIL operation. SHAEF, hard pressed in matters of supply, won a postponement until 15 July of the shifting of landing craft requested by AFHQ and indicated a desire not to release any aircraft unless General Wilson considered it absolutely necessary. Similar delays were requested on the release of warships required for ANVIL but permitted to be kept by SHAEF until after the taking of Cherbourg. Agreements relative to the shift of resources for an airborne operation were arranged in early July.[12]

As the commander in whose interest the landings in the Mediterranean were to be launched and as the future chief of the forces participating in ANVIL, General Eisenhower on 6 July outlined the objectives of the ANVIL operation for General Wilson. He described these as (1) containing and destroying forces that might otherwise oppose OVERLORD, (2) securing a major port in southern France for the entry of additional forces, (3) advancing northward to threaten enemy flanks and communications, and (4) developing lines of communications to support ANVIL forces and later reinforcements. These aims could be achieved by securing the

Marseille area and marching up the Rhône to Lyon. General Wilson was to retain the ANVIL command until SHAEF assumed the responsibility. The Mediterranean commander was also to have administrative charge of the ANVIL forces, including civil affairs in the area south and east of the departments of Doubs, Côte-d'Or, Nièvre, Allier, Puy-de-Dôme, Cantal, Aveyron, Tarn, and Haute-Garonne, and be prepared to maintain ANVIL forces beyond that area if SHAEF was unable to do so. In order to insure uniformity in civil affairs policy, General Wilson was asked to administer these matters in accordance with SHAEF's interim directive of 14 May 1944, which had been issued to the Mediterranean commander as a guide in civil affairs planning for southern France. Control of Resistance forces in the southern area of France was passed to General Wilson, but SHAEF retained responsibility for co-ordinating Resistance policy throughout France. SHAEF was to supply the Resistance forces in the south of France in order to develop maximum French aid for ANVIL. General Eisenhower's headquarters also undertook the task of co-ordinating publicity and psychological warfare in the ANVIL area.[13]

[11] Diary Office CinC, 1 Jul 44; CCS to AFHQ, COSMED 139, 2 Jul 44, SHAEF SGS 370.2/2 Operation from the Mediterranean in Support of OVERLORD, II.

[12] SHAEF to CCS, SCAF 54, 26 Jun 44; Memo, G-4 SHAEF for CAO, 26 Jun 44; Wilson to Br COS, MEDCOS 131, 24 Jun 44; Mtg, SHAEF, 26 Jun 44, relative to release of forces from OVERLORD for Mediterranean; ANCXF to NCWTF, 27 Jun 44; COMNAVEU to SHAEF, 19 Jun 44; ANCXF to SHAEF, 20 Jun 44; outgoing msg, COMNAVEU, 22 Jun 44; Memo for CofS, sgd Moore, 22 Jun 44. All in SHAEF SGS 370.2/2 Operation from the Mediterranean in Support of OVERLORD, II.

[13] SHAEF to AFHQ, S-55130, 6 Jul 44, SHAEF SGS 370.2/2 Operation from the Mediterranean in Support of OVERLORD, II.

General Wilson accepted most of the suggestions outlined by the Supreme Commander, but emphasized that his supply services were prepared only to support an advance 225 miles from the invasion area and would have to have additional outside aid if further demands were made on them. Besides preparing the ANVIL operation, General Wilson intended to press the attack in Italy to seize the line of the Po and then advance north of that river to secure the line Venice–Padua–Verona–Brescia.[14]

Meanwhile, the British Chiefs of Staff continued their opposition to ANVIL. Lest there be any doubt as to their attitude, they cabled Washington on 12 July that neither His Majesty's Government nor the British Chiefs of Staff considered Operation ANVIL the "correct strategy" for the Allies, and that they had given way only to dispel the view that the British were using delaying tactics to gain their point. They assured the U.S. Chiefs of Staff, however, that having accepted the decision they would do their utmost to make it work. Mr. Churchill wrote along a similar line to Mr. Hopkins on 19 July, saying: "We have submitted under protest to the decision of the United States Chiefs of Staff even in a theatre where we have been accorded the right to nominate the Supreme Commander. You can be sure we shall try our best to make the operation a success. I only hope it will not ruin greater projects."[15]

Mr. Churchill apparently by early July had given up hope of shifting the Allied effort from southern France. However, after the breakout in Normandy he cabled the President that, since the course of events in Normandy and Brittany had given good prospects that the whole of the Brittany peninsula would soon be in Al-

lied hands, they should consider switching ANVIL "into the main and vital theatre where it can immediately play the part at close quarters in the great and victorious battles in which we are now engaged."[16] He threw out the suggestion that they might find some point from St. Nazaire northward along the Brittany peninsula already liberated by U.S. troops where a landing could be made. The divisions assigned to ANVIL/DRAGOON could thus be brought in rapidly and sent into battle by the shortest route across France. The President, who had been absent since mid-July on a trip which took him to Pearl Harbor, apparently made no immediate reply, and Mr. Churchill next expressed his fears to Mr. Hopkins. The latter felt that supply problems involved in shifting the landings to the Brittany peninsula were insurmountable, and that the President would not agree to a change. Hopkins believed that the attack from the south would go much more quickly than expected and that "a tremendous victory" was in store for the Allies. The President shortly afterward sent a similar message, giving as his considered opinion: "ANVIL should be launched as planned at the earliest practicable date and I have full confidence that it will be successful and of

---

[14] Wilson to Eisenhower, F–69283, 6 Jul 44; Wilson to Eisenhower, FX 69883, 8 Jul 44; Wilson to Br COS, FX 69815, 8 Jul 44. All in SHAEF SGS 370.2/2 Operation from the Mediterranean in Support of OVERLORD, II.

[15] Br COS to JSM, 12 Jul 44, Eisenhower personal file; Prime Minister to Hopkins, 19 Jul 44, OPD Exec 10, 63b.

[16] Mr. Churchill actually used the new code name DRAGOON which had been chosen for ANVIL a few days before. Such changes were frequently made in the name of an operation in the fear that the original had become known to the enemy. In order to avoid confusion for the reader, the term ANVIL/DRAGOON will hereafter be used except in the case of direct quotations.

great assistance to Eisenhower in driving the Hun from France." [17]

Meanwhile, the Prime Minister made a final effort to change the views of the Supreme Commander. On 5 August, Mr. Churchill, meeting with General Eisenhower and Admirals Cunningham, Ramsay, and William G. Tennant, had warned of the great opportunity which would be missed if the ANVIL/DRAGOON forces were not moved from the Toulon area to Brest, Lorient, St. Nazaire, or perhaps even the Channel ports. Admiral Cunningham supported the Prime Minister against General Eisenhower, who was backed by Admirals Ramsay and Tennant. Holding the view that sound strategy required the Allies to force the Germans to fight on the maximum number of fronts, General Eisenhower adhered to the original plan. To make certain that no doubt existed as to his position, the Supreme Commander cabled Washington that he would not "under any conditions agree at this moment to a cancellation of DRAGOON." General Wilson also struck a blow at the Prime Minister's arguments at this point when he reported that, even though the French forces could be diverted to the Brittany ports without difficulty, the U.S. forces had started loading and any change would lead to delay. [18]

Despite these statements, the Prime Minister took up the question again with General Eisenhower in several interviews which proved unusually trying for the Supreme Commander. On 9 August, in a meeting at 10 Downing Street described by General Eisenhower as one of the most difficult sessions in which he engaged during the war, the Prime Minister pressed his point. Intimating that the United States was taking the role of "a big strong and dominating partner" rather than at-

tempting to understand the British position, the Prime Minister expressed his concern at the apparent indifference of the United States toward the Italian campaign. [19] Obviously "stirred, upset and even despondent," Mr. Churchill seemed to feel that the success of his whole administration would be involved in the failure to push General Alexander's drive to the north. General Eisenhower suggested that if Mr. Churchill had political reasons for backing a campaign into the Balkans he should take up the matter with President Roosevelt. The Supreme Commander was willing to change his plan of campaign if political considerations were to be paramount; on military grounds alone he felt he could not yield. Mr. Churchill continued to press his case. These arguments, however painful to General Eisenhower, did not change his views, and he again assured the War Department of his strong opposition to "a cancellation or a major modification of DRAGOON." [20]

With this new evidence that the United States would not yield, the British Chiefs of Staff on 10 August notified General Wilson that he was to proceed with

---

[17] Br COS to JSM, 5 Aug 44, Eisenhower personal file. Prime Minister to President, 742, 4 Aug 44; Hopkins to Prime Minister (given in Memo for SGS, 7 Aug 44); President to Prime Minister, 596, 7 Aug 44; Prime Minister to President, 7 Aug 44. All in OPD Exec 10, 63b. Summaries of three messages given in Sherwood, *Roosevelt and Hopkins*, pp. 810, 812–13.

[18] Butcher, *My Three Years With Eisenhower*, p. 635; Eisenhower to Marshall, FWD–12612, 5 Aug 44, Eisenhower personal file; Wilson to CCS, FX 79468, 5 Aug 44, AFHQ file; Eisenhower, *Crusade in Europe*, pp. 281–84.

[19] The quoted words are General Eisenhower's paraphrase.

[20] Eisenhower to Marshall, 9 and 11 Aug 44, Eisenhower personal file. Butcher, *My Three Years With Eisenhower*, p. 639, and Eisenhower, *Crusade in Europe*, pp. 281–84, reconstruct parts of the conversation.

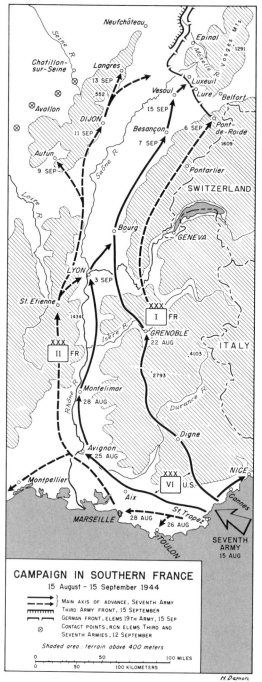

CAMPAIGN IN SOUTHERN FRANCE
15 August – 15 September 1944

⟶ } MAIN AXIS OF ADVANCE, SEVENTH ARMY
⟶ THIRD ARMY FRONT, 15 SEPTEMBER
⟶ GERMAN FRONT, ELEMS 19TH ARMY, 15 SEP
⊗ CONTACT POINTS, RCN ELEMS THIRD AND
      SEVENTH ARMIES, 12 SEPTEMBER

Shaded area : terrain above 400 meters

0   50   100 MILES
0   50   100 KILOMETERS

H. Damon

MAP 2

ANVIL/DRAGOON as planned, a directive which was confirmed by the Combined Chiefs of Staff on the following day—only four days before the landing.[21]

Deeply distressed by the interview of 9 August, General Eisenhower attempted to reassure the Prime Minister of the good faith and good will of the U.S. Chiefs of Staff. He denied that there was any intent on the part of anyone in the U.S. war machine to disregard British views or "cold-bloodedly to leave Britain holding an empty bag in any of our joint undertakings." In his concluding paragraphs, he stressed the degree of co-operation which had been achieved in the Allied staffs:

In two years I think we have developed such a fine spirit and machinery in our field direction that no consideration of British versus American interests ever occurs to any of the individuals comprising my staff or serving as one of my principal commanders. I would feel that much of my hard work over the past months had been irretrievably lost if we now should lose faith in the organisms that have given higher direction to our war effort, because such lack of faith would quickly be reflected in discord in our field command.

During all these months I have leaned on you often, and have always looked to you with complete confidence when I felt the need of additional support. This adds a sentimental to my very practical reasons for hoping, most earnestly, that in spite of disappointment, we will all adhere tenaciously to the concepts of control brought forth by the President and yourself two and one half years ago.[22]

Mr. Churchill quickly set the matter right on 15 August with this message:

Thank you for your kind letter of August 11. Many congratulations on brilliant opera-

---

[21] Br COS to AFHQ, 10 Aug 44; CCS to AFHQ, 11 Aug 44. Both in SHAEF cbl log.

[22] Eisenhower to Prime Minister, 11 Aug 44, Eisenhower personal file.

tions in Anjou and Normandy. There must have been a magnificent fight and logistic penetration of American turning movement will long excite wonder. Every good wish.[23]

The Landings and the Advance

General Wilson launched the long-awaited attack on the southern coast of France on 15 August. *(Map 2)* British,

GENERAL DE LATTRE DE TAS-SIGNY

GENERAL PATCH

French, and U.S. forces under Lt. Gen. Alexander M. Patch, commander of the Seventh U.S. Army, began landing that morning against light opposition in the area east of Toulon. French forces under Gen. Jean de Lattre de Tassigny, commander of French Army B, landed over the U.S. beaches on the second day and started their drive for Toulon and Marseille. General de Lattre commanded the

II French Corps in the assault and was subordinated to General Patch. It was understood that later he would revert to command of the French Army.[24]

At the time of the landings, *Army Group G* had eleven divisions with which to hold France south of the Loire. OKW had considered withdrawing General Blaskowitz' forces to a line nearer to the German bor-

[23] Prime Minister to Eisenhower, 15 Aug 44, Eisenhower personal file.
[24] The author has drawn some operational details of this chapter from the official history of the campaign in southern France prepared in the OCMH by Maj. James David T. Hamilton. See also *Report by the Supreme Allied Commander Mediterranean to the Combined Chiefs of Staff on the Operation in Southern France, August 1944* (Washington, 1946); Seventh Army Rpt of Opns, I; and Gen. Jean de Lattre de Tassigny, *Histoire de la Première Armée Française* (Paris, 1949). Two important German sources are *Der Westen* (Schramm) and MS # T–121 (Zimmermann *et al.*).

der, but had taken no action when the attack came. In the face of a major Allied offensive, OKW on 17–18 August ordered *Army Group G* to evacuate both the Atlantic and Mediterranean coasts except for the fortresses and ports. The *LXIV Corps,* which had been in charge of troops in southwestern France since *First Army* was withdrawn a few weeks before to build up a Seine defense line southeast of Paris, formed three march groups and withdrew eastward, south of the Loire, toward Dijon. *Nineteenth Army,* meanwhile, retreated northward through the Rhône valley toward the Plateau de Langres.[25]

The first two weeks of the Allied attack exceeded all expectations as to the speed with which the initial objectives were seized. The period saw two major ports, Toulon and Marseille, opened and more than 57,000 prisoners taken at the cost of 4,000 French and 2,700 American casualties. The only direct effect of the landings on the fortunes of OVERLORD seems to have been the cancellation of movement orders for the *338th Division,* which was already on its way to Normandy.[26] Indirectly, however, the scattering of enemy forces south of the Loire and the approach of Allied forces to the 12th Army Group's right flank meant the strengthening of General Eisenhower's position. More important to later operations in the north was the promise that the opening of Marseille would provide a new port through which men and supplies could be brought for a sustained drive into Germany. General Eisenhower, greatly pleased at the success of ANVIL/DRAGOON, was gratified still further when the Prime Minister, who had observed the landings, wired:

I watched this landing yesterday from afar. All I have seen there makes me admire the perfect precision with which the landing

was arranged and intimate collaboration of British-American forces.

Mindful of the difficulties which had preceded the operation, the Supreme Commander replied:

I am delighted to note in your latest telegram to me that you have personally and legally adopted the DRAGOON. I am sure that he will grow fat and prosperous under your watchfulness. If you can guarantee that your presence at all such operations will have the same effect that it did in this wonderful show I will make sure that in my future operations in this theater you are given a fleet of your own. I hope you will hurry back to us as I have many things to talk over with you. With warm and respectful regard. IKE.[27]

In early September the U.S. and French forces pushed northward toward Lyon and Dijon to prevent a junction between enemy forces from the south and southwest and to bar their escape routes to Germany. The enemy evacuated Lyon before the French and U.S. forces arrived there on 3 September, and Dijon fell to the French without a fight on the 11th. On the following day, French forces that had pushed beyond Dijon in the direction of the Third U.S. Army made a junction with OVERLORD units near Châtillon-sur-Seine.[28]

The junction of Allied forces spelled defeat for those enemy forces from southwest-

---

[25] *Armeegruppe G* (referred to hereafter as *Army Group G) KTB Nr. 2* and *Anlagen 1.VII–30.IX.44; OB WEST, KTB 1.–31.VIII.44; Der Westen* (Schramm); OB WEST, A Study in Command (Zimmermann *et al.*), written under the auspices of the Department of the Army Historical Division in 1946.

[26] *OB WEST, KTB 1.–31.VIII.44,* 15 Aug 44.

[27] Prime Minister to Eisenhower, 18 Aug 44; Eisenhower to Wilson for Prime Minister, 24 Aug 44. Both in Eisenhower personal file.

[28] The time and place of the first meeting like that of so many other junctions during the war is a subject of some controversy. Individual jeeploads of soldiers and at least one courier plane had sought out elements of the other of the approaching forces before

ern France still west of Dijon. Two of the three march groups which had started from the Atlantic area and other miscellaneous units passed Dijon before that city was captured, but the third unit, *Group Elster,* some 20,000 strong, including elements of the *159th Division* and a large number of noncombatant personnel (administrative personnel, Wehrmacht civilian personnel, auxiliary workers), proceeded more slowly and was cut off by the junction at Châtillon-sur-Seine. Continually harassed by the French Forces of the Interior and the XIX Tactical Air Command and cut off from Germany by the Third Army's advance, this group began negotiations for capitulation on 10 September and formally surrendered on the 16th. The final honor of accepting the surrender went to the Ninth U.S. Army, which had recently been assigned the Third Army's sector along the Loire. In recognition of the role played by the air forces in protecting the Allied right flank and in forcing the enemy surrender, the Ninth Army commander invited the commanding general of the XIX Tactical Air Command to take part in the ceremonies.[29]

Upon the link-up of General Eisenhower's forces with those advancing from the south, the direction of the French attack was changed to conform to the Supreme Commander's original views. The II French Corps suspended its advance northward and regrouped its forces between VI U.S. Corps (Lt. Gen. Lucian K.

Truscott) and the I French Corps. The U.S. forces seized Vesoul on 13 September, thus blocking the last escape route to Belfort in the U.S. zone. On 16 September General Truscott's corps occupied Lure and Luxeuil-les-Bains, which controlled two other important corridors to Germany, but was not in time to catch the main body of enemy forces. The U.S. divisions, as a result of supply shortages and stiffening enemy resistance, now came almost to a halt some fifteen miles short of the Moselle while awaiting relief by the II French Corps and the general regrouping of Allied forces.

On 15 September a major change in command had been made. By agreement between General Eisenhower and General Wilson, the forces from the Mediterranean passed to SHAEF control and were placed under the 6th Army Group (Lt. Gen. Jacob L. Devers) which became operational on that date. Control of French Army B, soon to be named First French Army, was given to 6th Army Group.

In the month which had passed since Allied forces stormed ashore in southern France, the forces of General Patch and General de Lattre had swept westward from the assault beaches to Avignon and northward up the Rhône valley for a distance of more than 400 air-line miles. Their rapid advance had forced the enemy to evacuate France south of the Loire, except for a few ports, and had inflicted heavy losses on *Army Group G.* Some consolation for the Germans remained in the fact that General Blaskowitz' skillful handling of the retreat had saved more than half of his forces. Despite this action, he

12 September, and reconnaissance elements of the OVERLORD and ANVIL/DRAGOON forces had met at Sombernon on the evening of 10–11 September. Seventh Army Rpt of Opns, I, 271–72; TUSA AAR, I, 69. *Report by the Supreme Allied Commander Mediterranean* prefers 11 September as the date of meeting; de Lattre, *Histoire de la Première Armée Française,* pp. 161–62, accepts the 12 September date.

[29] OB WEST, A Study in Command (Zimmermann *et al.*); *OB WEST KTB 1.-30.IX.44,* 5 and 9 Sep 44; *Conquer: The Story of Ninth Army, 1944–45* (Washington, 1947), pp. 47–50; TUSA AAR, I, 50.

was replaced on 21 September by General der Panzertruppen Hermann Balck, then commander of the *Fourth Panzer Army* on the Eastern Front. *Army Group G,* to which the *Fifth Panzer Army* had been transferred in the hope that it could deliver a counter-attack against the Third Army from the Plateau de Langres, by mid-September took up the protection of the left wing of the German line north of the Swiss border. The *Fifth Panzer Army* and part of the *First* *Army* were committed against the Third U.S. Army, and the battered *Nineteenth Army* was given the task of opposing the French and U.S. forces under General Devers.[30]

---

[30] *Fifth Panzer Army* was taken out of the line on 6 September 1944 and attached directly to *OB WEST;* on 11 September 1944 it was assigned to *Army Group G. First Army* was transferred from *Army Group B* to *Army Group G* on 8 September 1944.

CHAPTER XIII

Relations With the French, June–September 1944

The Supreme Commander had become painfully aware, long before D Day, that smooth relations with General de Gaulle and the French Committee of National Liberation were of critical importance to Allied operations. Involved in this question were such matters as the administration of civil affairs in liberated France, the command of French Resistance forces, and the establishment of a provisional government in Paris after its liberation. General Eisenhower was concerned, therefore, with Allied efforts to establish a working arrangement with the French Committee.

Civil Affairs

Civil affairs activities in France during the first phase of operations were under the general control of the 21 Army Group.[1] Not until the activation of a U.S. army group did SHAEF assume direct responsibility for these operations in the field. During the first weeks of the invasion, therefore, many of the decisions relative to the re-establishment of civil affairs administration in Normandy were handled directly at 21 Army Group. The fact that the British Government was more inclined to recognize the French Committee than was the United States may have sim-plified the task of General Montgomery's officers in dealing with the Gaullist representatives in Normandy.

In those civil affairs problems which required decisions at governmental levels, SHAEF was involved directly—the more so in cases that meant any implied recognition of the sovereignty of the French Committee, particularly in those instances where the Foreign Office and the State Department appeared willing to go farther than the President toward co-operation with de Gaulle. Where the matter affected military operations, the Supreme Commander was sometimes approached in the hope that he could help in finding a working solution to the problem.

An example of the type of case which came to General Eisenhower's attention was that relating to the issuance of invasion currency to Allied troops. Like many other French civil affairs questions this had been discussed by French and Allied representatives since 1943, and had bogged down on the issue of the sovereignty of the French Committee. In an effort to avoid depreciating French currency by issuing yellow-seal dollars and British Military Authority notes to the troops, as in Italy, the British and U.S. au-

---

[1] See above, p. 83.

thorities arranged in December 1943 to print special invasion money in Washington for the use of the armies. Before this could be done, the British Ambassador "unexpectedly" notified the State Department that his government preferred a French national currency issued by the French Committee of National Liberation. The immediate effect was to delay any decision on the issue for a number of weeks. To bring the matter to a head, the British Secretary of State for War, Sir James Grigg, appealed to General Eisenhower at the end of January 1944, reminding him that currency was "a vital if uninteresting necessity to successful operations." [2] If General Eisenhower had ever doubted the necessity of settling such problems promptly, he had sufficient reason to change his mind when they continued to reappear in the spring and summer of 1944.

In early May, General Eisenhower forwarded to Washington proposals based on preliminary discussions with the French Military Mission in London regarding the whole financial situation in France. After a period of three weeks, having received no direction on the problem, he proposed as "a solution of desperation" to issue a proclamation declaring the supplemental francs legal tender. The Supreme Commander and his chief of staff doubted their legal right to issue such a proclamation and feared it would be considered a flagrant violation of French sovereignty, but they felt they would have to take such action unless they received other instructions by 28 May.

Before this second proposal was received, General Eisenhower's program of early May had been approved in principle at "the highest American level," subject to certain specified conditions, and passed on to the Combined Chiefs of Staff for study. Among these conditions were the following: arrangements made with the French Committee of National Liberation must not preclude consultation with or the reception of aid from other representatives of the French people; authority for issuing supplemental francs belonged to SHAEF, and any statement of the French Committee of National Liberation would merely be a supporting announcement. [3]

No agreement had been reached with the French by the time General de Gaulle reached London shortly before D Day. He was dissatisfied when he found that limited quantities of supplemental francs in small denominations had actually been given to British and U.S. soldiers in the assault units, and that larger quantities were ready when needed to supplement the five and one-half billion metropolitan francs put at the disposal of Allied forces by the War Office. His anger at this assumption of what he considered to be a prerogative of the French Committee of National Liberation apparently influenced him to forbid the 180 French liaison officers trained for civil affairs duties to sail with the assault units on D Day. He finally relented sufficiently to permit twenty liaison officers to accompany Allied troops. [4]

President Roosevelt's announcement on 9 June that General de Gaulle would be welcome in Washington for a visit in late

---

[2] Grigg to Eisenhower, 27 Jan 44; Hilldring to Barker, 17 Dec 43; CCS to Eisenhower, 31 Jan 44. All in SHAEF SGS 123 Invasion Currency, I.

[3] Eisenhower to CCS for CCAC, VOG 32, 4 May 44; Eisenhower to CCS for CCAC, VOG 53, 25 May 44; Smith to McCloy, S–52510, 25 May 44; Hilldring to Holmes, 41408, 25 May 44 (written on 25 May, but not sent until the following day), SHAEF SGS 123 Invasion Currency, I.

[4] New York *Times*, June 8, 1944; Eisenhower to CCS, VOG 65, 9 Jun 44, SHAEF SGS 123 Invasion Currency, I.

June or early July raised some hope for an early agreement on currency and other questions. General de Gaulle dashed this hope almost immediately by his statement that no agreement existed between the French Committee and the United States and Great Britain regarding French co-operation in the administration of liberated France. He feared that General Eisenhower's address and proclamation to the French, which made no mention of General de Gaulle and the French Committee of National Liberation, foreshadowed "a sort of taking over of power in France by the Allies' military command." He warned that "the issuance of a so-called French currency in France without any agreement and without any guarantee from the French authority can lead only to serious complications." [5]

Mr. Churchill promptly urged President Roosevelt to make a decision on the currency question. While the Prime Minister did not believe that General de Gaulle would brand the invasion francs as counterfeit, as he was rumored to be ready to do, he feared that the Allies faced the alternatives of permitting de Gaulle to obtain new status as the price for backing the notes or of themselves guaranteeing the money. The President, with the tone of irritation he frequently showed where de Gaulle was concerned, suggested telling the French general that, if the French people would not accept the invasion currency, General Eisenhower would be authorized to use British Military Authority money and yellow-seal dollars. Therefore, if General de Gaulle encouraged the French to refuse invasion money, he would be responsible for the certain depreciation of the franc which would follow. The President opposed any effort to press General de Gaulle for a statement

supporting the new currency, but agreed that, if he wanted to issue something on his individual responsibility, he could put his signature on any currency statement "in any capacity that he desires, even to that of the King of Siam." [6]

The Allied press widely reported General de Gaulle's angry statements over invasion currency and his action relative to French liaison officers and apparently greatly exaggerated the difficulties which existed between the invasion forces and the French Committee. Some members of the Foreign Office pressed for a policy of greater co-operation with the committee. The U.S. Chiefs of Staff, who had gone to Europe on 9 June to visit the new beachhead and discuss further policy, became alarmed over the situation. They notified the President that, although he had the support of the Prime Minister on the French question, this was one matter on which Mr. Churchill could not dominate the Foreign Office or the Cabinet. The U.S. Chiefs considered the French situation unhappy at best and potentially dangerous in view of its possible effect on the French Resistance forces. [7]

Meanwhile, a 21 Army Group liaison officer reported a satisfactory situation in the British beachhead. The invasion currency was being accepted, and for the most part an enthusiastic welcome greeted the Allied forces. The liaison officer concluded from discussions with people in the area that the average man looked to de Gaulle "as the natural and inevitable

---

[5] New York *Times,* July 10, 11, 1944.

[6] Prime Minister to President, 686, 9 Jun 44; Prime Minister to President, 696, 10 Jun 44; Paraphrase of Msg, President to Prime Minister, 12 Jun 44, cited in Hilldring to Holmes, W–50351, 13 Jun 44. All in SHAEF SGS 123 Invasion Currency, I.

[7] Marshall, King, and Arnold to President, S–53809, 14 Jun 44, Eisenhower personal file.

leader of Free France." They were not clear, he added, as to whether or not they regarded de Gaulle as the head of a provisional government, but he was certain that if the general landed as head of such a government he would be accepted.[8]

The President, while not inclined to do any favors for de Gaulle, was willing to make full use of any organization or influence the general had which would aid the Allied military effort, provided the result was not to impose the French Committee on the French people by force of U.S. and British arms. General Marshall received this assurance in London about the time General de Gaulle was visiting Bayeux and Isigny and receiving a noisy welcome. By 16 June when the French chief returned to Algiers, he had strengthened his position with the French people in the liberated areas and with the British Government. Apparently aware of reports that the Prime Minister was under pressure to ask for outright recognition of the French Committee as the provisional government of France, de Gaulle left M. Pierre Vienot and several assistants behind to discuss civil affairs problems with British representatives. These officials opened negotiations on a civil affairs agreement similar to that concluded with Belgium before the invasion.[9]

Feeling certain of support in British and U.S. political circles as well as among military authorities on the beachhead, General de Gaulle spoke confidently in his address to the French Consultative Assembly at Algiers on 18 June. Speaking on the anniversary of the date he called the French people to arms in 1940, he stressed the efforts which the French had already personally expended for their liberation. Casting a glance at the British and U.S. Governments, he noted that France, hav-

ing had long experience with other countries, knew that foreign support would sometimes be given hesitantly, and that France's friends, however numerous, would not always give free and immediate aid. He informed the assembly of the steps he had taken to establish the committee's authority in liberated France. M. François Coulet had already assumed the office of Commissioner of the Republic for the Region of Normandy, thus becoming the representative of the committee in liberated areas with general administrative authority over prefectural, subprefectural, and municipal authorities. Coulet was directly responsible to General Koenig, but had the right of direct appeal to London or Algiers. Col. Pierre de Chevigne, another supporter of the committee, was territorial military governor of the subregion of Rouen. General de Gaulle further assured the assembly that General Koenig as commander of French forces under General Eisenhower conserved all the rights of recourse to French national authority that any other national commander had under an interallied system. He praised the strategic understanding of General Eisenhower "in whom the French Government had complete confidence for the victorious conduct of the common military operations."[10]

The tribute to General Eisenhower in a

---

[8] Lt Col D. R. Ellias, Preliminary Report on Reconnaissance of British Beachhead, 9–12 Jun 44, SHAEF SGS 014 France (Oct 43–Aug 44), Civil Affairs Dir for France, I.

[9] Notes on de Gaulle visit, 14 Jun 44; Roosevelt to Marshall, 14 Jun 44. Both in SHAEF SGS 092 France, French Relations, II. Holmes to McCloy, S–54099, 18 Jun 44; Holmes to McCloy, S–54530, 23 Jun 44. Both in Eisenhower personal file.

[10] Text of addresses to Consultative Assembly on 18 and 26 June 1944, de Gaulle, *Discours et Messages*, pp. 444–50; Smith to Hilldring, 4 Jul 44, SHAEF Civil Affairs CCS Dirs.

speech underlining French sovereignty indicated a willingness on the part of General de Gaulle to help prepare a favorable atmosphere for the talks he was to have with President Roosevelt in July. SHAEF representatives attempted in the meantime to conclude directly with General Koenig a working agreement on supplemental francs until a formal financial agreement could be made. On 4 July, General Smith informed the War Department of General Koenig's assurance that supplemental francs would be accepted even for taxes. The liaison officer problem had also been straightened out to a considerable extent. French military tactical liaison officers were attached to Allied army groups, corps, and divisions, and French administrative liaison officers were assigned to the French civil administration for civil affairs liaison between their various offices and the Allied forces. General Smith was especially pleased about the excellent relations that existed between the Allied commanders and General Koenig.[11]

General de Gaulle, accompanied by Gen. Emile Béthouart, French Chief of Staff, M. Gaston Palewski, Chief of the Civil Cabinet, and MM. Hervé Alphand and Jacques Paris of the French Foreign Office, arrived in Washington on 6 July. Both the President and the general made efforts to be affable, and their representatives set about arranging a satisfactory settlement of their differences. On 8 July, the State, War, and Treasury Departments sent a memorandum to the President suggesting that a civil affairs agreement similar to those concluded with Belgium, the Netherlands, and Norway be signed with the French Committee of National Liberation. The President informed the press on 11 July that the United States had

decided to consider the committee the dominant political authority of France until elections could be held to determine the will of the French people. The door was left open, however, for other groups in France to present conflicting claims to authority, with the understanding that the Supreme Commander, under his power to maintain peaceful relations in a military area, could make final decisions. Some press observers saw little change in this from the pre-D-Day state of affairs, except in the trend toward cordiality, but it was generally recognized that the situation had improved. General de Gaulle, on leaving Washington, expressed satisfaction with the talks he had held with the President. Lest there be any doubt of his intention to conserve the sovereignty of France, however, he declared in Ottawa on 11 July that it would be not only an error but an impossibility to exclude France from her true place among the great nations of the world.[12]

Some delays yet remained before the civil affairs agreements drafted separately in London and Washington could be concluded with the French. The Allies were to reach Paris before General Eisenhower and General Koenig signed them. However, the talks in Washington, as well as the friendly relationships between Generals Eisenhower and Smith and General Koenig, helped to mitigate a portion of the difficulties that existed in June. Improvised arrangements, already in effect in Nor-

---

[11] Smith to Hilldring, 4 Jul 44, SHAEF Civil Affairs CCS Dirs.

[12] Holmes, WD, to Smith, 8 Jul 44, SHAEF Civil Affairs CCS Dirs; Interview with press, 10 July 1944, in de Gaulle, *Discours et Messages;* New York *Times,* July 6–13, 1944; John J. McCloy, ASW, to Stimson (giving the text of message from Roosevelt to a Certain Naval Person [Churchill] in which the President informed Churchill of his decision), Diary Office CinC, 11 Jul 44.

mandy before the talks began, continued to work until more formal agreements could be put into effect.

Command of French Resistance Forces

The Supreme Commander instituted a major change in the command organization of the French Forces of the Interior shortly after D Day, not only to satisfy the French desire to exercise control over Resistance forces, but also to insure effective support of Allied operations by these units. General Koenig, commander of the French forces in the United Kingdom, had asked for such a command reorganization shortly before D Day. He pointed out that for almost four years the Resistance forces of France had carried on their work while the French headquarters in Great Britain had no share in the control of such activities. With D Day in sight and the prospect of the movement of thousands of French patriots toward the beachhead area, the French Committee of National Liberation wanted General Koenig to organize a headquarters of the French Forces of the Interior under the Supreme Commander to control these Resistance forces. General Koenig asked that all agencies dealing with the activities of the French Forces of the Interior be brought under one headquarters and that a French commander be appointed under the Supreme Commander to head the group.[13]

On 2 June, General Whiteley of SHAEF and General Koenig reached agreement, subject to General Eisenhower's concurrence, that Koenig would assume command of the French Forces of the Interior and act under the instructions of the Supreme Commander. The French general was to issue his directives through Special Force Headquarters. In addition, a tripartite regional staff under Colonel Vernon (Colonel Vernon's real name was Jean Ziegler) was set up within Special Force Headquarters to deal with all matters pertaining to France. The French Committee of National Liberation promptly approved these arrangements and announced that the French Forces of the Interior consisted of all fighting or service units participating in the fight against the enemy on home territory. The committee added that these forces were an integral part of the French Army and entitled to all the rights and privileges of regular soldiers.[14]

SHAEF issued General Koenig's directive as commander of French Forces of the Interior on 17 June. On the basic consideration that the French Forces of the Interior were to furnish maximum support to Allied operations on the Continent, the Supreme Commander directed General Koenig to delay the concentration of enemy forces in Normandy and Brittany by (1) impeding the movement of German reserves, (2) disrupting enemy lines of communications and rear areas, and (3) compelling the enemy to maintain large forces in his rear areas to contain resistance. General Eisenhower instructed Allied ground force commanders to ask for Resistance help in normal tactical operations according to priorities set by operational requirements. The initial efforts were to be aimed at the Normandy bridgehead and Brittany to delay or prevent the movement of enemy formations to these areas. Later, Resistance forces were to concentrate on other parts of

---

[13] Koenig to Smith, 24 May 44, sub: Organization of Comd of FFI, SHAEF SGS 322 FFI, Command and Control of French Forces of the Interior.

[14] Smith to Koenig, 31 May 44; Koenig to Smith, 9 Jun 44; Proclamation of French Republic Provisional Government, 9 Jun 44; Smith to Koenig, 12 Jun 44. All in SHAEF SGS 322 FFI, Command and Control of French Forces of the Interior.

France. The third priority was given to attacks on the enemy telecommunication system.[15]

General Eisenhower regularized the status of General Koenig on 23 June by announcing that the latter commanded the French Forces of the Interior with the status of any Allied commander serving under General Eisenhower. It was General Koenig's duty, consonant with the obligations of senior American and British commanders, to indicate if orders given him were "in serious conflict" with those issued by the French Committee of National Liberation. In such a case, it was the duty and prerogative of General Koenig to refer the matter to Algiers for policy guidance.[16]

The Supreme Commander indicated in July that Koenig would gradually relieve the Special Force Headquarters of its responsibilities in connection with French Resistance, and that SHAEF and Special Force Headquarters would aid him in working out a program for taking over these responsibilities. The shift was delayed, however, and not until 21 August was the staff of the French Forces of the Interior integrated in accordance with SHAEF's directive of 1 August. Maj. Gen. Harold Redman and Col. Joseph F. Haskell were appointed as deputies to General Koenig. Special Force Headquarters, Special Force detachments with army groups and armies, and a number of the Allied planning sections for Resistance operations were transferred to General Koenig's headquarters.[17]

Activities of French Resistance
June–August 1944

Long before control over French Resistance forces passed to General Koenig, those elements had proved their worth to the Supreme Commander's forces in France. At SHAEF's direction Special Force Headquarters on the night of 5–6 June ordered Resistance groups in France to put into effect D-Day plans for general harassing action and sabotage of railroads, highways, and telecommunications. Rail lines were damaged or destroyed in parts of northeast and southeast France. French partisans rendered valuable aid in delaying the movement of German units to the beachhead, particularly in the case of an armored division which was forced to take twelve days for its move from Toulouse to the beachhead. By the end of June, Special Force Headquarters declared that the results had "far surpassed" those generally expected. Whenever sufficiently armed, these forces had "displayed unity in action and a high fighting spirit." In Brittany, the French Forces of the Interior, strengthened by elements flown in from the United Kingdom, were speedily organized. They proved of great value in the early weeks of the invasion in furnishing information on enemy activities in this area to Allied intelligence units. In southeast France, the Resistance forces were particularly strong. By early July they controlled almost wholly the Vercors area and the eastern portion of the department of Ain, had a strong measure of authority in the departments of Indre, Haute-Vienne, and northern Dordogne, and were strong

[15] SHAEF Dir to Gen Koenig, 17 Jun 44, SHAEF SGS 322 FFI, Command and Control of the French Forces of the Interior.

[16] SHAEF Dir, 23 Jun 44, sub: Designation of Comdr of FFI, SHAEF SGS 322 FFI, Command and Control of the French Forces of the Interior.

[17] Notes of decisions made at mtg held at SHAEF, Whiteley, Koenig, *et al.*, 10 Jul 44, SHAEF SGS 322 FFI, Command and Control of French Forces of the Interior; SHAEF Dir to Koenig, 1 Aug 44; SHAEF G-3 Memo, 21 Aug 44, sub: Formation of Etat-Major FFI, SHAEF G-3 322-8 Operational Dir to SFHQ.

enough to hold specific positions for daylight drops of arms or troops in the Massif Central, Vosges, Morvan, Jura, and Savoie.[18]

In July the Resistance forces intensified their attacks on enemy rail movements. They carried on their chief activity against the enemy in Normandy south of the beachhead, in the Rhône valley, against lines of communications through the Toulouse Gap, and in the Paris–Orléans Gap. They had enlarged their control in the south of France to include parts of the Saône-et-Loire, Cantal, Gard, and the eastern parts of the Isère, Hautes-Alpes, and Basses-Alpes, but a violent German counterattack in the Vercors had dispersed the Resistance forces in that area. Special Force Headquarters estimated that by the end of July there were 70,000 armed Resistants in the south of France. In Brittany, these forces worked directly with U.S. units after the Allied breakout in late July. In Belgium during the same period, Resistance forces attacked railroads which could bring troops and supplies to Germans in northern France. Their work was hampered by their shortage of supplies, since only two planeloads were dropped in July. SHAEF approved plans for overt action in the Ardennes during the month.[19]

In Brittany, southern France, and the area of the Loire and Paris, French Resistance forces greatly aided the pursuit to the Seine in August. Specifically, they supported the Third Army in Brittany and the Seventh U.S. and First French Armies in the southern beachhead and the Rhône valley. In the advance to the Seine, the French Forces of the Interior helped protect the southern flank of the Third Army by interfering with enemy railroad and highway movements and enemy telecommunications, by developing open resistance on as wide a scale as possible, by providing tactical intelligence, by preserving installations of value to the Allied forces, and by mopping up bypassed enemy positions. Reporting on the work of these forces in Brittany, General Eisenhower later declared:

Special mention must be made of the great assistance given us by the F.F.I. in the task of reducing Brittany. The overt resistance forces in this area had been built up since June around a core of S.A.S. troops of the French 4th Parachute Battalion to a total strength of some 30,000 men. On the night of 4/5 August the Etat-Major was dispatched to take charge of their operations. As the Allied columns advanced, these French forces ambushed the retreating enemy, attacked isolated groups and strongpoints, and protected bridges from destruction. When our armor had swept past them they were given the task of clearing up the localities where pockets of Germans remained, and of keeping open the Allied lines of communication. They also provided our troops with invaluable assistance in supplying information of the enemy's dispositions and intentions. Not least in importance, they had, by their ceaseless harassing activities, surrounded the Germans with a terrible atmosphere of danger and hatred which ate into the confidence of the leaders and the courage of the soldiers.[20]

The Resistance forces interfered with the enemy retreat through the Rhône valley by denying him use of some of the railroads along the river, and by ambushing forces moving along the highways in that area. Some bands carried on guerrilla

---

[18] Rpt, SFHQ to SHAEF, 10th Monthly Rpt (for Jun 44), 10 Jul 44, SHAEF SGS 319.1/10 Monthly SOE/SO Rpts (SFHQ). For detailed study of this subject see The French Forces of the Interior, prep in French Resistance Unit, Hist Sec, ETOUSA, 1944, MS, Pt. II, Chs. I, II, OCMH files.

[19] Rpt, SFHQ to SHAEF, 11th Monthly Rpt (for Jul 44), 10 Aug 44, SHAEF SGS 319.1/10 Monthly SOE/SO Rpts (SFHQ).

[20] *Report by the Supreme Commander to the Combined Chiefs of Staff on the Operations in Europe of the Allied Expeditionary Force, 6 June 1944 to 8 May 1945* (Washington, 1946), p. 41.

warfare against enemy headquarters and supply depots in the south, while others sought to protect port facilities at Toulon, Marseille, and Sète against enemy destruction at the time of the Allied landings in those areas. In mid-August when it became clear that the enemy was preparing to evacuate field forces from France south of the Loire and west of the line Orléans–Toulouse–Tarbes, SHAEF gave the task of liberating that part of the area which lay outside the zone of Allied Force Headquarters to the French Forces of the Interior. The Resistance forces were directed to disrupt the movement of troops, annihilate petty garrisons and isolate larger ones, seize communications centers such as Limoges, Poitiers, and Châteauroux, capture airfields to allow the landing of supplies for the Resistance forces in the Massif Central, close the Spanish frontier to escaping German troops, and preserve port facilities and public utilities from destruction by the enemy. The forces in the south gave valuable assistance to the French Army in its attack on Marseille and Toulon, and later inflicted losses on enemy forces retreating northward. They were particularly active against Germans withdrawing from the Bordeaux area, and were an important factor in forcing the surrender of nearly 20,000 persons under Generalmajor Botho Elster. After the Allied forces swept to the Seine and beyond, the Resistance groups remained active along the Atlantic Coast in the sieges of German garrisons at St. Nazaire, La Rochelle, and Bordeaux.[21]

The Liberation of Paris

The Supreme Commander's desire to respect the sensibilities of the French and at the same time make certain that the enemy was driven from the French capital influenced his decisions of late August relating to the entry into Paris. In the incidents connected with these developments, one may also see the need of the French Committee for British and U.S. backing, the efforts of General de Gaulle to establish the French Committee's sovereignty in France, and the co-operative efforts of U.S. and French units in a common cause.

British and U.S. leaders had recognized as early as May 1943 that it was politically important to include a French division in the early campaigns to reconquer French soil. The Combined Chiefs of Staff agreed during the Washington Conference (TRIDENT), at the urging of President Roosevelt, that the possibility of adding a French division to the assault forces should be seriously considered. In mid-January 1944, General Morgan in discussing Allied plans for an entry into Paris said that it was "of paramount importance that amongst the first troops to enter Paris shall be Frenchmen." General Eisenhower accepted this suggestion and added that a unit large enough to be called a division should be brought from North Africa to co-operate with U.S. forces in northern France. Brig. Gen. Jacques-Philippe Leclerc's 2d French Armored Division was ultimately selected for this purpose. As a part of General Patton's forces, the unit was committed to action after the breakout and was active in the pursuit to the Seine.[22]

---

[21] The French Forces of Interior, Pt. II, Chs. I, II; *Conquer: The Story of Ninth Army*, pp. 49–50.

[22] 4th and 5th plenary sessions, 21, 23 May 43, CCS Final Rpt to President and Prime Minister, CCS 242/6, 25 May 43, TRIDENT Conf Min. Morgan to SHAEF G–3, 14 Jan 44; Record of conversation between General d'Astier de la Vigerie and General Eisenhower, 22 January 1944, by Comdr. Tracy B. Kittredge (with corrections and additions by General Eisenhower); SHAEF to Br COS, 28 Jan 44; Morgan to SHAEF G–3, 28 Feb 44. All in SHAEF SGS 381 France, French Participation in OVERLORD, I.

The Supreme Commander made no final decision relative to the taking of Paris until the Falaise battle. He had intended initially to bypass Paris and to pinch it out, hoping to postpone as long as possible the task of supplying the city. His views were passed on to General Montgomery, who declared on 20 August that the 12th Army Group should "assemble its right wing west and southwest of Paris and capture that city when the Commanding General considers the suitable moment has arrived—and not before. It is important that we should not attempt to secure Paris until it is a sound military proposition to do so. This is in accordance with the views and wishes of the Supreme Commander, and this policy will obtain unless and until he issues orders to the contrary." [23]

Resistance forces in Paris had in the meantime started a train of events which required a prompt decision by the Supreme Commander. On 15 August, the Paris police, railway workers, and other government employees took advantage of the Allied advance and the withdrawal of part of the enemy garrison from the city to call a general strike. As the movement spread through the city, Resistance forces asked Allied headquarters in London for aid and prepared a general insurrection in the French capital. On 19 August they seized the Prefecture of Police and issued a call for an uprising in the city. That evening, the German commander of the city, General von Choltitz, asked for a suspension of hostilities in order to examine the situation. He and Resistance representatives arranged a truce until noon, 23 August, in order that German forces west of the city could be withdrawn to points east of Paris without having to fight their way out of the capital. Resistance forces took advantage of the lull to seize the Ministry of Interior, the Hôtel de Ville, and other public buildings. [24]

As the insurrection in Paris spread, Resistance leaders attempted to get help from the Allies before the truce terminated on 23 August. When messages to London were delayed, the Resistance forces dispatched representatives to Allied forces nearest Paris. General de Gaulle, who had arrived in France from Algiers, told General Eisenhower on 21 August that he was concerned lest the disappearance of police forces and German units from Paris and the extreme shortage of food shortly lead to trouble in the capital. He believed it "really necessary to occupy Paris as soon as possible with French and Allied forces, even if it should produce some fighting and some damage within the city." He warned that if disorder occurred it would be difficult later to take things in hand without serious incidents which might ultimately hamper military operations. He nominated General Koenig as military governor of Paris to confer with General Eisenhower on the question of occupation in case the latter decided to proceed without delay. General Eisenhower, after talking to General Koenig, declared: "It looks

---

[23] Memo of info from CG, 12 A Gp, 23 Aug 44, atchd to V Corps FO 21 (photostat), *V Corps Operations in the ETO, 6 January 1942–9 May 1945* (printed in Paris, 1945), p. 200; 21 A Gp, Operational Situation and Dir, M–519, 20 Aug 44, SHAEF SGS 381 Post OVERLORD Planning, I (a). Compare 21 Army Group order with statement in Montgomery, *Normandy to the Baltic*, p. 172, to the effect that "Paris should be captured when General Patton considered that a suitable time had arrived." It seems, instead, that General Bradley was the commanding general. For General Patton's view on the entry into Paris, see his *War as I Knew It*, pp. 116–17.

[24] This and succeeding paragraphs, unless otherwise noted, are based on The French Forces of the Interior, Pt. II, Ch. II, Sec. 6, The Liberation of Paris.

now as if we'd be compelled to go into Paris. Bradley and his G–2 think we can and *must* walk in." [25]

While General Eisenhower was deciding that he would have to order Allied forces into Paris, representatives of the Resistance went to the Third Army headquarters and asked that Allied forces enter the capital. They were sent back to General Bradley's headquarters, where they reported that the French Forces of the Interior controlled all of the main city of Paris and the bridges leading to Paris from the west. Ammunition stocks were low, they added, and they feared that if Resistance forces were not promptly relieved shortly after noon on the 23d, "they might be severely dealt with by the Germans if the Germans decide to return to the city. . . ." General Eisenhower had already concluded that an Allied force should enter Paris as soon as possible after the armistice expired. He emphasized that no advance party was to be sent into the city until after that time, and that he did not want a severe fight to take place. General Bradley ordered the 2d French Armored Division to go into the city, while the 4th U.S. Division went along the southern limits of the French capital to seize crossings of the Seine south of Paris and to occupy positions to the south and southeast. He placed these operations under V Corps. [26]

On 24 August, General Bradley changed his initial orders and directed both the 2d French Armored and the 4th Divisions to enter Paris. Early on the following morning both units reported they had entered the city. They rapidly cleared out enemy resistance and forced the capitulation of General von Choltitz, who surrendered formally to General Leclerc at 1515. Shortly afterward, Maj. Gen. Leonard T. Gerow, the V Corps commander, established his tactical command post at the Hôtel des Invalides. Three days later he notified General Koenig that command of the city was being shifted to the French. The French general, named military governor of Paris by General de Gaulle some days before, noted in reply that he had assumed that command on 25 August and that the French authorities alone had handled the administration of Paris since its liberation. [27]

General Koenig's emphasis on the fact that the French were in control of their own affairs reflected General de Gaulle's determination to settle without delay the matter of the French Committee's authority. British and U.S. officials had discussed the possibility of de Gaulle's entry into Paris some days before, and there had been a disposition to delay his entry until some agreement could be reached. The French general settled the matter in mid-August by notifying General Eisenhower that he proposed to come from Algiers to France. The Supreme Commander, assuming that General de Gaulle planned to enter Paris and to remain in France, foresaw possible embarrassment if the French general arrived before the recognition of a French provisional government. The Combined Chiefs of Staff on 17 August said they had no objection to the proposed visit and instructed Eisenhower to follow his own proposal of receiving

---

[25] Ltr, de Gaulle to Eisenhower, 21 Aug 44, with penciled annotations by Eisenhower, SHAEF SGS 092 France, French Relations, II.

[26] Memo of info from CG 12th A Gp, 23 Aug 44 (photostat), *V Corps Operations in the ETO,* p. 200. Cf. Bradley, *A Soldier's Story,* pp. 390–92.

[27] Bradley, *A Soldier's Story,* p. 392. Ltr, Gerow to Koenig, 28 Aug 44; Ltr, Koenig to Gerow, 31 Aug 44. Photostats of both in *V Corps Operations in the ETO,* p. 209.

de Gaulle as commander of the French forces.[28]

SHAEF proposed that the French leader come by U.S. plane and land in London before proceeding to the Continent. Apparently suspecting that this was an attempt to keep him out of France rather than a measure to protect his plane from possible Allied attack, he announced that he was leaving in his own plane and would land in Cherbourg or Rennes. After a warning by General Eisenhower that Allied antiaircraft crews might not recognize the type of plane in which General de Gaulle would be flying, and a refusal to accept responsibility for his safety, the French commander agreed to delay his trip one day and to check over the English coast before landing at Cherbourg. He came by his own plane on 18 August and joined the 2d French Armored Division in time to enter Paris on 25 August.[29]

On 26 August, General de Gaulle directed Leclerc's forces to parade through Paris. This order was contrary to instructions of General Gerow, who feared that Germans or German sympathizers in the city might fire on the French troops. Later, when some shots were fired, General de Gaulle expressed his regrets, and General Koenig agreed to co-operate with the U.S. commander.[30]

In order to get General de Gaulle's impressions of the general situation in Paris and to show that the Allies had taken part in the liberation of Paris, General Eisenhower visited the French capital on 27 August. Wishing to have the British represented, he invited General Montgomery to accompany him, but the British commander felt unable to leave his troops at that time.[31] General Eisenhower recalls that during the visit General de Gaulle expressed anxiety about conditions in

Paris, and asked that two U.S. divisions be put at his disposal to give a show of force and establish his position. For this purpose, the Supreme Commander arranged for U.S. forces on the way to the front to march through Paris and be reviewed by Generals de Gaulle and Bradley. The 28th Division was sent through on 29 August on the way to the battlefront northeast of the city.[32]

On 29 August, General Eisenhower passed on to General Bradley a request from General de Gaulle that the 2d French Armored Division be left in Paris until other troops came up from the south. The Supreme Commander instructed the 12th Army Group commander to handle the matter as he thought best. General Bradley arranged for the French division to remain for the rest of August. On 3 September, General de Gaulle asked that Leclerc's force be sent eastward, saying that order and calm had been restored to the capital and it was desirable that

---

[28] CCS to Eisenhower, 17 Aug 44, Eisenhower personal file.

[29] Eisenhower to CCS (two msgs), 16 Aug 44; Wilson to SHAEF, 17 Aug 44; Eaker to de Gaulle, 17 Aug 44; Wilson to Eisenhower, 18 Aug 44. All in SHAEF cbl log.

[30] Col Norman H. Vissering to SHAEF, 262343 and 262357, Aug 44, SHAEF cbl log.

[31] Diary Office CinC, 26 Aug 44, entry written by General Eisenhower's British military assistant, Colonel Gault. Eisenhower to Montgomery, 26 Aug 44; Montgomery to Eisenhower, 27 Aug 44. Both in Eisenhower personal file.

[32] Eisenhower, *Crusade in Europe*, pp. 297–98. When this statement by General Eisenhower appeared, General de Gaulle denied that he had asked for such support. He declared that his position was strong, since Paris on 25 August had recognized the authority of the provisional government by unanimous and indescribable enthusiasm and that the move of American divisions through the French capital several days later had nothing to do with the re-establishment of national sovereignty. He had saluted the U.S. forces when they marched through the city but had "not at all asked for them." New York *Times*, December 7, 1948.

French troops be used in active operations. The French units, which had proudly carried their country's standard back to their nation's capital, returned to battle on 8 September.[33] Many months of battle lay ahead, but they were now able to feel that the period of defeats was at an end and that France, by her own efforts and the support of Great Britain and the United States, was on the road to victory and reconstruction.

---

[33] De Gaulle to Eisenhower, 26 Aug 44, SHAEF SGS 092 France, French Relations, II. Eisenhower to 12th A Gp comdr, 29 Aug 44; de Gaulle to Eisenhower, 3 Sep 44. Both in SHAEF cbl log. Movement order, 7 Sep 44, 2d French Armd Div Opn Orders.

CHAPTER XIV

The Pursuit Stops Short of the Rhine

In the three weeks between 18 August and 11 September, British and Canadian forces drove eastward from Falaise to the Seine, overran the flying bomb sites in the Pas-de-Calais, and wiped out the memories of Dieppe and Dunkerque. The First U.S. Army crossed the Seine, captured a large enemy force at the Mons Pocket, and dashed through Belgium. The Third Army swept through the Brittany peninsula, ran wild through the Argentan–Laval–Chartres area, and lent its forces to clear part of the First Army and British sectors while pushing other units south and east of Paris. By mid-September, General Eisenhower's troops had driven the enemy back to a line running along the Dutch border and southward along the German border to a point near Trier, and thence to Metz. In less than two weeks, the Allies had gone more than 200 miles from the Seine to the German border, clearing all northern France and the greater part of Belgium and Luxembourg. They had penetrated into the Netherlands and in places crossed the German frontier. From the south, U.S. and French forces had advanced more than 300 miles up the Rhône valley and helped to clear southern and southwestern France of the enemy. They had made contact with the right flank of General Bradley's army group on 12 Sep-

tember and were in process of establishing a line running southward from Metz by way of Epinal and Belfort to the Swiss border. By 15 September the vast bulk of occupied western Europe had been freed and the battle had been carried to German soil. *(Map IV)* These great events, coming in less time than it had taken to capture Caen and St. Lô, raised the hopes of the Allies and led them to believe that quick victory before winter was in their grasp. Instead, the great drive lost its momentum at the West Wall and a winter of hard fighting remained in the Vosges, the Huertgen Forest, the Ardennes, and in the plains of the Maas and the Roer.

The Situation at the End of August

Toward the end of August 1944, Allied intelligence agencies, aware of the desperate straits of the enemy and viewing constantly the increasing evidence of his demoralization, saw German defeat near at hand if the Allied attack could be continued and the enemy allowed no chance to regroup or strengthen his defenses. With these possibilities in mind, the SHAEF G–2 summary declared near the end of August: "The August battles have done it and the enemy in the West has had it. Two and a half months of bitter fighting have brought the end of the war in Europe within sight, almost within reach." A week later it described the German Army in the west as "no longer a cohesive force but a number of fugitive battle groups, disorganized and even demoralized, short of equipment and arms." The First Army chief of intelligence saw a thoroughly disorganized enemy and predicted that political upheaval in Germany might well occur "within 30 to 60 days of our investiture of Festung Deutschland." The Combined Intelligence Committee, which had foreseen possible German collapse in the fall of 1943, was certain in the first week of September that the German strategic situation had deteriorated to the point "that no recovery is now possible." Holding that neither the German government then in power nor any Nazi successor was likely to surrender, the committee saw collapse taking the form of piecemeal surrenders by field commanders. It concluded that "organized resistance under the control of the German High Command is unlikely to continue beyond 1 December 1944, and . . . it may end even sooner." [1]

This enthusiasm was not shared by all commanders or intelligence chiefs, nor was it borne out entirely by the situation in Germany. General Eisenhower had warned newspaper reporters against undue optimism in an interview on 20 August. His forces had advanced so rapidly, he felt, and supply lines were so strained that "further movement in large parts of the front even against very weak opposition is almost impossible." General Patton's chief of intelligence showed greater caution than either his colleague at SHAEF or his commander at Third Army. At a time when SHAEF was declaring the Germans no longer a cohesive force and General Patton believed he could cross the

German border in ten days, Colonel Koch declared:

Despite the crippling factors of shattered communications, disorganization and tremendous losses in personnel and equipment, the enemy nevertheless has been able to maintain a sufficiently cohesive front to exercise an overall control of his tactical situation. His withdrawal, though continuing, has not been a rout or mass collapse. Numerous new identifications in contact in recent days have demonstrated clearly that, despite the enormous difficulties under which he is operating, the enemy is still capable of bringing new elements into the battle area and transferring some from other fronts.

* * *

It is clear from all indications that the fixed determination of the Nazis is to wage a last-ditch struggle in the field at all costs. It must be constantly kept in mind that fundamentally the enemy is playing for time. Weather will soon be one of his most potent Allies as well as terrain, as we move east to narrowing corridors. . . . But barring internal upheaval in the homeland and the remoter possibility of insurrection within the Wehrmacht, it can be expected that the German armies will continue to fight until destroyed or captured. [2]

Developments in the Reich and among the German armies in the west gave grounds both for Allied optimism and for caution as to the enemy's ability to continue the fight. The enemy situation, extremely confused when the Falaise trap was closed, became chaotic after the retreat east of the Seine. By the end of August, Model, still attempting to direct both *OB WEST* and *Army Group B,* saw his position grow progressively worse as Allied

---

SHAEF Weekly Intel Summaries 23 and 24, 26 Aug and 2 Sep 44, SHAEF G–2 Rpts; FUSA G–2 Estimate 24, 3 Sep 44, Opns Rpts; Rpt of Combined Intel Com, Prospects of a German Collapse and Surrender as of 8 Sep 44, CCS 660/1, 9 Sep 44, OCTAGON Conf Min.

[2] TUSA G–2 Estimate 9, 28 Aug 44, TUSA AAR, II.

forces broke through the Somme–Marne–Saône line and threatened the line Meuse–Moselle. Hitler's reaction was to announce that Rundstedt had been recalled to the post of Commander in Chief West, that Model would retain *Army Group B,* and that the West Wall (Siegfried Line) position would be strengthened. On 3 September, Hitler admitted that exhaustion of the forces in the west and lack of immediately available reserves made it impossible to indicate positions other than the fortresses which could and must be held. He ordered instead that an attempt be made to gain the maximum amount of time for the organization and transfer of new divisions and the improvement of German defenses in the west. Forces on the north and in the center were to fight stubbornly for every foot of ground, while preventing the Allies from making any major envelopment. *Army Group G* was to gather a reserve force in the area of the Vosges which was initially to cover the retreat from southern France and then to strike deeply in the U.S. southern flank. Meanwhile, the *Chief of Army Equipment and Commander of the Replacement Army* was to retain responsibility for the defense of the West Wall from the Swiss border to Roermond. Efforts were also made to provide new units for the defense. *Army Group G* was instructed to use as replacements men from the ground, air, and naval elements that were then withdrawing from southern and southwestern France.[3]

On the following day, Model informed the Fuehrer that the forces in the west could hold only on the line Albert Canal–Meuse River–Siegfried Line extensions. This stand he said, would require at least twenty-five fresh divisions and an armored reserve of five or six panzer divisions. He asked for immediate reinforcements and

for ten infantry and five panzer divisions by 15 September. Von Rundstedt supported these views. The new Commander in Chief West reported on 7 September that *Army Group B* was worn out and that it had only 100 tanks in operating condition. Saying that the Allies had complete air superiority, that an airborne attack could be expected, and that a ground forces drive in the direction of Aachen seriously menaced his position in the north, he asked at once for five or preferably ten divisions with assault gun battalions and antitank weapons and emphasized the need of aerial support. He added that at least six weeks would be necessary to get the West Wall ready for defense, and requested more armor and weapons to protect his existing positions for that length of time.[4]

Hitler found himself hard pressed on the matter of reinforcements because of the situation in the east. The Allies were aided at this juncture, as they had been since June, by a sustained Russian drive along a front stretching more than 800 miles from Finland to the Black Sea. Beginning their offensive within a week after the landings in Normandy, the Red armies by 5 September had forced Finland to sue for peace, had driven to East Prussia, threatening to cut off enemy forces in the Baltic area, and had swept into Poland

[3] OI–SIR/39 (Scheidt); *Der Westen* (Schramm); Hitler's order of 1 Sep 44, *Nr. 773134/44.* Office of Naval Intelligence, Fuehrer Directives and Other Top-Level Directives of the German Armed Forces. 1942–1945. (Referred to hereafter as *ONI Fuehrer Directives.*) Fuehrer Directives is a selection of translated documents from German naval archives. Hitler's orders of 3 and 4 Sep 44 *(WFSt Op. Nr. 773189/44* and *OKW/WFSt Nr. 773222/44). Army Group B, Ia Fuehrerbefehle 17.VI.-25.IX.44.*

[4] Teletype, Model to Jodl, 4 Sep 44; Teletype, Rundstedt to Keitel, 7 Sep 44. Both in *Army Group B, Ia Lagebeurteilungen 20.V.-11.X.44.*

to the gates of Warsaw, where they stopped. In late August and early September they seized the Ploesti oil fields, forced the collapse of România, and turned Bulgaria to the Allied side. The Germans had to commit more than two million men on the Eastern Front as compared to approximately 700,000 in the west. Incomplete statistics indicate that the Germans suffered over 900,000 casualties on the Russian front during June, July, and August. The casualties inflicted by Soviet forces on the Germans prompted Mr. Churchill to tell the House of Commons in early August that the Russian Army had done "the main work of tearing the guts out of the German army." He added: "In the air and on the oceans we could maintain our place, but there was no force in the world which could have been called into being, except after several more years, that would have been able to maul and break the German army unless it had been subjected to the terrible slaughter and manhandling that has fallen to it through the strength of the Russian Soviet armies." [5]

The Russian efforts, tremendous though they were, rested heavily on material contributions of the United States, Great Britain, and Canada in the form of lend-lease. In the period October 1941 to 30 June 1944, the Allies had supplied nearly 11,000 aircraft, more than 4,900 tanks, and 263,000 vehicles, including trucks, jeeps, trailers, armored cars, and the like. The vehicles, equivalent to more than one-third the total number landed on the Continent for the United States forces until the end of the war, were of tremendous importance to the mobility of the Red Army. Indeed, it is estimated that by the middle of 1944 American trucks carried one half of the Russian supplies. It is worthy of note that the tanks would have

supplied the initial T/O requirements of more than 18 American armored divisions, and the trucks and other vehicles would have supplied the organic requirements of more than 110 armored or 125 American infantry divisions as then organized. [6]

A glance at the bill of casualties presented in the west could have given Hitler little encouragement. In three months of fighting, nearly 300,000 Germans were dead, wounded, and missing, while an additional force of more than 230,000 officers and men, of whom 85,000 belonged to the Field Army, had gone into the fortresses of

[5] Strength figures on German forces in the west and east in August–September 1944 are discussed by H. M. Cole in *The Lorraine Campaign* (Washington, 1950), pp. 29–43. Mr. Churchill's statement to the House of Commons was cited in 302 H. C. Deb. 1474 (Hansard's 1943–44).

[6] Office of Foreign Liquidation, Foreign Economics Section, Dept of State, Report on War Aid Furnished by the U.S. to the U.S.S.R., June 22, 1941–September 20, 1945; *Sixteenth Report to Congress on Lend-Lease Operations: For the Period Ended June 30, 1944* (Washington, 1944); War Department Field Manual 101–10, Organization, Technical and Logistical Data, 10 Oct 43 and 12 Oct 44 (organization of armored and infantry divisions); Historical Section, Headquarters, ETOUSA, *American Enterprise in Europe* (Paris, 1945); Transportation Corps Monthly Rpt, 31 May 45, and Consolidated Statistics of TC Ops in ETO, 1 Jan 42–8 May 45, contained in Historical Report of the Transportation Corps in ETO, Vol. VII (Apr–May–Jun 45).

The statistics on tanks and vehicles sent the Russians indicate the number actually shipped, less those lost or diverted elsewhere, prior to 1 July 1944. Undoubtedly part of these were still in the supply pipelines going into Russia, and were not available during most of the period in question.

Only organic transportation of the division is considered in the statistics relative to the number of U.S. divisions which could have been supplied from tanks and vehicles furnished the Red Army. It is clear that a number of vehicles far in excess of the divisional table of organization is essential to supply a division, depending on distance from a port, conditions of combat, and the like. By the same token the replacement factor for combat losses or normal wear on tanks would require a reserve of tanks beyond that mentioned.

western Europe to remain until the final surrender. The toll of high-level commanders—dead, removed, or captured—was heavy. Rommel, an army group commander, was badly wounded,[7] one army commander (Generaloberst Friedrich Dollmann) was dead, another (Hausser) badly wounded, a third (Eberbach) captured, and a fourth (Chevallerie) relieved. Three *OB WEST* commanders (von Rundstedt, von Kluge, and Model) had been relieved during the period, although Rundstedt was reinstated. Von Kluge, who had also been relieved of the *Army Group B* command, was dead by his own hand.[8]

German estimates of Allied strength gave even less comfort. Still heavily overestimating the opposing divisions, the enemy spoke at the end of the first week in September of 54 Allied divisions on the Continent.[9] Although the number was grossly exaggerated, even a more accurate listing would have been discouraging. General Eisenhower had at the moment some 38 divisions (20 U.S., 13 British, 3 Canadian, 1 Polish, and 1 French), and 5 to 8 U.S. and French divisions still under the Mediterranean commander were being landed in the south of France. The actual number still in the line or in support cannot be estimated precisely inasmuch as three divisions or more had been withdrawn for re-equipping. Nor is it clear how many men carried as wounded and missing during the period had returned to duty. Nevertheless, the number was still substantially in excess of the 700,000 men now in the enemy's forty-nine and a half divisions and attached units stationed in the west.[10]

Hitler refused to regard the situation as hopeless. New units were in the process of formation. OKW notified the Commander

in Chief West that he would get four infantry divisions between 13 and 25 September, and that in the period 15 to 30 September his forces would be reinforced by two panzer brigades, several antitank companies, former fortress battalions, and other reconverted units. An attempt was made to encourage *OB WEST* by pointing out that the Allies had been overoptimistic and that their boasts in late August both at home and in the field that the war was about at an end had proved false. Hitler pressed the work of strengthening the West Wall defenses, rushing workers and materials to the task. By 10 September more than 200,000 workers were engaged in construction on these fortifications. In a move to aid the defense efforts, OKW gave the Commander in Chief West jurisdiction over all branches of the Wehrmacht, control over the work on West Wall defenses, and permission to call on all

---

[7] Another army group commander, Blaskowitz, was soon to be relieved.

[8] SHAEF estimated German losses as of 29 August 1944 at 400,000. Memo, SHAEF G–2 for SAC, 29 Aug 44, SHAEF G–2 Intel on Germany GBI/o1–A/091–3. See Cole, *The Lorraine Campaign*, p. 31, for information on German casualties.

[9] Teletype, Rundstedt to Keitel, cited above, n. 4.

[10] Strength statistics for both Allied and enemy forces are open to question. The Allied order of battle for 1 September is given in SHAEF G–3 War Room Summary 87, 1 September 1944. Strength as of that period showed a cumulative total since 6 June of 826,700 in the British area and 1,211,200 in the U.S. area. These statistics do not include the U.S. and French forces pouring into southern France which were to total six French and three U.S. divisions by 15 September. Cumulative casualties since D Day (not including 6th Army Group figures) were over 200,000 (124,394 for the U.S. forces as of 30 August and 82,309 for the British and Canadians as of 31 August. With the exception of 36,486 dead (20,668 American and 15,818 British and Canadian) it is not clear how many of the 200,000 casualties had been returned to duty. (For cumulative casualties, see SHAEF G–3 War Room Summary 91, 5 September 1944.)

agencies in the western theater of war for aid.[11]

Indications that the enemy was determined to hold in the west appeared in a reprint of captured minutes of a meeting at the German Ministry of Propaganda on 4 September, circulated by 12th Army Group later in the month. The German representatives, anticipating the transportation difficulties of the Allies, predicted that the advance would soon be halted. In this event, they added, the Germans would be able to make use of new weapons then in preparation, and wait for the inevitable squabble which would arise between the Russians and the British over the Balkans. "It is certain," they said, "that the political conflicts will increase with the apparent approach of an Allied victory, and some day will cause cracks in the house of our enemies which no longer can be repaired." [12]

Allied Plans for an Advance to the Rhine

Against this background of enemy disorder and frantic attempts to re-establish a new defense line, Allied commanders were considering various plans for clearing northern France and Belgium and advancing to the German border and the Rhine. The SHAEF planners, at least a month before D Day, had outlined general strategy to be followed for the defeat of Germany after capture of the lodgment area. Recalling that the Supreme Commander had been charged with the task of undertaking operations "aimed at the heart of Germany and the destruction of her armed forces," the planners selected what they considered to be the chief target area of Germany and the best route by which this objective could be reached. They recognized Berlin as the ultimate

Allied goal but held that the city was "too far east to be the objective of a campaign in the West." Instead, they set their eyes on the Ruhr, saying that it was the only area in western Germany of vital economic importance, that an attack on the area would force the enemy to commit his main forces there and thus give the Allies a chance to bring them to battle and destroy them, and that capture of the area would have a tremendous effect on German morale.[13]

From the beginning, therefore, there was a SHAEF plan to angle the attack from the Seine in the direction of the Ruhr. This plan, it will be recalled, was based on the idea of a slow advance after a careful build-up at the Seine and a series of actions which would push the enemy forces back to the German frontier north of Aachen by D plus 330 (2 May 1945). It was considered dangerous to attack by a single route and thus canalize the advance and open it to a concentrated enemy attack. SHAEF decided in favor of "a broad front both north and south of the Ardennes," which would give the Allies the advantages of maneuver and the ability to shift the main weight of attack. If the enemy could be forced to extend his forces to meet threats in the Metz Gap and the Maubeuge–Liége areas and to maintain his coastal defenses along the Channel

---

[11] OI–SIR/39 (Scheidt); *Der Westen* (Schramm); Hitler's order of 7 Sep 44, *Nr. 0010783/44. ONI Fuehrer Directives.*

[12] Rpt of Conf of ministers at Ministry of Propaganda, 4 Sep 44, in Annex 2 to 12th A Gp Periodic Rpt 106, 19 Sep 44, 12th A Gp Periodic File, 28 Jul–Nov 44.

[13] This and the following paragraphs on the SHAEF plan are taken from SHAEF Planning Staff draft, Post NEPTUNE Courses of Action After Capture of the Lodgment Area, Main Objectives and Axis of Advance, I, 3 May 44, SHAEF SGS 381 Post OVERLORD Planning, I.

coast, his hold would be weakened along the whole front. In this circumstance, a deep penetration on both sides of the Ardennes or north of that area would force an enemy withdrawal from the Ardennes west of the Liége–Luxembourg line for a concentration to meet the Allied main thrust. In the light of these conclusions, the SHAEF planners recommended that the main line of advance be along the line Amiens–Maubeuge–Liége–the Ruhr, with a subsidiary attack on the line Verdun–Metz.

When the enemy began to retire from Normandy in confusion after mid-August, General Eisenhower returned to the pre-D-Day concept for the advance into Germany. While favoring a major thrust into the Ruhr area, he still wanted a secondary attack to the south of the Ardennes. Some observers felt that in holding to this view he was overlooking the fact that the bulk of the enemy forces, once held east of the Seine, had been committed in the Mortain and Falaise Gap areas and were no longer available to threaten any single line of advance which might be made to the northeast or to the east. To them, speed was needed to destroy the enemy before he could piece together enough of his shattered elements for a defense of the West Wall or the Rhine.

In mid-August, before it was clear that the German collapse west of the Seine would be as sweeping as it proved to be, Generals Bradley and Patton discussed a scheme for sending three corps across the Rhine near Wiesbaden, Mannheim, and Karlsruhe to end the war speedily. To them this was the shortest route into Germany and one that promised the best dividends. General Bradley thought that both First and Third Armies should execute the maneuver, whereas General Patton be-

lieved that the Third Army alone, if given sufficient supplies, could move to the Metz–Nancy–Epinal area and cross the German border in ten days. General Montgomery at the same time was considering an entirely different approach to the problem, an approach somewhat nearer the initial SHAEF concept than that of General Bradley and General Patton. Wanting as quickly as possible to clear the Pas-de-Calais coast with its V-bomb sites, to get airfields in Belgium, and to secure the port at Antwerp, Montgomery felt that the main drive should be made toward the northeast. In the belief that his own British and Canadian forces would be unable to accomplish all of these missions quickly, he proposed that part or all of General Bradley's forces should move northeastward with their right flank on the Ardennes, cutting the enemy lines of communications and facilitating the advance of the British forces.

The British and U.S. commanders, each conscious of the opportunities on his own front and desirous of seizing them quickly, favored single thrusts into enemy territory. One would have swung nearly all of the Allied force to the northeast; the other would have thrust the main U.S. forces almost due east.

On 22 August, General Eisenhower considered the various plans of his subordinates. He expressed his intention eventually to direct 21 Army Group north of the Ardennes while 12th Army Group advanced beyond Paris and prepared to strike just south of the Ardennes. At the moment, however, he had certain tactical requirements to consider. In order to aid 21 Army Group in carrying out its immediate missions of destroying forces between the Seine and the Pas-de-Calais, it was necessary, he felt, to reinforce the British army group with an entire airborne command and such other forces as might be required. He added that General Bradley's rate of advance east of Paris would depend on the speed with which ports in Brittany could be cleared and the Allied supply situation improved.[14]

General Montgomery on the 23d reminded the Supreme Commander that to sweep through the Pas-de-Calais to Antwerp he would need an entire U.S. army moving on his right flank. General Bradley argued that one corps would be sufficient for this purpose. General Eisenhower, although believing the British commander overcautious, acceded to his request in order to insure success. At the same time, he ordered General Bradley to use his remaining forces to clear the ports in Brittany, defend U.S. lines of communications against possible attacks from the Paris area, and amass supplies for an advance eastward toward Metz. Told by the services of supply that they could support the British advances through northern France and Belgium, Eisenhower wrote Montgomery: "All of us having agreed upon this general plan, the principal thing we must now strive for is speed in execution. All of the Supply people have assured us that they can support the move, beginning this minute—let us assume that they know exactly what they are talking about and get about it vigorously and without delay."[15]

In supporting General Montgomery's attack with a U.S. army, the First, General Eisenhower also allocated the bulk of 12th Army Group's gasoline to that army, thus depriving Third Army of the means of making a rapid drive to the east. It was a blow to the hopes of General Patton, who felt that the British commander had outargued the Supreme Commander.

Patton drew some solace from the fact that he still had seven good divisions going in the direction he and Bradley always wanted to go.[16] Furthermore, he still had eight days in which to advance before the drying up of his fuel supply led him to a temporary halt.

General Eisenhower in explaining his decision to General Marshall said that he had temporarily changed his basic plan for attacking both to the northeast and the east in order to help General Montgomery seize tremendously important objectives in the northeast. He considered the change necessary even though it interfered with his desire to push eastward through Metz, because 21 Army Group lacked sufficient strength to do the job. He added that he did not doubt 12th Army Group's ability to reach the Franco-German border, but "saw no point in getting there until we are in a position to do something about it."[17]

On 26 August, General Montgomery, still acting as commander of ground forces on the Continent, repeated the Supreme Commander's decisions to the Allied generals. He assigned the following tasks: the First Canadian Army was to clear the Pas-de-Calais; the Second British Army was to advance rapidly into Belgium; and the First U.S. Army was to support the British advance by driving forward on the Paris–Brussels axis to establish forces in the Maastricht–Liége area east of Brussels and the Charleroi–Namur area south of Brus-

---

[14] Eisenhower to Marshall, CPA 90235, 22 Aug 44, Eisenhower personal file.

[15] Eisenhower to Montgomery, 24 Aug 44, confirming agreements of the preceding day, SHAEF SGS 381 Post OVERLORD Planning, I; Bradley, *A Soldier's Story*, pp. 399–401; Eisenhower to Marshall, 5 Sep 44, Diary Office CinC.

[16] Patton, *War as I Knew It*, pp. 116–17.

[17] Ltr, Eisenhower to Marshall, 24 Aug 44, Eisenhower personal file.

TABLE 1—CASUALTIES CAUSED BY FLYING BOMB AND ROCKET ATTACKS ON THE UNITED
KINGDOM, 1944–45

	Number		Killed		Seriously Injured	
	Bombs [a]	Rockets [b]	By Bombs [a]	By Rockets [b]	By Bombs [a]	By Rockets [b]
Totals	5,890	1,054	5,835	2,855	16,762	6,268
In London	2,563	517	5,373	2,642	15,258	5,670
Elsewhere	3,327	537	462	213	1,504	598

[a] Between 12 June 1944 and 29 March 1945.
[b] Between 8 September 1944 and 27 March 1945.

sels. The 21 Army Group commander stressed a special British problem which had developed since mid-June in his reminder that a speedy advance would "bring quick relief to our families and friends in England by over-running the flying bomb launching sites in the Pas de Calais." [18] (*Table 1*)

General Bradley confirmed the broad outline of General Montgomery's directive but asked that the inter-army-group boundary be changed to give Brussels to the Second British instead of to the First U.S. Army. This shift was accepted by the 21 Army Group commander. In addition to making these arrangements for First Army, General Bradley directed the Third Army to complete the reduction of Brittany, protect the south flank of 12th Army Group, and prepare for a continuation of its advance to seize crossings of the Rhine between Mannheim and Koblenz.[19]

General Eisenhower's decision to shift the First U.S. Army northward temporarily during the British advance from the Seine to Antwerp was accompanied by a firm resolution to return as soon as possible to the early SHAEF policy of advancing toward Germany by routes north of the Ardennes and south of that area

through the Metz Gap. At the beginning of September, his planners began to study means by which one corps from the First Army could now be used to support a move of the Third Army toward the Saar and a move either up to the Moselle or toward Frankfurt while the remainder of the British and U.S. forces were going northeast. On 2 September at Chartres, General Eisenhower discussed future plans with

[18] Montgomery to army comdrs, M–520, 26 Aug 44, SHAEF SGS 381 Post OVERLORD Planning, I. Mr. Churchill at the beginning of August estimated that between 13 June when the first V-bombs were dropped on the United Kingdom and 1 August more than 5,700 robot bombs had killed nearly 5000 people, seriously injured 14,000, destroyed 17,000 homes, and damaged 80,000. Address by Mr. Churchill, August 2, 1944, 302 H. C. Deb. 1475 (Hansard's 1943–44). Postwar estimates indicate that between 12 June 1944 and 29 March 1945 nearly 5,900 bombs fell in the United Kingdom, killing over 5,800 people and seriously injuring nearly 17,000 more. In the period 8 September 1944 to 27 March 1945 more than a thousand rockets were to fall in the United Kingdom, killing 2,855 people and seriously injuring 6,268 more.

For efforts of SHAEF and the air forces to deal with the continued CROSSBOW threat in the summer of 1944, see Craven and Cate, *The Army Air Forces in World War II*, Vol. III, Ch. 15, "CROSSBOW—Second Phase." The authors indicate that U.S. bomber commanders and, to a lesser extent, British bomber chiefs opposed Air Chief Marshal Tedder's insistence on a continued bombing of V-weapon launching sites. The bomber commanders preferred to concentrate more heavily on German economy and support of

Generals Bradley, Hodges, and Patton. As a result of decisions made there, the 12th Army Group commander told his subordinates to prepare for an advance by the Third Army and one corps of the First Army toward Mannheim, Frankfurt, and Koblenz.[20]

General Eisenhower qualified his approval of the drive to the east with his statement that it would depend on the success of the northern thrust, which had prior claim on supplies. He also warned of the supply problems which might give trouble in the future and noted:

We have advanced so rapidly that further movement in large parts of the front even against very weak opposition is almost impossible. . . . The closer we get to the Siegfried Line the more we will be stretched administratively and eventually a period of relative inaction will be imposed upon us. The potential danger is that while we are temporarily stalled the enemy will be able to pick up bits and pieces of forces everywhere and re-organize them swiftly for defending the Siegfried Line or the Rhine. It is obvious from an over-all viewpoint we must now as never before keep the enemy stretched everywhere.[21]

From Field Marshal Montgomery's point of view, the scarcity of supplies provided no basis for a strategy of stretching the enemy everywhere.[22] Instead, he insisted that Allied resources were insufficient for two full-blooded attacks and that a compromise solution would merely prolong the war. He urged that the drive to the Ruhr be given full backing, saying, "We have now reached a stage where one really powerful and full-blooded thrust toward Berlin is likely to get there and thus end the German war." [23]

General Eisenhower replied that no re-allocation of existing resources "would be

[20] Memo, Nevins for Chief Ops A Sub-Sec G–3 SHAEF, 1 Sep 44, OCMH files; points of discussion at Chartres given in Notes on Meeting of Supreme Commander and Commanders, 2 Sep 44, 12th A Gp Military Objectives 371.3; Memo, G–3 SHAEF for CofS SHAEF, 3 Sep 44, SHAEF SGS 381 Post OVERLORD Planning I. General Patton says (War as I Knew It, pp. 120–24) that General Bull, the SHAEF G–3, refused to approve this plan on 30 August while on a staff visit to Bradley's advance headquarters. "We [Bradley and Patton] finally persuaded General Eisenhower" to approve the plan on 2 September. General Bull recommended the plan in a memorandum of 3 September in which he said that, in view of reported German weakness along the West Wall, the reduction of the size of Allied forces driving northeast of the Ardennes was not only practicable "but desirable . . . to maintain the speed of advance."

[21] Eisenhower to comdrs, FWD 13765, 4 Sep 44, SHAEF SGS 381 Post OVERLORD Planning, I; Eisenhower to Marshall, FWD 13792, 4 Sep 44, Eisenhower personal file.

[22] General Montgomery's appointment as field marshal was announced on 1 September. Mr. Churchill had informed General Eisenhower on 22 August that the promotion would be made to run from the termination of Montgomery's command of Allied assault forces. This the Prime Minister considered a necessary concession to British public opinion. He added that the promotion, which would make Montgomery outrank both Eisenhower and Bradley, would make no difference in the field marshal's position in regard to high-ranking U.S. officers. AMSSO to Eisenhower, 4891, 22 Aug 44, Eisenhower personal file.

[23] Montgomery to Eisenhower, M–160, 4 Sep 44, Eisenhower personal file. Compare this with the statement, Montgomery, *Normandy to the Baltic*, p. 193: "My own view was that one powerful, full-blooded thrust across the Rhine and into the heart of Germany, backed by the whole of the resources of the Allied armies, would be likely to achieve decisive results."

the Allied land battle as a better means of stopping the V-weapon attack. The authors conclude that the large-scale CROSSBOW operations during the period were a failure but that they offered firm evidence that "the Allies could respond too generously rather than too niggardly to whatever threats might arise to jeopardize the execution of the grand strategic designs so carefully prepared and so skilfully executed in the pursuance of one objective—defeat of the enemy in Europe." (P. 541.)

[19] 12th A Gp, Ltr of Instr 6, 25 Aug 44, 12th A Gp Rpt of Opns, V, 85–87; Ltr, Bradley to Montgomery, 26 Aug 44, 12th A Gp Military Objectives 371.3; Montgomery, *Normandy to the Baltic*, p. 208.

adequate to sustain a thrust to Berlin." Since the bulk of the German Army in the west had been destroyed, he went on, it was imperative to breach the Siegfried Line, cross the Rhine on a wide front, and seize the Ruhr and the Saar. Such a drive would give the Allies a stranglehold on two of Germany's chief industrial areas and largely wreck its ability to wage war. It would assist in cutting off the forces retreating from the south of France, give the Allies freedom of action, and force the enemy to disperse his forces over a wide front.[24] The Supreme Commander, while giving priority to Montgomery's advance to the northeast, thought it important to get "Patton moving again so that we may be fully prepared to carry out the original conception for the final stages of the campaign." As he saw it at the time, the logical move was to take advantage of all existing lines of communications in the advance toward Germany and to bring the southern wing of the OVERLORD forces on to the Rhine at Koblenz. At the same time, airborne forces would be used to seize crossings over the Rhine thus placing the Allies in a position to thrust deep into the Ruhr and threaten Berlin. The execution of these drives rested, he added, on speed, which in turn relied on maintenance—"now stretched to the limit."[25]

Field Marshal Montgomery argued that the maintenance question emphasized the need for putting all supplies behind one thrust into Germany. Believing "with all respect . . . that a reallocation of our present resources of every description would be adequate to get one thrust to Berlin," he asked General Eisenhower to reconsider his decision. SHAEF planners felt that Montgomery's view was optimistic. They suggested that a maximum of three Allied corps could be pushed to

Berlin by the end of September only if five corps were grounded in Normandy and Brittany, if Antwerp—captured on 4 September—and ports in the Pas-de-Calais were producing some 7,000 tons of supplies a day, and if an airlift was bringing in 2,000 tons daily.[26] Nonetheless, SHAEF made a considerable effort to provide additional support for Montgomery's battle. General de Guingand reported to his superior on 7 September that SHAEF had met 80 percent of the British requests for locomotives and rolling stock and that an increased allocation would be made. He added that the northern thrust was to have priority on air supply and would be allocated the airborne army as a means of capturing Walcheren Island and clearing the Schelde estuary in the hope of opening the approaches to Antwerp.[27]

The new allocations, while welcome, were much less than Field Marshal Montgomery thought necessary for a powerful thrust into Germany. Worse still, in his view, the Supreme Commander during the first week in September had authorized General Bradley to continue the attack to the east and to allocate additional fuel supplies to the Third Army. Under these authorizations, the 12th Army Group commander ordered crossings of the Rhine by the First Army near Cologne, Bonn, and Koblenz and by the

---

[24] Eisenhower to Montgomery, FWD 13889, 5 Sep 44, Eisenhower personal file.

[25] Memo for record, Eisenhower, 5 Sep 44, Diary Office CinC.

[26] Although Antwerp itself was seized almost intact, Germans on Walcheren Island and to the south of the Schelde estuary prevented ships from coming up the Schelde to Antwerp.

[27] Montgomery to Eisenhower, 7 Sep 44, Diary Office CinC; Plng paper, Logistical Implications of Rapid Thrust to Berlin, Sep 44, SHAEF G–4 Logistical Forecasts, Folder 13; Cbl ADSEC (21 A Gp CofS) to TAC HQ EXFOR (Montgomery), 7 Sep 44, SHAEF SGS 381 Post OVERLORD Planning, I.

Third Army in the vicinity of Mannheim and Mainz, and, if possible, near Karls-ruhe.[28]

General Eisenhower discussed the routes of advance and other problems with his army group commanders and the Allied naval commander on 9, 10, and 11 September. In the most important of the three conferences, he met with Air Chief Marshal Tedder, General Gale, and Field Marshal Montgomery on 10 September at Brussels. The Supreme Commander refused to consider what he called "a pencil like thrust" into the heart of Germany.[29] Since the Germans still had reserves, he believed that a single thrust on any part of the front would meet with certain destruction. General Eisenhower was unwilling, therefore, to stop operations in the south. He emphasized that his chief interest was in opening the port of Antwerp, but added that he was willing to defer this operation until an effort could be made to obtain a bridgehead over the Rhine at Arnhem and outflank the defenses of the Siegfried Line.[30]

General Patton's forces went forward rapidly, and on 14 September General Bradley was able to announce that Third Army had crossed the Moselle in force. Noting that the next forty-eight hours would indicate how fast Patton could go, the 12th Army Group commander added that if Third Army could not make any real progress northeast from the Metz area he would shift it to the north. But the Supreme Commander now relaxed his previous order to the point of saying that if Montgomery could go ahead on the maintenance promised him, and if Hodges could be kept fully supplied up to the time he reached his first principal objective, there was no reason "why Patton should not keep on acting offensively if conditions

for offensive action were favorable."[31]

These concessions to 12th Army Group, however hedged about with conditions, appeared to Field Marshal Montgomery to undermine plans for the approaching airborne operation near Arnhem and the campaign to open the port of Antwerp. To some members of his staff, the granting of permission for Patton to continue to drive to the east, while Montgomery was oriented toward the northeast, prevented any commander from landing a solid punch and weakened the center of the Allied line in the area of the Ardennes. To Field Marshal Montgomery's worried comments on the subject, General Eisenhower replied on the eve of the Arnhem operation: "I sent a senior staff officer to General Bradley yesterday to see that all of his forces and distribution of his supplies will coordinate effectively with this idea. While he had issued a temporary directive on September 10 that on the surface did not conform clearly to this conception of making our principal drive with our left, the actual fact is that everything he is doing will work out exactly as you visualize

[28] Bradley ltr of instructions to comdrs (in confirmation of previous verbal orders), 10 Sep 44, SHAEF SGS 381 Post OVERLORD Planning, I; Bradley, A Soldier's Story, pp. 410–14.

[29] It should be noted that Field Marshal Montgomery spoke of the thrust as "full-blooded." Inasmuch as his proposals involved the use of the Second British Army and two corps of the First U.S. Army for an advance between Arnhem and the Ardennes, his term "full-blooded" seems the more accurate description. General Patton's earlier proposal for an advance toward Berlin by two corps seems to conform more nearly to the term "pencil like."

[30] Notes on mtg at Brussels, 10 Sep 44, by Tedder, OCMH files; Eisenhower, Crusade in Europe, pp. 306–07.

[31] Bradley to Eisenhower, 12 Sep 44; Dir, Eisenhower to army comdrs, FWD 14764, 13 Sep 44. Both in SHAEF SGS 381 Post OVERLORD Planning, I. Bradley to Eisenhower, 14 Sep 44, 12th A Gp 371.3 Military Objectives, I; Eisenhower to Bradley, 15 Sep 44, Eisenhower personal file.

it." He added: "So Bradley's left is striking hard to support you; Third Army is pushing north to support Hodges; and Sixth Army Group is being pushed up to give right flank support to the whole."[32]

The Supreme Commander's emphasis on the opening of the port of Antwerp at the conference of 10 September may be said to mark a new phase in Allied operational planning. At the beginning of September, the stress had been on thrusts to the Rhine. This strategy had been encouraged by the capture of Antwerp on 4 September. But when it was clear that this prize was of no value until the enemy had been dislodged from his positions north and south of the Schelde estuary, stretching for some fifty miles to the sea, General Eisenhower gave priority to an operation to clear the estuary. After his conferences of 9, 10, and 11 September, he became confirmed in his view that "the early winning of deep water ports and improved maintenance facilities in our rear are prerequisites to a final all-out assault on Germany proper." He was influenced by the fact that the Allies were still supported logistically over the open beaches and that a week or ten days of bad weather in the Channel could paralyze the movements of the armies. He now ordered 21 Army Group to secure promptly the approaches to Antwerp and Rotterdam in addition to the Channel ports, 12th Army Group to reduce Brest, and 6th and 12th Army Groups to open lines from Marseille to the north.[33] In his insistence on deepwater ports, General Eisenhower was supported by the Combined Chiefs of Staff. From their conference at Quebec they had expressed their preference for the northern over the southern routes of advance into Germany and had stressed the necessity for opening the northwest ports, "particu-

larly Antwerp and Rotterdam, before the bad weather sets in."[34]

Before the Antwerp operation could be started, Field Marshal Montgomery carried out his offensive near Arnhem. With the end of that attack, the pursuit into Germany came to a full halt.[35] On other fronts, it had virtually come to a standstill by mid-September. A review of the logistical situation of the Allied forces in the preceding four to six weeks may help explain why the pursuit stopped short of the Rhine.

Logistical Reasons for the Halt

It is clear that the demands of four rapidly advancing armies, requiring as much as a million gallons of gasoline daily, overtaxed the Allied lines of communications, which extended in some cases as far back as Cherbourg and the invasion

[32] Montgomery to Eisenhower, M–181, 9 Sep 44; Montgomery to Eisenhower, M–192, 11 Sep 44; Eisenhower to Montgomery (comments on Montgomery's statements to Gen Smith), FWD 14758, 13 Sep 44; Eisenhower to Montgomery, 16 Sep 44. All in SHAEF SGS 381 Post OVERLORD Planning, I. Comments of members of 21 Army Group staff to author in series of interviews.

[33] Montgomery to Eisenhower, M–192, 11 Sep 44; Eisenhower to Montgomery, FWD 14758, 13 Sep 44; Dir, Eisenhower to army comdrs, FWD 14764, 13 Sep 44. All in SHAEF SGS 381 Post OVERLORD Planning, I.

[34] CCS to Eisenhower, OCTAGON 16, 12 Sep 44, SHAEF SGS 381 Post OVERLORD Planning, I. In discussing General Eisenhower's proposals of alternative routes into Germany, Field Marshal Brooke thought the northern route should be strengthened as much as possible. He asked for the most energetic efforts to secure and open the port of Antwerp as a valuable base for future operations on the northern flank. He felt there had not been enough emphasis on these two points. His proposed draft reply was the one sent General Eisenhower. CCS 172d mtg, OCTAGON (Quebec), 12 Sep 44.

[35] For discussion of the Arnhem operation, see below, Ch. XVI.

beaches. These limitations certainly made impossible a number of simultaneous drives through the Siegfried Line and also made doubtful the success of a single thrust beyond the Rhine. From the beginning of OVERLORD planning, the various staffs had recognized supply difficulties as one of their major problems. They had stressed, therefore, the necessity of capturing sufficient ports to provide adequate and easily accessible stores, emphasizing the vital importance of Cherbourg, Le Havre, and the ports of Brittany if a drive into Germany was to be sustained. The planners assumed, as a result, that the rate of the advance beyond the Seine would be much less rapid than the rate actually achieved. In procurement estimates of June 1944, designedly optimistic for purposes of planning, D plus 90 (4 September 1944) was set for reaching the Seine, D plus 200 (23 December 1944) the Belgian frontier, D plus 330 (2 May 1945) the German frontier north of Aachen, and D plus 360 (1 June 1945) the surrender.

Both the first and last of these dates proved pessimistic. The Third Army reached the Seine on D plus 75 (20 August 1944) and the surrender came on D plus 336 (8 May 1945). These predictions, later pointed to with pride by the Allied staffs, have tended to obscure the more important fact, so far as supplies were concerned, that on D plus 97 (11 September 1944), one week after they were expected to reach the Seine and some seven months before they were supposed to reach the German border north of Aachen, the Allies actually sent units across the Reich frontier. But it was in this period of the great pursuit between the Seine and Germany that supply and transport facilities proved hopelessly insufficient for the slashing attack which developed. True, in mid-

August, when the armies were beginning to be pinched for supplies, the planners changed their calculations. At that time British planners estimated that bridgeheads could be established over the Seine at Rouen in the period between 10 August and 10 September, and that after the latter date an advance could be made on Amiens. The SHAEF planners were less optimistic, holding that any advance in strength before October east of the Seine–Loire River line would have to be conducted mainly by British forces. They suggested that an advance in strength by U.S. forces beyond the Mantes-Gassicourt–Orléans line be delayed until late October. Because the Allies would have to feed the population of Paris if they took the city, the SHAEF planners favored postponing its capture until rail facilities were developed in Brittany and Normandy and the Seine ports were captured.[36] As late as 23 August, the 12th Army Group deputy chief of supply estimated that the British would be at the Seine on 1 September, the Somme on 15 September, and on other objectives (apparently northern France and Belgium) by 1 November. General de Guingand, 21 Army Group chief of staff, concurred with these estimates ex-

---

[36] SHAEF G-4 Post NEPTUNE Operations Administrative Appreciation, 17 Jun 44, SHAEF G-4 370.2 Post-NEPTUNE Operations Logistic Studies. 21 A Gp Plan, Development of Current Operations, 11 Aug 44; Air Staff SHAEF, Development of Operations from the Bridgehead to Secure Lodgment Area and Advance Beyond (21 A Gp Plans); SHAEF G-3 Plan, Post NEPTUNE Operations, 17 Aug 44, Sec. III, SHAEF G-3 Post OVERLORD Planning, 18008, 370-31. When the preliminary draft of the 21 A Gp Plan was received at SHAEF at the end of July, Group Captain Gleave, one of the SHAEF planners, indicated that, whereas SHAEF felt that the paper was too optimistic, Air Marshal Coningham considered the plan not bold enough. Gleave to SASO, AEAF, 2 Aug 44, SHAEF file Air Staff (SHAEF).

cept that he expected to gain the "other objectives" by 15 October.[37]

In mid-August as the tremendous possibilities of a rapid advance became evident, the Allied supply organizations made great efforts to provide the means for the offensives which were developing. Communications Zone troops were laying pipelines for carrying fuel, constructing at the peak as much as thirty to forty miles a day. Special emphasis was placed on the rapid restoration of railroad lines so that overburdened truck companies could be used more economically. At the height of supply difficulties in the last week of August, an emergency airlift and the Red Ball Express truck line were set up to deal with the gasoline shortages which became more acute as the advance continued beyond the Seine.[38]

The liberation of Paris, as SHAEF supply planners had feared, increased the heavy load thrown on the U.S. supply organization and interfered directly with the flow of fuel to combat elements. The additional burden came at a time when aircraft engaged in carrying fuel to the First Army were supposed to be returned to the Air Transport Command for training in preparation for forthcoming airborne attacks.[39] On 29 August, the 12th Army Group chief of civil affairs found that the French capital needed 2,400 tons of supplies daily and proposed that they be brought by air. General Bradley initially authorized 500 tons at the expense of military requirements, but added in another message the same day that additional information on supply requirements in the city required that a "total of 1500 tons daily regardless of cost to the military effort, be delivered at once."[40] The reassignment of aircraft to airborne training and the diversion of air tonnage to civil

affairs supplies coincided with the almost complete cessation of gasoline deliveries to the Third Army, which had been the chief beneficiary of the airlift since 25 August.

Another complication appeared as the armies moved farther to the east: the problem of constructing sufficient and proper airfields to receive the airplanes necessary to maintain the pace which was being set on the ground. The rapid advance of armored columns meant that the burden thrown on airfield construction agencies in the matter of materials, men, and time was much greater than the capacities of the organization which had been set up. The chief of staff of IX Engineer Command, which was charged with the task of building and maintaining airfields, gave eloquent testimony after the war on the problems confronting the Allies in their attempts to supply the rush to the Rhine. In analyzing the claim that General Patton could have gone to Germany in ten days, he declared:

Had Patton continued through the Saar Valley and the Vosges it must have been without close air support and with a very small contribution in the way of air supply beyond the Reims–Epernay line. We could have fixed up Conflans, Metz, and Nancy–Azelot in time to have done some good, but the next possible fields were at Haguenau and Strasburg with no fields except Trier be-

[37] Memo on conf with Maj Gen Miles Graham, 21 A Gp G–4, *et al.*, dtd 23 Aug 44, SHAEF 12th A Gp G–4 Papers, Drawer 11, Folder 11.

[38] Ruppenthal, *Logistical Support of the Armies*, discusses these efforts in detail. Mr. Royce L. Thompson of OCMH has prepared an exhaustive study of the gasoline shortages from the official reports of SHAEF, Communications Zone, and the army group, army, corps, and division files. This study is in OCMH files.

[39] See Craven and Cate, *The Army Air Forces in World War II*, III, 275–77.

[40] 12th A Gp to SHAEF *et al.*, QX 21026, 29 Aug 44; 12th A Gp to COMZ Fwd, QX 21043, 29 Aug 44. Both in SHAEF G–4 581.2 Transportation by Air of Supplies and Equipment, II (1944).

tween there and Koln–Maastricht Plain. I would not have liked to tackle the job of supplying Patton over the Vosges and through the Pfalz during that October. I don't doubt that we could have carried about 2 armored and one mtz. division up to Koln, but then where. Certainly not across the Rhine. A good task force of Panzerfaust, manned by Hitler youth could have finished them off before they reached Kassel.[41]

Whether a diversion of all supplies to Field Marshal Montgomery's forces would have enabled him to cross the Rhine before the enemy could reorganize his defenses cannot be finally settled. To let the 21 Army Group have all the support it wanted in late August would have meant stopping the Third U.S. Army near Paris, delaying a link-up between the OVERLORD and the ANVIL forces, failing to capture enemy elements retreating from southwestern France to Germany, and opening the right wing of the army to a possible enemy attack. If the Rhine could have been crossed while the enemy was still unprepared and the shock of that event had shaken the Reich into collapse or its armies into surrender, obviously these eventualities would not have mattered. If the single thrust across the Rhine had failed to smash German resistance, there is some doubt that the forces could have been maintained at full operational scale.

It is equally difficult to determine whether the diversion of all available supplies to General Patton would have permitted him to reach the Rhine in ten days or two weeks. On this subject, the Third Army chief of operations noted at the end of August 1944 that there was an indication that the army would necessarily have to slow its pace "to permit supply echelons to make adjustments that would enable them to keep up." This was attributed in part to the fact that the Third Army was

responsible for operations on fronts 600 miles apart, and responsible for a flank of over 1,000 miles which it was covering with less than two divisions plus the XIX Tactical Air Command.[42]

The failure of the Allies to realize their hopes of victory in late August may have followed in part from a deficiency of optimism on the part of OVERLORD planners.[43] The means of communication, built for a slower, more ponderous drive than that which developed, could not sustain the ten- or twenty-day pursuit that opened the way to the smashing of the enemy short of the Rhine. The original supply estimates emphasized the opening of the Brittany ports and Le Havre and the amassing of supplies west of the Seine before beginning a drive toward the Ruhr. The Brittany ports were still judged to be of primary importance as late as 1 September. By 9 September, when Generals Patton and Bradley discussed the matter, there had been a considerable change in opinion. General Patton later wrote: "We both felt that the taking of Brest at that time was useless, because it was too far away and the harbor was too badly destroyed. On the other hand, we agreed that, when the American Army had once put its hand to the plow, it should not let go. Therefore, it was necessary to take Brest."[44] At least three excellent divisions of the Third Army and valuable transport

---

[41] Ltr, Col Herbert W. Ehrgott to Ralph Ingersoll, 25 Jul 46, copy furnished by Ehrgott to Air Historical Section, U.S. Air Force.

[42] G–3 Summary for Aug 44, TUSA AAR, I. See also Cole, *The Lorraine Campaign*, p. 22. In his statement, "the iron rules of logistics were in full operation and . . . the Third Army, making an attack subsidiary to the Allied main effort, would be the first to suffer therefrom."

[43] This is discussed fully in Ruppenthal, *Logistical Support of the Armies.*

[44] Patton, *War as I Knew It*, pp. 127–28.

were heavily involved here at a time when troops and vehicles were desperately needed to the east.

In hardly any respect were the Allies prepared to take advantage of the great opportunity offered them to destroy the German forces before winter. The build-up of men and certain critical supplies in the United Kingdom, the arrival of divisions in France, the requisition and transport of civil affairs supplies, the organization for military government,[45] the rebuilding of rail lines, the laying of pipelines—virtually the whole intricate military machine was geared to a slower rate of advance than that required in late August. Unfortunately the period of the great opportunity lasted for only a few weeks and there was not sufficient time, however vast the effort, to make the necessary readjustments in the logistical machinery which would insure speedy victory.

In this period of confusion, of overstrained supply lines, of strident demands for many different courses of action, most of which would have been excellent had the means been available, the Supreme Commander decided to stick by his initial plan of making the main attack in the north, with a subsidiary advance in the south. In the first bold thrust across the Seine, when he wished to clear the Pas-de-Calais and capture Antwerp, he approved Montgomery's drive to the northeast and threw most of the First Army into support of the British advance. This required the allocation of most of the U.S. gasoline supplies to the First Army and brought the Third Army virtually to a halt just east of Paris. When by 5 September the supply situation eased slightly General Eisenhower agreed that the Third Army could resume its drive toward the Saar and Frankfurt and thus returned to the earlier SHAEF concept of a dual thrust. At the same time he sent all but one corps of the First Army northeastward in support of the main offensive. Within the next two weeks he was to offer the 21 Army Group commander the bulk of available locomotives and rolling stock, the transport of three U.S. divisions, and the resources of the airborne army. In these various decisions, he attempted to take advantage of any momentary opportunities for exploitation which might be offered, while clinging to the objectives laid down before D Day as vital to victory: seizure of industrial areas essential to Germany's continuance of the war, use of routes which offered the best opportunity for maneuver while stretching the enemy's forces over a broad front, and elimination of the maximum number of Germans west of the fortifications of the West Wall and of the Rhine.

---

[45] For example, policy on the issuance of occupation money for Germany was not settled until three weeks after the Allies had crossed the German frontier.

CHAPTER XV

Command Reorganization, June–October 1944

A number of changes in command arrangements affecting the Allied Expeditionary Force marked the period between the invasion of Normandy and the entry into Germany. These included the Supreme Commander's assumption of direct control of the forces in the field, the activation of new army group headquarters, the shifting of four additional armies to the Continent, the clarification of relations between SHAEF and U.S. theater staffs, and the reorganization of strategic and tactical air commands. (*Chart 5*)

The Ground Forces

General Eisenhower Takes Command

The Normandy invasion began under an arrangement by which General Montgomery was to command the ground assault forces until such time as the Supreme Commander should take personal control of operations in the field. The date of change-over was to be determined in part by the build-up of U.S. forces on the Continent; no shift appeared necessary so long as only one U.S. army was ashore. When, however, a second U.S. army should be required, the Supreme Commander proposed to bring forward a U.S. army group to co-ordinate the actions of the two U.S.

armies. He would then decide the point at which he should take over the task of co-ordinating the British and U.S. army groups.[1]

The Third U.S. Army, brought from the United States and put under the command of General Patton in late 1943, remained in England during the first weeks of the invasion while some of its divisions were sent to the Continent for initial use in the First Army. The plan for the breakout from the Cotentin peninsula required the employment of some of these units. At the opening of the attack on 25 July, General Eisenhower announced that, on a date set by General Bradley, the U.S. forces on the Continent were to be regrouped under the 12th Army Group.[2] An additional statement to the effect that U.S. assault forces were to remain under General Montgomery until General Eisenhower allocated a specific area of responsibility for

---

[1] Memo, Command and Organization after D Day OVERLORD, 1 Jun 44, SHAEF G–3 322.011–1 Command and Control of U.S./British Forces.

[2] This army group had initially been called 1st U.S. Army Group and had been commanded since October 1943 by General Bradley. For purposes of deceiving the Germans, it now became 12th Army Group. First U.S. Army Group was retained on paper and in the German imagination. As already noted, General McNair and, later, General DeWitt were appointed to head this paper army group to maintain the fiction.

CHART 5—OPERATIONAL CHAIN OF COMMAND, AEF, 1 SEPTEMBER 1944

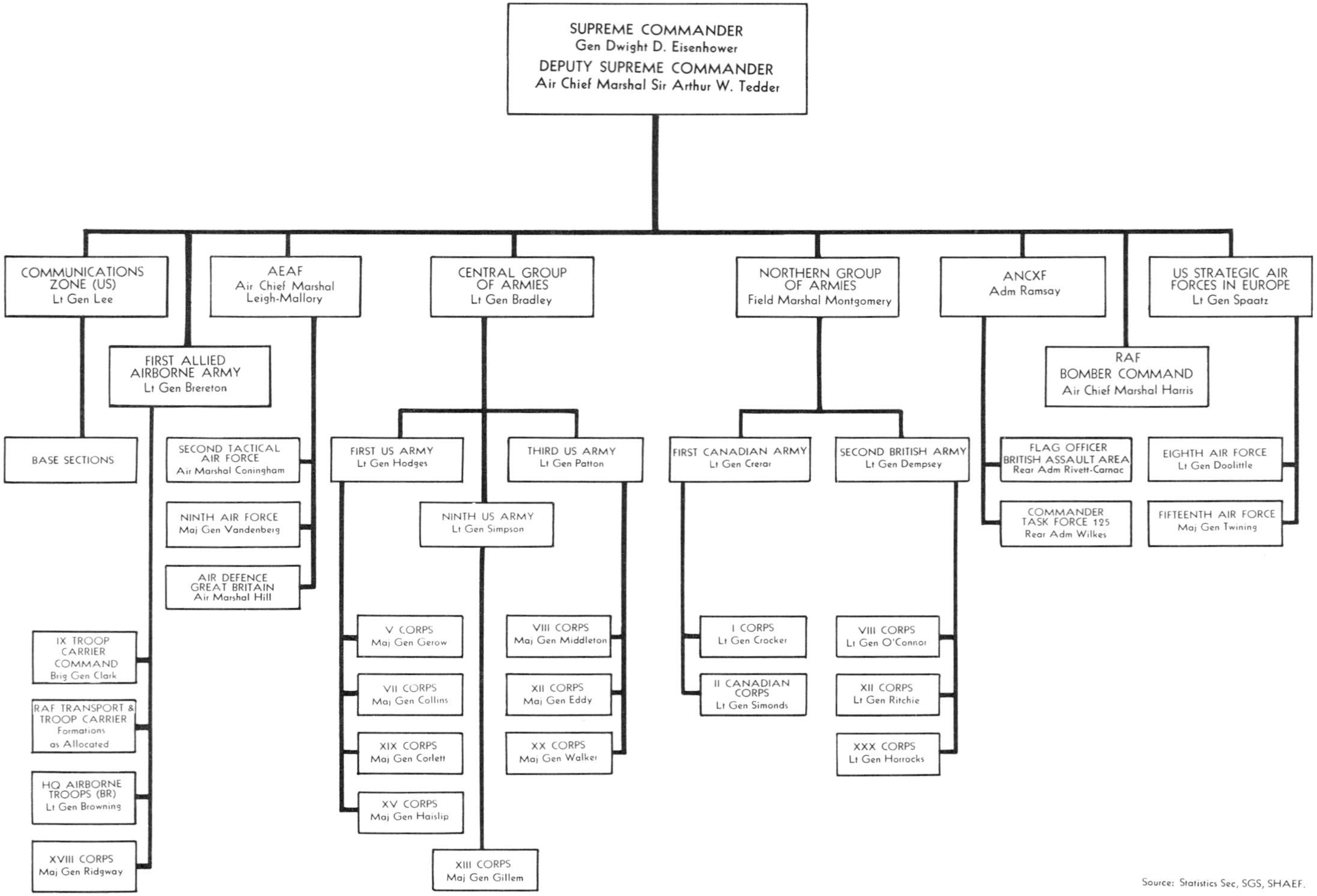

SUPREME COMMANDER
Gen Dwight D. Eisenhower
DEPUTY SUPREME COMMANDER
Air Chief Marshal Sir Arthur W. Tedder

COMMUNICATIONS ZONE (US)
Lt Gen Lee

FIRST ALLIED AIRBORNE ARMY
Lt Gen Brereton

BASE SECTIONS

IX TROOP CARRIER COMMAND
Brig Gen Clark

RAF TRANSPORT & TROOP CARRIER
Formation as Allocated

HQ AIRBORNE TROOPS (BR)
Lt Gen Browning

XVIII CORPS
Maj Gen Ridgway

AEAF
Air Chief Marshal Leigh-Mallory

SECOND TACTICAL AIR FORCE
Air Marshal Coningham

NINTH AIR FORCE
Maj Gen Vandenberg

AIR DEFENCE GREAT BRITAIN
Air Marshal Hill

CENTRAL GROUP OF ARMIES
Lt Gen Bradley

THIRD US ARMY
Lt Gen Patton

NINTH US ARMY
Lt Gen Simpson

FIRST US ARMY
Lt Gen Hodges

VIII CORPS
Maj Gen Middleton

XII CORPS
Maj Gen Eddy

XX CORPS
Maj Gen Walker

XIII CORPS
Maj Gen Gillem

V CORPS
Maj Gen Gerow

VII CORPS
Maj Gen Collins

XIX CORPS
Maj Gen Corlett

XV CORPS
Maj Gen Haislip

NORTHERN GROUP OF ARMIES
Field Marshal Montgomery

SECOND BRITISH ARMY
Lt Gen Dempsey

FIRST CANADIAN ARMY
Lt Gen Crerar

VIII CORPS
Lt Gen O'Connor

XII CORPS
Lt Gen Ritchie

XXX CORPS
Lt Gen Horrocks

I CORPS
Lt Gen Crocker

II CANADIAN CORPS
Lt Gen Simonds

ANCXF
Adm Ramsay

FLAG OFFICER BRITISH ASSAULT AREA
Rear Adm Rivett-Carnac

COMMANDER TASK FORCE 125
Rear Adm Wilkes

US STRATEGIC AIR FORCES IN EUROPE
Lt Gen Spaatz

RAF BOMBER COMMAND
Air Chief Marshal Harris

EIGHTH AIR FORCE
Lt Gen Doolittle

FIFTEENTH AIR FORCE
Maj Gen Twining

Source: Statistics Sec, SGS, SHAEF.

the U.S. army group immediately led to some confusion in the press.[3] Although the 12th Army Group became active on the Continent on 1 August and Montgomery channeled his orders to the U.S. armies through it, the 21 Army Group commander retained over-all control until 1 September.

This arrangement was valuable in that it permitted one commander to co-ordinate Allied forces during the period of the breakout and pursuit. But it led many people in Great Britain and the United States to overestimate the degree to which General Bradley's army group was subordinated to General Montgomery. Throughout August, General Montgomery continued as before to issue operational instructions to the U.S. forces, but he consulted General Bradley increasingly as a partner instead of a subordinate and gave him great latitude in directing the U.S. forces. General Bradley presented some of his plans directly to General Eisenhower. The difference in the command relationship which existed between the 21 Army Group and the U.S. forces in June and July and the arrangement in effect in August was largely that between the direction of an operation and the co-ordination of a joint effort.[4]

On the day General Bradley assumed command of 12th Army Group on the Continent, the Third U.S. Army became operational. The enemy was aware almost immediately that General Patton was in action and announced the news to the world, although the Allied press was forbidden to print any notice of the fact. Some of General Patton's subordinates criticized the ban severely, charging SHAEF with jealousy of their chief. SHAEF had explained its reason for this action in the memorandum of 25 July on command reorganization. Desiring to continue the threat against the Pas-de-Calais based on the suggestion that General Patton had an army group in the United Kingdom poised for an attack, SHAEF asked that the Third Army commander's presence on the Continent be kept secret until it was certain that the Germans had positively identified him. Since a common trick of the enemy was to announce the arrival of new units in the hope of getting a confirmation or denial, SHAEF waited several days before making a statement. When it did come, without any explanation of the reason for secrecy, the feeling was heightened that Supreme Headquarters had some ulterior reason for its silence.[5]

Scarcely had criticism of SHAEF's handling of the Patton story subsided when a greater uproar arose over the announcement of the activation of the new U.S. army group. In mid-August, as a result of a censor's error, press correspondents were allowed to announce that 12th Army Group had been activated and that General Bradley was now equal in authority with General Montgomery. Since the latter statement would not become true until General Eisenhower assumed direct command in the field, an arrangement scheduled for 1 September, SHAEF officials denied the statement without adding that the change would be made within a short time. Some London papers,

---

[3] Memo, Eisenhower for Bradley, 25 Jul 44, sub: Comd and Organization U.S. Ground Forces, SHAEF G–3 322.011–1 Command and Control of U.S./British Forces. The same file contains a letter from Bradley to Montgomery, 19 July 1944, suggesting this arrangement, and Montgomery's agreement.

[4] See above, p. 198, for Bradley's description of command relations.

[5] Memo, Eisenhower to Bradley, 25 Jul 44, SHAEF G–3 322.011–1 Command and Control of U.S./British Forces.

unaware of the projected command arrangements, sharply attacked the original statement, asking that persons responsible for it be punished and that an apology be made to General Montgomery. In the United States some newspapers lashed out at the command arrangements in Europe saying that British officers had been given the posts of ground, air, and naval commanders, thus reducing General Eisenhower to the role of figurehead. Fearing that this criticism would spread and be injected into Congressional debate, General Marshall wrote General Eisenhower that "The Secretary [Mr. Stimson] and I and apparently all Americans" were strongly of the opinion that it was time for the Supreme Commander to take direct command—at least of the U.S. forces. To this recommendation, already made by Tedder and Smith, General Marshall added: "The astonishing success of the campaign up to the present moment has evoked emphatic expression of confidence in you and Bradley. The late announcement I have just referred to has cast a damper on the public enthusiasm." [6]

General Eisenhower was startled by the reaction and indicated that General Bradley shared his feelings. Apparently irritated, he replied: "It seems that so far as the press and public are concerned a resounding victory is not sufficient; the question of 'how' is equally important." It would be a great pity, he agreed, if General Bradley were denied full credit for his brilliant work "merely because general instructions and policies he has pursued have been channeled through Montgomery." The current command arrangement, he noted, had been adopted because it was impossible to move Supreme Headquarters to the Continent until an adequate communications network could be secured to connect the United Kingdom and the Continent. While waiting for this development, General Eisenhower added, he had found it necessary to make one person responsible for the temporary control of ground forces in Normandy and had chosen General Montgomery on the basis of seniority and experience. In carrying out that task, the British commander had worked always under plans approved by the Supreme Commander, who made his influence felt by frequent visits to the battlefront. By 19 August, General Eisenhower was inclined to agree with the U.S. Chief of Staff that the time for a change was near at hand, and he hoped that the establishment of new communications would make possible the move of SHAEF to the Continent on 1 September. Even in the absence of such direct control, the Supreme Commander still felt justified in saying, "No major effort takes place in this Theater by ground, sea or air except with my approval and no one in the Allied Command presumes to question my supreme authority and responsibility for the whole campaign." [7]

Anticipating his assumption of direct control in the field, General Eisenhower had sent his headquarters commandant and the chief of the Signal Division to the Continent in early August to find a site which would have adequate communications for Supreme Headquarters. Toward the end of August, they decided that Jullouville, a small town just south of Granville at the base of the Cotentin peninsula,

---

[6] Marshall to Eisenhower, W–82265, 17 Aug 44; Surles to Eisenhower, 19 Aug 44. Both in SHAEF cbl log. Copies of articles in London *Daily Mirror*, Washington *Times-Herald*, and other papers in Diary Office CinC, 19 Aug 44; Eisenhower, *Crusade in Europe*, p. 300.

[7] Eisenhower to Marshall, CPA 90230, 19 Aug 44, SHAEF cbl log.

GENERAL SIMPSON. *(Photograph taken in 1945.)*

would serve. With this assurance, the Supreme Commander announced that he would assume direct operational control on 1 September with General Montgomery and General Bradley as respective commanders of the Northern and Central Groups of Armies.[8]

SHAEF became operational on the Continent on 1 September at Jullouville. Its forces, now consisting of two army groups (21 and 12th) and four armies, were soon augmented by another army group and three armies. One of these armies, the Ninth, which had been brought to the United Kingdom shortly before the invasion, became operational under Lt. Gen. William H. Simpson on 5 September 1944 and was assigned to the 12th Army Group. On that date General

Simpson took command of all forces in the Brittany peninsula which had been operating there under General Patton's command.[9] The other units, which were even then engaged in the battle for southern France, were shortly to be incorporated into General Eisenhower's command as the 6th Army Group.

Command of ANVIL/DRAGOON Forces

General Eisenhower had assumed before D Day that one U.S. and one British army group would be sufficient to control Allied forces on the Continent. He did not object, however, in July 1944 when the War Department suggested that the 6th Army Group be created to command the Allied forces that would land in the south of France. Both the War Department and Headquarters, North African Theater of Operations (NATOUSA), emphasized that this additional army group was needed to co-ordinate civil affairs and to assure U.S. control of the operation. The Supreme Commander also agreed to the selection of General Devers for the 6th Army Group post. To dispel a rumor that he was opposed to the appointment, he cabled Washington that, while he did not know General Devers well, all reports were that he was doing a fine job and had the faculty of inspiring troops.[10]

General Wilson, Supreme Commander in the Mediterranean, and General Eisenhower agreed before the landings in southern France that troops put ashore in that

---

[8] Eisenhower to all comds, 25 Aug 44, SHAEF cbl log.

[9] *Conquer: The Story of Ninth Army*, p. 21.

[10] Eisenhower to Marshall, 12 Jul 44, Eisenhower personal file.

area would ultimately be placed under SHAEF, but probably not until they had advanced in strength north of Lyon. Before that time General Eisenhower was to keep General Wilson informed of his scheme of action in order that the Mediterranean commander's campaign would conform to OVERLORD operations. SHAEF was not ready to take over the maintenance of the 6th Army Group immediately; reserve stocks of supplies in the Mediterranean could be used for some weeks to support the forces in southern France. General Eisenhower also proposed that Allied Force Headquarters retain responsibility for civil affairs in the south of France as long as that headquarters continued to supply the ANVIL/DRAGOON forces. These suggestions were accepted by General Wilson.[11]

The rapid advance of the ANVIL armies from the south and the sweep of the OVERLORD forces to the east in the opening days of September hastened SHAEF's assumption of the operational control of units coming from the south. At 0001, 15 September, in accordance with the order of the Combined Chiefs of Staff, the 6th Army Group became operational under the command of General Devers. It and the First French and Seventh U.S. Armies passed from Allied Force Headquarters to SHAEF. The Twelfth Air Force handed over the XII Tactical Air Command to the Ninth Air Force. For the moment, Allied Force Headquarters retained responsibility for the administration, logistical support, and maintenance of ANVIL/DRAGOON forces and civil affairs in the south of France.[12]

Fifteenth Army

Before the second U.S. army was com-

GENERAL GEROW. *(Photograph taken in 1948.)*

mitted in Normandy, the War Department made plans to activate a fifth U.S. army, the Fifteenth, which was ultimately to be added to the forces under the Supreme Commander's control. The army was activated at Fort Sam Houston, Tex., in August 1944. It began operations in the United Kingdom in late November of the same year. Toward the end of December the unit began moving to the Continent where it became operational on 6 January 1945. Ten days later General Gerow, com-

[11] Eisenhower to Marshall and Wilson, FWD 13445, 31 Aug 44; Wilson to Eisenhower, FX–91666, 3 Sep 44. Both in AFHQ CAO 1202, ANVIL (20–A 134 E). Eisenhower to Marshall, 31 Aug 44, Diary Office CinC.

[12] AFHQ to 6th A Gp, FX 24922, 14 Sep 44; SHAEF to 6th A Gp, FWD 14827, 14 Sep 44. Both in AFHQ CAO 1202 ANVIL (20–A, 134 E).

mander of V Corps, took command of the new army.[13]

SHAEF, ETOUSA, and Communications Zone in 1944

General Eisenhower's dual role of Supreme Commander and U.S. theater commander was accompanied by some complications in the handling of U.S. administrative and supply matters on the Continent in 1944–45. Basically the difficulty arose because General Eisenhower did not wish to set up a separate theater administrative staff. He realized that there existed a shortage of qualified staff officers and that it was necessary if possible to avoid establishing an additional staff. He tended frequently, therefore, to call upon U.S. members of the SHAEF G–4 Division as well as members of Headquarters, Communications Zone, for advice in administration and supply matters.[14]

In mid-January 1944, General Eisenhower had consolidated Headquarters, European Theater of Operations, U.S. Army, which was responsible for all U.S. forces in the theater, and Headquarters, Services of Supply, which had the chief responsibility for mounting and supplying the U.S. part of the operation. At the same time he appointed Maj. Gen. John C. H. Lee, the Services of Supply commander, as deputy theater commander with special responsibilities for administration and supply. General Lee's tasks included command of the Communications Zone troops in the United Kingdom and on the Continent, necessary activities in connection with static defense, and performance of additional duties delegated by the theater commander.[15]

Several problems soon developed out of the new arrangements. Combat commanders did not like the fact that the chief of the services of supply was in a position to control the inflow of reinforcements and supplies in such a way as to discriminate against the field forces. Since there was no other U.S. headquarters to act as an umpire, the U.S. members of the G–4 Division, SHAEF, sometimes found themselves acting as General Eisenhower's advisers in these matters. General Lee and his staff felt that the SHAEF G–4, General Crawford, was attempting to control all U.S. supply matters. Shortly before D Day, General Lee asked for a clarification of the whole command relationship. On D Day, General Smith drafted an order saying that General Eisenhower would use U.S. members of the SHAEF staff only in those purely U.S. matters which remained under his direct control.[16]

General Eisenhower found that he had to intervene personally in the matter in early June and again in mid-July. On the latter occasion, he emphasized that the determination of broad policies, objectives, and priorities affecting two or more major U.S. commands was the responsibility of the U.S. theater commander. He proposed to delegate part of these duties to the major commands—12th Army Group, Communications Zone, and USSTAF. General Eisenhower stipulated, however, that as theater commander he would utilize both the U.S. elements of the SHAEF staff and the chiefs of special and

---

[13] *History of the Fifteenth United States Army, 21 August 1944 to 11 July 1945* (apparently printed in Germany, 1946), pp. 6–18.

[14] Eisenhower note for author, Aug 51; Ltr, Lt Col Roy Lamson to Maj Gen Orlando Ward, Chief of Military History, 9 Aug 51. Both in OCMH files.

[15] Hq ETOUSA GO 5, 17 Jan 44. ETOUSA files.

[16] Ltr, Lee to Eisenhower, 29 May 44; Draft GO by Gen Smith, 6 Jun 44. Both in SHAEF SGS 322 ETOUSA, Organization and Administrative Command.

technical services of ETOUSA for advice.[17]

In order that no question should remain in the minds of his staff members, General Eisenhower on 21 July laid down the procedure for carrying out "so-called American administration in this *Allied* theater of operations." Communications with various U.S. headquarters on supply were to be channeled through the Communications Zone commander, since he retained all theater duties except decisions and policy on major differences among the principal U.S. commands. Because it was clearly impossible to separate U.S. and Allied matters completely, General Eisenhower added, he would habitually use "the senior U.S. officer in each of our several sections as an advisor on applicable U.S. matters, when the subject is of the type that requires the Theater Commander to take personal action." Although this arrangement, he noted, did not make SHAEF officers part of the theater staff, they were "convenient agents responsible to me for advice and where necessary, for following up something of particular importance." [18]

The new system failed to satisfy either the Communications Zone or SHAEF G–4 staffs. The former felt that the situation was unsatisfactory in that it separated the theater commander from his staff, required the expansion of U.S. personnel at SHAEF to handle supply matters, and weakened the position of Communications Zone relative to other U.S. commands in Europe which tended to look to SHAEF in administrative matters. Army group and army commanders were likewise dissatisfied with the arrangements of mid-July. The supply problems that developed in late August and early September, particularly the ammunition and gasoline shortages, led to strong criticism of Headquarters, Communications Zone. As a result, General Crawford, the SHAEF G–4, in mid-September asked that the U.S. members of the SHAEF staff be given "a considerably greater measure of supervision than [seemed] to be contemplated by existing orders." He did not mean that General Lee's staff should cease to function, but held that increased supervision by SHAEF was required in such matters as speeding up ammunition for U.S. units in the Brest peninsula, shifting U.S. supplies to the 21 Army Group, and allocating rolling stock. An alternative solution, he added, was to attach strong elements of Communications Zone to SHAEF to act directly under the Supreme Commander.[19] General Eisenhower did not take action on these proposals, and the same general organization continued to exist until the end of 1944. While the administrative system was marked by friction, its functioning was assured by the fact that Generals Eisenhower and Smith were sufficiently near Communications Zone to make sure that difficulties were held to a minimum and that their operational decisions were promptly implemented.

---

[17] Memo, DDE [Eisenhower] for CofS SHAEF, 18 Jul 44, issued 19 Jul 44 by Hq ETOUSA as Memo on Organization and Command of U.S. Forces, SHAEF AG 322.1 (ETO).

[18] Memo, Eisenhower for CofS SHAEF, 21 Jul 44, SHAEF SGS 322 ETOUSA, Organization and Administrative Command.

[19] [Robert W. Coakley], Organization and Command in the ETO, Pt. II of The Administrative and Logistical History of the ETO, Hist Div USFET, 1946, MS, II, 209–16; General Board Rpt 127, Organization and Functions of the Communications Zone, Ch. I, pp. 9–10; Crawford to CofS SHAEF, 18 Sep 44, SHAEF SGS 322 ETOUSA, Organization and Administrative Control. See also Ruppenthal, *Logistical Support of the Armies,* for a discussion of command organization in the European theater.

The Air and Naval Forces

Formation of the First
Allied Airborne Army

The establishment of the First Allied Airborne Army under SHAEF to co-ordinate the varied elements of air and ground forces essential for airborne operations on the Continent was one of the major command changes of 1944. Such co-ordination proved necessary because parachute and glider troops used in the airborne operations were part of the ground force organization, while the aircraft which carried the troops, furnished escorts, and resupplied the airborne units were under air force command. The problem became further complicated when both British and U.S. air and ground forces were involved. To simplify the command difficulties and make possible the thorough exploitation of airborne forces, the First Allied Airborne Army was created. (*Chart 6*)

Back of the formation of a special army headquarters to plan and carry out airborne operations was the campaign of the War Department for greater strategic use of airborne forces. Since February 1944, Generals Marshall and Arnold had reiterated to the Supreme Commander the importance of strategic employment of these units. General Eisenhower agreed with their views in principle, but, as has been observed, doubted the feasibility of using them strategically in the opening phases of the assault when it would be difficult if not impossible to open lines of communications to them. As the War Department continued to press for a strategic airborne operation using up to six divisions, it became evident that an airborne headquarters which could plan and execute such activities was necessary. On 20 May 1944, SHAEF set the period between 12 and 26 June as the time for the activation of such an organization. Two weeks later, SHAEF asked AEAF and the army groups for their reactions to a plan by which airborne divisions and necessary air forces would be brought under one organization for planning, command, and co-ordination. The 21 Army Group approved but asked that the activation be postponed until SHAEF assumed operational command of the ground forces. The U.S. army group disapproved on the ground that United States airborne troops should be controlled by a U.S. rather than an Allied command. On 20 June, General Eisenhower approved the organization of a combined United States–British Airborne Troop Command, established as a modified corps headquarters under a U.S. Army Air Forces officer with the rank of lieutenant general. The new headquarters was to be activated about the time SHAEF became operational on the Continent.[20]

In explaining his action to General Marshall, General Eisenhower declared that it was necessary because a suitable agency was lacking for joint planning between the troop carrier command and the airborne divisions. The airborne commander, he said, would be able to assume such responsibilities as joint training, development of operational projects, and logistical support of airborne operations until these functions could be taken over by normal agencies. If an airborne attack by two or three divisions took place in a

---

[20] Memo, SHAEF G–3 for CofS SHAEF, 20 May 44; SHAEF G–3 to FUSAG, 21 A Gp, and AEAF, sub: Establishment of Combined U.S.-Br Airborne Troops Hq, 2 Jun 44; 21 A Gp to SHAEF, 4 Jun 44; FUSAG to SHAEF, 8 Jun 44; AEAF to SHAEF, 8 Jun 44; Memo, Gen Smith for G–3, 20 Jun 44. All in SHAEF G–3 Formation of FAAA 17281/1/Airborne.

CHART 6—OPERATIONAL CHANNELS, FIRST ALLIED AIRBORNE ARMY, 28 NOVEMBER 1944

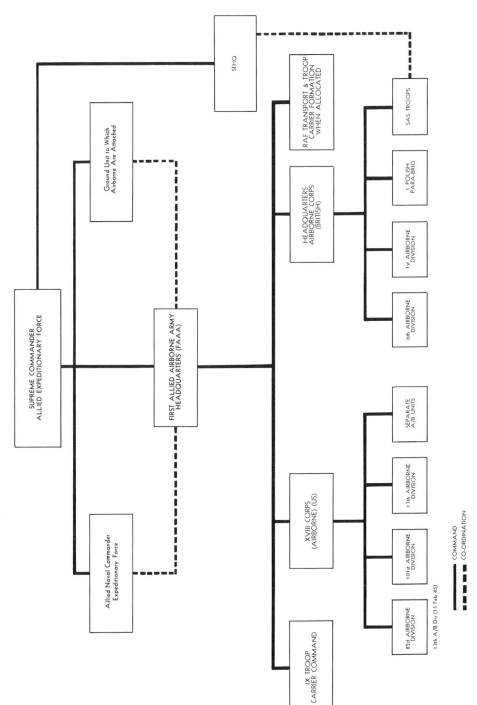

13th A/B Div (15 Feb 45)

COMMAND
CO-ORDINATION

Source: Statistics Sec, SGS, SHAEF.

single area, a temporary corps commander would be designated to conduct the fighting on the ground. He would operate under directives from the airborne headquarters until he joined the nearest army, which would then take operational and logistical responsibility for his units.[21] No persuasion seemed to be necessary so far as the U.S. Chief of Staff was concerned if one may judge by the Ninth Air Force commander's remark of mid-July that he knew "General Marshall had insisted on the creation of an airborne army."[22]

In mid-July both the AEAF and the Ninth Air Force commanders proposed changes in the airborne command scheme. Lt. Gen. Lewis H. Brereton, the Ninth Air Force chief, felt he should be given responsibility for airborne operations inasmuch as the major airborne troop carrier forces were American. The AEAF commander, Air Chief Marshal Leigh-Mallory, proposed that U.S. airborne forces be placed under a special corps commander and that both U.S. and British airborne troops be unified under one command. At the same time, he wished to limit the latter command to control of the ground forces, while reserving for AEAF responsibility for all air aspects of airborne operations.[23]

SHAEF replied with the reminder that General Eisenhower had studied the airborne problem for more than one and one-half years and that he felt the proposed reorganization the proper one. On 8 August, Supreme Headquarters announced the establishment of Combined Airborne Headquarters, and eight days later, at the suggestion of its new commander, it was renamed the First Allied Airborne Army. General Brereton was appointed chief of the new headquarters, and Lt. Gen. F. A. M. Browning, commander of the British

Airborne Corps, was named his deputy.[24] Placed under the new army were IX Troop Carrier Command, XVIII U.S. Corps (Airborne) headquarters, British Airborne Troops, including 1st Polish Parachute Brigade, and the Combined Air Transport Operations Room (CATOR). Royal Air Force Transport and Troop Carrier formations were placed under First Allied Airborne Army only when specifically allocated.[25]

At the request of AEAF, Supreme Headquarters announced on 18 August that the First Allied Airborne Army would control its own airlift, but that AEAF would retain the responsibility for supporting air operations. In September, the functions of General Brereton's command were further limited by an agreement that the First Allied Airborne Army would confine itself to outline planning and to operational command. Headquarters, Airborne Troops, though under the operational command of General Brereton, was

[21] Marshall to Eisenhower, W–56294, 26 Jun 44; Arnold to Spaatz and Smith, WX–61600, 7 Jul 44; Eisenhower to Marshall, S–55192, 8 Jul 44. All in SHAEF G–3 Formation of FAAA 17281/1/Airborne.

[22] Brereton, *The Brereton Diaries*, entry for 17 July 1944, p. 309.

[23] Ltr, Brereton to Eisenhower, 25 Jul 44, sub: Organization and Contemplated Opns of Air Army; Leigh-Mallory to Eisenhower, 17 Jul 44, sub: Organization of a Combined U.S.-Br Airborne Troop Hq. Both in SHAEF SGS 322 FAAA, Organization and Command FAAA.

[24] General Brereton's selection brought a general shift in which he was succeeded as head of Ninth Air Force by Maj. Gen. Hoyt S. Vandenberg, then Deputy Air Commander-in-Chief, AEAF. Vandenberg was replaced by Maj. Gen. Ralph Royce, Deputy Commanding General, Ninth Air Force.

[25] Memo, SHAEF for WO, Br COS, *et al.*, 8 Aug 44, sub: Reorganization of Airborne Forces; SHAEF dir to Brereton, 8 Aug 44; Brereton to SAC, 4 Aug 44; Memo by SHAEF G–3, 15 Aug 44; SHAEF memo, Redesignation of Combined Airborne Forces, 16 Aug 44; Smith to AEAF comdr, 18 Aug 44; SHAEF dir to AEAF and USAAFE, 9 Aug 44. All in SHAEF G–3 Formation of FAAA 17281/1/Airborne.

AIR CHIEF MARSHAL HARRIS

to have direct access to 21 Army Group or the War Office for administrative purposes. Air-transported formations were to remain under the command of ground formations concerned, being placed under the command of Headquarters, Airborne Troops, when necessary.[26]

Strategic Bomber Command

Among the command shifts of September, one of the most important was that involving the strategic air forces. This was made in accordance with the agreement of mid-April 1944 by which the Supreme Commander had assumed control of the strategic air forces supporting OVERLORD operations. It was clearly understood that, after the Allied forces had established themselves on the Continent, the Combined Chiefs of Staff would review the ini-

tial directive for the employment of the bomber forces and the method of their employment.[27] At the beginning of September, General Eisenhower was informed that changes in the air command arrangement would be made at the Combined Chiefs of Staff conference shortly to be held in Quebec. The Supreme Commander promptly urged that existing arrangements be continued. He recalled that

GENERAL VANDENBERG. *(Photograph taken in 1950.)*

the basic conception underlying the campaign was the possession of an overpowering air force which made feasible an other-

[26] Smith to AEAF, 18 Aug 44; Mtg at WO, 22 Sep 44, to discuss functions of FAAA, SHAEF G-3 Formation of FAAA 17281/1/Airborne.
[27] Memo, CCS for SAC, 27 Mar 44; Portal to Spaatz, 13 Apr 44; Air Ministry to Bomber Comd, 13 Apr 44. All in SHAEF SGS 373/1 Policy re: Control and Employment of USSTAF and Bomber Com-

wise impossible campaign. The air forces had lived up to expectations, virtually destroying the German Air Force, disrupting enemy communications, neutralizing beach defenses, aiding the ground forces to break through enemy lines, and fulfilling all other demands made on them. Meanwhile, the strategic air forces had been committed to the greatest extent possible on strategic targets and had prevented substantial rehabilitation of enemy industry and oil production. At present the ground forces were almost beyond the range of medium bombers, and in emergencies would require heavy bomber support. General Eisenhower said that he believed this emergency type of aid depended on the continuation of the existing command system. He added that General Spaatz shared his views on the existing system.[28]

At the Quebec meeting in mid-September, the Combined Chiefs of Staff ultimately decided that considerations in addition to those advanced by the Supreme Commander had to be taken into account. They concluded on 14 September that the Chief of the Air Staff, Royal Air Force (Portal), and the Commanding General, U.S. Army Air Forces (Arnold), should exercise control of all strategic bomber forces in Europe. The Deputy Chief of the Air Staff, RAF (Air Marshal Sir Norman H. Bottomley), and the Commanding General, United States Strategic Air Forces (Spaatz), were to provide control and local co-ordination through consultation.[29]

A new directive for the strategic air forces issued at this time undertook to in-

sure continuation of a broad strategic bombing program as well as adequate bomber support for General Eisenhower's ground operations. The over-all mission of the strategic air forces remained "the progressive destruction and dislocation of the German military, industrial and economic systems and the direct support of Land and Naval forces." The Supreme Commander's calls for aid in battle were to be filled promptly. The Combined Chiefs of Staff were to prescribe attacks in support of the Soviet ground forces.[30] The strategic air forces were to co-ordinate their activities with the operations of the tactical air forces, consulting as necessary the AEAF commander, who would normally co-ordinate air action in accordance with ground force requirements. In a list of priorities worked out by the strategic air force commanders in consultation with Air Chief Marshal Tedder, first priority for strategic bombing was given to the destruction of the petroleum industry with special emphasis on gasoline. Second priority targets were the German rail and water transportation systems, tank production plants and depots and ordnance depots, and motor transport production plants and depots.[31]

While General Eisenhower would have

---

[28] Eisenhower to Marshall and Arnold, FWD 13605, 2 Sep 44; Eisenhower to Arnold, FWD 13657, 3 Sep 44. Both in Eisenhower personal file.

[29] Portal and Arnold to USSTAF for Spaatz, 14 Sep 44; RAF London to Bottomley, OCTAGON 29, 14 Sep 44. Both in SHAEF SGS 373/1 Policy re: Control and Employment of USSTAF and Bomber Command.

[30] Portal and Arnold to USSTAF for Spaatz, 14 Sep 44; RAF London to Bottomley, OCTAGON 29, 14 Sep 44. Both in SHAEF SGS 373/1 Policy re: Control and Employment of USSTAF and Bomber Command.

[31] Bottomley to Bomber Comd, 25 Sep 44; Spaatz to SAC, 3 Oct 44, with attached dir for control of strategic air forces in Europe. Both in SHAEF SGS 373/1 Policy re: Control and Employment of USSTAF and Bomber Command.

---

mand. For description of the April arrangements, see above, p. 125. For general discussion of the shift in strategic air forces command see Craven and Cate, *The Army Air Forces in World War II*, III, 319–22.

preferred complete control of strategic air forces at SHAEF, he told General Marshall that the new arrangement would be satisfactory because of the "goodwill of the individuals concerned" and the assurances that his operations would be supported. He knew he could depend on the backing of General Spaatz, and he had found that Air Chief Marshal Harris was one of the most effective and co-operative members of the Allied team. The Supreme Commander added that the British bomber commander had not only met every request but had led the way in finding new ways and means for particular types of planes to be of use on the battlefield.[32]

Allied Expeditionary Air Force

Less than a month after the shift in the strategic air forces command, Air Chief Marshal Leigh-Mallory was appointed to command the Allied air forces in southeastern Asia, and the Allied Expeditionary Air Force was abolished. In September 1944, Admiral Lord Louis Mountbatten had sounded out General Eisenhower on the possibility of getting the AEAF chief released to head up the Southeast Asia air command. General Arnold opposed this shift on the ground that a U.S. and not a British airman should be named to the post. At the same time, the U.S. air chief was strongly in favor of abolishing Headquarters, Allied Expeditionary Air Force, which he felt no longer served any useful purpose. He found, however, that the chief difficulty in getting the headquarters abolished lay in finding a suitable appointment for Leigh-Mallory. General Eisenhower, when informed of this situation, cabled General Arnold:

Under present circumstances I agree we could get along without Leigh-Mallory's

Headquarters. The fact is, however, that through every day of this campaign Leigh-Mallory has proved his intense desire to co-operate and a very admirable grasp of the whole situation. Our plans for reorganization when and if he is detached will eliminate that headquarters and all the functions it has been performing will be centered right here at SHAEF. But you should not be under any misapprehension as to Leigh-Mallory's qualifications and attitude. Admitting that upon first glance he seems to be a bit difficult, he is one of the type that never ceases to develop and above all, he is a real fighter, which I like. He is an experienced and valuable officer.

There is no need to manufacture a job merely to get rid of Leigh-Mallory but on the other hand, as I explained above, if he is taken out of here for any reason I will not assign another man to his present title.

The initiative for Leigh-Mallory's eventual release came from the British Air Ministry. On 20 September, Sir Archibald Sinclair, Secretary of State for Air, pointed to decisions which had been made at Quebec relative to southeastern Asia and added that Air Chief Marshal Leigh-Mallory should go out to head the Allied air forces there as soon as possible. General Eisenhower asked for a delay until 10 or 15 October inasmuch as Leigh-Mallory was intimately mixed up with the heavy fighting then in progress.[33]

Allied Expeditionary Air Force was dissolved at 0001, 15 October 1944, shortly after Air Chief Marshal Leigh-Mallory

---

[32] Eisenhower to Marshall, 25 Sep 44, Eisenhower personal file. Harris, *Bomber Offensive*, pp. 214–16, indicates that his relations with SHAEF were extremely cordial.

[33] Arnold to Eisenhower, 6 Sep 44; Eisenhower to Arnold, 14 Sep 44; Sinclair to Eisenhower, 20 Sep 44; Eisenhower to Sinclair, 22 Sep 44. All in Diary Office CinC, 14, 20, and 22 Sep 44. For a summary of the discussion leading to the termination of AEAF, see Craven and Cate, *The Army Air Forces in World War II*, III, 620–22.

left for his new post.[34] SHAEF Air Staff was then set up under a Chief of Staff (Air), Air Vice Marshal Robb, then serving as SHAEF Deputy Chief of Staff (Air), to absorb the operational functions of AEAF and reallocate its responsibilities. Air Chief Marshal Tedder was assigned the tasks of co-ordinating the Allied tactical air forces and of stating the Supreme Commander's requirements for strategic bombing. Administrative functions previously exercised over Royal Air Forces by the AEAF commander were now given to the commander of 2d Tactical Air Force, while similar administrative control of U.S. forces remained in the hands of the USSTAF commander.[35]

Allied Naval Forces

The main task of the Allied naval forces under SHAEF was completed once the invading units in southern France had linked up with the troops from the OVERLORD area. Important duties still remained, however, in connection with such matters as guarding troop and supply ships in the Channel and off the southern coast of France and co-ordinating the efforts of the Allied naval forces with port reconstruction units in western Europe. Another major naval concern was planning for later campaigns, such as the opening of Antwerp and the crossing of the Rhine, which would require naval support.

Throughout the remainder of the war, the Allied naval commander and a small staff remained at SHAEF. Admiral Ramsay held the post of ANCXF until his death in a plane crash at the beginning of 1945. He was succeeded by Admiral Harold M. Burrough. After SHAEF had moved across the Channel in the early fall

of 1944, Admiral Kirk was established at that headquarters as head of the U.S. naval elements on the Continent.

Shifts in Locations of Supreme Headquarters

The numerous command changes between June and October 1944 had been accompanied by almost as many shifts in the locations of Supreme Headquarters. It will be recalled that on D Day the main force of SHAEF was located at Bushy Park near London and General Eisenhower had a small advance command post—SHARPENER—near General Montgomery's headquarters at Portsmouth. Later in June the Supreme Commander decided to enlarge the forward headquarters at Portsmouth. On 1 July, a tented camp capable of housing 400 officers and 1,000 enlisted men was opened.[36] Members from all the divisions of the headquarters were present, but G–2, G–3, and Secretary, General Staff, personnel predominated. Adequate telephone, teleprinter, and radio facilities kept the headquarters in close connection with the War Office, the War Department, and the army groups. Four daily flights in addition to the usual dispatch-rider letter service connected SHAEF Forward and SHAEF Main.[37]

---

[34] Leigh-Mallory was killed in November in a plane crash while en route to the Southeast Asia Command.

[35] SHAEF Memo, 14 Oct 44, sub: Command and Control of Allied Air Forces, SHAEF G–3 322.011–1 Ops A Command and Control of U.S./British Forces; Notes of mtg at SHAEF Fwd, 3 Oct 44, to decide RAF organization at SHAEF in place of AEAF, SHAEF SGS 322 SHAEF, Organization of SHAEF, I.

[36] This headquarters was known by the code name SHIPMATE. See movement orders to Portsmouth in SHAEF SGS 370.5/4 Location of Battle Hq AEF, and SHAEF SGS 370.5–1 Movement of SHAEF.

[37] Details on camps given to author by Maj. George S. Bare and Miss Mattie A. Pinette, formerly of Gen-

Plans made before D Day to establish SHAEF advance command posts near both U.S. and British army headquarters on the Continent were not fully carried out. On 7 August, however, General Eisenhower established a small advance headquarters, known as SHELLBURST, in a combined tent and trailer camp near Tournières, twelve miles southwest of Bayeux.

By the time of the move to Tournières, SHAEF officials were planning a move of the Forward Headquarters from Portsmouth to the Continent. The new headquarters was constructed on the grounds of *La colonie scolaire de St. Ouen,* a school on the outskirts of Jullouville. The largest building of the school housed the communications center, the War Room, and messes, as well as providing billets for female personnel. Offices were located in prefabricated huts, while officers and men were quartered in tents. The chief problem in establishing the headquarters was the installation of adequate communications for Supreme Headquarters at Jullouville, and for the nearby forward echelons of the Allied Expeditionary Air Force, the Allied Naval Expeditionary Force, the U.S. Strategic Air Forces, and the French command, which were located in and around Granville. Accommodations were provided initially at Jullouville for 1,500 officers and men, but they soon proved insufficient as signal units, supply detachments, and other groups needed by a large headquarters were brought in. While the

eral Eisenhower's staff. Chief sources for this section, unless otherwise noted, are: SHAEF SGS 370.5/4 Site Plans—Portsmouth; SHAEF SGS 370.5/4 Location of Battle Headquarters, I, II; SHAEF SGS 370.5–1 Movement of SHAEF; Intervs with Brig Gen Robert Q. Brown, Hq Commandant SHAEF, and Lt Col H. J. Rothwell, Camp Commandant SHAEF; Ltr, Maj Bare to author.

general and special staff divisions at SHAEF Forward numbered only some 318 officers and 478 enlisted men, the attached units ultimately pushed the total to 750 officers and 2,500 men. Movement to the new headquarters from Portsmouth began on 28 August, five parties coming by sea and air at staggered intervals. The small camp at Tournières was integrated in Forward Headquarters while Main Headquarters remained for the time being at Bushy Park.

By the time Forward Headquarters of SHAEF opened at Jullouville, the tide of battle had shifted from Normandy to points beyond the Seine. The situation gave rise to the criticism that the Supreme Commander was too far removed from the front lines at one of the most critical parts of the battle. Almost as soon as he reached Jullouville, he ordered preparations made to move both Forward and Main echelons of Supreme Headquarters nearer the combat zone. He had previously emphasized that when a second move was made, the headquarters should be near a major communications center. On no condition, however, was it to be in a large city, particularly Paris, where there were "too many temptations to go night clubbing." Versailles was ultimately chosen as the new site. On 6 September, General Eisenhower, who was attempting to keep in touch with his commanders by jeep and plane, directed that his headquarters move forward as soon as it could without inconveniencing the 12th Army Group, which had its headquarters located in that vicinity. The move was to include all organizations located near Jullouville and Granville. As soon as possible, SHAEF Main was to be brought from the United Kingdom. The headquarters began its move from Normandy to Versailles on 15

TRIANON PALACE HOTEL, *SHAEF Headquarters.*

September and opened there officially on the 20th.

Offices of the general staff divisions were established in the Trianon Palace Hotel near grounds of the Petit Trianon. Special staff sections were located in the Grandes Ecuries, and the Air Staff in the Petites Ecuries. Hotels Reservoir, Royale, and Vittel were also used. Enlisted men were billeted in Satory Camp, and officers in homes along the Seine between St. Cloud and St. Germain-en-Laye. New buildings had to be requisitioned continually as the number of assigned and attached units increased. General Vulliamy, the chief of the Signal Division, pointed out that within a week after the move the estimated figures were more than doubled.[38]

In accordance with his policy of keeping a small advance headquarters as near as possible to the army groups, General Eisenhower in early September directed that a camp be built forward of Versailles. This headquarters was opened on 19 September at Gueux about seven miles northwest of Reims, just off the Laon highway. As in Normandy it consisted of a small staff installed in tents and trailers. Instead of an orchard, the men used the grounds and clubhouse belonging to the Athletic Club of Reims. General Eisenhower continued to use this advance site until 17 February 1945 when the forward echelon of SHAEF moved to Reims. He, of course,

[38] An advance party of the Seine Base Section estimated before the move that SHAEF would ultimately require space for 2,000 officers and 10,000 enlisted men, and 750,000 square feet of office space.

retained offices in Versailles and in London.[39]

At the end of September, various echelons of SHAEF Main began their move from the United Kingdom to Versailles by air. The move was completed by 5 October. Rear Headquarters, SHAEF, consisting of approximately 1,500 officers and men, moved from Bushy Park to Bryanston Square in London on 9–10 October. A small contingent was located at Goodge Street Tunnel, which was now used as an underground storage place for important SHAEF records.

While at Versailles, SHAEF made great progress in improving its communications facilities. The French postal, telegraph, and telephone service (PTT) helped to establish the Paris Military Switchboard, which provided trunk service by connecting military exchanges in other centers to the Paris exchange via the French PTT system. To avoid confusion SHAEF took control of the main trunk telecommunications network and established the AEF Long Lines Control to allocate circuits in the rehabilitated French systems.[40] Radio communication between the Supreme Commander and his army group commanders was assured in early September by the establishment of several radio circuits known as REDLINE which were set up exclusively for messages to and from the Supreme Commander.

By 1 October, the Supreme Commander had gathered firmly into his hands the control of Allied forces from Holland to the Mediterranean and from the German frontier westward to the Atlantic. He commanded as well U.S. air and ground forces in the United Kingdom. Under his direct control he had one British, one Canadian, one French, one Allied airborne, and four U.S. armies as well as the British and U.S. tactical air forces. While he no longer controlled any part of the strategic air forces, he still had first call on them for necessary support of his ground operations. With his headquarters set up on the Continent and with an adequate radio and telegraphic link to his chief subordinates, he could now personally direct operations against the Third Reich.

---

[39] Details on this advance headquarters were furnished the author by Major Bare in a letter of 7 November 1949.

[40] Rpt of Signal Div, SHAEF, Vols. IV, V, OCMH.

CHAPTER XVI

Fighting in the North

The great drive across northern France and Belgium began to lose its momentum in the first week of September and was showing signs of coming to a halt by the middle of the month as Allied lines of supply became intolerably stretched. Shortly thereafter the Allies launched an airborne operation (MARKET-GARDEN) in the Netherlands in the hope of establishing a bridgehead across the Rhine before the enemy could reorganize his forces for an effective defense.

Background of Operations in the Netherlands

In agreeing to the operation MARKET-GARDEN, General Eisenhower seems to have been influenced not only by a desire to get a bridgehead across the Rhine but by the hope of utilizing the First Allied Airborne Army, which had been awaiting action since July and August. Aware that Generals Marshall and Arnold were both deeply interested in the strategic use of airborne forces, General Eisenhower had sought a suitable occasion for employing these resources. In mid-July he asked for an airborne plan marked by imagination and daring which would make a maximum contribution to the destruction of German armies in western Europe. The desire to implement such a plan helped to influence the foundation of the First Allied Airborne Army. When various factors delayed its organization, the Supreme Commander told General Smith: " . . . Brereton should be working in his new job instantly. Please inform him that I am particularly anxious about the navigational qualifications of the transport command crews. He is to get on this in an intensive way. He is to keep me in touch with his progress. There is nothing we are undertaking about which I am more concerned than this job of his. I want him on the ball with all his might." General Arnold in August asked General Eisenhower for a broad outline for the employment of airborne forces, noting that troop carrier planes were not "comparing at all favorably with combat plane missions (other than supply and training) accomplished and hours in the air." [1]

When it became clear that the First Allied Airborne Army would not be employed west of the Seine, the Deputy Supreme Commander and the SHAEF deputy G–3 proposed the strategic use of these forces in the area of Boulogne or Calais. [2] In addition, the SHAEF planners asked the airborne army to examine plans to employ airborne forces north of the Somme between the Oise and Abbeville, and north of the Aisne in the neighborhood of Soissons. Meanwhile, General Brereton completed plans for an operation to capture Boulogne. This was abandoned near the end of August when it became

---

[1] *The Brereton Diaries*, pp. 308–09, 322, 333.

[2] See above, p. 210.

apparent that the ground forces would by-pass or capture the city before the operation could be launched.

At this juncture, General de Guingand outlined for General Brereton the types of airborne operations 21 Army Group desired in the coming weeks. He reminded the First Allied Airborne commander that General Eisenhower, although willing to leave the specific operations up to Generals Montgomery and Brereton, was insistent that the airborne forces be used. The 21 Army Group chief of staff thought the airborne forces should speed the advance northeast across the Somme, prevent enemy elements in the coastal area from reinforcing the main line, and provide a reserve to clear the area when contact was made with troops advancing from the south. He suggested an operation in the Doullens area north of Amiens. General Brereton explained that, while his forces were at the disposal of General Montgomery, it was necessary first to decide on the advisability of particular operations. He ultimately refused the Doullens drop because he thought that a link-up of ground forces would occur within forty-eight hours. In view of the rapidity of the ground forces' advance, General Brereton proposed that all planning be discarded except that which aimed at action in the Aachen–Maastricht area. He pointed out that the armies were moving so swiftly that the airborne army could not keep up with them unless its transport was released from air supply operations.[3]

General Brereton not only opposed using airborne forces for operations which he believed the ground forces could perform, but he was showing concern over the Supreme Command's tendency to permit the Troop Carrier Command to be used for supply instead of its primary role of carrying soldiers. Almost solid opposition from ground commanders confronted General Brereton's recommendation that aircraft intended primarily for tactical airborne missions be released from the task of carrying supplies. "Inability to take advantage of the chance of delivering a paralyzing blow by airborne action," he insisted, "was due to lack of Troop Carrier aircraft which could have been made available immediately for airborne operations had they not been used for resupply and evacuation." He held that airborne planning should be conducted at the Supreme Commander's level. Along with General Arnold, he believed that the conception of the employment of the First Allied Airborne Army as a strategic force was not properly understood.[4]

After the operation to seize Boulogne was canceled, an air drop at Tournai (LINNET I) was planned. This was set aside, in turn, on the evening of 2 September by 21 Army Group as a result of adverse weather and delay. General Eisenhower and Air Chief Marshal Tedder on 3 September gave their backing to an operation planned for the Aachen–Maastricht Gap (LINNET II). The final decision on this project was left to Field Marshal Montgomery and General Bradley. General Brereton believed that the disorganization of the enemy required immediate launching of the operation. He declared that the operation should be mounted on 4 September or not at all. General Browning, deputy commander of the First Allied Airborne Army, protested that insufficient time had been given. When General

[3] Highlights of mtg at Hq 21 A Gp, 25 Aug 44, SHAEF FAAA, Plans for Operations. *The Brereton Diaries*, p. 336, gives General Brereton's reactions.

[4] *The Brereton Diaries*, p. 339; Arnold, *Global Mission*, p. 521; for a ground force view, see 12th A Gp G–4 AAR, Aug 44.

Brereton held to his resolution, General Browning tendered his resignation. The airborne army commander declared next day that only General Eisenhower could act upon the matter, and General Browning withdrew his letter. The entire problem was settled apparently as the result of the slowing of the ground battle; on 5 September LINNET II was canceled.[5]

Airborne planners devised eighteen different plans in forty days only to have many of the objectives overrun by the ground troops before any action could be taken. The schedule of operations had been disrupted temporarily in the last half of August when for an interval of nearly two weeks troop carrier aircraft were diverted to the supply of ground troops. Only after a strong reminder by General Brereton that these planes were needed for training in preparation for new operations were they withdrawn from supply activities. Even then, the air drops for which the troop carrier units had been withdrawn were canceled.

Meanwhile the airborne headquarters and the 21 Army Group were exploring other ways in which the airborne army might be used. By 5 September, Field Marshal Montgomery had decided in favor of an air drop of one and one-half divisions on 7 September to seize river crossings in the Arnhem–Nijmegen area (Operation COMET).[6] This operation was postponed from day to day and finally canceled on 10 September as a result of bad weather and stiffened enemy resistance. A decision was finally made to strengthen the attack and not to abandon it. First Allied Airborne Army was informed on the 10th that General Eisenhower and Field Marshal Montgomery wanted an operation in the general area specified in COMET. A decision was made

to enlarge the air drop to three and one-half divisions, to seize bridges over the Maas, Waal, and Neder Rijn at Grave, Nijmegen, and Arnhem (Operation MARKET), and to open a corridor from Eindhoven northward for the passage of British ground forces into Germany (Operation GARDEN).

Although some individuals at 12th Army Group and First Allied Airborne Army, and even some members of the 21 Army Group staff, expressed opposition to the plan, it seemed to fit the pattern of current Allied strategy. It conformed to General Arnold's recommendation for an operation some distance east of the enemy's forward positions and beyond the area where enemy reserves were normally located; it afforded an opportunity for using the long-idle airborne resources; it was in accord with Field Marshal Montgomery's desire for a thrust north of the Rhine while the enemy was disorganized; it would help reorient the Allied drive in the direction 21 Army Group thought it should go; and it appeared to General Eisenhower to be the boldest and best move the Allies could make at the moment. The Supreme Commander realized that the momentum of the drive into Germany was being lost and thought that by this action it might be possible to get a bridgehead across the Rhine before the Allies were stopped. The airborne divisions, he knew, were in good condition and could be supported without throwing a crushing burden on the already overstrained supply lines. At worst, General

---

[5] *The Brereton Diaries*, pp. 337–38, entries for 3, 4, and 5 September 1944.

[6] CofS 21 A Gp Conf, 5 Sep 44, 21 A Gp files; SHAEF G–3 Memo, 21 Oct 44, sub: Projected Abn Opns, SHAEF G–3 Future Opns 24533/Ops; SHAEF FAAA, Plan for Operation COMET. A list of operations is given in *The Brereton Diaries*, pp. 339–40.

Eisenhower thought the operation would strengthen the 21 Army Group in its later fight to clear the Schelde estuary. Field Marshal Montgomery examined the objections that the proposed route of advance "involved the additional obstacle of the Lower Rhine (Neder Rijn) as compared with more easterly approaches, and would carry us to an area relatively remote from the Ruhr." He considered that these were overriden by certain major advantages: (1) the operation would outflank the Siegfried Line defenses; (2) it would be on the line which the enemy would consider the least likely for the Allies to use; and (3) the area was the one with the easiest range for the Allied airborne forces.[7]

Operation MARKET was placed under General Browning's British Airborne Corps. Specifically, it provided for the 101st U.S. Airborne Division to seize key points on the highway between Eindhoven and Grave, the 82d U.S. Airborne Division to take bridges at Nijmegen and Grave, and the 1st British Airborne Division to capture the bridges at Arnhem. The 1st Polish Parachute Brigade was to reinforce this last effort. The 52d British (Lowland) Division was to be flown in later to strengthen the Arnhem bridgehead. While these attacks were under way, the Second British Army was to launch Operation GARDEN. The 30 British Corps was to spearhead a drive with the British Guards Armored Division and follow up its efforts with the 43d and 50th Divisions. The corps was to advance from the line of the Meuse–Escaut Canal along a narrow corridor from Eindhoven northward and push across the bridges which had been secured by airborne forces to Arnhem some sixty-four miles away. Thrusting thence to the IJsselmeer, nearly one hundred miles from the original jump-off

point, it was to cut off the escape route of the enemy in western Holland and then turn northeast into Germany. Meanwhile, the 12 and 8 British Corps on the flanks of the 30 British Corps were to advance in support of the attack.[8]

The boldness of the operation was apparent. Its success required a rapid advance by ground forces along a narrow corridor more than sixty miles from the advanced British positions at the Meuse–Escaut Canal, and several days of favorable flying conditions at a season when the weather in northwest Europe was normally bad.

Set over against the factors making for caution was the belief, still generally held at most Allied headquarters, that the enemy forces which had fled through northern France and Belgium would be unable to stop and conduct any sort of effective defense against the Allied armies. Limiting factors on continued Allied advances were believed to be based more on Allied shortages of supply than on the enemy's capacity to resist. Fairly typical of the Allied point of view was SHAEF's estimate of the situation a week before the Arnhem operation. Enemy strength

[7] 21 A Gp, Operation MARKET-GARDEN, 7–26 Sep 44, SHAEF FAAA; Bradley, *A Soldier's Story*, pp. 416–18. General Bradley says he objected strenuously to the plan but "I nevertheless freely concede that Monty's plan for Arnhem was one of the most imaginative of the war." Brereton, in a letter to General Ward, 10 June 1951, OCMH, says that he opposed the operation as planned (*The Brereton Diaries*, pp. 340, 342); Ltr, Brig Williams to author, 12 Aug 51; Arnold, *Global Mission*, p. 521; Eisenhower, *Crusade in Europe*, p. 307; Notes by Gen Eisenhower, 16 Jun 51, OCMH files; Montgomery, *Normandy to the Baltic*, p. 224. For an air force view of the operation see Craven and Cate, *The Army Air Forces in World War II*, III. 598–611.

[8] Hq Br Abn Corps, Allied Airborne Operations in Holland (Sep–Oct 44), SHAEF FAAA; outline plan for Operation COMET in same file; outline of Operation MARKET-GARDEN in SHAEF G–3 file.

throughout the west was listed at forty-eight divisions or approximately twenty infantry and four armored divisions at full strength.[9] This included four divisions which had to remain in the fortresses and three others outside the area of the Siegfried Line. SHAEF thus assumed that the immediate defense of the West Wall would be left to the 200,000 men who had escaped from France and an additional 100,000 who might yet escape from Belgium and southern France or be brought from Germany. This defending force, the SHAEF G–2 concluded, would not be greater than eleven infantry and four armored divisions at full strength. As to reinforcements, an estimate which was believed to be unduly fair to the enemy added a "speculative dozen" divisions which might "struggle up" in the course of the month. It was considered "most unlikely that more than the true equivalent of four panzer grenadier divisions with 600 tanks" would be found. The G–2 declared: "The Westwall cannot be held with this amount, even when supplemented by many oddments and large amounts of flak."[10] In the light of this and other similar assessments of the enemy situation, it would have been difficult for General Eisenhower or Field Marshal Montgomery, even in the face of logistical difficulties, to justify stopping the great pursuit without some effort to pierce or outflank the West Wall defenses.

The optimism reflected in SHAEF's intelligence estimate was also evidenced four days before the attack in the statement by Headquarters, Airborne Corps, that the enemy had few infantry reserves and a total armored strength of not more than fifty to one hundred tanks. While there were numerous signs that the enemy was strengthening the defenses of the river

and canal lines through Arnhem and Nijmegen, it was believed that the troops manning them were not numerous and were of "low category." The 1st British Airborne Division's report later described Allied estimates as follows: "It was thought that the enemy must still be disorganized after his long and hasty retreat from south of the River Seine and that though there might be numerous small bodies of enemy in the area, he would not be capable of organized resistance to any great extent." Only on the very eve of the attack was a warning note sounded. The SHAEF G–2 at that time declared that the "*9 SS Panzer Division,* and with it presumably the *10,* has been reported as withdrawing to the Arnhem area of Holland; there they will probably both collect new tanks from a depot reported in the area of Cleves."[11]

Supply difficulties intensified the problems of MARKET-GARDEN at the outset of planning. On 11 September, Field Marshal Montgomery notified General Eisenhower that the latter's failure to give priority to the northern thrust over other operations meant that the attack could not be made before 26 September. The Supreme Commander then sent his chief of staff to assure the 21 Army Group commander that 1,000 tons of supplies per day would be delivered by Allied planes and U.S. truck companies. Field Marshal Montgomery now reconsidered and set 17 September as the target day for the operation. To the Supreme Commander he wired: "Most grateful to you personally

⁹ See above, p. 248, for actual strength.

¹⁰ SHAEF Weekly Intel Summary 25, week ending 9 Sep 44, SHAEF G–2 file.

¹¹ Hq Abn Troops Operational Instruction 1, 13 Sep 44; 1st Abn Div AAR on Opn MARKET, Pts. 1–3. Both in SHAEF FAAA. SHAEF Weekly Intel Summary 26, week ending 16 Sep 44, SHAEF G–2 file.

and to Beetle for all you are doing for us." [12]

Despite the narrow margin of logistical support for MARKET-GARDEN, Field Marshal Montgomery now believed that, if weather conditions permitted full development of Allied air power and unhindered use of airborne forces, he had sufficient supplies to secure the Rhine bridgehead. Later, in reporting on the operation, he declared that it was necessary to shorten the time for building up supplies in order to prevent the enemy from reorganizing. He added: "After careful consideration it was decided to take this administrative risk, subsequently fully justified, and the actual date of the start of the operation was advanced by six days." To reduce the risk, the Field Marshal suggested on 14 September that U.S. forces create a diversion along the Metz–Nancy front during the period 14–26 September in order to pull the enemy away from Arnhem. Two days later he indicated that, inasmuch as the Third Army operations in Lorraine were producing a sufficient threat, no special feint was necessary. [13]

In order to get transport for the additional 500 tons which had to be hauled daily from Bayeux to Brussels during the MARKET-GARDEN operation, SHAEF ordered the newly arrived 26th, 95th, and 104th U.S. Infantry Divisions stripped of their vehicles, save those needed for self-maintenance. Using the freed vehicles, provisional units were substituted for more experienced U.S. truck companies on the Red Ball route, and the companies thus made available were then transferred to the British Red Lion route. By 8 October, at which time British supplies began to go by rail, these companies had hauled more than 18,000 tons of supplies. A daily average of 627 tons, about half of it British POL and the remainder U.S. supplies, was transported over the 306-mile forward route. [14]

The MARKET-GARDEN Operation

Operation MARKET-GARDEN started according to plan in the early afternoon of 17 September as elements of the 1st British and 82d and 101st Airborne Divisions began dropping near Arnhem, Grave, and Veghel. (Map 3) At approximately the same time, the 30 British Corps moved from a point north of the Meuse–Escaut Canal toward Eindhoven. In the largest airborne attack undertaken up to that time, the Allied forces landed with light losses. Soon afterward they ran into serious trouble. The general area of the southeastern Netherlands was held by the First Parachute Army (Generaloberst Kurt Student) which was in the process of consolidation when the airborne force struck. Though surprised by the airborne force and not prepared for an attack, General Student was able to draw on the II SS Panzer Corps, then regrouping northeast of Arnhem, and to bring up to Nijmegen the II Parachute Corps with several parachute

---

[12] Montgomery to Eisenhower, M–205, 16 Sep 44, SHAEF SGS 381 Post OVERLORD Planning, I; Montgomery to Eisenhower, M–197, 12 Sep 44, Eisenhower personal file. General Eisenhower had made clear that during the airborne operation the 500 tons delivered by airlift would have to be made up by emergency measures, since all available aircraft would be used in MARKET-GARDEN. Eisenhower to Montgomery, FWD 14758, 13 Sep 44, SHAEF SGS 381 Post OVERLORD Planning, I.

[13] SHAEF to 12th A Gp, FWD 14837, 14 Sep 44, SHAEF SGS 381 Post OVERLORD Planning, I; SHAEF to EXFOR (21 A Gp), FWD 15007, 16 Sep 44; Montgomery, Normandy to the Baltic, p. 220; 21 A Gp Rpt, MARKET-GARDEN, 17–26 Sep 44, SHAEF file.

[14] History of G–4, ComZ, ETO, prep by Hist Sec, G–4, COMZ, MS, Sec. III, Ch. 3, OCMH files.

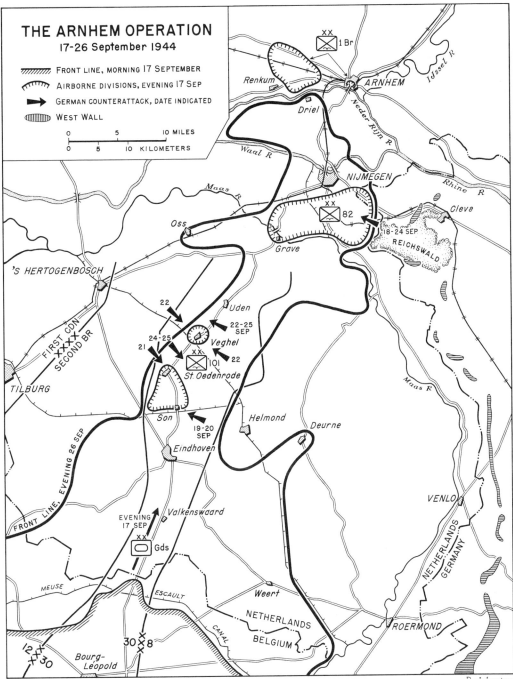

THE ARNHEM OPERATION
17-26 September 1944

- //////// FRONT LINE, MORNING 17 SEPTEMBER
- ^^^^^^^ AIRBORNE DIVISIONS, EVENING 17 SEP
- ➤ GERMAN COUNTERATTACK, DATE INDICATED
- ▥ WEST WALL

```
0        5        10 MILES
0    5       10 KILOMETERS
```

MAP 3

R. Johnstone

Kampfgruppen which were reorganizing near Cologne. Student was aided by a captured copy of the Allied attack order which reached him within two hours after the landing. An infantry division, en route to the area from the *Fifteenth Army* area at the time of the attack, was detrained and put into the attack against the 101st Airborne Division near Son. The enemy was also helped by the fact that Field Marshal Model, who had his *Army Group B* headquarters near Arnhem, was able to coordinate the fighting at Arnhem and Nijmegen. The defense was quickly organized and new forces brought up. The enemy sent all available combat aircraft to help his antiaircraft stop the Allied attack.[15]

Despite prompt and unexpectedly strong enemy reaction, the Allies made some gains during the first day. By midnight, the 101st and the 82d Airborne Divisions were well established near Eindhoven and Nijmegen. The 1st British Airborne Division, dropping some six to eight miles west of Arnhem, lost the effect of the initial surprise by landing too far from the objective. Elements of the division took the north end of the Arnhem highway bridge, which was still intact. Many miles to the south, British armored units, starting their advance in the early afternoon from the Meuse–Escaut Canal bridgehead, ran into heavy opposition from parachute and SS panzer troops. Even though progress was "disappointingly slow," the general feeling was one of optimism.[16]

For the next five days, increasingly bad weather and the arrival of German reinforcements upset Allied plans. The dropping of additional Allied units was delayed four hours on 18 September and resupply efforts were so disrupted that they were only 30 percent effective. Worse weather

on the 19th held up reinforcements for the 82d U.S. and 1st British Airborne Divisions. The 1st Polish Parachute Brigade, which was expected to arrive in the Arnhem area on the 18th, did not land until the 21st. Even then its drop zones had to be altered to points south of the Neder Rijn and only half of the force was put down near Arnhem. In the south, the 101st Airborne Division took Eindhoven on the 18th and the 82d Airborne, aided by the Guards Armored Division, seized railroad and highway bridges at Nijmegen on 20 September. The enemy, despite these setbacks, rushed sufficient units to the Nijmegen area to delay armored elements from reaching Arnhem.

The plight of the 1st British Airborne Division, desperate after the first day, was not "known to any satisfactory extent" at Headquarters, British Airborne Corps, until the 20th. Not only was it impossible to push through ground force aid as planned, but the rest of the division outside Arnhem was unable to join up with the small group holding the north end of the bridge. Efforts to reinforce the group were thwarted by bad weather. Resupply difficulties arose when the division was unable to capture its supply dropping zone. It could neither notify the air transport forces nor arrange for another supply site. As a result, the bulk of ammunition and supplies flown in fell into enemy hands. The group at the Arnhem highway bridge, unable to get ammunition, was forced to surrender on the 21st.

The other British airborne units near Arnhem, now shadows of their former

---

[15] MS # B–717, Supplement to Report by Oberst i. G. Geyer (Student); *Der Westen* (Schramm). *First Parachute Army* was assigned to *Army Group B* on 6 September 1944.

[16] Hq Br Abn Corps, Allied Airborne Operations in Holland (Sep–Oct 44), SHAEF FAAA.

strength, were cut off from the river and unable to get support from the air. Nevertheless they continued to fight in the hope that armor from the south could get through. The Guards Armored Division, advancing northward from Nijmegen on the 21st, was quickly stopped. The 43d Division was now brought up and its advanced brigade crossed the Nijmegen bridge on the morning of 22 September. On that day, the Guards Armored was forced to send back a mixed brigade to deal with an enemy attack on the supply corridor near Veghel well to the south of Nijmegen. On the same day, the 43d Division and the Polish Parachute Brigade linked up at Driel but became heavily engaged in a fight to keep the corridor open from Nijmegen to Driel. Only a small force of Poles succeeded in crossing the Neder Rijn on the evening of 22 September. By the evening of the 23d, the situation of the airborne forces near Arnhem was so critical that the commander of the Second British Army gave his approval for a withdrawal should it prove necessary.

On the morning of 25 September, the position of the 1st British Airborne Division had obviously become untenable. Acting under the authority previously granted, the division prepared to withdraw that night. Beginning at 2200, the British brought more than 2,000 of the division and recent reinforcements south of the Neder Rijn. Some 6,400 of those who had gone in north of the river were dead or missing.[17]

The Allies had failed in their effort to establish a bridgehead across the lower Rhine. They still retained, however, the important bridgeheads over the Maas and the Waal at Grave and Nijmegen. The British line had been extended nearly fifty miles northeast of the position of 17 Sep-

tember. The enemy showed his concern over these gains by the fury with which he attempted to eliminate the corridor and new bridgeheads held by U.S. and British forces. Field Marshal Montgomery found it necessary to retain the 82d and 101st U.S. Airborne Divisions in the line.[18] General Brereton opposed this action, warning that these divisions would be rendered unavailable for the future operations then being proposed by the 12th and 21 Army Groups. In the remaining weeks between 26 September and 5 November the two units suffered losses slightly greater than those sustained by them during the MARKET operation.[19]

Both Field Marshal Montgomery and General Brereton hailed the airborne phase of the operation as a success. They were correct insofar as the initial units landed in accordance with plan and held their bridgeheads at Nijmegen and Eindhoven. The failure to hold Arnhem, however, ended the possibility of a quick drive onto the north German plain, and the severity of the enemy reaction deprived the armies of any immediate airborne support for further drops along the Rhine. Numerous reasons were adduced for the failure of the operation to attain complete success. The 21 Army Group, in summarizing the reasons, concluded that under north European climatic conditions "an

---

[17] Hq Br Abn Corps, Allied Airborne Operations in Holland, p. 5.

[18] The Polish Parachute Brigade left the area on 7 October.

[19] *The Brereton Diaries*, pp. 361, 367–68. The 82d Airborne Division's casualties of 1,432 in the September operation were increased by 1,912, and the 101st Airborne Division's 2,110 were increased by 1,682 in the weeks following the initial action. Nearly 12,000 casualties were sustained by the British and U.S. airborne divisions, the troop carrier crews and pilots, and the air support groups between 17 and 25 September. Hq Br Abn Corps, Allied Airborne Operations in Holland.

airborne plan which relies upon linking the airborne forces dropped on D Day and dropping additional forces at D plus 1 is risky, since the weather may frustrate the plan." Field Marshal Montgomery was inclined to believe that good weather would have made possible a completely successful operation. The First Allied Airborne Army declared: "The airborne Mission . . . was accomplished. The airborne troops seized the fifty mile corridor desired by CinC, Northern Group of Armies, and held it longer than planned. The fact that the weight of exploiting troops was insufficient to carry them past Arnhem in time to take advantage of the effort does not detract from their success." A German analysis, captured by the Allies after the operation, concluded that the Allies' "chief mistake was not to have landed the entire First British Airborne Division at once rather than over a period of 3 days and that a second airborne division was not dropped in the area west of Arnhem." General Browning pointed to the fact that the almost total failure of communications prevented his headquarters from knowing the seriousness of the 1st British Airborne Division's situation until forty-eight hours too late. If he had known it sooner, he believed, it would have been possible to move the division to the area of Renkum, where a good bridgehead could have been held over the Neder Rijn, and the 30 British Corps would have had a chance to cross against little opposition. Undoubtedly, much of the trouble came because the 30 British Corps had to move some sixty-four miles to Arnhem over one main road which was vulnerable to enemy attack. Instead of the expected two to four days, nearly a week was required for the advance to Arnhem. It is possible that the operation would not have been under-

taken but for the Allied belief that the enemy between Eindhoven and Arnhem was weak and demoralized. One may readily believe that the Germans were right in concluding that the strength of the *II SS Panzer Corps* in the area was "a nasty surprise for the Allies." [20]

So far as the debate between proponents of the single thrust to the north or south of the Ardennes was concerned, the result at Arnhem settled nothing. To some partisans, the operation proved that Field Marshal Montgomery had been wrong in insisting on his drive in the north. Other observers thought that MARKET–GARDEN might have succeeded had the Supreme Commander halted all advances south of the Ardennes. To SHAEF, the outcome of the gamble to outflank the West Wall meant that all efforts would now have to be turned toward capturing the approaches to Antwerp and building up a backlog of supplies sufficient to resume an all-out offensive against Germany. For the Germans, their success in stopping the Arnhem thrust short of its objective meant additional time in which to reorganize their forces and prepare for the attack they knew would come. For the soldier, the dismal prospect of spending a cold winter in France, Belgium, or Germany was increased.

Discussion of Future Operations

While the Arnhem operation was still in the preparatory state, General Eisenhower and his subordinates had been examining

---

[20] Montgomery, *Normandy to the Baltic,* p. 243; Hq Br Abn Corps, Allied Airborne Operations in Holland; 21 A Gp Rpt, MARKET-GARDEN, 17–26 Sep 44, SHAEF files; Covering ltr, First Allied Airborne Army Operation in Holland (Sep–Nov 44), FAAA, 18 Dec 44, sub: German Analysis of Arnhem, SHAEF FAAA.

plans for future operations in Germany. A number of questions arose in the course of discussions between the Supreme Commander and the 21 Army Group commander which persisted until the spring of 1945. Several points of honest disagreement were found which involved not only divergent views as to proper strategy but also national interests of Great Britain and the United States. A study of these debates is essential to an understanding of the problems of coalition command.

Not only did General Eisenhower have to consider the strategy which he thought best, but he had to give due weight to the strategic and tactical views held by the chief military commanders of other nationalities under his command. As Supreme Commander and as the principal U.S. commander in the European theater, he sometimes gave orders to his U.S. army group and army commanders which they considered inimical to their interests. At the same time he appeared to be giving greater freedom of action and discussion of strategy to the British army group commander. This impression developed to some extent from the fact that while Field Marshal Montgomery was the leader of a British army group, and as such occupied the same level of authority as Generals Bradley and Devers, he was also the chief British commander in the field, in close contact with the British Chief of the Imperial General Staff and in a position to know and defend the British strategic point of view. Suggestions that he presented to the Supreme Commander might represent either ideas that the British Chiefs of Staff were expressing to the U.S. Chiefs of Staff or views of his own that would be backed by the British Chiefs in later meetings. In these cases it was not always possible for the Supreme Com-

mander to decide the matter simply by saying, "Here is an order: execute it."

Generals Bradley and Devers, on the other hand, while sometimes in control of larger forces and technically at the same level of command as the field marshal, did not have exactly the same position. The Supreme Commander was the chief U.S. military representative in Europe. It was he who was in contact with the U.S. Chiefs of Staff and it was his views on strategy which were expressed in Washington. His orders to the U.S. army groups had the full weight of both the Combined Chiefs and the U.S. Chiefs of Staff behind them.

In both the U.S. and British armies it was understood that proposed plans might be debated and various viewpoints developed. General Eisenhower encouraged this type of discussion and often invited criticism of his plans. It is possible, however, that he added to his own command problems by failing to make clear to Field Marshal Montgomery when the "discussion" stage had ended and the "execution" stage had begun. Associates of the British commander have emphasized that he never failed to obey a direct order, but that he would continue to press his viewpoints as long as he was permitted to do so. Perhaps the Supreme Commander, accustomed to more ready compliance from his U.S. army group commanders, delayed too long in issuing positive directions to Montgomery. Perhaps, anxious to give a full voice to the British allies, he was more tolerant of strong dissent from the field marshal than he should have been. Whatever the reason, some of his SHAEF advisers thought him overslow in issuing final orders stopping further discussion on Antwerp and closing debate on the question of command. It is difficult to sustain the charge that Montgomery willfully disobeyed orders. It is plausible to say that he felt he was representing firmly the best interests of his country and attempting to set forth what he and his superiors in the United Kingdom considered to be the best strategy for the Allies to pursue in Europe. When his statements on these matters were accompanied by what appeared to be a touch of patronage or cocky self-assurance, some members of the SHAEF staff viewed them as approaching insubordination. There is no evidence that General Eisenhower shared these views.

Because of the various elements involved in the discussions on policy in 1944 and 1945, any true account of the period is certain to give the impression of continual bickering between SHAEF and 21 Army Group. Indeed, a few people have concluded as a result that coalition command is virtually an impossibility. In this, as in many other cases, the vast number of cooperative efforts which raised only a few questions and arguments are too often overlooked or forgotten, by both the historian and the reader who turn rapidly through pages of dull agreement and seek out the more interesting paragraphs of controversy. If these last deserve considerable attention, it is for the good reason that the strength of coalitions is tested by controversies and trials.

On 15 September, General Eisenhower looked beyond the Arnhem attack and the Antwerp operation, which he expected to follow, to action that the Allies should take after they seized the Ruhr, Saar, and Frankfurt areas. He named Berlin as the ultimate Allied goal and said he desired to move on it "by the most direct and expeditious route, with combined U.S.-British forces supported by other available forces moving through key centres and occupying strategic areas on the flanks, all in

one co-ordinated, concerted operation." This was the nub of what was to be known as his "broad front" strategy. Having stated it, he virtually invited a debate by asking his army group commanders to give their reactions.[21]

Only the day before, Field Marshal Montgomery had given an indication of his views when he proposed that, once the Second British Army had an IJssel River line running from Arnhem northward to Zwolle near the IJsselmeer and had established deep bridgeheads across the river, the Allies should push eastward toward Osnabrueck and Hamm. The weight would be directed to the right toward Hamm, from which a strong thrust would be made southward along the eastern face of the Ruhr. Meanwhile, the Canadian Army was to capture Boulogne and Calais and turn its full attention to the opening of the approaches to Antwerp.[22]

In answer to General Eisenhower's invitation, the field marshal now repeated what one might call the "narrow front" view. Since it introduced new arguments relative to the logistical possibilities open to the Allied forces, it is worthy of quotation at some length. The 21 Army Group commander declared:

1. I suggest that the whole matter as to what is possible, and what is NOT possible, is very closely linked up with the administrative situation. The vital factor is time; what we have to do, we must do quickly.

2. In view of para. 1, it is my opinion that a concerted operation in which all the available land armies move forward into Germany is not possible; the maintenance resources, and the general administrative

---

[21] Eisenhower to army group comdrs, 15 Sep 44, SHAEF SGS 381 Post OVERLORD Planning, I.

[22] 21 A Gp General Operational Situation and Dir, M–525, 14 Sep 44, SHAEF SGS 381 Post OVERLORD Planning, I.

situation, will not allow of this being done *quickly.*

3. But forces adequate in strength for the job in hand could be supplied and maintained, provided the general axis of advance was suitable and provided these forces had complete priority in all respects as regards maintenance.

4. It is my own personal opinion that we shall not achieve what we want by going for objectives such as Nurnberg, Augsburg, Munich, etc., and by establishing our forces in central Germany.

5. I consider that the best objective is the Ruhr, and thence on to Berlin by the northern route. On that route are the ports, and on that route we can use our sea power to the best advantages. On other routes we would merely contain as many German forces as we could.[23]

Having stated his argument, Field Marshal Montgomery noted the alternatives. If General Eisenhower agreed that the northern route should be used, then the British commander believed that the 21 Army Group plus the First U.S. Army of nine divisions would be sufficient. Such a force, he added, "must have *everything it needed in the maintenance line;* other Armies would do the best they could with what was left over." If, he continued, the proper axis was by Frankfurt and central Germany "then I suggest that 12 Army Group of three Armies would be used and would have all the maintenance. 21 Army Group would do the best it could with what was left over; or possibly the Second British Army would be wanted in a secondary role on the left flank of the movement."

To his earlier arguments for a northern thrust, the field marshal had actually added a plea for an all-out thrust on either his or Bradley's front. This point was obscured by two observations. In one, he declared: "In brief, I consider that as TIME is so very important, we have got to decide what is necessary to go to Berlin

and finish the war; the remainder must play a secondary role. It is my opinion that three Armies are enough, if you select the northern route, and I consider, from a maintenance point of view, it could be done." In the second, his concluding statement, he indicated that the discussion was in accordance with general views expressed by telegram on 4 September, and he attached a copy of that telegram.

The views of both 4 and 18 September were at variance with General Bradley's estimate of the situation. While noting that terrain studies showed "that the route north of the area is best," he returned to the pre-D-Day view, which had been frequently repeated, that drives should be made to both the north and south of the Ruhr. He thought that the main southern attack toward the Ruhr should be made from Frankfurt and that this would require holding the Rhine from Cologne to Frankfurt. After both drives had passed the Ruhr, he proposed that one main spearhead be directed toward Berlin, while the other armies supported it with simultaneous thrusts. He added that while territorial gains were important there might be cases where the destruction of hostile armies should have priority over purely territorial gains.[24]

The Supreme Commander now had set before him two different plans of action. Apparently seeing in Montgomery's proposal nothing more than a restatement of his 4 September argument for a push to the north, he declared against a "narrow front" policy. While specifically accepting the Ruhr-to-Berlin route for an all-out offensive into Germany, he firmly rejected

---

[23] Montgomery to Eisenhower, 18 Sep 44, entry in Diary Office CinC for 20 Sep 44. Italics in original.
[24] Memo, Bradley for Eisenhower, 21 Sep 44, Eisenhower personal file.

Field Marshal Montgomery's suggestion that all troops except those in the 21 Army Group and the First U.S. Army should "stop in place *where they are* and that we can strip all these additional divisions from their transport and everything else to support one single knife-like drive toward Berlin." The Supreme Commander added: "What I do believe is that we must marshal our strength up along the western borders of Germany, to the Rhine if possible, insure adequate maintenance by getting Antwerp to working at full blast at the earliest possible moment and then carry out the drive you suggest." He denied that this meant that he was considering an advance into Germany with all armies moving abreast. Rather, the chief advance after the crossing of the Rhine would be made by Montgomery's forces and the First U.S. Army. But General Bradley's forces, less First Army, would move forward in a supporting position to prevent the concentration of German forces against the front and the flank. The Supreme Commander noted in passing that preference had been given to Field Marshal Montgomery's armies throughout the campaign while the other forces had been fighting "with a halter around their necks in the way of supplies." "You may not know," he continued, "that for four days straight Patton has been receiving serious counter-attacks and during the last seven days, without attempting any real advance himself, has captured about 9,000 prisoners and knocked out 720 tanks." [25]

He could not believe, said General Eisenhower in his letter of 20 September, that there was any great difference in his and the field marshal's concepts of fighting the battle against Germany. This opinion arose in part from his assumption that Montgomery was merely repeating his early September views.

The 21 Army Group commander now undertook to make quite clear the points on which the two disagreed. To the British commander, the Supreme Commander's acceptance of a main thrust in the north as the chief business of the Allies meant that men and supplies should be concentrated on the single operation. Always in favor of making sure of his position before attacking, he regarded as bad tactics any subsidiary action that would weaken the main offensive. To him the granting of permission to General Bradley or General Patton to move forces to the south meant that the right wing was being permitted to angle away from the proper direction of attack and that a battle might be brought on from which it would be impossible to disengage the forces in the south.

In some respects, Montgomery's arguments and fears were similar to those expressed by the U.S. Chiefs of Staff in their arguments with the British Chiefs concerning the Mediterranean campaign. General Marshall, in particular, had feared that no matter how much the British might favor OVERLORD the continual involvement of Allied forces in the Mediterranean would require ever-new commitments which would distract the Anglo-American forces from their major operation in northwest Europe. To Field Marshal Montgomery, the granting of a division or additional tons of fuel to General Patton meant not only that the Third Army commander was dealing in operations which did not contribute directly to the main attack, but that with the best faith in the world he was likely to get into new battles which would require further diversion of men and supplies from the

---

[25] Ltr, Eisenhower to Montgomery, 20 Sep 44, Eisenhower personal file.

main operation. It appears that 21 Army Group also believed that Patton would use any opportunity he had to bring on other engagements so that he would have to have additional support.[26]

There thus appears on occasion in the correspondence between General Eisenhower and Field Marshal Montgomery an intimation by the latter that the Supreme Commander, while committed to the northern operation, was prone to permit operations harmful to the northern thrust. Thus the constant recurrence of the theme: you have said let us go on the north but you have allowed certain departures from that operation. This was not only irritating to General Eisenhower, who believed that there were sufficient resources to carry on the additional secondary actions in the south, but it was alarming to Generals Bradley and Patton, who thought that their troops and stockpiles of material were being raided to support a British operation while they were relegated to a secondary role. Feelings were undoubtedly strong on both sides. But for the reasons previously mentioned the field marshal continued the discussion, while the U.S. commanders accepted the orders they were given and kept their complaints among themselves. At the same time, General Patton, if his war memoirs are to be accepted unreservedly, believed that since the Supreme Commander was too closely committed to Field Marshal Montgomery's plan of operations the Third Army had to make the greatest possible use of any loopholes in the Supreme Commander's orders to push the battle on its front.[27]

Field Marshal Montgomery on 21 September made clear his anxiety about the Supreme Commander's current policy. He declared:

. . . I can not agree that our concepts are the same and I am sure you would wish me to be quite frank and open in the matter. I have always said stop the right and go on with the left but the right has been allowed to go on so far that it has outstripped its maintenance and we have lost flexibility. In your letter you still want to go on further with your right and you state in your Para. 6 that all of Bradley's Army Group will move forward sufficiently etc. I would say that the right flank of 12 Army Group should be given a very direct order to halt and if this order is not obeyed we shall get into greater difficulties. The net result of the matter in my opinion is that if you want to get the Ruhr you will have to put every single thing into the left hook and stop everything else. It is my opinion that if this is not done you will not get the Ruhr. Your very great friend MONTY.[28]

In thanking Montgomery for clarifying the situation, General Eisenhower said that he did not agree with the 4 September view that the Allied forces had reached the stage where a single thrust could be made all the way to Berlin with all other troops virtually immobile. He did accept emphatically what the field marshal had to say on attaining the Ruhr and added:

. . . No one is more anxious than I to get to the Ruhr quickly. It is for the cam-

---

[26] General Patton's testimony has it that he proposed to do just that.

[27] This process, General Patton called the "rock soup method." He described it as follows: "In other words, in order to attack, we had first to pretend to reconnoiter, then reinforce the reconnaissance, and finally put on an attack—all depending on what gasoline and ammunition we could secure." Again, speaking of Field Marshal Montgomery's efforts to have all the U.S. troops halt while he attacked in the north, General Patton says: "In order to avoid such an eventuality, it was evident that the Third Army should get deeply involved at once, so I asked Bradley not to call me until after dark on the nineteenth." Patton, *War as I Knew It*, pp. 125, 133, 265.

[28] Ltr, Montgomery to Eisenhower, M–223, 21 Sep 44, Eisenhower personal file.

paign from there onward deep into the heart of Germany for which I insist all other troops must be in position to support the main drive. The main drive must logically go by the North. It is because I am anxious to organize that final drive quickly upon the capture of the Ruhr that I insist upon the importance of Antwerp. As I have told you I am prepared to give you everything for the capture of the approaches to Antwerp, including all the air forces and anything else you can support. Warm regard, IKE.[29]

The matters of Antwerp, the Ruhr, and future advances into Germany were all discussed by General Eisenhower and most of his chief subordinates at Versailles on 22 September. Unfortunately, the field commander most directly concerned, Field Marshal Montgomery, felt that because of operational demands he could not be present and sent his chief of staff to represent him. Had he been present, it is possible that later misunderstandings over priority for operations might have been avoided. The Supreme Commander, while interested in future drives into Germany, asked early in the conference for "general acceptance of the fact that the possession of an additional major deep-water port on our north flank was an indispensable prerequisite for the final drive into Germany." Further, he asked that a clear distinction be made between logistical requirements for the present operations which aimed at breaching the Siegfried Line and seizing the Ruhr and the requirements for a final drive on Berlin.[30]

In the course of the conference, Eisenhower also declared, "The envelopment of the Ruhr from the north by 21st Army Group, supported by 1st Army, is the main effort of the present phase of operations." He noted that the field marshal was to open the port of Antwerp and develop operations culminating in a strong attack on the Ruhr from the north. General Bradley

was to support these actions by taking over the 8 British Corps sector and by continuing a thrust, as far as current resources permitted, toward Cologne and Bonn. He was to be prepared to seize any favorable opportunity to cross the Rhine and attack the Ruhr from the south when the supply situation permitted. The remainder of the 12th Army Group (*i. e.*, the Third Army) was to take no more aggressive action than that permitted by the supply situation after the full requirements of the main effort had been met. The 6th Army Group was notified that it could continue its operations to capture Mulhouse and Strasbourg inasmuch as these would not divert supplies from other operations and would contain enemy forces that otherwise might be sent to the north. Pleased with the decision, General de Guingand wired the 21 Army Group commander that his plan had been given "100 per cent support." Although Field Marshal Montgomery had not been given command of the First U.S. Army as requested, he was permitted, as a means of saving time in case of emergencies, to communicate directly with General Hodges.[31]

General Eisenhower hoped that the conference of 22 September had cleared the air and that complete understanding had been reached which should hold at least until the completion of the effort to take the Ruhr. In outlining the decision to Field Marshal Montgomery, the Supreme Commander emphasized the way in

---

[29] Eisenhower to Montgomery, FWD 15407, 22 Sep 44, Eisenhower personal file.

[30] Montgomery to Smith, 21 Sep 44, Diary Office CinC; Mtg at SHAEF Fwd, 22 Sep 44, SHAEF SGS 381 Post OVERLORD Planning, I.

[31] Mtg at SHAEF Fwd, 22 Sep 44; Eisenhower to Bradley, FWD 15510, 23 Sep 44. Both in SHAEF SGS 381 Post OVERLORD Planning, I. De Guingand to Montgomery, ER/3, 22 Sep 44, Diary Office CinC.

which U.S. efforts were aiding the attack in the north. He was glad to grant additional aid by directing General Bradley to take over part of the British zone, but warned that the Allies "must not blink the fact that we are getting fearfully stretched south of Aachen and may get a nasty little 'Kasserine' if the enemy chooses at any place to concentrate a bit of strength." However, in view of the enemy's lack of transport and supplies, he felt that the Allied forces should be all right. In a gesture evidently meant to wipe out any unpleasant memories of former disagreements over policy, the Supreme Commander concluded:

Good luck to you. I regard it as a great pity that all of us cannot keep in closer touch with each other because I find, without exception, when all of us can get together and look the various features of our problems squarely in the face, the answers usually become obvious.

Do not hesitate for a second to let me know at any time that anything seems to you to go wrong, particularly where I, my staff, or any forces not directly under your control can be of help. If we can gain our present objective, then even if the enemy attempts to prolong the contest we will rapidly get into position to go right squarely to his heart and crush him utterly. Of course, we need Antwerp.

Again, good luck and warm personal regards.[32]

The decisions of 22 September had been made at a time when there was still some hope of holding the Arnhem bridgehead and perhaps outflanking the West Wall fortifications. Once this opportunity was gone, Field Marshal Montgomery sought to push one more operation toward the Rhine. While agreeing that the opening of Antwerp was essential to any deep advance into Germany, he proposed that he seize the opportunity to destroy the enemy forces barring the way to the Ruhr.

He suggested that, as the Canadian army cleared the approaches to Antwerp, the British army should operate from the Nijmegen area against the northwest corner of the Ruhr in conjunction with a First U.S. Army drive toward Cologne. These forces, he proposed, should seek bridgeheads over the Rhine north and south of the Ruhr. It was clear that all hope of "bouncing" over the Rhine had now been abandoned and that, instead of an initial long thrust toward Hamm and a subsequent U.S. drive toward Cologne, there would now be two converging attacks by the Second British and the First U.S. Armies against the western Ruhr.[33]

Unfortunately, all of these projects could not be carried out at once. The First Canadian Army's drive of 2 October to cut the isthmus leading from western Holland to South Beveland and to destroy enemy forces south of the Schelde estuary met strong resistance, and the convergent British-U.S. drives against the Ruhr had to be postponed. Field Marshal Montgomery found it necessary to commit British forces to aid the First U.S. Army, which had been unable to clear the area west of the Meuse. He said ammunition shortages had been responsible in part for these difficulties. With British forces committed west of the Meuse, Montgomery reported, his remaining forces were too weak to launch the main attack from the Nijmegen area against the northwest corner of the Ruhr. The British commander reminded General Eisenhower that in his view the existing command situation between the 21 Army Group and

[32] Ltr, Eisenhower to Montgomery, 24 Sep 44, SHAEF SGS 381 Post OVERLORD Planning, I.

[33] 21 A Gp Operational Situation and Dir, M–527, 27 Sep 44, 12th A Gp 371.3 Military Objectives, I; de Guingand to Smith, 26 Sep 44, SHAEF SGS 381 Post OVERLORD Planning, II.

the First U.S. Army was unsatisfactory.[34]

General Eisenhower agreed that the commitments of the 21 Army Group were far too heavy for its resources. As a remedy, he made two suggestions: the U.S. forces could take over the line Maashees–Wesel as a northern boundary, or they could transfer two U.S. divisions to Montgomery and establish the boundary farther to the south. He agreed that plans for a co-ordinated attack to the Rhine should be postponed until more U.S. divisions could be brought up. Six of these, he noted, were being held in staging areas on the Continent because of the lack of supplies to maintain them in the line. The Supreme Commander proposed that both army groups retain as their first mission the gaining of the Rhine north of Bonn and asked consistent support of the First U.S. Army's efforts to get its immediate objective at Dueren.[35]

The second of General Eisenhower's suggestions for strengthening the 21 Army Group was accepted. General Bradley arranged for an armored division to be sent northward at once and made available an infantry division which could be used in clearing the Antwerp area.[36] He reported that as a result of this action Field Marshal Montgomery had declared that he was "completely satisfied as to the command set-up in the north at that time and did not need any additional assistance."[37]

Apparently through the first week in October General Eisenhower had hoped that the 21 Army Group could clear the Schelde estuary while driving toward some of its other objectives. As the early days of the month passed without Antwerp's being opened to Allied shipping, he stressed increasingly the necessity of placing that objective first. A report of the British Navy on 9 October that the First Canadian Army would be unable to move until 1 November unless supplied promptly with adequate ammunition stocks prompted him to warn Field Marshal Montgomery that unless Antwerp was opened by the middle of November all Allied operations would come to a standstill. He declared that "of all our operations on our entire front from Switzerland to the Channel, I consider Antwerp of first importance, and I believe that the operations designed to clear up the entrance require your personal attention."[38] Apparently stung by the implication that he was not pushing the attack for Antwerp, the 21 Army Group commander denied the Navy's "wild statements" concerning the First Canadian Army's operations, pointing out that the attack was already under way and going well. In passing, he reminded the Supreme Commander that the conference of 22 September had listed the attack on the Ruhr as the main effort of the current phase of operations, and that General Eisenhower on the preceding day had declared that the first mission of both army groups was gaining the Rhine north of Bonn.[39]

The priority of the Antwerp operation was spelled out by General Eisenhower in messages of 10 and 13 October. In the former he declared: "Let me assure you that nothing I may ever say or write with

[34] Montgomery to Eisenhower, M–260, 6 Oct 44; Montgomery to Eisenhower, M–264, 7 Oct 44. Both in Eisenhower personal file.

[35] Eisenhower to 21 A Gp for Bradley (message undated but apparently written 8 October 1944), Eisenhower personal file.

[36] Both of these were to continue to be supported logistically by the U.S. supply services.

[37] Bradley to Hodges, 8 Oct 44, Eisenhower personal file.

[38] Eisenhower to Montgomery, S–61466, 9 Oct 44, Eisenhower personal file.

[39] Montgomery to Eisenhower, M–268, 9 Oct 44, Eisenhower personal file.

regard to future plans in our advance eastward is meant to indicate any lessening of the need for Antwerp, which I have always held as vital, and which has grown more pressing as we enter the bad weather period." Three days later, after Field Marshal Montgomery had suggested changes in the command arrangement to give him greater flexibility in his operations, General Eisenhower moved once more to dispel any doubts on the matter of Antwerp. In one of his most explicit letters of the war, he declared that the question was not one of command but of taking Antwerp. He did not know the exact state of the field marshal's forces, but knew that they were rich in supplies as compared with U.S. and French units all the way to Switzerland. Because of logistical shortages, it was essential that Antwerp be put quickly in workable condition. This view, he added, was shared by the British and U.S. Army Chiefs, General Marshall and Field Marshal Brooke, who on a recent visit to SHAEF had emphasized the vital importance of clearing that port. Despite the desire to open Antwerp, SHAEF had approved the operation at Arnhem and Nijmegen, which, while not completely successful, had proved its worth. But all recent experiences had made clear the great need for opening the Schelde estuary, and he was willing, as always, to give additional U.S. troops and supplies to make that possible. He added that he was repeating this in order to emphasize that the operation involved no matter of command, "Since everything that can be brought in to help, no matter of what nationality, belongs to you." [40]

Then in a strong declaration of policy, designed to end further discussion of a change in command, General Eisenhower presented his concept of "logical command arrangements for the future," saying that if Field Marshal Montgomery still classed them as "unsatisfactory" there would exist an issue which must be settled in the interests of future efficiency. "I am quite well aware," he said, "of the powers and limitations of an Allied Command, and if you, as the senior commander in this Theater of one of the great Allies, feel that my conceptions and directives are such as to endanger the success of operations, it is our duty to refer the matter to higher authority for any action they may choose to take, however drastic."

He agreed that for any one major task on a battlefield, "a single *battlefield* commander" was needed who could devote his whole attention to a particular operation. For this reason armies and army groups had been established. When the battlefront stretched, as it did now, from Switzerland to the North Sea, he did not agree "that one man can stay so close to the day by day movement of divisions and corps that he can keep a 'battle grip' upon the overall situation and direct it intelligently." The Allies were no longer confronted with a Normandy beachhead. Rather, the campaign over such an extended front was broken up into more or less clearly outlined areas of operations, of which one was the principal and the others of secondary nature. The over-all commander, in this case the Supreme Commander, then had the task of adjusting the larger boundaries, assigning support by air or by ground and airborne troops, and shifting the emphasis in supply arrangements.

For the immediate attack on the Ruhr, he felt that one commander should be re-

---

[40] See Eisenhower to Montgomery, 10 and 13 October 1944, Eisenhower personal file, for this and the succeeding four paragraphs.

sponsible, but it was not clear which commander would be in position to provide the strength of the task. At present, it appeared that the current commitments of the 21 Army Group would leave it with such depleted forces facing eastward that it could not be expected to carry out anything more than supporting movements in the attack on the Ruhr. He proposed, therefore, to give the task of capturing the Ruhr to the 12th Army Group with the 21 Army Group in the supporting role. Looking beyond the seizure of that objective, he noted that the 21 Army Group would be concentrated north of the Ruhr and thus be in a position to participate in the direct attack toward Berlin. Originally, he continued, he had hoped that the field marshal would take Antwerp and clear up the western coast of Holland rapidly and therefore be in a position to make a major attack on the Ruhr, an operation for which U.S. units would have been made available to the 21 Army Group. He had gathered from the recent conference, however, that Montgomery agreed with the view that the British army group "could not produce the bulk of the forces required for the direct Ruhr attack."

The Supreme Commander then turned his attention to the question of nationalism versus military considerations and reminded the 21 Army Group chief that there had never been any hesitation in putting U.S. forces under British command. He added:

It would be quite futile to deny that questions of nationalism often enter our problems. It is nations that make war, and when they find themselves associated as Allies, it is quite often necessary to make concessions that recognize the existence of inescapable national differences. For example, due to differences in equipment, it necessary that the 12th Army Group depend primarily upon a Line of Communications that is separate so far as possible from that of 21st Army Group. Wherever we can, we keep people of the same nations serving under their own commanders. It is the job of soldiers, as I see it, to meet their military problems sanely, sensibly, and logically, and while not shutting our eyes to the fact that we are two different nations, produce solutions that permit effective cooperation, mutual support and effective results. Good will and mutual confidence are, of course, mandatory.

Even before this message reached the 21 Army Group commander, Montgomery appears to have concluded that the First U.S. Army could not reach the Rhine and there was no reason for British forces to move alone toward the Ruhr. He had already dispatched the Second British Army to help the Canadian forces speed the opening of Antwerp. After receiving General Eisenhower's letter, the field marshal terminated the discussion of the Ruhr, Antwerp, and command arrangements with the assurance that "you will hear no more on the subject of command from me." He wrote:

I have given you my views and you have given your answer. I and all of us will weigh in one hundred percent to do what you want and we will pull it through without a doubt. I have given Antwerp top priority in all operations in 21 Army Group and all energies and efforts will now be devoted towards opening up the place. Your very devoted and loyal subordinate.[41]

The Battle for Antwerp

The full attention of 21 Army Group was focused on clearing the Schelde estuary in mid-October. The task, simple

---

[41] Montgomery to Eisenhower, M–77, 14 Oct 44; Eisenhower to Montgomery, 15 Oct 44; Montgomery to Eisenhower, M–281, 16 Oct 44. All in Eisenhower personal file. 21 A Gp Operational Situation and Dir, M–532, 16 Oct 44, 12th A Gp 371.3 Military Objectives, II.

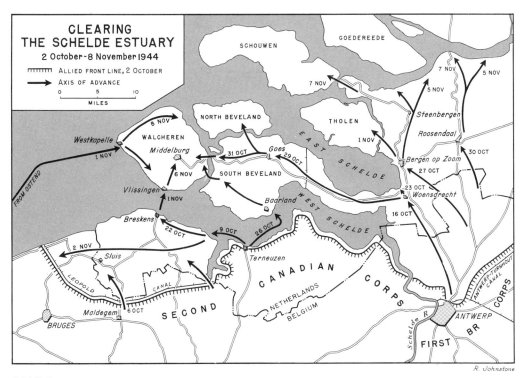

MAP 4

to state, was far from easy to execute. The enemy, intent on denying the Allies use of the tremendously important port of Antwerp, had reinforced the fortifications and coastal guns on the island of Walcheren, the South Beveland peninsula, and the mainland south of the Schelde estuary to prevent shipping from reaching the Allied-held docks at Antwerp. *(Map 4)*

Unfortunately for the Allies, the enemy had saved many of his troops in the area from destruction and had managed to strengthen his positions. General der Infanterie Gustav von Zangen, who had succeeded Generaloberst Hans von Salmuth as commander of the *Fifteenth Army* in late August, had managed to withdraw part of his troops from the Pas-de-Calais in good order and had established a defense line south of the Schelde estuary after the fall of Antwerp. To keep the escape route open for other retreating units, the commander had brought the division guarding the approaches to Antwerp down to the area of Ghent on 4 September. As quickly as other forces could be brought up, he put them into the line near Woensdrecht to protect the isthmus. By this means he was able both to block the Allied advance and to keep open an escape route to the north and east. On 6 September, after the forces to the west had been brought into Belgium, he ordered a general withdrawal northward across the Schelde estuary to Walcheren Island. Allied air activity harassed the move, but in a period of slightly more than two weeks an estimated 80,000 men and nearly 600 pieces of artillery together with supply vehicles, antitank guns, and assault guns, were withdrawn without major losses. During the remainder of September, while the Allies were heavily engaged in attacks on the Channel fortresses and at Arnhem and Nijmegen, the Germans built up their defenses in the areas directly south of the Schelde estuary, the area north of Antwerp, and on the isthmus near Woensdrecht.[42]

The initial task of clearing the Schelde estuary had been assigned to the First Canadian Army, while the Second British and the First U.S. Armies were driving toward the Ruhr. Now, as General Eisenhower pressed for the opening of Antwerp, the latter two armies put part of their forces at the disposal of General Simonds, commanding the Canadian army in the absence of General Crerar (in the United Kingdom on sick leave).[43] The Canadians began to drive north from the Antwerp–Turnhout Canal and the suburbs of Antwerp on 2 October. They took Woensdrecht fifteen days later after heavy fighting. On their right, troops of the 1 British Corps pushed north and northwest upon Roosendaal and Bergen op Zoom and assisted the Canadians in sealing off the South Beveland isthmus from the mainland on 23 October. Meanwhile, an especially bitter fight developed to the west in the area between the Leopold Canal and Breskens as the Canadians sought to clear the pocket directly south of the Schelde estuary. Breskens finally fell on 22 October, and the entire area was cleared by 3 November, yielding more than 12,500 prisoners.

The First Canadian Army began its attack for South Beveland on 25 October with an advance westward from Woensdrecht. On 25–26 October, British forces

sailed from Terneuzen and struck northward across the estuary. Making assault landings near Baarland, they drove across the island. By the end of 30 October, the Canadian and British forces had linked up, cleared South Beveland of the enemy, and sent a small column to North Beveland to put down any resistance that might be offered there.

The worst obstacle was still to be faced on Walcheren Island some fifty miles west of Antwerp. Here a garrison estimated at 6,000 to 7,000, well dug in and equipped with strong antiaircraft batteries and coastal defenses, maintained the last barrier between Allied shipping and Antwerp. General Simonds in September had originated and pressed, against the opposition of some airmen, a plan for bombing the dikes on Walcheren. While the scale of heavy bomber attacks, which began in the first days of October, was insufficient, the air efforts were responsible for breaching the dikes and forcing the enemy out of some of his low-lying positions. The main reliance for driving the Germans out of the island had to be placed, however, on seaborne assaults together with an attack from South Beveland.[44]

On the morning of 1 November, British Commandos from Breskens began landing near Vlissingen. A larger force made up of Royal Navy and British Commando units, mounted at Ostend, made a frontal assault on the strong undamaged

---

[42] MS # B–249, Battles of the *Fifteenth Army* in Northern France and Holland, 28 Aug–10 Nov 44 (Zangen); MS # B–475, Battles of the *Fifteenth Army* between the Meuse–Scheldt Canal and the Lower Meuse, 15 Sep–10 Nov 44 (Zangen); *Der Westen* (Schramm).

[43] Maj. Gen. C. Foulkes temporarily succeeded General Simonds as commander of the 2d Canadian Corps.

[44] Stacey, *The Canadian Army*, p. 228.

fortifications in the area of Westkapelle at the extreme western end of the island. The landing craft were particularly hard hit by enemy shore defenses. Despite heavy opposition, the force was successfully put ashore and started its eastward drive across the island. Meanwhile, the units which had landed from Breskens seized Vlissingen on 2 November. On the following day, the two forces linked up and began systematically clearing the enemy from the island. On 8 November, German resistance ended.[45]

The period 1 October to 8 November in the Antwerp sector had proved costly to both the Allies and the enemy. The forces under the First Canadian Army had suffered nearly 13,000 casualties, but they had inflicted much heavier losses on the enemy, whose casualties in prisoners alone totaled some 40,000.[46]

General Eisenhower was able to inform the Combined Chiefs of Staff on 3 November that the approaches to Antwerp had been cleared. Even as the last resistance was being rooted out on Walcheren Island, minesweeping activities began on the Schelde estuary. Some three weeks later, on 28 November, the first convoy of Allied ships reached the port of Antwerp.

[45] For general discussions of the battle for the Schelde estuary, see Stacey, *The Canadian Army*, Ch. XIV; Mongomery, *Normandy to the Baltic*, Ch. XIII.

[46] Stacey, *The Canadian Army*, p. 229. These figures were based on General Simonds' contemporary report to General Crerar, 22 November 1944. Compare statistics with those given in Eisenhower, *Crusade in Europe*, p. 327. The 10,000 German prisoners listed in the Eisenhower volume were apparently those taken on Walcheren and Beveland, while more than 27,000 Allied casualties were approximately those suffered along the entire 21 Army Group front from Walcheren to Nijmegen during the period. It should be recalled that operations to clear the Schelde estuary were controlled by the First Canadian Army but contained British, U.S., and Polish elements as well. More than 6,000 of the 13,000 casualties were Canadian.

CHAPTER XVII

The Battles of Attrition, September–December 1944

While the 21 Army Group, aided by the First Allied Airborne Army and elements of the First U.S. Army, carried out the attack on Arnhem and operations around Antwerp, the 12th (less First Army) and 6th Army Groups probed at German weakness and sought to wear down the enemy in the area between Belgium and the Swiss border. *(Map V)* Campaigns in late September and early October were based on the belief that Hitler's forces were still disintegrating and that some lucky push might find a soft spot in the opposing lines which would permit the Allies to advance to the Rhine before the dead of winter. Later, when it became evident that the Germans had reorganized their forces and had succeeded in manning the West Wall fortifications against the Allied offensive, General Eisenhower refused to accept a static policy for the winter, feeling that even minor advances were better than completely defensive tactics. "We were certain," he wrote after the war, "that by continuing an unremitting offensive we would, in spite of hardship and privation, gain additional advantages over the enemy. Specifically we were convinced that this policy would result in shortening the war and therefore in the saving of thousands of Allied lives." [1]

The Enemy Regroups

The enemy by mid-September had performed amazing feats in improvising units to hold the West Wall defenses and in creating an opposition which was often formidable. It is possible, as British and U.S. proponents of the single thrust to the Rhine argue, that these efforts were impressive only because the attempt to advance on a broad front enabled small groups of second- and third-rate troops to hold up the Allied advance. A complex of varying factors, however, as already indicated, entered into the Supreme Commander's decisions on these points. Whether the efforts of Field Marshal Model or General Blaskowitz or the so-called caution of the Allied command was responsible, it is clear that by the time of the Arnhem attack the Germans were in a position to meet with considerable force either a single or a double thrust by the Allies.

Three moves ordered by Hitler before the drive across northern France affected the Allied attacks of fall and early winter. By late July, the German leader had directed that eighteen divisions be formed for use against the Russians and the West-

---

[1] Eisenhower, *Crusade in Europe*, p. 323.

ern Allies. Two of these were sent to the west by 1 September. In midsummer approximately one hundred fortress infantry battalions, formerly used in the rear areas, were made available for battle. About four fifths of these were ultimately sent to the west. Some were in action by mid-September. More important still were twenty-five *Volks Grenadier* divisions, which Hitler had ordered organized in mid-August as a general reserve. These began to come into the line at the beginning of October and were supposed to be completely organized by 1 December. By 5 November eight of them had been sent to Field Marshal Rundstedt's forces, two were in the east, and the remaining fifteen in the Replacement Army.[2]

In actions that exerted pressure on the Germans south of the MARKET-GARDEN area in September, the First U.S. Army sent one corps across the Meuse above Liége to gain contact with the British at Maeseyck and start a drive toward Geilenkirchen. Another corps forced the Germans back into West Wall defenses southeast of Aachen before settling down to meager gains for the remainder of the month. The southernmost corps crossed into Germany, but made little progress. Even though the period was rather unproductive in results, it cost the First Army nearly 10,000 casualties.

The Third Army at the beginning of September was extended along a 450-mile (air-line) front from Brest to the Moselle. In order to leave the army free for activities toward the east, General Bradley on 5 September gave its missions of clearing the Brest peninsula and protecting the southern flank of the 12th Army Group to General Simpson's newly arrived Ninth Army. The VIII Corps, already engaged in the

Brest peninsula, was transferred from the Third to the Ninth Army and continued its attack under the new command. Three days later, General Simpson opened a three-divisional attack against Brest which cleared the city on 18 September. The last resistance in the Brest peninsula ceased on 21 September. In the course of fighting for the area, the Third and Ninth Armies took more than 37,000 prisoners and killed an estimated 4,000 Germans. The Ninth Army suffered approximately 3,000 casualties in the campaign. The port of Brest was too badly wrecked to be of any immediate value. Its port facilities, however, once considered vital to any Allied advance into Germany, were no longer essential to the Allies.

On the surrender of the Brest peninsula, the Ninth Army invested German-held ports on the Atlantic Coast, which were estimated to hold some 25,000 enemy troops. The task of besieging the cities was handed over to the 94th Division. This unit, with French Forces of the Interior elements, French naval units, and a French bomber squadron, undertook the containment of enemy forces spread along the southwest coast of France. At the close of September, the Ninth Army, which had also been receiving and processing divisions as they arrived on the Continent, was ordered into the line between the First and Third Armies, roughly in the area running from St. Vith to Bollendorf. U.S. activities in western France were then brought directly under 12th Army Group; the job of handling newly arrived troops was given to Communications Zone.

[2] Cole, *The Lorraine Campaign*, Ch. I; Rpt, *Uebersicht ueber die in Aufstellung und Umgliederung befindlichen Verbaende des Heeres u. Pz. Verbaende der Waffen SS (Stand 5.XI.44). OKH/Organisations Abteilung* (referred to hereafter as *OKH/Org.Abt.*)

The Third Army, almost completely halted at the end of August by gasoline shortages and increasing enemy opposition, resumed its advance on 4 September with the mission of crossing the Moselle and moving to positions on the Rhine. Preparations, unknown to the Third Army, had been initiated by Hitler and *OB WEST* as early as 28 August for a counterattack against the southern flank of the Allied forces. The initial proposal, which envisaged a blow in the Troyes sector and a penetration northward between the Seine and the Marne, was given up when General Patton's forces reached the Meuse on 3 September. Hitler on that day gave instructions to *OB WEST* for a different plan. This scheme, "the most ambitious to be advanced during the months between the Mortain counterattack and the Ardennes offensive," provided for the left wing of Hitler's forces *(Army Group G)* to cover the German retreat from southern and southwestern France and to strike against the extended south flank of the Third Army. Had the attack been effective, it could have prevented the junction of the Third and Seventh Armies and rolled up the right flank of the OVERLORD forces, pushing the Third Army back toward Reims and exposing the U.S. lines of communications.[3]

Hitler's deep interest in the proposed counterattack was shown by his promise of additional armored elements and by his personal selection of General der Panzertruppen Hasso von Manteuffel as head of the *Fifth Panzer Army,* which was to make the attack. Unfortunately for the enemy, the promised reinforcements were not delivered in sufficient quantities to influence the battle. Units were committed piecemeal, and the Americans were able to deal with them separately. On 13 September, before the German offensive could be mounted in the Neufchâteau–Mirecourt area, the 2d French Armored Division supported by the XIX Tactical Air Command inflicted a loss of sixty tanks on the enemy—one of the heaviest armored losses suffered by the Germans in northwest Europe in a single day. Five days later the enemy reluctantly undertook the task of eliminating the Third Army's bridgehead at Pont-à-Mousson and restoring the Moselle line north of Nancy. The reverses they suffered in that area were used by Hitler on 21 September as grounds for replacing Blaskowitz, the *Army Group G* commander, with General Balck. For ten days, in the face of recommendations from field commanders that the attack be stopped, Hitler ordered that it be continued. By the end of September the German threat to the Allied flank had been ended. Von Rundstedt now asked in vain for reinforcements to meet expected Third Army attacks. Instead, Hitler shifted forces northward to meet the Second British Army attack. On 1 October, the *Fifth Panzer Army* and the Third U.S. Army were both on the defensive.

The 6th Army Group forces, which had driven more than 400 miles in scarcely a month, came to an almost complete standstill in mid-September, although the Seventh Army, after regrouping, was able to send three divisions across the Moselle by the end of the month. Supply difficulties kept the First French Army virtually idle.

October Battles

The month of October, outside the 21 Army Group zone, was marked by two major actions by U.S. forces—the taking

[3] Cole, *The Lorraine Campaign,* pp. 190–219. Complete details on these plans and the results of the counterthrust are given in Chapters IV and V of Dr. Cole's volume.

of Aachen and the attack on Metz. The First Army on 29 September ordered its forces to conduct limited operations from the vicinity of Deurne, north of Maastricht, to protect the right flank of 21 Army Group, and to make a co-ordinated attack about 1 October with the mission of taking Dueren and Cologne. The two northern corps were directed to surround and capture Aachen and then push toward the Rhine. They attacked on 2 October, but met stubborn resistance from an enemy reinforced by units from the Arnhem area and other sectors of the Western Front and encouraged by Hitler's pleas for a last-ditch fight. A heavy bombardment by the IX Tactical Air Command between 11 and 13 October softened opposition, and the U.S. forces began house-to-house fighting inside Aachen on the 14th. Two days later the city was encircled and attempts to relieve it were beaten back. Continual daily poundings by Allied artillery and methodical clean-up operations in various parts of the city by U.S. infantry forced the garrison to surrender on 21 October.

To the south of General Hodges' forces, the Third Army on 2 October had launched an attack on the Metz fortifications. Part of Fort Driant was occupied after bitter fighting, but extremely heavy enemy resistance led the American forces to withdraw on 12 October. Reduced ammunition supplies at this point required postponement of a new offensive until November. An attack for Maizières-les-Metz, some six miles north of Metz, was carried on against stubborn opposition until the month's end, but for the most part the Third Army's activities during the last half of October were summarized under the head of "aggressive patrolling."

Supply difficulties and bad weather harassed 6th Army Group throughout the month of October. In addition to these problems, the First French Army had the tasks of integrating French Forces of the Interior into the Regular Army, and of "whitening" [4] the African divisions whose native members were unable to endure the cold of the Vosges. General Patch's forces during the month seized the high ground dominating the Meurthe valley in the St. Dié area and took nearly 6,000 prisoners. In the first half of October, General de Lattre attempted to advance north of the Vosges toward Colmar, but the increasing severity of the weather soon made it necessary to abandon this effort. General de Lattre so notified his commanders on 17 October and turned to the task of getting more men and supplies for his army.

As the weather grew progressively worse, General Eisenhower saw his forces at the West Wall slowed to advances of a few yards a day. Deprived of air and, sometimes, of armored support, the Allies endured severe hardship but produced little that was tangible in the way of ground won. No period saw more dogged fighting or required more stamina and physical tenacity on the part of the soldiers than that between late October and the end of December. It was a time of stockpiling supplies, of digging in, and of battling painfully to straighten the lines. This period more than any other of the war in northern Europe belonged to the foot soldiers. The high-level communiqués which day after day spoke of "actions confined to aggressive patrolling" were insufficient tributes to the fighting qualities of men who managed to exist and even advance a little in areas plagued with freezing rain, driving snow, record floods, endless stretches of mud, and biting cold. Until more supplies could be brought up,

---

[4] The process of replacing native members with whites.

strategic decisions were of little importance. At best there was talk of what could
be done later. Meanwhile, trenchfoot and
respiratory diseases took their toll of men
who came to understand more fully what
soldiers in the Russian and Italian theaters
had undergone in the winter battles of the
preceding years.

Before the difficulties of the campaign
became so thoroughly apparent, General
Eisenhower had been hopeful of pressing
a successful attack along the entire line. In
mid-October, as the British pressed their
battle to clear the approaches to Antwerp,
he anticipated a great increase in supplies
for November which would make it possible to push his offensive. His chief of intelligence, General Strong, saw November
as the month Hitler dreaded most. While
he believed that the German leader hoped
to launch some counterstroke about that
time, Strong concluded that attrition was
slowly reducing the enemy's power to attack. His policy of switching armor back
and forth between Aachen and Nijmegen
indicated that he had barely one hundred
tanks or just enough to deal with one
penetration at a time. SHAEF estimated
that on the relatively stable front between
Venlo and Nancy the Allies had taken an
average of 1,300 prisoners a day during
the period 10 September to 9 October.
This meant, if other casualties were set at
a normal proportion, that the enemy had
a casualty rate of 4,000 a day, "or one 'division' on his new standard every day or
two, through simple attrition in the line."
The result, the SHAEF G–2 believed, was
that the enemy was getting into the same
dangerous situation that had prevailed in
Normandy. "The dwindling fire brigade
is switched with increasing rapidity and
increasing wear and tear from one fire to
another." [5]

A number of considerations influenced
General Eisenhower to press his offensive
in late October. Not only did he desire to
continue to drain enemy manpower, but
he wanted to make certain that the Germans had no chance to move into better
positions and to build up their forces. He
was aware of many difficulties which lay
in his way, and the many different demands for men and supplies. The Schelde
estuary was still not open; Allied forces
were getting farther away from air bases
in the United Kingdom; and transportation problems were increasing as the
winter approached. Despite the repair and
improvement of rail systems, the matter
of transport remained critical. Two other
problems loomed increasingly larger. In a
series of inspection trips which he made to
most of the Allied units down to divisional
level during October, General Eisenhower
heard continually of shortages in ammunition and the lack of riflemen replacements.
The ammunition shortage was not merely
one of port capacity and distributional
facilities, but also one of inadequate production in the United States. [6] The manpower problem had arisen for several reasons, but prominent among them was the
fact that planners in the United States had
misjudged the role which riflemen were
going to play in the war and had put too
many men in branches other than the Infantry. Because of the time factor, the only
solution was a rigid comb-out of men in
the communications zone and the zone of
interior who might be readily reconverted
into foot soldiers. By the end of October a
study of such plans was under way in the

[5] SHAEF, G–2 Weekly Intel Summary 30, 15 Oct
44, SHAEF G–2 files.
[6] Eisenhower to Marshall, S–63259, 20 Oct 44,
Eisenhower personal file.

zone of interior and in the European Theater of Operations.[7]

Plans To End the War Quickly

On 20 October the Combined Chiefs of Staff in Washington decided to study the possibility of an all-out offensive that could conceivably end the war before the close of 1944. In the course of discussing with the Combined Chiefs the advisability of releasing the heretofore-secret proximity fuze for use in battle, General Marshall indicated that the release of secret weapons was bound up with their use to end the war speedily. In the light of an apparent agreement that the matter was the proper subject of a directive to the Supreme Commander, General Marshall instructed his staff to draft a memorandum on the subject to General Eisenhower. His advisers proposed that the Allies should make an all-out effort to defeat the German armies before 1 January 1945. This effort, they thought, would require release of weapons whose use had hitherto been restricted for security reasons and elimination of those strategic air force operations which did not effect an immediate reduction in German capabilities. It would also require commitment of strategic reserves and theater stockpiles without regard to their position by the end of the year, and would have a bearing on the continuation in action of units which otherwise would be withdrawn for rehabilitation and training for 1945 operations. General Eisenhower was informed that this draft was under consideration and was based on the assumption that Germany could be defeated in 1944 if the utmost use was made of all Allied resources. General Marshall added, "Be frank with me. I will accept your deci-

sion." General Eisenhower replied that he was as anxious as the Combined Chiefs of Staff to wind up the operation as quickly as possible. His logistical problems had become so acute, however, that all his plans had made the clearing of the approaches to Antwerp a *sine qua non* to the waging of the final all-out battle. He agreed that, with the divisions in the European theater and those on their way, there was a possibility that they might achieve the desired break.[8]

Changes were made in the original draft to emphasize that the Supreme Commander, Allied Expeditionary Force, and the Supreme Commander, Mediterranean, would consult together as to the way the latter could best aid the defeat of Germany by 1 January 1945. This referred in particular to the possible transfer of troops to France. The revised version was then submitted to the British Chiefs of Staff for their comments.[9]

On 29 October, the Joint Planning Staff of the British Chiefs of Staff Committee re-

[7] See study by Robert R. Palmer and William R. Keast, "The Provision of Enlisted Replacements" in Robert R. Palmer, Bell I. Wiley, and William R. Keast, *The Procurement and Training of Ground Combat Troops*, UNITED STATES ARMY IN WORLD WAR II (Washington, 1948). On both ammunition and manpower shortages, see Ruppenthal, Logistical Support of the Armies, Vol. II, now in preparation.

[8] Memo, G. C. M. (Gen Marshall) for Gen Handy and Gen Hull, 20 Oct 44, OPD 381 TS, Sec XVIII, Case 538/2; Draft of Dir to Eisenhower, Wilson, *et al.*, SS 316, 20 Oct 44, ABC 381 Strategy Sec Papers (7 Jan 43); Marshall to Eisenhower, W–50676, 22 Oct 44, SHAEF message file, Folder 27, Plans and Operations (13 May 44–23 May 45); Eisenhower to Marshall, S–63616, 23 Oct 44, Eisenhower personal file.

[9] The date of the revised document is not given. The major revisions seem to have been in the phrasing rather than the intent, although the provisions relating to strategic air forces were changed to say that these forces would act in accordance with the Supreme Commander's directions. OPD 381 TS, Sec XVIII, Case 538.

plied to the U.S. proposals. The planners concluded that the earliest date that could be suggested for the war's end was 31 January 1945, and the latest was 15 May 1945. Analyzing the proposed directive, they held that General Eisenhower's future actions were governed by the date Antwerp could be opened to shipping. To launch an all-out offensive before its opening, they added, "would be to court failure, and would probably have the effect of prolonging the war well into 1945." As to the means suggested by General Marshall to shorten the war, the members of the Joint Planning Staff had some reservations. They were inclined to question his proposal for changing the main air effort, feeling that the strategic air forces should continue to give top priority to oil targets. As a result of previous bombings, they pointed out, oil production had been reduced in September to about 23 percent of its preattack (April) level. If the attacks were suspended, the Joint Planning Staff believed, the enemy would be able to raise production to 50 percent of the preattack level within one month. The planners, noting that these targets would not absorb all the available strategic bomber forces, suggested the value of a series of heavy attacks on selected areas of the Ruhr. This effffort could also be aided by attacks on the German transportation system, with especial emphasis on barges and vulnerable points on canals. They added that General Eisenhower retained the right to call for direct bomber support of his land forces, but that he had agreed to reduce these demands as far as practicable. As for operations in the Mediterranean, the British felt that maximum pressure should be continued in that theater until the launching of the offensive in the west. They had already recommended release of the prox-

imity fuze for use against the enemy, and they welcomed the use of various psychological warfare and diversionary activities that would aid the Supreme Commander's battle.

The British Chiefs of Staff accepted these views of their planners and requested the U.S. Chiefs of Staff to withhold the proposed directive for the time being. General Marshall, therefore, on 1 November directed that nothing be done about the matter until further notice.[10]

While these plans were being discussed by the Combined Chiefs of Staff, the Allied air planners were discussing various campaigns for shortening the war by intensified air action. Under directives of September 1944, the strategic air forces had given first priority to the German oil industry and had placed enemy ordnance depots, armored fighting vehicle assembly plants, and motor vehicle assembly plants in the second priority list. At this time the German oil situation was believed to be desperate, but the Allied airmen feared that a few weeks of respite from Allied bomber attacks would permit the Germans to restore their oil production to 60 percent of the normal output. U.S. bomber experts considered this view confirmed in October when bad weather and commitments to support of land operations cut Eighth Air Force missions against

---

[10] Rpt, Jt Plng Stf, 29 Oct 44, sub: Plng Date for End of War With Germany, JP (44) 262 (Final); Rpt, Jt Plng Stf, 29 Oct 44, sub: Opns in Europe, JP (44) 275 (Final); Memo by Br Representatives, 31 Oct 44, sub: Immediate Supreme Effort in Western Europe; Memo, H.H.F. (Lt Col Harvey H. Fischer, member of Strategy Sec, Strategy and Policy Group, OPD) for Gen Roberts (Brig Gen Frank N. Roberts, Chief, Strategy and Policy Group, OPD), 1 Nov 44. Colonel Fischer said in his memorandum, "Chief of Staff has issued verbal instructions that nothing more should be done on this matter." All these papers are in ABC 384 Europe (4 Aug 43), Sec 1A.

oil targets. They estimated that the enemy oil output for October rose seven points or 30 percent of the preattack level. Meanwhile, discouraging results were coming in about the attacks on ordnance depots and assembly plants. Bad weather and the priority of oil targets left few days for attacks on the second-priority targets. As a result the airmen concluded in October that their attacks were clearly not having a decisive influence on the enemy's efforts to re-equip his armies. They were, therefore, aware of the inconclusiveness of these attacks when, in late October, General Marshall spoke of throwing all Allied efforts into an offensive to end the war against Germany by the end of the year.[11]

Against this background of somewhat disappointing results, Air Chief Marshal Tedder and the Air Ministry reopened the possibility of using the strategic air forces for attacks on railway centers and marshaling yards. Tedder had advocated this project successfully in the spring of 1944 and believed it to have been mainly responsible for paralyzing the rail system in northern France. He asked that the strategic air forces concentrate their principal attacks on the Ruhr with bombings of the rail centers, oil targets, canal systems, and centers of population. The SHAEF intelligence division gave the plan only qualified approval. Its chief, General Strong, agreed that the air and ground battle against Germany should be co-ordinated and felt that an attack on transport would probably give the best over-all effect. He believed, however, that oil targets should continue to have top priority and added that recent reports as to the decreased importance of the Ruhr in Germany's economy probably would require a reassessment of its worth. He thought that a future air offensive should probably be extended

to the whole enemy transportation system.[12]

Despite doubts among railway and intelligence experts as to the degree of success that the transportation scheme might obtain, top commanders, meeting at SHAEF near the end of October, decided that bombing of German transportation would be given priority second only to operations against synthetic oil plants. General Spaatz and Air Marshal Bottomley issued a directive to this effect on 28 October 1944.[13]

The proposals to end the war in 1944 by means of an all-out offensive had actually come too late to be effective. Such an attack could succeed only if it were made while the enemy was still disorganized. Once he had established himself in his defenses, the Allies had to get a port within a reasonable distance of the battle area in order to stockpile weapons and supplies for a new attack. Until Antwerp was open and matériel had begun to move through it, the granting of permission to use new weapons and to shift priorities would be of little value. The end of October found the battle for Antwerp still in progress. Since it would be nearly a month at best before ships would be unloading in that port, it appeared more reasonable during the remaining days of 1944 to concentrate on an attempt to reach and establish bridgeheads across the Rhine than to launch an offensive to end the war.

---

[11] Craven and Cate, *The Army Air Forces in World War II*, Vol. III, Ch. 18, "Autumn Assault on Germany."

[12] Deputy Supreme Commander's Notes on Air Policy To Be Adopted With a View to the Rapid Defeat of Germany, 25 Oct 44; Strong to Tedder, 28 Oct 44. Both in SHAEF G–2 Intel on Germany GBI/01–A/091–3.

[13] Craven and Cate, *The Army Air Forces in World War II*, III, 653.

The November Offensive

On 18 October, just before the Combined Chiefs of Staff had raised the question of launching a campaign to conclude the war in Europe before the end of 1944, the Supreme Commander and the 12th and 21 Army Group commanders met at Brussels to discuss a more modest program for November and perhaps December 1944. Since General Eisenhower had decided that the British and Canadian forces would have to concentrate during the next several weeks on the task of clearing the Schelde estuary, he concluded that the drive toward the Rhine, heretofore largely a 21 Army Group mission, should be assumed by the First and Ninth U.S. Armies. General Hodges was to attempt to establish a bridgehead south of Cologne, while General Simpson's forces protected his left flank between Sittard and Aachen. To the right of the First Army, General Patton's forces were to advance in a northeasterly direction in support of the main thrust. Meanwhile, General Devers' French and U.S. forces were to attempt to cross the Rhine in their sector.[14] For the first time since late August, the main thrust was given to the U.S. forces, and the Allied forces were oriented directly at and south of the Ruhr, instead of north of that area. If these various drives proved successful in establishing bridgeheads across the Rhine before the 21 Army Group was free to return to its missions, it would be impossible to return to the strategy which Field Marshal Montgomery had favored since late August and which the Supreme Commander had approved in its broad aspects.

In agreeing to this operation, which differed from that envisaged by the British Chiefs of Staff and the 21 Army Group commander, General Eisenhower followed his policy of closing up along as much of the Rhine as possible and of hitting the Germans at every possible point in order to keep them stretched. Nonetheless, he opened himself up to British suspicions that he was straying from his earlier strategic commitments.

The Supreme Commander on 28 October confirmed his decisions made ten days earlier at Brussels and pressed preparations by the Ninth and First U.S. Armies.[15] During the next two weeks he visited every division in the two armies and was pleased to find their morale good. His chief worry was the weather. It was so severe, he reported, that it was breaking a number of records which had stood for twenty-five to fifty years. Despite the problems of mud, rain, and fog, he retained his optimism and assured General Marshall that the Allies would yet make the Germans wish they had gone east of the Rhine when they withdrew from France. There still remained in his mind, however, considerable anxiety over the state of supplies—a concern expressed shortly after the opening of the November offensive in a public appeal for greater Allied efforts to keep industrial production at a maximum.[16]

[14] Decision reached at SAC's conf, Brussels, 18 Oct 44; SAC's dir confirming decisions of Brussels conf, SCAF 114, 28 Oct 44; Revisions in dir, SCAF 119, 2 Nov 44. All in SHAEF SGS 381 Post OVERLORD Planning, II.

[15] SAC's dir confirming decisions of Brussels conf, SCAF 114, 28 Oct 44, SHAEF SGS 381 Post OVERLORD Planning, II. The plan had to be changed at the beginning of November because of a limited offensive launched by the enemy against British forces on 27 October. Field Marshal Montgomery found it necessary to clear the area west of the Maas before advancing from the Nijmegen area between the Maas and the Rhine.

[16] Eisenhower to Marshall, 11 Nov 44, Eisenhower personal file; Eisenhower press conference, New York *Times*, November 22, 1944.

Two subsidiary attacks preceded the main November offensive. The first, ordered by First Army to secure the Schmidt area just north of important dams on the Urft and Roer Rivers, was launched by V Corps on 2 November. The Americans seized the town of Schmidt, but a sharp enemy reaction and supply difficulties forced them to withdraw and terminate the action.[17] On 12 November, the Second British Army moved eastward for the purpose of forcing the Maas in its area. Enemy resistance was not heavy, but minefields, mud, and bad weather delayed the advance. By 22 November, the British had succeeded in clearing the west bank of the Maas opposite Roermond.

The Ninth and First Armies launched the main offensive in the early afternoon of 16 November after an air preparation described as the largest "air-ground cooperative effort yet undertaken by the Allied air forces." The bombardment destroyed the center of Dueren and nearly wiped out nearby cities like Eschweiler and Juelich.[18] Two German divisions in the process of shifting positions were severely hit. In the Ninth Army's sector, ground forces made good progress during the first three days of the attack, but units in the First Army area had less success. The enemy used his West Wall fortifications effectively, particularly in the Huertgen Forest where poor road nets, often little more than forest trails, slowed or stopped armored advances. Infantrymen proceeding through the dense woods were subjected to the terrors of mines and artillery tree bursts. Rain and snow added to the difficulties and the misery of the combatants. Resistance stiffened along the entire front as the enemy brought up reinforcements, forcing a virtual stalemate on the U.S. units. A final spurt of action near the month's close

brought the Ninth Army to the Roer in most of its sector, while the First Army established a front on the line of the Inde and opened a drive toward the Roer in the Huertgen area. British efforts to make General Bradley's left flank more secure had continued through November, ending with the elimination of enemy positions near Venlo and with attacks east of Geilenkirchen in the first week of December.

In the Third Army's area, General Patton turned his attention both to the drive against the Saar and to the battle for Metz. His troops encircled Metz on 18 November and on the following day entered the city. Four days later, all enemy resistance in the city itself ceased, although the battle for the outlying forts continued. Meanwhile, other Third Army elements, advancing on the right, forced the enemy back into the Siegfried Line from Nennig to Saarlautern and reached the Saar at Hilbringen.

The 6th Army Group, cast only for a supporting role in November, gained several of the month's most important victories. The Seventh Army attacked as early as 13 November with the object of capturing Sarrebourg and forcing the Saverne Gap. Task forces of the 2d French Armored Division were sent to Saverne on 22 November. The division was next ordered to aid the drive on Strasbourg and opened an attack against that famous city on 23 November. Within a few hours armored elements had cleared the city and reached the Kehl bridge at the Rhine.

---

[17] A detailed account of this battle is given in Charles B. MacDonald and Sidney T. Matthews, *Three Battles: Arnaville, Altuzzo, and Schmidt*, UNITED STATES ARMY IN WORLD WAR II (Washington, 1952).

[18] The Eighth Air Force dropped more than 4,000 tons of bombs, and the RAF Bomber Command dropped nearly 5,700. Craven and Cate, *The Army Air Forces in World War II*, III, 631–32.

General de Lattre's First French Army on the extreme south flank also added a string of victories to the Allied list in the last two weeks of November. Starting on the 14th with the intention of forcing the Belfort Gap and driving the enemy from Alsace, the First French Army rapidly cleared the industrial area southwest of Belfort. I French Corps liberated Belfort, Altkirch, and Mulhouse between 18 and 25 November and then drove toward Colmar and Neuf-Brisach with the intention of crossing the Rhine near the latter city. The II French Corps, ordered to advance toward the center of Alsace and aid the advance to the north, linked up at Burnhaupt, ten miles west of Mulhouse, with the I French Corps, and caught a number of Germans in the trap. In their two weeks' battle, one of their hardest and most successful fights of the war, the French killed an estimated 10,000 Germans and took another 17,000 as prisoners. The First French Army's losses were estimated at more than 10,000.[19]

Allied Strategy Re-examined

The fighting in November, while bringing the Allies closer to the Rhine, proved costly and failed to achieve the hoped-for successes on the Ninth and First Army fronts. Field Marshal Montgomery discussed this outcome with General Eisenhower on 28 November, and two days later said that in his opinion the Supreme Commander's failure to implement his directive of 28 October was responsible for the situation. The October directive, the 21 Army Group commander recalled, ordered the main effort to be made in the north, the decisive defeat of the enemy west of the Rhine, the establishment of bridgeheads over the Rhine and IJssel

Rivers, and the deployment of Allied forces in strength east of the Rhine in preparation for the seizure of the Ruhr. "We have achieved none of this," the field marshal said, "and we have no hope of doing so. We have therefore failed; and we have suffered a strategic reverse." Montgomery continued:

3. We now require a new plan. And this time *we must not fail*. The need to get the German war finished early is vital, in view of other factors. The new plan *must not fail*.

4. In the new plan we must get away from the doctrine of attacking in so many places that nowhere are we strong enough to get decisive results. We must concentrate such strength on the main selected thrust that success will be certain. It is in this respect that we failed badly in the present operations.[20]

Closely connected with the request for a new plan was a renewed appeal for closer ground force co-ordination. Field Marshal Montgomery said:

5. The theatre divides itself naturally into two fronts; one north of the Ardennes and one south of the Ardennes. We want one commander in full operational control north of the Ardennes, and one south.

6. I did suggest that you might consider having a land force commander to work under you and run the land battle for you. But you discarded this idea as not being suitable, and we did not discuss it any more.

7. You suggested that a better solution would be to put 12 Army Group and 21 Army Group both north of the Ardennes, and to put Bradley under my operational command.

8. I said that Bradley and I together are a good team. We worked together in Normandy, under you, and we won a great victory. Things have not been so good since you separated us. I believe to be certain of success you want to bring us together again; and

---

[19] De Lattre, *Histoire de la Première Armée Française*, Pt. IV.

[20] Montgomery to Eisenhower, 30 Nov 44, Diary Office CinC. Italics in original.

one of us should have the full operational control north of the Ardennes; and if you decide that I should do that work—that is O. K. by me.[21]

To understand the field marshal's reference to strategic reverse, it is necessary to recall the earlier plans and his proposals. Before the Schelde campaign, it should be remembered, the Supreme Commander had put the main emphasis upon a thrust to the north—one in which the Allies would ultimately cross the Rhine north of the Ruhr.[22] With the shift of the British and Canadian forces to the Schelde estuary operation, the drive toward the Rhine had moved temporarily to the Ninth and First U.S. Army fronts with the main emphasis on the Bonn–Cologne area. If this orientation continued, the Allied forces would be in a position to cross the Rhine north of the Ardennes, but south of the Ruhr. They would absorb forces that would otherwise have been available for the 21 Army Group drive farther north. Thus, when the field marshal sharply criticized operations which had taken place in November, he was talking not merely of failures to advance to Bonn and Cologne, but of failures to continue in the northeast direction to which he and, he thought, SHAEF were committed. To get involved in operations which led away from that direction he considered faulty strategy, and to drive in the wrong direction, particularly without reaching the Rhine, was "a strategic reverse."

General Eisenhower, who interpreted the field marshal's reference to "a strategic reverse" as a general condemnation of past plans wrote Montgomery a letter in which he flatly contradicted the statement that they had failed. He summarized the successes of the campaigns up to

that point and defended firmly his recent broad front policy. His letter read in part:

I am not quite sure I know exactly what you mean by strategic reverse; certainly to date we have failed to achieve all that we had hoped to by this time, which hopes and plans were based upon conditions as we knew them or estimated them when the plans were made. The Ruhr is an important place, but let us never forget for one second that our primary objective is to defeat the Germans who are barring our way into Germany. The Ruhr itself was always given as a geographical objective, not only for its importance to Germany, but because it was believed that in that region the *German forces* would be largely concentrated to meet our attacks.

Specifically, I agree to the following:

a. We must determine how much profit there is in the continuation of our current attacks in the 12th Army Group area, and whether they give real promise of reaching the Rhine.

b. We must recast our future general plans in the light of conditions as they now exist.

c. We must choose the best line of attack to assure success, including the maintenance of deception lines.

I also stated that from my personal viewpoint, it would be simpler for me to have the battle zone divided into two general sectors, in each of which one individual could achieve close battle coordination. I expressed some doubt whether this zone should be divided on the basis of our rear areas or on the basis of natural lines of advance into Germany. There was some question in my mind whether the Ardennes or the Ruhr should mark the dividing line, if such a plan should be adopted.

I do not agree that things have gone badly since Normandy, merely because we have not gained all we had hoped to gain. In fact, the situation is somewhat analogous to that which existed in Normandy for so long. Our line as late as D plus 60 was not greatly different than what we hoped to hold in the first week, but I never looked upon the situation then existing as a strategic reverse, even

[21] *Ibid.*

[22] See above, p. 294.

though out of the circumstances of our long confinement in the narrow beach head have developed some of our greatest later difficulties. If we had advanced from the beginning *as we had hoped,* our maintenance services would have been in a position to supply us during the critical September days, when we actually reached the limit of our resources.

Moreover, I do not agree that more strength could have been thrown to the North than was actually maintained there during early September. Lines of communication in the north were so stretched that even delivery of five hundred tons to you at Brussels cost Bradley three divisions, the possession of which might have easily placed him on the Rhine in the Worms area.

We gained a great victory in Normandy. Bradley's brilliant breakthrough made possible the great exploitation by all forces, which blasted France and Belgium and almost carried us across the Rhine. Had we not advanced on a relatively broad front, we would now have the spectacle of a long narrow line of communication, constantly threatened on the right flank and weakened by detachments of large fighting formations. In addition, we would have had a similar picture in the south, stretching all the way from Marseilles to Dijon. As it is, we now have a rear that is cleared of the enemy. We can look to the front.

I have no intention of stopping Devers' and Patton's operations as long as they are cleaning up our right flank and giving us *capability of concentration.* On the other hand, I do not intend to push these attacks senselessly.

It is going to be very important to us later on to have two strings to our bow. Don't forget that you were very wise in making a provision for this at·Mareth, and it paid off.

* * *

I most definitely appreciate the frankness of your statements, and the usual friendly way in which they are stated, but I beg of you not to continue to look upon the past performances of this great fighting force as a failure because we have not achieved all that we could have hoped.

I am quite sure that you, Bradley, and I can remain masters of the situation and the victory we want will certainly be achieved. But we must look at this whole great affair stretching from Marseilles to the lower Rhine as one great theater. We must plan so when our next attack starts we will be able to obtain maximum results from all our forces, under the conditions now existing. IKE.[23]

Field Marshal Montgomery quickly pointed out that he had never intimated the work of the Allied forces had been a failure, but that he had said they had failed to carry out the directive of 28 October. General Eisenhower immediately sent his "prompt and abject apologies" for giving the letter an interpretation which the writer had not intended.[24]

Within a week after Field Marshal Montgomery had expressed to General Eisenhower his fears concerning Allied strategy, Mr. Churchill voiced similar anxieties to President Roosevelt. Conceding that current attacks had brought a number of splendid trophies such as Metz and Strasbourg, the Prime Minister nevertheless felt that the Allies "had definitely failed to achieve the strategic object we gave our armies five weeks ago." They had not reached the Rhine in the northern and most important sector of the front, and would have to continue the battle for many weeks before they could hope to do so. The British statesman was equally worried about the over-all strategic picture. He saw a marked degree of frustration in Italy, which he blamed in part on the diversion of forces to the landings in southern France; a large part of the enemy forces had escaped from the Balkan peninsula; the plans for Burma were not going well; and China had been eliminated as a

---

[23] Ltr, Eisenhower to Montgomery, 1 Dec 44, Eisenhower personal file. Italics in original.

[24] Ltr, Montgomery to Eisenhower, 2 Dec 44; Ltr, Eisenhower to Montgomery, 2 Dec 44. Both in Diary Office CinC.

combatant. He believed that the situation required another meeting shortly of the Allied leaders to discuss the future. Mr. Roosevelt, in the letter he drafted in reply, declared that he was less disappointed than the Prime Minister about results, partly because he had been less optimistic over the time element six months previously. The President said that he had bicycled over most of the Rhine terrain "in the old days" and, as a result, had never been as sanguine about the ease of getting across the river as had some of the Allied commanders. Despite disappointments, he believed that the agreed broad strategy was going according to plan. He reminded the Prime Minister that they were in the position of commanders in chief who had prepared their plans, issued their orders, and committed their resources to battle. "For the time being, even if a little behind schedule, it seems to me the prosecution and outcome of the battles lie with our Field Commanders in whom I have every confidence." He was heartened by the fact that the enemy was being chewed up, and that Allied supplies were being piled up for later offensives. "I still cannot see clearly when, but soon a decisive break in our favor is bound to come. [25]

General Eisenhower was keenly aware of the difficulties that faced his force. But he was pleased to find from his visits to various lower headquarters that everyone was "in surprisingly good heart and condition." In a report to General Marshall, he threw a little light indirectly on his own problems in a remark that the corps, army, and army group commanders were standing up well. Their good condition was due, he intimated, to the fact that they had to worry only about tactics and local maintenance "without . . . having to

burden themselves with politics, priorities, shipping and Maquis" on the one hand and without having to undergo the "more direct battle strains of a Division commander" on the other. The Supreme Commander was not hopeful of immediate success since the enemy was sending new divisions to the west, and he felt that much depended on the scale of the anticipated winter offensive of the Russians. He saw some hope in the fact that the enemy was badly stretched in the west and was forced to shift his units constantly to protect various points threatened by the Allies. To continue this strain, he proposed to keep up a number of limited attacks toward the Rhine, while preparing an all-out offensive. He frankly admitted that he was not overly optimistic about the immediate results of these thrusts since it appeared that unless "some trouble develops from within Germany, a possibility of which there is now no real evidence, [the enemy] should be able to maintain a strong defensive front for some time, assisted by weather, floods and muddy ground." [26]

The Allied air commanders were also pessimistic because of their fear that the German Air Force might stage a comeback in 1945. In the closing months of 1944 there was evidence that German fighters were steadily increasing in number, and there was some fear that the Germans might put their jet planes into the battle before the Allies. General Spaatz warned General Arnold in early November of the possibility of an upsurge in Ger-

---

[25] Churchill to Roosevelt, 844, 6 Dec 44; President to Leahy, proposed reply to Prime Minister (the President added "Clear with Marshall and King"), 8 Dec 44, OPD Exec, Leahy file.

[26] Ltr, Eisenhower to Marshall, 5 Dec 44, SHAEF SGS 381 Post OVERLORD Planning, II.

man air strength,[27] and Lt. Gen. James H. Doolittle indicated in midmonth that the Eighth Air Force might have to drop its strategic objectives in order to reconquer the enemy air forces. For the moment, however, the U.S. airmen continued to place their chief emphasis on the offensive against oil. This decision was reaffirmed on 5 December by top Allied commanders at SHAEF when they agreed to hold oil in first place, give second priority to carpet bombing in support of the ground forces, and make transportation bombing third in the list of targets.[28]

Despite evidence of Germany's staying power, the Allied commanders still hoped to launch an all-out offensive against the enemy in the early weeks of 1945. General Eisenhower, Air Chief Marshal Tedder, Field Marshal Montgomery, and General Bradley met at Maastricht on 7 December to discuss such a campaign. The 21 Army Group commander again presented his plan for a concentrated thrust across the Rhine north of the Ruhr while reducing operations on the rest of the front to containing actions. General Eisenhower once more declared that the Frankfurt area was suitable for an attack and that he did not propose to check the advance on General Patton's front. Field Marshal Montgomery seemed to feel that the argument was back at the same point it had reached in September. If attacks were made simultaneously in the north and south, he feared that neither would succeed. He held, therefore, that there was a fundamental difference between their views. General Eisenhower, apparently desiring to reconcile their points of view, insisted that they differed only as to the point of origin of the secondary thrust, since both agreed that the main attack would be made north of the Ruhr by the 21 Army

Group with the support of a U.S. army (the Ninth) of ten divisions. The Supreme Commander also denied that he and the field marshal differed fundamentally in their views on command. The 21 Army Group commander had again asked that all operations north of the Ardennes be placed under one commander. General Eisenhower maintained, as he had several times before, that command boundaries must be determined by the nature of the operations in front of the line and not by geographical features in the rear. Since the main operations were to be made north of the Ruhr, he thought that it was a better dividing line than the Ardennes.[29]

The Maastricht conference concluded with a decision by the Supreme Commander in favor of a major attack north of the Ruhr in 1945 with secondary attacks by U.S. forces farther to the south. To him this was what he had always favored. Believing that he had sufficient forces to support the northern thrust adequately and still mount a subsidiary attack, he saw no difference between his concept and that of the 21 Army Group commander. But to Field Marshal Montgomery, who believed that experiences of the past few months demonstrated the lack of sufficient resources for both attacks, the difference was between success and failure—and therefore fundamental. In terms of complete understanding and agreement, these viewpoints were never really reconciled. On the other hand, Gen-

---

[27] Craven and Cate, *The Army Air Forces in World War II*, III, 663, and n. 126, say that the German Air Force was numerically larger in December 1944 than it had ever been.

[28] Craven and Cate, *The Army Air Forces in World War II*, III, 657–66.

[29] Notes of mtg at Maastricht, 7 Dec 44, DSC/-TS.100/12, 8 Dec 44, SHAEF SGS 381 Post OVER-LORD Planning, II.

eral Eisenhower, with control of the U.S. forces and supplies that Field Marshal Montgomery deemed essential to the all-out attack in the north, was in a position to make his view prevail. For this reason, if for no other, there was never a deadlock between the two commanders in chief.

Action in December

The chief emphasis in early December was on preparations for an all-out offensive north of the Ardennes early in 1945. Since General Eisenhower wished to maintain pressure on the enemy and since he felt there were divisions and resources south of the Ardennes which would not be needed for this attack, he gave permission for the Third Army, supported by the Seventh Army, to prepare for an offensive against the Saar beginning on 19 December. He cautioned General Bradley that unless the operation made great progress it would have to be stopped after a week. In outlining the operation, SHAEF made clear that it was intended to aid the main effort in the north, and that any crossing of the Rhine south of the Moselle was to be restricted until the success of operations in the north was assured.[30]

North of the Ardennes, the British and U.S. commanders now attempted to improve their positions. Field Marshal Montgomery ordered a limited-objective attack in the Heinsberg area for this purpose early in December. In the Ninth Army sector, General Simpson's forces cleared up enemy pockets near Juelich and closed to the Roer at midmonth. To his right, General Hodges' forces advanced through the Huertgen Forest and reached the Roer. Unwilling to cross that river while the enemy held the dams on the Urft and the Roer to the south, and find-

GENERAL DOOLITTLE

ing that repeated air attacks could neither dislodge the enemy nor destroy the dams, General Bradley directed the First Army to launch an attack to seize this objective. The operation, which began on 13 December, was suspended three days later as the result of the Ardennes counteroffensive. Despite the limited nature of the First and Ninth Army attacks between 16 November and 16 December, the fighting was exceedingly bitter and costly. The Ninth Army suffered some 10,000 casualties, and the First Army, which was heavily hit in the Huertgen Forest area, had three divisions severely mauled and suffered over 21,000 casualties.

[30] Memo, G-3 SHAEF for CofS SHAEF, 12 Dec 44, sub: Future Opns; Memo, G-3 SHAEF for CofS SHAEF, 15 Dec 44, sub: Proposed Ltr to Gen Bradley. Both in SHAEF SGS 381 Post OVERLORD Planning, II.

Farther to the south, General Patton's forces crossed the Saar River in several places early in December and pressed their attack on Saarlautern. Back near Metz, other elements of the army took the last of the fortifications in that area on 12 December. Preparations were also pushed for the projected offensive of 19 December. The Seventh Army now reoriented its forces almost directly to the north to support this attack. The shift took away left-flank support from the First French Army, which was deeply involved at the moment in preparations for the capture of German-held ports along the southwestern coast of France (Operation INDEPEND-ENCE). Some compensation was made in the shift of two divisions, one American, to General de Lattre, but his forces were unable to carry out their mission of clearing the Colmar Pocket.[31] The French commander had to request that operations in western France be delayed and that two additional divisions be given the First French Army for operations in the Colmar area. He also asked General de Gaulle for French troops to fill vacancies in the existing divisions, pointing out that morale was deteriorating among the North African troops because they had seen their comrades die without any French troops to replace them.[32]

The Seventh Army on 7 December drove northward between the Sarre and the Rhine. By 16 December one corps had sent elements of all its divisions up to the German frontier, while another carried on a heavy fight for the strongly fortified area around Bitche. By the end of December, General Patch's forces held northern Alsace from the Third Army boundary,

just east of Sarreguemines, to the Rhine, and thence southward along the Rhine to the First French Army boundary some ten miles south of Strasbourg. General de Lattre held sectors along the Rhine both north and south of the enemy's Colmar bridgehead.

On the eve of the Ardennes counteroffensive, the Allies were preparing all along the line for main or secondary attacks toward the Rhine and beyond. Field Marshal Montgomery's long-range planning looked toward the crossing of the Rhine north of the Ruhr by the 21 Army Group supported by the Ninth Army. Meanwhile, the Ninth and First Armies pressed forward to the Roer and looked beyond to the Rhine—the Ninth Army as an integral part of the main thrust, and the First Army in a supporting role. Hence the main thrust was characterized as being north of the Ruhr, although the supporting attack extended the advance southward to the Ardennes. South of the Ardennes, the Third Army was poised for an offensive toward the Rhine. To its right, the Seventh Army was pushing up to the West Wall positions or to the Rhine. The First French Army was already established on the Rhine to the right and left of the enemy's Colmar Pocket. The only static area was the Ardennes, which was being held thinly so that troops could be committed to attacks elsewhere. It is clear that by mid-December the attitude of the Allies strongly favored the offensive.

---

[31] This was the first time in the war that a major U.S. unit was placed under French command.

[32] De Lattre, *Histoire de la Première Armée Française*, Ch. X.

CHAPTER XVIII

Relations With Liberated Countries

The liberation of France and Belgium and part of the Netherlands in the fall of 1944 presented to SHAEF and the Supreme Commander a number of problems in the administration of civil affairs which increased steadily until the end of the year. Because of the political factors involved, many questions which otherwise could have been settled at lower levels had to be handled by the Supreme Commander or his immediate subordinates. They found, of course, that the prompt and proper settlement of these difficulties was essential to smooth-running military operations in the liberated countries.

Relations With France

Civil Affairs Agreement With France

Not until 26 August, the day after the Allies entered Paris and more than two months after they had arrived in France, was a formal civil affairs agreement concluded with French authorities. This agreement, requested by General Eisenhower before D Day and agreed on in principle in Washington during General de Gaulle's visit there in July was not finally initialed in Washington until 15 August.[1] Shortly thereafter General Eisenhower was instructed to exchange

ratifications of the agreement with General Koenig on behalf of the United States while the British did the same at foreign minister level. Thus even at the moment of formal agreement, the United States held to its policy of dealing with the French at a military rather than a governmental level. The Combined Chiefs of Staff issued General Eisenhower their directive relative to civil affairs with France on 23 August and the formal exchange of ratifications was made at the Hôtel des Invalides on the 26th.[2]

The Combined Chiefs of Staff in their directive authorized the Supreme Commander to deal with the French Committee of National Liberation as the *de facto* authority in France. By the terms of the five memorandums which made up the

---

[1] See above, Ch. XIII.

[2] The contents of the following files are valuable on this phase of negotiations: SHAEF SGS 014.1 France, Civil Affairs Dir for France, I; and SHAEF G–5 702 Dirs—France. The agreement actually bears the date 25 August 1945. This was done to make it coincide with a Washington press announcement, after it became clear that General Koenig and General Eisenhower could not make the exchange in person on the 25th. The terms were transmitted by the Supreme Commander to the French commander by radio on the 25th and General Koenig arranged for his letter of exchange to bear that date. Interv with Gen Holmes, 5 Jun 47; photostatic copy of Ltr, Koenig to Eisenhower, 25 Aug 44, SHAEF G–5 730 Internal Affairs Branch.

civil affairs agreement, General Eisenhower was authorized to take all measures essential to the successful conduct of military operations. To simplify the administration of civil affairs in France, the French Committee of National Liberation agreed to the establishment of a forward zone and a zone of interior. In the former, a military delegate, appointed by the French Committee and acting in accordance with French law, was to carry out those measures deemed necessary by the Supreme Commander. In emergencies affecting military operations or where no French authority was available, the Supreme Commander could act alone. The Allied chief was also permitted to ask the French delegate to take action under the French Law of Siege. In the zone of interior, the French authorities had full power of administration, subject to military requirements of the Supreme Commander. The right of the Allies to use ports, fortified naval bases, and troop concentration points in the zone of interior was guaranteed.[3]

In matters pertaining to the exclusive jurisdiction of the Allied forces over their troops, the establishment of claims commissions, and the procedure for requisitioning supplies and services and the like, the agreement followed the lines already laid down in the earlier civil affairs memorandums concluded separately between the United States, Belgium, the Netherlands, and Norway, and between Great Britain and the same powers. One important memorandum—that dealing with paper currency issued for the use of Allied forces in continental France—settled a problem which had troubled the Supreme Commander in the early days of the invasion. The French Committee accepted this paper currency as if it had been issued by the Central French Treasury and agreed

that any similar currency issued in the future would be furnished by the French Treasury and put at the disposal of the Allied forces in the amount deemed necessary by the Supreme Commander. Another important memorandum was that dealing with censorship. By its provisions the Supreme Commander was to exercise strict military censorship in the forward zone. In the zone of interior, the French services agreed to consult the censorship authorities of SHAEF on all matters relating to military operations and to impose censorship instructions given by Supreme Headquarters. French authorities were to have no control over publications intended solely for Allied troops other than French.

SHAEF Mission (France)

Much of the work of dealing with the French was given by the Supreme Commander to the SHAEF Mission (France), which had been organized before the invasion for that purpose. The mission was to provide liaison between the French Government and Supreme Headquarters and was to furnish a staff to aid the French in dealing with civil affairs in liberated France. Maj. Gen. John T. Lewis, formerly commanding general of the Military District of Washington, headed the mission, and General Redman served as his British deputy. The mission was established in Paris on 3 September by Col. Alden K. Sibley. He, and later General Redman, served temporarily as head of the mission until General Lewis assumed command in mid-September.[4]

---

[3] For texts of the civil affairs memorandums see photostatic copy of agreement initialed in Washington, 15 August 1944, SHAEF G–5 702 Dirs—France.

[4] See the series of papers between dates 31 August 1944 and 8 September 1944 dealing with the establishment of the mission, in SHAEF SGS 322.01/5 SHAEF Mission (France).

General Eisenhower accredited General Lewis to General de Gaulle on 15 September and gave the head of the mission the task of representing the Supreme Commander in official dealings by SHAEF with the French *de facto* authority. The mission was to be the authorizing and screening agency when commands under SHAEF wished to establish contact with the "French authority." [5]

Shortly after the establishment of the SHAEF mission, General Koenig appointed Lt. Gen. Louis Koeltz as his personal liaison officer at SHAEF. SHAEF agreed to the arrangement after it had been made clear that he was merely to report to SHAEF the views of the French Government on questions put to it by SHAEF Mission (France). In particular, General Koeltz was charged with presenting to SHAEF the French views on military dispositions in regard to Germany as well as over-all plans for the use and armament of French forces. [6]

Problems Arising Out of the Move to Paris

The liberation of Paris and the re-establishment of French authority there were accompanied by a rush to the French capital of military and civilian personnel from outside the Continent. The groups involved were frequently of such importance that requests for transportation came directly to the SHAEF chief of staff and even to the Supreme Commander at a time when operational demands on them were extremely heavy. One of the first such problems arose in early September when General de Gaulle asked for aid in moving some 3,000 administrative officers from Algiers to the French capital. When SHAEF officials held that such "a mass immigration" was impossible and asked the French chief to set a priority for the movement of various echelons of this group, General de Gaulle protested to General Eisenhower that Supreme Headquarters was holding up the shift of French officials to Paris. The Supreme Commander denied any such intent, and repeated the request for a priority list according to which the transfer could be made. This was worked out by 11 September and General Eisenhower ordered that the 100 most important officers be brought immediately by air, and the remainder as and when an opportunity offered. The movement was finally completed by 1 November. [7]

Special requests to the SHAEF chief of staff and his deputies for movements of various Allied civilian groups and individuals to the French capital multiplied

[5] SHAEF dir to Gen Lewis, 15 Sep 44, SHAEF Mission (France) file, France Mission 091.112–1, I. SHAEF to Lewis, 28 Mar 45, sub: Amendment to Dir; SHAEF to Lewis, 22 Feb 45, sub: Amendment to Dir. Both in SHAEF SGS 322.01/5 SHAEF Mission (France).

Among the important sections of SHAEF Mission (France) and their chiefs were the following: G–5 Section, Brigadier S. S. Lee; Naval Division, Vice Adm. Alan G. Kirk; Air Division, Air Commodore Lord Arthur Forbes; and Rearmament Division, Brig. Gen. Harold F. Loomis. Later Brig. Gen. Jack W. Wood became head of the Air Division, retaining Air Commodore Forbes as his deputy. Brig. Gen. John A. Appleton, Director General, Military Railways, and Chief, Military Railways Branch, G–4 Division, SHAEF, was later made available to the G–4, SHAEF Mission (France), for consultation on railway matters. Stf Memo 16, SHAEF Mission (France), 14 Oct 44; Ramsay to Lewis, Ramsay to Kirk, 13 Oct 44; Organization, SHAEF Mission (France), Mar 45. All in SHAEF SGS 322.01/5 SHAEF Mission (France).

[6] Memo, SHAEF for SHAEF Mission (France), 15 Sep 44, Sub: Liaison With French National Authority; Juin to Smith, 18 Sep 44; Juin to SHAEF Mission (France), 28 Sep 44; Instr atchd to Ltr, Juin to Lewis, 28 Sep 44; Lewis to Smith, 29 Sep 44, with Smith's note, "I have no objection. If you have none, I suggest we accept Gen Koeltz on this basis." All in SHAEF SGS 322.01/21 French Military Mission (Liaison With the French).

[7] See extensive correspondence on the subject throughout September and October 1944 in SHAEF SGS 092 France, French Relations, III.

after mid-September. Indicative of this type of problem, which frequently took the time of SHAEF officials at the highest level, was the request of an Allied embassy for the movement of seventeen members of its staff plus Italian enlisted men, Arab houseboys, and several French and Belgian civilians and their chauffeurs. This plea was brought to the attention of at least three high-ranking members of SHAEF. General Morgan, to whom the problem was ultimately presented, approved the movement of members of the staff but ruled out the additional attached personnel.[8]

Businessmen as well as officials sought admittance to the French capital. This question of entry was aired in late September by the London *Daily Mail.* The newspaper alleged that British officials were being held up when they attempted to go to Paris, whereas U.S. businessmen were arriving in the uniforms of Red Cross workers or junior officers and being given special priority. These charges, though not substantiated, were brought to General Smith's attention by the SHAEF Public Relations Division, which suggested that a fixed policy on the transportation of civilians to Paris be made public. At this point SHAEF also investigated the appearance of an advertisement of a U.S. firm on a billboard along the Champs-Elysées shortly after the Allied forces entered the city. When it was found that a Red Cross representative had acted as intermediary between U.S. and French advertising agencies, SHAEF ordered the man returned home. The Red Cross organization concurred in the action.[9]

The Supreme Commander was especially concerned about the movement of U.S. personnel into Paris. In England, he had insisted that his own headquarters be moved out of London, and he held that so far as possible military headquarters should stay out of large cities. Despite this often-expressed view, Headquarters, Communications Zone, moved its forward echelon from areas near Cherbourg to Paris during the early days of September before the Supreme Commander was aware of the shift. Army commanders charged that vital gasoline supplies were used in the move, and that the headquarters was out of touch with the supply situation at a time when its control was critically needed. The commanding general of Communications Zone, General Lee, held that the headquarters had to be moved forward in order to keep in touch with the supply situation, and he believed it necessary to go into the chief communications center of France.

Advance parties of General Lee's headquarters requisitioned most of the hotels and buildings occupied by the German forces in Paris and asked for additional billets. General Koenig on hearing that 8,000 officers and 21,000 men were to settle in the city pointed out that they would require more hotels than Paris possessed. He objected to the requisitioning of schools for billets and suggested that a great part of the U.S. force be located outside the city. General Smith agreed that schools should not be requisitioned, and General Eisenhower promptly prohibited the establishment of any Allied headquarters within the area of Paris without his specific approval. Shortly thereafter a member of his personal staff reported unfavorably on the rapid increase of U.S. personnel in the

---

[8] Truscott to Morgan, 11 Sep 44; Morgan to AF 1 and 2, 12 Sep 44. Both in SHAEF SGS 092 France, French Relations, III.

[9] Gen Allen to Gen Smith, S–60275, 21 Sep 44; Barker to CofS SHAEF, 14 Oct 44, SHAEF SGS 014.1 Paris, Civil Affairs in Paris, I.

city, their dress, discipline, and conduct. He noted in particular, that members of the supply organization were engaged in black market activities near the Arc de Triomphe.

General Eisenhower then issued the Communications Zone commander a sharp order to stop the entry into Paris of every individual not needed there for essential duty, and to send away everyone whose presence was not necessary. He added that the initial move had been made without his knowledge and that he was permitting the headquarters to remain only because of the difficulty of making a shift at that stage of operations. He characterized the influx of U.S. personnel, including the members of General Lee's headquarters, as "extremely unwise" and insisted that the situation be corrected as quickly as possible without interfering with the operations of fighting units.[10]

To give force to this directive, General Smith in October held a conference with members of the SHAEF staff and Communications Zone and got a promise that the latter would release one fourth of its 167 hotels and Seine Base Section would release all but twenty of its 129 hotels in the city. Nevertheless, the number of requests by U.S. units for building space in the Paris region continued to increase. M. François Coulet, delegate for interallied relations to the SHAEF Mission (France), protested in mid-December that nearly all available premises had been occupied, and that the French people were beginning to think that U.S. Army demands were in excess of those made by the Germans. The Ardennes counterattack within the same week effectively ended complaints on this score for a time.[11]

The overcrowding of Paris was increased when U.S. and British leave cen-

ters were established there. By 1 February 1945, 8,400 U.S. and 700 British soldiers were reaching the city daily on seventy-two-hour passes. Studies at that time indicated that more than 21,000 persons belonging to U.S. units were located in an area bound by a road net approximately fifteen miles from the geographical center of Paris. Troops in the Seine Section outside this zone and the Department of the Seine pushed the total to over 160,000. SHAEF in March 1945 sought once more to move part of this force outside the Department of the Seine, but found the task impossible. The situation had not been greatly improved at the close of the war. Even after redeployment began, the Allies were unable to vacate billet space rapidly enough to meet French needs.[12]

French Rearmament

One of the chief problems in the fall of 1944 was the rearmament of French forces. The United States and Great Britain, as already indicated, had begun to rearm French troops long before the cross-Channel attack. The United States had taken on this task in North Africa,[13] had largely equipped the forces that fought in Italy, and then had furnished supplies for French forces in the OVERLORD and ANVIL operations. By the fall of 1944 eight divi-

[10] Koenig to SHAEF Fwd Liaison Sec, 9 Sep 44; Smith to Koenig, FWD 14542, 11 Sep 44; Eisenhower to ANCXF, USSTAF, AEAF, et al., FWD 14637, 12 Sep 44; Sibley to Crawford, 12 Sep 44; Eisenhower to Lee, FWD 15033, 16 Sep 44. All in SHAEF SGS 014.1 Paris, Civil Affairs in Paris, I.

[11] Conf, Gen Smith with members of SHAEF, COMZ, et al., Paris, 20 Oct 44; Coulet to SHAEF Mission, 11 Dec 44. Both in SHAEF SGS 014.1 Paris, Civil Affairs in Paris, I.

[12] Rpt to SHAEF as of 1 Feb 45, SCAEF to ANCXF, et al., 8 Mar 44, SHAEF SGS 014.1 Paris, Civil Affairs in Paris, I.

[13] See above, p. 150.

sions equipped by the Allies were in France. Once the liberation of France had been completed, the French authorities pressed for Allied approval of a program, outlined before D Day, for arming liberated manpower. Assuming that a large number of men of military age would be liberated shortly after the invasion of the Continent, the French had asked for aid in raising new divisions. SHAEF explained that its main need was not for fighting men, but for some 172,000 men (of whom 140,000 would be French) to guard lines of communications and maintain internal security. These troops, who would require far less equipment than regular fighting units, would be in a position to relieve fighting men who otherwise would have to be assigned to such duties.[14]

The French authorities stressed the importance to national morale of arming mobilized personnel as soon as possible. General Grasett, the SHAEF G–5, agreed that the failure to use French liberated manpower in fighting units might have a serious psychological effect on other troops at the front. He warned that the French would never be convinced that maintaining internal security and furnishing unskilled labor in base areas constituted appropriate tasks for their men of military age. General Eisenhower replied that his immediate need was for internal security and garrison troops, but said that he was willing to make an effort to equip a few Commando-type units for combat action. The problem of the proper use of liberated manpower had not been settled at the time of the landings in southern France in mid-August.

The manpower question became more pressing in September 1944 as the rapid sweep of Allied forces across northern France and up the Rhône valley made

available thousands of Frenchmen of military age. The French high command set about the task of organizing two new divisions from these troops, and spoke of raising the number to five. This figure, the French indicated, had been accepted in principle during General de Gaulle's visit to Washington in July 1944. General Marshall then asked that the matter be settled by the Combined Chiefs of Staff.

To deal with questions affecting the French metropolitan forces, the Combined Chiefs of Staff in the fall of 1944 moved to Paris the Joint Rearmament Commission, a Franco-American group which had been organized in December 1942 to deal with the rearmament of the French. In October the group became the Rearmament Division, SHAEF Mission (France). Brig. Gen. Harold F. Loomis, who had headed the commission in North Africa, remained its chief. In December, British members were added to the group and the new integrated staff section was made responsible for rearmament questions concerning all liberated countries in Europe.[15]

---

[14] This section, save where otherwise noted, is based on Dr. Marcel Vigneras' The Rearmament of the French Forces in World War II, now in preparation for the series UNITED STATES ARMY IN WORLD WAR II.

[15] The Rearmament Division was charged with the following duties: (1) to set up and implement ground and air rearmament programs which the Combined Chiefs of Staff had approved or might approve in SHAEF's sphere, (2) to provide inspection and training groups for the formation of approved units, (3) to co-ordinate within SHAEF and with the nation concerned all demands for rearmament of units not in approved rearmament programs, (4) to keep the staff sections of SHAEF and missions to foreign governments informed regarding rearmament programs and proposals for rearmament put forward by various nations. SHAEF to SHAEF Mission (France), 22 Dec 44, sub: Inclusion of Disarmament Div in SHAEF Mission (France); SHAEF to all concerned, 29 Dec 44, sub: Rearmament Div, SHAEF Mission (France). Both in SHAEF SGS 322.01/5 SHAEF Mission (France).

The slowing of the Allied offensive in September 1944 and the growing lack of infantry replacements led General Eisenhower at the end of October to re-examine the possibility of equipping additional French divisions. In September, he had doubted that new divisions could be equipped and trained in time to be of value in the campaigns in northwest Europe, but he now asked that the matter be reopened. He suggested raising two additional French divisions and increasing the liberated manpower ceiling from 172,000 to 460,000. This new figure included 243,000 Frenchmen. The revised estimate was intended to take care of new manpower commitments such as those needed for territorial command headquarters, the *gendarmerie, garde mobile,* labor battalions, and the like.

In mid-November 1944, the French submitted a proposal to SHAEF for equipping eight new divisions. At SHAEF's insistence the proposal was revised to meet SHAEF's needs for security and line-of-communications troops and forwarded to the Combined Chiefs of Staff. That group, despite SHAEF's declaration that all or any part of the plan would be of great value to the Allied forces, did not act upon it immediately. The proposal was still pending when the enemy counteroffensive of mid-December made Allied manpower a major problem.

Recognition of the French Provisional Government

President Roosevelt was disappointed in his hope that the French Committee would be satisfied with the *de facto* recognition provided in the August agreement. On 30 August 1944, General de Gaulle proclaimed the establishment in Paris of the Provisional Government of the French Republic. Two weeks later he announced that elections to determine the form of the French government would be held as soon as French sovereignty had been restored, her territories liberated, and the French war prisoners and deportees returned to their homes.[16]

In mid-September the U.S. political officer at SHAEF, Mr. Samuel Reber, warned the State Department that failure to grant early recognition to the French Provisional Government might cause it to lose prestige and leave it poorly equipped. The Supreme Commander, when asked in October by the U.S. Chiefs of Staff for his recommendations, urged formal recognition of the de Gaulle group as the provisional government of France. This opinion, which coincided with views already held by many European countries, apparently found ready acceptance in Washington. On 23 October, the United States, the Soviet Union, Great Britain, and some five other nations recognized the French Provisional Government headed by General de Gaulle. A French zone of interior in which civil rather than military authority would prevail was proclaimed the same day. The United States named Mr. Jefferson Caffery, who was acting as the American diplomatic representative "near the de facto authority of France," as ambassador to the new government. As their ambassador, the British named Mr. Duff Cooper. Shortly afterward, General Eisenhower and the head of the SHAEF Mission (France) were told to rely on these two representatives, rather than the British and U.S. political officers at SHAEF,

---

[16] De Gaulle, *Discours et Messages,* pp. 485–86.

for political advice on French affairs.[17]

The proclamation of a French zone of interior on 23 October 1944 followed negotiations of more than a month between General de Gaulle and SHAEF representatives. During late September and early October, SHAEF and French authorities selected the departments to be included in the new zone and exchanged assurances that the civil affairs agreement signed in August would remain in effect in this area. The Supreme Commander on 13 October suggested that the French Government declare that a zone of interior existed within the boundaries of the following departments: Seine-Inférieure, Oise, Seine-et-Marne, Yonne, Nièvre, Saône-et-Loire, Rhône, Ardèche, and Gard. The French made clear that military zones would be established along the Atlantic coast where German resistance still existed.[18]

The zone of interior was not enlarged until 1945. Shortly after the New Year, the SHAEF deputy G–3 suggested that SHAEF extend it before the French asked for such action, and thus anticipate their complaint that concessions were made only after repeated requests.[19] Headquarters, Communications Zone, strongly objected to this proposal, pointing to the various difficulties which would arise in regard to Allied control of railroads, the requisitioning of billets and hospitals, and other administrative questions. SHAEF postponed a decision for the moment and called conferences to settle some of the existing administrative problems. General Morgan, acting in place of the SHAEF chief of staff, held that the difficulties cited would exist whether or not the zone of interior was extended, and he directed the SHAEF G–3 to study the expansion of the zone to include all of France except Alsace-Lorraine. Before the study could be completed, General Juin asked for an enlargement of the zone of interior, but requested less than SHAEF was prepared to give. SHAEF staff members thought the French had purposely omitted departments along the frontiers in the fear that the Ministry of War would have to surrender its control of these regions to the Ministry of the Interior.[20] SHAEF approved the French proposals, subject to the proviso that the agreements of 25 August should not be affected. The Atlantic and Dunkerque areas, where the Germans were still resisting, were to continue to be military zones, and hospitals and other military and supply installations in the new zone of interior were to remain in Allied hands.[21] The new zone of interior, expanded to include the departments of Pas-de-Calais, Somme, Aisne, Marne, Aube, Haute-Marne, Côte-d'Or, Drôme, Vaucluse, Bouches-du-Rhône, and Var, was announced on 24 April 1945.[22]

Shortly after conclusion of the armistice with the enemy in May 1945 the French Government asked that all France be in-

[17] SHAEF Fwd (Reber) to WD for State Dept for Dunn, FWD 14734, 13 Sep 44; JCS to Eisenhower, W–47959, 17 Oct 44; Eisenhower to JCS, S–63111, 20 Oct 44. All in SHAEF SGS 092 France, French Relations, III.
[18] Eisenhower to Juin, 13 Oct 44; Eisenhower to A Gp and COMZ comdrs, 13 Oct 44; Juin to Eisenhower, 18 Oct 44, and related papers, Sep–Oct 44. All in SHAEF SGS 371 France, Zone of the Interior, I.
[19] Memo, Whiteley for CofS SHAEF, 10 Jan 45, SHAEF SGS 371 France, Zone of the Interior, I.
[20] Memo, G–2 SHAEF for G–3 SHAEF, 24 Mar 45; Morgan to G–3 SHAEF, 5 Mar 45; Larkin (Deputy CG COMZ) to SHAEF, 14 Mar 45. All in SHAEF SGS 371 France, Zone of the Interior, I.
[21] Smith to Juin, 11 Apr 45, SHAEF SGS 371 France, Zone of the Interior, I.
[22] SHAEF to AGWAR for CCS, FWD 19789, 23 Apr 45, SHAEF SGS 371 France, Zone of the Interior, I.

cluded in the zone of interior, but added that the frontier departments were to remain in the hands of the War Ministry rather than being transferred to the Ministry of the Interior. SHAEF did not object to this extension, asking only that existing arrangements relating to accommodations, transportation, airfields, and ports be confirmed. The extension was put into effect by the French on 13 July 1945.[23]

Dissolution of the French Resistance Forces

With the liberation of Paris, the French Committee of National Liberation as well as SHAEF became aware of the need of bringing the French Forces of the Interior under the control of the newly established French authority. Fearful of the danger to public order which might come from irresponsible partisan bands after the liberation, General Koenig as early as 11 August issued instructions for receiving volunteers from the French Forces of the Interior into the French Regular Army. Two weeks later General de Gaulle decreed that elements of the Resistance forces likely to participate in coming operations were to be regularly drafted into the Army as the territory in which they fought was liberated. On 28 August he dissolved the high command of the underground forces in Paris and gave its duties to the commanding generals of the different military regions into which France was divided. The commanding generals of existing units were authorized to accept all volunteers from the French Forces of the Interior as replacements or as members of new units. Volunteers were also to be accepted to fill the needs of the *gendarmerie, garde mobile,* and other local police and defense elements. Units were to be activated to keep order in the rear areas and were

held liable to combat duty at the discretion of the commanding officers of the military regions. Further decrees ruled that all the men who had voluntarily fought the enemy during operations leading to the liberation of national territory belonged to the French Forces of the Interior. They were held to constitute an integral part of the French Army and were subjected to Army regulations. Existing FFI units were to be reorganized immediately into separate infantry battalions or so far as practicable into similar units of other arms.[24]

SHAEF, vitally interested in all measures looking toward the establishment of order in France while military operations were in progress, was especially concerned about the reactions of Resistance forces to General de Gaulle's orders. The Military Resistance Committee (COMAC) immediately criticized the decree as unfavorable to a national, popular, and democratic army. This reaction, which SHAEF thought might have been politically inspired, also appeared to rest on the feeling of many Resistance leaders that their personal deserts would be overlooked once they were integrated into the Regular Army. Many of the Resistance leaders had acquired high rank in the FFI and resented being placed under Regular Army officers who had been less active during

---

[23] Bull to SHAEF divs, 15 May 45; SHAEF to A Gps *et al.,* 31 May 45; Morgan for Smith to Juin, 6 Jun 45; SHAEF Memo, Extension of the Zone of the Interior, in France, 2 Jul 45; SHAEF to CCS, SCAF 479, 13 Jul 45. All in SHAEF SGS 371 France, Zone of the Interior, I.

[24] Koenig, General Instructions, Organization of the FFI, 11 Aug 44; de Gaulle decision, 28 Aug 44; Minister of War A. Diethelm to Dept of CofS and CGs Military Regions, 28 Aug 44, Ministry of War decree on organization of FFI, 19 Sep 44; Ministry of War decree on status of FFI, 20 Sep 44. All in SHAEF SGS 322 FFI, Command and Control of FFI.

the war. In addition, many members of the Resistance preferred to remain under their former commanders. General de Lattre understood this reaction and made an effort to absorb the FFI elements into his army with the least damage possible to the *esprit de corps* that they had developed. Many members of the FFI gave up their arms and returned to their homes, while 137,000 ultimately joined the 250,000 Regular forces of the Army of the Rhine and the Danube. In parts of Brittany, however, where few Allied troops were left after the rapid advance to the east, Resistance members insisted on retaining their arms to deal with enemy groups that had been overrun.

In September, the French authorities, fearing trouble from Communist-inspired troops, asked SHAEF to divert elements of the First French Army to disaffected areas to preserve internal stability. Operational requirements made it impossible for General Eisenhower to grant this request, but he agreed to recommend that the Mediterranean Supreme Commander send French forces from his theater to France where they could be used for keeping order. SHAEF, he emphasized, desired that order be preserved in France, and by French, not by Allied, authorities. In mid-October General Lewis reported that, while danger of excesses by extremist elements of the FFI still existed, the worst period of disorganization had passed. As late as February 1945, however, General de Gaulle asked for the withdrawal of several large French units from the Army zone for reconstitution and training and to insure that contact was maintained "between certain regions of the country and its organized army." Despite fears of possible trouble, the dissolution of the Resistance forces throughout France was ac-

complished for the most part without incident.[25]

After the official dissolution of the French Forces of the Interior in the liberated areas of France, General Koenig remained in command of these forces in enemy-occupied areas. He was directed on 23 November to relinquish this control at the end of the month, and the French Forces of the Interior in occupied areas were ordered to come under the local military regional commanders. The section of the former FFI headquarters in London, which had remained in operation to deal with Resistance activities in nonliberated France, was also ordered to close on 1 December.[26]

Relations With Belgium

Civil affairs problems in Belgium differed in some respects from those in France but were no less difficult to settle. King Leopold was in captivity, but the legal government of Belgium, headed by Prime Minister Hubert Pierlot, was returned to power in Brussels by the Allies very shortly after the city was liberated. As a matter of fact, the first task of Maj. Gen. G. W. E. J. Erskine (Br.), head of the SHAEF Mission (Belgium), was to arrange speedy passage for members of the Belgian Government

---

[25] PWD Intel Sec, Special Rpt (France) 10, 9 Oct 44, SHAEF SGS 322 FFI, Command and Control of FFI. Juin to Eisenhower, 11 Sep 44; Bull to 6th A Gp, 19 Sep 44; de Gaulle to Eisenhower, 21 Sep 44; Memo, Eisenhower for CofS, 22 Sep 44; Eisenhower to de Gaulle, 25 Sep 44; 6th A Gp to SHAEF, B–16713, 26 Sep 44; de Gaulle to Eisenhower, 15 Feb 45. All in SHAEF SGS 475/2 France, Employment of French Forces, I and II. Rpt, Gen Lewis to SAC, Progress Rpt 3, 19 Oct 44, SHAEF SGS 219 French Mission Fortnightly Reports, 1/23, I; SHAEF Mission (France) to SHAEF G–2, 6 Dec 44, SHAEF Mission (France) AG 091.711–5 (Fr) Combined, II.

[26] SHAEF Mission (France) AG 091. 711–5 (Fr) Combined, II.

and Parliament to Brussels in time for the opening of Parliament on 19 September 1944.[27] Once this was settled satisfactorily, he gave his aid to the solution of a number of pressing problems, such as rushing the release of a Belgian franc note issue prepared by the Bank of England, disarming the Resistance forces, establishing an armed *gendarmerie* to keep order, and arming Belgian forces to protect Allied lines of communications.[28] As in France, the SHAEF Mission had no desire to interfere in the control of internal affairs but intended to help the existing government prevent any disorders that were likely to interfere with Allied operations.

Belgian Resistance Forces

SHAEF's two main interests in Belgium in the fall of 1944 were the rapid establishment of order and the raising of special battalions to support the Allied forces. These measures were closely tied up with the dissolution of the Resistance forces in Belgium, which were believed to be infiltrated by left-wing sympathizers opposed to the Pierlot government. The situation was somewhat delicate in view of the valuable contributions made by the Resistance forces to the liberation of Belgium. The underground units had numbered an estimated 30,000 effective members at the time the Allies reached the Belgian border and rapidly increased their forces as the enemy was driven eastward. While the depletion of stores in August had reduced their activities somewhat in the period before 1 September, they had made a valuable contribution after that date. When the Allies crossed the border, they sent Special Air Service forces to aid the Resistance units that were proving to be especially useful in the southern Ardennes

and in the Hainaut Province. Placed under Maj. Gen. Yvan Gerard Gerard at the end of August, the Resistance elements aided the Allied advance in particular by mopping up isolated pockets of Germans and by protecting the flanks of the Allied armies.[29]

In asking that the Resistance forces be dissolved, the Pierlot government desired first of all to establish order. In addition, however, it hoped to draw on these elements for manpower to increase the *gendarmerie,* strengthen the Regular Army, and organize special battalions for the Allies. SHAEF was especially interested in this last objective. In September, U.S. units had used Belgian forces of the interior in the drive across Belgium, but they could not employ them in Germany unless they became part of the Belgian Army. SHAEF favored the Belgian Government's effort to dissolve the Resistance organizations and integrate their members into Regular Army and police units. As a step toward this end General Eisenhower joined the Belgian Government in inviting the populace to surrender all arms and military equipment. A delay by many in accepting this invitation heightened the government's apprehension. On 29 September, the Supreme Commander, in an Order of the Day recognizing and praising the great contributions of the Resistance forces to Belgium's liberation, said that they could now best serve their country by turning in their weapons and waiting for instructions as to the part they

---

[27] General Erskine's deputy was Col. John B. Sherman (U.S.).

[28] Rpt, Erskine to SHAEF (Morgan), 15 Sep 44; SHAEF to Erskine, 15 Sep 44. SHAEF SGS 322.01/6 SHAEF Mission (Belgium).

[29] Rpts, SFHQ to SHAEF, Monthly Rpts 12 and 13 (Aug and Sep 44), 10 Sep and 10 Oct 44, SHAEF SGS 319.1/10 Monthly SOE/SO Rpts SFHQ.

could play in the coming fight against Germany. The *Front de l'Indépendence,* which represented many of the Resistance organizations, anticipated this request by announcing that until its program was accomplished it would not disarm. *La Nation Belge,* one of the conservative newspapers of Brussels, was amused by General Eisenhower's suggestion that the Resistance forces should surrender their arms on the ground that they were urgently needed for other purposes. It commented: "Others besides ourselves will catch the humor of the lecture; it is not for nothing that General Eisenhower is from Mark Twain's country. It is absolutely American, and now we may expect the Belgians, who are supposed to have a sense of humor, will respond by deferring without delay to a bit of advice that is not the less imperative for having been given in a fatherly fashion." [30]

Many Resistance elements retained their arms and remained outside regular Belgian police and military organizations. SHAEF representatives pressed the question of raising special battalions at a meeting in Brussels on 10 October with officers of the 12th Army Group and the Belgian Ministry of National Defense. The Belgians made a commitment to raise forty-four battalions for the Allied forces, and SHAEF agreed to request equipment from the War Office for the units which were to be enrolled in the Belgian National Army. Belgian representatives declared that the required number of men, some 62,000 in all, would be raised even if conscription had to be used. Of this number, approximately 35,200 were to go to the forty-four battalions, 17,000 into labor groups, and 10,000 to the *gendarmerie.* [31]

SHAEF Mission (Belgium) reported a non-co-operative attitude on the part of the Resistance forces, adding that this re-action was a mixture of opposition to the government, resentment over food and coal shortages, and a feeling that they were not being properly rewarded for their efforts. Near the end of October, General Erskine warned the Supreme Commander that the continued existence of an armed Resistance force, now estimated at 70,000, as opposed to some 6,000 members of the police and *gendarmerie,* made possible serious rioting which would cause a breakdown of government. General Eisenhower, concerned over the possible effect of such a development on military operations, reminded the Belgian Premier that the carrying of arms, except by those specifically authorized to do so by army group commanders, could no longer be permitted in the zone of the armies. The Belgian Government now called on civilians to turn in their weapons to the nearest *gendarmerie* barracks and receive a disbanding indemnity. Resistance forces were also invited to enlist in the Regular Army. [32]

The Supreme Commander made a formal visit to Brussels on 9 November and spoke before the Belgian Parliament and at a ceremony honoring the Belgian unknown soldier. His appearance was believed to be helpful to the government.

---

[30] Rpt, Belgian Press Opinion, 3 Oct 44, Daily Summary of Newspapers (hereafter cited as Belgian Press Opinion), SHAEF G–5 hist file 17.02 Mission to Belgium, Final Rpt, I. The author has relied on SHAEF SGS 016/1 Summary of Decisions, II, for statements relative to the proclamation of 29 September 1944. It should be noted that the author has followed SHAEF reports on developments in Belgium in 1944–45, and has used reports of the SHAEF Mission (Belgium) in his interpretations of events.

[31] Mtg at SHAEF Mission (Belgium), 10 Oct 44, SHAEF SGS 322.01/6 SHAEF Mission (Belgium).

[32] Erskine to SHAEF, 21 Oct 44, SHAEF G–5 132.02 Mission to Belgium; Belgian Press Opinion; Eisenhower to Belgian Prime Minister, 27 Oct 44, summarized in SHAEF SGS 016/1 Summary of Decisions, II.

Four days later the Ministry of National Defense set 18 November as the date for demobilizing the Resistance forces. The temporary permission of 13 September giving members of the Resistance groups the right to bear arms was withdrawn. In the meantime, anticipating possible trouble on 18 November, SHAEF officials drew up a directive which, while disavowing any desire to interfere in Belgian affairs, instructed General Erskine to take full precautions to secure Allied installations and lines of communications in Belgium. He was to intervene only if the Belgian Government called for aid, or if strikes, riots, and picketing made such action necessary to safeguard military operations. Independent action was to be taken only in an extreme emergency. Requests for military assistance from the Allies were to be in writing and, if possible, to have government approval.[33]

The Resistance representative and the two Communist members of the Pierlot cabinet resigned in protest against the government's decree of 13 November. When this action was followed by a demonstration against the government, General Erskine conferred with the three former ministers and reminded them that the necessities of war and military operations required that no unauthorized person should bear arms. He requested formally that the Resistance forces turn their arms over to the government and avoid incidents which might bring conflicts with the Allied forces. He emphasized that the Allies would support the Ministry fully. The three former ministers now joined General Erskine in a statement designed to avoid clashes between the Resistance and Allied forces. Some Belgian newspapers expressed regret that Allied representatives had been called in to settle a problem which the Belgian Government should have handled. Shortly after the meeting of General Erskine with the disaffected ministers, the Resistance groups agreed to collect all arms and hand them in to the "inter-allied authorities." [34]

Strong feeling against the government nevertheless persisted. On 25 November a demonstration was organized in the Rue de la Loi near the chief government building in Brussels. Anticipating trouble, British commanders in Brussels had ordered their forces to stand by to give aid to the Belgian Government. Allied armored vehicles were moved near the government buildings but took no part in breaking up the demonstration. The Communist press in Belgium quickly protested the government's action against the demonstrators and reprinted with glee a London *News Chronicle* editorial saying that the incident showed the unpopularity of the Pierlot government, which was holding its authority with the support of the Allied high command. The London *Times* warned that it would be disastrous if the Allies exposed themselves to the charge of favoring or boycotting this or that ideology or of maintaining in power a group of ministers that had no substantial backing in popular opinion and would be likely to disappear once the army was withdrawn. General Erskine found it necessary to explain that he had ordered an alert of Allied forces in the city because of the possible effect a flare-up would have on the Allied lines of

---

[33] Text of ministerial decree, 13 Nov 44, App. B (Capt. A. W. Williams, Historical Summary of Events in Belgium from Liberation to July 45), SHAEF G–5 hist file 17.02 Mission to Belgium, Final Rpt, I; Dir on internal security in Belgium, 18 Nov 44, SHAEF G–5 132.02 Mission to Belgium. The directive was apparently signed on 17 November 1944 and General Erskine seems to have known of it on that date.

[34] Belgian Press Opinion, 17, 19 Nov 44.

communications. The Belgian episode, which coincided with British intervention in Greece, brought formal questions in the House of Commons as to Allied policy in liberated countries. Mr. Churchill made clear that General Erskine represented and was directly responsible to the Supreme Commander. He added, "I have no hesitation in saying not only did we obey General Eisenhower's orders, but we thought these orders wise and sensible."[35]

The demonstration of 25 November was followed by an attempt on the part of left-wing elements to organize a general strike. Before it made any progress the workers' committee voted to return to work in order not to interfere with the Allied war effort. Attacks on the government continued until the German counteroffensive of mid-December 1944. At that point the *Front de l'Indépendence* offered the complete backing of the Resistance units to the Allied military authorities. The Allies preferred not to reactivate these forces, but rather to make use of the Belgian Regular Army. The immediate effect of the German attack was to bring demands from nearly all elements of the Belgian press for unified action against the Germans. It brought as well new problems such as the care of refugees from the Ardennes area, and increased damage to homes arising from the intensification of the flying-bomb attacks.

Civil Defense and Food

One of the tragedies of the war was that Belgium, which was liberated quickly and with comparatively little loss, later suffered heavily from German flying bombs and from the German counteroffensive of December 1944. Even before the port of Antwerp was cleared for traffic in late fall

of 1944, the enemy had opened a V-bomb attack on it in the hope of making it unusable. Beginning 13 October 1944, the Germans turned on Belgium much of the fury they had once vented on England. These attacks continued until the end of March 1945, but seemed to be at their heaviest about the time of the German counteroffensive. In six months, more than 5,000 bombs fell in Belgium causing casualties of more than 8,000 dead and missing, and 23,584 wounded. The blow fell heaviest on the provinces of Antwerp and Liége. In Antwerp the bombs hit two thirds of the houses, seriously damaging or wholly destroying more than one fifth of them. In Liége the percentage of serious damage was even greater. The attacks laid a heavy burden on SHAEF civil and operational units. Besides keeping the port of Antwerp in operation, they had to aid the Belgians in maintaining civilian defense, in meeting fire-fighting emergencies, and in solving health problems.[36]

The SHAEF Mission (Belgium) and civil affairs authorities of the Allied forces were also troubled by the problem of supplying Belgium with food. From SHAEF's standpoint, an adequate food supply was needed to prevent demonstrations, to get coal mined, and to maintain the ports in full operation. General Erskine in late November became particularly worried because of SHAEF statements that sufficient civil affairs supplies had been delivered in November for the rest of the year and no

---

[35] Details of these events can be found in the New York *Times*, November 26, 30, December 2, 3, and 8, 1944, and in Belgian Press Opinion.

[36] Address of Commissioner for the Defense of the Civil Population, History of Fire and Civil Defense in Belgium, 16 Jun 45, App. F (Summary of V1 and V2 Attacks in Belgium), Civil Defense—Antwerp, SHAEF G-5 hist file, Mission to Belgium 17.02, Final Rpt, I.

more were available for Belgium in December. Food supplies were very short and he feared that the Allies would be charged with breaking their promises. At his urging, SHAEF on 6 December authorized a special allotment of ten thousand tons of supplies for December at the expense of other commitments.[37]

The German counteroffensive in the Ardennes made the shortage of food even more acute. This shortage was blamed for a strike of dock workers at Antwerp in January 1945, and General Erskine warned that additional troubles might follow. Not only were further strikes among dock workers and coal miners likely but a danger of disorders along the Allied lines of communications threatened. General Erskine reported in mid-February that the government recently formed by M. Achille van Acker might be seriously weakened if food shortages continued. The general urged, therefore, that a strenuous effort be made to replace Belgian losses in the Ardennes resulting from enemy action, that a reserve stockpile of one month's imports be established, that plans be approved to increase supplementary rations for workers, and that the Belgian Government be pressed to the limit to carry out its part in the collection and distribution of food. Even before this report came in, General Eisenhower had informed the Combined Chiefs of Staff of the situation. Explaining that the arrival of supplies from the United States and the United Kingdom was falling behind schedule, he urged that 100,000 tons of civil affairs supplies be made available immediately from stocks in the United Kingdom to offset the shipping lag. The state of affairs created in Belgium and the Netherlands by the delay was "sufficiently serious to warrant Civil Affairs requirements being treated

as a matter of operational urgency." The Combined Chiefs of Staff met the emergency in Belgium by releasing 55,000 tons of supplies from stocks in the United Kingdom, and by assuring the Supreme Commander that part of the supplies from the United States would soon arrive. They reminded General Eisenhower, however, that the chief cause for the serious situation lay in SHAEF's failure to present its requirements to the Combined Civil Affairs Committee until late in December. To prevent recurrence of similar crises, SHAEF now asked the Belgian Government to make estimates of requirements running into the following November. A special effort was made by SHAEF in March and April to insure that these would be met.[38]

Besides its other duties, the SHAEF Mission (Belgium) had the responsibility of representing the Supreme Commander in Luxembourg. SHAEF had initially planned to set up a separate mission for that country and had issued a directive to Brigadier S. O. Jones in September 1944 as head of the mission. When the Allied forces halted on the eastern borders of Luxembourg, thus leaving the country in the forward zone of operations, SHAEF decided to withdraw the mission. After 1 December 1944, SHAEF was represented through the Luxembourg Civil Affairs Detachment. In April 1945, General Erskine was directed to assume responsibility for Luxembourg, and Col. F. E. Fraser, head of the civil affairs detach-

---

[37] Erskine to Smith, 25 Nov 44; Smith to Erskine, 6 Dec 44. Both in SHAEF SGS 014.1 Civil Affairs Dir for Belgium, I.

[38] Erskine to CofS SHAEF, 18 Feb 45; SHAEF to CCS, SCAF 210, 14 Feb 45; CCS to SHAEF, FACS 143, 23 Feb 45; Ltr, Smith to CCS and CCAC, 28 Apr 45. All in SHAEF SGS 014.1 Belgium, Civil Affairs Dir for Belgium, II.

ment in that country, was designated as deputy. In May 1945, in order to avoid confusion with other civil affairs detachments in Luxembourg, Colonel Fraser's unit was redesignated SHAEF Mission (Luxembourg) with General Erskine as chief and Colonel Fraser as deputy.[39]

Relations With the Netherlands

The Supreme Commander issued a directive to Maj. Gen. J. K. Edwards (Br.) as head of the SHAEF Mission (Netherlands) in mid-September 1944, but the establishment of the mission was postponed as the clearing of the country was delayed. Brig. Gen. George P. Howell (U.S.) was appointed deputy chief of the mission at the end of September, and an advance detachment was sent to Brussels shortly thereafter. No formal accreditation of the SHAEF mission was made to the Netherlands Government until early December when an advance detachment of that government began to move to Dutch soil.[40]

Because the Netherlands Government was located in London during most of the fall of 1944, some of the most important issues affecting the Netherlands were brought directly to the British Foreign and War Offices instead of to SHAEF. The Netherlands Government intervened with the British in October when SHAEF proposed to bomb Vlissingen in preparation for an attack to clear the Schelde estuary. As a result of Dutch opposition, the British Government banned all bombing of the city unless it was authorized by the Combined Chiefs of Staff. General Eisenhower, when informed of this action, made clear his desire to spare the Dutch city, but added that it would be a serious matter to withhold this aid from the Canadian

Army and thereby aid the enemy. This argument was enough to overcome the doubts of the British Chiefs of Staff. They now declared that, although every effort should be made to spare noncombatants, the view of the Supreme Commander in such matters must prevail. Despite this approval, the bombing scheduled for 1 November did not take place.[41]

In early October, Queen Wilhelmina of the Netherlands and her Prime Minister, P. S. Gerbrandy, appealed to the President and the Prime Minister to approve shipments of food and medical supplies through the Swedish Red Cross to occupied portions of the Netherlands. Both Mr. Churchill and Mr. Roosevelt held that the matter was a military responsibility. General Eisenhower voiced no objection to the proposal. Before it could be implemented, however, proposals were brought forward for sending a Red Cross ship from Lisbon, for air-dropping food on the three principal cities in occupied Netherlands, and for sending an International Red Cross ship from Basel down the Rhine to Arnhem and Rotterdam.

---

[39] See entire contents of SHAEF SGS 322.01/4 SHAEF Mission (Luxembourg).

[40] See entire file, SHAEF SGS 322.01/7 SHAEF Mission (Netherlands). In January 1945, General Edwards was succeeded as head of the mission by Maj. Gen. John G. W. Clark (Br.). The latter retained his headquarters in Brussels until April 1945 when he was given permission to move the mission to Breda. During April another change came in the command of the mission: General Howell had to be returned to the United States because of ill health and was replaced by Col. John Griffith. After the surrender of Germany, the SHAEF mission moved to The Hague. Shortly after its arrival there it absorbed Headquarters, Netherlands District, which had been set up by the British, and retained duties and responsibilities of that headquarters with regard to the relief of the Netherlands until the end of June 1945.

[41] Br COS to Eisenhower, 30 Apr 44; Eisenhower to Br COS, 31 Oct 44; Br COS to Eisenhower, 31 Oct 44. All in SHAEF cbl log. Ltr, Col Stacey to author, Aug 51.

General Eisenhower, near the end of October, approved the sending of Swedish relief ships or a ship from Lisbon even at the risk that some of the supplies would be taken by the enemy. The air dropping of supplies he opposed, since there was no way of assuring that they would reach the civilian population. He ruled out the dispatching of a ship from Basel down the Rhine on operational grounds, agreeing with the British Chiefs of Staff that such action would interfere with Allied air attacks on German river traffic. The fact that the Germans readily accepted the latter plan was considered to be sufficient indication that it played into their hands.[42]

Arrangements made to move supplies from Sweden broke down soon afterward because the Netherlands Red Cross lacked sufficient transportation to distribute supplies. In December a new plan was worked out by which two Swedish ships would bring their cargoes from Göteborg to Delfzijl where barges would pick them up and take them to points of distribution. An arrangement was reached with the Germans in the third week of January for this movement. The ship from Lisbon was to move to Göteborg at this time but was to wait until there was evidence that the supplies of the first ship were delivered.[43]

The Dutch faced not only the problem of feeding the inhabitants of the occupied regions of their country, but also the burden of distributing civil affairs supplies for the liberated areas. They were forced to cut the daily ration below that in effect during the enemy occupation. As in France, complaints were voiced in the liberated areas that the Allied forces were feeding German prisoners and refugees better than they did the liberated peoples. In mid-December Prime Minister Gerbrandy proposed in a letter to the Su-

preme Commander that the relief of the Netherlands be given first priority—even over the slogan of "defeat the Germans first." He asked that the Netherlands Government be permitted to handle those details of relief work which it could do best and that 21 Army Group be instructed to consult the Netherlands Government on matters relating to relief planning. General Eisenhower, who found the letter "quite moving," directed that the Dutch be kept informed and be consulted on all matters relating to relief. By the close of the year, the Dutch Prime Minister believed that some progress had been made, but the head of the SHAEF mission reported that members of the Netherlands Government felt that they had had little information of any practical progress since 21 Army Group had been made responsible for relief activities. He recommended that the Netherlands Government and its Navy and Military Administration be represented in all relief planning. Inasmuch as the greater part of the Netherlands remained in the hands of the enemy until the end of the war, it was not possible until then to find a satisfactory solution to the food problem. As a result, some of the

---

[42] Msg, Queen Wilhelmina to President Roosevelt, 8 Oct 44, and President to Queen Wilhelmina, 26 Oct 44 (both quoted in JCS to Eisenhower, W–52805, 26 Oct 44); Maj Desmond Morton to Gen Smith, 12 Oct 44; Foreign Office to Br COS, 5 Oct 44; Br COS to Eisenhower, 6322, 27 Oct 44; Eisenhower to Br COS, S–64652, 30 Oct 44; Eisenhower to CCS, SCAF 115, 29 Oct 44; Eisenhower to Br COS, S–61325, 7 Oct 44; Br COS to Eisenhower, 6479, 3 Nov 44; Eisenhower to Br COS, S–65384, 4 Nov 44; Eisenhower to Br COS, S–65714, 6 Nov 44; Eisenhower to CCS and Br COS, SCAF 132, 15 Nov 44. All in SHAEF SGS 014.1 Netherlands, Civil Affairs Dir for Netherlands, I.

[43] Br COS to JSM, 7277, 12 Dec 44; Eisenhower to Br COS, S–71810, 21 Dec 44; Br COS to SHAEF, 7499, 22 Dec 44; Br COS to JSM, 499, 19 Jan 45. All in SHAEF SGS 014.1 Netherlands, Civil Affairs Dir for Netherlands, II and III.

peoples of occupied regions of the Netherlands were near the point of starvation when the war came to a close.[44]

Allied Public Information Activities in the Liberated Countries

SHAEF attempted to improve relations with liberated countries and to encourage the spirit of resistance in occupied areas by means of a program of radio broadcasts, publication of newspapers, and distribution of Allied magazines and books. SHAEF's Psychological Warfare Division devoted much of its effort to these public information activities.

The division used its facilities effectively in the early days of the invasion to give warnings to inhabitants living near the invasion coasts. Beginning on D Day, the Voice of SHAEF warned citizens near the Channel coasts to leave the area.[45] In the days that followed, SHAEF broadcast evacuation warnings and frequently directed the dropping of leaflets shortly before heavy air raids. The warnings applied not only to areas subject to bombardment but also to the coastal waters of Denmark, Norway, the Netherlands, Belgium, and France where action might take place. Announcements advising fishermen to stay in port were made until 10 August.

SHAEF's Psychological Warfare Division also informed inhabitants in liberated countries of the way in which they could aid the Allied armies, countered rumors which might be spread, and rendered assistance to liberated governments in reconstituting their media of public information. The division entrusted these efforts to its Allied Information Service (AIS). The advance group of this agency landed in Cherbourg in early July 1944 and at the request of the First Army as-

sumed part of the public information activities in the Normandy area. The AIS established civilian press and radio service in Cherbourg and aided the civilian radio program in Rennes. Representatives of the service entered Paris on 25 August and continued their work there until shortly before the end of the war, although some AIS functions were gradually transferred to civilian agencies. In the Low Countries and Denmark, three Psychological Warfare consolidation teams were established to work with the SHAEF missions and SHAEF co-ordinated their work. In Norway, civilian agencies handled most of the information activities with the aid of the Psychological Warfare Division.

The tasks of the Allied Information Service were also extended to displays of photographs and charts depicting the Allied war efforts, distribution of publications, photographs, and motion pictures, and the servicing of newspapers in the liberated area.

In an effort to acquaint the French people with Allied war efforts, civilian agencies prepared fifteen posters which the mayors of French cities were given to distribute as they saw fit. In Paris, the Allied Information Service opened an exhibit room at the Place de L'Opéra for the display of photographs, charts, and posters outlining the war activities of the United Nations. The exhibit attracted nearly a

---

[44] Prince Bernhard to CofS SHAEF, 1 Nov 44; Gerbrandy to Eisenhower, 16 Dec 44; Smith to Gerbrandy, 22 Dec 44; Eisenhower to Gerbrandy, 23 Dec 44; Edwards to Morgan, 27 Dec 44. All in SHAEF SGS 014.1 Netherlands, Civil Affairs Dir for Netherlands, I and II. See below, Chapter XXIV, for negotiations near the end of the war between General Smith and Seyss-Inquart relative to the feeding of the population of occupied Netherlands.

[45] The Voice of SHAEF was the name applied to special broadcasts from SHAEF in the name of the Supreme Commander.

quarter-million people between mid-October and mid-December 1944. The interest evinced by the Parisians induced the Allied Information Service to send similar exhibits to twenty-seven French cities between December 1944 and the end of the war. More than seven million people registered at the exhibits during this period.

Also effective in the liberated areas was the sale at low prices of both the English texts and French versions of American and British books. Two illustrated publications—*Voir* (American) and *Cadran* (British)—were prepared as well. Later, digest-type magazines made up of selections from British and American publications were put on sale. Between the distribution of the first publications in France on 10 July 1944 and the end of the war more than 15,570,000 copies were sold.

To provide information in France in June 1944, psychological warfare teams with the British and American armies printed news sheets at Bayeux and Isigny. Later a daily newspaper was printed at Cherbourg. The project, started by the First Army Psychological Warfare Team, was turned over to the Allied Information Service in July 1944. Wall news bulletins were printed and sent to the smaller towns for display. These activities proved unnecessary in Paris inasmuch as fourteen Resistance papers were in circulation there when the city was liberated. The number increased tremendously within a few weeks. The Allied Information Service aided these publications by distributing newsprint, special articles, and photographs.

The SHAEF Psychological Warfare Division and the Allied Information Service helped service strategic radio activities, operated mobile transmitters, assisted civilian radio broadcasting in the liberated areas, and ultimately operated the static transmitter at Luxembourg. Although the original work of mobile broadcasting was done by army group teams, the Psychological Warfare Division tended to take over this function in rear areas. In Cherbourg, the Psychological Warfare Division furnished the transmitter and ran a purely Allied station. In Rennes, Paris, and other cities where the transmitters were still available, the division supplied equipment to put them into operation and furnished material for broadcasts.

The most important work performed by the radio section of the Psychological Warfare Division during the war was that of operating Radio Luxembourg after its capture in September 1944. This station, which had a 150-kilowatt transmitter, had been damaged by the Germans before they left the city, but psychological warfare experts of 12th Army Group started repairs almost immediately after arriving in Luxembourg. On 3 October 1944, personnel from the SHAEF Psychological Warfare Division, acting under an agreement signed by the Allies and Luxembourg in May 1944, took over the station. The first daily SHAEF news program went on the air on 10 November 1944, and a complete program was gradually built up which ultimately ran twelve hours a day. The station was off the air from 20 to 30 December as a result of the German attack in the Ardennes.

Other Aid to Liberated Peoples

Assistance in re-establishing and maintaining public order, rearming of the *gendarmerie* and the equipping of security and line-of-communications troops, and the restoration of public information facilities were only a few of the civil affairs activities in which SHAEF agencies participated. Much of the actual work was performed by civil affairs detachments with the army groups, armies, and corps, but SHAEF gave its full support to the speedy restoration of civil government by establishing uniform procedures and policies, by allocating transportation and scarce supplies, by co-ordinating military and civil requirements, and by acting as intermediary between the civilian governments and the subordinate military authorities.

CHAPTER XIX

Program for Germany

The means of hastening German surrender by other than military efforts, the government of occupied areas of Germany while the war was still in progress, and the method of dealing with Germany after the final surrender constituted problems that concerned SHAEF as well as the governments of the United States, Great Britain, the USSR, and France. The Supreme Commander and his headquarters were frequently called on for suggestions as to Allied policy in regard to Germany. Sometimes SHAEF on its own initiative outlined possible solutions for Allied consideration, and on other occasions it implemented the policy laid down by higher authority. Throughout the war, the Allied governments were slow in reaching final conclusions on a program for Germany. The reasons were not far to seek. First of all, three, and later, four, nations with somewhat disparate aims had to agree on a policy—always a slow process. Various agencies in the individual Allied nations, especially in the United States, had to be consulted on postwar policy. Finally, there were often jurisdictional disagreements among the European Advisory Commission, the Combined Civil Affairs Committee and other units set up to handle problems relating to Germany. The result of the delays was that the Supreme Commander was frequently without official policy to guide him at the time he most needed it.[1]

Efforts To Induce German Surrender

Allied planners were hopeful from the start of planning for OVERLORD in the summer of 1943 that the enemy might collapse or be induced to surrender before or shortly after the invasion. It will be recalled that three RANKIN plans were outlined to deal with developments in the case of collapse, of withdrawal from the occupied areas, and of outright surrender.[2] While hopes of German surrender before D Day were almost completely discarded by the first of 1944, the Allied military planners believed that the German people were weary of war and disgusted with their Nazi leaders and that a proper appeal to them might bring a revolt or at least weaken the German will to resist.

Unconditional Surrender Formula

In planning propaganda appeals to the German people, the SHAEF planners found themselves handicapped by the unconditional surrender formula announced by President Roosevelt at Casablanca. He

[1] See above, Ch. IV. For relations of the European Advisory Commission and other Allied agencies, see Philip E. Mosely, "The Occupation of Germany, New Light on How the Zones were Drawn," *Foreign Affairs*, XXVIII (July, 1950), 580–604. Mr. Mosely was political adviser to Ambassador John G. Winant on the European Advisory Commission from June 1944 to August 1945.

[2] See above, Ch. V.

and the Prime Minister had later issued explanatory statements which removed any suggestion of Allied terrorism or acts of vengeance directed at the whole German people, but they had not succeeded in evolving a version of the formula which Allied propagandists could use to persuade the German people to seek peace.[3]

SHAEF planners feared that the Germans would put up a last-ditch fight in preference to accepting unconditional surrender. General Barker, the G–1, in January 1944 held that it would be a grave mistake to treat unconditional surrender as "our irreducible demand," and General McClure, responsible for psychological warfare against the enemy, asked that he be permitted at least to distinguish between the German leaders and the people in propaganda aimed at the enemy.[4]

SHAEF fears were shared in Washington where Secretaries Hull and Stimson, who had already expressed disapproval of unconditional surrender terms, tried to get the President to modify his formula. Intelligence reports in Washington and London indicated in the early weeks of 1944 that enemy leaders were using fear of Allied demands to strengthen the resistance of their people. The U.S. Chiefs of Staff in March urged the President to restate his demands in a way that would reassure the German people, but Mr. Roosevelt preferred to let the matter stay as it was at the time. And there were good reasons advanced in favor of his stand. General Hilldring, War Department director of civil affairs, doubted that the United Nations could afford to bind themselves by a pact to treat the enemy in any specific manner, and Mr. John J. McCloy, Assistant Secretary of War, suggested that it was not unconditional surrender but fear of the Red Army which kept the Ger-

mans fighting. Although it is possible that these views did not reach the President, he was probably aware of Mr. Churchill's view that the Allies should avoid any specific statement of terms which would permit the Germans later to claim they were tricked.[5]

In mid-April 1944, Generals Eisenhower and Smith impressed on Under Secretary of State Edward R. Stettinius, Jr., who was then in London, the need of clarifying the principle of unconditional surrender. They felt that by making clear to the German people the basis on which they would be treated after surrender the Allies could create a willingness on the part of the population to give up and perhaps also induce a German Badoglio to take steps leading to surrender. They asked for a joint statement by the United States, Great Britain, and the Soviet Union defining unconditional surrender and guaranteeing law and order in the Reich. Once a beachhead was established in northwest Europe, they added, the Supreme Commander should issue a statement recapitulating the terms of surrender and calling on the enemy to lay down his arms. If such a step was not taken, General Smith indicated, the Allies would find it impossible to exploit the advantages which would be gained from the effect of a successful landing. The President was apparently unmoved by these suggestions,

---

[3] Churchill, *The Hinge of Fate,* pp. 685–91; Cordell Hull, *The Memoirs of Cordell Hull* (New York, 1948), Vol. II, Ch. 13.

[4] Memo, Barker for McClure, 27 Jan 44, SHAEF SGS 322.01 Publicity and Psychological Warfare; Interv with Gen McClure, 29 Mar 47.

[5] Hull, *Memoirs,* Vol. II, Ch. 13; Notes on mtg of McClure, Peake, Phillips, *et al.,* 11 Feb 44, McClure jnl. JIC Paper, 19 Feb 44; JCS 718/1, 16 Mar 44 with atchd papers (memos by Hilldring and McCloy); Memo, JCS for President, 25 Mar 44. All in ABC 387 Germany (18 Dec 43), Sec 3.

saying only that any reply should have his approval before being sent. Mr. Hull interpreted this statement to mean that the President was holding strongly to his unconditional surrender stand. Three weeks later, Mr. Roosevelt did yield to Russian and British pressure for modifications of unconditional surrender so far as it affected the German satellite countries, and agreed that some latitude could be shown in surrender settlements with Bulgaria and Românĭa.[6]

General Eisenhower, though eager to remove exaggerated fears of the German people, nonetheless believed that terms of capitulation should include the surrender of the armed forces of the Axis powers and the handing over of designated political and military leaders for trial. For the rest, he favored the declaration, "The masses of the population in the Axis countries will be expected and required to take up again their normal pursuits of peace in order that conditions of starvation and privation may be ameliorated." He recognized that any such declaration had to meet the demands of the Soviet Union, which was likely to insist on using several million Germans after the war, and that a statement to this effect would play into the hands of German propagandists. Unless the problem could be overcome in some way, he thought it best to drop the whole matter of attempting to state Allied demands.[7]

A statement to meet the Supreme Commander's requirements was prepared in General McClure's office in late May, touched up by Mr. Robert Sherwood and put into final shape by Mr. Phillips, political officer at SHAEF. President Roosevelt at this time agreed that a declaration could be made to the German people which would place the chief stress on the

inevitability of their defeat. The British War Cabinet and the Prime Minister disapproved this suggestion. Mr. Churchill was quoted as saying that any declaration to the German people which omitted their war crimes would be subject later to enemy charges of Allied bad faith, but that listing of such crimes would be likely to terrify the Germans and lead them to fight the more fanatically. The Prime Minister on 24 May, in an address to the House of Commons, had gone as far as he cared to go with the statement that, while unconditional surrender gave the enemy no rights, it relieved the Allies of none of their duties. "Justice," he added, "will have to be done and retribution will fall upon the wicked and the cruel."[8]

The invasion of France thus began without any action on SHAEF's request for a concrete statement of war aims which would weaken enemy resistance to the Allied landings. The only concession by Washington and London was that something might be done later when Allied operations met with "a large measure of success."[9] Plans were discussed in June

[6] Stettinius to Hull, 14 Apr 44, Diary Office CinC; Hull, *Memoirs*, II, 1578; Wallace Carroll, *Persuade or Perish* (Boston, 1948), pp. 319–20.
[7] Eisenhower to CofS SHAEF, 20 May 44, Diary Office CinC. This seems at variance with the statement of Fred Smith in "The Rise and Fall of the Morgenthau Plan," *United Nations World*, I (March, 1947), 32–37, that General Eisenhower either suggested parts of the Morgenthau plan or agreed with its broad implications. (Mr. Smith was a member of Secretary Morgenthau's staff in 1944.) See Eisenhower, *Crusade in Europe* p. 287.
[8] Memo prepared for PWD (unsigned), 29 May 44, with notations by Peake and Phillips, SHAEF SGS 091.412/3 Psychological Warfare Against Germany, I; Churchill, address to House of Commons, 24 May 44, text in Louise Wilhelmine Holborn, ed., *War and Peace Aims of the United Nations* (Boston, 1943–48), p. 497; Hull, *Memoirs*, II, 1580.
[9] Notation by Phillips on Memo prepared for PWD (unsigned), 29 May 44, SHAEF SGS 091.412/3 Psychological Warfare Against Germany, I.

and July for the presurrender period of German occupation and for the posthostilities period, but in mid-August nothing besides "unconditional surrender" had yet been devised. An attempt by the Office of War Information to draw up a paper for guidance on long-range propaganda for Germany was challenged by the War Department on the ground that it suggested a soft treatment of the enemy. The policy of "nonfraternization" and the impression on the Germans of their war guilt were said to be the fundamental principles of War Department policy. In making this explanation, General Hilldring took exception to OWI's statement that the end of the war meant the end of German suffering and the beginning of reconstruction economically, culturally, and socially.[10]

From the standpoint of SHAEF's psychological warfare campaign to persuade the enemy to surrender, the situation was worsened in September 1944 when word leaked out that Secretary of the Treasury Morgenthau had persuaded President Roosevelt and the Prime Minister at Quebec to approve a plan to convert Germany "into a country primarily agricultural and pastoral in character." Under strong pressure from the Secretaries of State and War, the President said that he had never intended to accept a proposal for making a wholly agricultural nation out of Germany. No public statement was made to this effect and the idea continued to persist in administration circles and in German propaganda. The *Voelkischer Beobachter,* in a typical press reaction, warned: "The German people must realize that we are engaged in a life and death struggle which imposes on every German the duty to do his utmost for the victorious conclusion of the war and the frustration of the plans of destruction planned by these can-

nibals." The *Berliner Morgenpost* called it a "satanic plan of annihilation," and the *12 Uhr Blatt* declared that the "aim of these conditions, inspired by the Jews, is the annihilation of the German people in the quickest way." The enemy henceforth was to couple these themes and those relating to unconditional surrender with claims that Allied occupation authorities in Germany were carrying out a reign of terror.

General McClure, trying to get a propaganda policy which would at least gain the backing of Germans in areas already occupied by Allied forces, was told by the War Department that he should follow the general line laid down by the President in an address on 22 October. In it Mr. Roosevelt insisted that there would be no bargain with "Nazi conspirators," to whom should be left no shred of control nor a single element of military power or military potential. He had brought no charge against the German race and he had assured the German people that they would not be enslaved.[11]

The War and State Department instructions were more valuable in getting German co-operation in areas already occupied than in helping to break the will to resist of those Germans not yet conquered. General Eisenhower explained this difference on 20 November when he asked as a matter of urgency that a means be found to reduce enemy resistance. He noted that it was based on the iron discipline of the

[10] *Ibid.;* WD G–2 to CAD, 17 Aug 44, and CAD to G–2, 26 Aug 44; both in CAD 091.412 (2–25–43), Sec 1.

[11] Memo, Stettinius for President, 27 Oct 44, containing statement of Winant to State Dept, 17 Oct 44, concerning PWD proposals, CAD 091.412 (2–25–43), Sec 1. McCloy to Smith, W–52734, 26 Oct 44; Smith to McCloy, S–64199, 27 Oct 44; McCloy to Smith, WX–56779, 3 Nov 44. All in SHAEF SGS 091.412/3 Psychological Warfare Against Germany, I. Carroll, *Persuade or Perish,* pp. 326–29.

Wehrmacht and the stranglehold of the Nazi party, and on successful enemy propaganda which was convincing the German people that unconditional surrender meant the complete devastation of Germany and its destruction as a nation.[12]

At the suggestion of the Combined Chiefs of Staff, the President in late November proposed a statement assuring the enemy that the Allies were not seeking to devastate or destroy Germany. Reservations were then made by Prime Minister Churchill and the War Cabinet, who feared that such a statement, if made during a period of comparative stalemate, might be interpreted as a sign of Allied weakness. Mr. Churchill added that the Germans feared, not Allied occupation, but conquest by the Russians. He suggested that the Allies go along as they were until winter arrived. "In the meantime," he concluded, "I shall remain set on unconditional surrender which is where you put me." General Eisenhower, when informed of this reaction, agreed that the joint proclamation should follow an operation universally recognized as a definite success.[13]

After the failure of the Allies to agree in October or November 1944 on a statement regarding unconditional surrender which could be released to the German people, the British Chiefs of Staff set up a committee to discuss arrangements for a plan to break enemy morale. General McClure represented SHAEF in meetings of the group. Apparently it could arrive at no satisfactory formula. The question was later discussed at Yalta, and a statement on Allied aims was issued at the conclusion of the conference. President Roosevelt, Mr. Churchill, and Marshal Stalin on 11 February 1945 declared: "It is our inflexible purpose to destroy German militarism

and nazism and to insure that Germany will never again be able to disturb the peace of the world. . . . It is not our purpose to destroy the people of Germany, but only when nazism and militarism have been extirpated will there be hope for a decent life for Germans, and a place for them in the comity of nations."[14] With this explanation of the meaning of unconditional surrender, SHAEF had to be content.

Psychological Warfare Appeals to the Enemy

Because SHAEF had no success before D Day in getting a definition of "unconditional surrender" that would appeal to the German people, it had to direct its chief efforts at the German soldier. The Psychological Warfare Division made a special attempt to persuade the individual fighting man that it was no disgrace to surrender after he had fought courageously in the field.

In early propaganda activities during the static period of hedgerow fighting, teams attached to combat units aimed special appeals at groups of Germans who were outnumbered and threatened with annihilation. To persuade the enemy of his hopeless position, the teams used statements in German describing the actual tactical situation. Many of their efforts

[12] Eisenhower to CCS, S–67648 (SCAF 134), 20 Nov 44, SHAEF SGS 091.412/3 Psychological Warfare Against Germany, I.

[13] Marshall to Eisenhower, W–66936, 22 Nov 44; Roosevelt to AGWAR for Eisenhower, 25 Nov 44; Churchill to Eisenhower, 26 Nov 44; Eisenhower to Churchill, 26 Nov 44; Eisenhower to Marshall, CPA 90359, 27 Nov 44. All in Eisenhower personal file.

[14] Br COS to JSM, 6845, 25 Nov 44; Smith to Ismay, S–68298, 25 Nov 44. Both in SHAEF SGS 091.412/3 Psychological Warfare Against Germany, I; Statement of Allied aims, February 11, 1945, *War and Peace Aims of the United Nations*, pp. 20–21.

were successful. In Brittany, the psychological warfare teams concentrated their efforts on the fortress garrisons. At St. Malo, the psychological warfare teams were directed to study various surrender appeals previously used, including the one issued to Lt. Gen. Jonathan M. Wainwright by the Japanese at Corregidor. The enemy was told that no humiliation could be attached to a surrender in the face of overwhelming odds. This particular appeal met with no success. A more effective propaganda device during the periods of heavy fighting was the *Passierschein*, or safe-conduct pass, which carried the signature of General Eisenhower and gave instructions on how German soldiers could surrender. This safe-conduct leaflet, which was dropped or fired into enemy lines, carried the seals of Great Britain and the United States, and declared in both German and English: "The German soldier who carries this safe conduct is using it as a sign of his genuine wish to give himself up. He is to be disarmed, to be well looked after, to receive food and medical attention as required, and to be removed from the danger zone as soon as possible." While no one can be certain of the leaflet's effectiveness in inducing the enemy to surrender, more prisoners saw it than any other propaganda leaflet and a large number who surrendered had been carrying their copies for several weeks in case they should decide to give up.[15]

When the Allied forces approached Germany, the Voice of SHAEF urged all foreign workers in Germany to leave factories at the earliest opportunity, to boycott those among them who were in liaison with the Germans, and to avoid any unorganized action. They were advised to remain as the German Army withdrew, to prevent the retreating forces from destroying installations if possible, and to gather information about the enemy which would be of value to the Allies. Another campaign reminded the German people that it was dangerous to remain in areas subject to bombing and warned them against committing atrocities against Allied prisoners and foreign workers.[16]

After the occupation of the first captured cities of Germany began, the SHAEF Psychological Warfare Division attempted to offset charges of Allied mistreatment of Germans and to dispel other fears of Allied occupation policy. To aid this program, the division used a newspaper, *Aachener Nachrichten*, which had been started initially by 12th Army Group's Psychological Warfare Section. This, the first newspaper published under Allied auspices in Germany, ultimately attained a circulation of 52,000.

In October 1944, seeing the unlikelihood of getting a suitable revision of the unconditional surrender formula for propaganda purposes, General McClure turned his attention to a campaign designed to get German support for Allied military government in the occupied areas. In November, the War and State Departments suggested a number of aims for SHAEF to follow in this effort. These stressed the advantage of Allied rule over that of the Nazis, the fact that responsibility for German suffering lay on the Nazis, and the assurance that the average German would be allowed to live and work without molestation if he obeyed Allied regulations and committed no crimes. SHAEF told the various Allied psychological warfare units at lower level of these aims on 16 November, adding that no ap-

---

[15] The author has relied heavily for this and other information in this section on Psychological Warfare Division (SHAEF), *An Account of Its Operations*.

[16] Voice of SHAEF broadcasts 27–32, 5–13 Sep 44, translation given in PWD (SHAEF), *An Account of Its Operations*, pp. 120–22.

peals were to be made to the Germans in the nonoccupied areas but that they were to be informed of the way in which Allied military government actually functioned in those German areas then occupied by the Allied armies.[17]

In accordance with a SHAEF directive of 20 October on "Propaganda Treatment of Military Government," General McClure and his staff now prepared thirteen broadcasts to explain the nature of military government to the Germans. Beginning on 4 December, the programs were given daily until completed by the British Broadcasting Corporation, American Broadcasting Station in Europe, and Radio Luxembourg. The broadcasts stated the major points of the Allied military government program: steps for destroying the Nazi regime, the assumption of local government by the Allied commanders, changes in economic controls, termination of oppressive laws, and the like. No effort was made to hide the severity of military occupation, but the announcements made evident an intention to establish a system in accord with "the dictates of humanity, justice, and civilized standards." [18]

The leaflet war against the Germans which had been carried on intensively before the invasion was greatly increased after 6 June. Making use of planes, artillery, and, occasionally, agents, the Allied psychological warfare agencies distributed newspapers and millions of leaflets to the enemy forces, as well as news sheets to the peoples in occupied countries. In June 1944, the Allied air forces dropped nearly five million copies of a newspaper for German troops, two and a half million periodicals, and approximately six million strategic and thirty-five and a half million tactical leaflets on the enemy. These did not include those fired from artillery and disseminated by hand. Copies of leaflets distributed in languages other than German totaled more than thirty-eight and a half millions.[19]

The Allies made a special drive in late July to distribute a bulletin reciting the details of the 20 July attempt to kill Hitler. On the evenings of 23 and 24 July, planes dropped nearly four million leaflets about the subject on the enemy front in Normandy and distributed nearly three quarters of a million newspapers giving the information. Evidence that these and other leaflets were effective was seen in efforts of German commanders to prevent their men from reading the propaganda. Radio denials and special orientation programs designed to answer the leaflets indicated that the Allied program was feared by the enemy.[20]

The Germans naturally retaliated with their own leaflets and radio appeals. An analysis of the line they were taking in the fall of 1944 showed that the Germans were attempting to play off the various Allies against each other, stressing particularly the coming struggle between the Russians and the West. In their efforts to counteract the effect of Allied appeals, the enemy propagandists said that by inflicting heavy casualties on the Allies the German Army would gain more favorable peace terms for the Reich. The German soldier was

[17] Psychological Warfare Policy and Info Memo 7, 16 Nov 44, SHAEF SGS 091.412 Propaganda; Carroll, *Persuade or Perish*, pp. 328–29.

[18] Statements by Spokesmen of Military Government, 25 Nov 44 (texts of military government proclamations), SHAEF SGS 091.412/3 Psychological Warfare Against Germany, I.

[19] Psychological Warfare Rpt 7, 17 Jul 44, SHAEF SGS 091.412 Propaganda, I.

[20] The Leaflet Propaganda Front, Report on Special Operations During OVERLORD (atchd to Gen McClure's communication slip of 4 Aug 44); McClure to CofS SHAEF, 29 Aug 44; Goebbels Gives Leaflet Warning, 30 Sep 44. All in SHAEF SGS 091.412 Propaganda, I.

told it was better to die than to live in a conquered Germany.[21]

In the course of the German counteroffensive in the Ardennes, the Psychological Warfare Division stopped its appeals for German surrender and turned instead to exaggerated statements of what the enemy expected to gain. SHAEF broadcasts emphasized that Hitler had promised to take Liége, Namur, and Verdun before Christmas. The Allies hoped thereby to magnify the disillusionment of the enemy once the counteroffensive was defeated.[22]

In the final days of the war, the psychological warfare agencies made new leaflet appeals to the German civilian and to foreign workers in Germany. Civilians in the battle zones were told to evacuate danger areas, to evade service in the *Volkssturm,* and to avoid needless destruction of their homes. Foreign workers were advised by leaflets to practice sabotage or malingering, to refuse to work in munitions factories, and to spread rumors. Instructions were given to displaced persons both in leaflets and in a four-page newspaper called *SHAEF* which was printed in several languages. At one time, small fuze incendiaries were dropped to foreign workers with instructions on how to use them in sabotage operations (BRADDOCK II). By the time the war ended, the Allied air forces had dropped nearly six billion leaflets. Of this number three and a quarter billions were distributed between 6 June 1944 and 8 May 1945.[23]

Military Government of Germany

While the Allies were conducting military operations against the enemy and searching for means to induce him to surrender, they were also confronted with the task of establishing policy and procedures for governing occupied German territory during the presurrender period. It was essential to devise a program that would restore sufficient order in the occupied areas to avoid interference by the conquered populace with military operations and that would possibly offset the dire warnings of German propagandists as to the fate of their people who fell into Allied hands. Such a program was simpler than the long-range military government programs then being planned for the postwar period. Until the war's end, SHAEF and its army groups needed a program that would combat starvation and disease, destroy all vestiges of Nazi control, prevent local guerrilla warfare, and set the basic machinery of community life to functioning again.

By the time SHAEF started to operate in January 1944, a number of agencies were already engaged in planning for Allied military government in Germany. The War Department had charged its Civil Affairs Division with the task of planning for U.S. military occupation in the Reich in both the presurrender and posthostilities periods. In Great Britain, the British Chiefs of Staff had established the Post Hostilities Planning Sub-Committee to do a similar job for them. The British, in the spring of 1944, went further and established a Control Commission Military Section under Maj. Gen. Charles A. West to provide and train the staffs of various

---

[21] See Rpt of U.S. Legation at Bern, 23 Nov 44; summaries of German propaganda in PWD news digests, SHAEF SGS 091.412 Propadanda, I.

[22] PWD guidance bulletin, 20 Dec 44–1 Jan 45, SHAEF SGS 091.412 Propaganda, I.

[23] PWD (SHAEF), *An Account of Its Operations,* pp. 159, 167, 53. Of the nearly six billion leaflets, some 57 percent were dropped by U.S. air forces. For a description of their activities, see Craven and Cate, *The Army Air Forces in World War II,* III, 494–98.

British missions for posthostilities work. Meanwhile, both the Foreign Office and the State Department had committees busy studying postwar problems.

As early as November 1943, Headquarters, COSSAC, had submitted to the various Allied commands in the United Kingdom a civil affairs–military government plan for Europe. Based on existing military government manuals, the outline was very general. As soon as the G–5 Division of SHAEF was formed, it continued the planning which had been started under COSSAC. A German country unit was established by the division in March 1944 to prepare a handbook on military government for the Reich. The SHAEF G–3 Division was already at work on similar matters, having established a Post-Hostilities Planning Sub-Section of its Plans Branch to work in liaison on these problems with the British service ministries, the U.S. advisers to the European Advisory Commission, and the appropriate agencies of ETOUSA. In the absence of a directive from the Combined Chiefs of Staff, this subsection and other SHAEF agencies began preparing papers on such questions as armistice terms, displaced persons, prisoners of war, disarmament, martial law, control of German courts, and co-ordination of movement and transport facilities. These papers ultimately became the bases of the so-called ECLIPSE memorandums.[24] In March 1944, a SHAEF study on the armistice and posthostilities period, dealing with various problems which would confront the Supreme Commander between the end of hostilities and the termination of SHAEF, listed some thirty-eight studies either planned or in preparation for this interim period. By the end of April some seventy-two studies were being made.[25]

Presurrender Directive

General Eisenhower, in an effort to get some positive guidance on which to base the burgeoning plans of his civil affairs agencies, asked the Combined Civil Affairs Committee in the spring of 1944 for a definitive directive on military government. The CCAC informed him that the European Advisory Commission was working on a directive and program for Germany. In view of the fact, however, that SHAEF would need some guidance before the members of the commission could reach an agreement, the CCAC initiated a directive for the presurrender period, with the understanding that it would be subject to amendment by the European Advisory Commission. The directive was approved informally by the Combined Chiefs of Staff and dispatched to the Supreme Commander on 28 April 1944. The European Advisory Commission later circulated it for Soviet examination.[26]

The presurrender directive for Germany and for those parts of Austria which might be overrun by the Allied Expeditionary Force granted the Supreme Commander supreme legislative, executive, and judicial authority in all areas occupied by his troops. It declared that

[24] ECLIPSE was a name given in November 1944 to posthostilities plans for Germany. The original code name, TALISMAN, was changed after it was reported to be known to the enemy.

[25] Much of this section is based on Office, Chief Historian, EUCOM, Planning for the Occupation of Germany, compiled and written by Martin P. Detels, Jr., Col A.R.C. Sander, Francis Chase, and Joseph Starr, 1947, MS, OCMH files; and on [Richard M. Welling] Germany: Plans and Policies (Bk. VI of History of the Civil Affairs Division, War Department Special Staff, World War II [until March 1946]), MS, OCMH files.

[26] Welling, History of the Civil Affairs Division, Bk. VI.

military government was to be an Allied undertaking and was to be administered in the interests of the United Nations. No political agencies or political representatives of Great Britain and the United States were to have part in military government, and representatives of civilian agencies of the two countries and of the United Nations Relief and Rehabilitation Administration (UNRRA) were to participate only when the Combined Chiefs of Staff should so decide on the recommendation of the Supreme Commander.[27]

The Allied commander in chief was directed to discourage fraternization between Allied troops and the Germans in occupied areas. He was to take sweeping measures to dissolve the Nazi organization and system of government and to eliminate the General Staff and prevent its revival. Besides maintaining law and order and restoring "normal conditions among the civilian population as soon as possible, in so far as such conditions would not interfere with military operations," he was to make clear that the occupation was intended to destroy Nazism and Fascism. On the more constructive side, the Supreme Commander was to free Allied prisoners of war and place them under military control pending other disposition; permit freedom of speech, press, and worship, subject to military exigencies and the prohibition of Nazi activities; and establish local government, making use of Germans or of Allied officials according to the decision of the Supreme Commander. If SHAEF forces entered Austrian territory, they were to follow political aims fundamentally different from those in effect in Germany, since the Allied purpose in Austria was liberation. Fraternization was to be permitted and political activity given greater latitude.[28]

At the end of May 1944 the presurrender directive to General Eisenhower was completed with the approval of a Financial Guide for Germany and an Economic and Relief Guide for Germany. Where possible the Supreme Commander was to work through existing German administrative and economic machinery in carrying out his program, keeping in mind the necessity of removing the Nazis from power.[29]

Allied Zones of Occupation

With the presurrender directive out of the way, Allied planners in the United States and Europe were able to return to the outlining of zones of occupation in Germany, a subject they had been discussing since the summer and fall of 1943. COSSAC in its initial proposals for the occupation of Europe in case of German collapse had assumed that Allied troops would have to take the responsibility for disarming enemy forces in the occupied countries and returning them to Germany. Occupation zones were outlined, therefore, in France, Belgium, the Netherlands, Norway, and Denmark in addition to Germany, and the United States was made

---

[27] UNRRA was an organization created by the United Nations in 1943 to aid refugees and displaced persons in former Axis-occupied countries in Europe and Asia.

[28] CCS Memo for SAC, 28 Apr 44, CCAC 014 Germany (11–15–43), Sec I. As presented by CCAC to CCS for approval this paper carried the number CCAC 69/5. The same document when forwarded by the Combined Chiefs of Staff was given the number CCS 551.

[29] Financial Guide for Germany, App. C, and Economic and Relief Guide for Germany, App. D, CCS 551/2, 24 May 44 (approved as CCS 551/3, 31 May 44), CCAC 014 Germany (11–15–43), Sec I. Modifications were made in the financial guide by CCS 551/5, 31 Aug 44, SHAEF G–5 hist file, 1 (CCS) and 1A (CCS Dirs).

responsible for France, Belgium, and southern Germany.[30] President Roosevelt, however, as a result of his difficulties with General de Gaulle, had become reluctant to have any more political dealings with French authorities than necessary and wanted to avoid any responsibility for France. This feeling apparently influenced him, at least in part, in favor of a northern zone of occupation in Germany which would permit the United States to supply its troops through north German rather than through French ports. He also insisted that the United States should have Berlin.[31] At Quebec and again at Cairo the conferees discussed these matters without reaching any final conclusions.

The President in February 1944 said that he wanted to stay out of the problems of southern Europe after the war, adding that it was out of the question for the United States to have the postwar burden of reconstructing France, Italy, and the Balkans. This he considered another reason why the United States should have a northern rather than a southern zone of occupation. Arguing that the British were far more interested than the United States in southern Europe, he saw no reason why they should not take an occupation zone in that area. He emphasized that the United States would be only "too glad" to take its troops out of all Europe as soon as the British were ready to take over. In this, he was merely repeating his statement of the previous fall that the United States' postwar occupation would probably consist of about one million troops and last for about two years.[32]

In mid-February 1944 General Eisenhower had suggested to the War Department that the United States refuse to take any responsibility for any specific area in Europe. Instead, he proposed that respon-

sibility be accepted only so long as orders and policies were issued through the Combined Chiefs of Staff. In the event that Great Britain desired some specific area, the United States should withdraw its occupation forces. He justified this idea on the ground that, since the United States had to furnish a large share of the relief, it should "be strongly represented in the *whole* controlling system." Again at the end of March, he opposed proposals for separate U.S. and British military government administrations in Germany. He believed it practical to have British occupation troops in one zone and U.S. in another with a combined administrative body functioning in both. This view was not approved in Washington where the President and the Joint Chiefs of Staff held that the United States should have the northern zone of Germany. They also had the feeling that no impression should be given to the Soviet authorities that they were being confronted with a combined British-American view before being consulted.[33]

General Eisenhower returned to his theme just before D Day. He believed that the President had not distinguished between a complete and arbitrary division of Europe into separate British and U.S. zones on the one hand, and a complete amalgamation of British and U.S. units on

---

[30] See below, page 351, for details relating to the Russian zone of occupation.

[31] Mtg, President and JCS, at sea, 19 Nov 43.

[32] *Ibid.*; Memo by T.T.H. (Handy), 19 Nov 43, sub: RANKIN, OPD Exec 9; CCS 134th Mtg, 4 Dec 43, SEXTANT Conf Min; CCS 143d Mtg, 28 Jan 44; CCS 144th Mtg, 4 Feb 44; Memo, President for Actg Secy State, 21 Feb 44, ABC 384 Northwest Europe (20 Aug 43), Sec 1B.

[33] Eisenhower to Marshall, 15 Feb 44; Handy to Eisenhower, 21 Feb 44. Both in OPD Exec 9, Bk 15. Winant to Secy State, COMEA 50, 30 Mar 44; proposed draft of cable from Marshall to Eisenhower, 2 Apr 44, CAD 210.31.

the other. There was no question that the bulk of the forces of the two armies should be divided because of operational necessity, and because of convenience in handling supply and administration. The chief point was whether a sharp line would be drawn between the two or whether over-all Allied control should continue. General Eisenhower believed it would be easier for the Combined Chiefs of Staff to operate through an Allied commander than through independent commanders. There was also the danger that, instead of having a solid front, the British and U.S. area commanders would find themselves trying to settle all questions on a British versus U.S. basis, thus giving the Russians a chance to side with one at the expense of the other.[34] This argument did not change the policy in Washington.

The President continued to sit tight in regard to occupation zones through June and July. In early August the Russians in the European Advisory Commission raised the question of zones and asked that they be settled between Britain and the United States as soon as possible. The State Department proposed that the United States accept the southern zone of Germany in exchange for British promises to take over the occupation of France, Italy, and the Balkans, if necessary, and to grant the United States sufficient ports in the Low Countries and Germany to permit supply and evacuation of U.S. troops without dependence on French ports. The State Department suggested that the northern area might have "a great many headaches" and quite a bit of shooting. The President said he was unable to understand why any discussion was necessary with the Russians since an agreement had been made that they might police that part of Germany in which they had expressed a desire to exercise control. As to the general question of

the zones of occupation, he said he merely awaited an agreement by the Prime Minister that U.S. troops would police northwest Germany.[35]

When mid-August arrived without any final decision on the zones, General Eisenhower declared that he would have to approach the problem on a purely military basis and send his forces in with the 21 Army Group on the left. This action, of course, meant that British forces would be occupying Belgium, Holland, and northwest Germany, while U.S. forces would be in the south.[36] The necessity of having some arrangement made by the European Advisory Commission before Allied forces entered Germany may have led that body to hasten its approval of the text of a protocol between the United States, Great Britain, and the USSR on 12 September providing for the boundaries of the three zones of occupation. Even the protocol did not decide whether the United States or Great Britain would have the northwest or southwest zone of Germany. It merely noted the boundaries and said that the allocation of zones would be settled by joint agreement.[37]

---

[34] Memo, Eisenhower for CofS SHAEF, 20 May 44, used as basis for Ltr, Eisenhower to Marshall, 27 May 44, Diary Office CinC. In an entry of 27 May, Captain Butcher explained that some historian might read into the general's letter a desire to continue as Allied commander in chief. He noted that, while General Eisenhower had indicated he would like the job of ridding the world of the German General Staff and all it stood for, he also wanted to get on with the war so he could "get home and go fishing." Butcher thought he was merely being consistent in urging unity of command.

[35] Stettinius to President, 2 Aug 44; President to Stettinius, 3 Aug 44. Both in OPD Exec 10, Item 63c.

[36] SHAEF to WD, FWD 12936, 17 Aug 44, CCAC 014 Germany (11–15–43), Sec 2.

[37] Approval of text of protocol between U.K., U.S., and USSR on zones of occupation in Germany and administration of Greater Berlin, 12 Sep 44 (photostat of signed agreement), CCAC 014 Germany (11–15–43), Sec 2.

On the day that the Combined Chiefs of Staff examined the question in Quebec, Admiral Leahy explained the military reasons why the United States should have the northwest zone. Admiral King, however, took the view that it would be easier for the United States to occupy the southwest zone of Germany if at the same time arrangements could be made to evacuate American troops and to supply occupation forces through the northern German ports. The question was referred to President Roosevelt and Mr. Churchill. The President now agreed that the British forces would "occupy Germany west of the Rhine and east of the Rhine north of the line from Coblenz following the northern border of Hessen and Nassau to the border of the area allocated to the Soviet Government." The United States was to occupy Germany east of the Rhine and south of the British zone eastward to the Russian zone. The British zone thus included the Ruhr, the Rhineland north of Koblenz, and the northern German ports, while the Americans had Bavaria, the Saar, and the Rhineland south of Koblenz. The USSR occupied the rest of Germany with the exception of Berlin, which was to be held on a tripartite basis. At President Roosevelt's insistence, the United States received control of the ports of Bremen and Bremerhaven and the necessary staging areas in their immediate vicinity. U.S. forces were also to have access to the western and northwestern seaports and passage through the British-controlled area.[38] Final ratifications by the governments were not completed until 6 February 1945, by which time U.S. and British forces were already carrying out military occupation functions in western Germany. Approximately a week later, at the conclusion of the Yalta Conference, the Allies announced that France would be invited to take a zone of occupation, and that its boundaries would be worked out by the four powers through their members on the European Advisory Commission.[39]

Postsurrender Preparations

While discussions were in progress on zones of occupation, SHAEF turned its attention to the preparation of handbooks and directives for postsurrender military government of Germany. The British had already taken independent action in April and May 1944 by establishing the British Control Commission Military Section under General West to provide and train the cadres of various British missions for posthostilities work.[40] General Eisenhower and his staff in June 1944 recommended that the United States take similar action, and in August the U.S. Chiefs of Staff formally established the U.S. Group Control Council (Germany) to act in close liaison with similar British and Soviet groups. Brig. Gen. Cornelius W. Wickersham, representative of SHAEF at European Advisory Commission meetings, was selected as acting deputy to the chief U.S. representative on the Control Council and placed in charge of organizing the U.S. group.[41]

General Eisenhower announced in late August that during the presurrender period the U.S. control group would be re-

[38] CCS 172d Mtg, 12 Sep 44; CCS 176th Mtg, 16 Sep 44. Both in OCTAGON Conf Min.

[39] See below, pp. 464–65.

[40] SHAEF G–4 Weekly Rpt 1, Administrative Planning for Post-Hostilities Period, 3 Aug 44, SHAEF G–3 312.1–2 Post Hostilities Planning, Bundle O.

[41] Mtg, SHAEF G–5, 13 Jun 44; Memo by SAC, 19 Jun 44; Smith to JCS, 20 Jun 44. All in SHAEF G–5 803 Internal Affairs Branch, Military Govt in Germany, Gen Corres, Jacket 2. ETOUSA GO 80, 9 Aug 44; Rpt, U.S. Group Control Council, 1–15 Sep 44, G–5 hist file 17.05 German Country Unit and U.S. Control Council.

sponsible to him as U.S. theater commander, and the British group would be responsible to the British Government. In the initial stage after surrender, the British and U.S. control groups were to function together under the Supreme Commander—but not under SHAEF. The agreed policy of Great Britain, the United States, and the USSR was to be passed on to the Supreme Commander through the Combined Chiefs of Staff. General Eisenhower was to use the Control Commission/Council as his normal channel of communication to the German central authority. The SHAEF G–3 was to coordinate posthostilities planning.[42]

The British in early September proposed instead that General Eisenhower use the Control Commission/Council in framing occupation policy, referring any disagreements to the Combined Civil Affairs Committee (London). The Supreme Commander indicated his willingness to have the U.S. and British control agencies represent their separate governments but preferred that they appeal disagreements to the Combined Chiefs of Staff. Pending decisions by the Combined Chiefs, he added, the Supreme Commander's decision "must be binding." He reaffirmed his intention of establishing the nucleus Control Commission/Council in Berlin as soon as conditions permitted and of using it in his communications with the central German authority. He insisted, however, that no such authority could be given the Anglo-American group until stability and adequate communications had been established in Berlin.[43]

General Eisenhower defined his policy even more firmly in a memorandum to his army group commanders on 15 November 1944. He declared that, during the period between the surrender of Germany and the termination of combined command, he would retain ultimate responsibility in its widest sense for control of the German forces, military government, and disbandment and disarmament. To prevent any divergence of policy in the U.S. and British spheres of occupation, no agreements on policy were to be made between army groups and their respective control commissions without SHAEF's concurrence.[44]

The question of French participation in combined control groups for Germany arose in September when General de Gaulle indicated that he wanted French troops to take part in operations in Germany. The Combined Chiefs of Staff agreed to General Eisenhower's proposal that during the period of combined command the German occupation should be on a strictly Allied basis and that U.S., British, and French forces should be employed in accordance with military requirements and without regard to political factors. In November, the Combined Chiefs of Staff suggested that until Germany was defeated the participation of the French should be limited to forming part of the U.S. and British military government teams. Such a suggestion, Eisenhower warned, would lead to violent reactions on the part of the French. He pointed to plans then under way for conducting a French military government school under SHAEF supervision, and suggested that he be permitted to use French military government teams in

---

[42] SHAEF Stf Memo 104, 23 Aug 44, SHAEF G–5 803 Internal Affairs Branch, Military Govt in Germany, Gen Corres, Jacket 2.

[43] SHAEF to CCS, FWD 13854, 5 Sep 44, CCAC 014 Germany (11–15–43), Sec 2.

[44] Eisenhower to A Gp comdrs, 15 Nov 44, SHAEF G–5 803/3 Internal Affairs Branch, Military Govt in Germany, Relationship With Control Commission/Council.

those areas occupied by the French. Apparently this permission was granted, for the French military government school was subsequently opened and its first teams were placed under 6th Army Group in mid-March 1945.[45]

Policy and Directives for Occupation of Germany

By the time the Allied armies were established in the Normandy beachhead, various British and U.S. agencies were drawing up handbooks, manuals, and directives for the occupation of Germany. By June, the German country unit of SHAEF had prepared the first draft of a Handbook for Military Government in Germany, the British Control Commission Military Section had started a manual on disarmament, SHAEF G–1 was preparing a Handbook for Unit Commanders (Germany), and SHAEF G–5 was drafting a directive to guide army group commanders when they entered enemy territory. Early drafts of many of these texts were circulated in Supreme Headquarters and occasionally sent to service ministries in London and to interested branches of the State, Treasury, and War Departments in Washington. By late June, General Hilldring, War Department director of civil affairs, had seen SHAEF papers dealing with preparations for the presurrender and posthostilities periods and had reminded General Smith that the European Advisory Commission was charged with formulating recommendations for the German surrender and for the control and occupation of Germany after its defeat or surrender. He added that no agreements had yet been made as to the duration of military government in Germany or the type of organization to be established after the cessation of military government.[46] In the absence of any specific directive or guidance, the SHAEF agencies and divisions continued to make plans, and in August had drafts of a handbook and directives to army group commanders for the initial stages of military occupation ready for distribution.

On 17 August, General Eisenhower warned the War Department that the Allied forces might begin their occupation of Germany sooner than had been expected. Less than a week later, after the Falaise Gap was closed and shortly before Paris fell, he called for guidance on Germany. Plans for occupation of the Reich, he said in a cable to the Combined Chiefs on 23 August, were being based on the presurrender directive, but the directive rested on the assumption that the Allies would have to fight their way into Germany and that they would have behind their lines enemy territory in which the military forces would have to re-establish law and order and be responsible for the economic well-being of the people. It also assumed that ultimately there would be a mass surrender of the German Army, and that some central authority would be left. Now, however, it appeared that no single surrender would take place and the Allied

---

[45] Eisenhower's msg and CCS reply appended to CCAC 140/2, 10 Oct 44, CCAC 014 Germany (11–15–43), Sec 3. CCS to Eisenhower, WX 58337 (FACS 106), 6 Nov 44; Eisenhower to CCS, S–66513 (SCAF 129), 12 Nov 44. Both in SHAEF G–5 803 Military Govt in Germany, General Correspondence, Jacket 1. For French military government units and schools, see SHAEF Mission (France) AG 091.711–1(Fr), through 30 September 1944.

[46] Planning for the Occupation of Germany, OCMH files; Hilldring to Smith, 1 Jul 44, CAD 014 Germany (7–10–42), Sec 7. Among the SHAEF papers that Hilldring had seen were SHAEF/21540/1/Ops, sub: PS SHAEF (44) 10—Primary Disarmament of the German Forces, and SHAEF/21542/Ops, sub: PS SHAEF (44) 9—Preparation for the Surrender and Post-Hostilities Middle Period, 29 Apr 44.

forces might find a chaotic Germany in which guerrilla warfare and civil war could be expected. In such a case it would be impossible to control or save the economic structure of the country. If this were true, the Supreme Commander, added, he felt that he could not take responsibility for the control and support of the German economic structure.[47]

The Civil Affairs Division of the War Department had anticipated General Eisenhower's earlier warning of 17 August by suggesting that the Combined Civil Affairs Committee draft a statement of general policies for SHAEF's guidance if the German surrender came before a detailed postsurrender directive could be issued.[48] On 23 August, representatives of the British Chiefs of Staff in Washington, recognizing the complications which had arisen from the fact that the European Advisory Commission had reached no agreement on a great number of directives, urged the Combined Chiefs of Staff to give the Supreme Commander guidance relative to the military government of Germany in the early stages of the postsurrender period. Fearing that the handbook and directives under preparation by SHAEF might conflict with Allied policies, they asked that General Eisenhower's instructions to his army groups coincide with British and U.S. postwar plans. They also requested that the Supreme Commander be instructed as to his proper relationship with the U.S. and British elements of the Group Control Council and Control Commission, suggesting that these agencies be directed to aid SHAEF in military government and in case of disagreement to submit their differences to the Combined Civil Affairs Committee (London) rather than to the main committee in Washington.[49] The Combined Chiefs of Staff now

proposed that General Eisenhower be told to continue his planning along the lines indicated in his cable of 23 August and noted that appropriate directives would be issued him in due course.[50]

Before any final arrangements could be made, President Roosevelt intervened decisively. Draft copies of the Handbook for Military Government in Germany had been submitted for comment to the Foreign Office, the Civil Affairs Division, and other government agencies. One copy had found its way to the President, apparently through the Treasury Department. Mr. Roosevelt, in a strong memorandum to Secretary Stimson on 26 August, described the handbook as "pretty bad" and directed that it be withdrawn if it had not been sent out. The handbook displeased the President because of its emphasis on seeing that the governmental machinery of Germany ran efficiently and on retaining the highly centralized German administrative system unless higher authority directed otherwise. He disliked the statements that military government officers would see to it that needed commodities and stores were imported, industrial plants converted from war to consumer goods production, essential economic activities subsidized where necessary, and German foreign trade reconstructed with priority for the needs of

---

[47] SHAEF to WD, FWD 12936, 17 Aug 44, CCAC Germany (11–15–43), Sec 2; Eisenhower to CCS, FWD 13128 (SCAF 68), 23 Aug 44, SHAEF G–5 803 Internal Affairs Branch, Military Govt in Germany, General Correspondence, Jacket 2.

[48] Memo by Dir CAD, CCAC 119, 15 Aug 44, CCAC 014 Germany (11–15–43), Sec 2.

[49] Memo by Br COS representative, CCS 658, 23 Aug 44, CCAC 014 Germany (11–15–43), Sec 2. The proposed directive appears in the CCAC files as CCAC 119/1, 24 Aug 44.

[50] Memo, CCS for CAD, 24 Aug 44, CCAC 014 Germany (11–15–43), Sec 2.

the United Nations. President Roosevelt expressed displeasure because so many Americans and Englishmen held that the people of Germany were not responsible for the war, a view he insisted was not based on fact. "The German people as a whole must have it driven home to them," he declared, "that the whole nation has been engaged in a lawless conspiracy against the decencies of modern civilization." If they needed food beyond what they had, to keep body and soul together, they should be fed with soup from Army kitchens, but he was unwilling to start a Works Progress Administration, a Civilian Conservation Corps, or a Public Works Administration for Germany when the Army of Occupation entered on its duties.[51]

This memorandum got immediate results. The War Department directed SHAEF to suspend its handbooks on Germany and its directives to army group commanders, since they were strenuously objected to on the highest United States level and were in many respects inconsistent with the presurrender directives. There were British objections as well, the War Department indicated. General Smith called attention to the difficult position in which this order left Supreme Headquarters and added that SHAEF could not do business on an informal basis in matters of such importance. He asked that instructions to suspend the handbook and directives be issued by the Combined Chiefs of Staff. This request had already been anticipated and instructions were on the way by the time General Smith's cable was received.[52]

The Combined Civil Affairs Committee, in view of the likelihood that Allied troops would shortly be in Germany and the possibility that Germany would soon

collapse, was stirred to action. It decided to inform the Supreme Commander that, if Germany surrendered before he received a directive to guide him in that contingency, he might carry on military government under the existing presurrender directive. This action was suspended, however, when the Supreme Commander requested permission to comment on the new instructions before they were issued.[53] Later in the same day, the Combined Civil Affairs Committee notified General Eisenhower that he might issue presurrender interim directives based on directives of the Combined Chiefs of Staff. It instructed him, however, to block out of the handbook all directives that assumed a policy of general economic or administrative rehabilitation. As for posthostilities guidance, the committee informed him that a directive to meet the needs of that period was then under consideration.[54]

SHAEF sent final drafts of its German directive and handbook to Washington, pointing out that they had been prepared in accordance with the presurrender directives but modified to meet the possibility that there would be chaos in Germany when the Allied armies arrived. SHAEF officials added that they had neither the

---

[51] Memo, President for Secy War, 26 Aug 44, CAD 014 Germany (7–10–42), Sec 8.

[52] Telephone conversation, Hilldring, Marcus, and Boettiger with Sherman, 28 Aug 44; Smith to Hilldring, FWD 13405, 30 Aug 44; Hilldring to Holmes, 30 Aug 44; WD to SHAEF, WAR 89024 (GOV 100), 29 Aug 44. All in CCAC 014 Germany (11–15–43), Sec 2. Hilldring to Smith, W–89253, 31 Aug 44, SHAEF AG 014.1–1 Germany, Military Govt. The War Department message of 29 August 1944, 90024 (GOV 100), was received on 31 August.

[53] Notes on mtg in Mr. McCloy's office, 29 Aug 44; SHAEF to WD, FWD 13496 (SCAF 70), 1 Sep 44; CCS to SHAEF, WAR 24564 (GOV 103), 2 Sep 44. All in CCAC 014 Germany (11–15–43), Sec 2.

[54] CCAC to Eisenhower, WAR 24569 (GOV 102), 1 Sep 44, CCAC 014 Germany (11–15–43), Sec 2.

facilities nor the time to block out of the handbook passages relating to general economic provisions and rehabilitation, and suggested they be permitted to issue the handbook and directive with covering notes stating categorically that the commanders were not to apply the offending provisions.[55]

The Supreme Commander issued his interim directive to 21 and 12th Army Groups on 10 September 1944, delegating to Field Marshal Montgomery and General Bradley responsibility for executing his policy in their zones. As soon as they occupied any part of Germany, they were to establish military government. SHAEF was to set policy for the distribution of relief and rehabilitation supplies to Allied displaced persons in Germany and for the distribution of supplies, approved by the Combined Chiefs of Staff, to the civil population of Germany. On request of the army group commanders, SHAEF was to furnish military government staffs, detachments, and experts. The army group commanders were empowered in their areas to enforce the terms of surrender and to take necessary steps to maintain order and wipe out the traces of Nazism.[56]

Meanwhile, SHAEF's draft handbook and proclamations were undergoing careful scrutiny in Washington. The U.S. members of the Combined Civil Affairs Committee felt that the handbook should be rewritten to insure that (1) no steps beyond those necessary for military purposes should be taken for the economic rehabilitation of Germany; (2) no relief supplies except the minimum necessary to prevent disease and disorder that might interfere with military operations should be imported or distributed; and (3) no Nazi, Nazi sympathizer, nor Nazi organization should be continued in office for purposes

of convenience or expediency. The Supreme Commander's proposed proclamation to the German people was to be changed so as to carry no implication that Germany was to be treated as a liberated country. The Supreme Commander was informed that, if he could not hold up distribution of the handbook until changes could be made, he should issue it with a covering note to the effect that it would not be used during the postsurrender period of military government. Apparently without waiting for any further order, the SHAEF G–5 on 15 September directed the army group commanders to insert a fly leaf in all copies of the interim directive and handbook for military government stating that the three basic principles mentioned above were to be applied and adding that the directive would apply only to the presurrender period.[57]

SHAEF's proposed proclamation to the Germans on military government was reviewed next in Washington. The first paragraph led to considerable discussion. After some examination to make certain that the German word for "conquerors" did not give the impression that the Allies were "looters," British and U.S. officials examined the statement that the Nazi rule would be overthrown "as in other countries liberated from the horrors of Nazi tyranny." This seemed to the Combined Chiefs of Staff to leave the impression that Germany was to be treated as a liberated country. After exchanging cables with

[55] SHAEF to CCS, FWD 13851 (SCAF 73), 5 Sep 44, CCAC 014 Germany (11–15–43), Sec 2.

[56] SHAEF Interim Directive for Military Government of Germany, 10 Sep 44, SHAEF AG 014.1–1 Germany, Military Govt.

[57] Hilldring to Holmes, W–29982, 13 Sep 44; SHAEF G–5 to A Gp comdrs and COMZ, FWD 14955, 15 Sep 44. Both in SHAEF AG 014.1–1 Germany, Military Govt.

Washington over a period of approximately two weeks, and after reprinting the proclamation three times to incorporate changes, SHAEF released it to the press on 28 September. The key paragraph now read:

The Allied Forces serving under my Command have now entered Germany. We come as conquerors, but not as oppressors. In the area of Germany occupied by the forces under my Command, we shall obliterate Nazism and German militarism. We shall overthrow the Nazi rule, dissolve the Nazi Party and abolish the cruel and oppressive and discriminatory laws and institutions which the party has created. We shall eradicate that German militarism which has so often disrupted the peace of the world. Military and party leaders, the Gestapo and others suspected of crimes and atrocities, will be tried, and if guilty, punished as they deserve.[58]

The proclamation permitted no doubt on the part of the Germans that Allies intended to annihilate the Hitlerian system. Although the softening phrases of the original draft had been stricken from the document, the omission of unconditional surrender from the statement permitted the Germans some hope as to the effects of the occupation.

Another question raised by the Supreme Commander concerning his occupation policy was also dealt with in September. It will be recalled that in August General Eisenhower had expressed the fear that he would be unable to support the German economic system and had asked to be relieved of his responsibility in that connection. The War Department was inclined to accept his recommendation, but the British representatives in Washington were unable to agree that collapse of the whole economic structure was inevitable. They urged that the Supreme Commander do his best to carry out the

policy prescribed in the presurrender directive. In order to deal with the impasse, General Hilldring, in a message which he also sent to the British, suggested that General Eisenhower recall his original request and note that he felt the contingencies he had discussed could be adequately handled under the provisions of his presurrender directive. General Hilldring suggested that the cable be so worded that it would not require an answer. SHAEF promptly complied, thereby disposing neatly of at least one topic of transatlantic correspondence.[59]

The SHAEF staff was gratified to hear in September that the Combined Civil Affairs Committee was examining the text of a posthostilities directive. Unfortunately, SHAEF had to wait until the end of the fighting for specific instructions. The delays were based in particular on the inability of the British and the U.S. Chiefs of Staff to agree on the type of document which should be issued. The British representatives in the Combined Civil Affairs Committee believed, for example, that General Eisenhower could get along for some time after the defeat of Germany on the basis of his presurrender directive. Even when drafts were submitted to the committee, considerable divergence developed among the various representatives as to what should be included. It is not surprising to find, therefore, that not until late in April 1945 was a posthostilities directive approved. This had not reached SHAEF on the day the armistice was signed at

---

[58] SHAEF Fwd to CCS and CCAC, VOG 134, 28 Sep 44, and other correspondence and cables of 15–28 September, SHAEF AG 014.1–1 Germany, Military Govt.

[59] Hilldring to Holmes, WAR 31224, 15 Sep 44; SHAEF to WD, SCAF 88, 18 Sep 44, CCAC 014 Germany (11–15–43), Sec 3.

Reims. General Eisenhower reminded the Combined Chiefs of Staff at that time that he was still operating under directives limited in application to the presurrender period. He considered the issuance of a new directive unnecessary, however, since policies developed under the postsurrender drafts did not differ markedly from those set down in the presurrender documents. In the absence of a new directive, he proposed to continue his current policies and directives until the termination of the combined command. On 11 May 1945, President Harry S. Truman approved the directives of the U.S. Chiefs of Staff for General Eisenhower as commander in chief of the United States Forces of Occupation regarding the military government of Germany. This document, which was to guide General Eisenhower in his activities as U.S. commander after the dissolution of SHAEF, was dispatched on 15 May 1945.[60]

[60] SHAEF to WD, FWD 16012, 27 Sep 44, CAD 014 Germany (7–10–42), Sec 9; CCAC 45th Mtg, 12 Oct 44, CCAC 014 Germany (11–15–43), Sec 3; SHAEF to WD, SCAF 362, 7 May 45; IPCOG 1/4, 11 May 45; Note by Secretaries on Directive to CinC, U.S. Forces of Occupation, Regarding the Military Government of Germany, 26 Apr 45; JCS to Eisenhower, WAR 83249, 16 May 45. All in CCAC 014 Germany (11–15–43), Sec 8.

CHAPTER XX

The Winter Counteroffensives

The German Plan

While the Allies were pressing their offensive toward the Rhine in the fall of 1944, Hitler was planning an attack in the Ardennes region to roll up and destroy Allied forces north of the line Antwerp–Brussels–Bastogne. Conceived by the Fuehrer at the beginning or middle of September, the counteroffensive was intended as a crippling blow to slow or stop the Allied advance.[1]

The first weeks of September saw few developments that would justify German hopes for success. The enemy made an attempt to roll back the southern flank of 12th Army Group and the month ended without his regaining the initiative in that area. Elsewhere, Hitler's generals had managed to improvise defenses that interfered with Allied plans for a quick breakthrough to the Rhine. Despite this success, Field Marshal von Rundstedt, who had returned as Commander in Chief West at the beginning of September, was not optimistic. In a report written after the war, he recalled that in his contemporary estimate of the situation he predicted that the main Allied thrust would skirt Aachen and aim at northern Germany and Berlin. He believed that most of the U.S. forces, once they approached the German border, would wheel in a northeasterly direction, advance across the line Trier–Aachen in the direction of the Cologne–Ruhr area,

and then proceed toward northern Germany. In this case, southern Germany would fall automatically even if attacked only by minor forces.[2]

Hitler was much more hopeful. On 13 September 1944, he ordered the *Sixth Panzer Army* constituted with the idea of using it in a counteroffensive against the Allies.[3] During the next ten days, he ordered two panzer corps disengaged from battle and transferred to the new army. About the same time, he outlined his proposals to Jodl, asking for plans to implement his general scheme. Jodl presented

---

[1] Considerable confusion exists as to the sense in which the terms *counterattack* and *counteroffensive* were used during this period. Although there are instances where no clear line of demarcation can be drawn, the term *counterattack* properly applies to a tactical situation in which a defending force reacts to an enemy attack with an offensive action pursuing limited objectives. It is carried out mostly by local reserves and is limited in scope and duration. The term *counteroffensive* belongs rather to the realm of strategy. It denotes an operation mounted on a large scale, often involving commitment of strategic reserves, and capable of affecting the further development of the whole campaign. The primary aim of a counteroffensive is complete reversal of the situation created by the attacker and seizure of the initiative from the enemy.

[2] Field Marshal von Rundstedt's undated "Critique" which precedes MS # 1–121 (Zimmermann *et al.*). The author is indebted for the greater part of the information in this chapter relating to German plans and operations to Mrs. Magna E. Bauer of the Office of the Chief of Military History who not only did the basic research in the German documents but carefully checked the completed narrative for errors.

[3] The primary mission of the *Sixth Panzer Army* was to supervise the rehabilitation of the armored divi-

his draft on 11 October; it was formally described to von Rundstedt and Model on 1 November. While the Commander in Chief West may have received some hint of these preparations before that time, it is clear that he was not the originator of the "Rundstedt counter-offensive." [4]

The plan called for *Army Group B* to attack with twenty-nine or thirty divisions [5] in the area of the Ardennes with the objective of destroying Allied forces north of the line Antwerp–Brussels–Bastogne and thereby bringing about a decisive change in the over-all situation. These efforts were to be co-ordinated with those of *Army Group H,* [6] which was located north of *Army Group B. Army Groups G* and *Oberrhein,* south of *Army Group B,* were ordered to tie up Allied forces. The initial break-through was to be aided by Operation *GREIF,* in which German officers and men dressed in U.S. uniforms and driving U.S. vehicles were to spread confusion by issuing false orders and by seizing bridges and key points. They were to be aided by some 800 parachutists who were to be dropped in the Malmédy area. [7]

Although Hitler's advisers were less hopeful than he about the prospects of the counteroffensive, they agreed it should be attempted. Keitel and Jodl declared after the war that, while the counteroffensive involved some risks, it was necessary to make an effort in late 1944 to check the threat of an Allied break-through from Aachen toward Cologne. Von Rundstedt and Model believed that, if surprise could be achieved and the attacking forces supplied, there was a chance for its success. Both doubted that the forces available were strong enough for the operation. For this reason Model, who was to command *Army Group B* in the attack, proposed and von Rundstedt approved a "little solution" involving a pincer movement around Aachen to cut off the Allied forces in that area. Model continued to urge it as late as 10–11 December, but Hitler rejected it. Despite the doubts of von Rundstedt and the commanders of the units involved, they thought that the Ardennes area was suitable for attack. They believed the attempt worth making, although they doubted whether more than half the distance proposed could be covered with the resources available. If the first half of the counteroffensive succeeded, they could then decide whether the rest of the plan was feasible. [8]

---

[4] MS # A–862, The Preparations for the German Offensive in the Ardennes, September–16 December 1944 (Schramm). A full account of the enemy preparations will be given in the chief study on the counteroffensive—Hugh M. Cole, The Ardennes, now in preparation for the UNITED STATES ARMY IN WORLD WAR II series.

[5] Elements of twenty-eight divisions were actually used.

[6] In October 1944 it was decided to organize a new army group headquarters, so as to relieve *Army Group B* of a part of its load. On 29 October *Army Group Student* assumed command of *Fifteenth Army, Armed Forces Commander Netherlands,* and *First Parachute Army. Army Group Student* was renamed *Army Group H* on 11 November, with Student as army group commander.

[7] See Enclosure No. 2 to letter from Jodl to the chief of staff of *OB WEST,* Generalleutnant Siegfried Westphal, entitled *Grundgedanken der Operation "Wacht am Rhein",* 1 Nov 44. *OB WEST, KTB Anlage 50 1. VII.-31.XII.44;* MS # A–862 (Schramm). On 26 November 1944 Reichsfuehrer SS Heinrich Himmler was designated *Oberbefehlshaber Oberrhein* and was ordered to take command of all Army, Air Force, and SS elements on the east bank of the Rhine between Bien Wald and the Swiss border.

[8] MS # A–862.

---

sions, both SS and Army, which were earmarked for the Ardennes counteroffensive. In view of the mixed composition of its staff the *Sixth Panzer Army* was sometimes referred to as the *Sixth SS Panzer Army.* Allied intelligence officers usually identified it as such. However, in nearly all official references to it as late as April 1945 by the OKH and the army groups under which it served, it is designated as *Sixth Panzer Army.*

To hide their intentions the Germans worked out elaborate deception plans. All preparations were to be made under the guise of a counterattack against the Allied drive toward the Rhine. Only a small number of high-ranking officers were permitted to know the details of the plan, and the defensive nature of the preparations was stressed. All movements of German forces assigned for the counteroffensive were arranged to fit into the deception plan. The newly activated *Sixth Panzer Army* was not to be brought into the line until the eve of the attack, and all of its movements to the front were to be made by night. Both the *Fifth* and *Sixth Panzer Armies* were given fake names, and other units were shifted or renamed in order to confuse the Allies. To make certain that no slip-ups would occur, some of the units earmarked for the attack were left off situation maps at even the highest headquarters.[9]

The deception plans were to play an important part in the surprise gained by the enemy. In this effort the Germans were aided not only by the plausibility of their story but also by the fact that the Allies, now that they were on German soil, no longer had the excellent local information and certain other types of intelligence that had been available in France and Belgium.

Allied Estimate of Enemy Intentions

In their December preparations to launch a drive toward the Rhine, the Allies had concentrated forces north and south of the Ardennes, leaving that area thinly held by one corps over a seventy-mile front. As troops were sent from the Ardennes to the north, General Eisenhower had pointed out that they were getting stretched and there was a danger

of a "nasty little Kasserine," but he did not change his dispositions. General Bradley believed that he could afford to take a risk in the area in order to mount a strong attack against the enemy. In making these decisions, the commanders were taking a type of calculated risk common in all battles or campaigns where a given force lacks sufficient troops to concentrate at the point of main attack and still hold strongly elsewhere. The decision to concentrate north and south of the Ardennes was made because those areas provided the best routes of advance into Germany, but there were also adequate grounds for choosing the Ardennes as the area to be weakly held. Although the enemy had come through the Ardennes in 1870 and again in 1940, the terrain was not suited for mobile warfare, particularly in the winter months when bad weather was likely to make the poor road net even less valuable than usual.

While the Germans prepared the Ardennes counteroffensive, the Allies made use of normal intelligence sources such as air reconnaissance, captured documents, prisoner interrogation, and patrol reports. They also had some information from OSS agents, but this varied from army to army.[10] From the sources available, the Allied intelligence sections predicted rather accurately that the enemy lacked the means of preventing the Allies from

---

[9] See Order, OKW to *OB WEST*, signed by Jodl, 5 Nov 44. *OB WEST, KTB Anlage 50 1.VII.-31.XII.44;* MS # A–862 (Schramm); MS # A–896, *OB WEST—34 Questions, 1 Sep–8 May 45 (Westphal).*

[10] The Ninth and Third Armies had OSS detachments, but all except a small section of the one at First Army had been withdrawn on the recommendation of that headquarters when the 12th Army Group became operational. Thereafter the OSS detachments formerly at First Army operated from army group level. 12th A Gp Rpt of Opns, III, 136–37; Interv with Col B. A. Dickson, 6 Feb 52.

reaching the heart of Germany and destroying her military might, and that the enemy would make his major stand west of the Rhine. They were also able to locate most of the enemy units and to plot their general movements.

The various intelligence sections published these estimates in weekly and, at some levels, daily summaries. Because there was a time lag between the reception of information and its publication and because some information was too highly classified to be circulated, the published estimates were supplemented by daily reports at conferences of the commanders and their staffs and by personal reports to the commanders. Few, if any, records were kept of these meetings, and it is necessary to depend heavily upon the printed estimates for the views of the intelligence chiefs. With certain qualifications, however, it is safe to make use of these sources. Inasmuch as no major change was made in the general conclusions about enemy capabilities in the estimates of October and November, it may be assumed that these represent generally the thinking of the intelligence sections of that period.

For December, when the nature of the warnings becomes important, it is necessary to know what additional information was given. In the absence of a record of the oral briefings, one can do little more than apply a rule of thumb test: was the warning of such weight that the commander found it necessary to make any immediate changes in his tactical dispositions? This test must naturally be used with caution since the intelligence officer's warnings may have been ignored by his commander. It may normally be assumed, however, that no commander intentionally permits his forces to be overwhelmed. The problem of judging the nature of intelli-

gence warnings is an exceptionally thorny one, particularly when they are given orally and when they are later involved in controversy. The intelligence chief tends to give a number of alternative capabilities which the enemy may develop, and since he is obliged to emphasize the maximum effort the enemy may make he often hits on all the courses of action the enemy can possibly take. In such a case, he is able to claim later that he forecast the enemy's action accurately. The commander, accustomed to rather gloomy forecasts, has to have something more than an array of enemy capabilities if he is to continue battle at all. At this point he wants an intelligence officer to give him a precise statement as to the action the enemy seems most likely to take. The ideal intelligence report would be one which would say that a force of a specific number of divisions is likely to strike within a given period along a particular front to carry out a particular mission. The prospects are slim, however, that any intelligence officer, short of getting a copy of the operational orders from the enemy commander in chief, could make such a report. The most that any commander expects is an approximation of that type of information.

In the case of the Ardennes, some intelligence officers believed that they provided such warning to their superiors and that either the intelligence sections at higher echelons or the commanders themselves ignored it. With the reminder that the materials at hand are incomplete, that there were a number of important oral briefings which may have contradicted the information given in daily or weekly summaries, and that the chief commanders involved, Generals Eisenhower and Bradley, have assumed full responsibility for any errors of judgment made in the Ardennes, the question of what the intelligence reports said about enemy intentions and what the Allied commanders did about them can be explored.

As early as 1 October, the SHAEF G–2 reported that the *Seventh Army* was withdrawing armor from the line and that a panzer army would soon emerge to give *Army Group B* the same type of armored support which the *Fifth Panzer Army* gave *Army Group G*. As the enemy withdrawals continued later in the month, leaving the Ardennes dangerously short of troops, SHAEF concluded that a reshuffle of enemy forces was under way to strengthen *Army Group B* around Aachen. This view was seconded by the estimates of the army groups and armies in the north.[11]

SHAEF concluded near the end of October that the Germans would soon be able to collect a reserve of panzer and parachute units with which they could attack the Allies—probably in the north. The 12th Army Group predicted that if the enemy was left free until 1 December he would be able to build a powerful striking force, and named the area near Paderborn and Muenster as the possible site for training and organizing its armored elements. SHAEF added that Hitler was preparing this panzer force in Westphalia for action against the Allies in November. The principal doubt revolved around whether it would be used for a counterattack after the launching of an Allied offensive or for a spoiling attack. In the opinion of the 12th Army Group, the enemy's most serious capability was a counterattack with armored reserves against any Allied break-through toward the Rhine in the Ninth and First Army sectors. The 21 Army Group saw in German activities the possible forerunner of an attack which would act as an "emo-

tional counterblast to the memories of 11 November."[12]

By the end of the first week in November, a German deserter had reported that panzer units then re-forming in Westphalia were part of the *Sixth Panzer Army*. In releasing this statement, SHAEF also revealed that the *Fifth Panzer Army,* identified on SHAEF maps as having been in the line the preceding week, had not been heard of for some weeks.[13]

By mid-November there was evidence that activities in Westphalia were accompanied by enemy troop movements east of the area from the Ruhr to Luxembourg. Impressed by the "truly colossal effort" which the enemy had made in forming or re-creating at least five panzer and five parachute divisions during September and October, SHAEF concluded that the enemy's hand was dealt for "a final showdown before the winter." On the assump-

---

[11] SHAEF Weekly Intel Summaries 28–30, weeks ending 1, 8, and 15 Oct 44; 12th A Gp Weekly Intel Summary 9, week ending 7 Oct 44; 21 A Gp Intel Review 163, 8 Oct 44; FUSA G–2 Estimate 33, 17 Oct 44; TUSA G–2 Periodic Rpt 130, 19 Oct 44.

Much of this material comes from a detailed study made by Mr. Royce L. Thompson of OCMH of intelligence reports of 12th and 21 Army Groups, First, Third, and Ninth Armies, V and VIII Corps, and the seven divisions stationed in the area hit by the German counteroffensive. The study covered the period 1 September–16 December 1944. The author has carefully examined the weekly and periodic reports issued by SHAEF, the army groups, and armies for this period.

[12] SHAEF Weekly Intel Summaries 31–32, weeks ending 22, 29 Oct 44; 12th A Gp Weekly Intel Summaries 11–12, weeks ending 21, 28 Oct 44; 21 A Gp Intel Review 165, 30 Oct 44; FUSA G–2 Estimate 34, 31 Oct 44; TUSA G–2 Periodic Rpts 134, 137, 138, 139, and 141, for 23, 26, 27, 28, and 30 Oct 44; NUSA G–2 Periodic Rpt 52, 26 Oct 44.

[13] SHAEF Weekly Intel Summary 33, week ending 5 Nov 44; 12th A Gp Weekly Intel Summary 13, week ending 4 Nov 44; FUSA G–2 Periodic Rpt 149, 5 Nov 44; TUSA G–2 Periodic Rpt 149, 7 Nov 44; NUSA Periodic Rpt 65, 9 Nov 44; 21 A Gp Intel Review 166, 10 Nov 44.

tion that the enemy was organizing a reserve to repel an Allied offensive, SHAEF
decided it was logical for the Germans to
use their new panzer army against Allied
thrusts building up north of the Eifel (a
northeastern prolongation of the Ardennes).[14]

In general, the 12th Army Group
reached the same conclusions. The enemy
was deemed capable of reinforcing his
units west of Cologne with all available
armored reserves for (1) an attack on the
north flank of the Ninth Army or the
south flank of the VII Corps, or for (2) a
counterattack against any further eastward advance by the Allies toward
Cologne. The First Army G–2 was somewhat more positive in his view that the
enemy would stake everything on an offensive in the west. His estimate declared:

It is believed that this entire front has been
stiffened to hold against an Allied offensive
while he launches his blow in the north,
probably between Aachen and Venlo, with
the possible scheme of maneuver of a penetration to the west and southwest on both
banks of the Meuse. Although his immediate
stocks of fuel are probably ample, it may be
difficult for him to maintain a sustained
offensive.[15]

In these early summaries, the Allied intelligence chiefs clearly assumed that,
since the Germans knew of the Allied
intention to push toward the Ruhr, they
had built an armored force to cope with it.
Anxieties about the strength of a counterstroke were dispelled by the belief that bad
weather and fuel shortages would interfere with anything more serious than a
spoiling attack.[16] Instead of being alarmed
at the moment about any danger to the
thinned-out Ardennes region, General
Bradley, when told of the enemy concentrations, worried chiefly about the struggle
he expected between the Roer and the
Rhine. He told General Smith that he
would prefer a counterattack in November since the Allies could kill the Germans
more easily if they would come out of their
holes.[17]

The illusion that the Germans were preparing to meet an Allied attack toward
the Ruhr persisted through November.
Correctly, the intelligence sections identified the movement of panzer divisions on
their way from Westphalia to the Duesseldorf–Cologne area. By 20 November, they
agreed that the *Sixth Panzer Army* was west
of the Rhine prepared to defend the Roer
River line and prevent Allied thrusts to
the Rhine. Three of the *Fifth Panzer Army's*
five divisions were reported to be behind
the enemy front in the Aachen sector. This
report seemed to confirm the opinion that
here the Allies should find "Rundstedt's
only two panzer armies fighting side by
side to deny [them] the approaches to the
most vital sector of Germany—the Ruhr."
The First Army believed that the enemy
"lost a big advantage in not being able to
put in a spoiling attack prior to the commencement of the present Allied offensive." Before the Germans could go over
to the offensive, they would now have to
wait until a soft spot developed on the

---

[14] SHAEF Weekly Intel Summary 34, week ending 12 Nov 44.

[15] 12th A Gp Weekly Intel Summary 14, week
ending 11 Nov 44; FUSA G–2 Estimate 35, 12 Nov
44.

[16] The Allied error as to fuel shortages was caused
in part by a misreading of captured documents
which showed the enemy to be making drastic efforts
to conserve gasoline. These documents, as SHAEF
admitted later, were assumed to indicate an immediate critical shortage of fuel rather than an all-out
effort to build sufficient reserves for an attack. SHAEF
Weekly Intel Summaries 37 and 38, weeks ending 3
and 10 Dec 44. Some intelligence officers were later
inclined to blame what they called overoptimistic Air
Force estimates of the destruction of German oil
reserves.

[17] Bradley, *A Soldier's Story*, pp. 441–42.

Allied front or until an Allied attack was stopped as the result of heavy losses.[18]

In December, the Allied intelligence sections showed uneasiness as the enemy shuffled his divisions between the northern and southern parts of his front. They tended increasingly to predict that the enemy was planning an attack, perhaps before Christmas, but they never positively settled on the Ardennes as the place of attack. During the week ending 3 December, SHAEF spotted various tank movements from the Rhine toward Bitburg in the Eifel—opposite the Ardennes. Considerable activity was noted in this area, but the arrival of new units seemed to be balanced by the withdrawal of others. The 12th Army Group concluded that the enemy's policy was to use the newly arrived units in the Ardennes sector opposite the thinned-out VIII Corps sector in order to be able to shift the more experienced troops to more critical sectors. The First Army also announced the movement of troops to the Bitburg area but added, "During the past month there has been a definite pattern for the seasoning of newly-formed divisions in the comparatively quiet sector opposite VIII Corps prior to their dispatch to more active fronts." The VIII Corps, against which the enemy was to launch the full fury of his armored attack, paraphrased this view six days before the attack: "The enemy's present practice of bringing new divisions to this sector to receive front line experience and then relieving them out for commitment elsewhere indicates his desire to have this sector of the front remain quiet and inactive." In the last hours before the attack, the corps hinted at suspicious activity in the area, but its last periodic report before the attack, issued on 15 December, indicated that enemy capabilities showed no change.[19]

The SHAEF intelligence chief in the final weeks before the enemy counteroffensive became worried over enemy movements toward the Ardennes and the Strasbourg area and gave some warning to both General Eisenhower and General Bradley.[20] On 10 December, the Third

[18] SHAEF G–2 Intel Summary 35, week ending 19 Nov 44; 12th A Gp Intel Summary 15, 18 Nov 44; FUSA G–2 Periodic Rpt 163, 20 Nov 44; TUSA G–2 Periodic Rpt 158, 16 Nov 44 (reprints SHAEF Intel Summary 34 on enemy capabilities); NUSA G–2 Periodic Rpt 74, 18 Nov 44; FUSA G–2 Estimate 36, 20 Nov 44.

[19] SHAEF Weekly Intel Summary 37, week ending 3 Dec 44; Intel Rpt at 12th A Gp CGs briefing, 7 Dec 44; 12th A Gp G–3 Sec Rpt, Dec 44; FUSA G–2 Estimate 37, 10 Dec 44; VIII Corps G–2 Estimate 12, 9 Dec 44; VIII Corps Periodic Rpts 175–81, 9–15 Dec 44.

[20] General Strong, in a letter to the author, 31 August 1951, says: "At these meetings [chief of staff's morning conferences at SHAEF] daily for a period of at least a fortnight before the attack, I called attention to the possible three uses of the reforming Panzer Army (a) to go to Russia; (b) to counter attack an Allied penetration; (c) to stage a relieving attack through the Ardennes. . . . Course (c) so impressed General Smith that he asked if General Bradley was aware of this possibility. I replied in the affirmative but nevertheless General Smith instructed me to go to 12 AG and see General Bradley personally and warn him. This would be about the first week in December. I saw General Bradley personally for about ¾ hour and he told me he was aware of the danger but that he had earmarked certain divisions to move into the Ardennes area should the enemy attack there. . . ." General Smith in an interview with the author, 1 November 1951, declared: "General Strong . . . said the attack might come in the Ardennes or east of the Vosges whenever the Germans had a prediction of six days of bad weather. He didn't know which would be the real attack. As a consequence of this I sent him to see Bradley and Bradley said let them come. . . ." Lt. Col. Roy Lamson, SHAPE Historian, in a letter to the author, 26 September 1951, cites General Eisenhower as saying that "the possibility of a break through was certainly made known to him by General Strong." Eisenhower said he had discussed the situation in detail with General Bradley but had decided to keep moving rather than build up in defensive line. See also Eisenhower, *Crusade in Europe*, pp. 338–40. Cf. Bradley, *A Soldier's Story*, pp. 461–64.

Army became strongly impressed by the withdrawal of German elements from the line. This reserve, which included two panzer divisions, might enable the enemy "to mount a spoiling offensive in an effort to unhinge the Allied assault on *Festung Deutschland.*" By the 13th, the Third Army believed that the enemy was planning a counteroffensive in which the armor of the *Sixth Panzer Army* would be used in the area between Aachen and Dueren.[21]

Perhaps the most frequently quoted intelligence estimate of this period and the one commonly regarded as the most accurate was that issued by the First Army on 10 December. Some observers, who believe that this estimate and the later additions to it gave a sufficient basis for expecting the 16 December attack, have advanced various reasons why these warnings were unheeded. They cite the fact that relations between the First Army chief of staff and chief of operations, on the one hand, and the chief of intelligence, on the other, were not always as close as they should have been. Others state that some coolness or jealousy existed between the 12th Army Group and First Army G–2's. Still others say that the First Army G–2's predictions were sometimes discounted because he tended to identify units on the Western Front which were known to be elsewhere.[22] For present purposes it is sufficient to find whether or not the forecasts of an impending enemy attack were of such a nature as to cause the First Army commander and the commanders above him to order a change in the dispositions of the U.S. forces to meet an attack in the Ardennes.

The 10 December estimate began with a general summary of the current situation. It indicated that since the last report of 20 November 1944 the enemy had stub-bornly contested every foot of ground in the First Army zone. "He has defended," it continued, "with one Armd, one Para, one Pz Gren and eighteen Inf Divs. 116 Pz Div is now out of the line for repair, 3 Pz Gr is about due, ten Inf Divs have been consolidated into four for a net loss of six, one Inf Div was dissolved and a further Div, 3 Para, is badly mauled." The enemy was reported to be intensifying his defenses back of the line of the Roer and along the line of the Erft. "His armored reserve," the estimate added, "appears to be quartered in houses and barns along the railroads generally in a semi-circle from Duesseldorf to Koblenz, with Koeln [Cologne] as the center point." To the First Army G–2 it seemed plain that the enemy's "strategy in defense of the Reich is based on the exhaustion of our offensive to be followed by an all-out counterattack with armor, between the Roer and the Erft, supported by every weapon he can bring to bear."[23]

The First Army estimate mentioned some evidence of a build-up in the Bitburg–Wittlich area (an area from which

---

[21] TUSA G–2 Periodic Rpts 186–88, 14–16 Dec 44.

[22] The author has discussed this problem at some length with the G–2's of SHAEF, 12th Army Group, 21 Army Group, First Army, and with one or more staff members of each G–2 Division at these headquarters. While some effort was made by the principals to discount the effect of the personalities involved, there seems little doubt that some personality conflicts, and sometimes a tendency to question the validity of predictions, existed between the 12th Army Group and First Army G–2's. There was apparently a disposition at lower headquarters to feel that SHAEF's intelligence estimates were not always up to date. On the other hand, it is clear that G–2 staff members at the working levels frequently had close personal relationships which made up for any difficulties that existed between the chiefs of the sections. Therefore, it is easy to overestimate the influence of difficulties between the headquarters or within any headquarters.

[23] This and the succeeding paragraphs relating to the 10 December estimate are taken from FUSA G–2 Estimate 37, 10 Dec 44.

part of the counteroffensive was launched on 16 December), where *Panzer Division Grossdeutschland* and *Panzer Lehr Division,* or some of its elements, were reported to be. A captured order asking for German soldiers speaking "the American dialect" to report to Skorzeny's headquarters by 1 November for special training was taken as an indication that special operations for sabotage and attacks on Allied command posts and vital installations were in progress.[24] First Army intelligence officers were impressed by the fact that morale among freshly captured prisoners of war was unusually high and that they appeared eager to return to the battle for Germany. These and other factors made it apparent that

von Rundstedt, who obviously is conducting military operations without the benefit of intuition, has skilfully defended and husbanded his forces and is preparing for his part in the all-out application of every weapon at the focal point and the correct time to achieve defense of the Reich west of the Rhine by inflicting as great a defeat on the Allies as possible. Indications to date point to the location of the focal point as being between Roermond and Schleiden, and within this bracket the concentrated force will be applied to the Allied force judged by the German High Command to be the greatest threat to successful defense of the Reich.[25]

These conclusions hit accurately on many details of the enemy build-up. The signs, such as improved enemy morale and the organization of teams consisting of soldiers speaking American, all pointed toward increased enemy activity. At the same time, the First Army chief of intelligence was somewhat wide of the mark in several of his estimates. The bracketing of the focal point of attack between Roermond and Schleiden, which covered part of the Second British Army's front, all of the Ninth Army's front, and less than half of the First Army's front, was less precise than the information General Hodges needed if he was to make a major shift of his troops to the south. The southernmost line indicated by this prediction was slightly north of the Ardennes area where the counteroffensive took place. The placing of the armored reserve in the vicinity of Cologne, while fairly correct, made it possible that the front of attack would be considerably north of the Ardennes. Like his fellow intelligence chiefs, the First Army G–2 indicated that the enemy would send his concentrated forces against those Allied forces which most strongly

---

[24] SS Obersturmbannfuehrer Otto Skorzeny commanded a unit known as *Panzer Brigade 150,* which was to use U.S. Army uniforms and equipment to spread confusion behind the Allied lines.

[25] The Roermond–Schleiden concentration estimate was based, according to Col. B. A. Dickson, the First Army G–2, on air reconnaissance information which was tabulated by First Army on 8 December. A photograph of the map, marked "Study of Enemy Armd Reserves, 8 Dec 44," shows priority one, two, and three targets on these reserves. In the area above a line drawn Gemuend–Muenstereifel–Sinzig–the Rhine, an area somewhat to the north of that struck by the enemy on 16 December, there are twenty-six first-priority and three third-priority targets. In the area below that line—or one corresponding more closely to the Ardennes area—there were ten first-priority (four at the Rhine and one at Mayen), twelve second-priority, and two third-priority targets. According to these maps, therefore, the chief concentration of armored reserves was much nearer Cologne and Aachen than the area where the attack took place. First Army correctly identified on its front elements of fourteen divisions which ultimately attacked in the Ardennes. It located the *Sixth Panzer Army* in an area between Muenchen-Gladbach (on the Second British and Ninth Army front) in the north and Remagen–Blankenheim in the south. Colonel Dickson holds that the fact that 50 percent of the targets were south of Cologne showed that the attack could be expected in the Ardennes area. (Interv with Dickson, 6 Feb 52.) It could, of course, also show that an attack could be expected in the Aachen area, which is what prisoner-of-war rumors cited by First Army on 15 December indicated.

threatened Germany. These were definitely north of the Ardennes.

The First Army report came close to the truth with its identification of one armored division and elements of another in the Wittlich–Bitburg sector. Unfortunately for First Army's later claim of accurate prophecy, the estimate ended by destroying part of the effect of its warning. Speaking of German strategy, the First Army intelligence chief said:

The restoration of the West Wall is still a probable strategic objective. . . . The enemy has let his situation in both the upper Rhine and south of the Moselle deteriorate while still conserving reserves between Duesseldorf and Koeln. Von Rundstedt apparently is accepting defeats in the south rather than compromise his hope of a decisive success in the north. This would appear to be the keynote of his strategy in the defense of the Reich west of the Rhine. During the past month there has been a definite pattern for the seasoning of newly-formed divisions in the comparatively quiet sector opposite VIII Corps prior to their dispatch to more active fronts. The enemy is well aware of the tactical "ace" which he holds in the Roer River dams. Our recent attempts to breach the dam walls by air bombardment, as yet unsuccessful, have served to emphasize our own concern with the flooding of the Roer valley. The enemy has reacted by building up his forces on the route of approach to the Schwammenauel and the Urfttalsperre, the key dams in this system of barrages. Besides the divisions in the Sixth Panzer Army, the enemy has 2 Pz and 116 Pz Divs conditionally available for local counterattacks in the defense of the dams, in addition to at least two Volks-grenadier divisions which are available from the VIII Corps sector.

The importance of the Roer dams to both the Allies and the enemy seems to have outweighed other factors when the First Army intelligence chief drew his conclusions as to possible enemy capabilities. Four of these were listed. In the first, the enemy was considered capable of continuing his defense of the line of the Roer north of Dueren, his present lines west of the Roer covering the dams, and the West Wall to the south. Next, he was considered capable of "concentrated counterattack with air, armor, infantry and secret weapons at a selected focal point at a time of his own choosing." A third capability was defense of the line of the Erft and retirement east of the Rhine. Last, he was capable of collapse or surrender. The first of these conclusions, reflecting a static defense by the enemy plus a build-up in threatened areas like those near the Roer dams, was regarded as current. Number 3 was described as probable if enemy counterattacks proved unsuccessful, and number 4 was spoken of merely as a possibility. The important capability was number 2. Here, where the First Army intelligence chief had an opportunity to pin down the point of attack, he, like his fellow intelligence officers, failed to qualify as a completely accurate prophet. To his commander, who needed to know what changes in troop dispositions on First Army's front were required as a result of enemy activities, he reported:

. . . The exercise of capability 2a(2) [the capability referring to a counteroffensive] is to be expected when our major ground forces have crossed the Roer River, and if the dams are not controlled by us, maximum use will be made by the enemy of flooding of the Roer in conjunction with his counterattack.

As reasons for his conclusion, he added:

The enemy is apparently reconciled to the loss of Alsace and to defending behind the upper Rhine. He is now fighting in the Saarlautern area and along the Saar River in defensive action similar to that in the Aachen sector. There is no disposition to retire behind the Rhine except where he has been forced to do so, and this occurred in a sector where his West Wall is east of the Rhine. The continual building up of forces to the west of the Rhine points consistently to his staking all on the counteroffensive as stated in capability 2a(2).

Despite these intimations that something might happen before the end of the year, there were few indications that at those headquarters most involved—VIII Corps, First Army, 12th Army Group, and SHAEF—the counteroffensive of 16 December was expected by the commanders concerned.[26] It is necessary, in this connection, to determine what the various commanders and their staffs were doing to prepare against an attack in the last days before the counteroffensive.

At SHAEF, the Supreme Commander, although aware of the predictions of his chief of intelligence, was not sufficiently impressed by the imminent danger to the Ardennes area to stress its defense at the expense of other sectors. Instead his attention was turned on 14 December to the Colmar bridgehead sector. In order to eliminate this enemy salient, which was keeping eight Allied divisions busy, General Eisenhower authorized General Devers to suspend the operation then being prepared by the First French Army against enemy garrisons on the Atlantic coast of France (Operation INDEPENDENCE) and use the forces thus released against the Colmar bridgehead.[27] On the morning of 15 December, the SHAEF G–3 briefing officer, though presumably aware of the current intelligence estimates, said that there was nothing to report from the Ardennes sector.[28]

The 12th Army Group, which had shown some uneasiness earlier, declared on 12 December, "It is now certain that attrition is steadily sapping the strength of German forces on the western front and

that the crust of defenses is thinner, more brittle and more vulnerable than it appears on G–2 maps or to troops in the line."[29] At 21 Army Group, it was assumed that von Rundstedt, known to be a cautious commander, would not risk his panzer divisions forward of the Cologne–Bonn area until the Allied drive beyond the Roer had advanced to the point that Model's army group could not deal with it or until the position of the Allies was such that an abrupt counteroffensive would put an end to their prospects for the winter. There was certainly no sense of imminent attack at that headquarters: General de Guingand, the chief of staff, went to the United Kingdom on 15 December, and Field Marshal Montgomery asked General Eisenhower on the same day if he had any objection to his going to the United Kingdom the following week.[30]

---

[26] General Brereton in *The Brereton Diaries*, p. 387, says that his G–2 came closer than any other chief of intelligence to predicting the attack. Apparently in view of the fact that no airborne units were then in the line, the estimate went without notice.

[27] SHAEF to Devers, S–70750, 14 Dec 44; Gen Bull, Memo for CofS SHAEF, 14 Dec 44. Both in SHAEF SGS 381 Post OVERLORD Planning, II.

[28] Notes of conf, 15 Dec 44, in notes of Allied Air Commanders Conf, Nov 44–May 45, Air Staff (SHAEF) files 505.39–2, Air Hist Archives.

[29] 12th A Gp Summary 18, 12 Dec 44. Some 12th Army Group intelligence officers attribute the sweeping language of this report to the fact that they had just decided that they should make their reports more dramatic in order to get them read. They therefore got a former journalist, Maj. Ralph McA. Ingersoll, to put some color in the 12 December report. Its language was less guarded as a result. See also Ltr, Brig Gen Edwin L. Sibert to Williams, 11 Dec 44, 12th A Gp 371.3 Military Objectives, III, in which the 12th Army Group chief of intelligence speaks of the enemy's weak position. General Sibert in a statement to the author, 11 May 1951, said that while the letter bore his signature, it was drafted by someone else and merely reflected the current intelligence reports.

[30] 21 A Gp Intel Review 168, 3 Dec 44, Eisenhower personal file; de Guingand, *Operation Victory*, p. 425; Ltr, Montgomery to Eisenhower, 15 Dec 44, Eisen-

The First Army, which on 10 December spoke of a counterattack when the Allies had crossed the Roer, issued several supplementary reports before the 16th. Two days before the attack it reprinted VIII Corps' report of a German woman's statement that equipment and troops were being massed in the area of Bitburg. The presence of engineers with bridging equipment suggested to the First Army the possibility of offensive action. The First Army estimate declared on 15 December:

> Reinforcements for the West Wall between Dueren and Trier continue to arrive. The identification of at least three or four newly re-formed divisions along the Army front must be reckoned with during the next few days. Although the enemy is resorting to his attack propaganda to bolster morale of the troops, it is possible that a limited scale offensive will be launched for the purpose of achieving a Christmas morale "victory" for civilian consumption. Many PWs now speak of the coming attack between the 17th and 25th of December, while others relate promises of the "recapture of Aachen as a Christmas present for the Fuehrer."

VIII Corps reports that an abrupt change of routine of enemy personnel opposite 9th Armored Division strongly suggests that new troops may have arrived in that area. (Comment: Very likely a recently arrived Volks-grenadier Division coming in to relieve 212 Volksgrenadier Div.) [31]

In this report, the First Army had come close to an exact date for the counteroffensive although spoiling the accuracy of the prediction by mention of a "limited scale offensive" and the recapture of Aachen. Moreover, its comment on the VIII Corps suggestion that new troops had arrived in its area seemed to say only that routine relief was in progress. These conclusions may help to explain why, although 17 December was spoken of as a possible date for the attack, the First Army chief of intelligence was on leave in Paris, on the 16th, when the Germans attacked.[32]

There is little evidence that First Army's intelligence estimates brought any important changes in the dispositions of corps or divisions in First Army to meet a possible counteroffensive.[33] Rather than sending additional forces into the VIII Corps sector, where the brunt of the German counteroffensive fell, the First Army on 13 De-

hower personal file. Field Marshal Montgomery in his letter jokingly enclosed a statement for £5 for a bet made on 11 October 1943 in which General Eisenhower had wagered that the war would end before Christmas 1944. General Eisenhower on 16 December replied in the same jesting vein, "I still have nine days, and while it seems almost certain that you will have an extra five pounds for Christmas, you will not get it until that day." Eisenhower to Montgomery, 16 Dec 44, Eisenhower personal file. Bradley quotes Field Marshal Montgomery as saying in an estimate published at 21 Army Group on 16 December 1944: "The enemy is at present fighting a defensive campaign on all fronts; his situation is such that he cannot stage major offensive operations. . . ." General Bradley says that if he had been preparing an estimate on that day he would have said the same thing. Bradley, *A Soldier's Story*, p. 460.

[31] FUSA G–2 Periodic Rpt 189, 15 Dec 44.
[32] Colonel Dickson in an interview with the author on 6 February 1952, said he had already given all the warnings he could to the First Army commander, the chief of staff, and the chief of operations. He added that he had been without any leave since the Normandy operations and that when he was offered a short leave in Paris on the 15th he was so much in need of a rest that he decided to risk being away from his headquarters when the attack came. He was summoned to 12th Army Group headquarters the following day and returned to First Army by way of VIII Corps on the 17th.
[33] This statement was confirmed by General Hodges, in an interview with the author, 12 January 1950. His chief of intelligence, General Hodges said, had noted movements of the enemy into the Ardennes sector, but "all of us thought they were getting ready to hit us when we crossed the Roer." He added, "You know my intelligence chief was on leave when the attack came; he wouldn't have been if he had expected an attack." Colonel Dickson in his interview with the author on 6 February 1952 recalled, on the contrary, that General Hodges, after reading the 10 December prediction, asked General Bradley for two extra divisions and was refused.

cember took a combat command from the 9th Armored Division, the VIII Corps' reserve, and gave it to the V Corps, which was preparing to launch an attack. The V Corps made little use of the combat command, however, and the First Army listed it on 15 December among other units to be returned to parent organizations. No sense of urgency seems to have prompted this move, inasmuch as the combat command was not notified to move until the following morning, and it did not actually go into action until the morning of 17 December.[34] Lt. Gen. Troy H. Middleton, VIII Corps commander in December 1944, pointed out after the war that there could have been no great alarm about his weakened front, since he had been directed in December to simulate the movement of additional units into his area in order to draw enemy divisions to his front. He had carried out part of these activities early in the month and was told to resume the program later, but he was relieved of this responsibility when the Germans struck on 16 December.[35]

The army group commander most concerned, General Bradley, has written that nothing short of "an unequivocal indication of impending attack in the Ardennes could have induced me to quit the winter offensive," and that he received no such indication. He insists that, while the First Army's observations could have been interpreted to suggest the possibility of an enemy counteroffensive, they were not convincing enough to lead him to postpone his attack.

Nor [he adds] was my own G-2 at Army Group, Brigadier General Sibert, sufficiently impressed by these reports to come to me with a warning. By this time I commanded almost three quarters of a million men on a 230-mile front. It was impossible for me even

to scan the intelligence estimates of subordinate units. As a consequence, I looked to my own G-2 and to the Army commanders to keep me informed on the enemy's capabilities. Hodges neither spoke to Middleton, one of his own corps commanders, of any premonitions in the Ardennes, nor did he telephone me in advance of the offensive. Indeed no one came to me with a warning on the danger of a counterattack there.[36]

In analyzing the intelligence situation before the Ardennes counteroffensive, one may well ask what additional information the Allies would have needed to predict the 16 December attack. In many ways their information was highly accurate. Most of the units which made up the panzer armies had been spotted days and even weeks before the attack. Air reconnaissance, while hampered at times by bad weather, had marked the steady stream of men and supplies westward across the Rhine.[37] Despite the clever deceptive measures of the enemy, the Allied intelligence experts had correctly analyzed most of the German dispositions and, in the closing hours before the counteroffensive, were aware of shifts toward the Ardennes area and of the arrival of new units in the zone of VIII Corps. But with all this, they

---

[34] A detailed study of the movement of this combat command was made for the author by Mr. Royce Thompson of OCMH.

[35] Ltr, Gen Middleton to Theater Historian, 30 Jul 45. A file on this operation may be found in Combat Interview File 350, AG Records.

[36] Bradley, *A Soldier's Story*, pp. 461–64. Compare General Bradley's last statement above with General Strong's recollections, n. 20, above, and Bradley's statement to General Smith, p. 374, below. The question seems to have been one of the strength of General Strong's warning. This, indeed, seems to be the point at issue throughout. It is clear that nearly all the intelligence chiefs did feel that an attack in the Ardennes was possible, but the question is how clear and effective they made this warning in discussing the matter with commanders.

[37] Craven and Cate, *The Army Air Forces in World War II*, Vol. III, Ch. 19.

did not convince Generals Eisenhower, Bradley, Hodges, and Middleton, the commanders whose forces were to take the brunt of attack, that an attack by two panzer armies in the Ardennes area about the middle of December was imminent enough to force any change in existing Allied plans. The commanders were loath to move their troops about from point to point to meet every possible threat, since such action would disrupt all of their offensive plans and reduce their activities to the construction of countermoves against the enemy. Perhaps as important in their consideration as this element were several factors which lessened their fear of possible enemy attacks: (1) the Allied emphasis on offensive rather than defensive action; (2) the conclusion that the enemy was straining every nerve to stop the Allied attack against Cologne and the Ruhr and would be likely to attack when the Allies had crossed the Roer; (3) the erroneous belief that von Rundstedt, a reasonable and cautious man, was controlling strategy in the west; (4) the view that Germany's fuel shortage would make any enemy offensive unsuccessful; and (5) the conviction that any attack the enemy was capable of mounting would lead only to a quicker German defeat.

The Attack

The Germans hit the First Army front in the early morning of 16 December. The *Sixth Panzer Army* attacked south of Monschau with the mission of seizing the Meuse bridges between Liége and Huy. *(Map 5)* Its ultimate objective was the Albert Canal in the area between Maastricht and Antwerp. Farther south, the *Fifth Panzer Army* attacked in the direction of St. Vith and Bastogne. It was to sweep across

the Meuse between Andenne and Givet to the vicinity of Brussels and Antwerp, with the mission of forestalling Allied counterattacks in the rear of the *Sixth Panzer Army* anywhere between Antwerp and Givet. While the initial main thrusts were in progress, the *Seventh Army* protected the southern flank of the attacking forces. The *Fifteenth Army,* meanwhile, provided cover for the northern flank of the counteroffensive and launched a series of holding attacks to tie up U.S. forces in that area. According to German plans, it was also to seize the first opportunity to encircle and wipe out the Allied forces in the Aachen salient with a concentrated attack. *Army Group H,* between the attacking *Army Group B* and the North Sea, was ordered to prepare for a subsidiary attack to be made as soon as the development of the situation should permit. *Army Group G,* south of the attacking forces, was to repel any further advances of the Allies in that area. Both army groups, as well as *Army Group Oberrhein* were ordered to support the main attack by following up any retrograde movement of the Allies.[38]

The smashing blow against the First Army front drove back five U.S. divisions in the Ardennes area. The surprise gained by the attack and the disruption of communications rapidly created such widespread confusion along the front that the extent of the enemy action was not known for several hours at higher headquarters. More than four hours after the first assault, no report of it had been received at the 12th Army Group. At the 0915 briefing at General Bradley's headquarters, the repre-

---

[38] Operation order of *Army Group B*, 9 Dec 44. *OB WEST, KTB Anlage 50 1.VII.-31.XII.44; OB WEST, KTB 1.-31.XII.44,* 15 to 18 Dec 44; FUSA Rpt of Opns, 1 Aug 44-22 Feb 45, Vol. I. Cole, The Ardennes, will give the detailed operational story of the counteroffensive.

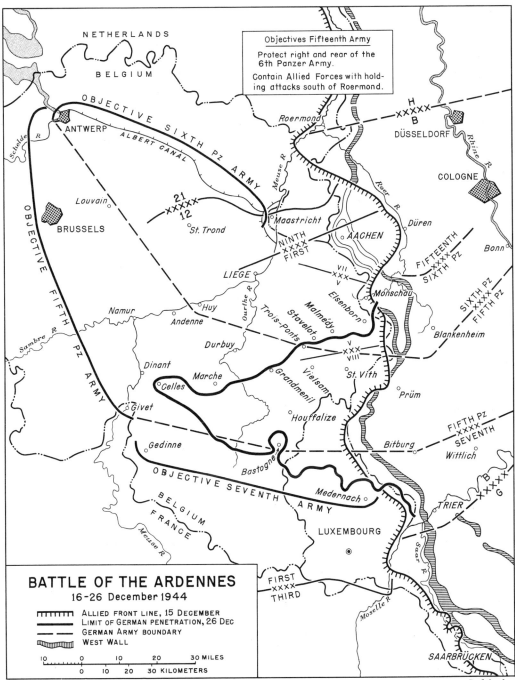

Objectives Fifteenth Army

Protect right and rear of the 6th Panzer Army.

Contain Allied Forces with holding attacks south of Roermond.

NETHERLANDS

BELGIUM

OBJECTIVE SIXTH PZ ARMY

Roermond

ALBERT CANAL

ANTWERP

Schelde R.

Meuse R.

Roer R.

H
XXXXX
B

DÜSSELDORF

Rhine R.

COLOGNE

OBJECTIVE FIFTH PZ ARMY

Louvain

21
XXXXX
12

St. Trond

BRUSSELS

Maastricht

NINTH
XXXX
FIRST

AACHEN

Düren

Bonn

FIFTEENTH
XXXX
SIXTH PZ

SIXTH PZ
XXXX
FIFTH PZ

LIEGE

VII
XXX
V

Namur

Huy

Andenne

Ourthe R.

Trois-Ponts

Malmédy

Stavelot

Elsenborn

Monschau

Blankenheim

Sambre R.

Durbuy

V
XXX
VIII

Dinant

Marche

Celles

Givet

Grandmenil

Vielsam

St. Vith

Prüm

Houffalize

FIFTH PZ
XXXX
SEVENTH

Gedinne

Bastogne

Bitburg

Wittlich

OBJECTIVE SEVENTH ARMY

Medernach

B
XXXXX
G

TRIER

BELGIUM
FRANCE

Meuse R.

LUXEMBOURG

Saar R.

FIRST
XXXX
THIRD

Moselle R.

SAARBRÜCKEN

BATTLE OF THE ARDENNES
16-26 December 1944

 ALLIED FRONT LINE, 15 DECEMBER
LIMIT OF GERMAN PENETRATION, 26 DEC
GERMAN ARMY BOUNDARY
WEST WALL

10   0   10   20   30 MILES

0   10   20   30 KILOMETERS

MAP 5

sentative of the operations group reported no change on the VIII Corps front, and the intelligence representative added merely that the move of the *326th Division* northward "might be the answer to the numerous vehicular movements in the northern VIII Corps sector." In the early afternoon, the First Army and the 12th Army Group learned of captured orders which indicated that a desperate all-out effort had been launched against the Allies.[39]

News of the attack reached General Bradley at Supreme Headquarters on the afternoon of 16 December while he was in conference with General Eisenhower and members of the SHAEF staff. The 12th Army Group commander recalls that General Smith said: ". . . you've been wishing for a counterattack. Now it looks as though you've got it." General Bradley, in turn, replied: "A counterattack, yes, but I'll be damned if I wanted one this big."[40] Generals Eisenhower and Bradley at once conferred and ordered reinforcements to the threatened area. Two armored divisions, one north and one south of the Ardennes, were directed to close into the threatened sector. General Bradley then instructed his army commanders to alert the divisions they had free for employment in the Ardennes area.[41]

Meanwhile, the SHAEF staff searched for reserves to throw into the battle. The question was an old one to SHAEF, which since 20 November had been trying to locate enough units to form a reserve corps. General Eisenhower had wanted to build up such a force in the event that he needed to reinforce a success north or south of the Ardennes, but he had been unable to get much beyond the point of asking the army groups what divisions they could make

available for such a purpose.[42] The SHAEF reserve on the Continent consisted only of the XVIII Corps (Airborne), whose two divisions had only recently been withdrawn from the Netherlands to Reims for refitting. On the 17th SHAEF alerted these units to move to the threatened sector. Bastogne, because of its excellent road net, was selected as the point where the units would be committed.[43] By the time they arrived, the 12th Army Group had made dispositions for the defense of Bastogne and ordered the airborne units to positions north of the town. Ultimately the 82d Airborne Division was sent to the north flank of the Ardennes sector, while the 101st was moved into Bastogne where a combat command of the 10th Armored Division was already established. The Supreme Commander on the 17th also ordered an armored and an airborne division to the Continent.[44]

As reports of the German counteroffensive began to pour into Supreme Head-

---

[39] 12th A Gp briefings, 16 Dec 44, 12th A Gp files; Msg, V Corps to FUSA, 1244 hours, 16 Dec 44, in FUSA G-2 Jnl, 1450 hours, 16 Dec 44. V Corps reported receiving the information from 99th Division at 1350, 16 Dec 44.

[40] Bradley, *A Soldier's Story,* pp. 449–50; Diary Office CinC, 17 Dec 44.

[41] Memo by Eisenhower, 23 Dec 44, Diary Office CinC. Almost the same statement, describing the action, appears in the Diary Office CinC, 17 Dec 44. These two statements are cited in *Crusade in Europe,* p. 344. Cf. Bradley, *A Soldier's Story,* pp. 464–65.

[42] G-3 Plng Stf Memo, Possibilities of Mutual Reinforcement, 20 Nov 44; Eisenhower to Bradley and Devers, 3 Dec 44. Both in SHAEF SGS 381 Post OVERLORD Planning, II.

[43] General Smith had agreed to the selection of Bastogne by General Whiteley, deputy G-3, according to Smith's statement to the ETO Historical Division, 14 September 1945. In a statement made to the author on 8 May 1947, General Smith recalled that General Strong also aided in the selection.

[44] Memo by Eisenhower, 23 Dec 44, Diary Office CinC.

quarters, there was no inclination to underestimate the gravity of the situation or to deny that the enemy had achieved complete surprise. Air Chief Marshal Tedder, in a statement made shortly after the attack, said that Supreme Headquarters had been caught unawares. He attributed the surprise to the fact that the SHAEF intelligence section, while stating that the Germans were holding the *Sixth Panzer Army* in reserve, had failed to indicate that any early use was to be made of it. General Spaatz, in answer to a query by General Arnold as to the part played by air reconnaissance before the breakthrough, cabled that the counteroffensive had "undoubtedly caught us off balance." He paid tribute to the cleverness of the Germans in shifting their forces in a manner which hid their intentions, and added that bad weather had seriously interfered with air reconnaissance activities.[45] General Eisenhower believed that there had been a failure to evaluate correctly the strength of the forces that the enemy could thrust through the Ardennes. He pointed out to General Marshall that "all of us, without exception, were astonished at the ability of the Volkssturm [*sic*] divisions to act offensively." [46]

Even as the first decisions were being made at Supreme Headquarters, First Army units were putting up strong defensive actions which forced the Germans to withdraw in the *Fifteenth Army* sector and slowed the drives of the two panzer armies, thus upsetting completely the timetable of the enemy commanders. The German high command had hoped that by taking advantage of surprise they could put part of their force across the Meuse by the end of the second day. This ambitious program was thwarted in the early hours of the attack when Allied units, falling back slowly

near Monschau and in front of St. Vith, delayed the enemy sufficiently to give time for reserves to be sent up. The slowing of the *Sixth Panzer Army* advance persisted and was ultimately to have its effect on the more successful *Fifth Panzer Army* drive, which required the movement of the right wing forces as a screen. The *Seventh Army,* in charge of flank protection to the south, made little progress. *Army Group H,* north of the attack front, reported no changes. In the area of *Army Group G,* south of the attacking forces, the Germans were able to hold their own against strong Allied pressure.

On 18 December, the third day of the attack, Hitler ordered a basic change in plans.[47] He canceled the subsidiary attack for which the *Fifteenth Army* had been alerted and which Rundstedt had ordered to start on 19 December. Instead, all available forces were to be used to help the two panzer armies push through the breaches already opened. Von Rundstedt gave the necessary orders. He also urged the *Seventh Army* to increase its efforts so as to create full freedom of maneuver for *Fifth Panzer Army.* Moreover, now that the supplementary attack by *Fifteenth Army* would no longer take place, the Germans considered an attack farther north of much greater importance. *Army Group H,* on the British front, received orders to intensify preparations for an attack to be

---

[45] Tedder memo, 17 Dec 44, OCMH files. Arnold to Spaatz, 30 Dec 44; Spaatz to Arnold, 7 Jan 45. Both in Air Staff SHAEF files, USSTAF Incoming Msgs 519.800.1.

[46] Eisenhower to Marshall, S–71794, 21 Dec 44, Eisenhower personal file.

[47] General Smith in a statement to the author, 1 November 1951, says that Jodl, shortly after the war, told him he realized on the third day of the attack that it had failed. Rundstedt shared this view (see below, p. 384).

launched on short notice over the Waal and lower Meuse.[48]

In the first two days of the German attack, the Allies still thought it might be nothing more than an effort to pull forces away from their offensives then being planned. On the evening of 18 December, however, General Bradley informed General Patton that the situation appeared worse than initially believed. He had received the impression, he added, that General Eisenhower intended to give the VIII Corps to Third Army and would shortly launch a new offensive.[49] The Supreme Commander, apparently believing that part of the 12th Army Group could stop the German attack while the rest joined the 21 Army Group in a renewed offensive, seriously thought of launching an attack with all the forces north of the Moselle. He considered having the 21 Army Group attack southeast from the Nijmegen area between the Rhine and the Meuse, while the 12th Army Group checked the enemy, secured the lines of communications along the line Namur–Liége–Aachen, relieved the 21 Army Group east of the Meuse, and launched a counteroffensive converging on the general area Bonn–Cologne. Then the 6th Army Group, reinforced by four divisions from the 12th Army Group, was to take over part of the 12th Army Group's zone, moving northward to a line running from St. Dizier to Thionville and thence along the Moselle.[50]

These long-range plans underwent considerable changes by the time Allied commanders conferred at Verdun the following morning. Apparently influenced by growing evidence that the enemy was making an all-out attack toward the Meuse, General Eisenhower placed the immediate emphasis on checking that drive. He opened the Verdun conference by asking that his commanders show him nothing but cheerful faces. Actually, they all appeared to be calm and one of them, General Patton, expressed enthusiasm over the prospect of trapping the enemy and cutting him to pieces. In view of the major thrust then under way in the Ardennes sector and the possibility of an attack in the Trier sector, the Supreme Commander limited his proposed offensive to counterthrusts on either side of the enemy salient in the Ardennes. In areas not vital to this main purpose, he declared, he was ready "to yield ground in order to insure the security of essential areas and to add strength to [the Allied] counteroffensive." He now directed the 6th Army Group to move forces to Saarlautern where it would defend against any major penetration. Subject to securing essential lines of communications, General Devers was to be prepared to yield ground rather than endanger the integrity of his forces. General Bradley was to check the enemy's advance east of the Meuse and, in conjunction with Field Marshal Montgomery's forces, launch an attack against the enemy salient. The British forces were also ordered to stop the enemy in their area east and south of the Meuse, paying par-

---

[48] MS # A–858, The Course of Events of the German Offensive in the Ardennes, 16 Dec 44 to 14 Jan 45 (Schramm); *OB WEST, KTB 1.-31.XII.44,* 18 to 20 Dec 44.

[49] Gen Patton, Notes on Bastogne, entry for 18 Dec 44, TUSA AAR; Diary, Brig Gen Hobart R. Gay, TUSA CofS, 18 Dec 44, OCMH files. General Betts, deputy G–2 of SHAEF, in a letter to the author, 5 September 1951, says that it was "almost a week before we realized that Hitler, in fact, was out to split the Allied Armies apart." General Bradley in *A Soldier's Story,* p. 455, says that when he first got news of the attack he thought it a spoiling attack to force a halt on Patton's advance into the Saar.

[50] Eisenhower to 12th A Gp and 6th A Gp, S–71400, 1900 hours, 18 Dec 44, SHAEF cbl log; also Diary CinC, 18 Dec 44.

ticular attention to securing the line of the Meuse from Namur to Liége.[51]

By these measures the whole front south of the Moselle passed to strict defense. General Devers, who received one division instead of the four originally intended for him, was ordered to push farther north than initially planned and take over most of Third Army's sector. General Patton in the meantime prepared to move north with six divisions, take over the VIII Corps, and organize a major attack against the south flank of the German penetration on 22 or 23 December. The general plan now required the plugging of holes in the Allied line in the north and the co-ordination of attacks launched from south of the German penetration.[52]

Having started forces in the direction of the Ardennes sector, the Supreme Commander next turned to the task of massing a reserve force for use in stopping further enemy attacks or in renewing an Allied offensive. For this purpose, he not only halted offensives directed toward the Rhine but considered the possibility of shortening his line. On the 19th, he asked Field Marshal Montgomery to examine the situation on his northern flank with a view "to the possibility of giving up, if necessary, some ground in order to shorten our line and collect a strong reserve for the purpose of destroying the enemy in Belgium." On the following day, he told General Bradley that the Allies must not let the fear of losing ground around Aachen deter them from adopting the best line of defense. He directed the 12th Army Group commander to choose the line he could hold most cheaply and effectively, no matter how far back he had to go to establish it. In these statements, he apparently intended the line of the Meuse to mark the limit of withdrawal.[53]

Field Marshal Montgomery had been in the process of moving the 30 British Corps northward and had already taken steps to use this force of three infantry divisions, one armored division, and three armored brigades to protect his southern flank. On 17 December, he ordered reserve divisions of this corps, the only Allied reserve then available, to go into positions west of the Meuse. Two days later, he directed the corps to stop all northward movement and to assemble in the Louvain–St. Trond area where it would be in a position to aid where needed. Later, by moving elements of this corps into First Army positions along the line of the Meuse, Montgomery made it possible for General Hodges to commit all of his forces against the enemy.[54]

While General Patton was engaged in the herculean effort of disengaging his troops from battle in the Saar, completely changing their direction, and throwing them into the Ardennes battle, and while Field Marshal Montgomery was taking measures to aid the U.S. forces north of the Ardennes, General Hodges' forces in the Bulge fought desperately to halt the German drive or at least check its speed. The enemy in this period moved ever

[51] Eisenhower, *Crusade in Europe*, p. 350; Patton, Notes on Bastogne, entry for 19 Dec 44, TUSA AAR; Patton, *War as I Knew It*, p. 190; Eisenhower to A Gp comdrs, S–71724, 20 Dec 44, SHAEF cbl log.

[52] Patton, *War as I Knew It*, p. 191; Patton, Notes on Bastogne, entry for 19 Dec 44; Eisenhower, *Crusade in Europe*, p. 351; Eisenhower to Marshall for CCS, SCAF 149, 19 Dec 44, Eisenhower personal file.

[53] Eisenhower to Montgomery, S–71591, 19 Dec 44, Eisenhower personal file; Air Marshal Robb's notes on a meeting of airmen in the Supreme Commander's office, 1000 hours, 20 December 1944 (with penciled notes by General Eisenhower), in OCMH files; Eisenhower, *Crusade in Europe*, p. 350.

[54] Montgomery, *Normandy to the Baltic*, pp. 280–81; Comments by Hist Sec, Cabinet Office, to the author, 10 Jul 51.

closer to St. Vith and Bastogne, smashing some First Army units and isolating others. In the face of powerful attacks, the U.S. forces succeeded in improvising effective counterattacks. U.S. armor delayed the enemy in the area of St. Vith until new positions could be established to the west. On the north flank of the break-through, First Army forces in one of the most critical battles of the campaign held the Elsenborn ridge, the village of Butgenbach south of the ridge, and the Malmédy–Stavelot line against repeated attacks by elements of the *Sixth Panzer Army,* thus buying time needed by the Allied forces.

Despite the prompt reaction of the Allied units to the German threat, the enemy columns continued to forge westward. On the evening of 19 December, General Strong, the SHAEF chief of intelligence, feared that the Germans would soon drive a wedge between General Bradley's forces, making it impossible for him to retain contact with First U.S. Army from his advanced headquarters in the city of Luxembourg. He confided these anxieties to General Whiteley, the deputy chief of operations, and the two went to General Smith with the proposal that Field Marshal Montgomery be given command of U.S. forces north of the Ardennes. The SHAEF chief of staff initially rejected the proposal but, on being told that there had been no close contact for two days between the 12th Army Group and the First Army, agreed to make the recommendation to General Eisenhower. Sometime in the course of the evening, General Smith telephoned General Bradley to discuss the proposed shift. The 12th Army Group commander doubted that the change-over was necessary, but was mainly concerned because it might discredit the American command. This reaction was indicated in

his statement: "Certainly if Monty's were an American command, I would agree with you entirely. It would be the logical thing to do." He also admitted that if the British commander was in charge of all operations north of the Ardennes, he might be more inclined to use his reserve forces against the enemy. Field Marshal Montgomery was apparently notified unofficially the same evening that a change in command would be made. The formal shift was made the following day when the Supreme Commander put Field Marshal Montgomery in temporary command of all forces north of the Ardennes.[55] *(Chart 7)*

General Eisenhower subsequently justified the shift on the ground that the salient north of the Ardennes had become one battlefront "with a single reserve which might be called upon to operate in support either of the British and Canadian Armies or of the American Ninth and First Armies." Prime Minister Churchill immediately approved the action, saying that the arrangement would make the British reserve instantly available for use wherever needed, regardless of previously defined zones. It led, however, to great resentment on the part of many Americans, particularly at Headquarters, 12th Army Group, and Third Army.[56]

---

[55] The shift was also accompanied by an agreement between representatives of SHAEF, USSTAF, and the Ninth Air Force to place the two tactical commands then in support of the U.S. forces north of the Ardennes under the operational control of Air Marshal Coningham, commander of the tactical air forces in support of the 21 Army Group. Enough fighter-bombers were shifted from the north to bring up to ten groups the air forces supporting General Patton. Robb, Notes on mtg, 20 Dec 44, OCMH files.

[56] Montgomery, *Normandy to the Baltic,* p. 281; Intervs with Strong, 12 Dec 47, Whiteley, 18 Dec 46, Smith, 8 May 47, and Bradley, 6 Nov 46; Eisenhower, *Crusade in Europe,* p. 355; Bradley, *A Soldier's Story,* pp. 475–77; Robb, Notes on mtg, 20 Dec 44, OCMH files. The bitter feeling which existed at the two U.S. head-

CHART 7—OPERATIONAL CHAIN OF COMMAND, AEF, 18 DECEMBER 1944

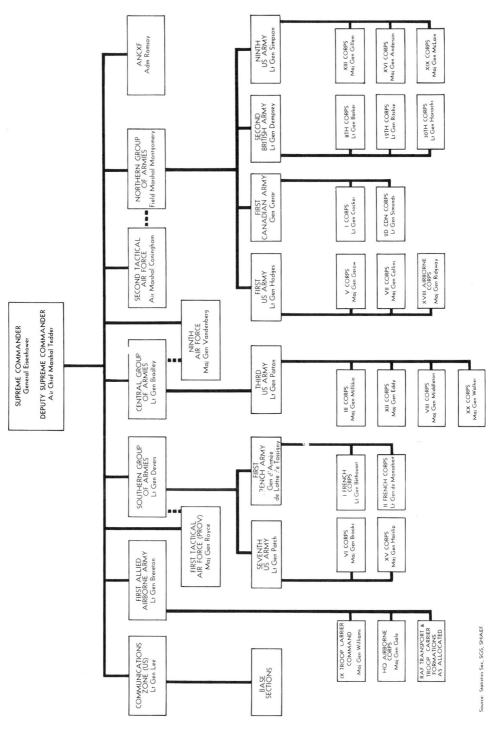

Source: Statistics Sec, SGS, SHAEF

General Bradley in his postwar memoirs indicated that he saw in the shift evidence of considerable nervousness at SHAEF over developments in the Ardennes. He also called attention to SHAEF's orders for the destruction of bridges over the Meuse in case of withdrawal as another such indication.[57] The orders to destroy the Meuse bridges, hedged about with many restrictions to avoid precipitate destruction by the guards, were similar to directions normally issued when enemy tanks were located in positions from which they could reach a river line. It is true that SHAEF sent hurry-up messages to Washington asking for more men and supplies, that the Supreme Commander was willing to give up territory in order to shorten his line and amass a strategic reserve, and that a personal bodyguard was assigned to General Eisenhower to protect him against an alleged assassin band under Skorzeny. These measures could have been attributed to nervousness, panic, or, perhaps more plausibly, to reasonable precaution.

On receiving instructions to take command, Field Marshal Montgomery called Generals Hodges and Simpson to a conference at First Army headquarters, where he issued orders for reorganization of the battle. The Ninth Army took over part of First Army's zone. General Collins, who relinquished the area and the divisions which Ninth Army brought under its control, was given a reserve force of one armored and two infantry divisions and told to assemble them near the northwest corner of the German salient (Durbuy–Marche), where he was to be available for operations to blunt the enemy advance or for later counterthrusts. The Third Army extended its boundary northward to a line running from Givet to St. Vith. Montgomery was hopeful at the close of the day that the situation could be restored, and he said he saw no reason at the moment "to give up any of the ground that [had] been gained in the last few days by such hard fighting."[58]

With the increase of Allied efforts against the enemy and the reorganization of the Allied command, General Eisenhower took steps to encourage his commanders and soldiers. In a special Order of the Day he pointed to the opportunities presented by the enemy's action:

By rushing out from his fixed defenses the enemy may give us the chance to turn his great gamble into his worst defeat. So I call upon every man, of all the Allies, to rise now to new heights of courage, of resolution and of effort. Let everyone hold before him a single thought—to destroy the enemy on the ground, in the air, everywhere—destroy him! United in this determination and with unshakable faith in the cause for which we fight, we will, with God's help, go forward to our greatest victory.[59]

On the same day, he recommended to General Marshall the promotions of Generals Bradley and Spaatz, pointing out that the time was particularly opportune in the case of the former. He added that the 12th Army Group commander had

---

quarters is reflected in books like Ralph Ingersoll's *Top Secret* (New York, 1946), Robert S. Allen's *Lucky Forward: The History of Patton's Third U.S. Army* (New York, 1947), and Patton's *War as I Knew It*. The strong animus toward SHAEF which prevailed at the two headquarters among junior officers, even before the Ardennes developments, was the subject of a special report by a War Department observer in early December 1944. It is interesting to note that while staff members of 12th Army Group and Third Army thought that SHAEF was unduly influenced by 21 Army Group, a number of officers at 21 Army Group fancied that Generals Bradley and Patton had the inside track to the Supreme Commander.

[57] Bradley, *A Soldier's Story*, pp. 475–76.
[58] Montgomery to Eisenhower, M–384, 20 Dec 44, Eisenhower personal file.
[59] Eisenhower, *Crusade in Europe*, pp. 354–55.

"kept his head magnificently and . . . proceeded methodically and energetically to meet the situation. In no quarter is there any tendency to place any blame upon Bradley." [60]

On the 22d, General Eisenhower notified Field Marshal Montgomery that he was sending messages of encouragement to Generals Hodges and Simpson. General Eisenhower pointed out that unless the First Army commander became exhausted he would always wage a good fight. He added that he wished Field Marshal Montgomery to keep in touch with his subordinates and let him know of any changes which should be needed on the United States side. [61] This last was apparently in answer to an earlier statement of Field Marshal Montgomery's that some changes in command might become necessary because of physical exhaustion, but that he was unwilling to relieve U.S. commanders personally. General Smith told him that should this action become necessary it would be done by the Supreme Commander. On the evening of the 22d, Montgomery reported that while Hodges had originally been a bit shaken, very tired, and in need of moral support, he was improving. [62]

The Supreme Commander was encouraged personally by messages from Washington and London in the days following the German counteroffensive. The Prime Minister cabled General Eisenhower on 22 December that as a mark of confidence in the Supreme Commander's leadership, the British intended to find an additional 250,000 men to put at his disposal. About the same time, General Marshall said that orders had been given that General Eisenhower was to be left free to give his entire attention to the fighting. The U.S. Chief of Staff added: "I shall merely say now that you have our complete confidence." [63]

The emphasis north of the Ardennes during the first week of the German offensive was necessarily on defensive measures. Heavily hit and badly stretched, General Hodges could do little more than meet enemy attacks as they developed and hope that he could get a reserve for later use in an effective counterstroke. South of the Ardennes, however, Generals Bradley and Patton were moving rapidly to strike at the enemy penetrations. General Patton was notified on 19 December that he was to throw his main weight to the north. Two days later he had broken off his battle in the Saar area and was attacking toward Bastogne. In what General Bradley has described as "one of the most astonishing feats of generalship of our campaign in the West," General Patton swung the bulk of the Third Army on a ninety-degree angle and moved it north from fifty to seventy miles into the new attack. His forces were met by enemy air attacks and by stubborn resistance that delayed the relief of Bastogne. [64]

SHAEF meanwhile struggled to build a reserve force to deal with further enemy counteroffensives or to be committed in an Allied offensive. The SHAEF staff feared that, without some plan for building a reserve, U.S. divisions would be committed piecemeal. General Eisenhower, though positive that Bastogne would be held, di-

---

[60] Eisenhower to Marshall, S–71794, 21 Dec 44, Eisenhower personal file.

[61] Eisenhower to Montgomery, S–71982, 22 Dec 44, Eisenhower personal file.

[62] Smith to author, 8 May 47; Montgomery to Eisenhower, M–389, 22 Dec 44, Eisenhower personal file.

[63] Churchill to Eisenhower, 22 Dec 44, SHAEF cbl log; Marshall to Eisenhower, W–81088, 23 Dec 44, Eisenhower personal file.

[64] Bradley, *A Soldier's Story*, pp. 472–74; TUSA Rpt of Opns, Vol. I.

rected that Allied counterattacks beyond that point be postponed for the moment. He thought that General Patton might persuade General Bradley to authorize a Third Army attack at once aimed at going "right through" without waiting for the fully co-ordinated counteroffensive.[65]

Forces for the Allied attack were gathered from a number of points. By 24 December, priorities had been set for the speedy movement of one armored and three infantry divisions from the United Kingdom to the Continent, and the shipment of units in the United States already earmarked for the European theater was accelerated. By Christmas, one British division had passed to First U.S. Army control and three other British divisions held the west bank of the Meuse from Givet to Liége. On 21 December, General Lee had ordered supply units to defend crossings of the Meuse and to defend vital installations within the Communications Zone. Two days later, General de Gaulle alerted security units of the four military regions of northeastern France and ordered them to move at once to positions on the Sambre and the Meuse. These units were to be reinforced as soon as possible by troops from the zone of interior and by part or all of a French infantry division. Maj. Gen. André Dody was placed in charge of the French forces defending the line of the Meuse.[66]

As the enemy continued his drive toward the Meuse, Field Marshal Montgomery, who had been hopeful on 20 December that no ground would have to be given up, expressed both optimism and pessimism. He reported on the 22d that Ninth Army had been ordered to get two divisions into reserve and that efforts were being made to establish a similar reserve for First Army. He added, "First

Army is now reorganized and in good trim and we will fight a good battle up here." On other matters he was less hopeful. "From information available here," he noted, "I am not optimistic that the attack of Third Army will be strong enough to do what is needed and I suggest Seventh German Army will possibly hold off Patton from interfering with the progress westwards of Fifth Panzer Army. In this case I will have to deal unaided with both Fifth and Sixth Panzer Armies. . . ."[67]

The 21 Army Group commander became worried on the 23d when it seemed clear that the *Fifth Panzer Army* was swinging northwestward and trying to envelop VII Corps to the west. He was "disturbed at the weak local arrangements, particularly in infantry, of most of the divisions in the First and Ninth Armies." He reported that the V Corps divisions were understrength by some 7,000, mostly in infantry, and asked if something could be done to get replacements "for this serious discrepancy."[68]

When enemy pressure increased on the right flank of the First Army, Field Marshal Montgomery decided he would have to shorten the front. On Christmas Day he ordered the 82d Airborne Division to withdraw from the salient it held in the Vielsalm area west of St. Vith and come back to the general line Grandmenil–

---

[65] Robb, Notes on mtgs in SAC's office, 21 Dec 44, OCMH files.

[66] Msgs, SHAEF to COMZ and ETOUSA, 18–23 Dec 44; Lee to all base secs, EX–76867, 21 Dec 44. All in SHAEF cbl log. FUSA Rpt of Opns, Aug 44–Feb 45, Vol. I. De Gaulle to Minister of War, 23 Dec 44; Dody to Bradley, 29 Dec 44; Bradley to Dody, 3 Jan 45. All in 12 A Gp 322.011 Commanders and Command Relations, I.

[67] Montgomery to Eisenhower, M–389, 22 Dec 44, Eisenhower personal file.

[68] Montgomery to Eisenhower, M–390, 23 Dec 44, Eisenhower personal file.

Trois-Ponts. He also ordered the British 51st Division to move from the Ninth to the First Army reserve on the 26th.[69]

The British commander discussed the Allied situation with General Bradley on the 25th and indicated that he could not pass over to offensive action at the moment. The 12th Army Group commander said he hoped to get to Bastogne but doubted his ability to go farther without replacements. In reporting this reaction to the Supreme Commander, Montgomery added that the Allies, if they intended to take the initiative from the Germans, would need more troops. Unaware that SHAEF was even then in the process of sending a message promising 17,000 replacements to the First and Third Armies by the end of December, the British commander indicated that additional troops could be found only by withdrawing Allied forces from salients and holding shorter fronts. He suggested that this aspect of the problem be examined on the southern front.[70]

These reactions left Bradley with the feeling that the 21 Army Group commander had adopted a purely defensive attitude. The U.S. general now asked that American forces north of the Ardennes be returned to him and suggested that 12th Army Group headquarters be moved to Namur where it could assure co-ordination of the U.S. forces.[71]

The U.S. commanders attacked vigorously the suggestion of even a limited withdrawal. Generals Hodges and Collins expressed their disapproval, and, when the matter was left to them to resolve, decided to stay where they were. General Patton's staff insisted that the Saar positions should be held, saying that a withdrawal would have serious psychological effects on the soldiers who had taken the

area. The Third Army commander himself was strongly opposed to any pulling back. General Bradley at this point wrote General Hodges and outlined his views. While making clear that he had no control over the First Army and that his letter was not to be considered as a directive, the 12th Army Group commander said that he viewed with misgivings any plan to give up terrain which might be favorable for future operations. Aware that the First Army had been hard hit, he nevertheless believed that the enemy divisions had also suffered heavily and were now weaker than General Hodges' forces.[72]

General Bradley's optimism was justified by conditions within the German

---

[69] Montgomery to Eisenhower, M–394, 25 Dec 44, Eisenhower personal file.

[70] Montgomery to Eisenhower, M–396, 25 Dec 44, Eisenhower personal file. SHAEF's message on replacements, dated 25 December 1944, reached Montgomery the following day. Note, Br Hist Sec to author, 23 Apr 52.

[71] Air Marshal Robb's notes on a meeting in General Smith's office, 26 December 1944, give General Bradley's reactions as reported by General Smith. Field Marshal Montgomery, according to Patton, *War as I Knew It*, p. 203, had told General Bradley that First Army could not attack for at least three months and that the only offensive effort that could be made would be that of Third Army, which the British commander considered too weak. It would be necessary, therefore, to fall back to the line of the Saar–Vosges or to the Moselle to get a sufficient number of divisions for the attack. Bradley, *A Soldier's Story*, pp. 480–81, says only: "Although I had hoped Montgomery would soon join our counter-attack with one from the north, I found him waiting expectantly for one last enemy blow on the flank. Not until he was certain that the enemy had exhausted himself, would Montgomery plunge in for the kill. Disappointed at the prospect of further delay, I headed back to St. Trond."

[72] Patton, *War as I Knew It*, pp. 203–05, has the full memorandum. Bradley to Hodges, 26 Dec 44, 12th A Gp 371.3 Military Objectives, IV. The question of his withdrawal will be treated at length in Cole's *The Ardennes*.

armies. Their attack, whose success had been staked on surprise and speed, had now lost the effect of surprise and was falling more and more behind schedule. The *Sixth Panzer Army* had failed to break through the Monschau–Malmédy area. St. Vith had held out three times as long as the Germans had anticipated, and Bastogne, which had been expected to fall the second day of the offensive, stubbornly held out after the Germans had surrounded it. Field Marshal von Rundstedt claimed after the war that he was aware by the third day of the attack that he could not achieve his assigned objectives. He added that, when OKW insisted on pushing the counteroffensive, his answer was that his forces must start preparing to defend the territory they had already taken.

Whatever Rundstedt replied at the time, he was probably not as hopeful as Hitler and his advisers. On 26 December they believed that *Army Group B* could thrust forces across the Meuse if the *Seventh Army* forces could regain their equilibrium in the south, if Bastogne could be taken, and if the *Fifth* and *Sixth Panzer Armies,* in a co-ordinated effort in the center, could destroy Allied forces between the Ourthe and the Meuse north of the line Marche–Dinant. With these objectives in mind, they proposed to order the *Fifth Panzer Army,* already far in the lead, to turn off to the northeast as soon as it reached the Meuse so as to outflank the Allied forces east of the river and attack them from the rear, while the *Sixth Panzer Army* continued a vigorous attack to the west and northwest. A supplementary thrust by *Fifteenth Army* farther north near Dueren, intended to hold the U.S. forces in the salient around Aachen, was considered very desirable but canceled as being too costly. The Germans, hopeful of tying up U.S. forces south of the Ardennes, had ordered *Army Group G* to prepare an attack from Bitche against U.S. forces in the Wissembourg area. Apparently realizing that these various efforts would ultimately force the cancellation of long-standing plans for a supplementary attack by *Army Group H* in the north, the German high command nevertheless continued preparations for a time on paper at least, possibly as a means of deceiving the Allies. In reality, the German estimates at the time were based on reports which had been superseded by events. The front commands at the three crucial points must have known on the 26th that their efforts had failed.[73]

The German situation was destined to grow worse. The fog, which had interfered with air activity since the beginning of the attack, lifted on 23 December and the Allied air offensive was renewed. Allied planes immediately rushed supplies to beleaguered units like those in Bastogne and opened powerful attacks against enemy armored columns and supply lines. The steady roar of hundreds of Allied aircraft over the threatened area brought renewed hopes to the hard-pressed forces that their Christmas would be a thankful one.[74] A symbol of the changed situation for the Allies was the arrival on 26 Decem-

---

[73] See study by Magna E. Bauer and Charles von Luettichau, Key Dates During the Ardennes Offensive, 1944, OCMH files.

[74] Craven and Cate, *The Army Air Forces in World War II,* III, 690–92. The 9th Bombardment Division of the Ninth Air Force sent out more sorties on 23 December than it had since the battles in Normandy. It dispatched 624 bombers in the course of the day. The day also saw attack by 417 heavy bombers of the Eighth Air Force and 696 fighter-bomber sorties. In the period 23–31 December, Ninth Air Force, with two Eighth Air Force fighter-bomber groups under its temporary operational control, flew 10,305 sorties.

ber at Bastogne of advance elements of General Patton's tanks, which had broken through from the south.

On the same day, miles to the west near Dinant, First Army armored formations smashed the enemy's most ambitious bid to reach the Meuse. Other German drives were turned back near Celles. Enemy armored units had outrun their supplies, and their stalled vehicles jammed the roads and became easy prey to the Allied bombers. By the 28th, as a heavy snowfall slowed enemy armor, Germans were in the process of pulling back. General Patton ordered his forces to push northward to Houffalize and to continue their march toward St. Vith. General Hodges at the same time moved his units southward with the object of linking up with these Third Army forces. The first phase of the enemy counteroffensive had been brought to an end and the second begun. The enemy drive to the Meuse had been effectively stopped. But the enemy still had to be driven back from Luxembourg and Belgium.[75]

Preparations for an Allied Attack

On 28 December General Eisenhower and Field Marshal Montgomery met at Hasselt, Belgium, to plot an Allied offensive against the enemy.[76] The British commander insisted that a reserve be created to deal with other enemy counteroffensives and to launch an Allied counterattack. He emphasized the need of pressing the fight against the enemy in order to prevent von Rundstedt from withdrawing armored forces to build a reserve. Planning to strengthen his front and reorganize his forces, he proposed to start a drive on New Year's Day or shortly thereafter if the enemy had made no attack by that time.[77]

Proposals for a Ground Commander

In discussing the new drive against the enemy, Field Marshal Montgomery suggested that the Allied forces in this offensive be placed under the control of one commander. This renewal of an old proposal was accompanied by a reminder that failure had attended the Supreme Commander's previous dependence on coordination of British and U.S. forces rather than definite operational control. To anyone made sensitive by British press criticisms of late December, it might have appeared that the British were making use of the early reverses in the Ardennes to register a lack of confidence in the Supreme Commander's direction of operations. In

---

[75] FUSA Rpt of Opns, Vol. I; TUSA Rpt of Opns, Vol. I; Bradley, *A Soldier's Story*, pp. 481–82; Entry dtd 26 Dec 44 in *OB WEST*, *KTB 1.–31.XII.44*.

[76] The meeting had been slightly delayed because of the bombing of General Eisenhower's special train—in the railway yards near Paris—on 26 December. The trip to Hasselt was complicated because of the heavy guard given General Eisenhower as a result of a report that German forces under Colonel Skorzeny had slipped through the American lines to Paris with the object of killing key Allied commanders (Eisenhower, *Crusade in Europe*, pp. 359–60). German plans for the Ardennes offensive do not indicate that Skorzeny's forces were intended to carry out such a mission.

Field Marshal Montgomery's plane was also bombed during the course of the Ardennes battle. General Eisenhower immediately put his own plane at the field marshal's disposal. De Guingand's plane was also destroyed.

[77] The draft of a letter from Eisenhower to Montgomery, 29 December 1944, Eisenhower personal file, recapitulates the points discussed at the meeting. (A note in General Eisenhower's writing says "probably not sent.") It accords generally with the general's recollections in *Crusade in Europe*, pp. 360–61, although it cites 1 January 1945 instead of 3 January as the date of Field Marshal Montgomery's proposed drive. General de Guingand in meetings at SHAEF on 31 December denied that Montgomery had committed himself firmly to an attack on 1 January, but said it might be made on the 2d or 3d. Robb, Notes on CofS and SAC confs, 31 Dec 44, OCMH files.

reality nothing was said at this time that had not been stated on various other occasions by the 21 Army Group commander and his advisers. Undoubtedly he was emboldened by the fact that the Supreme Commander had given him command of U.S. forces north of the Ardennes in December, and he pressed this point home. Montgomery held that the key to future success lay in the assignment of all available offensive power to the northern line of the advance to the Ruhr and the establishment of one-man control of the whole tactical battle in the north.[78]

SHAEF, the War Department, and the U.S. commanders in Europe were opposed to leaving forces north of the Ardennes under the 21 Army Group. On learning that the London press was predicting such a move, General Marshall cabled General Eisenhower:

My feeling is this: under no circumstances make any concessions of any kind whatsoever. You not only have our complete confidence but there would be a terrific resentment in this country following such action. I am not assuming that you had in mind such a concession. I just wish you to be certain of our attitude on this side. You are doing a fine job and go on and give them hell.[79]

Conscious of this backing, and of General Bradley's strong feelings about the current command arrangements, the Supreme Commander said that he was willing to leave one U.S. army with the 21 Army Group on the basis of military necessity and as a token of confidence in the British commander but would go no further.[80] General Eisenhower added that he was disturbed because of the field marshal's predictions of failure unless his views were met in detail. Thanking the 21 Army Group commander for his "frank and friendly counsels," the Supreme Commander declared that he would deplore "the development of such an unbridgeable gulf of convictions between us that we would have to present our differences to the CC/S. The confusion and debate that would follow would certainly damage the good will and devotion to a common cause that have made this Allied Force unique in history."[81]

Several of General Eisenhower's closest advisers at SHAEF now counseled him to force a showdown with the 21 Army Group commander. General Smith, who favored such a course, discussed frankly with Montgomery's chief of staff the difficulties which were arising. General de Guingand, in turn, informed his chief of the strong feelings which existed on the subject at SHAEF and warned that in a showdown someone would have to go and it would not be the Supreme Commander. Field Marshal Montgomery, who seemed

---

[78] Montgomery to Eisenhower, M–540, 29 Dec 44, Eisenhower personal file.

[79] Marshall to Eisenhower, W–84337, 30 Dec 44, Eisenhower personal file.

[80] General Eisenhower had indicated in a meeting with his staff on 30 December that he proposed to return First Army to General Bradley when the situation was restored in the Ardennes. In the course of the conference, the Supreme Commander's advisers agreed that Montgomery had quickly restored the situation in the First Army area, straightened out the army and brought order out of disorder. When it came to the need for offensive action they felt he was far behind Bradley. They feared his alleged overcareful policy would cause the Allies to miss a chance to inflict a severe defeat on the enemy in the immediate future. While the group referred specifically to Field Marshal Montgomery's policy during the Ardennes fight, it is not unfair to say that it represented generally SHAEF's attitude toward the 21 Army Group commander. Discussions at meeting based on Air Marshal Robb's notes on Supreme Commander's conference, 30 December 1944. It should be noted that Generals Smith, Strong, and Whiteley and Air Marshal Robb usually met with General Eisenhower during this period.

[81] Eisenhower to Montgomery, 31 Dec 44, Eisenhower personal file.

to be genuinely surprised at the strong feeling engendered by his views, discussed with de Guingand the necessary action for changing the existing situation. On 31 December, in a letter designed to clear the air, the British commander wrote General Eisenhower expressing distress if the previous letter had proved upsetting. He conceded that there were probably many factors involved in the command question which he did not know about, and pledged his 100 percent co-operation in backing any decision the Supreme Commander might make.[82]

Aware, perhaps, that Field Marshal Montgomery's requests coming on the heels of criticism of the Supreme Commander in the London press might be construed as a lack of faith in General Eisenhower's leadership, the Prime Minister in early January assured the President that His Majesty's Government had complete confidence in the Supreme Commander and acutely regretted any attacks which had been made on him. "He, Montgomery, Bradley, and Patton," Churchill wrote, "are closely knit and it would be a tragedy to break this group which has already for a year given results beyond the dreams of military avarice." He added that British troops were ready at all times to carry out General Eisenhower's orders. The Prime Minister extended his cordial congratulations on the gallantry of U.S. troops, particularly at Bastogne, and declared that the 7th Armored and the 1st and 9th Divisions had performed the "highest acts of soldierly devotion at heavy personal sacrifice."[83]

Field Marshal Montgomery and the British Chiefs of Staff revived the command question on at least two other occasions, but the possibility of its being seriously considered by General Eisenhower

was pretty effectively killed by the reactions of U.S. commanders to an interview given the Allied press by Field Marshal Montgomery on 7 January 1945. Members of his staff had feared that there might be an unfavorable reaction and had attempted to prevent the press conference or at least tone down the statements of their chief. He insisted, however, that something had to be done to counteract British press criticisms of General Eisenhower and other U.S. commanders.

The British commander made a lengthy analysis of the Ardennes battle and paid tribute to the U.S. soldier as "a brave fighting man, steady under fire, and with the tenacity in battle that stamps the first class soldier." To the fighting qualities of these men, he said, was due the basic credit for stopping Rundstedt. The field marshal made a strong appeal for full backing for the Supreme Commander, saying that he personally was devoted to General Eisenhower and was grieved by the uncomplimentary articles concerning him which had appeared in the British press. He pleaded for Allied solidarity, declaring, "Anyone who tries to break up the team spirit of the Allies is definitely helping the enemy."[84]

Read in its entirety, the statement justified the New York *Times*'s editorial comment: "No handsomer tribute was ever paid to the American soldier than that of Field Marshal Montgomery in the midst of combat."[85] But it was his tone and what his chief of staff characterized as a "what

---

[82] De Guingand, *Operation Victory*, pp. 432–45; Montgomery to Eisenhower, M–406, 31 Dec 44, Eisenhower personal file.

[83] Paraphrase of Msg, Churchill to Roosevelt, 7 Jan 45, in Memo, Leahy for Marshall *et al.*, 8 Jan 45, OPD Exec 9, Bk 24, Item 1539.

[84] New York *Times*, January 8, 1945.

[85] New York *Times*, January 9, 1945.

a good boy am I" attitude that offended General Bradley and his subordinates.[86] Passages of the interview singled out by the 12th Army Group commander were these:

When Rundstedt attacked on December 16, he obtained a tactical surprise. He drove a deep wedge into the center of the United States First Army and the split night have become awkward; the Germans had broken right through a weak spot, and were heading for the Meuse.

As soon as I saw what was happening I took certain steps myself to ensure that if the Germans got to the Meuse they would certainly not get over that river. And I carried out certain movements so as to provide balanced dispositions to meet the threatened danger; these were, at the time, merely precautions, i. e. I was thinking ahead.

Then the situation began to deteriorate. But the whole allied team rallied to meet the danger; national considerations were thrown overboard; General Eisenhower placed me in command of the whole Northern front.

I employed the whole available power of the British Group of Armies; this power was brought into play very gradually and in such a way that it would not interfere with the American lines of communications. Finally it was put into battle with a bang and today British divisions are fighting hard on the right flank of the United States First Army.

You have thus the picture of British troops fighting on both sides of American forces who have suffered a hard blow. This is a fine Allied picture.

The battle has some similarity to the battle that began on 31 August 1942 when Rommel made his last bid to capture Egypt and was "seen off" by the Eighth Army.[87]

The 12th Army Group commander and his staff, already sensitive because of the shift in command, were exasperated, if not outraged, by the interview. Their feelings were further roused a few days later when a German station broke in on a BBC channel and, imitating a British broadcast, criticized the handling of the battle by U.S. commanders. Mr. Brendan Bracken, chief of British press affairs, immediately branded the broadcast as false and expressed British confidence in General Eisenhower and the U.S. forces. But much damage had been done to U.S.-British command relations.[88]

General Bradley believed that SHAEF might have settled the whole matter at the time of the initial shift in command, if it had made clear the fact that the whole shift was temporary. By mid-January, he felt that the confidence of the U.S. soldiers and of the U.S. public in their commanders was at stake. He further argued that U.S. public opinion would not permit the battle south of the Ardennes to be neglected, and he emphasized the political importance in the United States of giving the next major offensive to a U.S. commander. When General Eisenhower mentioned the matter of a ground forces commander, General Bradley flatly said if he were placed under Field Marshal Montgomery's command he would ask to be relieved.[89]

Weeks after the Montgomery interview, General Eisenhower was still getting strong reactions from his U.S. commanders and the U.S. press. He later declared, "No single incident that I have ever encountered throughout my experience as an Allied commander has been so difficult to combat as this particular outburst in the papers." [90] Aware of these feelings, the

[86] De Guingand, *Operation Victory*, p. 434.
[87] New York *Times*, January 8, 1945. This version is slightly different from that in Bradley, *A Soldier's Story*, pp. 484–85. It is possible that Bradley's was taken from the BBC broadcast which he mentions.
[88] Bracken to Smith, RR–15103, 10 Jan 45, SHAEF cbl log.
[89] Bradley, *A Soldier's Story*, pp. 487–88.
[90] Eisenhower to Bradley, 16 Jan 45; Eisenhower to Marshall, 8 Feb 45. Both in Eisenhower personal file.

Prime Minister had already done his best to set the record straight. On 18 January, in summarizing for the House of Commons the state of Allied fortunes throughout the world, he paid a great tribute to the U.S. commander and the U.S. forces in the Ardennes. Part of his statement follows:

I have seen it suggested that the terrific battle which has been proceeding since 16th December on the American front is an Anglo-American battle. In fact, however, the United States troops have done almost all the fighting and have suffered almost all the losses. They have suffered losses almost equal to those on both sides in the battle of Gettysburg. Only one British Army Corps has been engaged in this action. All the rest of the 30 or more divisions, which have been fighting continuously for the last month, are United States troops. The Americans have engaged 30 or 40 men for every one we have engaged, and they have lost 60 to 80 men for every one of ours. That is a point I want to make. Care must be taken in telling our proud tale not to claim for the British army an undue share of what is undoubtedly the greatest American battle of the war and will, I believe, be regarded as an ever famous American victory.[91]

After describing the manner in which the battle had been carried on, Mr. Churchill sternly warned: "Let no one lend himself to the chatter of mischief-makers when issues of this momentous consequence are being successfully decided by the sword." Despite his generous words and timely warning, the shift in command during December continued to rankle in the minds of the U.S. commanders. General Eisenhower could scarcely have ignored this factor in the debates which followed relative to making the main drive on Field Marshal Montgomery's front and on the question of placing additional U.S. troops under 21 Army Group command.

Even while General Eisenhower was faced with sharp American reactions to Montgomery's temporary assumption of command of all Allied troops north of the Ardennes, the British Chiefs of Staff were proposing the appointment of a single ground force commander for the remainder of the war. They argued, in defense of this suggestion, that General Eisenhower was too heavily occupied with matters of supply, political complexities, and the like to handle ground force operations. The Supreme Commander, when notified of this recommendation, declared that the Ruhr was the logical dividing line between the British and U.S. army groups, and that there was no way in which a ground forces commander could secure better co-ordination or direction of the battle than could the Supreme Commander. Rather the ground commander would merely complicate matters by getting involved in questions of allocations of men and supplies and the development of communications—matters which properly belonged to the Supreme Commander. While disavowing any nationalistic viewpoints, General Eisenhower emphasized that the establishment of two ground commanders, one on either side of the Luxembourg area, would put forty-five to fifty U.S. divisions and fourteen British divisions under the 21 Army Group for an offensive task; the other commander would be left with a defensive task only. He considered such a plan illogical and, with the personalities involved, one that would not work well. He conceded only that, in view of the size of the ground forces, it would be convenient if the Deputy Supreme Commander were

[91] 407 H.C. Deb. (Hansard's 1944–45), pars. 415–18.

a ground force rather than air force officer.[92]

General Marshall feared that General Eisenhower's closing remark meant that he was weakening under heavy British pressure to put one of their officers in charge of the ground forces. Recognizing that the Supreme Commander needed someone to visit forward units and keep contact with top ground commanders, he offered to send an officer from Washington for the job and suggested that General Eisenhower get a British officer as well. General Eisenhower replied that he would strenuously object to a deputy for ground operations and that he would consider only a deputy without portfolio who would be directly responsible to the Supreme Commander. His present deputy, he added, was "a loyal, splendid man," whose only difficulty arose from the unwillingness of senior ground commanders to take his opinion on purely ground matters. Advice in these matters was available, however, from General Smith, who was highly respected in all echelons, and from General Bull, who was sent frequently to the lower headquarters. The Supreme Commander proposed to bring to his headquarters Maj. Gen. Lowell W. Rooks, formerly of AFHQ, who, together with General Whiteley, would stay on the road constantly.[93]

The ground commander question cropped up again in mid-February when the British asked if General Eisenhower would accept Field Marshal Alexander as his deputy. The Supreme Commander reminded Field Marshal Brooke that he had previously said he would take a replacement for Air Chief Marshal Tedder if the latter were assigned elsewhere. In case of a change, he could not accept "any intermediary headquarters, either official or

unofficial in character," between himself and the army group commanders. General Eisenhower called attention to controversies over command which had arisen in January and warned that if the newspapers attempted to describe Alexander's appointment as the establishment of a new ground command he would have to issue a formal statement that might hurt the feelings of the British officer and give the press "another opportunity to indulge in futile but nevertheless disturbing arguments." In standing firm on this issue, General Eisenhower was aware that he now had the backing of Field Marshal Montgomery. The latter, who felt that an intermediate command or any interference with the "clear line of authority extending from . . . [Eisenhower] . . . to him should be carefully avoided," was described by the Supreme Commander as being "most emphatic in insisting that the command arrangements I have made are as nearly perfect as circumstances, including diverse nationalities, will permit." [94]

Mr. Churchill, on seeing these statements, became disturbed at what he interpreted as an intention to reduce the position of Deputy Supreme Commander if a change was made. General Eisenhower reassured him on this point and pointed out his strong affection for Field Marshal Alexander. "Moreover," he went on, "far from regarding this problem from a British versus American viewpoint, my whole effort is to exercise the authority of my office so as to weld and preserve the sense of

[92] Eisenhower to Marshall, S–74437, 10 Jan 45; Eisenhower to Marshall, S–74461, 10 Jan 45. Both in Eisenhower personal file.
[93] Marshall to Eisenhower, W–90175, 11 Jan 45; Eisenhower to Marshall, S–74678, 12 Jan 45. Both in Eisenhower personal file.
[94] Eisenhower to Brooke, 16 Feb 45, Eisenhower personal file.

partnership that to my mind is absolutely essential to the winning of the war and to our common welfare." [95]

Field Marshal Montgomery added his voice to General Eisenhower's in early March, suggesting that the command set-up be left as it was and warning that a change would merely raise a storm and put everything back.[96] This attitude on the part of one who had formerly stoutly favored something like a ground commander pretty effectively settled the matter. In a conference with Eisenhower and Tedder on 5 March, the Prime Minister agreed that the decision regarding command arrangements belonged entirely to General Eisenhower. Thus the command situation was left as it had been arranged in January. The Ninth U.S. Army remained under the 21 Army Group for the Rhineland battle, but the other U.S. forces stayed under General Bradley or General Devers. General Eisenhower cabled General Marshall on 14 March, "I suppose you know the Prime Minister has withdrawn his suggestion of making any change in my deputy." [97]

Allied Manpower Difficulties

Discussions of command had been accompanied by Allied efforts to solve the manpower problem, which had been intensified by heavy U.S. losses in the opening days of the Ardennes counteroffensive.[98] At a time when the number of soldiers in the U.S. Army stood at the highest in the history of the United States, riflemen available for front-line duty were in short supply. This scarcity in the midst of plenty was due not only to the difficulty of working out a year or two in advance the proper allotment of manpower among the various services and their branches but also to the increasingly heavy losses among riflemen.[99]

The British manpower situation, which had been strained even before the invasion in June 1944 as a result of heavy commitments around the world and the losses in four years of fighting, was much worse than that of the U.S. forces. Some existing units had to be broken up to fill ranks which had been thinned during the battle for Antwerp. The French, who had a potentially rich source of manpower, were in no position to give immediate aid to the Allies. For some months they had urged the activation of new divisions, but the Allies, needing the supplies and equipment they would have had to give to the new units, had postponed any action on the matter.

The Ardennes crisis forced the Allies to re-examine their resources. Mr. Churchill, as already pointed out, had ordered special measures to get another quarter of a million men. General Eisenhower, who on the eve of the Ardennes attack had directed his rear echelon headquarters to comb out their ranks for men fitted for combat, demanded redoubled efforts in that direction. At the end of December, he reminded the Combined Chiefs of Staff of the possibility of raising additional units from Belgian, Polish, and French manpower sources. He emphasized particu-

[95] Ltr, Eisenhower to Prime Minister, 25 Feb 45, Eisenhower personal file.

[96] Montgomery to Eisenhower, 4 Mar 45, Eisenhower personal file.

[97] Eisenhower to Marshall, 14 Mar 45, Eisenhower personal file.

[98] See below, p. 396.

[99] Kent Roberts Greenfield, Robert R. Palmer, and Bell I. Wiley, *The Organization of Ground Combat Troops*, UNITED STATES ARMY IN WORLD WAR II (Washington, 1946), Mobilization of the Ground Army, pp. 189–98, 242–44. See above, Ch. XVII, p. 306. See also Ruppenthal, Logistical Support of the Armies, Vol. II, now in preparation.

larly that the French should be able to form five of a proposed eight divisions by 1 May 1945. The Combined Chiefs of Staff accepted in principle the task of equipping eight additional French divisions plus 460,000 line-of-communications and security troops (of whom 243,000 would be French). They added, however, that they had to await the outcome of the Ardennes battle before making a decision as to the supplies which could be made available.[100]

General Eisenhower's pleas to the War Department, backed by appeals of the Prime Minister to the President, may have spurred efforts already under way to meet the manpower crisis in Europe. The Joint Chiefs of Staff shortly after receiving news of the Ardennes had moved up the sailing date of three infantry, one airborne, and three armored divisions so that they would leave in January and early February. Two infantry divisions, not previously intended for the European theater, were allocated at once to General Eisenhower and listed for mid-February departure. In addition, General Marshall initiated a comb-out of the defense commands and other installations in the United States, Alaska, and Panama.[101]

In authorizing these various moves, the Joint Chiefs of Staff had allocated every available unit. The President was informed that once these had sailed all divisions would have left the United States for overseas theaters. It was therefore necessary for General Eisenhower to make drastic efforts to find additional troops in his own theater. On 6 January 1945, General Marshall proposed that a War Department manpower expert come to Europe to survey the situation there. After the finger had been pointed at available men, the Chief of Staff continued, a "tough

hatchetman" with rank should be sent over to force the rear echelon commanders to give up the soldiers in their commands fit for combat duty. General Eisenhower welcomed these proposals, asking that the two men be sent ahead. He outlined other possible ways to alleviate the manpower shortage. These included the opening of a major Russian offensive that would force the Germans to stop shifting troops to the west, the bringing of several divisions from Italy, and the speedier development of French units. He also indicated that the Army could not "deny the Negro volunteer a chance to serve in battle" and, as a final suggestion, asked if the Marines might be willing to turn over 100,000 men to the European theater.[102]

To expedite the search for replacements in the European theater, General Eisenhower appointed Lt. Gen. Ben Lear, then chief of the Army Ground Forces, as deputy theater commander with special duties for personnel and morale. Later, he gave General Barker, the SHAEF chief of personnel, an increased measure of control over U.S. personnel policy. These grants were both restricted by the fact that the theater chiefs of services continued to serve under the Commanding General, Communications Zone. Despite difficulties some progress was made in getting addi-

---

[100] Eisenhower to WD, 30 Dec 44; WD to SHAEF, 30 Dec 44. Both in COMZ Cbls, ETO Adm. Ruppenthal, Logistical Support of the Armies, and Vigneras, French Rearmament, contain detailed discussions of this problem.

[101] Marshall to Eisenhower, W-88482, 8 Jan 45, Eisenhower personal file; Memo, Leahy for President (undated but apparently in answer to Churchill cable of 7 January 1945), OPD Exec 9, Bk 24.

[102] Marshall to Eisenhower, W-87829, 6 Jan 45; Marshall to Eisenhower, W-88777, 8 Jan 45; Eisenhower to Marshall, S-74003, 7 Jan 45. Eisenhower personal file.

tional men for the combat units.[103]

Closely allied to the question of manpower was that of supplying front-line forces. Combat commanders believed that Headquarters, Communications Zone, was not only getting a lion's share of men who came from the United States but also was taking too large a percentage of critical supplies. In asking for a careful check on manpower, General Marshall also insisted that the supply situation be examined. In January he sent Lt. Gen. Brehon B. Somervell, the Army Service Forces chief, to look into the functioning of the supply services. Marshall made clear that in taking this step he was not implying that the commander of Headquarters, Communications Zone, was unfitted for his post. Rather he wished to find if there was any basis for the complaints being made by front-line commanders. He warned that they must not be allowed to feel that they were suffering heavily and working with reduced forces while the rear echelon elements continued to operate with "plenty of fat meat." After careful study, General Somervell suggested a number of ways for improving the work of the Communications Zone, but he made no recommendations for a radical change of command.[104]

The turn of the tide in the Ardennes battle and the renewal of the Allied offensive there toward the end of January eased the pressure on the Allies with regard to men and supplies. While never having as much of either as they would have liked, the combat commanders found that for the most part they were now able to get ahead with the job.

The Allies Take the Initiative

On 10 January, Field Marshal Montgomery and General Bradley issued orders for a co-ordinated attack on 13 January in the Ardennes, which was designed to trap the enemy or to drive him back into Germany.[105] The offensive's first objective was the link-up of Allied forces at Houffalize. (Map 6) Once this was completed, the Allies were to execute a major thrust from the north to retake St. Vith and the nearby high ground in an effort to deny the enemy lateral ground communications through St. Vith and to eliminate most of the enemy salient between the Elsenborn area and the First Army's southern boundary. Before the big push started, attacks were already under way. The Third Army had been maintaining a continuous offensive since 22 December, vigorous Allied aerial attacks had been hitting the enemy, and the First Army attack that began on 3 January had been making some progress. At mid-January, however, a fully co-ordinated, full-scale offensive was launched. With the opening of this attack, the Allies seized the initiative, and they were not to relinquish it again.[106]

Shortly before the Allies began their drive in the north, their forces were heavily attacked in the Vosges mountains and in the Strasbourg area. General Bradley feared that SHAEF might stop the Third Army attack in the Ardennes area in order to deal with this southern thrust. He be-

---

[103] Hq ETOUSA GO 5, 23 Jan 44; Interv with Gen Lear, 3 May 48.

[104] Marshall to Eisenhower, W–87829, 6 Jan 45; Marshall to Eisenhower, W–88777, 8 Jan 45. Both in Eisenhower personal file. Hq ASF 200.02 Gen Somervell's Inspection Trip to the ETO 333. See Ruppenthal, Logistical Support of the Armies, Vol. II, for full discussion of this matter.

[105] This attack, envisaged by the Allies in late December, had become obvious to the enemy by 28 December, as shown by an entry of that date in the *OB WEST KTB.*

[106] A detailed account of the Allied attack will be found in Cole, The Ardennes.

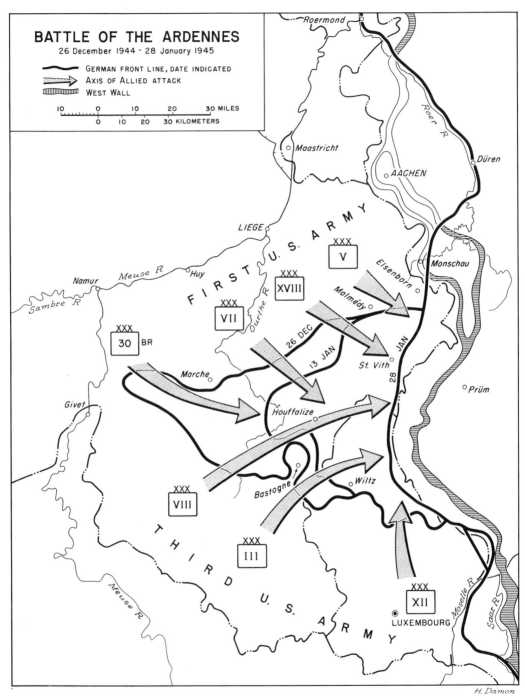

BATTLE OF THE ARDENNES
26 December 1944 - 28 January 1945

GERMAN FRONT LINE, DATE INDICATED
AXIS OF ALLIED ATTACK
WEST WALL

10   0   10   20   30 MILES
0   10   20   30 KILOMETERS

Roermond

Maastricht

AACHEN

Düren

Roer R.

LIEGE

FIRST U.S. ARMY

XXX
V

Monschau

Eisenborn

Meuse R.

Huy

XXX
XVIII

Malmédy

Namur

XXX
VII

26 DEC

13 JAN

St. Vith

28 JAN

Sambre R.

Ourthe R.

Prüm

XXX
30 BR

Marche

Houffalize

Givet

XXX
VIII

Bastogne

Wiltz

XXX
III

THIRD U.S. ARMY

Meuse R.

XXX
XII

LUXEMBOURG

Moselle R.

Saar R.

H. Damon

MAP 6

lieved that the army should stay on the offensive. General Patton, unimpressed by attacks on his XX Corps front in the south, strongly criticized what he called the strictly defensive views of SHAEF.[107] Supreme Headquarters was worried about the situation to the south and wanted to form a SHAEF reserve, but it did not interfere with the opening of the attack.

There was adequate basis for concern over the Alsatian counteroffensive. But the enemy's efforts in the Ardennes were at an end. As early as 3 January, Field Marshal Rundstedt had informed his commanders that there was no prospect for the success of the Ardennes attack as planned. On 8 January, Hitler authorized limited withdrawals of his forces in that area, including the movement of nearly all of the *Sixth Panzer Army* to an area northeast of St. Vith and east of Wiltz where Allied counterattacks were expected. On the following day, the armored units of the *Sixth Panzer Army* were ordered out of the line and sent to a rest area in the rear of *Army Group G.* Five days later, a general withdrawal to a line east of Houffalize was approved.[108]

As the German units started withdrawing, the Allied forces pressed in toward Houffalize. They took the town on the 15th, and elements of the First and Third Armies linked up on the following day. In accordance with earlier arrangements, SHAEF now readjusted the Allied command setup. Control of the First Army was handed back to General Bradley at midnight of 17 January, while the Ninth Army was directed to remain under Field Marshal Montgomery for his attack toward the Rhine.[109] In anticipation of this shift in command, the 21 Army Group commander had already expressed his admiration to General Bradley for the work of the U.S. forces. He wrote:

My Dear Brad

It does seem as if the battle of the "salient" will shortly be drawing to a close, and when it is all clean and tidy I imagine that your armies will be returning to your operational command.

I would like to say two things:—

First: What a great honour it has been for me to command such fine troops.

Second: how well they have all done.

It has been a great pleasure to work with Hodges and Simpson: both have done very well.

And the Corps Commanders in the First Army (Gerow, Collins, Ridgway) have been quite magnificent; it must be most exceptional to find such a good lot of Corps Commanders gathered together in one Army.

All of us in the northern side of the salient would like to say how much we have admired the operations that have been conducted on the southern side; if you had not held on firmly to Bastogne the whole situation might have become very awkward.

My kind regard to you and to George Patton.

Yrs very sincerely,
B. L. Montgomery[110]

The U.S. forces now redoubled their pressure on the Germans, who fell back "with skill and dogged fighting" toward Germany. The skill of their ground troops was no match, however, for continuous attacks from the air. Despite bad flying weather, the Allied air forces kept up their strikes against the enemy columns.[111] Any

---

[107] Diary, Gen Gay, 11, 14 Jan 45, OCMH files.

[108] MS # C–020, *Ausarbeitung, Die Deutsche Wehrmacht in der letzten Phase des Krieges,* 1 Jan–7 May 45 (Schramm). This manuscript was prepared from the draft *OKW/WFSt* records and daily notes in 1948.

[109] Bradley, *A Soldier's Story,* p. 492.

[110] Montgomery to Bradley, 12 Jan 45, Eisenhower personal file. A copy of the original was sent to General Eisenhower with the covering note: "It has been a very great honour for me to command two American armies."

[111] Particularly striking were the results gained by the air forces on 22 January—a day in which the XIX Tactical Air Command claimed over 1,100 motor vehicles destroyed and another 536 damaged. The

TABLE 2—ESTIMATED CASUALTIES IN THE ARDENNES

Force	Total	Killed	Wounded	Missing
Total Allied	76,890	8,607	47,129	21,144
Total U. S.	75,482	8,407	46,170	20,905
First U. S. Army	39,957	4,629	23,152	12,176
Third U. S. Army	35,525	3,778	23,018	8,729
30 Br. Corps (to 17 Jan)	1,408	200	969	239

Source: G–3 SHAEF to G–2 SHAEF, 2 Feb 45, SHAEF G–3 file Battle of the Ardennes GCT/370–49/Ops A.

hopes the Germans had of bettering their situation by transferring forces from the east were dashed by the opening of the Russian offensive on 12 January. On 20 January, as the situation worsened in both east and west, Hitler notified von Rundstedt to be prepared to send the *Sixth Panzer Army* with four SS panzer divisions and the two Fuehrer brigades to the Russian front. Reichsfuehrer SS Himmler was transferred at the same time from *Army Group Oberrhein,* which he had commanded since November 1944, to *Army Group Weichsel* in the east. Von Rundstedt was also ordered to regroup his forces to meet an expected Allied thrust to the Ruhr. One by one the gains so quickly taken were given up to the Allies, while troops and matériel desperately needed for the defense of the Roer and the Rhine were smashed by ground and air forces as the retreating columns clogged the road nets of the Ardennes. By 28 January 1945, all the ground which the Allies had lost to the enemy in the Ardennes counteroffensive had been retaken.

In simple bookkeeping terms, one cannot be sure of the cost to the enemy in men. The First U.S. Army estimated that by mid-January von Rundstedt had lost one fourth of the men with whom he opened the 16 December attack, as well as one half of the vehicles. Some Allied estimates ran as high as 103,900 casualties, excluding nonbattle losses and including more than 24,000 killed and 16,000 prisoners. Enemy estimates were somewhat lower. In one case, a figure of 92,234 total casualties is mentioned; in others, the figure is fixed at 81,834 including 12,652 dead. Enemy claims of 125,000 casualties inflicted on Allied units have proved to be greatly exaggerated. Nonetheless, the cost to U.S. forces was heavy. Statistics furnished General Eisenhower at the beginning of February 1945, while undoubtedly only approximations, give an idea of the considerable losses taken by the Allied forces. *(Table 2)* The estimates indicate that the twenty-nine U.S. and four British divisions employed at one time or another in the Ardennes area sustained 76,780 casualties, of which nearly 40,000 were in the First Army, 35,525 in the Third Army, and 1,408 in the 30 British Corps. If the lowest German estimate of enemy losses can be taken as correct, the casualties were

enemy air force made its most vigorous attack on 1 January 1945, using about 700 planes. Craven and Cate, *The Army Air Forces in World War II,* III, 709–10, 665.

roughly the same on both sides. The great difference was—and of this the Germans were thoroughly conscious—the Allies could replace their losses in men and matériel; the enemy could not.[112]

The Attack in Northern Alsace

While General Eisenhower was still reorganizing his forces to drive the enemy from the Ardennes, he was faced with another German attack in Alsace. It came at a time when he was attempting to form a reserve force from the army group in the threatened region and forced him to consider a withdrawal from part of Alsace. This, in turn, raised a political issue between the Supreme Commander and the French Government.

Hitler had considered a counteroffensive in northern Alsace in the fall of 1944, but had put it aside in favor of the Ardennes operation. When that counteroffensive began to go badly and when he realized that the U.S. forces in the area had been shifted northward to aid First Army, he again turned his attention to Alsace. There *Army Group G's First Army* and *Army Group Oberrhein's Nineteenth Army* opposed General Devers' Seventh U.S. and First French Armies. The Germans on 24 and 25 December formulated plans for an operation called *NORDWIND*. They planned to attack from West Wall positions near the boundary of northern Alsace and drive east and west of Bitche toward the Saverne Gap lying directly to the south. German forces that were to cross the Rhine north of Strasbourg and enemy units from the Colmar bridgehead were supposed to link up with the northern force east of the Vosges mountains. If this maneuver succeeded, U.S. units in the northeastern Alsatian salient would be cut

off, Strasbourg endangered, and the French forces near Colmar threatened with defeat.[113] *(Map 7)*

When the Seventh U.S. Army intelligence section on 26 December estimated that the enemy might attack northern Alsace between 1 and 3 January, General Devers flew to Paris to discuss the situation on his front. General Eisenhower and his staff, still preoccupied with the Ardennes battle, apparently repeated their previous advice that the 6th Army Group commander be prepared to give ground rather than endanger the integrity of his forces. As a result of the conference with SHAEF officials, General Devers ordered General de Lattre and General Patch to remain on the defensive. He listed three intermediate positions to which the forces in northern Alsace could fall back. At the same time he asked his commanders to hold Strasbourg and Mulhouse if possible.[114]

As signs of a possible German attack multiplied, General Devers asked the Supreme Commander to leave with the 6th Army Group the units earmarked for SHAEF reserve until the threat to northern Alsace disappeared or until the Sev-

---

[112] FUSA Rpt of Opns, Vol. I; MS # A–858, Schramm, *Course of Events of the German Offensive in the Ardennes; The War in the West* 01–SIR/39 (Scheidt), p. 109; MS # C–020, *History of the Armed Forces* (Schramm), p. 108. The figures in Table 2 represent a hasty compilation prepared for General Eisenhower during the action. For a postwar summary of the Ardennes–Alsace campaign casualties, see below, Table 3. For tabular summaries of Allied strength and casualty figures during entire period of the war, see Appendix E.

[113] Seventh Army History, II, Ch. XXII; *Army Group G, KTB Nr. 3b 1.-31.XII.44*, 21 to 25 Dec 44; MS # C–020 (Schramm). The tactical control of *Nineteenth Army* had been transferred from *Army Group G* to *Army Group Oberrhein* on 7 December 1944.

[114] 6th A Gp, Ltr of Instr 7, 28 Dec 44, and other entries in 6th A Gp Opn Rpts, Dec 44.

GENERAL JUIN

enth Army could build a reserve of its own.[115]

Before SHAEF had a chance to answer the request, the enemy had acted. Striking just before midnight on 31 December, the German forces drove southward from their West Wall positions against the Seventh U.S. Army in the area south of Bitche. This attack was executed in two main drives, of which the western one was halted after two days of fighting, while the eastern one pressed forward to the western passages of the Vosges. The enemy, however, was still short of the Saverne Gap on 5 January.

The Question of Strasbourg

General Eisenhower, in the face of the new attack, had to decide whether or not to fall back to new positions in northern Alsace. As early as 26 December, he had considered the possibility of shortening his line in that area in order to get a SHAEF reserve. In discussing the matter with his advisers at that time, he had said that he might have to bring his forces back to the Vosges mountains, thus leaving Strasbourg exposed to the enemy. When Tedder questioned the wisdom of the action, the Supreme Commander said that he had been willing to consider the measure only because of the great need for a strategic reserve. He agreed that it would be a disappointment to give up ground, but added that the area then held by General Devers was not the one in which the 6th Army Group commander had been told to put his weight.[116]

The hint of a withdrawal from Strasbourg was especially unwelcome to the French. General Juin, Chief of Staff of the Ministry of Defense, when informed on 30 December that a withdrawal might be necessary, strongly disapproved the suggestion and spoke of placing newly organized FFI units at Devers' disposal to defend the Strasbourg area. Despite this reaction and the reluctance of the 6th Army Group commander to give up the territory, General Eisenhower on 1 January ordered General Devers to shorten his line in northeastern Alsace and to hold the Alsace plain with reconnaissance and observation forces only. This order, which the French might have accepted on purely military grounds, was politically unacceptable. Strasbourg, lost to the French

[115] 6th A Gp Weekly Intel Summary 15, 30 Dec 44; 6th A Gp Opns Rpts, Dec 44; SUSA G–2 Estimate 6, 29 Dec 44; SUSA Diary, 14 Aug 44–31 Jan 45; Devers to SHAEF, 31 Dec 44, 6th A Gp Opns Rpts, Dec 44.

[116] Air Marshal Robb, Notes of mtg in SAC's office, 26 Dec 44, OCMH files; SUSA Rpt of Opns, Vol. II; 6th A Gp Opns Rpts, Dec 44.

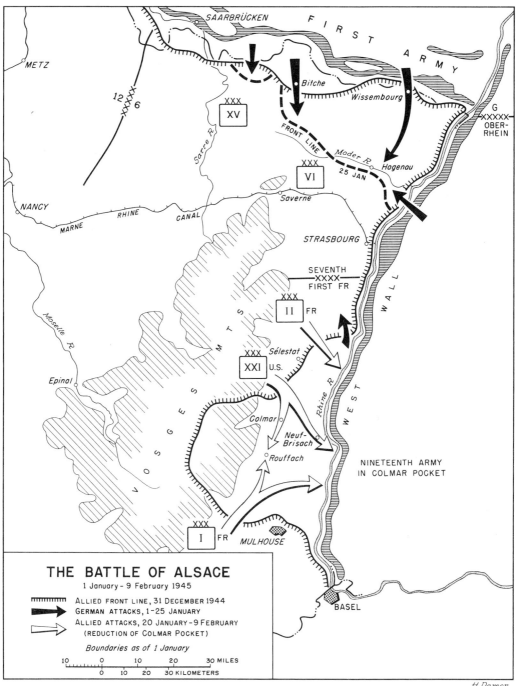

METZ

SAARBRÜCKEN

FIRST ARMY

12 XX 6

XXX
XV

Bitche

Wissembourg

G
XXXXX
OBER-
RHEIN

FRONT LINE 25 JAN

Moder R.

Hagenau

XXX
VI

NANCY

MARNE

RHINE

CANAL

Sarre R.

Saverne

V
O
S
G
E
S

M
T
S

STRASBOURG

SEVENTH
XXXX
FIRST FR

Moselle R.

Epinal

XXX
II FR

XXX
XXI U.S.

Sélestat

Rhine R.

W
E
S
T

W
A
L
L

Colmar

Neuf-
Brisach

Rouffach

NINETEENTH ARMY
IN COLMAR POCKET

XXX
I FR

MULHOUSE

BASEL

THE BATTLE OF ALSACE
1 January - 9 February 1945

━━━━ ALLIED FRONT LINE, 31 DECEMBER 1944
➡ GERMAN ATTACKS, 1-25 JANUARY
⇨ ALLIED ATTACKS, 20 JANUARY-9 FEBRUARY
   (REDUCTION OF COLMAR POCKET)

Boundaries as of 1 January

10 ___ 0 ___ 10 ___ 20 ___ 30 MILES
0 __ 10 __ 20 __ 30 KILOMETERS

MAP 7

from 1870 to 1918 and again from 1940 to its liberation in 1944, could not be handed back to the enemy without severe political repercussions. On 1 January, General de Gaulle expressed his anxiety over the proposed withdrawal and General Juin asked that the order be reconsidered. Next day, in a stormy session with General Smith, General Juin indicated that the French might remove their forces from General Eisenhower's control if the Supreme Commander persisted in his plan to withdraw. When on 3 January General Patch passed on the order for forces under his command to evacuate Strasbourg, the French military governor of the city, General Schwartz, warned of the terrible reprisals the Germans would take against inhabitants of Strasbourg in case of withdrawal and added that he could not undertake any such action without a direct order from the French Government.[117]

General de Gaulle went further on 3 January and declared that the deliberate evacuation of Alsace and part of Lorraine without a fight would be a major error from both the military and the national points of view. He informed the Supreme Commander that General de Lattre was being advised "to defend with the French forces he had the position he [was] at present occupying and to equally defend Strasbourg, even if the American forces [withdrew] on the left."[118]

General Eisenhower discussed the withdrawal from Strasbourg with his staff on the morning of 3 January, apparently before receiving General de Gaulle's protest against that measure. Once the withdrawal to the Vosges had been made, the Supreme Commander said, Allied armor should still be able to operate in the Alsace plain north of Strasbourg to delay or stop an enemy advance on that city. He

thought that the bulk of the Allied forces would have to come back from northeastern Alsace, and that they should send out mobile elements to give warnings of the enemy's advance. General Eisenhower and his advisers examined in particular the grave political repercussions of the withdrawal. They realized that the action could mean a breaking away of the French from the Allies. Opinions were expressed that more than 100,000 inhabitants would have to be evacuated from Strasbourg and that 300,000 to 400,000 inhabitants of the area would be subject to possible reprisals by the Germans. The staff concluded that the Prime Minister, who was scheduled to arrive at Versailles that afternoon, would have to be briefed on the necessity of the withdrawal, since General de Gaulle would probably raise with him the question of Strasbourg.[119]

Shortly after making his protest to General Eisenhower on 3 January, General de Gaulle appealed to President Roosevelt and to Mr. Churchill to stop the withdrawal. The Supreme Commander was apparently unaware of this action at the time of his morning conference that day.[120] The President promptly refused to act in

---

[117] 6th A Gp Ltr of Instr 7, 28 Dec 44; 6th A Gp Opns Rpts, Dec 44, p. 98; Air Marshal Robb, Notes on mtgs in SAC's office, 1, 3 Jan 45, OCMH files; Schwartz to Patch, 3 Jan 45, SUSA Diary, Vol. II.

[118] Eisenhower to de Gaulle, 2 Jan 45; de Gaulle to Eisenhower, 3 Jan 45; Eisenhower to de Gaulle, 5 Jan 45. All in Diary Office CinC. Citation of the de Gaulle letter is from the translation prepared for General Eisenhower. This copy does not show the exact time the message was written or received. It is likely that it arrived after the morning meeting held by the Supreme Commander and his staff, but before the conference of Generals Eisenhower and de Gaulle in the afternoon.

[119] Robb, Notes on mtg in SAC's office, 3 Jan 45, OCMH files.

[120] Caffery to State Dept and President from de Gaulle, 3 Jan 45, Diary Office CinC. Sometime during the day Ambassador Caffery gave the mes-

the matter and notified the Secretary of State, through whom the appeal was sent, that the question was a military one and should be taken up with General Eisenhower. The Prime Minister flew to Versailles from the United Kingdom on the 3d. He had lunch with the Supreme Commander and afterward sat in on a conference attended by Field Marshal Brooke and Generals Eisenhower, Smith, Whiteley, and Strong. Still later in the day he was present at General Eisenhower's conference with Generals de Gaulle and Juin.[121]

Before his meeting with de Gaulle on the afternoon of 3 January, General Eisenhower had decided to modify his initial plans for withdrawal "to the extent of merely swinging the Sixth Corps back from its sharp salient with its left resting in the Vosges and its right extending southward generally towards Strasbourg." This change was accepted by General de Gaulle when it was presented. The Prime Minister did not intervene in the discussion but approved the new arrangement, saying that he appreciated the concern of the French leaders over the possible political effects of a withdrawal from Strasbourg.[122]

The change of orders in regard to Strasbourg led to considerable uncertainty at army level where several sets of completely contradictory instructions were received in the course of a few hours. Strasbourg was virtually undefended for a part of one day. On SHAEF's change of its initial order, General Devers accepted the Seventh Army suggestion that a position be established along the Maginot Line and the Rhine River and that several successive

lines be organized to which withdrawal could be made later if it became necessary.[123] The city itself was never again left unprotected.

Indications of U.S. withdrawals between the lower Vosges and the Rhine may have been responsible for a decision of the enemy to turn his main attention from the area of Bitche to points farther east. Starting on 4 January, the Germans attacked south of Wissembourg, and on 5 January other units drove across the Rhine north of Strasbourg. More attacks south of Strasbourg followed on 7 January.

---

[121] Marshall to Eisenhower, 7 Jan 45; Eisenhower to Marshall, S–73871, 6 Jan 45. Both in Eisenhower personal file. Entry in Diary Office CinC, 3 Jan 45; statements of de Gaulle and Juin to author. General Eisenhower told General Marshall in a message of 6 January 1945 that the Prime Minister's presence in Paris on 3 January was purely coincidental.

[122] Eisenhower to Marshall, S–73871, 6 Jan 45, Eisenhower personal file; entry in Diary Office CinC, 3 Jan 46. In the fall of 1945, several French newspapers reported that General Eisenhower had changed his order under pressure from the Prime Minister. Mr. Churchill at that time informed General Eisenhower that he was willing to issue a contradiction of the story, if the U.S. commander thought it worth while. Eisenhower said that no statement was necessary, but took the occasion to remind Mr. Churchill that the latter, with his usual confidence, had left the settlement of the matter to the Supreme Commander. General Eisenhower said that he had been convinced by General de Gaulle that the political developments which would follow a partial withdrawal in Alsace would lead to a deterioration of the situation in the rear areas far in excess of the value of getting one or two divisions for the SHAEF reserve. In 1949, when the city of Strasbourg gave Mr. Churchill an award for having saved the city in January 1945, the former Prime Minister confirmed a statement that he had flown to France on General de Gaulle's appeal, but paid tribute to General Eisenhower "as that great American soldier who was willing to assume additional risks rather than expose the people of Strasbourg to German vengeance." Churchill to Eisenhower, 8 Nov 45; Eisenhower to Churchill, 9 Nov 45. Both in Eisenhower personal file. New York *Times*, August 16, 1949.

[123] SUSA Rpt of Opns, Vol. II, Ch. XXII.

---

sage to General Eisenhower. The Ambassador, in accepting the message for transmittal, told de Gaulle he would take this action. Caffery to President and Secy State, 3 Jan 45, OPD 381, Sec I.

TABLE 3—U. S. BATTLE CASUALTIES, ARDENNES–ALSACE, 16 DECEMBER 1944–25 JANUARY 1945

Type	Total	Divisions	Nondivisional Units
Total	a 104,944	88,165	16,779
Killed in action	15,982	12,340	3,642
Wounded in action	62,372	53,216	9,156
Captured	23,554	20,102	3,452
Returned to duty from missing in action	b 2,802	2,333	469
Died while missing in action	234	174	60

a These data do not include nonbattle casualties due to frost bite, injuries behind the lines, sickness, and other casualties not resulting from enemy action.

b Early compilations in 1945 of casualties showed more than 20,000 as missing in action. In subsequent months and years most of these were found to have been captured, killed in action, or wounded in action. As a result, casualty accounting adjustments reduced the missing-in-action totals and increased the appropriate categories.

Source: The Adjutant General, Strength Authorization Branch, 1951–52.

Between 8 and 25 January, the enemy fought stubbornly to extend his gains from the bridgeheads, and the U.S. forces found it necessary to establish alternate lines to which they could retire. (Table 3) The French were made responsible for the defense of Strasbourg during the period.[124]

6th Army Group Counterattack

Toward the end of January, General Eisenhower released five U.S. divisions and 12,000 service troops from the SHAEF reserve to 6th Army Group. A U.S. corps was placed under General de Lattre to help him reduce the Colmar Pocket. The Supreme Commander, wanting to see the Germans pushed out of this salient and across the Rhine, pressed the French to reduce the pocket promptly. In so doing he repeated an appeal that he had made earlier in the month. He reminded General de Gaulle of the need of keeping French infantry units at full strength and said that it might be easier

to get equipment for new French divisions if it were possible to show that those in existence were being properly maintained. In a conference with General Juin on 23 January, the Supreme Commander again referred to the importance of the campaign in Alsace and expressed the hope that the French forces would be inspired to excel their own former records.

The French leaders reacted sharply. On being told of the conversation, General de Gaulle expressed surprise at the "severity of a judgment" he believed directed solely at the French command. General Juin, in a conference on the following day, reminded the Supreme Commander that since November the length of the First French Army's front had been doubled without any proportionate increase in reinforcements. Despite this fact, the French had not lost any ground and were even then developing an offensive in the face of problems of terrain, weather, fatigue, and

[124] Army Group G, KTB Nr. 4 1.I.–28.II.45, 4 to 7 Jan 45.

insufficient resources. It was difficult in view of these conditions, he said bluntly, to avoid a comparison "between the valiant efforts they furnish and the goings-on in the neighboring Army [apparently the Seventh] further to the North." General Juin asked that the problem in Alsace be treated as an army group question and not as something solely French. He added: "If errors have been committed, and they are divided, the fact remains, nevertheless, that the important thing today is that you win the battle of Alsace as you have won the battle of the Ardennes. That, in my opinion, as I told you yesterday, should be your sole preoccupation of the moment." [125]

General Eisenhower promptly disclaimed any intention of casting reflections on the French efforts and repeated that never as an Allied commander had he "compared unfavorably the troops and leaders of one nationality with respect to any other." He also accepted General Juin's suggestion that the matter be thoroughly discussed with General de Gaulle. The ensuing conference, like several others held previously between the Supreme Commander and the French leader, was extremely frank but devoid of recriminations. General Eisenhower made clear that he had no intention of criticizing or minimizing the contributions of the army of any particular nationality, but wished to impress on every member of the First French Army the critical significance of the offensive to clear the Colmar Pocket. He wanted the French to carry out the Alsatian operation with the same punch that they had used in Italy, the south of France, and the Belfort drive. General de Gaulle reminded the Supreme Commander that the French forces were tired as a result of the long period they had

been kept in the lines. He agreed to try to instill into them the drive and will essential to the success of the operation, but reminded General Eisenhower that Allied infantry strength was weak, artillery support was not sufficient to insure the success of large-scale operations, air reinforcement was diminished because of bad weather, and the enemy was resolved to fight a last-ditch battle. In the light of these factors, he believed that the troops could undertake only local actions in the near future. At the same time, he thought that sufficient units could be built up in the rear of these forces for a large-scale attack. The Supreme Commander nodded assent to this analysis and made clear that he was doing his best to get equipment for additional French divisions. He expressed his appreciation for the straightforward discussion with General de Gaulle, inasmuch as "a frank exchange of views on little problems that seemed at the moment to be difficult always led to a mutually satisfactory understanding." [126]

While these talks over the role of the French were in progress, the enemy had made a final attack against the Allied positions in northern Alsace. The Seventh Army repelled this drive on 25 January and regained the initiative which it held for the remainder of the war. Hitler, at this point, desiring to hold his reserves for further defensive efforts, suspended attacks in the lower Vosges and lower Alsace. While the Seventh Army held firmly in the Sarre valley and made minor gains in the area flooded by the Moder, the First French

---

[125] Ltr, Juin to Eisenhower, 24 Jan 45; Eisenhower to Juin, 24 Jan 45. Both in Eisenhower personal file.
[126] Résumé of conversation, Eisenhower and de Gaulle, 25 Jan 45 (made by Lt Col L. E. Dostert), Diary Office CinC, 26 Jan 45.

Army opened its attack to clear the Colmar Pocket. On 29 January, General de Lattre sent his U.S. corps against Colmar, which fell four days later. The French forces, which had pushed steadily eastward, linked up with U.S. units on 5 February to split the Colmar Pocket. Von Rundstedt, already authorized by Hitler to withdraw from the area when it proved necessary, now pulled back and ordered his forces east of the Rhine. As the Germans started withdrawing, the French and U.S. forces quickly cleared the Colmar Pocket, completing their task on 9 February. In northern Alsace and eastern Lorraine, the Seventh Army started a drive on 17 February to straighten its lines, establishing a foothold on German soil just south of Saarbruecken at the month's end. In the meantime to the left of the Seventh Army, Third Army units had driven through the Orscholz Switch Line to points east of Sarrebourg and south of Trier, occupying a considerable portion of German soil.

Effects of the German Counteroffensive

The battles between 16 December and 9 February in the Ardennes sector and in Alsace inflicted heavy losses on the enemy. By coming out of their established positions from which the Allied troops had tried so painfully to eject them, the Germans had lost men and matériel they could not replace. Despite these reverses, they still managed to maintain some of their fighting spirit. Even as they were withdrawing, the Nazi hierarchy organized the old and the very young into *Volkssturm* units, talked darkly of "Werewolf" units which would strike terror into invading forces, and hoped that the diminishing numbers of the fanatical faithful would be sufficient to rally the others to fight for the homeland. So far as the Allies were concerned, the enemy had done his worst and had failed. There could now be little doubt of the ultimate result. The question was: how great would be the price and how long the struggle?

CHAPTER XXI

The Battle for the Rhineland

The enemy counteroffensive in the Ardennes halted the Allied advance but did not stop preparations for later attacks. While the main energies of the Supreme Commander were directed toward shifting his forces to parry the German thrusts, his staff continued to work on plans for clearing the area west of the Rhine, for crossing the Rhine, and for advancing eastward into Germany. From the end of December on, General Eisenhower turned his attention increasingly to these operations.

Russian Plans

In planning for winter and spring offensives, the Supreme Commander found that much depended on the date and scale of the Red Army's anticipated winter offensive. The appearance of German divisions transferred to the Western Front from Hungary and East Prussia increased his problems and made it difficult to know how to plan, and he had little indication from the Russians of their intentions.[1] Marshal Stalin, for his part, did not fail to seek information regarding the plans of the Western powers. On 14 December, in talking with Ambassador Harriman, the Soviet chief asked about General Eisenhower's future moves. Harriman said that the SHAEF forces were preparing to push to the Rhine and that they desired to operate in concert with the Russians. For this

reason, he added, the Supreme Commander needed to be informed about developments on the Eastern Front. Stalin replied that he would consult with his staff and would probably be able to give some information in about a week. He noted that bad weather had prevented the Red Army from making the best use of its superiority in artillery and air power, but a winter offensive, he assured the Ambassador, would be launched.[2]

Apparently the Russian leader's answers were not passed on directly to General Eisenhower, for on 21 December, a week after Harriman's talk with Stalin, the Supreme Commander asked the Combined Chiefs of Staff for information from the Russians. He spoke again of the recent tendency of the Germans to move divisions from the east to the west. "The arrival of these divisions," he declared, "obviously influences the events in my area and if the trend continues it will affect the decisions which I have to make regarding future strategy in the west. . . . If, for instance, it is the Russian intention to launch a major offensive in the course of this or next month, knowledge of the fact would be of the utmost importance to me and I would condition my plans accordingly. Can any-

---

[1] Eisenhower to Marshall, 5 Dec 44, SHAEF SGS 381 Post OVERLORD Planning, II.

[2] Mil Mission Moscow to WD, M–22052, 17 Dec 44, OPD cbl files (TS).

thing be done to effect this coordination?"[3] The general proposed to send to Stalin a high-ranking officer of the SHAEF staff who would be prepared to tell the marshal of forthcoming Allied plans and in return receive information on the Red Army.

President Roosevelt, in response to this request, on 23 December asked Marshal Stalin to receive a SHAEF staff officer to discuss the situation in the west and its relation to the Russian front. The President added that the situation in Belgium was not bad, but that it was necessary to see what came next. The Russian leader promptly agreed to the proposed conference.[4]

The War Department's announcement that Marshal Stalin would receive a SHAEF representative also informed the Supreme Commander of suggestions made by the Russian leader to Mr. Churchill during the latter's Moscow visit in October 1944 and to Mr. Harriman in December. On both occasions the marshal had spoken of a possible transfer of Allied forces from Italy to the Balkans to join the Russians near Vienna. At the October meeting he had inquired about the possibility of an Allied advance through Switzerland to outflank the West Wall, and in the December conversation he had spoken casually of a possible break-through by General Devers' forces to the east to link up with the Red Army's left flank.[5] The Combined Chiefs of Staff in their instructions for the SHAEF representatives removed entirely from the realm of discussion the question of breaching Swiss neutrality. The suggested break-through by General Devers' forces toward Vienna was vetoed as conflicting with the northern drive into Germany then being planned. In the matter of sending forces from Italy to the Balkans, a plan which the Allies had already considered for some time, the Combined Chiefs of Staff showed greater interest. They suggested that General Alexander or his representatives might be sent to Moscow later for a conference on that subject. So this matter too was removed from the list which Eisenhower's representatives could discuss.[6]

The SHAEF party, consisting of Air Chief Marshal Tedder, General Bull, and Brig. Gen. Thomas J. Betts, after delays caused by bad weather and aircraft difficulties, finally arrived in the Russian capital on 14 January. Marshal Stalin received the three officers on the following night and at once informed them that the long-awaited Russian offensive, some 150

---

[3] SHAEF to WD, SCAF 155, 21 Dec 44, OPD cbl files (TS). Not only does this letter indicate that General Eisenhower was apparently unaware of Marshal Stalin's statement that he would probably have some information in a week, but General Marshall's letter giving details of the proposal for a link-up of Allied forces in southeastern Austria was not sent until 25 December.

[4] Marshall to Eisenhower, WX–82070, 25 Dec 44, Eisenhower personal file; Marshall to Eisenhower, FACS 118, 26 Dec 44, OPD cbl files (TS).

[5] Marshall to Eisenhower, WARX–82070, 24 Dec 44, Eisenhower personal file. Mil Mission Moscow to WD, M–22149, 24 Dec 44; Mil Mission Moscow to WD, MX–22154, 25 Dec 44. Both in OPD cbl files (TS). Maj. Gen. John R. Deane, head of the U.S. Military Mission to Moscow, said that Stalin had spoken of General Devers' move only casually, and that mention of it had been included to emphasize that Stalin's thinking was apparently directed toward joint action between the Red Army and the Western forces.

[6] CCS to Eisenhower, FACS 119, 29 Dec 44, SHAEF G–3 312.3–1 Correspondence and Communication with the Russians; Prime Minister to President, 31 Dec 44, OPD 336 (TS), Sec I. Mr. Churchill's suggestion of 31 December that General Alexander join the SHAEF group going to the Russian capital in order to discuss the Balkan operation appears to have been dropped as the result of Field Marshal Wilson's statement to the Combined Chiefs of Staff (MEDCOS 228, 8 Jan 45) that he would soon have to go on the defensive in Italy.

to 160 divisions in strength and intended to last from two to two and one-half months, had been launched on 12 January with the mission of reaching the line of the Oder. The Russian leader declared that the attack, which had been under preparation for more than a month, had been delayed until the weather was more favorable but that he had decided to launch it speedily in view of Allied difficulties in the west. The attack had come, of course, two weeks after the German offensive had been stopped in the Ardennes.[7] *(Map 8)*

The Russian chief showed great interest in General Eisenhower's plans and offered advice on how to proceed. While agreeing that the Ruhr was the best place to attack, he noted that the enemy would also be aware of that fact and would be on guard. He recommended that SHAEF amass a strategic reserve of some ten divisions for any further offensive, but, when told that this could be collected only at the expense of a withdrawal from Strasbourg, he admitted that such a move would be of great military and psychological value for the enemy.

Informed by Air Chief Marshal Tedder that SHAEF's chief interest, now that the offensive was started, was in the ability of the Red Army to harass the Germans from mid-March to late May, Stalin said he could not promise a full-scale offensive throughout that period but would use units organized for the purpose to stir up the enemy and prevent him from moving to the Western Front. In commenting on the Germans, the Russian leader declared that they had more stubbornness than brains and that the Ardennes attack was very stupid. He saw no possibility of German surrender before summer, however, since there was no leader around whom op-

position against Hitler could coalesce.

While taking credit for applying pressure on the Eastern Front to aid the western advance, Stalin revealed that he was well aware of his own interest in exerting such pressure. In parting, he told the SHAEF representatives that although he had no treaty with the Western Allies he considered it a proper, sound, and selfish policy for all of them to help one another in time of difficulties. It would be as foolish for him to stand aside while the Germans annihilated the Allies, he added, as it was wise for the Allies to prevent the enemy from crushing the Russians.

Allied permanent representatives in Moscow were pleased with the results of the meeting, which they described as one of the most successful conferences ever held between Allied and Russian representatives in Moscow. They credited Air Chief Marshal Tedder's direct approach with much of this success.[8]

Formulation of Allied Strategy

At the end of December 1944, the Supreme Commander had decided that once

---

[7] This and the four succeeding paragraphs are based on Memo of conf with Marshal Stalin, 15 Jan 45, Smith papers; Mil Mission Moscow to Eisenhower, 18 Jan 45 (quoted in Br COS to JSM, 19 Jan 45), Eisenhower personal file; Intervs with Air Chief Marshal Tedder and Gen Betts; Harriman to Eisenhower, 17 Jan 45, Diary Office CinC, 28 Jan 45.

[8] The direct approach to the Russians was recommended to General Eisenhower by General Marshall about the time of the meeting in Moscow. Speaking of a letter of congratulation which the Supreme Commander had forwarded through the War Department a short time before, the U.S. Chief of Staff declared: "In future I suggest that you approach them [the Russians] in simple Main Street Abilene style. They are rather cynically disposed toward the diplomatic phrasing of our compliments and seem almost to appreciate downright rough talk of which I give a full measure." Marshall to Eisenhower, 17 Jan 45, Eisenhower personal file.

SITUATION IN EUROPE
15 January 1945

AREA UNDER GERMAN CONTROL
AREA UNDER ALLIED CONTROL
NEUTRAL COUNTRIES

0   100   200   300   400   500 MILES
0   500 KILOMETERS

R. Johnstone

MAP 8

the Ardennes salient was reduced he would return the First Army to General Bradley and direct the 12th Army Group commander to open a drive with the First and Third Armies in the direction of Pruem and Bonn. The 21 Army Group would retain the Ninth Army and resume preparations for a major drive to the Rhine directed north of the Ruhr. South of the Ardennes, the front below the Moselle was to remain strictly on the defensive.[9]

In suggesting that the First and Third Armies should push toward the Rhine south of the Ruhr, General Eisenhower again raised the question of where the weight of the Allied attack should be pressed home, an issue long debated between him and Field Marshal Montgomery. On 10 January, the British Chiefs of Staff asked formally for a review of his strategy by the Combined Chiefs of Staff. Insisting that there would not be sufficient strength for two main attacks, the British asked that one major thrust be selected and that only those forces not needed for this purpose be used for other operations. This approach would rather effectively rule out any action by the Third Army. Further, they urged that all activities for the remainder of the winter bear a direct relation to the main front for the spring offensive, a suggestion which if accepted could conceivably stop the entire operation then being considered by General Bradley. The British Chiefs recommended that the Supreme Commander be asked to submit by the end of January reviews of the progress of his operations to date, the effects of the Ardennes counteroffensive on his forces, and his plans for the late winter and spring.[10]

With these actions, the British Chiefs of Staff entered the debate which previously had been carried on mainly by General Eisenhower and Field Marshal Montgomery. In presenting their questions, they appeared to be in the position of championing Montgomery against his superior. If the U.S. Chiefs of Staff so interpreted the British action, the question could easily become one of whether the Supreme Commander was to be upheld rather than one of which strategy was better. Inasmuch as Field Marshal Montgomery's program would have to be adopted over General Eisenhower's protest and since British strategy depended on the shift of at least two U.S. armies to British command, it was doubtful from the outset that the consent of the U.S. Chiefs of Staff could be obtained.

General Eisenhower's Replies

The Supreme Commander was aware of the British views before the formal request was made and had his arguments ready for submission before being asked for them. In replies sent to General Marshall on 10 January, he reiterated many of the points which he had made to Field Marshal Montgomery in November and December 1944. In the first he defended the broad front policy, saying that in order to concentrate a powerful force north of the Ruhr for the invasion of Germany he had to have a firm defensive line which could be held with minimum forces. With such a line, the Allies could threaten the enemy at various points and make easier an invasion in the north. But unless the Allies held the Rhine "substantially" throughout its length, he warned, the enemy with his West Wall de-

---

[9] Eisenhower to Montgomery, and atchd outline plan, 31 Dec 44, Eisenhower personal file.
[10] Marshall to Eisenhower, W–89338, 10 Jan 45, Eisenhower personal file.

fenses would be in a position to concentrate for further counterattacks against the Allied lines of communications. Despite a desire to close to the Rhine, he added, top priority had been given the area north of the Ardennes during late October and November and only secondary actions had been permitted south of that area. He had authorized subsidiary actions in the Saar valley with units which could not profitably be used in the north in the hope that they might drive the enemy across the Rhine in that area. In the last few days before the Ardennes counteroffensive, when rugged and flooded terrain had strongly limited the 21 Army Group's offensive action, he had permitted General Patton to make one more effort to reach the Rhine.[11]

General Eisenhower declared that he was bewildered at British insistence on assurances as to the northern thrust. He repeated that there had never been any doubt of placing his main strength north of the Ruhr and putting that effort under one commander. To the suggestion that his strong concentrations of forces south of the Ruhr did not square with his pledge to put everything possible in the northern thrust, the Supreme Commander replied that he had been told initially by Field Marshal Montgomery that only twenty-five divisions could be sustained in an attack through the northern area. After "almost arbitrary action" on the part of SHAEF, he added, the 21 Army Group commander had sought means of using a larger force.

On two matters, General Eisenhower conceded, definite differences had developed between himself and Field Marshals Brooke and Montgomery. These British officers seemed to consider it logical to advance into Germany on the front from Bonn northward, while leaving the rest of the Allied front south of that position relatively static. In Eisenhower's opinion, the Ardennes counteroffensive showed that, without a strong natural line, the Allies, if they remained static in the south, would have to use more divisions there than they were willing to take away from the major offensive. A second argument had arisen over the point from which the Allies should launch the principal attack in support of the main thrust in the north. The British favored the area Bonn–Cologne. Eisenhower held that the country east of this area was very unfavorable for action, and cited arguments by General Bradley and others in favor of the Frankfurt area. He repeated that it was his intention to make a secondary attack, designed only to force the dispersal of enemy troops and to permit the Allies to use all possible crossings and lines of communications. The U.S. commander said he would accept loyally any decision of the Combined Chiefs of Staff as to the proper place for attack, but warned that unless their long defensive flank was situated firmly on an easily defended line the Allies would have to immobilize more troops than they could afford.[12]

These arguments failed to persuade the British Chiefs of Staff, even as similar statements had failed to convince the 21 Army Group commander that a main thrust in the north and a secondary attack in the south were compatible. The difficulty seemed to develop mainly because of their feeling that any secondary action in which General Patton was concerned would probably become a major

---

[11] Eisenhower to Marshall, S–74461, 10 Jan 45, Eisenhower personal file.
[12] Eisenhower to Marshall, S–74437, 10 Jan 45, Eisenhower personal file.

one. They feared, first, that the stockpile of resources would be diminished and, second, that a successful limited attack might develop into a larger drive which would force the commitment of the main Allied force in an area less productive of results than the north. The whole argument turned, as did the earlier one on the same subject, on whether or not the Supreme Commander in backing these limited attacks would seriously weaken or make impossible the main offensive. On this question, the various commanders could not agree, and there was no immediate decisive result in the field that would give a pragmatic answer to the problem.

In the absence of such an answer, other factors could not be ignored. On the one hand, there was the Ardennes counteroffensive which, in the opinion of many British observers, showed the danger of the broad front policy. On the other hand, U.S. commanders were convinced that public opinion in the United States demanded a major thrust in the area south of the Ardennes. No matter how many arguments might be demonstrated in behalf of the British position, it was difficult for the Supreme Commander to continue shifting U.S. troops to the 21 Army Group and at the same time refuse to U.S. commanders, who had made sweeping advances in the previous summer and who felt that they had been cheated of a Rhine crossing at that time by concessions to the British commander, the chance to make at least small-scale assaults in their area. General Eisenhower's dilemma was stated succinctly in December by one of his key British advisers. This officer, while favoring the northern thrust, explained that the Supreme Commander had twice said "no" to Generals Bradley and Patton while giving preference to the north. Since decisive

results were gained in neither case, it was becoming increasingly difficult for him to say "no" to his U.S. commanders again.

The next problem of importance was the strength necessary to defeat the enemy in western Europe. To the Allied commander in mid-January it appeared that a weak and ineffectual Russian offensive, a partial enemy withdrawal from Italy to the west, and a continued enemy withdrawal from Norway to the west would make it possible for the enemy to keep a maximum of one hundred divisions on the Western Front and prevent a spring offensive. Lacking these conditions, the Germans could maintain only about eighty understrength divisions. To oppose these forces, the Supreme Commander estimated that the Allies by spring would have eighty-five divisions, with five to eight new French divisions in the process of being trained and equipped and with the existing eight French divisions brought to full combat strength.[13]

The chief problem confronting the Allies at the moment, General Eisenhower believed, arose from the enemy's frontier defenses. These formidable positions enabled the Germans to concentrate safely for counterattacks. The Supreme Commander insisted on a good natural line for the defensive parts of the Allied front, saying that for the most part it should be the line of the Rhine, although at some points he felt that it might not be worth the effort to eliminate "the extremely strong but constricted bridgeheads." In these statements, General Eisenhower showed the effect of the Ardennes counteroffensive on his thinking. Before 16 December, he had still been

---

[13] This and the succeeding five paragraphs are based on Eisenhower to Marshall, S–75090, 15 Jan 45, Eisenhower personal file.

willing to take a chance on a sudden thrust in some sector in the hope of getting a break-through to the Rhine; now he talked more of closing up to the Rhine along the entire front before attempting to force a crossing. This development in thinking, while perhaps owing something to the earlier "broad front" theory, probably owed more to the Ardennes attacks. It may also have marked some concession to General Bradley's wish to make limited advances south of the Ardennes. Not to be overlooked is the fact that in November and December the main hope had been to keep pushing in the hope that something might work before winter closed in; in January all eyes were turned toward spring when it might be possible to undertake an all-out offensive again.

The Supreme Commander next considered whether the eighty-five divisions available in the spring would be enough to win the war in the west. He believed they might be if the Russian offensive went well. But, he added, this strength was not sufficient to permit the Allies to depend entirely on one plan of action. If, for example, the enemy concentrated his forces north of the Ruhr, it might be impossible to break through in that area. The forces available for such an attack would, of course, be conditioned by the defensive requirements of the Allied forces. If they were on the line of the Rhine at the time the offensive started, twenty-five divisions would suffice for the defense and reserve, and fifty-five divisions would be available for attack. If the line remained where it was in January, short of the Rhine in the area north of Alsace, the defensive force and reserve would have to be increased by twenty divisions and the offensive forces reduced by the same amount. Even the elimination of the Colmar Pocket, with

the rest of the line remaining the same, would give only ten more divisions for the offensive. Since thirty-five divisions were needed for a full-scale offensive in the north, General Eisenhower reasoned that a line short of the Rhine would leave him only just enough divisions for the main offensive and without any of the twenty divisions he wanted for a secondary attack in the Frankfurt area. With little prospect of getting this number of divisions, he found it increasingly desirable to destroy the German forces west of the Rhine and to close up to the Rhine all along the front. This move, he believed, would be even more necessary should the Russian drive fail or prove ineffectual.[14]

In the final installments of his letters on strategy for coming operations, General Eisenhower visualized the first phase as the destruction of enemy forces west of the Rhine and closing to the Rhine along most of its length. He proposed first to launch a series of operations north of the Moselle to destroy the enemy and then to close to the Rhine north of Duesseldorf. Next he would direct his main efforts toward destroying the enemy on the remainder of the front west of the Rhine.[15] The second phase of operations, coming after the Allied forces had closed to the Rhine, would include attempts to seize bridgeheads over the Rhine between Emmerich

---

[14] These views were strongly presented in his message to Montgomery, 17 January 1945, Eisenhower personal file.

[15] This and the following paragraph are taken from Eisenhower to CCS, SCAF 180, 20 Jan 45, SHAEF SGS 381 Post OVERLORD Planning, III. This message had been anticipated to an extent by a SHAEF Planning Staff Memo on Future Operations (Final Draft), 23 Dec 44, SHAEF G-3 file G-3 18019 Plans Future Operations—1945, I. Eisenhower had also outlined the three phases of future operations in a letter to Marshall, S-74461, 10 January 1945, Eisenhower personal file.

and Wesel in the north and between Mainz and Karlsruhe in the south. These objectives attained, the Allied forces would then open phase three, advancing from the lower Rhine into the plains of northern Germany and from the Mainz–Karlsruhe area to Frankfurt and Kassel.

Running through the plans for these separate phases was a continued emphasis on a much broader plan of attack than that advocated by the British Chiefs of Staff or Field Marshal Montgomery. To General Eisenhower, a crossing in the south would permit the Allies to seize the Saar basin, an area of major industrial importance, and would give them the major airfields in the Frankfurt–Giessen area. More important, it would give greater flexibility to his plan. A single main thrust in the north would possibly be met by a major enemy concentration of forces. Developing the attack from the south would allow the Allies, if necessary, to shift the main weight from north to south, and would give them several different means of developing their attack once they reached the Kassel area. At that point, they could thrust northward to cut communications out of the Ruhr, they could drive northeast toward Berlin, or they could advance eastward toward Leipzig.

Discussion of Strategy by the Combined Chiefs

The answers of the Supreme Commander did not allay the fears of the British Chiefs of Staff. To them, the continuous emphasis on closing to the Rhine and the stress on a thrust in the Frankfurt area made the main offensive in the north impossible. They decided, therefore, that the question would have to be examined further by the Combined Chiefs of Staff be-

fore the Yalta Conference in early February. The issue came to a head in late January 1945, shortly before the meeting with Marshal Stalin.

En route to Yalta, General Marshall, wishing to get General Eisenhower's views but realizing that it would be difficult for the Supreme Commander to leave his headquarters for an extended period, asked that Eisenhower meet him at Marseille. Marshall there discussed future Allied plans and assured Eisenhower that he would back the SHAEF strategy. He also made clear that he would not accept a ground commander, saying that if such a step were approved he would not remain as Chief of Staff.[16]

The Combined Chiefs of Staff stopped at Malta on 30 January to review Allied strategy for northwest Europe before proceeding to the Yalta Conference. Generals Smith and Bull of Supreme Headquarters presented the plans of the Supreme Commander. The British Chiefs of Staff feared that General Eisenhower would make no effort to cross the Rhine, even in the north, until all territory west of the river was clear of the enemy. They were not satisfied by General Smith's view that his chief would not delay a crossing (1) if resistance was such that an attempt to clear the west bank would take until midsummer or (2) if the delay interfered with a chance to seize a bridgehead and cross in strength on the northern front. General Smith wired General Eisenhower that the British wanted written assurance that the main effort would be made in the north and that

---

[16] The meeting at Marseille was apparently held on 27 January, although there is some confusion in accounts. See Butcher, *My Three Years With Eisenhower*, pp. 751–52; and Edward R. Stettinius, Jr., *Roosevelt and the Russians: The Yalta Conference* (Garden City, N. Y., 1949), p. 35; Notes on conf with Gen Marshall, 28 Jan 45, Diary Office CinC.

the Rhine crossing would not be delayed until the entire area west of the river was cleared. He also sent the draft of a statement suggested by General Marshall which declared that the SHAEF plan was: "(A) To carry out immediately a series of operations north of the Moselle with a view to destroying the enemy and closing the Rhine north of Duesseldorf. (B) to direct our efforts to eliminating other enemy forces west of the Rhine which still constitute an obstacle or a potential threat to our subsequent Rhine crossings operations." The Supreme Commander accepted this phrasing and then added: "You may assure the Combined Chiefs of Staff in my name that I will seize the Rhine crossings in the north just as soon as this is a feasible operation and without waiting to close the Rhine throughout its length. Further, I will advance across the Rhine in the north with maximum strength and complete determination immediately the situation in the south allows me to collect necessary forces without incurring unreasonable risks." On 2 February, the Combined Chiefs of Staff accepted the Supreme Commander's plan as explained by his cable.[17]

General Eisenhower had met the two objections of the British mentioned by General Smith by saying that the main effort would be in the north and that he would not delay the crossing until the entire area west of the Rhine was cleared— but it is doubtful that his statements were entirely what they wanted. The way was still open for continuing operations south of the Ruhr and south of the Moselle which Field Marshal Montgomery regarded as directly prejudicial to his operations. Since two questions were subject to various interpretations—namely, (1) what German forces constituted a potential

threat to subsequent operations; (2) at what time could forces be collected in the south without incurring unreasonable risks—there was still the possibility of future misunderstandings. With the U.S. Chiefs of Staff solidly behind the Supreme Commander, it seemed clear that it was his interpretation which would prevail.

The meeting at Malta also saw the end of proposals to intensify the Allied effort in the Mediterranean. In the summer and fall of 1944, these had taken the form of suggestions by Mr. Churchill, but not by the British Chiefs of Staff, to shift some Allied forces into the Balkans. The U.S. Chiefs of Staff,[18] opposed to operations which they considered to be mainly political, were firm in the belief that no U.S. troops should be used in that area, but they were not inclined to oppose British activity there if the forces used were not needed to assure victory elsewhere.[19] The chances that any Allied divisions would be available for such operations were dimin-

---

[17] CCS 182d Mtg, 30 Jan 45, at Malta; CCS 183d Mtg, 31 Jan 45, at Malta. Smith to Eisenhower, Cricket 18, 30 Jan 45; Eisenhower to Smith, S-77211, 31 Jan 45; Smith to Eisenhower, 2 Feb 45. All in Eisenhower personal file.

[18] It should be noted that Lt. Gen. Mark W. Clark, commander of the Fifth U.S. Army in Italy and later of the 15th Army Group, favored the Churchillian position. See Clark's *Calculated Risk* (New York, 1950), pp. 367–72.

[19] The U.S. Joint Staff Planners had said in August 1944: "While the United States has no interest in Southeast Europe, this area is of vital interest to the British. . . . It is to our best interests to support Great Britain in any Southeast operations insofar as is consistent with our established policies." JWPC 259/7, Preparations for Next Allied Staff Conference (War against Germany), 26 Aug 44, ABC 337 (14 Sep 44), Sec 1; cf. JCS 1034, War Against Germany, 4 Sep 44, same file. In September, Lt. Gen. Thomas T. Handy, Assistant Chief of Staff, OPD, said that if the Fifth U.S. Army was to be left in the Mediterranean it should be used "in a campaign to the northeast of the Adriatic pointed towards Vienna and de-

ished in October 1944 when the military situation in Italy worsened. General Wilson reported that it was impossible for him to go into the Balkans unless he had three new divisions, but the U.S. Chiefs of Staff felt that nothing important could be gained by this diversion of forces. They proposed instead that elements of the Fifth U.S. Army be transferred from Italy to northwest Europe where they could influence the main offensive and that the U.S. amphibious resources in the Mediterranean be sent to the Pacific. Prime Minister Churchill now entered the discussion with proposals which seemed intended to justify his previous policy in that area. He talked with the Mediterranean commanders and reported that he "was much distressed by their tale." In a cable to the President, Mr. Churchill recalled his bitter fight against the southern France operations, remarking, "It seems so much was taken away from our Italian front against Germany as just to deny a complete victory in this theater." He asked the President to deflect to the Fifth U.S. Army two or three U.S. divisions intended for northwest Europe and reiterated his confidence in the plan for capturing the Istrian Peninsula—a plan "in accordance with over all strategic objective, namely the expulsion from or destruction in Italy of Kesselring's army." When the President refused on the ground that the divisions were needed for the main battle in northwest Europe and for resting battle-weary units there, Mr. Churchill discussed with the Mediterranean commanders the pos-

sibility of landing forces through Adriatic ports cleared by Yugoslav Partisans and advancing up the Adriatic coast. He spoke of a possible amphibious assault against Trieste or Fiume.[20]

The United States was willing to reopen the Balkans question only on the condition that the situation in Italy or northwest Europe improved to the extent that surplus forces might become available for the proposed campaign. The situation in both these areas had not improved sufficiently by late January 1945 to justify diverting forces from those theaters. Reports at that time from Field Marshal Alexander, who had replaced Field Marshal Wilson in the Mediterranean when the latter went to Washington to head the British mission there,[21] indicated that his forces were tired out and that he was abandoning the offensive. He had enough artillery ammunition for only fifteen days in attack. When that was expended, he

---

signed to destroy German forces, and definitely not to influence the political situation in the Balkans." Memo, T.T.H. (Handy) for CofS, n.d. (about 15 Sep 44), sub: Note for Conf with President, ABC 337 (14 Sep 44), Sec 1.

[20] Cbl, Wilson to Br COS, MEDCOS 201, 9 Oct 44; Gen Hull to Smith, WAR 45060, 11 Oct 44, WD cbl log; Memo, JCS for President, n.d. (penciled notation "Gen McNarney okayed 1030 14th Oct. Also Adm King, Gen Arnold."), ABC 384 Mediterranean (26 Oct 43), Sec 1–A; Cbl, Churchill to President, 793, 11 Oct 44, Incl to JCS 1096, Additional U.S. Divisions for the Mediterranean Theater, 11 Oct 44. Marshall to Eisenhower, WAR 47746, 17 Oct 44; Cbl, Wilson to CCS, MEDCOS 205, 24 Oct 44. Both in WD cbl log. JP (44) 277 (Final) Operations in the Mediterranean Theater; MEDCOS 205, 29 Oct 44, ABC 384 Mediterranean (26 Oct 43), Sec 1; CCS 677/3 Future Operations in the Mediterranean, 17 Nov 44; Memo, McFarland for Leahy, King, Arnold, 16 Nov 44, ABC 384 Mediterranean (26 Oct 43), Sec 1–A. This and the two following paragraphs dealing with the question of the Balkans have been condensed from a detailed draft written by Dr. Gordon A. Harrison for inclusion in another volume of the U.S. ARMY IN WORLD WAR II series. On his decision not to include the material in his volume, he placed his draft and his notes at the disposal of the author.

[21] Field Marshal Wilson succeeded Field Marshal Dill, who had died a short time before.

said, he might have difficulty in containing the enemy and would not be able to follow up an enemy withdrawal. In northwest Europe, the German counteroffensive had inflicted heavy losses on General Eisenhower's forces and faced him with the need for additional replacements. Instead of being able to give up divisions from his front to Italy, he needed whatever Field Marshal Alexander could spare. Suggestions of an immediate transfer of units from Italy to the north were dropped, however, by General Eisenhower when he was told that such a step involved the risk of losing some of the existing Allied positions in Italy, including Leghorn and Florence. He did ask that the bulk of the Twelfth Air Force be transferred at once to support General Devers' 6th Army Group.[22]

Another factor affecting the decision on the Balkans was the Russian offensive, which had begun on 12 January. In two weeks, the Red Army was reported to have cut off some thirty German divisions in Latvia, and it was assumed that the Germans were so disorganized that they could not make a strong stand short of the Oder. This drive relieved pressure on the western fronts in Italy and northwest Europe and made unnecessary any thrust into central Europe from the south. By the time of the Malta Conference at the end of January, it was clear that the Allies had to work out a co-ordinated offensive from the west. They also had to speed up operations in order to prevent the enemy from shifting forces from the west to the east and in order to take advantage of the reductions in the enemy forces which had already taken place in the west. When Field Marshal Brooke presented these points at the meeting, the Combined Chiefs of Staff agreed almost without discussion to order

the immediate transfer of three divisions from Italy to northwest Europe and the shift of two more as soon as they could be released from operations then under way in Greece. On 2 February, the Combined Chiefs sent a directive to this effect to Field Marshal Alexander, saying that it was their intention "to build up the maximum possible strength on the western front and to seek a decision in that theater." Besides moving these ground forces, Field Marshal Alexander was to move two fighter groups at once to northwest Europe and to prepare to move as much more of the Twelfth Air Force as could be spared without hazard to his mission in the Mediterranean. For reasons which do not appear in the official records, it was decided that the five divisions should be British and Canadian and that the Fifth U.S. Army should remain in Italy. These withdrawals, which were to be made between the first of February and mid-March, meant that the Allies would have to pass permanently to the defensive in Italy and concentrate on limited attacks and deception to contain as many German units as possible, while preparing to take advantage of any German weakening or withdrawals.[23]

---

[22] Alexander to Br COS and JSM (for JCS), MEDCOS 237, 23 Jan 45, WD cbl log; M05, Note on transfer of forces from Italy to northwest Europe, 10 Jan 45, 0100/12–D AFHQ G–3 Plans Sec 41/2 Mediterranean Future Opns and Strategy, Dec 44– Jun 45 (92344F), Serial 36. McNarney to Marshall, E–85295, 12 Jan 45; Eisenhower to Marshall, S–7509, 15 Jan 45. Both in WD cbl log.

[23] Deane to Bissell, 22487, 27 Jan 45, WD cbl log; JCS 1237, Strategy in Northwest Europe, 29 Jan 45; CCS 183d Mtg, 31 Jan 45; CCS 182d Mtg, 30 Jan 45; CCS 185th Mtg, 2 Feb 45; Min, Malta Conf, in ARGONAUT Conf Min; CCS to Alexander, CRICKET 3A, 2 Feb 45, WD cbl log; Eisenhower to CCS, SCAF 204, 8 Feb 45, Eisenhower personal file; CCS to Alexander, FAN 501, Incl to CCS 773/3, Operations in the Mediterranean, 17 Feb 45.

Looking Toward the Rhine

First and Third Army Attacks

On 18 January, the day after the First Army's return to General Bradley's command, General Eisenhower directed the 12th Army Group commander to continue his offensive "to take advantage of the enemy's present unfavorable position in the Ardennes, inflict the maximum losses on him, seize any opportunity of breaching the Siegfried Line and, if successful, advance northeast on the axis Prum–Euskirchen." Bradley was to press this attack with "all possible vigor" as long as there was a reasonable chance of achieving a decisive victory. If the assault could not succeed, he was to be prepared to pass to the defensive in the Ardennes sector and shift his attack to the sector of the Northern Group of Armies. This action, while not expected to supersede General Montgomery's preparations farther north, was an attempt to take advantage of the momentum already gained against the enemy in the First Army sector without a pause for regrouping.

General Eisenhower's orders introduced one element of uncertainty into the plans then being made by Field Marshal Montgomery for an attack by the First Canadian Army between the Maas and Rhine (Operation VERITABLE), and a thrust northeastward by the Ninth U.S. Army to link up with the Canadians on the Rhine (Operation GRENADE). The Ninth Army, which had been reduced to two corps and five divisions by withdrawals during the Ardennes fight, needed new units from First and Third Armies for its operation. Field Marshal Montgomery had asked that General Simpson's forces be increased to sixteen divisions, but General Eisen-

hower had decided that twelve was the maximum to be assigned. These were not forthcoming, of course, as long as General Bradley's advances continued in the south. If, therefore, the First Army advance continued to be successful, Montgomery might have to launch Operation VERITABLE without Ninth Army's supporting attack. For several days between mid-January and the end of the month, the forces in the north continued preparations without knowing whether there would be an operation GRENADE. To prepare against delays in the event that the First Army attack bogged down, the Supreme Commander directed Field Marshal Montgomery and General Bradley to have plans for the offensive toward the Rhine north of Duesseldorf ready for launching whenever he decided not to continue with the First Army attack.

At the end of January, General Bradley's forces had pushed the enemy back to the West Wall in their sector. At that time, the 12th Army Group commander wanted to drive through the Eifel region to the Rhine, but his forces were beginning to meet delays and there was little evidence that they could achieve the immediate decisive success which General Eisenhower had stipulated as a condition of a continued advance in that area. He was not surprised therefore on 1 February to find that VERITABLE and GRENADE "were on" and that his own attack was to stop. VERITABLE was to be launched on 8 February, and GRENADE on the same day or two days later. General Bradley began at once to shift units to Ninth Army for its operation, and prepared to go on the defensive except for an attack by First Army units to clear the Roer Dam area. On 2 February, he asked both Hodges and Patton what they could accomplish with the forces they had after transferring divisions to Ninth Army. When told that they thought they might continue to advance until 10 February, he agreed that they could keep up a push until that time.[24]

Given some latitude as to the time for stopping his attack, General Bradley decided to permit General Patton to make limited advances in the Eifel region north of the Moselle. The matter was kept quiet so as not to draw objections from Field Marshal Montgomery. As a result, General Patton thought that he and General Bradley were "putting something over" on SHAEF.[25] Field Marshal Montgomery apparently became aware that something was afoot, and this may have been responsible for some of his protests that the operations in the north were not being properly backed.

German Difficulties

Since the end of December the enemy situation had greatly deteriorated. Not only had the German forces been thrown back in the west with considerable loss in men and matériel, but their losses in territory and men to the Red Army after the Russian drive began in mid-January were even heavier. SHAEF reported at the end of January that Marshal Konstantin K. Rokossovski had moved northward from Warsaw to the Baltic in an advance which isolated East Prussia from the Reich, while other Russian armies were driving into the eastern half of the province. Marshal Ivan S. Konev forced his way westward across the south of Poland to the Oder and established several bridgeheads. The industry of Upper Silesia suffered heavily from this advance. Between these two forces, Marshal Georgi K. Zhukov smashed westward from Warsaw through Łódź and past Poznań, outstripping the armies on his flanks and sending spearheads to points within one hundred miles of Berlin. The Red armies went more slowly in the south, actually meeting a German counteroffensive in Hungary, but for the most part they overwhelmed the enemy forces. The third week of their attack found advance elements of Marshal Zhukov's forces at points on or near the Oder 280 miles west of the positions they had left near Warsaw on 12 January. In air-line distances, they had averaged fourteen miles a day.[26] The offensive had a twofold effect on the battle in the west. The loss of the Silesian industries forced the Germans to rely more heavily on the Ruhr and Saar plants, and the pressure of the Russians meant that no reinforcements would be available from the Eastern Front for use against the Allies.[27]

The gravity of the German situation in the west was thoroughly evident to Field Marshal von Rundstedt. He was especially fearful that the Allies, in pursuing their main objective of crossing the Rhine, would bypass the West Wall and roll up the German positions from the rear. He had no fuel reserves and he felt that his ammunition stockpiles were only one third

---

[24] Bradley, *A Soldier's Story*, pp. 495–97. Notes on Conf with Gen Bradley, Brig Gen A. Franklin Kibler, 1 Feb 45; Notes on Conf, Gen Bradley with comdrs First, Third, Ninth Armies, at Hq First Army, Gen Kibler, 2 Feb 45. Both in 12th A Gp 371.3 Military Objectives, VI.

[25] Bradley, *A Soldier's Story*, p. 501. General Bradley says that General Eisenhower had agreed to the action without the knowledge of the 12th Army Group or Third Army staffs. There is no documentary evidence on this incident in General Eisenhower's papers. Cf. Patton, *War as I Knew It*, p. 235.

[26] SHAEF Intel Summary 45, week ending 28 Jan 45; SHAEF Intel Summary 46, week ending 4 Feb 45. Both in SHAEF G–2 files.

[27] SHAEF Intel Summary 46, week ending 4 Feb 45; SHAEF Intel Summary 47, week ending 11 Feb 45. Both in SHAEF G–2 files.

of what he needed. In particular, he lacked reinforcements for his units. Of his three army groups, *Army Group H,* which had the task of protecting the German north flank, was in the best position. Troops were sent to it from other front sectors and from the rear, and it had the *First Parachute Army,* a unit of comparatively high combat value, at full strength. *Army Group B* was in a less fortunate position. Its extended front was held by twenty-five divisions of which all but six had been heavily battered in the Ardennes fighting. The actual strength per kilometer was estimated by the· Germans at twenty-six infantrymen, one to two artillery pieces, and less than one antitank gun. The entire army group had fewer than 200 armored vehicles. *Army Group G,* which had been roughly handled by U.S. and French troops in the south, was apparently even more depleted than its northern neighbor.[28]

SHAEF Establishes a Forward Headquarters

In preparation for the drive toward the Rhine and beyond, General Eisenhower ordered that a forward echelon of his headquarters be established nearer the front. Before this time, a small advanced command post had been set up for him at Gueux near Reims, and later, as the Allied forces moved forward, two Supreme Headquarters Advance Conference Establishments had been opened near Luxembourg and Spa.[29] As early as October 1944, Verdun, Reims, Luxembourg, Liége, Metz, and Spa were all considered as possible sites for the new forward headquarters. The initial decision to move to Luxembourg was changed in early December, and Reims was selected instead. This move was postponed as a result of the

Ardennes counteroffensive, but in mid-February preparations were made to carry it out.

On 18 February 1945, the advance party of SHAEF Forward began its move from Versailles to Reims. Two days later the transfer was completed, and the new headquarters opened at the Collège Moderne et Technique de Garçons, Ecole Supérieur de Commerce.[30] The Collège building had been constructed in 1931 by the Department of the Marne for the technical training of French boys ten to nineteen years of age. It was a modern, three-storied, red brick structure capable of holding some 1,500 students. The general staff was located in the school while other divisions were in the Conservatory of

---

[28] MS # B–147, *Army Group H,* 10 Nov 44–10 Mar 45 (Col Rolf Geyer, G–3 [*Ia*] of *Army Group H*); MS # A–964, *Die Folgen der Ardennen-Offensive* and MS # A–965, *Die Kaempfe der Heeresgruppe B nach der Ardennen-Offensive bis zum Rueckzug ueber den Rhein,* 25 Jan–21 Mar 45 (both by Generalmajor Karl Wagener, Chief of Staff of *Fifth Panzer Army* and later of *Army Group B*); MS # B–026, Effects of Ardennes Offensive on *Army Group G* and MS # B–600, *Army Group G,* 25 Jan–21 Mar 45 (both by Hausser).
On 27 January 1945 the headquarters of *Oberbefehlshaber Oberrhein* was transferred to the Eastern Front as *Army Group Weichsel* with Himmler as army group commander. *Army Group G* on 28 January took command of the former *Oberbefehlshaber Oberrhein* sector and troops. On the same date Hausser replaced Blaskowitz as army group commander. On 29 January General Blaskowitz replaced Student as commander of *Army Group H* while Student took command of *First Parachute Army.*
[29] The Advance Conference Establishments served "as convenient meeting places for senior commanders and senior Supreme Headquarters, AEF, staff officers. Messing, overnight accommodation and telephone communications [were] furnished in each SHAC on a limited scale." Ltr, Gen Whiteley, G–3 SHAEF, 8 Dec 44, SHAEF SGS 322 SHAEF Advance Conference Establishments.
[30] This is the name which appears over the main entrance. SHAEF records identify the school as Ecole Professionelle and Ecole Pratique de Commerce et d'Industrie, which apparently are names of schools of the college.

SHAEF AT REIMS. *German prisoners pass the Allied headquarters.*

Music and an office building at 1 Rue Tal-leyrand. Hotels provided billets for offi-cers, and the Caserne Jeanne d'Arc and Caserne Colbert housed enlisted person-nel. As in the case of earlier locations, esti-mates for space needs at Reims proved too low as new detachments were brought to Supreme Headquarters. Near the war's end, SHAEF Forward had increased to 1,200 officers and 4,000 men, or nearly double the original estimate of required strength.[31]

Allied Operations, January–February 1945

In shifting the main attack at the end of January from the First Army front to the north, General Eisenhower had instructed General Bradley to use a force of two or three divisions to seize the dams on the Urft and Roer Rivers which had been a threat to the Allied advance since the pre-vious fall. *(See Map V.)* It had been realized for some months that, so long as the Germans held the Schwammenauel Dam and the smaller barriers above it, they could open the discharge valves and flood the Roer valley at any time the Allies started an attack north of it. Attempts to destroy the dams by bomber attack in the winter of 1944 had proved futile. An of-

---

[31] Chief sources: Interv with Brig Gen Robert Q. Brown, SHAEF Hq commandant, Dec 45; Interv with Prof. M. Fauvet, instructor in the college at Reims, Dec 46. SHAEF SGS 370.5/4 Location of Battle Hq SHAEF, II.

fensive to take the dam by ground action had been launched on 13 December, but it was stopped after the enemy breakthrough on the 16th. On 4 February, the First Army undertook the task of seizing the Schwammenauel barrier. Five days later, as U.S. units pushed down to the dam from positions north of it, the Germans released the pent-up waters of the Roer. Two weeks were to pass before the flood waters subsided along the Roer valley, but the danger that the enemy would open the dams while an attack was in progress was ended.

While the First Army dealt with the Roer dams, Field Marshal Montgomery readied his attack in the north. The British commander proposed to destroy German forces in the area between the Maas and the Rhine from the Nijmegen bridgehead south to a line from Juelich to Duesseldorf. (Map VI) To carry out this plan, he intended to send the First Canadian Army, made up of thirteen British and Canadian divisions, southeastward from Nijmegen to the line running from Geldern to Xanten and then clear the entire area to the Rhine. Shortly thereafter, the Ninth Army with its twelve divisions was to cross the Roer River in the area between Juelich and Linnich and head for the Rhine between Duesseldorf and Moers. Later, the Second British Army, with a U.S. corps allotted to it, was to push eastward between the other two armies to Rheinberg and the west bank of the Rhine in that area.[32] Both General Crerar's and General Simpson's forces were faced by unfavorable terrain. The units under the First Canadian Army had to attack through the Reichswald and the flooded valleys of the Maas, the Niers, and the Rhine, while the Ninth Army was confronted by the flood waters in the Roer valley.

General Crerar opened his attack in the early morning of 8 February after a heavy air and artillery preparation. Floods delayed his advance, forcing his units in some areas to use amphibious vehicles in their attacks. As a result, they did not clear the Reichswald until 13 February. The second phase of his offensive, the capturing of enemy positions south of the Reichswald near Goch, was completed between 18 and 21 February.

Before General Crerar opened the third phase of his attack, the Ninth Army, whose operation had been postponed some two weeks until the flood waters of the Roer could subside, joined the battle. At 0245 on 23 February, General Simpson sent his assault forces across the Roer. Enemy artillery and the swiftness of the current gave the men in the assault boats some trouble, but by the close of the day they established a bridgehead across the river. Especially helpful during the crossing was the XXIX Tactical Air Command, which flew more sorties in the course of the day than it had on any previous day of the war. General Simpson strengthened his bridgehead and then began to push out to the east and northeast while building up his forces for a large-scale breakout. At the end of the month, he ordered his armor into the action. The enemy in the meantime had started withdrawing from the Roermond–Venlo area in order to escape an outflanking movement by the Ninth Army. As Army Group H pulled its units back toward the Rhine, towns in the Roermond area which had previously put up a lively defense began to surrender with little or no opposition. Hitler ordered his forces to

[32] 21 A Gp dir, M–548, 21 Jan 45, Eisenhower personal file; Stacey, The Canadian Army, pp. 237–38; Montgomery, Normandy to the Baltic, p. 184.

continue to hold positions west of the Rhine until defenses could be constructed east of the river, but this edict proved increasingly difficult to obey as the Ninth Army forces pushed eastward toward Duesseldorf and northward toward Geldern and Wesel.[33]

Under General Eisenhower's order to provide right-wing protection for the Ninth Army's eastward drive, the First Army made a simultaneous crossing of the Roer on the morning of 23 February. Armored elements crossed the following day and drove rapidly eastward to the Erft, where they paused on 28 February, giving the Ninth Army adequate assurance that its right flank was secure while it was driving toward the north.

Farther to the south, General Patton had been pushing his limited advances. Just to the right of the First Army, the Third Army advanced astride the Moselle across a series of flooded, heavily defended streams. By the end of February, it had opened a path up the Pruem valley toward the Rhine, had eliminated a salient known as the Vianden Gap, had cleared the triangle of land between the Saar and the Moselle, and had passed through most of the West Wall defenses in its zone to points within three miles of Trier.

As the tempo of the Third Army advance accelerated, General Patton became increasingly impatient to stage a break-through on the 1944 scale. On 20 February he pressed General Bradley to give him additional divisions for an attack in the area of Trier and the Saar. He pointed out that the great proportion of U.S. troops in Europe were not fighting and warned that "all of us in high position will surely be held accountable for the failure to take offensive action when offensive action is possible." General Bradley agreed that advances were possible in the

Third Army sector, but added that higher authority had decided to make the thrust elsewhere. He reminded General Patton: "Regardless of what you and I think of this decision, we are good enough soldiers to carry out these orders." Indicating that the First and Third Armies were to play the major role in the next big attack, Bradley suggested that the present opportunity be used to refit and retrain troops so that they would be able to deliver a decisive blow when the proper moment came.[34]

On 1 March, Generals Eisenhower and Bradley visited General Simpson to discuss further plans for his army. The Supreme Commander was especially interested in the Ninth Army's plans to seize a Rhine bridge intact. While this objective was not achieved, General Simpson's forces did succeed on 2 March in reaching the Rhine in the vicinity of Neuss. On this, the ninth day of his attack, General Simpson reported that seven of his twelve divisions had nothing to do. He proposed, therefore, making a surprise crossing of the Rhine. Field Marshal Montgomery indicated that he preferred the planned assault of the Rhine on a broad front between Rheinberg and Emmerich. The Ninth Army completed its main mission on 5 March, having uncovered the Rhine from Duesseldorf to Moers. In its seventeen days of fighting it had driven fifty miles with fewer than 7,300 casualties, while killing an estimated 6,000 Germans and taking some 30,000 prisoners.[35]

General Crerar later declared that the Ninth Army "attack led to the strategic defeat of the enemy." He added, however,

[33] MS # B–147 (Geyer).

[34] Patton to Bradley, 20 Feb 45; Bradley to Patton, 21 Feb 45. Both in 12th A Gp 371.3 Military Objectives, VI. See an earlier complaint by General Patton in his *War as I Knew It,* p. 240.

[35] *Conquer: The Story of Ninth Army,* Ch. V.

that it did not have any immediate effect on the hard battle which his troops had to face between the Roer and the Rhine. That it did not was due apparently to a shift of enemy units northward during the period before the Ninth Army offensive. As a result, bitter resistance met General Crerar's forces on 26 February when they opened the third phase of their operation in an offensive toward Xanten. While these units were delayed by stiffened enemy opposition near Xanten, First Canadian Army elements farther southwest linked up with Ninth Army units at Geldern and made parallel drives for the Rhine, clearing all organized resistance in their zone between the Maas and the Rhine. The cost of clearing the northern area had not been light for the British and Canadian forces involved. In a little less than a month, they had suffered nearly 16,000 casualties, one third of them Canadian. More than 23,000 Germans had been captured in the fight.[36]

With forces under the 21 Army Group securely anchored on the Rhine, it was possible in March for General Bradley to open an offensive in his sector to clear the enemy from the area north of the Moselle. A plan for this operation had been submitted to General Eisenhower at his request at the end of February and had been approved by him. General Bradley proposed to complete his current operation in support of the Ninth Army, to invest Cologne from the north and to advance from the northwest and west to secure the Koblenz sector, and to close to the Rhine in the entire zone north of the Moselle.[37]

General Bradley opened his new offensive on 1 March. To the right of the Ninth Army, General Hodges' forces made new crossings of the Erft, and rapidly exploited their bridgeheads. They shattered the right wing of the *Fifteenth Army* and cut it

off from Cologne and Duesseldorf. General Hodges pressed forward toward the Rhine, entering Euskirchen on 4 March. His armored elements, which were roaring toward Cologne, broke into the defenses of the great cathedral city on the 5th; on the following day they reported it almost cleared.

To the south of Cologne, General Hodges gave other units of his army the mission of pushing to the Rhine and then turning southward to cross the Ahr and make contact with the Third Army elements which, now unleashed, were driving to the north. The advantages of seizing a bridge across the Rhine were discussed, but apparently no one entertained more than a vague hope that the opportunity could be found. Apparently no specific order was issued for such an action, and no plan was outlined for such an eventuality.[38]

U.S. armored elements drove into the town of Remagen in the early afternoon of 7 March and discovered that the near-by

[36] Stacey, *The Canadian Army,* pp. 247–54. Stacey estimates that the Canadian and U.S. attacks together cost the Germans about 90,000 killed, wounded, and captured.

[37] Ltr, Eisenhower to Bradley, 20 Feb 45; Memo, Bull for CofS SHAEF, 27 Feb 45; Note, on draft letter of 28 February 1945, that oral notification of approval had been given Bradley. All in SHAEF SGS 381 Post OVERLORD Planning, III. 12th A Gp Ltr of Instr 16, 3 Mar 45, confirming oral instructions previously issued and outline of operations plans dated 23 February 1945, 12th A Gp Rpt of Opns, Vol. V.

[38] Combat interviews of 2d Information and Historical Team with staff members of First Army, III Corps, and 9th Armored Division (MSS 300, 340, and 341) in March 1945 indicate considerable divergence on the matter of intentions. The official journals do not show any specific orders on the subject, and the men who took the bridge near Remagen indicate that they were given none before reaching the town. As late as the morning of 7 March, a First Army staff officer made clear that the III Corps mission to proceed southward after reaching Remagen remained unchanged. The question will be considered at length in The Rhineland and Central Germany, a volume in preparation for this series.

Ludendorff Bridge across the Rhine was still intact. They reported this fact to their commander, Brig. Gen. William M. Hoge, who promptly ordered his men to take the bridge. It had not been destroyed at that time because the guards appointed to blow it up were waiting for German units still west of the Rhine to cross. As the first U.S. elements reached the bridge, the guards exploded demolition charges, creating a crater at the west end of the structure which prevented vehicles from crossing. A small American patrol now went forward to cut the wires of remaining demolition charges. Rushing across the bridge in the face of fire from the eastern towers of the bridge and from the far shore, the men quickly reached the east bank of the Rhine and established positions.

Reports were hurried rearward to higher headquarters asking for instructions to meet the unexpected development. Each commander confirmed the action taken by his subordinate and asked further instructions from his superior. When the report reached General Bradley, he ordered General Hodges to throw everything he had across the Rhine to exploit his bridgehead. The 12th Army Group commander discussed the situation with the SHAEF chief of operations, General Bull, who was visiting General Bradley's headquarters. The SHAEF officer, aware of heavy Allied commitments to a crossing farther to the north, suggested that General Eisenhower be consulted as to the number of divisions to be diverted before any further action was taken. A call was thereupon made to the Supreme Commander, who enthusiastically approved General Bradley's dispositions. On 8 March, he informed the Combined Chiefs of Staff that the railway bridge at Remagen had been captured and added: "Bradley is rushing troops to secure ade-

quate bridgehead with the idea that this will constitute greatest possible threat as supporting effort for main attack." [39]

While other First Army units cleared the west bank of the Rhine from Sinzig northward to the Ninth Army boundary, those in the bridgehead east of the river sought to expand their sector. By 12 March, the First Army held a twenty-three-kilometer front east of the Rhine and was employing three infantry divisions and part of an armored division in the area. By the time of the crossing in the north, about ten days later, the sector had been extended north to the Sieg River on both sides of Siegburg, east to the autobahn which ran toward Frankfurt, and south to Neuwied. Meanwhile the enemy had made frantic efforts to wipe out the bridgehead. Reinforcements were brought from north and south of the area and committed piecemeal in a desperate effort to stop the flow of U.S. forces across the river. The Luftwaffe launched a number of savage attacks against the bridge itself, but it was successfully defended by massed Allied antiaircraft units stronger by 50 percent than the number of such elements used by Allied forces the previous year to protect the Normandy beaches. The bridge, weakened by direct hits from long-range artillery, at length collapsed but not until the engineers had put in their own bridges.

While the First Army was seizing its Rhine bridge and enlarging its sector east of the river, the Third Army was also driving to the Rhine. General Bradley's plan of late February directed General Patton to (1) secure bridgeheads over the Kyll

[39] Eisenhower to WD, SCAF 223, 1234 hours, 8 Mar 45, SHAEF SGS 381 Post OVERLORD Planning, III. See Eisenhower, *Crusade in Europe*, p. 379; Butcher, *My Three Years With Eisenhower*, pp. 767–68; and Bradley, *A Soldier's Story*, pp. 510–13.

and concentrate his forces for further advances to the east, (2) prepare an attack from the Kyll to seize the Mainz–Koblenz area and, if the enemy was weak, to secure a Moselle bridgehead to the southeast, and (3) clear the enemy from the area between the Moselle and the Ahr and link up with the right flank of the First Army. In early March, General Patton pushed armored elements in the Eifel toward the Rhine. By 11 March they had eliminated the German forces in the Eifel and the Allied forces held the Rhine from Emmerich to Koblenz.

To the south of Third Army, General Devers' armies next entered the picture. General Eisenhower on 8 March had ordered the 6th Army Group, which had remained quiet since clearing the Colmar bridgehead in early February, to prepare for offensive action as soon as the 12th Army Group completed its operations in the north. General Patch's forces, with one French corps attached, were to attack in the general direction of the valley of the Blies and Homburg–Kaiserslautern–Worms with the objective of breaching the West Wall, destroying the enemy in its zone, and seizing a bridgehead east of the Rhine in the Worms area.[40] The First Allied Airborne Army was ordered to prepare an airborne operation should it be necessary for the support of the 6th Army Group's Rhine crossing. The First French Army was to defend the Rhine along its front during the Seventh Army operation, and the Third Army was to aid General Patch's forces in his offensive in the Saar. General Eisenhower arranged for coordination by the Seventh and Third Armies during their operations by directing the two army commanders to deal directly with each other in matters regarding the form, method, location, and timing of attacks.[41]

The Saar–Palatinate triangle, which was to be attacked by elements of the Seventh and the Third Armies in this March offensive, was bounded by the Rhine, the Moselle, and the Lauter–Sarre line. It was marked by four major terrain features—the Rhine valley, the Haardt mountains, the Saarbruecken–Kaiserslautern–Worms corridor, and the Hunsrueck mountains—and contained the valuable Saar basin. Despite the importance of the area, *Army Group G* could not get the forces needed to defend it. The three armies in the general area were extremely weak, the *First Army* having lost an estimated 30 to 50 percent of its strength in the February fighting, and the *Seventh Army* having been severely shaken in the Ardennes. The *Nineteenth Army*, which was transferred to direct *OB WEST* control in early March, was reduced to "absolute impotence," inasmuch as it had lost all of its combat units and now consisted mainly of ineffective *Volkssturm* and security units. The 6th Army Group chief of intelligence believed that there was no doubt that the Germans would be forced east of the Rhine, and that General Hausser's only decision was how many Germans he wished to leave in Allied hands west of the river.[42]

General Patch, supported by the XII Tactical Air Command, opened his battle for the Saar on 15 March from the north-

[40] This operation was named UNDERTONE.

[41] SUSA Rpt of Opns, Vol. III; TUSA Rpt of Opns, Vol. I.

[42] 6th A Gp G-2 Weekly Intel Summary 26, 17 Mar 45, 6th A Gp AAR, Mar 45. This summary agrees with SHAEF and Third Army summaries of the period as well as with estimates made later by enemy commanders in the area. See also MS # B-026 (Hausser); MS # B-500, Defense of the Upper Rhine Front in the Karlsruhe–Basel Sector, and Fighting Withdrawal by the *Nineteenth Army*, to the Alps, up to the Capitulation, 22 Mar–5 May 45 (Col Kurt Brandstaedter, Chief of Staff of *Nineteenth Army*). *Seventh Army* was transferred from *Army Group B* to *Army Group G* on 2 March 1945.

ern Alsace area through which the enemy had made his counteroffensive of early January. Aided by Third Army drives north of it, the Seventh Army drove its right more than twenty miles in the first five days of the attack against isolated and ineffective resistance. Its center and left, battling the fortifications of the West Wall, made less progress. Meanwhile, General Patton's armored elements swept across the enemy rear in the Palatinate triangle. Some of his units seized Koblenz, and others smashed through Bad Kreuznach toward Mainz. By 18 March, the Third Army was threatening the Frankfurt corridor between Mainz and Worms. A rapid move by General Patton's forces to St. Wendel in the rear of the Saar fortifications helped overcome enemy resistance in that area, and aided the Seventh Army to enter Saarbruecken on 19 March.

In the light of the Third Army's swift moves, General Eisenhower on 17 March at a meeting of army group and army commanders at Lunéville had arranged for General Patton to assume some of the Seventh Army's objectives. Fearing that faulty liaison between the two armies might permit some of the enemy in the Saar to escape, the Supreme Commander directed them to prepare, if necessary, to merge the command posts of the two armies. But the two commanders concerned assured him that this move would not be needed.[43]

Even as the Allied commanders explored new ways of strengthening their attack against the enemy, the *Army Group G* commander pleaded for permission to withdraw his forces east of the Rhine. Initially, he was told to hold in place, but as the U.S. pressure increased he was permitted to send the *Seventh Army* staff across the river. General Patch's forces gained greater momentum in the meantime and broke through the West Wall positions on 20 March. They made contact with Third Army elements on the following day. By 25 March the Saar–Palatinate triangle had been overrun, and the Seventh Army had started its preparations for a Rhine crossing.[44]

North of the Seventh Army, General Patton had sent his units forward with great effect; on 21 March he announced that his three corps had reached the Rhine. They cleared Landau and Mainz on the 22d, and shortly before midnight elements of the army began an assault crossing of the Rhine near Oppenheim. Before daylight of the 23d six battalions of infantry had been put across the river at the cost of twenty-eight casualties. Nearly a day ahead of Montgomery in the north, Patton had his Rhine crossing.[45]

The First French Army, which had carried out a defensive mission during the Seventh Army operation, contributed significantly to General Patch's battle. General Devers' order of 10 March had shifted armored and artillery elements to the Seventh Army and had held other armor in the 6th Army Group reserve for the operation. On the 18th, General de Lattre asked that a part of his forces be returned so that the French might play a still larger role in the offensive. Instead, General Devers formed a special task force consisting of a French infantry and a French armored division and attached it to a U.S. corps, with the understanding that the

---

[43] Patton, *War as I Knew It,* p. 262; SUSA Rpt of Opns, III, 720.

[44] MSS # B-026 and # B-600 (both by Hausser); MS # B-703, The Fighting of *Army Group G* in the West. The Final Battle in Central and Southern Germany until Capitulation, 22 Mar-6 May 45 (Col Horst Wilutzky, G-3 [*Ia*] of *Army Group G*).

[45] Patton, *War as I Knew It,* pp. 266-67, 272-74.

task force would revert to the First French Army when the line of the Erlen was reached. Meanwhile, General de Lattre's forces were charged with defending the Rhine from Drusenheim south, a considerable task for the French commander's four divisions.[46]

General de Lattre's wishes were gratified on 19 March when elements of the special task force crossed the Lauter and entered German territory. Electrified by the thought of fighting on the soil of the enemy after years of hated German occupation, the French forces rushed forward against heavy opposition to establish their flag firmly on the territory of the Reich. General de Lattre underlined 19 March as "a great day for French hearts." Almost immediately, he asked General Devers for an enlarged zone along the Rhine that would give the French better sites for crossing and permit them to capture some well-known German city. The 6th Army Group commander promptly shifted the interarmy boundary north to include Speyer in the French zone.[47]

The Crossing of the Rhine in the North

With the clearing of the Saar–Palatinate triangle, General Eisenhower's forces had closed to the Rhine from Arnhem to the Swiss border and had concluded the most difficult part of the battle for Germany. (Chart 8) The West Wall which had barred the Allied advance in September had now been left behind, and the days of painfully slow advances through mud, ice, and snow were ended. German units, shattered in the Ardennes fighting, lacked the strength to stop the onrushing Allied forces whose numbers increased daily. Meanwhile, the air war constantly gained in intensity. Despite the

increase of enemy jet-propelled aircraft and indications that the enemy's productive capacity had still not been destroyed, the Germans did not have the means in March to block the tremendous air strength being thrown against their industrial centers. By the end of the month the Allied strategic bombers were almost out of targets.[48]

The German position in late March was obviously critical. Toward the end of the month, SHAEF intelligence declared that *Army Group G* had been driven back across the Rhine with twelve of its divisions virtually destroyed. The Allies had taken more than 100,000 prisoners since crossing the Moselle, raising the total in the Rhineland battles to more than 250,000. These prisoners together with the killed and wounded amounted to the strength of more than twenty full divisions. The so-called divisions in the west now numbered over sixty, but four of them were only divisional staffs, eleven were Kampfgruppen, seven were described as remnants, and others were drastically weakened. They equaled only some twenty-six complete divisions. Allied strength by this time had risen to eighty-five divisions, five of them airborne and twenty-three armored. On all fronts there was dismal news for the enemy. In Upper Silesia the Russians had launched a new offensive which gained twenty-five miles on a thirty-mile front in its first day, and there were rumors of a fresh drive in Hungary. The Allied air of-

---

[46] Ltr of Instr 11, Devers to de Lattre and Patch, 10 Mar 45; Modification of Ltr 11, Devers to de Lattre and Patch, 18 Mar 45, and notes on plng. All in 6th A Gp AAR, Mar 45.

[47] De Lattre, *Histoire de la Première Armée Française*, Chs. XIII and XIV; 6th A Gp Ltr of Instr 12, 27 Mar 45, 6th A Gp AAR, Mar 45.

[48] For the story of air activities in this period, see Craven and Cate, *The Army Air Forces in World War II*, Vol. III, Ch. 20.

CHART 8—OPERATIONAL CHAIN OF COMMAND, AEF, 27 MARCH 1945

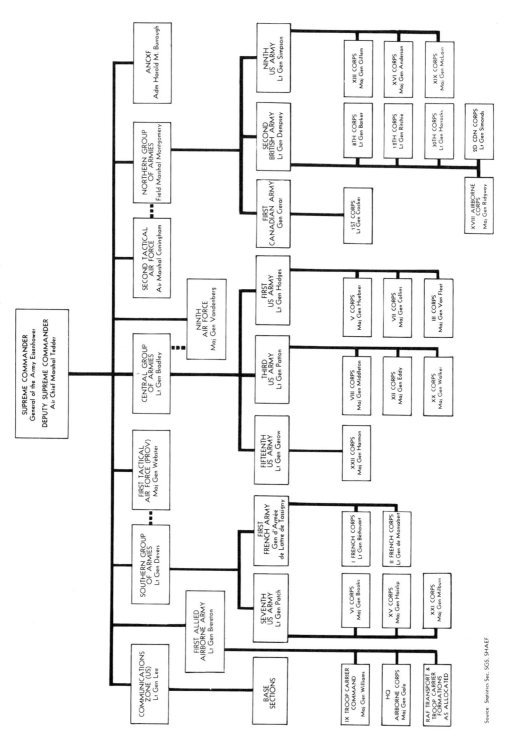

Source Statistics Sec. SGS, SHAEF

fensive against oil, which had been started at General Spaatz's insistence in the preceding spring, had virtually destroyed the fuel reserves of the Reich. Air attacks on railroads and bridges disrupted transportation, while round-the-clock bombings of the great German cities brought home daily to the enemy the futility of continuing the war. The Allied air forces set new records for air strikes nearly every day, making as many as 11,000 sorties in one twenty-four-hour period.[49] By the end of March, the German Army could no longer be considered a major obstacle. Nevertheless, the Allied intelligence chiefs could see no chance of surrender as long as Hitler and Himmler continued to control the destinies of the Reich. The Allies were committed, therefore, to "a systematic annihilation of the German armed forces."[50]

The enemy, already mortally wounded west of the Rhine, made some attempt to protect the river line. This task fell to the new Commander in Chief West, Field Marshal Kesselring, former commander in Italy, who took Rundstedt's place shortly after the Allies captured the Remagen bridge. Staff members of *Army Group H* thought that the British might attack south of Arnhem to roll up the Rhine defenses and then turn to the east or assault across the Rhine between Emmerich and the Ruhr. They believed that an airborne operation to facilitate this crossing might be made northeast of Wesel. Canadian forces were expected to attack the *Twenty-Fifth Army* as a means of protecting the British northern flank while U.S. forces crossed south of Wesel. Of the two alternatives, the crossing near Emmerich seemed to *Army Group H* the more likely. With this in mind, the commander assigned the *Twenty-Fifth Army* a long frontal sector which included the area between

Arnhem and Emmerich. The stronger *First Parachute Army* was to defend the region most seriously threatened by British and U.S. forces—the area between Rees and Dinslaken. Expecting the Allied offensive to come quickly, the *Army Group H* commander hastily tried to strengthen his defenses. To the south, *Army Group B,* which had been preoccupied with the Remagen bridgehead since early March, was in no position to stop an attack. Much weaker still was *Army Group G,* whose *Seventh Army* had virtually ceased to exist.[51]

While Kesselring struggled to get his forces ready for the Allied attack, General Eisenhower waited confidently for the start of his offensive. Field Marshal Montgomery's careful preparations north of the Ruhr had left nothing to chance. The Allied Naval Command, headed by Admiral Harold M. Burrough, which had busied itself mostly with supply matters since the completion of the landings in southern France, was asked to aid in preparing an amphibious assault.[52] A Navy detachment was added to the planning group for the Rhine crossing in November, and small landing craft were made available for the operation. General Brereton and his First Allied Airborne Army staff set to work to plan a major airborne attack east of the Rhine to insure the success of the crossing.

---

[49] Craven and Cate, *The Army Air Forces in World War II,* Vol. III, Ch. 20. See also MS # C-020 (Schramm).

[50] SHAEF Intel Summary 53, week ending 25 Mar 45; SHAEF daily G-3 War Room summary, 25 Mar 45.

[51] MS # B-414, *Army Group H (OB NORDWEST)* 10 Mar-9 May 45 (Col Rolf Geyer, G-3 [Ia] of *Army Group H* and later of *OB NORDWEST*); MS # B-593, The Battles of *Army Group B* on the Rhine up to its dissolution, 22 Mar-17 Apr 45 (Wagener); MS # B-703 (Wilutzky).

[52] Admiral Burrough had succeeded Admiral Ramsay, who had been killed at the beginning of January 1945 in a plane crash near Paris.

Near the end of January 1945, Field Marshal Montgomery issued specific orders for the Rhine crossing. His initial plan called for General Dempsey's Second British Army, with a U.S. corps attached, to force crossings at Rheinberg, Xanten, and Rees. This directive "flabbergasted" General Simpson, who was given no command role in the crossing. He was especially disturbed because U.S. forces in the attack would have to pass through the Second British Army's zone. The Ninth Army commander took up the matter with General Dempsey, and after several lengthy discussions the two commanders recommended that Field Marshal Montgomery revise his plans to give the Ninth Army a larger role in the operation. On 4 February, the 21 Army Group commander instructed General Simpson to make a crossing at Rheinberg while General Dempsey launched assaults at Xanten and Rees.[53]

In early February, Field Marshal Montgomery set 15 March as the target date for the crossing.[54] A SHAEF directive of 8 March changed this date to the 24th and outlined the main features of the operation. Field Marshal Montgomery spelled out these instructions in a directive dated 9 March to Generals Dempsey, Crerar, and Simpson. The mission of the 21 Army Group was described as the crossing of the Rhine north of the Ruhr to secure a firm bridgehead with a view to developing operations to isolate the Ruhr and penetrate more deeply into Germany. The Ninth Army was to cross the Rhine south of Wesel, protect the 21 Army Group's right flank, and develop the bridgehead south of the Lippe. The Second British Army, aided by U.S. airborne forces, was to capture Wesel and secure the bridgehead north of the Lippe.[55]

ADMIRAL BURROUGH

Air preparations to isolate the battlefield began two weeks or more before the actual crossing. In addition to attacking the area bounded generally by the line Bonn–Siegen–Soest–Hamm–Muenster–Rheine–Lingen–Zwolle, the British and American airmen hit bridges all the way from Bremen to Cologne. The air strikes interfered with traffic between the Ruhr and the rest of the Reich, seriously im-

---

[53] *Conquer: The Story of Ninth Army*, Ch. VI; Montgomery, *Normandy to the Baltic*, Ch. XVII.

[54] The operation by this time had been named Operation PLUNDER.

[55] 21 A Gp Orders for the Battle of the Rhine, M–559, 9 Mar 45, 12th A Gp 371.3 Military Objectives, VI. General Eisenhower's original dir to comdrs, SCAF 224, 8 Mar 45; Supplementary dir, Eisenhower to comdrs, SCAF 231, 13 Mar 45, SHAEF SGS 381 Post OVERLORD Planning, III.

peding efforts to reinforce the threatened area.[56]

The Second British Army started its Rhine assault at 2100 on 23 March, after a heavy artillery preparation. Elements of two corps speedily crossed the river, several advance groups making the trip in seven minutes. While some units turned toward Rees, others, after a preparatory bombing, attacked Wesel. The Ninth Army, in the meantime, had set its forces in motion, Generals Eisenhower and Simpson watching from a church tower while the artillery preparation was being made. At 0200 on 24 March, Ninth Army elements began crossing south of Wesel, completing the operation with comparative ease. So little effort was required to overrun the enemy forward positions that Ninth Army historians described the operation as more an engineering task than a tactical maneuver. General Simpson's losses during the first day were extremely light for such an operation—41 killed, 450 wounded, and 7 missing.[57]

General Eisenhower was an interested spectator later during the morning of 24 March when the First Allied Airborne Army launched Operation VARSITY. Elements of two airborne divisions, one U.S. and one British, flown from bases in France and the United Kingdom, began to land at 1000 in the British zone north of Wesel. More than 14,000 soldiers were flown in or parachuted.[58] In this, perhaps the most successful Allied airborne operation in Europe, British and U.S. forces quickly established their positions. Elements of one division joined up with British infantry elements by midafternoon; the other division made contact with British Commandos about noon and was on its objective by dark. Initial losses were slight, but stiffening opposition increased

the casualties of the two airborne units. At the end of three days, the U.S. airborne division had lost 1,584 and the British division 1,344.[59]

By the end of the first day's fighting, the Allies had established a firm bridgehead running as much as six miles in depth. British and U.S. forces had made a junction in Wesel, but fighting was still in progress in the town. Losses tended to be light along the front, although opposition in the British sector was heavier than that on the Ninth Army front. While hardly any German aircraft were seen during the first day in the bridgehead, some harmless raids were made during the night against Allied bridge sites. Fighter-bombers of the XXIX Tactical Air Command in the Ninth Army sector had their biggest day of the war to date, and the 2d Tactical Air Force also contributed heavily to the battle.[60]

On the second day of fighting, Prime Minister Churchill, Field Marshals Brooke and Montgomery, and General Simpson crossed the Rhine to inspect the new bridgehead.[61] They found engineers busily engaged in bridging the river, and the infantry steadily pressing eastward.

South of the 21 Army Group, forces of

---

[56] Montgomery, *Normandy to the Baltic*, p. 322.

[57] *Conquer: The Story of Ninth Army*. Ch. VI; Montgomery, *Normandy to the Baltic*, Ch. XVII. A special study of the British operation has been made: British Army of the Rhine, *Operation PLUNDER* (printed in Germany, 1947).

[58] *Conquer: The Story of Ninth Army*, p. 247. *The Brereton Diaries*, p. 414, gives the number of men dropped as 4,978 British and 9,387 American.

[59] *The Brereton Diaries*, p. 414.

[60] *Conquer: The Story of Ninth Army*, p. 252.

[61] Eisenhower, *Crusade in Europe*, p. 390, gives the date of this crossing as 24 March, the first day of the battle. The New York *Times*, March 26, 1945, and *Conquer*, p. 252, give the date as 25 March. *BBC War Report, 6 June 1944–5 May 1945* (London, 1946), p. 333, gives text of broadcast on 25 March which says the group crossed that day.

Generals Bradley and Devers were also on the move. The Third Army was ordered on 25 March to exploit its crossings over the Rhine, seize the line Hanau–Giessen, and be prepared to continue the advance toward Kassel. On the following day, the Third Army units seized a bridge intact across the Main near Frankfurt and entered the outskirts of that city. By 29 March, they had made contact with the First Army units in the vicinity of Wiesbaden and had cleared Frankfurt of the enemy. The Third Army was now directed to advance on the Hersfeld–Kassel area and drive the Germans east of the Hohe Rhoen mountains–Werra River– Weser River line. Rugged and wooded terrain gave some trouble, but the lack of effective enemy opposition permitted U.S. armor to gain up to thirty miles a day at the end of March. By 2 April, bridgeheads had been established across the Werra in several places and elements of the Third Army were in the city of Kassel. The distance between advanced elements of Allied and Russian troops was now less than 250 miles.

Once the forces in the north had established their bridgehead, the signal was given for crossings of the Rhine in the 6th Army Group area. The Seventh Army launched its attack north and south of Worms at 0230 on 26 March. Despite a sharp enemy reaction north of the city, four divisions were across the river by the end of the second day of the attack. At this time, the Seventh Army estimated that there were only 6,000 enemy combat effectives on its front, and indicated that the Germans were apparently confused as to the location of some of their troops. The U.S. army pushed the attack vigorously and crossed the Main in several places on the 29th. Opposition that developed east

of the Main at the close of the month temporarily slowed General Patch's advance in that area. Other Seventh Army forces crossed the Rhine at Mannheim and entered Heidelberg at the beginning of April.

These successes of the U.S. forces alarmed General de Lattre. He had been told on 27 March to prepare to cross the Rhine near Germersheim with the mission of seizing Karlsruhe, Pforzheim, and Stuttgart, but had been given no date for his attack. Fearing that the Seventh Army would soon advance into the area earmarked for the French offensive, he prepared to attack at the first opportunity, and General de Gaulle encouraged him in these efforts. Interpreting Allied delay in establishing a French zone of occupation as an indication of unwillingness to recognize French claims, de Gaulle was determined to seize a sector along the Rhine. He wired General de Lattre that a rapid crossing of the Rhine by the First French Army was "a question of the highest national interest." Before receiving this message, the French army commander had already set the date of his assault for the evening of 30–31 March, saying that his decision was conditioned not by the degree of preparation needed but by the situation caused by the U.S. advance. To the surprise of General Devers, who sent word to the French commander on 30 March to speed up his plans for an offensive, General de Lattre announced that he would make a crossing the following morning.[62]

Despite the shortness of time for preparation and the lack of sufficient assault boats, French forces were put across the

---

[62] 6th A Gp Ltr of Instr 12, 27 Mar 45, 6th A Gp AAR, Mar 45; de Lattre, *Histoire de la Première Armée Française*, pp. 489–91.

Rhine near Speyer in the early morning of 31 March. Other elements crossed the same day near Germersheim. Toward noon French troops met U.S. armored units that had already driven into the area de Lattre was supposed to clear. The French general felt that his haste had been justified inasmuch as "twenty-four hours later, the push of fourteen divisions of Patch's army in the direction of the Pforzheim Gap would have condemned us to a secondary role in the invasion of the Reich." [63]

The 6th Army Group advances inflicted fresh losses on *Army Group G's* already disorganized forces. By 3 April, the *Seventh Army* was thrown back through the Thueringer Wald. *Army Group G* found it necessary at this juncture to take over the *Nineteenth Army* from *OB WEST,* which could not regain contact with the army. OKW, seemingly unaware of the gravity of the situation, demanded that a counterattack be sent against the Allies, although it was unable to make available any additional troops. Instead of sending replacements, OKW relieved commanders. The army group chief of staff was removed on 2 April, and the commander in chief two days later. General der Infanterie Friedrich Schulz, formerly on the Eastern Front, succeeded to the command of *Army Group G.* Hitler demanded that the *First Army* prepare to attack northward to cut off the U.S. forces that had pushed to Wuerzburg. He asked for two weeks' time in which to prepare jet-propelled fighters and "miracle weapons" for use against the Allies. *Army Group G,* now the only high-level organization in southern Germany,

could do nothing except carry out a planned withdrawal to the Franconian and Swabian Albs and then to the Danube.[64]

The Supreme Commander was deeply gratified by the successes won by his forces in the Rhineland. Feeling that his broad front policy had been vindicated, he wrote General Marshall on 26 March:

Naturally I am immensely pleased that the campaign west of the Rhine that Bradley and I planned last summer and insisted upon as a necessary preliminary to a deep penetration east of the Rhine, has been carried out so closely in accordance with conception. You possibly know at one time the C.I.G.S. [Field Marshal Brooke] thought I was wrong in what I was trying to do and argued heatedly on the matter. Yesterday I saw him on the banks of the Rhine and he was gracious enough to say that I was right, and that my current plans and operations are well calculated to meet the current situation. The point is that the great defeats, in some cases almost complete destruction, inflicted on the German forces west of the Rhine, have left him with very badly depleted strength to man that formidable obstacle. It was those victories that made possible the bold and relatively easy advances that both the First and Third Armies are now making toward Kassel. I hope this does not sound boastful, but I must admit to a great satisfaction that the things that Bradley and I have believed in from the beginning and have carried out in the face of some opposition from within and without, have matured so splendidly.[65]

---

[63] De Lattre, *Histoire de la Première Armée Française,* p. 499.

[64] MS # B–703 (Wilutzky).

[65] Ltr, Eisenhower to Marshall, 26 Mar 45, Eisenhower personal file. Eisenhower, *Crusade in Europe,* p. 372, gives a much more extensive account of Field Marshal Brooke's statement than that quoted in this letter, which is cited as the source.

CHAPTER XXII

The Battle for the Ruhr

By the end of March General Eisenhower's armies had crossed the Rhine in force and were prepared to encircle the Ruhr and to open offensives toward the Elbe. Before undertaking these operations, however, the Supreme Commander made some changes in earlier plans both as to the direction of the main thrusts and the forces allocated for them.

A Change of Plans

Shortly before the attack at Arnhem in September 1944, General Eisenhower had studied the strategy for Allied forces to follow once they crossed the Rhine and had concluded that the main thrust should go from the Ruhr to Berlin. Supporting forces to accompany this thrust would move forward in "one coordinated, concerted operation." Recognizing that Berlin might be in the hands of the Russians before the Allies could reach the Elbe, he suggested that in such a case, instead of making a concentrated drive toward the German capital, the 21 Army Group might take the Hannover area and the ports near Hamburg, the 12th Army Group part or all of the Leipzig–Dresden area, and the 6th Army Group the Augsburg–Munich area.[1]

At the end of December when General Eisenhower assigned the Ninth Army to Field Marshal Montgomery for the drive to the Rhine in the area of the Ruhr, the spectacular Russian drives of the summer of 1944 had come to an end and there appeared to be a chance that some months might elapse before the Red armies reached Berlin. It is possible that at that time the Supreme Commander may have intended to let the British retain the Ninth Army for the main drive toward Berlin. By the end of March when the Allied forces had crossed the Rhine, the changed situation in both the east and the west prompted him to reconsider his earlier plans. Marshal Stalin's full-scale offensive, launched in mid-January, had driven the Germans back on the Oder. By 11 March, SHAEF intelligence sources indicated that Marshal Zhukov's spearheads were at Seelow, only twenty-eight miles from Berlin. Despite hurried German preparations to defend the city, there seemed to be little chance that it could hold out against a Russian attack.

Once Berlin was ruled out, there were strong reasons for making the main attack south and east of the Ruhr. There, with the Ruhr cleared, lay the remaining important industrial areas of western Germany. For a number of months, as the Ruhr took heavy poundings from Allied

---

[1] Eisenhower to Bradley, Montgomery, and Devers, 15 Sep 44, SHAEF SGS 381 Post OVERLORD Planning, I.

bombers, the enemy had been moving important factories to other parts of the Reich. SHAEF intelligence experts who had suggested in October that the Ruhr was losing its industrial importance believed that, even with it in Allied hands, "Germany would still be in possession of the bulk of her engineering and armament manufacturing facilities—at least those sections engaged on processing . . . equipment." SHAEF also suggested that emphasis be placed on offensives to interfere with rumored enemy plans to build a National Redoubt in the mountainous area running from western Austria as far north as the lakes below Munich and as far south as the Italian lakes. While there was some feeling in Allied circles that the Redoubt existed more in propaganda than in fact, Washington was sufficiently impressed for General Marshall to suggest at the end of March that U.S. forces attack from Nuremberg toward Linz or from Karlsruhe toward Munich to prevent the enemy from organizing resistance in southern Germany.[2]

Although never made explicit, other factors undoubtedly played some part in influencing the Supreme Commander's final decision. The surprise crossings of the Rhine at Remagen and Oppenheim before the main assault in the north and the rapid exploitation of this advantage in the two areas had placed General Bradley's forces in a position to play a major role in the sweep through Germany. These unexpected strokes of fortune caught the public imagination, particularly in the United States, and reinforced the 12th Army Group commander's request for a larger part in the drive to the Elbe than he had played in reaching the Rhine. It seems probable that General Eisenhower also

desired to let the 12th Army Group see what it could do. He knew that the Montgomery interview of January 1945 still "rankled" in General Bradley's mind, and that General Marshall felt that the work of commanders like General Bradley and General Hodges had been neglected by the press.

At the end of March, the Supreme Commander took special pains to underline the contributions of these two officers. Of General Bradley, he said:

He has never once held back in attempting any maneuver, no matter how bold in conception and never has he paused to regroup when there was opportunity lying on his front. His handling of his army commanders has been superb and his energy, commonsense, tactical skill and complete loyalty have made him a great lieutenant on whom I can always rely with the greatest confidence. I consider Bradley the greatest battle-line commander I have met in this war.

Of Hodges, he wrote that from the end of February "his drive, clear-headed and tactical skill have shone even more brightly than they did in his great pursuit across France, in which First Army's part was the most difficult given to any United States formation but brilliantly and speedily executed, often against much resistance." General Eisenhower added that he had no desire to detract from the work of other commanders, all of whom had performed "in a splendid manner," but he felt that the First Army's work had been overlooked in the headlines and that others had received credit for things that Bradley and Hodges were primarily responsible for. In the light of this belief, it

---

[2] SHAEF Weekly Intel Summary 51, 11 Mar 45, SHAEF G–2 file. Marshall to Eisenhower, W–59315, 27 Mar 45; Eisenhower to Marshall, FWD 18273, 28 Mar 45. Both in Eisenhower personal file.

is not surprising to find him giving the main offensive to them.[3]

On 28 March, after Field Marshal Montgomery had outlined plans for the 21 Army Group together with the Ninth U.S. Army to drive to the Elbe in the area north of Magdeburg, General Eisenhower announced that General Bradley's forces would make the main offensive east of the Rhine. The Supreme Commander approved existing arrangements, whereby the Ninth Army, while still under 21 Army Group command, and the First Army were to encircle the Ruhr. On completion of that mission, the Ninth Army was to revert to the 12th Army Group, which was to assume the tasks of mopping up and occupying the Ruhr, and making the major Allied thrust along the axis Erfurt–Leipzig–Dresden to link up with the Russians. Thus the decisive role, which Field Marshal Montgomery had planned for his forces, and to which he believed the Combined Chiefs of Staff had given general sanction, was changed.[4] Instead, the lesser task of protecting General Bradley's northern flank during the offensive in central Germany was given to him, although he was to have the use of the Ninth Army if he needed it after the Allies had reached the Elbe. To the south of the 12th Army Group, General Devers was ordered to protect the right flank of the main advance and he prepared to move through the Danube valley to link up with the Russians.[5]

Undoubtedly disappointed at General Eisenhower's decision, Field Marshal Montgomery asked permission to keep the Ninth Army until his forces reached the Elbe, since he felt that a shift at the moment would delay the great movement which was developing. The Supreme Commander held firm to his decision, ex-plaining that General Bradley would need elements of both the Ninth and First Armies to clear the Ruhr before starting his push to the Elbe. Further, since the 12th Army Group commander intended to bring up the Fifteenth U.S. Army to assume the occupation duties of the First and Ninth Armies in the Rhineland, he would need control of the three armies in order to co-ordinate their relief.[6]

Encircling the Ruhr

The operation to encircle the Ruhr was basically unaffected by the changes announced by the Supreme Commander on 28 March, since the First Army attack

---

[3] Marshall to Eisenhower, WX–57751, 23 Mar 45; Eisenhower to Marshall, FWD 18341, 30 Mar 45. Both in Eisenhower personal file. Field Marshal Montgomery in *Normandy to the Baltic*, p. 210, suggests that the change was made "as a result of the general enemy situation, and particularly in view of the rapid American success following the seizure of the Remagen bridge. . . ."

[4] See preceding chapter for the discussion by the Combined Chiefs of Staff at Malta. It appears that General Eisenhower's explanatory statement relative to his future operations applies to the field marshal's thrust across the Rhine north of the Ruhr and not to the advance after the encirclement of the Ruhr.

[5] Eisenhower to CCS, 27 Mar 45; Montgomery to Eisenhower, M–562, 27 Mar 45; Eisenhower to Montgomery, FWD 18272, 28 Mar 45; Eisenhower to Devers, 26 Mar 45. All in Eisenhower personal file. 21 A Gp Ltr of Intentions, M–563, 28 Mar 45, SHAEF SGS 381 Post Overlord Planning, III.

[6] Montgomery to Eisenhower, M–562/1, 27 Mar 45; Eisenhower to Montgomery, FWD 18389, 31 Mar 45. Both in Eisenhower personal file. The Fifteenth Army, headed by Lt. Gen. Leonard T. Gerow, had become operational on 6 January 1945. Its main purpose was to handle occupation duties for the other American armies. Among the other duties which it held at various times in 1945 were controlling the SHAEF reserve, surveying the line of the Meuse with a view to assuming responsibility for its defense, planning the occupation of the Bremen–Bremerhaven enclave, planning the organization of the Berlin District headquarters, and assuming on 31 March 1945 from the 12th Army Group the responsibility for containing enemy forces in Lorient and St. Nazaire. *History of the Fifteenth Army*.

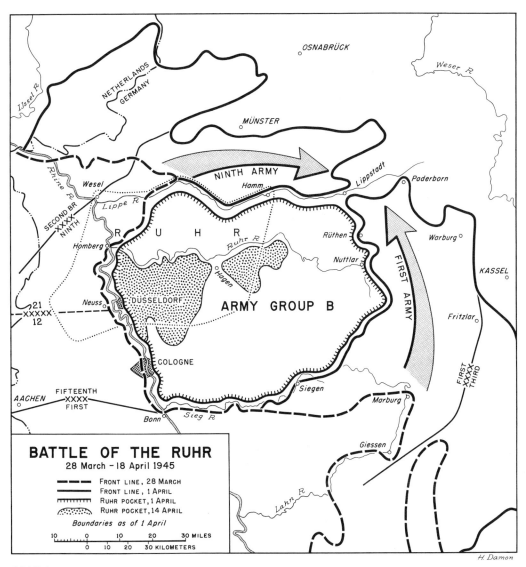

MAP 9

south of the area was already under way and making good progress, and little was needed except co-ordination between it and the Ninth Army offensive. On the 28th the 12th Army Group changed the First Army's planned advance northeast of Kassel to a drive almost directly north

from positions already attained on the Siegen–Giessen line, and on the 29th General Simpson ordered his forces to establish contact with General Hodges' forces then attacking toward Paderborn. *(Map 9)*

Allied progress in the Ruhr area had been aided greatly by the enemy's miscalculations and by the general deterioration of his position east of the Rhine. Field Marshal Model, the *Army Group B* commander, had shifted his forces shortly before the crossings of 24 March to meet an anticipated drive to the north by U.S. forces from the Remagen bridgehead. He was thus out of position to meet any attack directed eastward. Model counterattacked to close gaps on his army group's front, and he attempted to bring up some reserves, but the First Army's armored attacks of 25 March began to break through his positions before any reinforcements could arrive. He failed in his efforts to halt the advance on a line of resistance between the Sieg and the Lahn and soon found that he was virtually out of touch with his disorganized forces. Worse still, his army group lost all connection with *Army Group G* to the south, and there was danger that the Allied advance in the north, which seemed to proceed "like a peacetime maneuver, executed with all technical means of modern warfare," would soon separate his forces from the army group in the north. On 27 March, when he suggested withdrawing part of his forces behind the Sieg while holding on the Rhine front, he was informed that Hitler, trying to organize a new army east of the Ruhr, had prohibited on pain of death any further withdrawals or loss of inhabited localities.

On Model's north, *Army Group H* was hard hit by the 21 Army Group crossings, and its collapse appeared to be a matter of days. In that event, an Allied thrust eastward into central Germany and northward in the direction of Bremen and Hamburg seemed possible. Seeking to restore its position, *Army Group H* suggested that it be allowed to withdraw from the areas threatened by encirclement. It asked permission to stop the First Army's break-

through of *Army Group B,* which was endangering its southern flank, to establish a Weser River defense position, and to withdraw troops and supplies from most of the Netherlands in order to use them in building up a new defense front in the northeast tip of the country. OKW rejected these requests, ordering all forces to hold in place with the means available. Except for the promise of some training units from Denmark, there appeared to be little prospect for reinforcements.[7]

Forbidden to withdraw to new positions, and unable to build up tenable positions when they were forced to fall back, the Germans could neither stop nor escape the relentless advance of Allied forces. Armored elements of the First and Ninth Armies, intent on a link-up, made contact on 1 April at Lippstadt, just west of the agreed-on junction point of Paderborn, to complete what General Eisenhower has described as "the largest double envelopment in history."[8] Caught in the Ruhr Pocket were *Army Group B,* with most of the forces in its *Fifth Panzer* and *Fifteenth Armies,* and elements of *Army Group H's First Parachute Army.* Seven corps and the major elements of nineteen divisions plus some 100,000 antiaircraft personnel were included in an enemy force which totaled nearly one third of a million men. The pocket comprised nearly 4,000 square miles between the Sieg River in the south and the Lippe River in the north, measuring some fifty-five miles from north to south and seventy miles from east to west.[9]

---

[7] MS # B–593 (Wagener); MS # B–414 (Geyer); MS # C–020 (Schramm).

[8] *Report by the Supreme Commander*, p. 104.

[9] FUSA Rpt of Opns, 23 Feb–8 May 45, Vol. I; *Conquer: The Story of Ninth Army*, p. 269.

The Ruhr Pocket

The Supreme Commander returned the Ninth Army to the 12th Army Group on 4 April. In anticipation of the move, representatives of First and Ninth Armies had already set an interarmy boundary along the line of the Ruhr River–Nuttlar–Ruethen–Paderborn and agreed that General Simpson's forces were to clear the industrial area north of the Ruhr River, while the First Army took the rugged terrain to the south.

Inside the pocket, Field Marshal Model dismissed the possibility of surrender so long as he could pin down Allied forces that might be used elsewhere, but he discounted the possibility of getting large groups out of the area in the face of Allied air and armored attacks. As for the chances of holding the pocket for any length of time, he found that rations were estimated to be sufficient to supply the troops and civil population in the area for three or four weeks and that there was ammunition for two to three weeks if a major battle could be avoided. Some fuel was available for vehicles. The area was fairly well suited for defense, protected as it was on three sides by the Lippe, Rhine, and Sieg Rivers. The army group commander attempted initially to reinforce the eastern sector of the pocket in the hope that aid could be brought into that area from the east or that his forces might break out in small groups, but these hopes diminished steadily after the fall of Muenster and Gotha in the first week of April. For the most part, the troops of *Army Group B* offered little resistance and pulled back when faced by a strong attack. Fears that they might adopt a scorched earth policy as they withdrew brought pleas from German industrialists that the remaining resources of the area be spared. There is evidence that OKW orders for widespread destruction of plants and communications were read and not passed on by Model in this period.[10]

At the beginning of April, Secretary of War Stimson made efforts to spare the Ruhr industrial facilities any further loss, expressing fears about the economic future of Europe if more damage was inflicted on the Ruhr. He wondered if it was necessary for military purposes to destroy the remaining industry in the area. Admirals Leahy and King questioned whether General Eisenhower should be bothered with that problem in the midst of his battle, but General Marshall decided to seek an unofficial opinion. In so doing he avoided any effort to limit the Supreme Commander's future action and said that it was assumed that he would proceed in "the manner best adapted to the security and rapidity of the thrusts into Germany." The U.S. Army Chief of Staff added that he had no views on the subject "except that I think the fat is probably in the fire and whatever the political conclusions it is too late, too impracticable to take any action for such reason." General Eisenhower, who regarded "the substantial elimination of the enemy forces in the Ruhr as a military necessity" was nonetheless preparing to bypass the built-up areas as much as possible and to avoid useless or unnecessary damage to existing industrial facilities. Great damage had already been done by heavy bombers, but he realized that the remaining assets should be preserved. He noted that, save for support of tactical operations, air attacks had virtually ceased.[11]

---

[10] MS # B–593 (Wagener); MS # C–020 (Schramm).

[11] Marshall to Eisenhower, W–64236, 6 Apr 45; Eisenhower to Marshall, FWD 18697, 7 Apr 45. Both in SHAEF cbl log.

In preparation for the final offensive to destroy the German armies in the pocket, the Fifteenth U.S. Army on 1 April took over the occupation duties of the First and Ninth Armies on the west bank of the Rhine from Bonn to Neuss. It was directed to extend its defensive sector on the west bank to Homberg by 5 April and be prepared to occupy, organize, and govern the Rheinprovinz, Saarland, Pfalz, and Rheinhessen as the eastward advance of the Allied forces uncovered these areas.[12]

Two corps of the First Army and one corps and part of another of the Ninth Army on 6 April undertook the task of reducing the Ruhr Pocket, while the remainder of the two armies drove toward the Elbe. Two days later, advance elements of the two armies driving from the north and south of the pocket linked up. Pressing from the north, east, and south, the Allied divisions by mid-April had reduced the territory held by the enemy to an area with a twenty-eight mile diameter. Available ammunition and food had now decreased to an estimated three days' supply, but Field Marshal Model still rejected suggestions by members of his staff that he capitulate. Despite this resolution, he could not stop the U.S. armies. On 14 April, General Simpson's forces ended all German resistance north of the Ruhr River and General Hodges' units divided the forces remaining south of the river into two main pockets.

In the face of these disasters, OKW ordered *Army Group B* to break out of the pocket. The message was read and simply filed, for the events of the day had made action useless. On 15 April, the First Army broadened the point of contact with the Ninth Army at the Ruhr and turned both to the west and east to crush the remaining opposition. With defeat obviously a few days or hours away, the Germans adopted a novel procedure to avoid formal capitulation. On the morning of 17 April, they announced the dissolution of *Army Group B*. The extremely young and the very old soldiers were dismissed from the service and told to return home. The remaining officers and men were told they could stay to be overrun and then surrender, could try to make their way home in uniform or civilian clothes and without weapons, or try to break through to another front. Field Marshal Model thus did not have to take responsibility for a surrender. He disappeared from the scene shortly thereafter and no trace of him was subsequently found, although members of his staff testified that he committed suicide.[13]

Organized resistance in the Ruhr district ended on the morning of 18 April. In the approximately three weeks since they had encircled the area, Allied forces had taken more than 317,000 German prisoners, including twenty-four generals and an admiral. The enemy's token resistance had not interfered effectively with the Allied sweep to the east. Although parts of four corps had to be left to deal with the pocket, General Bradley's forces raced on without major difficulty to the Elbe.[14]

---

[12] FUSA Rpt of Opns, 23 Feb–8 May 45; *History of the Fifteenth Army*, pp. 39–50.

[13] MS # B–593 (Wagener); MS # C–020 (Schramm); Daily Sitrep West, 16 Apr 45. *OKH Operations Abteilung, KTB* (Draft) *16–24.IV. 45*, 17 Apr 45.

[14] FUSA Rpt of Opns, 23 Feb–8 May 45; *Conquer: The Story of Ninth Army*, Ch. VII.

CHAPTER XXIII

The Drive to the Elbe

The battle for the Ruhr, however great the number of men involved, was but an episode in the campaigns of April which saw most of western and central Germany overrun and occupied by Allied forces. In less time than it took to bring resistance to an end in the pocket, elements of one army reached the Elbe, and others were within a few days of a junction with the Russians and entry into Czechoslovakia and Austria. As victory appeared only a few weeks away, the tactical considerations of the battle for Germany began to recede and political factors to take their place. But, ironically, the very period in which political guidance was perhaps the most needed was the one in which only the field commander could exercise real control. The British Chiefs of Staff tried doggedly to inject a note of political realism into the situation, but found that remote control of a battlefield stretching from the North Sea to the Italian Alps was well-nigh impossible, especially when the U.S. President and the U.S. Chiefs of Staff preferred to leave the final stages of the battle in the hands of the Supreme Commander.

Shall It Be Berlin?

In no respect was the difference in British and U.S. viewpoints more clearly shown than in the case of Berlin. The Supreme Commander in mid-September had looked on the German capital as his ultimate objective, but by late March he had decided to direct his main drive toward Leipzig instead to link up with the Russians. This decision displeased the British because it meant the abandonment of Berlin as the objective and minimized the 21 Army Group's share in the offensive. It was made more unpalatable when on 28 March General Eisenhower asked the Allied military missions in Moscow to inform Marshal Stalin of his change in plans. The British Chiefs of Staff felt that the Supreme Commander, in informing the Russians directly of his decision, had not only made a political mistake but had also exceeded his powers. They promptly proposed that the Allied missions in Moscow be told to hold up delivery of later amplifications of SHAEF plans. If the Russians had already received these plans, the British said, they should be asked to delay their answer until the Combined Chiefs of Staff could discuss the matter.[1]

Sharply rejecting the British proposal as one that would discredit or at least lower the prestige of a highly successful commander in the field, the U.S. Chiefs of Staff said that any modification in the initial communication should be made, if at all, by the Supreme Commander, whose

---

[1] Eisenhower to Mil Mission Moscow, SCAF 252, 28 Mar 44, SHAEF SGS 373.5 Bomb line, Liaison, and Co-ordination of Fronts, I; Memo by Br COS (Plan of Campaign in Western Europe), CCS 805, 29 Mar 45, ABC 384 Europe (5 Aug 43), Sec 1–D. Eisenhower to Prime Minister, FWD 18334, 30 Mar 45; Prime Minister to Eisenhower, 2072, 31 Mar 45. Both in Eisenhower personal file.

proposals they found to be in line with agreed-on strategy and with his initial directive. In what might be interpreted as a dig at the strategic views of the British Chiefs of Staff and Field Marshal Montgomery, they pointed to the battle in the Rhineland as a vindication of the Supreme Commander's military judgment. There, while the northern drive was making good, the secondary drive, which General Eisenhower had insisted on against British opposition, had achieved an outstanding success and had made it possible for the Northern Group of Armies to accelerate its drive across the north German plain. The U.S. Chiefs were willing to ask the Supreme Commander for an amplification of his plan and for a delay of further messages to Moscow until he had heard from the Combined Chiefs of Staff, but they indicated that any change in their view that his ideas were sound was unlikely. Rather, they believed that the battle for Germany had reached the point "where the commander in the field is the best judge of the measures which offer the earliest prospects of destroying the German armies or their power to resist." [2]

The British were dismayed by the U.S. Chiefs' reaction. The Prime Minister assured both President Roosevelt and General Eisenhower that the British had no intention of disparaging or lowering the prestige of the Supreme Commander, and that their reaction had been prompted by their concern over plans and procedures which apparently left the fortunes of a million British troops to be settled without reference to British authority.[3] He added that he felt the U.S. Chiefs of Staff had done less than justice to British efforts in the war. The British had suffered severe losses in holding the hinge of the attacks at both Caen and Wesel, but because of the

nature of their task they had not shown the spectacular gains made by the U.S. forces. He favored an advance to the Elbe at the highest speed, but hoped that the shift in direction would not destroy the weight and momentum of Montgomery's drive and leave the British forces in an almost static condition along the Elbe when and if they reached it.

Turning now from Eisenhower's plans as they affected the 21 Army Group, the Prime Minister spoke of the political factors involved in a failure to drive to Berlin. He declared:

Having dealt with and I trust disposed of these misunderstandings between the truest friends and comrades that ever fought side by side as Allies, I venture to put to you a few considerations upon the merits of the changes in our original plans now desired by General Eisenhower. . . . I say quite frankly that Berlin remains of high strategic importance. Nothing will exert a psychological effect of despair upon all German forces of resistance equal to that of the fall of Berlin. It will be the supreme signal of defeat to the German people. On the other hand, if left to itself to maintain a siege by the Russians among its ruins and as long as the German flag flies there, it will animate the resistance of all Germans under arms.

There is moreover another aspect which it is proper for you and me to consider. The Russian armies will no doubt overrun all Austria and enter Vienna. If they also take Berlin, will not their impression that they have been the overwhelming contributor to our common victory be unduly imprinted in their minds, and may this not lead them into a mood which will raise grave and formidable difficulties in the future? I therefore consider that from a political standpoint we

---

[2] Memo by JCS, CCS 805/2, 30 Mar 45, ABC 384 Europe (5 Aug 43), Sec 1–D.

[3] Churchill to Eisenhower, 2072, 31 Mar 45; Churchill to Eisenhower, 2096, 2 Apr 45. Both in Eisenhower personal file. Churchill to Roosevelt, 931, 1 Apr 45, Incl to CCS 805, 29 Mar 45, ABC 384 Europe (5 Aug 43), Sec 1–D.

should march as far east into Germany as possible and that should Berlin be in our grasp we should certainly take it. This also appears sound on military grounds.[4]

Both the President and the Supreme Commander denied any American intent to underestimate British contributions to the campaigns in northwest Europe. Mr. Roosevelt explained that the U.S. insistence on upholding the Supreme Commander was an enunciation of a well-known military principle rather than an anti-British reaction. The unfortunate impression that the U.S. Chiefs had reflected on the performances of the 21 Army Group arose, he thought, from the U.S. Chiefs' failure to stress factors such as military obstacles and the strength and quality of opposing forces which had contributed to the difficulties facing Field Marshal Montgomery's forces. The President said he could not see that the Supreme Commander's plans involved any far-reaching change from the plan approved at Malta. He expressed regret that the Prime Minister should have been worried by the phrasing of a formal paper, but regretted even more that "at the moment of a great victory we should become involved in such unfortunate reactions."[5]

General Eisenhower, "disturbed, if not hurt" at the suggestion that he had any thought of relegating the British forces to a restricted sphere, assured the Prime Minister that "nothing is further from my mind and I think my record over two and one-half years of commanding Allied forces should eliminate any such idea." The current offensive had been selected as the one which would contribute most effectively to the disintegration of the remaining enemy forces and the German power to resist. Once the Allies reached the Elbe, he thought it probable that U.S.

forces would be shifted to Field Marshal Montgomery, who would then be sent across the river in the north and to a line reaching at least to Luebeck on the Baltic coast. If German opposition crumbled progressively, there seemed to be little difference between gaining the central position and crossing the Elbe. If resistance stiffened, however, it was vital for the Allies not to be dispersed. Inasmuch as British and Canadian forces were to advance in exactly the same zones that had been planned by Field Marshal Montgomery, Eisenhower saw no reason why the role, actions, or prestige of those forces should be materially decreased by the shift of the Ninth Army from Montgomery's to Bradley's command. The maximum extent to which the plans might be affected was in a possible short delay in making a powerful thrust across the Elbe. As for the drive to Berlin, the Supreme Commander made no promises. If it could be brought into the Allied orbit, he declared, honors would be equally shared between the British and U.S. forces.[6]

Although his suggested plan for Field Marshal Montgomery to retain the Ninth Army and to march to the Elbe and then to Berlin had not been accepted, Mr. Churchill said that changes in the earlier strategy were fewer than he had initially believed. He assured the President that relations with General Eisenhower were still of the most friendly nature and concluded with what he described as one of his few

---

[4] Churchill to Roosevelt, 931, 1 Apr 45, Incl to CCS 805, 29 Mar 45, ABC 384 Europe (5 Aug 43), Sec 1–D.

[5] Draft of msg, President to Prime Minister (with notation "Dispatched as is per White House"), in reply to msg of 1 Apr 45, ABC 384 Europe (5 Aug 43), Sec 1–D.

[6] Eisenhower to Churchill, FWD 18428, 1 Apr 45, Eisenhower personal file.

Latin quotations: *"Amantium irae amoris integratio est."* The War Department promptly turned this happy token of restored good relations into English— "Lovers' quarrels are a part of love"—and sent it to General Eisenhower.[7]

Mr. Churchill's words ended the discussion over the 21 Army Group's past contributions to Allied victory and its role in future campaigns, but did not dispose of the question of Berlin and the relations of the Western Allies with the USSR. Made suspicious by the alacrity with which Marshal Stalin agreed to General Eisenhower's decision to drive for Leipzig instead of Berlin and by Russian agreement that Berlin was no longer of strategic importance, the British Chiefs of Staff urged that this phase of the Supreme Commander's program be reconsidered. Since they felt that it was primarily a matter more of political than of military importance, they asked that the Combined Chiefs of Staff remind the Supreme Commander of the desirability of taking Berlin. Apparently wishing to avoid any further communications to Moscow on the subject before the Combined Chiefs could pass on it, the British also asked that a proper procedure for communicating with the USSR be laid down for SHAEF. They stressed that proper channels for dealing with the Russians were from heads of states to heads of states, and from high command to high command, and they indicated their belief that sufficient time existed for normal channels to be used.[8]

The U.S. Chiefs of Staff pointed to the eight days which had been consumed in discussions over General Eisenhower's announcement of plans on 28 March as evidence that committee action could not effectively deal with operational matters at the speed they were then developing. "As the situation stands today," they de-clared, "the center is a pocket, the right is rapidly moving and the left is making progress. Overnight, this situation may change. Even now air forces are overlapping in their offensive against the enemy. Only Eisenhower is in a position to know how to fight his battle, and to exploit to the full the changing situation." Nor were they disturbed by General Eisenhower's failure to send his plans to Marshal Stalin through the Combined Chiefs of Staff. His message to the Red leader had gone to him as head of the Soviet armed forces and not as head of the state and, therefore, was not outside normal channels. While it was true that he could have dealt instead with the Red Army Chief of Staff, experience had shown that any attempt to get decisions on a level lower than Stalin's met interminable and unacceptable delays. Instead of agreeing to bar direct dealings with the Russians, the U.S. Chiefs of Staff proposed that the Supreme Commander be authorized to communicate directly with the Soviet military authority on all matters requiring co-ordination of Russian and Allied operations.[9]

On the broader political question of getting to Berlin before the Russians, the U.S. Chiefs of Staff reacted as they had done formerly in regard to proposals of Balkan operations. Their view was that the busi-

---

[7] Churchill to Roosevelt, 933, 5 Apr 45; Marshall to Eisenhower, W–64244, 6 Apr 45, Eisenhower personal file.

[8] Memo by representatives of Br COS, CCS 805/4, 4 Apr 45, and Incl A, Mil Mission Moscow to WD (Msg, Stalin to Eisenhower), MX–23588, 1 Apr 45, ABC 384 Europe (5 Aug 43), Sec 1–D.

[9] Memo by JCS, CCS 805/5, 6 Apr 45, ABC 384 Europe (5 Aug 43), Sec 1–D. General Eisenhower was informed of this memorandum and of the British note which prompted it in Marshall to Eisenhower, W–64349, 6 Apr 45, Eisenhower personal file. SHAEF G–3 Division said on 11 April 1945 that the cable constituted authority for the Supreme Commander to communicate directly with the Soviet high command. The secretary of the general staff thought that suffi-

ness of the armed forces was to get the war ended as soon as possible and not to worry about the matter of prestige which would come from entering a particular capital. Militarily there was the strongest basis for such a view. At the time, when it appeared clear that the U.S. forces could not possibly outrace the Russians for the German capital, when it was already known that the Russian occupation would reach far west of the Elbe and that anything taken by the Allies east of that river would have to be evacuated,[10] when the Allies still faced a strong foe in the Pacific against whom it was then supposed that Russian help would be needed, there was little disposition on the part of the U.S. Chiefs of Staff to push to Berlin. The President, who at Yalta had made concessions in various parts of the world to the Russians apparently to insure their aid against Japan, would probably not have agreed with the U.S. Chiefs had they taken the opposite view. It is not clear whether the matter was ever presented to Mr. Roosevelt, who was then at Warm Springs, Georgia, where he was to die in less than a week. The U.S. Chiefs of Staff in a statement of their views which may have reflected the President's thinking, said, "Such psychological and political advantages as would result from the possible capture of Berlin ahead of the Russians should not override the imperative military consideration, which in our opinion is the destruction and dismember-

ment of the German armed forces." [11]

General Eisenhower had discussed the military considerations involved in the drive to Berlin with General Bradley shortly after the Allies had crossed the Rhine. Impressed by the fact that nearly two hundred miles separated the Allied bridgehead from the Elbe, and that fifty miles of lowlands, covered by streams, lakes and canals, separated the Elbe from Berlin, the 12th Army Group commander had said that it might cost 100,000 casualties to break through from the Elbe to Berlin. Viewing Berlin as a political prize only, and not wishing to take a U.S. army from his front in order to reinforce a drive by Field Marshal Montgomery to reach Berlin, he said that the estimated casualties were "a pretty stiff price to pay for a prestige objective, especially when we've got to fall back and let the other fellow take over." [12]

---

[10] This did not apply to Berlin, which was to be held jointly by the Western Allies and the Russians. It is questionable that the knowledge of the zones constituted the main factor in SHAEF's thinking at the time. General Eisenhower wrote in 1948:

"I already knew of the Allied political agreements that divided Germany into post-hostilities occupational zones. . . .

. . . .

"The future division of Germany did not influence our military plans for the final conquest of the country. Military plans, I believed, should be devised with the single aim of speeding victory; by later adjustment troops of the several nations could be concentrated into their own national sectors." *Crusade in Europe*, p. 396. See also below, pp. 463–66.

[11] Memo by JCS, CCS 805/5, 6 Apr 45, ABC 384 Europe (5 Aug 43), Sec 1–D.

[12] Bradley, *A Soldier's Story*, pp. 535–36. In a significant statement, General Bradley says of this reaction: "Had Eisenhower even contemplated sending Montgomery ahead to Berlin, he would have had to reinforce that British flank with not less than one American Army. I could see no political advantage accruing from the capture of Berlin, that would offset the need for quick destruction of the German Army on our front. As soldiers we looked naively on the British inclination to complicate the war with political foresight and nonmilitary objectives." Pp. 535–36.

---

cient authority had already been granted in the Combined Chiefs of Staff cable of December authorizing the Supreme Commander to send representatives to Stalin (CCS to SHAEF, FACS 118, 26 Dec 44, OPD cbl files [TS]). To make certain that no objection would be made on political grounds, SHAEF section chiefs were instructed to send all cables in future to the Soviet high command and not directly to Marshal Stalin. Nevins to DAC G–3, 11 Apr 45; Nevins to DAC G–3, 12 Apr 45; DAC G–3 to Sec Chiefs, 15 Apr 45. All in SHAEF G–3 321.3–1 Correspondence and Communication with the Russians.

The Supreme Allied Commander in-formed the Combined Chiefs of Staff on 7 April of his reluctance to make Berlin a major objective now that it had lost much of its military importance. It was much more important, he felt, to divide the enemy west of the Elbe by making a cen-tral thrust to Leipzig, and to establish the Allied left flank on the Baltic coast near Luebeck to prevent Russian occupation of Schleswig-Holstein. His indication of wil-lingness in the case of Luebeck to carry on an operation to forestall the Russians did not mean that he was weakening on his decision as to Berlin. He said that, if after the taking of Leipzig it appeared that he could push on to Berlin at low cost, he was willing to do so. "But," he added:

I regard it as militarily unsound at this stage of the proceedings to make Berlin a major objective, particularly in view of the fact that it is only 35 miles from the Russian lines. I am the first to admit that a war is waged in pursuance of political aims, and if the Com-bined Chiefs of Staff should decide that the Allied effort to take Berlin outweighs purely military considerations in this theater, I would cheerfully readjust my plans and my thinking so as to carry out such an oper-ation.[13]

Admiral Leahy has written that there is no evidence in his notes that the Com-bined Chiefs of Staff ever took up the ques-tion of the move on Berlin, and there seems to be little doubt that the decision was left by them to the Supreme Com-mander.[14] Despite the feeling of the Brit-ish, the way had been left open to a purely military decision on Berlin. That decision was made clear by the Supreme Com-mander on 8 April when Field Marshal Montgomery requested ten U.S. divisions for a main thrust toward Luebeck and Berlin. Betraying a note of impatience, General Eisenhower declared: "You must

not lose sight of the fact that during the advance to Leipzig you have the role of protecting Bradley's northern flank. It is not his role to protect your southern flank. My directive is quite clear on this point. Naturally, if Bradley is delayed, and you feel strong enough to push out ahead of him in the advance to the Elbe, this will be to the good." Agreeing that the push to Luebeck and Kiel should be made after the Elbe had been reached, he asked how many U.S. divisions Montgomery would need for that operation omitting Danish operations and the push to Berlin. Of the taking of the German capital the Supreme Commander said: "As regards Berlin I am quite ready to admit that it has political and psychological significance but of far greater importance will be the location of the remaining German forces in relation to Berlin. It is on them that I am going to concentrate my attention. Naturally, if I get an opportunity to capture Berlin cheaply, I will take it."[15]

The Berlin question was raised once more before the Russians captured the city. On that occasion, a U.S. commander, General Simpson, having reached the Elbe, suggested that he be permitted to go to the German capital. The Supreme

[13] Eisenhower to Marshall, FWD 18710, 7 Apr 45, Eisenhower personal file. Many of the points were stated in an earlier message, Eisenhower to Marshall, SHAEF 260, 31 Mar 45, ABC 384 Europe (5 Aug 43), Sec 1-D.
[14] Leahy, *I Was There,* p. 351. General Eisenhower in a letter to the author, 20 February 1952, said, "So far as my memory serves, I believe it is correct that the 7 April message was not answered by the Combined Chiefs of Staff."
[15] Montgomery to Eisenhower, M-568, 6 Apr 45; Eisenhower to Montgomery, 8 Apr 45. Both in Eisen-hower personal file. Field Marshal Montgomery re-plied: "It is quite clear to me what you want. I will crack along the north flank 100 per cent and will do all I can to draw the enemy forces away from the main effort being made by Bradley." Montgomery to Eisenhower, M-1070, Eisenhower personal file.

Commander instead ordered that he hold on the Elbe while turning his units northward in the direction of Luebeck and southward toward the National Redoubt area. In informing the War Department of this action, General Eisenhower said that not only were those objectives vastly more important than Berlin but that to plan for an immediate effort against Berlin "would be foolish in view of the relative situation of the Russians and ourselves. . . . While it is true we have seized a small bridgehead over the Elbe, it must be remembered that only our spearheads are up to that river; our center of gravity is well back of there." [16]

The Area and the Enemy

The Allied drives from positions east of the Rhine to the Elbe were channelized to a considerable degree by four main geographical zones: the Northern Lowland, the Loess Belt, the Central Upland, and the Bavarian Plateau. *(Map VII)* The first, through which elements of the Canadian and British armies advanced, extends westward into the Low Countries and eastward into Poland with its northern border on the North Sea and Denmark, and its southern border south of Berlin. The northwest sector of the region is extremely flat. The Loess Belt, which was invaded by Second British Army and some elements of the Ninth and First Armies, lies between the Ruhr and the Elbe and is drained by the Weser and the Leine. It is mainly undulating and marked by open country, hedgeless fields, and absence of streams at its western end, west of Kassel. The Central Upland, through which most of the First Army and a part of Third Army traveled, covers the central part of Germany. It consists of "forest highlands, low wooded scarps and open treeless plateaus." The Bavarian Plateau, a large triangular region lying between the Alps to the south, the Schwaebische Alb to the northwest, and the Bavarian and Bohemian forest uplands to the northeast, consists in the west of open arable lands marked with woods, marshes, and lakes, and in the east of rolling country. Elements of the Third, Seventh, and First French Armies went through these sectors.

After considering these terrain features, SHAEF planners concluded as early as September 1944 that it was possible for the enemy to set up defenses along the river lines in the north, in the central mountains east of Frankfurt and Karlsruhe, and along prepared positions in the forest areas of the south. Through most of the mountain barriers, however, there were roads that, except in the heavy snows of the higher mountainous areas, were passable throughout the year. It was fairly clear to SHAEF that the enemy could make little use of terrain features east of the Rhine to stop an Allied offensive toward the Elbe. [17]

Despite the defensive limitations of the central German terrain, it still offered more serious resistance to the Allied advance on most fronts than did the German Army. The disorganization and weakness of the enemy forces which had been observed before the crossings of the Rhine became constantly greater as the beaten units splintered and fell back without any prepared positions behind which they could regroup or conduct a defense. As a consequence of this and other factors SHAEF intelligence summaries became

---

[16] Eisenhower to Marshall, 15 Apr 45, Eisenhower personal file; Bradley, *A Soldier's Story*, pp. 537–39.

[17] SHAEF G–3 Appreciation, Factors Affecting the Advance Into Germany After the Occupation of the Ruhr, 24 Sep 44, SHAEF SGS 381, Post OVERLORD Planning, I.

increasingly optimistic after the beginning of April. They spoke of the little opposition offered by an "apathetic and supine" citizenry, and named the task of distributing foodstuffs to the inhabitants of captured towns and cities as the chief problem confronting the Allies. The possibility that German armed forces might fortify an area in western Austria, the National Redoubt, was not completely discounted, but the Allies tended to minimize the threat as their forces continued the advance into central Germany. By mid-April there was evidence that all but the most fanatic Nazis had given up hope of escaping decisive defeat. The intelligence experts assumed that any optimism the enemy might have rested on his belief in three possibilities: (1) friction between the Allies and the Russians when they met in central Germany; (2) a possible fight in the National Redoubt throughout the winter; and (3) the emergence of a large-scale guerrilla movement throughout the country.[18]

The Nature of the Pursuit

The campaign from 1 April until the end of the war is likely to be cited frequently in the future because it is replete with perfect "book" solutions to military problems. It was possible in most cases for commanders to set missions for their forces, allot troops and supplies, and know that their phase lines would be reached. Only when objectives were taken far before the hour chosen were the timetables upset. By its very nature, therefore, the great pursuit across central Germany may mislead the student who attempts to draw lessons of value for future campaigns. Allied superiority in quality of troops, mobility, air power, matériel, and morale was

such that only a duplication of the deterioration of enemy forces such as that which existed in April 1945 would again make possible the type of slashing attack that developed. Units were able to leave their supply bases far behind, to ask that gasoline supplies be delivered by air some miles beyond the positions they then held, to ignore wide gaps on their flanks, to leave in their rear enemy units which surpassed them in numbers, to roam far and wide in enemy territory without any adequate intelligence of the enemy situation, to let their main lines of communications become jammed with German civilians and liberated peoples—and still be certain that the enemy would give little trouble. Only in the last days when the Allied advance reached the edge of the dwindling airfields of the Reich did the Luftwaffe manage to mount occasional small attacks. At best, these merely proved annoying at bridge sites, and did little to stop even the small jeeploads of advance parties which sometimes went ahead of the armor into enemy-held towns.

The enemy fell apart but waited to be overrun. A German high command virtually ceased to exist and even regimental headquarters had difficulty in knowing the dispositions of their troops or the situation on their flanks. In those instances where unit commanders still received Hitler's messages to hold their positions, they tended to ignore them as having little relationship to the realities of their situation. Expedients such as the calling up of *Volkssturm* units proved futile. These last hopes of Hitler's army readily laid down their arms except in a few cases where their resistance was stiffened by SS elements. And

---

[18] JIC Political Intel Rpt, 6 Apr 45; Rpt on the National Redoubt, 10 Apr 45; Political Intel Rpt, 14 Apr 45. All in SHAEF G–2 JIC SHAEF (45) papers.

the general public, which might have furnished cadres for guerrilla warfare, proved uninterested in partisan activities. Near the war's end, civilians in many cities sent word that they were ready to surrender and asked that bloodless entries be made into their towns. Frequently they begged the German military commander of their area to evacuate his troops before the Allies arrived, and in a few instances they actually helped the Allied troops force the local German commander to surrender. The favorite color of enemy towns that April was "tattletale grey" as windows were filled with symbols of surrender.

The great pursuit makes a fascinating story. In a few weeks Allied unit journals chronicled the names of the great German cities, making a catalogue of conquests which no previous invader from the west had ever compiled in so short a time. Each army could boast of thousands of prisoners and square miles captured and nearly every unit could cite its triumphal parades by the score. Even small psychological warfare teams or prisoner of war interrogation units could sometimes claim to have been first in a village; individual jeeploads of soldiers stored up material for reminiscences about how they nearly reached Berlin or Prague before the Red Army. So rapid was the pursuit that official accounts varied greatly. In one sector of a large city, one division would be fighting hotly against some rear guard group, while elsewhere in the same city another Allied division would be marching in without any resistance. A town that may have been undefended when the first Allied reconnaissance elements announced their entry sometimes suddenly became the center of a short but bitter fight as German units from points west of the town were caught withdrawing through it.

In the eighteen days required to close and destroy the Ruhr Pocket the Allied forces north and south of that area roared on to the Elbe, often against no opposition, adding thousands of square miles and hundreds of thousands of prisoners to the total territory and men taken. The situation was best described by hackneyed allusions to the great flood of men and tanks that poured through the lands of the enemy. These, while diverted occasionally by a strong point, reached out to every main channel of communication and engulfed the straggling armies, which, attempting to reach a place of safety, found themselves outraced by the torrent which had burst forth from west of the Rhine. Enemy strong points, except in the Ruhr Pocket and the Harz mountains, were of little effect in slowing the Allied armies which inundated the mountain passes, the plains, and the lowlands of the Reich. In their wake was left the wreckage of war, the wandering hordes of displaced persons, liberated prisoners, and German families returning to their homes, clogging the road nets and threatening to hold back the great motor columns which streamed on relentlessly. Those who attempted to stop the Allies took on the appearance of anxious levee workers who toil frenziedly to raise a new barrier of sandbags even as the waters lap at their feet, knowing that nothing save a miracle can make their belated efforts succeed. Apparently feeling that they could not stem the tide, the Germans in most sectors made a half-hearted resistance and then merely waited until the flood rolled over them.

Operations in the North

Because of the wide dispersion of General Eisenhower's forces in April, he was usually able during this period to intervene directly only in those cases where inter-army-group shifts were required, a major change in the direction of an army group or army was needed, or a command question with political overtones was involved. Even army group, army, and corps commanders had difficulty in knowing the exact whereabouts of their units at any particular time of the day. For the purposes of this narrative it is necessary to show only the main outlines of the campaigns of the various army groups and the points at which the Supreme Commander intervened to an important degree.

Field Marshal Montgomery, it will be recalled, had planned a major drive toward the Elbe by the Second British, First Canadian, and Ninth U.S. Armies. On the withdrawal of the Ninth Army, the 21 Army Group commander indicated that the mission of General Crerar's army was still to open a supply route through Arnhem, to drive northward to clear the northeastern and western Netherlands, and to move along the coastal belt on the Second British Army's left to take the Emden–Wilhelmshaven peninsula. General Dempsey's army was still to drive for the line of the Elbe in his sector and reduce the ports of Bremen and Hamburg.[19]

The Second British Army scheme of maneuver, once the drive to Berlin was ruled out, was conditioned by the course of the lower Elbe and the location of the north German ports. The Elbe, which flows almost due north through the area in which the Ninth and First Armies were attacking, takes a sharp turn to the northwest near Wittenberg. In attempting to clear the left bank of the river, therefore, the eastbound British columns once they reached the Weser and the Aller turned sharply to the left and ended by driving

almost due north to hit the Elbe. Units on the extreme left, especially on the Canadian Army front, were directed almost due north from the beginning of their attack. This shift also put the main body of the British Army on the Elbe just south of Hamburg and in a position to drive across the base of the Jutland peninsula to the Baltic. By this means it could cut off an enemy retreat from Denmark and Schleswig-Holstein and prevent the area from falling into Soviet hands.

The attack to the Elbe was fairly uneventful by past standards of fighting, the right wing bridging the Weser on 5 April and sweeping on to the Elbe whose left bank it cleared by the 24th. Columns in the center and the left met much stiffer resistance, particularly along the Dortmund–Ems Canal, but by 26 April they had pushed up to the Elbe south of Hamburg, cleared Bremen, and sent columns toward the naval base of Cuxhaven.

On the British left, the First Canadian Army was in the process of moving northeast, due north, and west. Driving from a bridgehead near Emmerich, one column established a bridgehead over the Ems on 8 April and advanced against some of the stiffest resistance met in the north during this period against the naval bases at Emden and Wilhelmshaven. To the west, another column driving due north from Emmerich linked up with Special Air Service units, which had been dropped well into the rear of the German lines, and drove rapidly to the North Sea. By the end of the third week in April, all enemy resistance in the northeastern Netherlands, save for small pockets along the Ems estuary, had been eliminated. These re-

---

[19] Montgomery, *Normandy to the Baltic*, pp. 328–38; 21 A Gp, Operational Dir M–563, 28 Mar 45, General Board files, 21 A Gp Operational Dirs.

maining groups surrended by 3 May.

On the extreme left of the Canadian line, newly arrived troops from Italy crossed the Neder Rijn on 12 April, cleared Arnhem two days later, and reached the IJsselmeer on the 18th. Operations aimed at clearing the rest of the western Netherlands were halted on 22 April after the German high commissioner for the Netherlands, Arthur Seyss-Inquart, said that if the Canadians would halt east of the Grebbe line, he would not flood the area.[20] With his forces firmly established on the west bank of the Elbe, Field Marshal Montgomery prepared his offensive toward Luebeck to seal off the Jutland peninsula. General Eisenhower had looked on this operation approvingly in early April as one proposal with political implications which he was willing to back. Knowing of Mr. Churchill's interest in the matter and desiring to make good on his earlier promise to give Montgomery anything that was needed for an attack to the north once the Allies reached the Elbe, he sent General Bradley to check on the 21 Army Group's requirements and later went himself to ascertain that everything required for the operation's success was made available by SHAEF. Told that a U.S. corps and part-time use of the railway bridge at Wesel were sufficient, the Supreme Commander at once made available the U.S. airborne corps and the desired logistical support. Later, when the condition of roads in the British area and the necessity of building up administrative support of the attack led to delays, General Eisenhower called Montgomery's attention to the growing fluidity of the German defense in front of the Red Army and re-emphasized the need of a rapid thrust to Luebeck. He recalled the Prime Minister's keen interest in the operation and

made clear that all of SHAEF's resources were available to insure the speed and success of the action. The field marshal reminded Eisenhower that his plans for driving to Luebeck had been changed by the shift of the Ninth Army to the 12th Army Group, and that he was doing the best he could with what he had left. To keep the record straight, the Supreme Commander informed the British and U.S. Chiefs of Staff of his past efforts and his present intentions of giving all possible aid for the push northward.[21]

The Second British Army established bridgeheads across the lower Elbe on 29 and 30 April, and on 1 May started a series of drives that rapidly cleared the area. One armored column advanced thirty miles on the 2d and entered Luebeck without opposition, while another went forty miles northeastward to enter Wismar a few hours before the Russians. The campaign for the Baltic area ended on 3 May when Hamburg surrendered without a fight.[22]

The Main Thrust to the Elbe

While the 21 Army Group drive in the north turned to the left to follow the curve

[20] Seyss-Inquart's full title was: Reichskommissar fuer die besetzten niederlaendischen Gebiete.

[21] Eisenhower to Montgomery, FWD 18389, 31 Mar 45; Eisenhower to Montgomery, 9 Apr 45; Eisenhower to Marshall, 27 Apr 45; Eisenhower to Brooke, 27 Apr 45. General Marshall, in a message beginning "Don't let this message bother you," made one of his rare inquiries on a tactical action when the airborne allotment was made. Pointing to the heavy fighting the 82d Airborne Division had undergone, he asked if "your staff people keep in mind the percentages of casualties suffered by various divisions in relation to their assignments at this final stage of the war." General Eisenhower made clear that all assignments were made in the interest of speed and economy of fuel and transportation. Marshall to Eisenhower, W–75411, 1 May 45; Eisenhower to Marshall, 2 May 45. Both in SHAEF cbl log.

[22] Montgomery, *Normandy to the Baltic*, pp. 343–45.

of the Elbe, General Bradley's offensive tended to turn toward the right. The direction of his drive was influenced to a degree by the southeastward bend of the Elbe south of Dessau, but to a greater extent by the orientation of the Central and Southern Groups of Armies toward Bavaria and Austria to clean out the enemy in the Redoubt region. The chief delays in the Ninth and First Army sectors came in the Ruhr Pocket area and in the Harz mountains. The clearance of the Ruhr occupied elements of two corps of each army during most of the month. In the Harz mountain fight, elements from a corps of each army had to be committed for more than a week. This latter fight had developed at the end of the first week in April when OKW ordered the enemy forces in that area to hold their positions as a base of future operations for the new *Twelfth Army* then being organized east of the Elbe. Before anything except some of the army's staff could arrive, the German forces in that sector had been overwhelmed.

Save in these two fights, the two armies were concerned more with supplies than with the enemy during April. The First Army, having a longer axis of advance than General Simpson's forces, was particularly hampered by the long truck haul from the Rhine, and the problem became more difficult with each mile that the army pushed eastward. Some forward elements were more than 280 miles from the Rhine and were forced to undertake some round-trip hauls in excess of 700 miles. This situation was improved somewhat on 7 April with the completion of the first rail line east of the Rhine, but it was not eased completely until the end of the war.

Having left strong forces behind to crush the enemy in the Ruhr, the two U.S.

armies pushed forward from positions north and south of that sector during the first week in April. The Ninth Army, having the shortest distance to go to reach the Elbe, attained its objective a week after starting its offensive. On the evening of 11 April, General Simpson's advance armored spearheads climaxed the day's drive of fifty-seven miles by dashing to the Elbe near Magdeburg. On the 12th, the day of President Roosevelt's death, they established a bridgehead over the river, while further north other elements entered Tangermuende just fifty-three miles from Berlin. A second bridgehead was established south of Magdeburg on the 13th in the face of enemy air attacks. The enemy, hoping to forestall a possible break-through from the northernmost bridgehead toward Berlin, counterattacked on 14 April and forced the U.S. troops back across the river in that sector. The southern bridgehead held firm. While some elements of the First Army were being slowed temporarily in the Harz mountain area, its southern columns drove forward through Leipzig on the 18th and advanced toward the Mulde.

On reaching the Elbe, General Simpson raised with General Bradley the possibility of pushing on to Berlin. The 12th Army Group commander, who had already advised General Eisenhower against the move and who knew of SHAEF's view that the central forces should stop on the Elbe until other objectives were taken to the north and south, directed the Ninth Army commander to hold in place on the line of the river and await contact with the Red Army. The retention of a bridgehead over the Elbe was left to his discretion. The following week was spent, therefore, in clearing the enemy from the army zone west of the Elbe.

MEETING AT THE ELBE. *Brig. Gen. Charles G. Helmick and Maj. Gen. Clarence R. Huebner of the U.S. V Corps meet with Soviet representatives near Torgau, Germany.*

Meanwhile, Generals Eisenhower and Bradley were drawing a stop line for the First Army forces. Since in most of the zones then held by General Hodges the Elbe swung out sharply toward the east, it was necessary to find another line farther to the west so that there would not be an extended salient to the right of the Ninth Army. This was found in the Mulde River, which runs into the Elbe at Dessau. In accordance with a 12th Army Group order of 12 April which stipulated that forces of the First Army were not to advance east of the Mulde without permission of its commander, General Hodges on 24 April declared that only small U.S. patrols were to cross that river. His stop

order was broad enough to permit forces much larger than a normal patrol to cross the river. On 25 April, three of these roving units made contact with Red Army forward elements at the Mulde, at the Elbe, and beyond the Elbe. The first formal meeting between U.S. and Russian divisional commanders took place near Torgau on the following day.

To the right of the First Army, General Patton's forces had been advancing southeast against little opposition since early April. Except for heavily wooded areas in the Thueringer Wald, the terrain through which Third Army now moved was unsuitable for defense. Opposition was swept away, and by 11 April the army was reporting that it was not meeting any semblance of resistance. On that day, General Bradley set a restraining line for General Patton's forces a little to the west of the Czechoslovakian border. On the 14th, elements of the army raced forward to points within ten miles of the Czech frontier. They were now ordered to regroup in preparation for a new mission which would take them into Czechoslovakia and southward into Bavaria and Austria. Patrols crossed into Czechoslovakia on the 17th, but the army's main activities in the next few days were concerned with the sideslipping of units southward while the First Army took over part of the sector in the north. On the 22d the drive southeastward in the direction of the Danube and the Austrian border picked up full speed. Gains of fifteen and twenty miles a day became common along the entire line and were made at extremely low costs in men. The Third Army, reporting its casualties on 23 April, indicated that its losses were the smallest of any day of battle to that point: three killed, thirty-seven wounded, and five missing. It had taken nearly 9,000 prisoners.

General Patton's forces broke through hastily improvised defenses on the Isar and the Inn at the close of April and crossed into Austria to seize Linz on 4 May. A day later, the Third Army took over part of the First Army's sector and one of its corps as General Hodges started preparations to move his headquarters to the United States, where it was to be reconstituted for duty in the Pacific.[23] Some of Patton's forces were sent at once into Pilzen, which was already in the hands of the Czech Partisans. In accordance with recent arrangements worked out between General Eisenhower and the Red Army

high command, General Bradley now ordered the Third Army to advance to a line running north and south through České Budějovice (Budweis)–Pilzen–Karlsbad and be prepared to advance eastward.[24] The surrender at Reims came before General Patton's forces had pushed up to the new boundary at all points. They made contact with the Russians on the 8th, but there was a delay of several days before the Red Army closed up completely to the inter-Allied boundary.

6th Army Group Operations

The 6th Army Group offensive, while subsidiary to General Bradley's offensive in the north, was nonetheless crucial to the entire Allied attack. Not only were General Devers' northern units expected to give flank protection to the right wing of Patton's army, but other elements were to seize the Augsburg–Munich area, clear the sector just north of the Swiss border, drive into Austria, and ultimately link up with Allied forces in northern Italy.

General Devers' forces, like those of the army group to the north, swung to the southeast. The sharp turn southward of the Third Army between the Czech border and Nuremberg cut off the Seventh Army from any further advance to the east and Patch's force had to move almost due south from Nuremberg. This turn was accompanied by an even more abrupt reorientation of the First French Army.

The Seventh Army's chief fight in the period came in early April against enemy positions along the line of the Neckar.

---

[23] The First Army's other two corps were shifted to the Ninth Army on 6 May.

[24] See below, p. 469.

CHART 9—OPERATIONAL CHAIN OF COMMAND, AEF, 1 MAY 1945

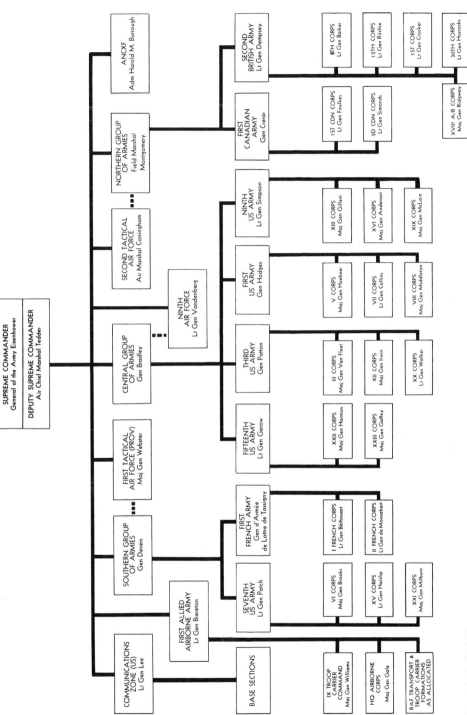

Source: Statistics Sec, SGS, SHAEF.

After a nine-day battle, it swept on to Nuremberg. The Germans resisted fanatically for three days, but the city succumbed on the 20th. In the course of this action, the Third Army, which was beginning to turn southward across the Seventh Army's front was given some twenty-five percent of the sector initially intended for General Patch's forces. Meanwhile, the First French Army, which had seized Karlsruhe on 3 April and pushed east and south into the Black Forest (Schwarz Wald) as well as southward along the east bank of the upper Rhine, was sending a column to aid in taking Stuttgart. U.S. forces enveloped the city, while the French cut it off from enemy elements in the Black Forest. The two Allied forces then joined up on 22 April and the city fell to the French on the following day.

After the fall of Nuremberg, General Eisenhower ordered General Devers to shift the Seventh Army into southern Bavaria and the Tirol to make certain that the enemy did not establish a National Redoubt in that region. General Devers sent the French Army, now considerably blocked by this broad turn across its front, toward Ulm and the Danube in its sector. On 22 April, elements of both armies crossed the Danube, becoming entangled as they tried to operate in the area around Ulm. The action from this point on was marked less by enemy opposition than by traffic jams on the roads in Bavaria. The period also saw evidence of resistance on the part of German civilians against any further continuance of the war by the military leaders. At Augsburg, when the military commander refused to heed civilian pleas to surrender, civilian parties led Seventh Army elements to his command post. Near the month's end, as U.S.

elements started the encirclement of Munich, an underground group, aided by a small band of German soldiers, in a premature coup arrested the Nazi governor of Bavaria and seized the radio station of Munich in an effort to surrender the city before serious fighting started. The coup proved abortive, but the city, which General Eisenhower termed "the cradle of the Nazi beast," surrendered on 30 April after an action in which three infantry divisions, two armored divisions, and a cavalry group all claimed to have had a hand.

At the beginning of May, General de Lattre began clearing the Austrian province of Vorarlberg near Lake Constance, while General Patch drove from Munich southward through the Inn valley toward Italy and southeastward to Salzburg. With the aid of Austrian Partisans, who acted as guides, Seventh Army units pushed to the Brenner Pass and took Brenner shortly after midnight on the morning of 4 May. Later in the morning, they made contact with advance elements of the Fifth U.S. Army coming up from northern Italy. In the Salzburg area, trouble developed when Seventh Army found it necessary, because of the mountainous area in its left-wing sector, to push into the Third Army zone. In order to avoid a tie-up of forces or the opening of a gap through which the enemy could escape, General Eisenhower on 2 May arranged with Generals Bradley and Devers to switch Salzburg from the Third Army to the Seventh Army zone. After an advance, which was described as "less a combat problem than a motor march . . . ," the city surrendered on 4 May. A few hours later, the Allies completed the last important action in the area, the capture of Berchtesgaden. *(Chart 9)*

CHAPTER XXIV

The Drive to the Elbe (Continued)

As the Supreme Commander's armies drove to the Elbe, SHAEF was confronted with a variety of developments. These included such diverse items as Allied attempts to feed the people in occupied areas of the Netherlands, difficulties with the French over the occupation of Stuttgart, discussions with the Russians on liaison and a line of demarcation between Western and Russian forces, the death of Hitler, and Admiral Doenitz' assumption of power in Germany.

Aid for the Netherlands

In the closing week of April, the Allies suspended their operations in the western Netherlands to permit representatives of the Supreme Commander and of the Nazi high commissioner in the Netherlands, Seyss-Inquart, to discuss procedures for feeding the population in the occupied area of that country. This problem had concerned the Western powers since the Arnhem operation in the fall of 1944. Food shortages had resulted partly because of an embargo imposed by Seyss-Inquart in retaliation for a Dutch slow-down and stoppage of railway traffic in the occupied area. After considerable negotiations, some food had been brought in through the Swedish Red Cross and from

Switzerland in January 1945. In the same month SHAEF sent representatives to Eindhoven to discuss the relief problem with Dutch medical experts. After other meetings at London and Brussels, doctors and trained personnel were selected to handle treatment of individuals in an advanced stage of starvation. In April, despite the aid of Red Cross agencies and severe rationing, the food situation threatened to become disastrous. As food stocks reached their lowest ebb, and as the Germans hinted they would flood the country in case of an attack, the Netherlands Government-in-exile appealed to the Allies for help. Meanwhile, Seyss-Inquart discussed with Doctor Hirschfeld, Secretary-General of Economics, various means of avoiding catastrophe in the Netherlands. The Reichskommissar indicated that he might be willing to open negotiations on the subject with Allied authorities, and this word was passed on to London. On 19 April, Prime Minister Churchill asked the authorities in Washington for their opinions. The U.S. Chiefs of Staff, doubting that the Germans would carry out their threats against the Dutch, pointed to the dangers of tampering with the unconditional surrender formula and possible unfavorable Russian reactions. They asked that nothing be done without previous consultation with the Russians and General Eisenhower. The Supreme Commander when asked for his views declared that something must be done to aid the Dutch even at the risk of interfering with military operations. He approved discussions with Seyss-Inquart, subject to Russian concurrence. If no agreement could be reached, he felt that the First Canadian Army would have to be used to aid the people of the occupied area.[1]

General Eisenhower, increasingly concerned over the Dutch situation, warned the German commander in the Netherlands that he would be punished if the Germans intensified Dutch suffering. Hostilities were suspended on the morning of 28 April, and General de Guingand and Brigadier E. T. Williams of the 21 Army Group staff proceeded to Achterveld to meet German representatives. The British officers presented Allied plans for aiding the population of the Netherlands, but the meeting foundered when the Germans indicated that they did not have authority to agree to anything. General de Guingand then insisted that they return in forty-eight hours with Seyss-Inquart or, at least, with his full authority to act.[2]

On 30 April, Seyss-Inquart and his staff met an Allied delegation which included Generals Smith and Strong of SHAEF; Maj. Gen. Ivan Susloparoff, who had been authorized by Moscow to represent the USSR in the talks; General de Guingand and Brigadier Williams of the 21 Army Group; Maj. Gen. A. Galloway, British commander of the Netherlands District; and Prince Bernhard, commander in chief of the Netherlands forces. Arrangements were worked out for dropping food from Allied planes at some ten points. In addition, one road was to be opened to trucks, and food ships were to be received at Rot-

terdam. On 1 May, in accordance with these agreements, Allied planes began relief operations. SHAEF broadcasts informed the inhabitants where to pick up supplies and warned the enemy not to interfere with the air drop. On the following day, trucks crossed from the liberated Netherlands into the occupied zone. Full-scale rescue efforts could not be undertaken, however, until after the armistice.[3]

While discussing the matter of aid to the Dutch, General Smith attempted to impress on Seyss-Inquart the hopelessness of the German situation in the Netherlands and suggested that the time was ripe for a truce or unconditional surrender. The Reichskommissar agreed with the argument, but said that as long as German civil and military authorities in the Netherlands were in touch with Berlin they would have to leave matters of surrender to their superiors. He also argued that the Germans in the Netherlands should continue to fight as long as any government existed in Germany. General Smith, who had dealt politely with Seyss-Inquart during the earlier interview, now threatened him with punishment if his policies caused further loss of life in the Netherlands. The Reichskommissar admitted his obligations to lighten the burden on the Dutch and promised to do what he could to help them. He also asked

---

[1] *Malnutrition and Starvation in Western Netherlands, September 1944–July 1945* (The Hague, 1948), pp. 5–45. Marshall to Eisenhower, W–70055, 19 Apr 45; Eisenhower to Marshall, FWD 19562, 20 Apr 45. Both in Eisenhower personal file.

[2] Eisenhower to Marshall, 23 Apr 45; Eisenhower to Marshall, 27 Apr 45. Both in Eisenhower personal file; de Guingand, *Operation Victory*, pp. 445–49; Ltr, Brig Williams to author, 22 Sep 51.

[3] Memo, Smith for Eisenhower, 1 May 45, Diary Office CinC, 1 May 45; de Guingand, *Operation Victory*, pp. 450–51; Interv with Brig Williams, 30–31 May 47. Stacey, *The Canadian Army*, p. 268, says that 510 tons of food were dropped as early as 29 April.

for a safe-conduct to go to Germany to discuss the matter of a truce and possibly an over-all surrender in the Netherlands. On the grounds that he could surrender if he wished to do so, and further that he had radio contact with Berlin and could get necessary instructions by that means, his request was refused.[4]

The Stuttgart Incident

After Stuttgart was enveloped by forces of the Seventh Army, the First French Army took the city. On the day before it fell, General Devers had redrawn the boundary lines in his sector to give Stuttgart to General Patch's forces. His purpose was to prevent U.S. and French units from becoming entangled and to provide proper lines of communications for his armies. General de Gaulle, however, apparently thought that the U.S. commander was more interested in getting the French out of this important German city than in the effective working of Seventh Army's supply lines. He decided therefore that until France was definitely assigned a zone of occupation by the Allies he should hold on to what he had. He indicated to General de Lattre that a political and not a military matter was involved and that this was a case where French forces were not answerable to General Eisenhower or General Devers. Consequently, when U.S. forces moved into Stuttgart on 24 April to relieve French units in the city, they found the French polite but determined not to leave. When General Devers for a second time directed the First French Army to evacuate the city, General de Gaulle issued the following order to General de Lattre:

I require you to maintain a French garrison at Stuttgart and to institute immediately a military government. . . . To eventual observations [of the Americans] you will reply that the orders of your Government are to hold and administer the territory conquered by our troops until the French zone of occupation has been fixed between the interested Governments, which to your knowledge has not been done.

General de Lattre thereupon informed the 6th Army Group commander that he could not hand over the city but added that Stuttgart could be used by the 6th Army Group.[5]

On an appeal from the 6th Army Group that its authority was being flouted, General Eisenhower protested officially to General de Gaulle, saying that the city was urgently needed as a link in the Seventh Army's supply line. He expressed concern at the French use of the issue to force political concessions by the British and U.S. Governments and declared:

Under the circumstances, I must of course accept the situation, as I myself am unwilling to take any action which would reduce the effectiveness of the military effort against Germany, either by withholding supplies from the First French Army or by other measures which would affect their fighting strength. Moreover, I will never personally be a party to initiating any type of struggle or quarrel between your government and troops under my command which can result only in weakening bonds of national friendship as well as the exemplary spirit of cooperation that characterized the actions of French and American forces in the battle line. Accordingly I am seeking another solution for the maintenance of the Seventh Army.

Eisenhower put on record a firm statement of his belief that "the issuance direct

---

[4] Memo, Smith for Eisenhower, 1 May 45, Diary Office CinC, 1 May 45; de Guingand, *Operation Victory*, pp. 451–53; Interv with Williams, 30–31 May 47.

[5] De Lattre, *Histoire de la Première Armée Française*, pp. 565–70.

to the First French Army of orders based on political grounds which run counter to the operational orders given through the military chain of command, violates the understanding with the United States Government under which French divisions armed and equipped by the United States were to be placed under the Combined Chiefs of Staff whose orders I am carrying out in this theater of operations." It became his duty, he said, to refer the matter to the Combined Chiefs of Staff with a statement that he could "no longer count with certainty upon the operational use of any French forces they may contemplate equipping in the future." He regretted that he had no knowledge of the negotiations between the French and Allied governments concerning a French zone of occupation. "Consequently the embarrassment I am experiencing in supplying and administering the Seventh U.S. Army, and in coordinating military operations involving the First French Army seems to me the more regrettable." [6]

General de Gaulle disposed of the initial protest with a reminder that the presence of French headquarters in Nancy and Metz had not been an obstacle to "General Patton's magnificent successes." He admitted that the difficulty which had arisen had been none of the Supreme Commander's doing. It was due rather to the lack of agreement and liaison between France and the Allied governments "on that which relates to the war policy in general and in particular to the occupation of German territory." The French Government, not being able to integrate its views with those of the Allies, had to put them forward separately. Since the French had no part in the meetings of the Combined Chiefs of Staff, decisions taken by this group failed to take into account French

national requirements. This situation had resulted, de Gaulle said,

in forcing me, personally—although to my great regret—to step in sometimes, either with respect to plans or their execution. You are certainly aware, that while agreeing to place French operational forces in the western theater under your Supreme Command, I have always reserved the right of the French Government eventually to take the necessary steps in order that French Forces should be employed in accordance with the national interest of France which is the only interest that they should serve.

He pointed out that arms for these forces had come in under lend-lease and that French services were given in return, and he recalled the sore point that no new French divisions had been completely equipped by the United States since the beginning of operations in the west "in spite of all that had appeared to have been understood a long time ago." He expressed his appreciation for the part General Eisenhower personally had played and said he hoped that a fine spirit would continue between French and U.S. forces in the field. General Eisenhower, in thanking de Gaulle for the courtesy of a very full explanation, declared that he understood the French chief's position. ". . . while I regret," the Supreme Commander went on, "that you find it necessary to inject political considerations into a campaign in which my functions are purely military, I am gratified to know that you understand my situation and attitude." [7]

In Washington, President Truman said he was shocked at the implications of General de Gaulle's action, and concerned be-

---

[6] Eisenhower to de Gaulle, 28 Apr 45, SHAEF cbl log.

[7] Eisenhower to CCS, 2 May 45 (Text of Ltr, de Gaulle to Eisenhower, 1 May 45, and Reply, Eisenhower to de Gaulle, 2 May 45), SHAEF cbl log.

cause reports of the incident that had reached the United States from French sources were likely to result in a storm of resentment. If the time had come when the French Army was to be considered as carrying out only the political wishes of the French Government, then the command structure would have to be rearranged. General de Gaulle expressed his wish that such situations would not arise, and indicated that they could be avoided easily if France's allies would only recognize "that questions so closely touching France as the occupation of German territory should be discussed and decided with her." This unfortunately had not been the case "in spite of my repeated request." [8]

So far as General Eisenhower was concerned, the incident had already been closed by the withdrawal of U.S. troops from Stuttgart. The war was so near its end that any inconvenience in keeping his supply lines open was annoying but not serious. Soon after the episode, the Allies agreed on a French zone of occupation and a part for France in the control machinery for Germany, thus meeting de Gaulle's main demands.

Avoiding Clashes With the Russians

In the war in northeast Europe, as in any coalition war where allied and associated powers are driving headlong toward each other through enemy territory, there existed by the end of March the danger that within a few weeks or even days clashes might arise between friendly ground forces. Such collisions could and did happen between units fighting side by side when proper co-ordination or liaison was missing. The danger was much greater in the case of the Russians and the Western powers because there was no direct

wire communication and the battle had reached the point that even division commanders were not always sure within twenty to forty miles where their forward elements could be located at a given moment. This difficulty did not become acute among the ground forces until early April 1945, but it had been causing troubles between the Soviet and British and U.S. air forces since the previous summer and fall. Efforts made since the time of the June 1944 landings to work out solutions to these problems had been complicated by the lack of agreements on such matters as the drawing of bomb lines, the nature of lines of demarcation, the procedure to be followed when contact was imminent, withdrawal of various troops to their proper zones of occupation, and the question of advancing beyond an agreed line of demarcation when it seemed essential to save friendly occupied peoples from German fury.

The Soviet leaders could not rid themselves of their fears of the Western capitalist powers or, perhaps, of their recollections that allies could suddenly become enemies. Throughout the war, therefore, they were unwilling to trust the Western powers with much information concerning the Red Army's activities. This closed door resulted in an unwillingness on their part to permit the establishment of real liaison machinery between the East and West or, where they had consented to some such arrangement, a tendency to render it unworkable by repeated delays. Some political co-operation had been worked out between the British and the Russians after the German invasion of the USSR, and between the Amer-

---

[8] Paraphrase of President Truman's and General de Gaulle's messages cited in Diary Office CinC. The Truman letter is also in Marshall to Eisenhower, W–76554, 3 May 45, SHAEF cbl log.

icans and the Russians after the negotiation of the lend-lease agreement in 1941, but systematic efforts to co-ordinate Russian plans and those being made for the invasion of Europe came only at the close of 1943. U.S. and British military missions in Moscow, headed respectively by General Deane and Lt. Gen. G. LeQ. Martel (replaced in March 1944 by Lt. Gen. M. B. Burrows, and in March 1945 by Admiral E. R. Archer), undertook to keep the Russians informed of the daily operations of the Western powers and to get some information in return on the actions of the Red forces. Shortly after the Normandy landings, an arrangement was made by which the Allies furnished the Soviet Government outlines of General Eisenhower's proposed operations and, when necessary, his plans for the future. The Russians, in return, gave the Allied military missions in Moscow advance copies of the Red Army communiqués a short time before their release to the press. For any serious attempt to co-ordinate military activities, the Supreme Commander had to indicate his wishes to the Combined Chiefs of Staff for transmittal to the military missions in Moscow and then to the Red Army Chief of Staff. On a matter of any importance, the communication was passed on to Marshal Stalin. If his answer was favorable, the whole process was repeated in reverse. In the early days of ground operations, this matter of holding partners at arm's length was merely exasperating. But as the war neared an end the problem became potentially dangerous.[9]

Attempts had been made to co-ordinate the boundaries of occupation zones for Germany by the creation of the European Advisory Commission late in 1943. This body had started on its task early in 1944.

Meanwhile, the Allies had tried to work out other effective methods of operational liaison. Marshal Stalin mentioned in June 1944 the possibility of a combined military staff for this purpose, and the Combined Chiefs of Staff went so far as to talk of the possibility of establishing a tripartite committee in Moscow with consultative and advisory powers to aid in co-ordinating operational and strategical matters. For some reason, Marshal Stalin in September postponed discussion of the matter on the pretext that he did not wish to discuss it until General Burrows was replaced as head of the British Military Mission in Moscow. This officer was withdrawn in the following month, but no permanent replacement was named until March 1945. The consultative committee was never established.[10]

General Eaker, worried in June about the need of co-ordinating attacks by his Mediterranean air forces and the Russian air forces over targets in southeast Europe, had sent an air representative to Moscow to meet daily with a member of the Russian General Staff to adjust air operations. In November the question of co-ordinating air and ground force actions became serious when U.S. fighters, attacking what they considered to be a German column in Yugoslavia, were charged with killing a Russian lieutenant general and several soldiers. The U.S. Chiefs of Staff promptly apologized but urged that more effective liaison be established. The Russians not only reacted unfavorably to this pro-

---

[9] The author has relied to a considerable extent on General Deane's *The Strange Alliance*. Many of the pertinent documents cited by Deane may be found in SHAEF SGS 373.5 Bomb-line, Liaison, and Co-ordination of Fronts, I, and SHAEF SGS 380.01/1 Exchange of Information on Operations Between the Allies and Russia, I.

[10] Deane, *The Strange Alliance*, pp. 142–54.

posal but stopped efforts at informal liaison which one of their army commanders had worked out with the Mediterranean air forces. When the matter dragged on into December 1944, General Eaker adopted the procedure of informing the Russians of the bomb line he intended to observe and leaving up to them the responsibility for co-ordination. To his surprise, they made no protest.[11]

In northwest Europe, the matter of air liaison was somewhat more complicated. When Red Army advances into Poland threatened to bring Soviet columns into the area being attacked by air forces from the west, General Deane suggested a bomb line which would run some fifty to a hundred miles west of the Russian lines. The Soviet representatives, apparently with the purpose of barring the British from dropping supplies to Poles loyal to the London Polish Government-in-exile, made a counterproposal of a line which would have prevented General Spaatz's forces from going east of Berlin. No agreement on this suggestion had been reached before the meeting at Yalta.[12] At the conference in the Crimea, the Western powers again raised the question, but the Russian representatives showed little disposition to reach an agreement. When General Marshall warned of possible repetitions of the bombing in Yugoslavia, Gen. Alexei Antonov, the Red Army Chief of Staff, said that the difficulty there was due not to the lack of liaison but to mistakes in navigation. The Russians persisted in their demands for a rigid bomb line which could be changed only occasionally, and they asked that the Allied bombing forces submit for clearance twenty-four hours before the attack lists of targets on the Russian front. The Combined Chiefs of Staff thereupon decided to continue General Eaker's ar-

rangement of giving the Russians advance notice of proposed operations and letting the Soviet forces do the co-ordinating. Finally, in March 1945, the Russians agreed to the initial Allied suggestion at Yalta whereby the bomb line moved daily in accordance with Red Army advances. The Western powers agreed not to attack a zone within 200 miles of the Russian positions without giving the Soviet commanders twenty-four hours' notice. The suggestion by the Russians that silence on their part would be regarded as disapproval was not accepted. They had the responsibility, therefore, of specifying which, if any, of the proposed targets were within the forbidden zone.[13]

As the Russians continued to drive toward the west, a formal agreement on lines of demarcation and zones of occupation became necessary. The European Advisory Commission had discussed these matters in London early in 1944. A British plan for dividing Germany into three zones, in virtually the same form that was ultimately accepted, was presented in January 1944. This proposal, which brought Russia well to the west of the Elbe, was accepted by the USSR rep-

[11] Deane, *The Strange Alliance*, 135–39. CCS to Wilson, FAN 454, 20 Nov 44; Mil Mission Moscow to CCS, MX–21802, 22 Nov 44; Wilson to CCS, NAF 817, 24 Nov 44; CCS to Wilson, FAN 458, 24 Nov 44; JCS to Deane, WX–67900, 24 Nov 44; Wilson to CCS, NAF 820, 27 Nov 44; CCS to Deane and Archer, WX–69568, 28 Nov 44; Wilson to CCS, NAF 822, 30 Nov 44. All in SHAEF SGS 373.5 Bomb-line, Liaison, and Co-ordination of Fronts, I.
[12] Spaatz to Arnold, Sp–163, 28 Nov 44. SHAEF approved this statement. SHAEF to CCS, SCAF 140, 3 Dec 44, SHAEF SGS 373.5 Bomb-line, Liaison and Co-ordination of Fronts, I; Deane, *The Strange Alliance*, pp. 138–39.
[13] 1st, 2d Tripartite Mtgs, Yalta, 5, 9 Feb 45, ARGONAUT Conf Min; Extract, CCS 188th Mtg, 9 Feb 45, SHAEF SGS 373.5 Bomb-line, Liaison and Co-ordination of Fronts, I; Deane, *The Strange Alliance*, p. 139.

resentative in February and apparently satisfied the Civil Affairs Division of the War Department. Toward the end of February, representatives of the Civil Affairs Division proposed a new plan by which the three occupation areas would meet at Berlin. The proposal was regarded as vague and unworkable, and work on the zones came to a stop until April 1944 when the President authorized his representative in London to approve the broad outlines of the initial British proposal for the zones of occupation. He objected only to the suggestion that the United States should occupy a zone in the south of Germany and asked instead for occupational duties in the north.[14] His insistence on this point held up final agreement on the protocol dealing with zones of occupation until after the second Quebec conference, when he finally accepted a zone in the south of Germany. Not until September 1944 did the European Advisory Commission send its protocol on zones of occupation to the three governments chiefly concerned. Even then final approval was delayed because the British and U.S. representatives could not reach agreement on U.S. entry rights in the Bremerhaven area. This matter was settled in November, and the revised protocol was approved by the British government in December 1944.[15]

In January 1945, the U.S. Ambassador to Great Britain, John Winant, became disturbed over the fact that the United States and the Soviet Union had still not formally approved the zones of occupation. He expressed his concern to Mr. Hopkins when the latter was on his way to the Allied meetings at Malta and Yalta, and said he feared that, if no agreement was reached soon, the Russians might continue to advance westward after they had crossed the border of the zone outlined for

them. Secretary of State Stettinius, and Foreign Secretary Eden discussed the question at Malta on 1 February and agreed to urge the Combined Chiefs of Staff to reach an immediate decision on the German occupation zones. Later that day, General Marshall and Field Marshal Brooke, after talking over the matter with Stettinius and Eden, authorized the dispatch of a cable informing the European Advisory Commission that the British and U.S. Governments had now approved the protocol of the zones of occupation. This action was taken apparently without reference to the President. Stettinius indicates that, when Roosevelt arrived at Malta on 2 February, he "seemed greatly relieved when I told him that General Marshall and Field Marshal Brooke had finally approved the plan for the German zones of occupation and that Eden and I had sent instructions to our representatives on the European Advisory Commission in London."[16]

The agenda of the Yalta Conference included for discussion the question of final agreement on the zones of occupation. Actually, of course, as far as the boundaries were concerned, the United States and Great Britain had made the decision before the conferees reached Yalta. The point which remained to be settled at the conference was whether or not France would be given a zone. In a meeting of the President and Marshal Stalin on 4 February, the Soviet leader seemed to concur with the tripartite zone arrangement outlined by the European Advisory Commission but was disinclined to admit

---

[14] See above, Ch. XIX, pp. 349–51.

[15] Philip E. Mosely, "The Occupation of Germany, New Light on How the Zones Were Drawn," *Foreign Affairs*, XXVIII (July, 1950), 580–604.

[16] Stettinius, *Roosevelt and the Russians*, pp. 56, 63, 69.

France. This matter was thoroughly explored on 5 February, and Marshal Stalin ultimately agreed with some reluctance to the British and U.S. plan to give France a zone in western Germany. Stalin made clear that it would not be at the expense of the Russian sphere. Soviet approval of the European Advisory Commission's protocol was given on 6 February. The fact that agreement had been reached was announced as part of the final report issued at the close of the Crimean conference.[17] This fact gave rise to the belief that the zones of occupation were worked out at Yalta. Historically, it is of value to note that the zones as finally drawn were initially outlined months before Yalta by representatives of the political authority of the United States, Great Britain, and the USSR. Final approval of the zones involved both the political authorities and the Combined Chiefs of Staff.[18]

The zones, drawn on the basis of equalizing population and resources among the occupying powers, did not correspond with military requirements as far as a stopping place was concerned. Part of the Russian zone ran well to the west of the Elbe, and it was not logical for the troops of the Western powers to stop their advance at the edge of that area leaving the German forces unbeaten within the zone until the Red Army could close the gap. It became clear, therefore, that the various armies from the east and west should continue to advance until they actually linked up or until they reached some clearly recognizable line of demarcation shortly before a junction was imminent. General Eisenhower indicated in early April that it was not practical to restrict operations on either side by a demarcation prepared in advance. Rather, both sides should be free to advance until contact was made. He

suggested that thereafter, subject to operational needs, either the Red Army or SHAEF could request the other to withdraw behind the interzonal boundaries set up by the European Advisory Commission. The British Chiefs of Staff opposed on both political and military grounds any mention of the interzonal boundary for purposes of defining areas while hostilities were still in progress. They suggested instead that the armies should stand in place until they were ordered to withdraw by their governments.[19]

The British suggestion immediately evoked objections from the U.S. War and State Departments. Officials of the European and Russian Affairs Divisions of the Department of State were said to believe "that for governments to direct movement of troops definitely indicated *political* action and that *such movements should remain a military consideration* at least until SHAEF is dissolved and the ACC (Allied Control Commission) is set up [italics in original]." The British proposal, they feared, might inspire the Russians to race for remaining German areas in order to acquire as many square miles as possible before the war ended. This interpretation, members of the War Department believed, meant that the Department of State preferred "a straight military solution to the problem. That is, for General Eisenhower to plan to move American and British troops when the operations allowed to respective American and British zones, co-ordinating such movements with the local Russian

[17] Stettinius, *Roosevelt and the Russians*, pp. 101–02, 126–27, 129; Mosely, *op. cit.*, p. 599.
[18] For earlier views of General Eisenhower on the division of Germany, see above, Ch. XIX, pp. 349–50.
[19] Eisenhower to CCS, SCAF 264, 5 Apr 45; Br COS to JSM, COS (W) 748, 11 Apr 45. Both in SHAEF SGS 373.5 Bomb-line, Liaison, and Co-ordination of Fronts, I.

commanders or, if necessary with Marshal Stalin through General Deane and Admiral Archer." [20]

The Combined Chiefs of Staff had already directed General Eisenhower to restate his proposal to the effect that, since it did not seem practicable during hostilities to restrict operations or areas by a demarcation line prepared in advance, both fronts should be allowed to advance until contact was imminent. Thereafter, the division of responsibility would be agreed upon by army group commanders. General Eisenhower, who as late as 11 April had cited five new encounters between U.S. and Russian planes as evidence that some arrangement was needed to prevent serious incidents, hastened to send the revised message to Moscow.[21] General Antonov questioned the proposal on the ground that it seemed to change the occupation zones already agreed upon by the governments. Although reassured by representatives of the military missions that it referred only to tactical areas, he insisted on confirmation from General Eisenhower. Antonov said it was his understanding that upon completion of tactical operations the Anglo-American forces would withdraw from the Soviet zone of occupation previously assigned. This assurance was given by the Supreme Commander on 15 April.[22]

The Combined Chiefs of Staff spelled out their policy more completely on 21 April when they suggested that both sides halt as and where they met, the line being subject to adjustments made by local commanders to deal with any remaining enemy opposition. After the cessation of hostilities, the Western forces were to be disposed in accordance with military requirements regardless of zonal boundaries. So far as permitted by the urgency of the situation, the Supreme Commander was to obtain approval of the Combined Chiefs of Staff before making major adjustments in boundaries. Within these limits he was free to negotiate directly with the Soviet General Staff through the Allied missions to Moscow. In case political and military problems of high importance to the British and U.S. Governments arose during the progress of the campaign, he was to consult the Combined Chiefs of Staff before reference to the Russians, unless he felt the delay was unacceptable "on vital military grounds." These instructions were repeated to the army group commanders by General Eisenhower on the day of their receipt.[23]

The decision to permit units to continue to advance until contact was imminent still left open the question of how they were to recognize each other. It was recalled in Washington that clashes had arisen in Poland in 1939 when the advance forces of the German and Soviet armies had met, and that the situation was ironed out only when the Germans withdrew.[24] General Eisenhower, who had been aware since Normandy days of how difficult it was to keep in touch with flying

[20] Memo, G.A.L. (Brig Gen George A. Lincoln) for Gen Hull, 13 Apr 45, sub: Military Contacts With the Russians, CCS 805/7 and CCS 805/8, OPD 381, Sec V.

[21] CCS to SHAEF, FACS 176, 12 Apr 45; Eisenhower to CCS, SCAF 274, 11 Apr 45; Eisenhower to Mil Mission Moscow, SCAF 275. All in SHAEF SGS 373.5 Bomb-line, Liaison, and Co-ordination of Fronts, I.

[22] Mil Mission Moscow to Eisenhower, MX–23875, 14 Apr 45; Eisenhower to Mil Mission Moscow, SCAF 282, 15 Apr 45. Both in SHAEF SGS 373.5 Bomb-line, Liaison, and Co-ordination of Fronts, I.

[23] CCS to Eisenhower, FACS 191, 21 Apr 45; Eisenhower to Comdrs, 21, 12th, 6th A Gps, 21 Apr 45. Both in SHAEF SGS 373.5 Bomb-line, Liaison, and Co-ordination of Fronts, I.

[24] WD Memo, with covering note by Maj Gen Clayton L. Bissell, G–2, German Line of Demarca-

armored columns as they raced ahead of virtually all communications, attempted to work out in mid-April a system of signals and markings whereby the various forces could identify themselves and avoid firing on each other.[25]

On 21 and 22 April, General Eisenhower took more specific steps to avoid clashes with the Red Army. Besides outlining the procedure laid down by the Combined Chiefs of Staff for the Western forces to follow when they approached Soviet units, he also added details of his future plans and asked the Red commanders for theirs. He repeated previous statements about his intention to stop his central forces on the Elbe and to turn his armies to the north and south to clear out enemy pockets there. It was clear that the northern forces would cross the Elbe and hit at the enemy at the base of the Jutland peninsula, and that his forces in the south would drive through the Danube valley into Austria. Eisenhower did not explain, but it was apparent, that these would continue to advance until they met the Red forces. On the central front, where initial contact seemed most likely, he had chosen the Elbe–Mulde line as one easily identified and desirable between the two forces. This could be changed, he added, if the Russians wished him to push on to Dresden. He believed that after making the first contact the principal purpose should be to establish a firm link between the two armies, preferably along "a well-defined geographical feature," before a firm mu-

tual adjustment on the basis of the local tactical situation. He proposed, therefore, that necessary adjustments and the definition of operational boundary lines be made between the Russian and Allied army group commanders most concerned.[26]

In an unusually prompt reply, the Soviet command indicated on 23 April that orders had already been issued in conformity with the procedure suggested by the Western powers for making contact. The Soviets also accepted the line of the Elbe and the Mulde as a common border. Moscow declared the following day that the Soviet command contemplated both the occupation of Berlin and the clearing of German forces from the east of the Elbe north and south of Berlin and from the Vltava (Moldau) valley. This answer bothered the British Chiefs of Staff. Fearing that the Russians might be trying to apply the line of the Elbe to the north as well as the center of the SHAEF line, they asked the Supreme Commander to make the distinction clear to the Russians.[27]

After the formal link-up of Allied and Soviet units on 26 April, numerous other meetings followed rapidly along the entire front. From the announcement of the first contact, SHAEF made a special effort to establish close liaison with the

---

tion Between Anglo-American and Soviet Operations, 22 Mar 45, OPD 381, Sec IV. This memorandum, which apparently was never passed on to General Eisenhower, was interesting in that it suggested a line of demarcation closely resembling the one along the Elbe later drawn by General Eisenhower. The Saale was used south of the Elbe rather than the Mulde, however.

[25] Eisenhower to Mil Mission Moscow, SCAF 284, 17 Apr 45; Mil Mission Moscow to Eisenhower, MX–23992, 21 Apr 45. Both in SHAEF SGS 373.5 Bomb-line, Liaison and Co-ordination of Fronts, I.

[26] CCS to Eisenhower, FACS 191, 21 Apr 45; Eisenhower to Mil Mission Moscow, SCAF 292, 21 Apr 45; Eisenhower to Mil Mission Moscow, SCAF 298, 22 Apr 45. All in SHAEF SGS 373.5 Bomb-line, Liaison, and Co-ordination of Fronts, I.

[27] Eisenhower to Mil Mission Moscow, SCAF 299, 23 Apr 45; Mil Mission Moscow to Eisenhower, MX–24032, 24 Apr 45; Mil Mission Moscow to Eisenhower, MX–24055, 25 Apr 45; Br COS to JSM, COS (W) 801, 25 Apr 45. All in SHAEF SGS 373.5 Bomb-line, Liaison, and Co-ordination of Fronts, I.

Soviet forces, carefully checking on tanks and troops in forward areas before permitting air strikes to be made.[28]

General Eisenhower's efforts to stop on a well-defined geographical line ran into certain political objections by the British Chiefs of Staff. Near the end of April they pointed out that the Western powers could derive remarkable political advantages by liberating Prague and as much of the rest of Czechoslovakia as possible. They agreed that this effort·should not be allowed to detract from the force of the drives toward the Baltic and into Austria, but proposed that the Supreme Commander take advantage of any improvement in his logistical situation to advance into Czechoslovakia. General Marshall, in passing these views on to General Eisenhower for his comments, declared: "Personally and aside from all logistic, tactical or strategical implications I would be loath to hazard American lives for purely political purposes."[29]

This statement, startling as it may have seemed later, was in accord with the policy followed by the U.S. Chiefs of Staff throughout the war: to place everything behind those offensives which would most quickly bring military victory. The war was now virtually at an end in Europe—at a place where the Russian advance would soon clean out the remaining Germans. If the war in Europe and the Pacific was intended solely for the purpose of defeating the Germans and the Japanese, then there was no point in continuing to use U.S. forces to seize objectives that could easily be taken by the Red Army. Especially was this true at a time when it still seemed necessary to send troops from the European theater to the Pacific theater and when it appeared that Soviet aid might be needed to crush the enemy in the Far East. This observation, of course, raises the question of what should have been the war aims of the Western Allies in 1945 and enters a realm of strategy and politics beyond the province of the Supreme Commander. His directive as given by the U.S. and British Chiefs of Staff was to "undertake operations aimed at the heart of Germany and the destruction of her armed forces." At no time did his military and political superiors define his mission as the maintenance or restoration of the balance of power in central and eastern Europe.

General Eisenhower showed that he understood General Marshall's meaning in his reply. He said that the first priority of his offensive should go to the northern thrust toward Luebeck and Kiel, a move he had already said was intended to forestall the Russians, and to the southern drive toward Linz and the Austrian Redoubt. If additional means were available, he planned to attack enemy forces that were still holding out in Czechoslovakia, Denmark, and Norway. He thought that the Western powers should deal with the enemy in Denmark and Norway, but concluded that the Red Army was in perfect position to clean out Czechoslovakia and would certainly reach Prague before the U.S. forces. He assured General Marshall: "I shall not attempt any move I deem militarily unwise merely to gain a political prize unless I receive specific orders from the Combined Chiefs of Staff."[30] Such orders were never given and, according to Admiral Leahy's notes on meetings of the Combined Chiefs of Staff, the matter, like

---

[28] Eisenhower to Mil Mission Moscow, SCAF 317, 27 Apr 45, SHAEF SGS 373.5 Bomb-line, Liaison, and Co-ordination of Fronts, I.

[29] Marshall to Eisenhower, W–74256, 28 Apr 45, SHAEF cbl log.

[30] Eisenhower to Marshall, FWD 20225, 29 Apr 45, SHAEF cbl log.

the question of whether to take Berlin, was never considered by them. When, a short time later, the Prime Minister discussed a slightly different phase of the question—the one involving readjustment of occupation zones—President Truman made clear that matters of that nature should be left to the commander in the field.[31]

The Supreme Commander on 30 April informed the Russians fully of his plans to advance to the east. He explained that, while operational positions were being adjusted along the Elbe and Mulde in the center, he would launch an operation across the lower Elbe to establish a firm operational east flank on the approximate line Wismar–Schwerin–Doemitz, the exact position to be adjusted locally by the commanders on the spot. From the headwaters of the Mulde southward, he intended to hold a line approximately along the 1937 frontiers of Czechoslovakia in the Erz Gebirge and Boehmer Wald. Later, the Allied forces could advance to Karlsbad, Pilzen, and České Budějovice. On the southern flank, he proposed an advance to the general area of Linz, from which forces would be sent to clear out any resistance to the south. He thought a suitable line on this front would be the main north-south highway line east of Linz and thence along the valley of the Enns. If at any time the situation required his forces to advance farther, he would take such action as permitted by the situation.

The USSR indicated its full agreement with these proposals. On 4 May, however, when General Eisenhower again spoke of his willingness to move forward after the occupation of České Budějovice, Pilzen, and Karlsbad to the line of the Elbe and the Moldau to clear the west bank of these rivers, General Antonov expressed strong dissent. To avoid "a possible confusion of forces," he asked General Eisenhower specifically "not to move the Allied forces in Czechoslovakia east of the originally intended line, that is, Ceski-Budejovice, Pilzen, Karlsbad." He added significantly that the Soviet forces had stopped their advance to the lower Elbe east of the line Wismar, Schwerin, and Doemitz at the Supreme Commander's request, and that he hoped General Eisenhower would comply with Russian wishes relative to the advance of U.S. forces in Czechoslovakia. General Eisenhower assured the Soviet commander that he would not move beyond the line suggested.[32] By this action he left Prague and most of Czechoslovakia to be liberated by the Red forces. Except for minor adjustments of boundaries and the closing up to lines of demarcation, operations of the Western Allies were at an end.

The End of Hitler

The month of April, which saw the Western Allies drive from the Rhine to the Elbe and complete a junction with advance elements of the Red Army in central Germany, also witnessed the fall of Berlin and the suicide of Hitler. Before these last two events had been consummated, however, the Fuehrer had attempted to provide for the continuance of his government, first, in the event that part of the Reich was cut off from his headquarters and, second, in the event that death claimed him. He tried also to

---

[31] Leahy, *I Was There*, pp. 349, 350, 382.
[32] Eisenhower to Mil Mission Moscow, SCAF 349, 6 May 45; Eisenhower to Mil Mission Moscow, SCAF 323, 30 Apr 45; Mil Mission Moscow to Eisenhower, MX–24166, 4 May 45; Mil Mission Moscow to Eisenhower, MX–24193, 5 May 45. All in SHAEF SGS 373.5 Bomb-line, Liaison, and Co-ordination of Fronts, I and II.

direct the defense of Berlin and to arrange for punishment of those former trusted colleagues and servants whom he now accused of treason.

The precise moment when Hitler realized that he had no prospect of avoiding complete defeat at the hands of the Allies is not clear. Orders throughout the early part of April indicate that he was still determined to hold to every foot of ground and insisted on fighting to the last at a time when a number of his commanders and political associates were contemplating surrender. Apparently hoping that the death of President Roosevelt in mid-April might help his cause, he issued an order of the day asking for resistance to the "deadly Jewish-Bolshevist enemy" and declared, "At the moment when fate has removed the greatest war criminal of all times from this earth the turning point of this war will be decided." [33]

Hitler was sufficiently aware of ominous developments to know that his forces might soon be divided by a link-up of his enemies which would make it impossible for him to keep close control of all sections of Germany. He decided that if he was in the southern zone when this occurred Admiral Doenitz would command in the north. If the Fuehrer was in the northern zone, then Field Marshal Kesselring was to command in the south. Hitler reserved to himself the right to announce the time when this arrangement would go into effect.[34]

He recognized the difficulty of holding Berlin indefinitely and apparently planned to send his ministers and their staffs to various points in southern Germany where he would join them for a final defense of the Reich. The bulk of the ministerial staffs had left for the south by mid-April, and only the ministers and a few of their aides

remained in Berlin. Hitler continued to postpone a definite decision on evacuating the capital until Russian advances made it too dangerous for the chief ministers to leave by the highways south of Berlin. It was decided instead that they should go to some safe place north of the city and fly south from there. During the evening of 20–21 April and throughout the following day, ministers and their staffs slipped out of Berlin to Eutin, about halfway between Luebeck and Kiel, and near the site of Doenitz' future headquarters.[35]

Marshal Hermann Goering, heir designate to Hitler's post, discussed the matter of a shift south with the Fuehrer on 20 April, Hitler's birthday. In what proved to be the last conference of the two Nazi leaders, Goering said that he or the Luftwaffe chief of staff, General der Flieger Karl Koller, should be in southern Germany to provide unified command for the almost defunct Luftwaffe. Upon Hitler's reply that Koller was to remain and that Goering could leave, the Reichsmarschall hastened to his string of cars, loaded and

---

[33] Hitler's order of 15 Apr 45 (*Chef Genst.d.H./B. Nr. 3064/45*). *ONI Fuehrer Directives*.

[34] For general information on the period from 20 April to 20 May 1945 the author has made use of *Entwurf Weissbuch* (May 1945) and annexes in file *OKW, Politische Angelegenheiten* (referred to hereafter as German White Book 1945). Intended as a defense of Doenitz' interim government, the unsigned paper is accompanied by numerous documents and comports in most particulars with other accounts of this period. Despite its possible bias, it is nonetheless valuable for the period. The author is indebted to Mr. Detmar Finke of Foreign Studies Branch, OCMH, for research in and translation of German documents used in this and the remaining chapters of the book. Hitler's order naming Doenitz and Kesselring was apparently drawn up about 10 April and issued 15 April 1945. See Extract from the Naval War Diary, Part A, 20 Apr 45. *ONI Fuehrer Directives*, 15 Apr 45.

[35] Memo, *Vermerk ueber die Absetzung der Fuehrungsstaebe der Obersten Reichsbehoerden*, late Apr 45, by Staatssekretaer Kritzinger. Annex to German White Book 1945.

waiting, and departed for Berchtesgaden.[36]

The growing exodus from the capital now gained momentum. The Soviet advance had forced OKW to leave its wartime offices at Zossen and move to Wannsee, a western suburb of the capital, on the night of 20–21 April. The headquarters immediately began to leave for Strub near Berchtesgaden. Keitel, Jodl, and a small staff remained behind.[37]

Admiral Doenitz was the next to go. He had been told on the 20th that he was to organize the defense in the northern sector. At the suggestion of Keitel, who was worried about the deterioration of the situation around Berlin, Doenitz discussed the matter with Hitler on the 21st and was told that he should leave very shortly. The admiral and his staff departed from Berlin in the early morning of 22 April and reached their new headquarters in Ploen the same day.[38]

While attempts were being made to establish elements of the government in other parts of the Reich, Hitler was trying to save Berlin. Reports on the 21st indicated that the attack he had previously ordered Obergruppenfuehrer und General der Waffen SS Felix Steiner to launch from points north of Berlin toward the south had failed to materialize. All efforts in that direction succeeded only in drawing German strength from the north where the Red Army had broken through. The failure of Steiner's corps to attack on the 22d and reports of other reverses apparently forced Hitler for the first time to admit that prolongation of the war was hopeless. Hitler's decision, as reported by Jodl to Koller, was to remain in the city, take over its defenses, and shoot himself at the last moment. The German leader said that he could not take part in the fighting for physical reasons and that he could not

run the danger of falling into the hands of his opponents when only wounded. He added that he was not the man to carry on negotiations with the Allies—a task, he said, for which Goering was far better fitted than he. Keitel, Jodl, Martin Bormann, Chief of the Party Chancellery, and later Doenitz and Himmler, all tried to get Hitler to change his mind, but he refused. Instead he told Keitel, Jodl, and Bormann to go south and conduct operations from there. They, in turn, declined.[39]

Jodl now proposed that some of the troops fighting against the Western Allies be thrown into the fight for Berlin and that OKW conduct the operation. Hitler agreed, and Keitel went to the headquarters of the *Twelfth Army*, fighting near the Elbe, to oversee the planned shift of forces from west to east. The remaining members of the OKW in Berlin now moved a few miles north of the city to Krampnitz. On 23 April, Keitel and Jodl attended the situation conference at the *Reichskanzlei*, where they saw Hitler for the last time. Thereafter, being cut off from Berlin, they and the small OKW staff with them moved north by stages to a point near Flensburg on 3 May 1945.[40]

[36] Rpt by Koller, A.D.I. (K), Rpt No. 349/1945, 12 Jul 45, British Air Ministry (referred to hereafter as Koller Rpt). This account, based on his personal diary, was dictated by General Koller while he was a prisoner of war in Britain. A later, slightly different, version was published as *Der Letzte Monat* (Mannheim, 1949).

[37] MS # C–020 (Schramm); *OKW, KTB 20.IV.–19.V.45*, 20, 21 Apr 45. The OKW *KTB*, which recorded the last days of the OKW, was kept by Maj. Joachim Schultz, a disabled officer assigned to that headquarters in the spring of 1945. The official account plus his own recollections of the events of that period formed the basis for his book *Die Letzten 30 Tage* (Stuttgart, 1951).

[38] German White Book 1945.

[39] Koller Rpt; Schultz, *Die Letzten 30 Tage*, pp. 21–23.

[40] *Ibid.*

Informed by General Koller on 23 April that Hitler had made up his mind to stay and die in Berlin, Goering asked the Chief of the Reich Chancellery, who was also at Berchtesgaden, if he should assume control of the government under the circumstances. It was decided that he should radio Berlin for instructions, saying that if he received no answer by the late evening of that day he would take charge of the affairs of the Reich. Goering also radioed Keitel and Reichsminister Joachim von Ribbentrop asking that they join him unless they received orders to the contrary from Hitler. The Fuehrer, considering these actions treasonable, now had Goering and his entourage arrested and ordered Generaloberst Hans Juergen Stumpff, head of *Air Force Reich,* to close all airports in the northern area in order to prevent any further moves of personnel to the south. Hitler next demanded Goering's resignation as head of the Air Force and appointed in his place Generalfeldmarschall Robert Ritter von Greim.[41]

Jodl on 24 April gave the armed forces their first indication of the policy to be followed during the remaining days of the war. Senior commanders in the west, southwest, and southeast were told that the fight against Bolshevism was the only thing that now mattered and that loss of territory to the Western Allies was of secondary importance.[42] Other directives issued on the 24th and 25th regulated the over-all chain of command. OKW, which absorbed the *Army General Staff (Operations Group),* became responsible for the conduct of operations on all fronts. Keitel personally reserved for himself the control of all army units in the northern area,[43] and also of *Army Groups South* and *Center* on the Eastern Front. General der Gebirgstruppen August Winter was to organize all the

resources of the southern area for further resistance[44] and Field Marshal Kesselring, Commander in Chief West, was to take or retain control of *OB SUEDWEST* (Italy), *OB SUEDOST* (the Balkans), *Army Group G,* and the *Nineteenth Army.* The primary mission of the armed forces was defined as the re-establishment of a connection with Berlin to defeat the Soviet troops in that area.[45]

These efforts at reorganization were taking place on paper while the Red Army was bypassing Berlin to the north and the south and starting to encircle the *Ninth Army* southeast of Berlin. On 25 April, the *Twelfth Army,* which was holding the Elbe against the U.S. thrust, was ordered to join the *Ninth Army* and attack northward to break the Soviet hold on

---

[41] Interrogation of Goering, CCPWC # 32/DI–7, 15 Jun 45; Koller Rpt; Hist Div Interrogation of Dr. Hans Heinrich Lammers, chief of the Reich Chancellery, 17 Jul 45; German White Book 1945. According to Goering, he and his family were imprisoned at Mauterndorf on 26 April. On 30 April a radiogram from Martin Bormann ordered the SS guards to execute all of the traitors of 23 April. The officer in charge did not recognize Bormann's authority and refused to carry out the order. Goering was released on Kesselring's order on 5 May and on 7 May surrendered to U.S. troops.

[42] Rad, Jodl to Kesselring and others, 24 Apr 45. *OKW, Befehle an die Truppe (Kapitulation) 13.IV.–20.V. 45* (referred to hereafter as *OKW, Befehle 13.IV.–20.V.45).* This file is exceedingly valuable on the period from mid-April to mid-May inasmuch as most of the messages were personally initialed by Keitel and Jodl and frequently have their corrections, changes, and comments.

[43] Units under Keitel's control were *Armed Forces Commander Denmark; Armed Forces Commander Norway; OB NORDWEST* (formerly *Army Group H); Twelfth Army; Army Group Weichsel; Army Group Kurland;* and *Army Ostpreussen.* For style of designating German theater commands, see above, Ch. X, n. 7.

[44] Winter, Deputy Chief Armed Forces Operations Staff (OKW/WFSt), arrived in the southern area on 24 April and took control of OKW, Operations Staff B (Fuehrungsstab B), the same day.

[45] Dir sgd Hitler, 24 Apr 45; Dir sgd Keitel, 26 Apr 45. Both in *OKW, Befehle 13.IV.–20.V.45.*

that city. Despite a belief that U.S. forces might seize this opportunity to drive toward Berlin, the *Twelfth Army* commander ordered attacks on American forces stopped and said that shooting would be resumed only in case of an attack by them. Only small forces were left to guard the Ninth U.S. Army bridgehead south of Magdeburg.[46]

OKW also ordered the Commander in Chief Northwest to bring as many troops as possible from the 21 Army Group front to a point east of Hamburg. To the southeast of Berlin, *Army Group Center* was directed to aid the *Ninth* and *Twelfth Armies'* attacks toward the north. Many of these orders had little connection with reality, since the forces involved were too badly scattered to be organized for an attack. Hitler, after some qualms about weakening the area in the northwest, approved the measures being taken to help Berlin and on 26 April expressed satisfaction over the results achieved by his forces.[47]

Any pleasure that Hitler may have felt on 26 April was certainly dissipated by the news that came on the 28th. General Winter sent gloomy tidings of an uprising in upper Italy, a report of Mussolini's arrest by the Partisans, and an attempted coup in Munich. There was also the distressing rumor that armistice negotiations were being initiated by commanders in Italy. Worse still was the report that the *Ninth Army's* attack toward Berlin had failed and that its units had not held firm. A state of nerves was possibly responsible for Keitel's decision on that day to remove Generaloberst Gotthard Heinrici from the command of *Army Group Weichsel* because Heinrici had independently ordered withdrawals on his front.[48]

By 30 April, Keitel had to admit that the relief of Berlin had failed and that the

city was facing its final fight. He ordered all units in the northern area to be concentrated so that connections could be maintained with Denmark. The armies in the south were directed to close all their fronts in a big ring and to undertake the task of saving as many men and as much land as possible from the Red Army. When they could no longer get instructions from the north, they were to fight to save time and to beat down all tendencies toward political and military disintegration. To co-ordinate activities in the south, Keitel now subordinated *Army Group South* to *Army Group Center*. Doenitz at this point was setting on foot plans to save the forces facing the Soviet troops east of Berlin by removing them to the west by sea.[49]

These efforts to retrieve something from the ruins were, of course, carried on independently of Hitler, who was cut off from his armies and chief commanders and waited in Berlin for the Red Army. During the evening of 28 April and the early hours of the following day, he discussed with his advisers in the command post in Berlin the naming of a successor. He expelled Goering and Himmler from the Nazi party and stripped them of any claim

---

[46] MS # B–606, The Last Rally: Battles Fought by the German *Twelfth Army* in the Heart of Germany, Between East and West, 13 Apr–7 May 45 (Col Guenther Reichhelm, Chief of Staff of *Twelfth Army*).
[47] OKW Communiques, 25, 26 Apr 45. *OKW, Wehrmachtberichte, 1.IV.–9.V.45;* Tel, Jodl to *OB NORDWEST,* 26 Apr 45; Tel, Hitler to Jodl, 26 Apr 45; Tel, Jodl to Hitler, 26 Apr 45; Sitrep, Konteradmiral Hans Voss to Doenitz, 26 Apr 45; Dir, Jodl to Winter, 27 Apr 45; Rad, Jodl to *Twelfth Army, Army Group Weichsel,* and *Ninth Army,* 27 Apr 45. All in *OKW, Befehle 13.IV.–20.V.45.*
[48] Tel, Winter to OKW/WFSt, 27 Apr 45; Rad, Winter to Jodl, 28 Apr 45; Sitrep Ninth Army, 28 Apr 45; Rad, Jodl to *Reichskanzlei,* 29 Apr 45; Tel, Keitel to Heinrici, 28 Apr 45; Rad, Keitel to Krebs, 30 Apr 45. All in *OKW, Befehle 13.IV.–20.V.45.*
[49] Rad, Keitel to Winter, 30 Apr 45. *OKW, Befehle 13.IV.–20.V.45;* German White Book 1945.

they had to the succession.[50] On the 29th he drew a will in which he appointed Grand Admiral Doenitz as head of the German state and Supreme Commander of the Armed Forces. On 30 April, when it became clear that no German defense against the Red advance was possible, Hitler committed suicide.[51]

Later in the evening, Bormann notified Admiral Doenitz that the latter had been appointed Hitler's successor and was to take all measures necessary to meet the existing situation. Bormann had planned to go to Doenitz' headquarters, but for some reason he did not notify the admiral at that time of Hitler's death. Not until 1 May was Doenitz finally told that Hitler was dead. He was notified that copies of the will were on the way to him and to Generalfeldmarschall Ferdinand Schoerner, commander of *Army Group Center,* and that Bormann would come to Doenitz' headquarters at Ploen to give him full details of the existing situation. Doenitz was to choose the form and time of communicating to the public and troops the news of Hitler's death and the grand admiral's succession.[52]

Doenitz announced Hitler's death to the armed forces and the German people in the late evening of 1 May. On the following day he called a conference of his chief military and political advisers to choose between two courses—surrender-

ing at once or continuing the attempt to save what they could from the Russians.[53]

---

[50] Hitler was apparently aware of Himmler's efforts to negotiate a surrender with the Western Allies. For Himmler's activities, see below, pp. 476–77.

[51] H. R. Trevor-Roper, *The Last Days of Hitler* (New York, 1947), Chs. VI, VII. Much of the volume is based on interrogations made by Trevor-Roper of individuals who were with Hitler shortly before his death. Trevor-Roper describes efforts made during the afternoon and evening of 30 April to arrange an armistice or truce with Marshal Zhukov, who was notified of Hitler's death. The Soviet commander is said to have terminated the conference with demands for unconditional surrender of the German forces and of the individuals who were in Hitler's final command post. See also Hitler, *Mein politisches Testament,* 29 Apr 45. The original of Hitler's political testament is filed in Record Group 218, Records of the Joint Chiefs of Staff, National Archives.

[52] When no copy of the will arrived, Doenitz took steps to establish the authenticity of the messages informing him of his appointment as Hitler's successor and of the instructions in the will. A group headed by *Flottenrichter* (Fleet Judge Advocate) Doctor Schattenberg interrogated all personnel on duty in the communications and coding rooms at Ploen who saw or handled the messages of 30 April and 1 May and had them declare under oath that these were the exact messages they saw. The texts and testimony are in Minutes of the Hearing Relative to Messages Dealing With Hitler's Successor, 6 May 45. *OKW, Hitler's Tod–Doenitz Nachfolger, Funksprueche, 28 IV.– 6.V.45.*

[53] The three top advisers suggested by Hitler— Bormann as Party Minister, Seyss-Inquart as Foreign Minister, and Goebbels as Chancellor—were of course unavailable. Bormann disappeared, Seyss-Inquart was prevented by the British from leaving the Netherlands, and Goebbels imitated his master by committing suicide. Doenitz appointed Reichsminister Graf Schwerin von Krosigk as Foreign Minister on 2 May and left the other posts unfilled at the time.

CHAPTER XXV

The German Surrender

At the beginning of May, the Western Allies and the USSR had virtually destroyed the German fighting machine and were engaged in the task of mopping up the disorganized elements remaining in central Germany. In the week of fighting that remained, while Hitler's successor debated his best course of action and sent representatives to sound out the Western Allies, individual enemy commanders made piecemeal surrenders along a wide front.

Early Peace Feelers

Informal steps toward peace had been taken in mid-January 1945 when Foreign Minister von Ribbentrop on his own initiative sent Dr. Werner von Schmieden to Bern and Dr. F. Hesse to Stockholm to make contact with Allied representatives for the purpose of discussing a negotiated settlement. Von Schmieden found it impossible to establish proper connections, and Hesse reported that his efforts were ruined because of publicity concerning his mission.[1]

More substantial overtures, looking to final surrender of German forces in Italy, were made in early February by representatives of the German command in northern Italy, who arranged for meetings in Switzerland with Allied agents. Allied authorities in Italy promptly informed the Russians of these talks and asked them to nominate officers to attend future peace conferences if they should be arranged. Despite this frank approach, Marshal Stalin became disturbed as the talks in Switzerland progressed. As his suspicions deepened, he became worried over a possible peace settlement between the Western powers and Germany which would leave the enemy free to continue the war against the Red Army. He protested strongly to Mr. Roosevelt and, when the latter assured him that nothing was being done against the USSR's interest, declared that the President was not being kept informed by his generals. Mr. Roosevelt characterized the statements given Stalin by his informants as "vile misrepresentations." So strong were the feelings engendered that some Allied leaders wondered at the time if the purpose of the German negotiators was to split the anti-Nazi forces. Delays in the negotiations ultimately postponed any final action in Italy until the last week of the war, with the result that the surrender activities had no direct effect on the war in northwest Europe. However, the suspicion aroused in the mind of Marshal Stalin and his ad-

[1] Interrogation of Dr. Werner von Schmieden, Secretary of Legation in German Foreign Office, 16 Aug 45, WD G-2 file; testimony of Fraeulein Margarete Blank, Ribbentrop's secretary, *International Military Tribunal Nuremberg* (Nuremberg, 1947), X, 193–94.

visers created an atmosphere of distrust which was to surround most of the peace negotiations in northwest Europe.[2]

The first important overtures in northwest Europe were made by members of Himmler's staff. On 2 April Brigadefuehrer Walter Schellenberg of Himmler's Intelligence Service, apparently speaking only for himself and without Himmler's authority, approached Count Folke Bernadotte, head of the Swedish Red Cross. Bernadotte, who was in Germany attempting to get Norwegian and Danish prisoners released into the custody of Sweden, was asked if he would discuss with General Eisenhower the possibility of arranging a capitulation. The count refused to act in this capacity, insisting that Himmler would have to take the initiative. Schellenberg pointed to possible developments in Germany which might shake Hitler's position, and said that in such a case Himmler wanted Bernadotte to go to General Eisenhower and ask for the negotiation of a surrender. The Swedish nobleman declared that he would go to the Supreme Commander only after Himmler announced: (1) that he had been chosen as German leader by Hitler; (2) that the Nazi party was dissolved; (3) that the Werewolf organization had been disbanded; and (4) that all Danish and Norwegian prisoners had been sent to Sweden.[3]

Count Bernadotte's conditions were not met and the Schellenberg suggestion was not passed on to SHAEF. Not until mid-April were peace feelers concerning the surrender of forces in northwest Europe communicated to the Supreme Commander. At this time, reports came from agents in Denmark that Generaloberst Georg Lindemann, German armed forces commander in Denmark (*Wehrmachtbefehlshaber Daenemark*), was willing to surrender the army there, but would not include SS and police units. Although the Supreme Commander authorized efforts through unofficial channels to get additional details of the proposal, he forbade Allied officers to be present at the conversations. In reporting this action to the Combined Chiefs of Staff, he suggested that the USSR be informed. Later information indicated that General Lindemann would continue fighting, but that commanders in Norway and in northern German cities such as Bremen would consider surrender. The Combined Chiefs of Staff, therefore, on 21 April informed the Soviet Government that unconditional surrender of large-scale enemy forces was a growing possibility and suggested that accredited representatives of all three allies be made available to the headquarters on each front for the purpose of observing negotiations for surrender. The USSR was asked to designate such representatives both at SHAEF and at AFHQ. General Deane and Admiral Archer were authorized to represent the United States and Great Britain at Soviet headquarters. The Soviet high command readily agreed to the suggestion, saying that the names of

[2] General Eisenhower was kept informed of the progress of negotiations in Italy through messages from AFHQ and CCS. They are outlined in messages between 27 February and 2 May 1945 in SHAEF SGS 387/1 Germany. Two articles by Forrest Davis, "The Secret History of a Surrender," *The Saturday Evening Post*, September 22 and 29, 1945, were based on an unpublished OSS story of the negotiations. For the Russian reaction see Stettinius, *Roosevelt and the Russians*, pp. 315–16; James F. Byrnes, *Speaking Frankly* (New York, 1947), pp. 56–58; and Leahy, *I Was There*, pp. 329–35.

[3] Count Folke Bernadotte, *The Curtain Falls: Last Days of the Reich* (New York, 1945), pp. 86–94.

their appointees would be submitted later.[4]

Himmler again entered the picture on the evening of 23 April in a conference, arranged by Schellenberg, with Count Bernadotte at the Swedish consulate in Luebeck. Himmler began the conference by saying that the Germans were defeated, that Hitler would soon be dead, and that he (Himmler) was ready to order a capitulation on the Western Front. Count Bernadotte doubted that an offer to surrender on one front only would be acceptable to the Allies, but he agreed to forward the proposal if Himmler would promise to surrender forces in Denmark and Norway. The SS leader approved this suggestion and wrote the Swedish Foreign Minister that he wished to act through the count. The Swedish Foreign Minister, who shared his fellow countryman's skepticism concerning the acceptability of a surrender on the Western Front alone, nonetheless arranged a meeting between Bernadotte and the British and U.S. ministers in Sweden, Sir Victor Mallet and Mr. Herschel Johnson, who dispatched Himmler's offer to their governments. Mr. Churchill relayed the information by transatlantic telephone to President Truman and the U.S. Chiefs of Staff on the afternoon of 25 April, the day that Soviet and U.S. patrols met near Torgau. The President, while emphasizing his desire to end the war quickly, declared he could accept only an unconditional surrender on all fronts and one made in agreement with the Soviet Union and Great Britain. This information was relayed to Marshal Stalin.[5] General Eisenhower expressed his satisfaction with the reply and informed General Marshall that the Prime Minister had agreed that the peace overture was an

attempt by the enemy to create a schism between the Allies. "In every move we make these days," said the Supreme Commander, making his position clear, "we are trying to be meticulously careful in these regards."[6]

During the discussion of Himmler's offer, reports of the possibility of a separate surrender in Norway and Denmark continued to be received in Supreme Headquarters, and an arrangement was discussed in Sweden for removing German soldiers to that country where they could be held for the Allies until the end of the war. SHAEF informed army group commanders that they could receive surrenders of forces facing their fronts but that anything more extensive had to be submitted to the Supreme Commander. It will be remembered that at the close of April General Smith, while discussing with Seyss-Inquart a truce which would permit the Dutch population to be fed, had also suggested that the Reich Commissioner surrender the forces in the Netherlands.

While peace negotiations were still in the talking stage in northwest Europe, the long-drawn-out negotiations in Italy were brought to a close. After a comic-opera interlude in which Kesselring removed the Commander in Chief Southwest and his chief of staff and ordered their arrest, and

---

[4] SFHQ to EXFOR (21 A Gp), RLB 629, n.d.; EXFOR to SFHQ, n.d.; SHAEF to SFHQ, FWD 19147, 14 Apr 45; WO to SHAEF, MI–14/33/17/45, 19 Apr 45; Troopers to SHAEF, 86992–MI–14, 21 Apr 45; CCS to Mil Mission Moscow, FACS 190, 21 Apr 45; Troopers to SHAEF, 87289–MI–14, 21 Apr 45; SHAEF to Mil Mission Moscow (draft approved 22 Apr 45); Mil Mission Moscow to CCS, MX–24031, 24 Apr 45. All in SHAEF SGS 387/1 Germany, I.

[5] Bernadotte, *The Curtain Falls*, pp. 104–16; Trevor-Roper, *Last Days of Hitler*, pp. 133–36, Leahy, *I Was There*, pp. 354–55.

[6] Eisenhower to Marshall, FWD 20032, 27 Apr 45, Eisenhower personal file.

in which the deposed officers brought about the arrest of their successors, the German forces in Italy signed surrender agreements on 29 April. Representatives of Generaloberst Heinrich-Gottfried von Vietinghof genannt Scheel, Commander in Chief Southwest, who had been restored to his position by Kesselring, and Obergruppenfuehrer und General der Waffen SS Karl Friedrich Wolff agreed to terminate hostilities at 1200, 2 May 1945. Their surrender affected part of Carinthia, the provinces of Vorarlberg, Tirol, and Salzburg, as well as all of Italy except that part of Venezia Giulia which is east of the Isonzo. The surrender removed the last threat from General Eisenhower's southern front and spelled the doom of German forces remaining in the Balkans.[7]

Doenitz Appraises the Situation

Admiral Doenitz and his advisers canvassed the German position completely on 2 May. Agreeing that the military situation was hopeless, they decided that their main effort should be to save as many Germans as possible from the Red armies. They said they would continue to fight on against the British and U.S. forces only to the extent that they interfered with German efforts to elude the Soviets. Otherwise, the German armies would attempt to avoid combat on the Western Front and strive to escape further bombing attacks. It was recognized that the goal of capitulation on one front only was difficult to achieve at the highest levels because of agreements which existed between the Western powers and the USSR, but efforts were to be made to arrange surrender at army group levels and below. In view of Seyss-Inquart's report that General

Smith, at discussions on the same day relative to the truce in Holland, had left the way open for armistice negotiations, Doenitz authorized the Reich Commissioner for the occupied portion of the Netherlands to examine the situation. One of the main problems was that of taking necessary measures to save the forces of Schoerner and Generaloberst Dr. Lothar Rendulic in the Bohemian area. The military situation there was said to be good, inasmuch as the area could be held another three weeks if supply and ammunition could be brought in. Doenitz was uncertain as to the wisdom of ordering an immediate withdrawal, since he believed there would be considerable losses in the process. He thought Bohemia might make a good bargaining point, and he desired to explore the possibilities of making a political arrangement with the Allies. The Reich Protector of Bohemia and Moravia, Staatsminister Karl Hermann Frank, and Schoerner's chief of staff were ordered to come to Doenitz' headquarters for discussions before a final decision should be made.[8]

The German military situation in the north was worsened on 2 May by the break-through of the British from Lauenburg to Luebeck and of the U.S. forces to Wismar. These actions closed "the last gate" through which the Germans could be brought back from the Mecklenburg–Pomerania area. Doenitz held that further fighting in northwest Europe against the Allied powers had now lost its purpose. Making use of a British offer to spare Hamburg as an opening for negotiations,

---

[7] For a brief outline of the surrender in Italy, see Eisenhower to A Gp Comdrs *et al.*, FWD 20479, 3 May 45, SHAEF SGS 387/1 Germany. The Commander in Chief Southwest had been placed under Kesselring's command on 25 April 1945.

[8] German White Book 1945.

he announced that the city would not be defended. He offered to send a delegation headed by Generaladmiral Hans Georg von Friedeburg, who had succeeded Doenitz as head of the Navy, and Generalleutnant Eberhardt Kinzel, chief of staff to Generalfeldmarschall Ernst Busch, Commander in Chief Northwest, to discuss peace negotiations with Field Marshal Montgomery on the following day. On the evening of 2 May, Doenitz moved his headquarters from Ploen to Flensburg, just south of the Danish border.[9]

On 3 May, Doenitz again reviewed the German military situation. Staatsminister Frank, present from Bohemia, was not sanguine about the Czechoslovak situation, since he felt that a revolt, which might occur at any time, would make it difficult to hold the protectorate. As possible solutions for strengthening the situation there until the Germans in Bohemia could be saved, he suggested that (1) Prague be declared an open city, (2) possibilities be explored of sending German and Czechoslovak emissaries to General Eisenhower to get favorable capitulation terms in that area, and (3) the Reich government be moved to Bohemia. The third course had been previously considered, but Doenitz opposed it, believing the situation too uncertain. Instead orders were sent to Prague to prepare a plan for defense.[10]

The situation in southern Germany and Austria was reported as being much worse than in Bohemia. Staatssekretaer Franz Hayler declared that only in upper Austria was there any true control by the government. Troops and administration in the south showed signs of disintegration and there were numerous indications of opposition by the public to the Army. Hayler noted that the old Bavarian flags were reappearing in the south and that

there were evidences of an Austrian freedom movement among the Tyrolean *Volkssturm*. He characterized a putsch which had been attempted in Munich as symptomatic of feeling in the south. On top of these pessimistic reports Doenitz received on 3 May a request from Field Marshal Kesselring that he be permitted to treat with the U.S. forces in his sector. Doenitz at once empowered the field marshal to conclude with the 6th Army Group an armistice applying to German forces between the Boehmer Wald and the upper Inn, and asked him to determine how far the U.S. forces intended to advance eastward. Doenitz said he felt the Germans should be pleased every time U.S. and British forces, rather than Soviet forces, occupied a part of Germany. He agreed that the over-all situation demanded capitulation on all fronts, but held that the Germans should not consider it at the moment since it would mean delivering most of the forces east of the Elbe to the Russians.[11]

True to his determination to surrender only to the Western Allies, Doenitz explored further the situation in northwest Europe, in the hope of finding something to offer the British and U.S. commanders. He found some encouragement in Norway and Denmark. Since both those countries wished, now that liberation was near, to avoid any action which would bring reprisals, Doenitz considered there would be no revolt there. Therefore, he ordered his commanders to present a

---

[9] Other members of the German delegation were Konteradmiral Gerhard Wagner and Maj. Hans Jochen Friedel. See *OKW, Kapitulationsverhandlungen 2.V.–11.V.45; German White Book 1945;* Schultz, *Die Letzten 30 Tage.*

[10] German White Book 1945.

[11] German White Book 1945; Rad, Doenitz to Kesselring, 3 May 45. *OKW, Befehle 13.IV.–20.V.45.*

strong front in these countries and directed that efforts be continued to resolve the Norwegian question through Swedish mediation. He approved Seyss-Inquart's efforts to explore peace possibilities in the Netherlands, but directed the continuance of the combat mission. He gave specific instructions that the Netherlands should not be flooded further. The Commander in Chief Northwest was informed that a delegation was on its way to British headquarters to discuss an armistice and that he should prevent a fast Allied breakthrough to and over the Kiel Canal before negotiations could be concluded. *Armeegruppe Mueller* was set up on 4 May to protect this area.[12]

Piecemeal Surrenders

Meanwhile discussions with Field Marshal Montgomery had begun. Admiral Friedeburg and his party had been instructed to promise that Hamburg would not be defended, and they were to try to secure the 21 Army Group commander's permission for German troops, including the *Third Panzer, Twelfth,* and *Twenty-first Armies,* to retire west of the Elbe. They also wanted permission to pass German civilian refugees through the British lines to Schleswig-Holstein. Such terms the army group commanders were not allowed to grant. As early as August 1944, the Combined Chiefs of Staff had issued a short document which outlined instructions to cover possible capitulations by German forces surrendering as units through their commanders. This document, apparently the basis of the surrender instruments used by the 21 and 6th Army Groups, rested on three main principles: (1) terms of capitulation were unconditional and had to be clearly and expressly

limited to the immediate military objects of local surrender; (2) no commitment of any kind was to be made to the enemy; and (3) capitulation was to be made without prejudice to and was to be superseded by any general instrument of surrender which might be imposed by the United States, the United Kingdom and the USSR.[13] Therefore, when Field Marshal Montgomery indicated to General Eisenhower that overtures for negotiations were being made, the Supreme Commander declared that only unconditional surrender would be accepted. He added that an offer to give up Denmark, the Netherlands, the Frisian Islands, Helgoland, and Schleswig-Holstein could be considered as a tactical matter and the surrender accepted. Any larger offer, such as a proposal to give up Norway or forces on another front, would have to be handled at Supreme Headquarters. One element in this decision was the fact that General Susloparoff had been informed of peace developments and had been told that in the event of the larger surrender Soviet representatives would be present.[14]

In accordance with these instructions, Field Marshal Montgomery refused to accept the withdrawal into his zone of German troops then on the Soviet front, although he said that individual soldiers would be accepted as prisoners of war. The field marshal added that he personally would not turn over these prisoners to the USSR. The enemy emissaries, lacking

---

[12] German White Book 1945; Schultz, *Die Letzten 30 Tage;* Tel, Keitel to *OB NORDWEST,* 4 May 45. *OKW, Befehle 13.IV.–20.V.45.*

[13] CCS to Eisenhower and Wilson, FACS 57 (FAN 395), 16 Aug 44, SHAEF SGS 387/1 Germany, I.

[14] Eisenhower to CCS, SCAF 327, 2 May 45; Eisenhower to CCS, SCAF 333, 3 May 45. Both in SHAEF SGS 387/1 Germany, Policy and Incidents of Local German Surrender.

any power to negotiate further, reported to Doenitz that only unconditional surrender would be accepted and that fleeing civilian refugees could not be admitted. Doenitz, in the belief that further fighting in northwest Europe was useless and that a partial capitulation in the west would gain time against the Red armies, agreed to the surrender of forces on Montgomery's front on his terms. Further, the admiral instructed von Friedeburg to get in touch with General Eisenhower with the hope of negotiating for further partial capitulation. He was to explain to the Supreme Commander why surrender on all fronts was not possible. As evidence of good faith toward the West, Doenitz told U-boat commanders to halt their activities, forbade any incidents in Norway, and ordered the release of King Leopold of the Belgians.[15]

On the afternoon of 4 May, German representatives appeared at the 21 Army Group headquarters at Lueneburg Heath with authority from Doenitz and Keitel to capitulate unconditionally on the British front. They signed an instrument of surrender to become effective at 0800, 5 May, which provided for the "surrender of all German armed forces in Holland, in northwest Germany including the Frisian Islands and Heligoland and all other islands, in Schleswig-Holstein, and in Denmark, to the C.-in-C. 21 Army Group. This to include all naval ships in these areas. These forces to lay down their arms and surrender unconditionally." The terms stipulated that the capitulation was independent of and would be superseded by any general instrument of surrender to be imposed on behalf of the Allied powers and applicable to the German armed forces as a whole.[16]

The same day, 4 May, also saw the end of operations of the *Twelfth* and *Ninth Armies* at the Elbe. The Red drive south of Berlin had threatened the extinction of the *Ninth Army,* but some 25,000 to 30,000 of its troops, without weapons and almost totally demoralized, made their way to the *Twelfth Army* about 1 May. Strong Soviet thrusts near the Elbe now made clear that the overrunning of the forces east of the river was a matter of a few days. On the morning of 3 May, General der Panzertruppen Walter Wenck instructed one of his corps commanders, General der Panzertruppen Maximilian Reichsfreiherr von Edelsheim, to discuss with representatives of the Ninth U.S. Army the surrender of the *Twelfth Army* and the remaining elements of the *Ninth Army*. General Wenck's 100,000 troops, now about 40 percent unarmed, were accompanied by many women and children fleeing from the Soviet zone. General von Edelsheim opened negotiations on 4 May at Stendal, asking that the Ninth Army permit the peaceful crossing of the Elbe by noncombatant personnel and civilians and the honorable surrender of other troops. The Ninth Army representatives, pointing to U.S. obligations to the USSR, refused to accept a mass surrender and forbade the civilians to cross the river. They agreed that individual soldiers might come over and surrender to U.S. units, and they apparently did not enforce too sternly the ban against civilians. Although they denied permission to build a bridge across the Elbe or to repair the damaged structure at Tangermuende, they did allow the use of damaged bridges. These and ferries

---

[15] German White Book 1945.
[16] See Montgomery, *Normandy to the Baltic,* pp. 347–49; de Guingand, *Operation Victory,* pp. 453–55. Terms of treaty in SHAEF SGS 387.4-4 Surrender Orders GCT.

were quickly pressed into service. By the close of hostilities on 7 May, the main body of General Wenck's forces and elements of the *Ninth Army* had crossed the Elbe and surrendered individually to U.S. forces. German estimates of the number who thus gave themselves up to the Ninth U.S. Army vary from 70,000 to 100,000.[17]

There is no evidence that this action on the part of Ninth Army or similar actions by other forces later was based on any policy or directive prescribed by higher headquarters. So far as SHAEF was concerned, the heads of the British and U.S. Governments and the Combined Chiefs of Staff had laid down the policy that any mass surrenders must be made simultaneously on both fronts. The way had been left open to commanders at lower levels to accept the surrender of units immediately opposing them or of individuals who came into British and United States lines to give themselves up.

In southern Germany and western Austria also, the war was moving swiftly to a close. Under Admiral Doenitz' authority to conclude a truce with the 6th Army Group for the area between the Boehmer Wald and the upper Inn, Field Marshal Kesselring on 4 May notified SHAEF of his readiness to send his chief of staff to Salzburg to discuss surrender terms. General Eisenhower declared that unless the offer included all enemy forces in *Army Groups Center, South, E,* and *G,* and all outlying garrisons, and all forces facing the Red Army, the Germans should send their representative not to SHAEF but to the 6th Army Group. Accordingly, General Schulz, commander of *Army Group G,* sent forward a delegation headed by General der Infanterie Hermann Foertsch, commander of the *First Army.* The Germans were brought to the Thorak estate at Haar

near Munich. There they met Generals Devers, Patch, and Haislip and on 5 May signed an instrument of surrender to become effective at 1200, 6 May. Included in the unconditional surrender were all elements under *Army Group G.* In spite of this surrender, some SS troops fought on, and one minor engagement ensued near Woergl when SS men attempted to retake Itter Castle, where important French prisoners had been held, after the original German garrison had surrendered it to the Americans. The original garrison helped to beat off the SS attack, and the garrison commander was killed in the process.[18]

General der Panzertruppen Erich Brandenberger, commander of the *Nineteenth Army,* came to Innsbruck where on 5 May he signed an instrument of surrender handing over those parts of the provinces of Tirol, Vorarlberg, and Allgaeu up to the Italian frontier which were under the jurisdiction of the *Nineteenth Army* commander. Hostilities were to cease by 1800, 5 May. Lt. Gen. Edward H. Brooks, commander of the VI U.S. Corps, representing General Devers and General Patch, signed for the United States Army, and Col. T. Demetz (Chief of Staff), representing General de Lattre, signed for the First French Army. Complications arose, how-

---

[17] MS # B–220, Capitulation Negotiations between the *Twelfth (German) Army* and the Ninth (American) Army, which took place at Stendal on 4 May 1945 (Edelsheim); MS # B–606 (Reichhelm); *Conquer: The Story of Ninth Army,* p. 329.

[18] Tel, Doenitz to Kesselring, 4 May 45, *ONI Fuehrer Directives;* Alexander to 6th Army Group, FX–69791, 3 May 45; Eisenhower to Alexander, 3 May 45; Eisenhower to Mil Mission Moscow and CCS, FWD 20635, 5 May 45; Eisenhower to CCS, FWD 20674, 5 May 45. All in SHAEF SGS 387/1 Germany. SHAEF SGS 387.4–4 SHAEF/21542/2 Surrender Orders GCT contains one of the original copies of the surrender specification signed by Foertsch. See also 6th Army Group diary.

ever, because General der Infanterie Hans Schmidt of the *Twenty-fourth Army* had previously made contact with the First French Army and arranged to negotiate the surrender of his forces. Just before the interview was to take place, his army was attached to General Brandenberger's and his forces were surrendered with those of the latter. Holding that the capitulation of the *Twenty-fourth Army* had not been made, General de Lattre ordered hostilities continued against General Schmidt's forces. He demanded that General Brandenberger take immediate measures required for the *Twenty-fourth Army* to surrender directly to the French. Fighting continued between French forces and General Schmidt's units until 7 May, when General Devers issued a cease fire order. The Seventh Army completed its activities on 8 May with the seizure of von Rundstedt, Generalfeldmarschall Wilhelm Ritter von Leeb, Generalfeldmarschall Wilhelm List, Kesselring, and Goering, and the liberation of King Leopold.[19]

After Brandenberger capitulated, Keitel had instructed Kesselring to assume command of *OB SUED*. With OKW, *Operations Staff B*, he was to take over *Army Groups Center, South,* and *OB SUEDOST. Army Group South,* which lay between Schoerner *(Center)* and Generaloberst Alexander Loehr *(OB SUEDOST),* and was renamed *Army Group Ostmark* (Austria). Kesselring and his subordinates were ordered to conduct operations so that time could be won in order to save as much of the civilian population as possible from the Soviet forces. If the Bohemian front could not be held against superior enemy attacks, forces in the east were to retreat in a southwesterly direction with the goal of bringing the "valuable human material" of the army groups out of the Rus-

sian zone.[20] On 6 May, Kesselring was ordered to make no further resistance to any penetration of U.S. forces eastward into the Protectorate of Bohemia and further south.[21]

General Schulz's surrender of 5 May was followed on the same day by a request from General Loehr, Commander in Chief Southeast, for permission to surrender his forces in the Balkans to Field Marshal Alexander. Loehr held that he could thus save Austria from Bolshevism, but he added that Austria's separation from Germany must be taken for granted. Doenitz on 5 May banned the Werewolf organization and warned *Air Group Reich,* which threatened to go underground, that such an action would harm the Reich more than it would help. He forbade the destruction of factories, land and water communications, railroads, bridges, and supplies except where combat made it necessary.[22]

Preliminary Talks With SHAEF

Meanwhile, arrangements had been made for Admiral von Friedeburg to pro-

---

[19] Typewritten copy of surrender document and of General de Lattre's Special Order 2 to General Brandenberger of 6 May 1945 in SHAEF SGS 387.4–4 SHAEF/21542/2 Surrender Orders GCT. See also discussion in SUSA Rpt of Opns, Vol. III, for the Seventh Army's story of the surrender.

[20] Rad, Jodl to *Fuehrungsstab B, H.Gr. Mitte, Chef des Generalstabes H.Gr. Mitte,* 4 May 45. *OKW, Befehle 13.IV.–20.V.45.*

[21] Rad, Keitel to Kesselring, 6 May 45. *OKW, Kapitulationsverhandlungen 2.V.–11.V.45.*

[22] Copies of tels, Loehr to Doenitz, 2 and 5 May 45. *OKW, Befehle 13.IV.–20.V.45;* German White Book 1945. Rad, Kinzel to Jodl and note by Jodl, 5 May 45; Tel, Keitel to *Luftflotte Reich* and others, 5 May 45. Both in *OKW, Befehle 13.IV.–20.V.45.* Loehr intimated that as the senior German officer coming from Austria he might be able to aid in the organization of Austria.

ceed to Supreme Headquarters at Reims on 5 May to open negotiations for the surrender of the remaining forces in the west. The Germans still hoped to gain time in which to bring their troops facing the Russians into the western zone. Realizing this, General Eisenhower cabled Moscow of his intention to inform the German emissaries that they must surrender all forces facing the Red Army to the Russians. The surrender was to be purely military and entirely independent of political and economic terms which would be imposed on Germany by the heads of the Allied governments. The Supreme Commander believed it highly desirable for the surrender on the Eastern and Western Fronts to be made simultaneously, and indicated that he would invite General Susloparoff to attend negotiations looking toward surrender of the enemy in the west. As an alternative he suggested that the Soviets send a party to Supreme Headquarters empowered to act for them. General Antonov replied, "The Soviet Command does not object to the plan of surrender set forth in the letter in the event that Doenitz accepts the condition of simultaneous surrender to the Soviet forces of those German troops which face them." In the event that Doenitz refused this condition, the Russians considered it desirable to discontinue negotiations with his representative. General Antonov added, "General Suslaparoff is authorized to take part in the surrender negotiations with the representative of Doenitz since it is not possible to send other officers in view of the shortness of time." In informing the Combined Chiefs of Staff of this arrangement, General Eisenhower said that a paragraph would be added by which the enemy agreed to make the surrender on both fronts simultaneously.[23]

When proposals for surrender first began to be discussed at the end of April, the question arose as to the nature of the surrender terms to be used. Details of a surrender instrument had been worked out by the European Advisory Commission and approved by the representatives of the United States, Great Britain, and the USSR in late July 1944. The document had been sent to SHAEF, but it was apparently viewed as a draft and not as a final proposal. Several things intervened before May 1945 to confuse its status. One was the fact that when the French were invited to join the European Advisory Commission near the end of 1944 they asked that the protocol for the instrument of surrender be changed to include them as a signatory. This step was delayed until shortly before the final surrender. The second complicating factor came at the Yalta Conference when the three great powers, without informing France, added the word "dismemberment" to provisions for complete disarmament and demobilization as possible steps in the pacification of Germany. Although French representatives learned indirectly of the change, they had not been notified officially of the amendment at the beginning of surrender negotiations. The European Advisory Commission on 1 May 1945 changed the protocol of the original surrender instrument to include France as a signatory, but did not make clear which set of surrender terms was to be used. When, therefore, SHAEF looked about for terms of capitu-

---

[23] Eisenhower to Mil Mission Moscow, FWD 20614, 4 May 45; Mil Mission Moscow to Eisenhower, M–24184, 5 May 45. Both in Eisenhower personal file. Eisenhower to CCS, SCAF 340, 5 May 45, SHAEF SGS 387/1 Germany, Policy and Incidents of Local German Surrenders, I.

lation to present to the Germans, it found not one set but two.[24]

On 4 May, General Smith told Ambassador Winant that no authoritative copy of the surrender instrument had been sent to SHAEF by the Combined Chiefs of Staff nor had the four governments delegated SHAEF power to sign that instrument. The Ambassador agreed that the authority had not been given but said that copies of the documents prepared by the European Advisory Commission were available for SHAEF's use. On 5 May, Mr. Winant was notified that SHAEF had decided to use a briefer form of unconditional surrender which had been drawn up at that headquarters. SHAEF believed, the Ambassador gathered, that it could obtain an acknowledgment by the enemy of complete defeat with the least controversy and delay by this means. Both the Prime Minister and General Smith, to whom Winant appealed when he found that the new draft had omitted certain important points contained in the older document, assured the Ambassador that SHAEF's terms did not preclude the later use of the surrender instrument or declaration which the European Advisory Commission had drawn up. At the Ambassador's suggestion, article four was added to the SHAEF instrument to make that point clear. SHAEF received no other objections to the use of its draft, and it was presented to the Germans for their signature at Reims.[25]

Surrender at Reims

General Eisenhower was informed on the evening of 4 May that German representatives would be flown to Reims from 21 Army Group headquarters the following morning. In preparation for the nego-

tiations, he told General Smith that there would be no bargaining with the Germans and stipulated that he would not see them until after the surrender terms were signed. General Smith and General Strong, who had handled the Italian surrender in 1943, were chosen to discuss terms with the Germans. To assure the Soviets that nothing underhanded was being done, General Eisenhower gave instructions that General Susloparoff and Lt. Col. Zenkovitch be called to Supreme Headquarters before the Germans arrived.[26]

In addition to notifying General Susloparoff of approaching negotiations, General Eisenhower kept Moscow informed of the developments at Reims and asked if

---

[24] A valuable summary of this background is given in Philip E. Mosely, "Dismemberment of Germany: The Allied Negotiation from Yalta to Potsdam," *Foreign Affairs*, XXVIII (April, 1950), 487–98. See also Winant to Secy State, 10 Jun 44; EAC Mtg, 25 Jul 44; Gen Vincent Meyer, Military Adviser EAC, to Gens Hilldring and Strong, 14 Oct 44; Winant to Secy State, 7 Nov 44; Memo, French delegation for EAC, 29 Dec 44, CAD 334 EAC, Sec II.

[25] A message conveyed by Mr. Robert Murphy to General Smith on 12 May 1945 reviewed the discussions and actions relative to the surrender terms between 4 and 6 May 1945. It may be found in SHAEF SGS 381/7 Germany, Policy and Incidents of Local German Surrenders, II. A similar account is given in Professor Mosely's article, "The Occupation of Germany," pp. 495–97. This differs from an account given by General Smith in his *My Three Years in Moscow* (Philadelphia and New York, 1950), p. 20. The author in dealing with the instrument of surrender received helpful suggestions from Mr. Denys Myers of the State Department who made a special study of the subject, and from Mr. Richard Welling, formerly of the Civil Affairs Division, who made available his unpublished study on the subject.

[26] The fullest account of the surrender negotiations is given in Butcher, *My Three Years With Eisenhower*, pp. 821–26. General Smith has given his recollections in "Eisenhower's Six Great Decisions," *The Saturday Evening Post*, July 13, 1946. General Eisenhower has a brief account in *Crusade in Europe*, pp. 425–26. See also Gen. François Sevez, "Reims 1945," *Revue Historique de l'Armée*, September 1948, pp. 75–78.

the Soviets wished to add to or modify the demands which had been presented. Further, General Eisenhower asked whether they desired "the formality of signing to be repeated before any other Russian representatives" at any other place they might care to designate, and whether they wished to participate in the more formal ratification meeting to follow. This message was handed to Soviet liaison representatives in Moscow by members of the Allied military missions, but no direct contact could be established with authorized members of the Red General Staff, who were said to be absent in the country as a result of the Russian Easter week end. This meant a delay in any reply Moscow might make, and was possibly responsible for the fact that General Antonov's request that the surrender ceremony be held in Berlin was not made until after the signing at Reims.[27]

Bad weather on the morning of 5 May interfered with the landing of Admiral Friedeburg and his party at Reims. They had to be landed at Brussels and driven by car to Supreme Headquarters. Shortly after 1700, the Germans arrived at Reims and were taken to General Smith's office. On coming before the SHAEF chief of staff, Admiral Friedeburg proposed to surrender the remaining German forces on the Western Front. General Smith informed him of General Eisenhower's refusal to continue discussions unless the Eastern Front was also included in the surrender offer. To make clear the hopelessness of the enemy situation, the SHAEF chief of staff displayed maps of the existing enemy situation as well as special maps on which some imaginary attacks had been projected. The German emissary was impressed, but he declared that he lacked authority to surrender on both fronts.

After studying a copy of the proposed Allied terms, Friedeburg cabled Admiral Doenitz asking that he be given permission to sign an unconditional and simultaneous surrender in all theaters of operations or that the chief of OKW and the commanders of the air and naval forces be sent to Reims for that purpose.

General Eisenhower's strong stand shocked the members of the German high command when they received Friedeburg's report. Doenitz found the demands unacceptable and decided to send Jodl, strong opponent of surrender in the east, to explain why over-all capitulation was impossible. His resolution was strengthened on the morning of 6 May by news of an uprising in Prague, which ended any hope of a political solution of the problem in Czechoslovakia and made virtually impossible the withdrawal of Schoerner's forces. Doenitz directed his staff to continue to try to save as many Germans as possible from the Soviets, while keeping rigidly to the terms of any armistice concluded with the Western powers.

General de Guingand and Brigadier Williams of Field Marshal Montgomery's staff brought General Jodl from their headquarters to Reims on Sunday evening, 6 May. After being briefed by Admiral Friedeburg, he opened negotiations with General Smith and General Strong. Concluding after more than an hour of discussion that the Germans were merely dragging out the talks to gain time for their forces in the east, the Allied officers

---

[27] Eisenhower to Mil Mission Moscow, SCAF 345, 5 May 45; Eisenhower to CCS, SCAF 346, 5 May 45; Msgs from Friedeburg cited in Eisenhower to CCS, SCAF 347, 5 May 45; Eisenhower to Mil Mission Moscow, SCAF 348, 0031 hours, 6 May 45; Mil Mission Moscow to Eisenhower, M–24197, 6 May 45. All in SHAEF SGS 387/1 Germany, Policy and Incidents of Local German Surrenders, I.

put the problem before the Supreme Commander. His reaction was that unless the Germans speedily agreed to the terms of surrender "he would break off all negotiations and seal the Western Front preventing by force any further westward movement of German soldiers and civilians." This answer was also reported to General Susloparoff, who was not sitting in on the meetings with the Germans. General Jodl, faced with General Eisenhower's threat, wired Admiral Doenitz for authority to make a final and complete surrender on all fronts, saying that he saw no other alternative except chaos.[28]

Admiral Doenitz characterized the Supreme Commander's demands as "sheer extortion." He felt impelled nonetheless to accede to them because Jodl, who only the day before had strongly opposed surrender of the forces in the east, now insisted that this was the only way out for the Reich. The grand admiral was consoled somewhat by the reflection that he could save many of the troops in the east during the forty-eight-hour period before the capitulation went into effect. Shortly after midnight he instructed Keitel to wire: "Full power to sign in accordance with conditions as given has been granted by Grand Admiral Doenitz."[29] When this message arrived at Reims, activities were transferred from General Smith's office to the War Room, where the final signing was to take place.

Sentimental newspapermen gave the American public a misleading picture of the building in which the peace terms were signed with their dispatches saying that the capitulation ceremonies took place in the "little red schoolhouse of Reims." Actually, the Ecole Professionelle et Technique de Garçons—a modern, three-storied, red brick building—had more floor space than the Hotel Trianon Palace which had housed the General Staff of SHAEF at Versailles. The War Room, it is true, was not very large. Approximately thirty feet square,[30] it was a small recreation hall where the students had played ping-pong and chess. Huge maps covered the walls, showing the location of all Allied divisions and supply units, the main airfields, results of air operation, data on transportation and supply, weather conditions, progress of daily operations, casualties, and the like. For the signing, the room had been filled with the equipment of the seventeen photographers and newsmen who had been chosen to represent the Allied press at the ceremony. A large table, which teachers had used in grading their papers, stood in the center of the room. Here about 0200, 7 May, General Jodl, Admiral Friedeburg, and the former's aide, Maj. Friedrich Wilhelm Oxenius, were brought before Generals Smith, Morgan, Bull, Sevez,[31] Spaatz, Strong, and Susloparoff,

---

[28] Eisenhower to CCS, SCAF 354, 2144 hours, 6 May 45; Jodl to Doenitz, 6 May 45. Both in SHAEF SGS 387.1 Germany, Policy and Incidents of Local German Surrenders, I. Copy of Rad, Jodl to Keitel, 6.V.45. *OKW, Kapitulationsverhandlungen 2.V.–11.V.45.*

[29] German White Book 1945; Rad, Keitel to Jodl and others, 7 May 45. *OKW, Kapitulationsverhandlungen 2.V.–11.V.45.*

[30] Actually 27 feet 10 inches by 32 feet except for a small offset in one corner.

[31] After negotiations with the Germans began, General Eisenhower asked the French to send a representative to attend the signing. General de Gaulle had already named General de Lattre on 4 May to sign for France when a capitulation should be made, but he found that there was not sufficient time to get de Lattre to Reims. He therefore named Maj. Gen. François Sevez to act in the place of General Juin, chief of the French General Staff of National Defense, who was then attending the United Nations conference at San Francisco. Sevez, *op. cit.*, p. 75.

Admiral Burrough, Air Marshal Robb, Colonel Zenkovitch, and Lieutenant Cherniaev.[32] When asked by General Smith if they were ready to sign, the Germans replied in the affirmative. General Jodl affixed his signature to the two documents placed before him, and they were then signed by General Smith for the Supreme Allied Commander and by General Susloparoff for the Soviet high command. General Sevez of the French Army signed as witness. The time was noted as 0241, 7 May 1945. At this point General Jodl rose and said: "General: With this signature the German people and German armed forces are, for better or worse, delivered into the victor's hands. In this war, which has lasted more than five years, both have achieved and suffered perhaps more than any other people in the world. In this hour I can only express the hope that the victor will treat them with generosity."[33]

The text of the Act of Military Surrender signed by General Jodl follows:

1. We the undersigned, acting by authority of the German High Command, hereby surrender unconditionally to the Supreme Commander, Allied Expeditionary Force and simultaneously to the Soviet High Command all forces on land, sea, and in the air who are at this date under German control.

2. The German High Command will at once issue orders to all German military, naval and air authorities and to all forces under German control to cease active operations at 2301 hours Central European time on 8 May and to remain in the positions occupied at that time. No ship, vessel, or aircraft is to be scuttled, or any damage done to their hull, machinery or equipment.

3. The German High Command will at once issue to the appropriate commanders, and ensure the carrying out of any further orders issued by the Supreme Commander, Allied Expeditionary Force and by the Soviet High Command.

4. This act of military surrender is without prejudice to, and will be superseded by any general instrument of surrender imposed by, or on behalf of the United Nations and applicable to GERMANY and the German armed forces as a whole.

5. In the event of the German High Command or any of the forces under their control failing to act in accordance with this Act of Surrender, the Supreme Commander, Allied Expeditionary Force and the Soviet High Command will take such punitive or other action as they deem appropriate.

Signed at Rheims at 0241 on the 7th day of May, 1945.

On behalf of the German High Command.

JODL.

IN THE PRESENCE OF

On behalf of the Supreme Commander, Allied Expeditionary Force

W. B. SMITH

On behalf of the Soviet High Command

SUSLOPAROFF

F. SEVEZ

Major General, French Army

(Witness)

General Jodl also signed the following statement:

It is agreed by the German emissaries undersigned that the following German officers will arrive at a place and time designated by the Supreme Commander, Allied Expeditionary Force, and the Soviet High Command prepared with plenary powers, to

---

[32] These were the members of the delegation at the table. In addition, Captain Butcher and several other members of the SHAEF staff were present. Most photographs of the group omit General Strong, who acted as interpreter for the Germans during the ceremony.

[33] Butcher, *My Three Years With Eisenhower*, pp. 832–33. Information as to the building and War Room is based in part on an interrogation of a member of the faculty of the school and on measurements of the room made by the author in 1946. Detailed specifications of the War Room and its maps have been made by the Historical Properties Branch of the Department of the Army.

SURRENDER AT REIMS. *In the War Room of SHAEF headquarters the Allies accept the unconditional surrender of the German high command. General Jodl (center foreground) prepares to sign the surrender documents. He is shown accompanied by Admiral Friedeburg of the German Navy, and Major Oxenius. Allied officers shown receiving the surrender are (left to right) General Morgan, General Sevez, Admiral Burrough, General Smith, General Susloparoff and General Spaatz.*

execute a formal ratification on behalf of the German High Command of this act of Unconditional Surrender of the German armed forces.

    Chief of the High Command
    Commander-in-Chief of the Army
    Commander-in-Chief of the Navy
    Commander-in-Chief of the Air Forces [34]

After signing, General Jodl was taken to General Eisenhower, who asked if the German officer thoroughly understood all the provisions of the document. When Jodl replied affirmatively, the Supreme Commander warned him that he would be held accountable officially if the terms of the surrender were violated. Jodl was also made responsible for seeing that the German commanders appeared in Berlin to accomplish the formal surrender to the Western Allies and to the USSR.[35]

---

[34] Photostatic copies of the original documents in SHAEF SGS 387/1 Germany, Policy and Incidents of Local German Surrenders, I. The originals are at the time of writing on exhibit at the U.S. National Archives building in Washington. The original battle map from the SHAEF War Room may also be found there.

[35] Eisenhower, *Crusade in Europe,* p. 426.

At 0324 General Eisenhower cabled the Combined Chiefs of Staff, "The Mission of this Allied Force was fulfilled at 0241, local time, May 7th, 1945, Eisenhower." He followed this with an official notification to the Soviet high command, emphasizing the agreement of the Germans to send representatives to a place chosen by General Eisenhower and the Soviets to execute a formal ratification. A delay of two hours in the handing of the latter message to the Russians ensued because they refused to meet the British and U.S. representatives sooner.[36]

Ceremony at Berlin

In answering General Eisenhower's telegram of 6 May which asked if the Soviet authorities wished to send representatives to a place other than Reims or make other arrangements, General Antonov declared that Admiral Doenitz, despite his offers to surrender, was still ordering German troops to fight against Red forces in the east. The note called attention to changes in the language of the proposed instrument of surrender which had been made at Reims before the final signing. In wiring Moscow on 6 May, General Eisenhower had spoken of a truce, a term stricken out several hours later when the Germans agreed to unconditional surrender. Another Soviet request—for the enemy to send emissaries to ratify the terms of surrender—had already been complied with. The USSR also asked that certain phrases from the European Advisory Commission draft be added. Finally, General Antonov, the Red Army Chief of Staff, asked that the signing of the act of military surrender take place in Berlin and indicated that Marshal Zhukov would represent the Red Army.

This message, dated 6 May but not handed to General Deane in Moscow for transmittal until 7 May, declared that the Soviets desired only one signing of the document and did not concur with the suggestion that preliminary signing be held with Susloparoff representing the Russians. General Deane and Admiral Archer expressed the belief that General Eisenhower would not agree to any delays which would unnecessarily risk the loss of more lives. They might have added that any delay granted the Germans would have helped them in their desire to remove troops from the Soviet front. General Eisenhower quickly replied that the Western powers had adhered scrupulously to their agreement of no separate truce. He had offered to keep pushing toward the Red forces, and had restrained his forces only at their request. While a brief instrument of surrender had been signed at Reims before the arrival of the Russian note, provision had been made for the representatives of the German high command to report for a more formal signing. He indicated his willingness to go to Berlin on 8 May at a time specified by Marshal Zhukov for this ceremony, but added that if bad weather prevented his arrival the British and U.S. heads of the missions in Moscow were to go to Berlin to represent him.[37]

General Eisenhower's initial intention to go to Berlin was questioned by some

---

[36] Eisenhower to Mil Mission Moscow, SCAF 359, 7 May 45; Eisenhower to CCS Br COS, and Mil Mission Moscow, SCAF 357, 7 May 45; Mil Mission Moscow to Eisenhower, MX–24202, 7 May 45. All in Eisenhower personal file.

[37] Mil Mission Moscow to Eisenhower, MX–24200, 7 May 45; Eisenhower to Mil Mission Moscow, SCAF 361, 7 May 45. Both in Eisenhower personal file. See also Deane, *The Strange Alliance*, pp. 168–69.

members of his staff who saw no necessity of repeating the signing. When Mr. Churchill also raised objections, the Supreme Commander appointed as his representative Air Chief Marshal Tedder, who was accompanied by a delegation that included Generals Spaatz, Strong, Bull, and de Lattre, and Admiral Burrough. General Deane and Admiral Archer traveled from Moscow to sign for the Supreme Commander if his party was unable to arrive. The German representatives were Field Marshal Keitel, Admiral von Friedeburg, and General Stumpff.[38] The parties from the west arrived in Berlin before noon and were taken to the grounds of the Military Engineering College at Karlshorst, a suburb about ten miles southeast of the city's center. A meeting between Tedder and the Russian representative was delayed until four in the afternoon since Zhukov had to wait for the arrival of Andrei Y. Vishinsky from Moscow before starting discussions.

Even before the formal meeting, difficulties arose over the matter of protocol. General de Lattre had discovered shortly after his arrival that the French flag had been omitted from the group displayed in the surrender hall and demanded that one be added. Since no French flag was available, the Russians made one, erring initially in designing a Dutch instead of a French banner. The proper flag was ultimately completed in time for the final ceremony. Another matter, that of the signing of the surrender instrument, was not so easily arranged. General de Gaulle in directing General de Lattre to sign for France had said that he would sign as a witness in case the document was signed by General Eisenhower. If the Supreme Commander was not present, then de Lattre was to insist on being treated in the same way as the British representative, unless the latter signed in the place of General Eisenhower. General de Lattre, on explaining his instructions to Tedder during the afternoon, was told that he and General Spaatz would sign as witnesses— a proposal to which Zhukov apparently agreed. The arrangement was upset, however, when Vishinsky arrived and said that de Lattre could sign, since his signature would publicly acknowledge the resurrection of France, but that Spaatz could not participate inasmuch as Air Marshal Tedder represented both the U.S. and British forces. General Spaatz insisted on signing if the French general was included, while General de Lattre stood on his instructions and declared that if he went back to France without having signed the capitulation of the Reich he would deserve to hang. Air Marshal Tedder promised to support his right to sign and returned to argue the matter with the Soviets. For several hours the question was debated, Zhukov holding there was no logical need for the witnesses. Tedder replied that it was not a matter of logic but that there had to be a name to represent 40,000,000 Frenchmen and another name to represent 140,000,000 Americans. He added that SHAEF had to represent three flags while the Russians had to consider only one. Near the end of the discussion, when Vishinsky looked at his watch, Tedder took advantage of the situation to say, "Yes, we aren't getting any vodka and food are we?" The Russian representative left the room shortly afterward and returned with a suggestion that the names of

---

[38] Eisenhower, *Crusade in Europe*, pp. 427–28; Butcher, *My Three Years With Eisenhower*, p. 835; Tedder to author, 13 Feb 47.

the witnesses be placed on a slightly lower line than those of the principals. This arrangement, promptly accepted, ended a discussion which had lasted from the afternoon until nearly midnight.[39]

With the settlement of the matter of protocol, the representatives of the Western powers and the USSR were ready to receive the Germans. The Act of Military Surrender to be presented to the Germans differed from that signed at Reims in only a few particulars, and these had been settled fairly quickly during the afternoon. Where the Reims document spoke of the Russian party as "the Soviet High Command," the Berlin document used "the Supreme High Command of the Red Army." To paragraph two, which enjoined the Germans to cease active operations on 8 May and remain in the positions occupied at that time, the new document added: "and to disarm completely, handing over their weapons and equipment to the local allied commanders or officers designated by the Representatives of the Allied Supreme Command." To the injunction that no damage was to be done to naval, marine, and air craft, the Berlin Act added: "and also to machines of all kinds, armament, apparatus, and all the technical means of prosecution of war in general."[40]

In preparation for the final signing, the representatives of the victorious armies approached their places at the main table. Marshal Zhukov sat in the center, placing Air Marshal Tedder to his immediate left. General Spaatz and then General de Lattre sat at Tedder's left. When Admiral Burrough started to take the seat at Zhukov's right, he found it taken by someone he did not recognize. It was Vishinsky, at whose right the admiral sat during the ceremonies.[41] Toward midnight, Marshal

Zhukov called the meeting to order and asked that the German representatives be brought in. Field Marshal Keitel, Admiral Friedeburg, and General Stumpff, together with their aides, now came forward and were questioned as to their understanding of the document and their powers to capitulate. Air Chief Marshal Tedder then asked if they were ready to sign. On answering that they were, they were handed copies of the Act of Military Surrender. General de Lattre noted with pleasure the change in seating which placed him just at Keitel's elbow when the field marshal wrote his name. When the Germans completed signing at approximately 2330 hours, Marshal Zhukov and Air Marshal Tedder penned their names on behalf of their respective commands, and General Spaatz and de Lattre were called forward to sign as witnesses. A comic touch was added when it appeared that despite the long dispute over their right to sign neither had a pen. The ceremony was completed at approximately 2345, and Marshal Zhukov gave orders for the Germans to depart. Keitel, bemonocled and carrying his marshal's baton, strode out of the hall, keeping the air of arrogance which had unfavorably

---

[39] De Lattre, *Histoire de la Première Armée Française*, pp. 600–603; Air Chief Marshal Tedder to author, 13 Feb 47. Deane, *The Strange Alliance*, p. 177, says that Tedder initially objected to de Lattre's signing. However, both Tedder and de Lattre indicate that Tedder backed de Lattre's demand.

[40] Deane, *The Strange Alliance*, pp. 175–76. Photostat of signed Act of Military Surrender given in SHAEF SGS 387/1 Germany, I.

[41] It is interesting to note that neither Butcher nor de Lattre mentions Burrough's presence, and that Deane says that the naval representative was Admiral Ramsay—Burrough's predecessor, who had been killed five months before. Admiral Burrough, in a letter of 6 February 1951, gave the author the above details.

SURRENDER AT BERLIN. *Field Marshal Keitel prepares to sign unconditional surrender documents. He is shown with General Stumpff (left) and Admiral Friedeburg (right) as German staff officers observe the proceedings.*

impressed the delegations throughout the proceedings.[42]

Before the signing of the surrender document at Berlin, President Truman and Prime Minister Churchill had announced the surrender at Reims. Their statement had been preceded by a series of frantic cables between London, Washington, and Moscow relative to the proper procedure to be followed in making the announcements, and by a breach of SHAEF censorship which led to the suspension of the Associated Press correspondent who represented his group at the surrender in Reims.[43] In announcing the Reims capitulation to the Combined

Chiefs of Staff, General Eisenhower had recommended a simultaneous statement from the three capitals at 1500 on Tuesday, 8 May, proclaiming 9 May as V-E

---

[42] The author has used for these details the accounts of Deane, *The Strange Alliance,* Ch. X; Butcher, *My Three Years With Eisenhower,* pp. 836–44; and de Lattre, *Histoire de la Première Armée Française,* pp. 597–606. The accounts while not always corroborative are in agreement on most points. In the case of the time of surrender, the author has followed that set by Air Chief Marshal Tedder in his official notification to General Eisenhower. In his cable sent at 0122, 9 May 1945, Air Marshal Tedder declared that the surrender was signed between 2315 and 2345. De Lattre and Deane both place the surrender one hour later. Newspaper accounts for the most part agree with the later time.

[43] See Appendix A.

Day. He warned that, while no release of any kind would be made from the European theater until after the announcement by the three powers, most of the orders to troops would go in the clear, and it would be impossible to prevent millions of individuals in France and neutral countries from learning the facts. "It is believed hopeless," he said, "to keep this secret until Tuesday." He suggested that the governments might consider it well to announce the surrender as soon as they could agree among themselves.[44] When the Soviets indicated their desire to have a signing in Berlin, however, he changed his original recommendations, "since manifestly it would be extremely unwise to make any announcement until the Russians are thoroughly satisfied." [45]

On the evening of 7 May, President Truman notified Marshal Stalin that if the time was acceptable to everyone he would make the announcement in Washington at 0900, 8 May, corresponding to the 1500 hour, Greenwich time, which General Eisenhower had suggested. General Antonov, not convinced that the Germans intended to surrender, held that a premature announcement would prove embarrassing and asked that the announcement be postponed until after the signing at Berlin or until 1900 Moscow time, 9 May. No word came officially from Marshal Stalin to President Truman. Meanwhile, Prime Minister Churchill had pressed for an announcement at 1800, 7 May, London time, or noon at Washing-

ton and 2000 in Moscow. President Truman, feeling that he had committed himself to 8 May, declined to go along unless Marshal Stalin consented to a change. Then followed a series of long-distance communications between the three capitals as efforts were made to get changes in the arrangements. When the Soviets finally declared that they could not advance the hour, the British and U.S. Governments decided to make the announcements on 8 May at the time initially suggested by General Eisenhower. The USSR waited until 0200 on 9 May, after the signing at Berlin, before making the surrender public.[46]

To the man in the street and the soldier on the battlefield the question of how the announcement of the signing at Reims and Berlin reached the world did not matter. For them the significant things were that the war which had started in Europe in the fall of 1939 was ended, and that the final offensive against Japan could now get under way. The time was not far off when they could return to the pursuits of peace.

---

[44] Eisenhower to CCS, SCAF 358, 7 May 45, SHAEF SGS 387/1 Germany, I. In an earlier message (Eisenhower to CCS, SCAF 356, 7 May 45) the Supreme Commander had urged an announcement at the earliest hour co-ordination could be arranged.

[45] Eisenhower to CCS, SCAF 360, 7 May 45, SHAEF SGS 387/1 Germany, Policy and Incidents of Local German Surrenders, I.

[46] Deane, *The Strange Alliance*, pp. 171–73; Leahy, *I Was There*, pp. 357–64. Admiral Leahy gives the text of the telephone conversation between himself and Mr. Churchill concerning arrangements.

CHAPTER XXVI

The Last Phase

The last phase, marking the period between the German surrender at Reims on 7 May and the dissolution of Supreme Headquarters on 14 July 1945, falls into two periods. The first, which saw the closing out of the former enemy commands, was ended on 5 June when representatives of France, Britain, the Soviet Union, and the United States met at Berlin to assume joint authority in Germany for their governments. The second, prolonged until 14 July, consisted of winding up the loose ends of combined responsibilities and preparing the way for a change-over from the Supreme Command to separate national headquarters in western Germany.

During both periods, General Eisenhower found it necessary to play several roles. As U.S. theater commander, he was occupied with the redeployment of U.S. forces to the United States and the Pacific theater. As leader of the victorious armies in the west, he was called on to make numerous appearances in European capitals and at home (he left for the United States on 16 June and did not return until mid-July just before the formal dissolution of SHAEF). As Supreme Commander, he had the task of separating the U.S. and British elements of his combined staff so that an easy transition might be made from an integrated headquarters to separate national forces. Finally, as the representative of his country on the Allied

Control Council in Berlin and as commander of U.S. Forces in Germany, he was occupied with tasks of Allied military government, an assignment he delegated in the period covered by this volume to his deputy for military government, Lt. Gen. Lucius D. Clay.

Initial Measures

The Supreme Commander's task in the first weeks after the German surrender consisted of instituting immediate disarmament and control of German forces to prevent the renewal of hostilities, enforcing the terms of surrender by maintaining a strategic air threat and occupying strategic areas on the Continent, establishing law and order as far as possible, and initiating measures to complete the disarmament and control of the German forces. At the same time, he took preliminary steps for the relief and evacuation of Allied prisoners of war and displaced persons and gave such aid to programs for the relief and rehabilitation of liberated countries as did not interfere with military objectives.[1] These tasks continued until control passed from the Su-

---

[1] The task of returning the forces of the Western powers to their respective zones was also listed for performance in the early weeks but had not been completed when SHAEF was dissolved.

preme Commander to the quadripartite military government at Berlin or until they were turned over to the national commanders in the French, British, or U.S. zones of occupation.[2]

In its initial planning for the occupation of Germany, SHAEF had prepared a number of detailed orders to be presented to the high-level headquarters of the German Army, Navy, and Air Force at the time of surrender. On finding a few days before the German surrender that the enemy's Army and Air Force headquarters either were powerless or had ceased to exist, General Eisenhower decided to present the Germans with only that part of the surrender orders which dealt with naval units. He then handed over to his army group commanders the task of issuing detailed orders to German commanders for the disarmament of their forces. Admiral Burrough, at the time of the signing at Reims, issued a detailed order to Admiral Friedeburg concerning the German Navy, and General Smith gave a briefer order to General Jodl to the effect that local German Army and Air Force commanders on the Western Front, in Norway, the Channel Islands, and in pockets that might still exist were to hold themselves in readiness to receive detailed instructions from the Allied commanders opposite their fronts.[3]

One of the chief means of insuring the prompt surrender and disarmament of German forces was, obviously, to establish firm control over the government of Admiral Doenitz. Less than seven hours after the surrender at Reims, members of the SHAEF staff had met with the German group at Reims and arranged for the exchange of liaison parties between Supreme Headquarters and the German headquarters at Flensburg. The SHAEF repre-

sentatives accepted General Jodl's proposal to reunite the southern and northern sections of OKW which had been divided in late April, and agreed to permit reliable elements of the Wehrmacht to keep their arms for a short period to maintain order and safeguard property.[4]

On the return of Jodl and Friedeburg to Flensburg, Admiral Doenitz and his advisers thoroughly explored with them the question of whether or not they should remain in power as agents of the Allied forces. The arguments for ending the regime immediately were strong. The government was manifestly impotent, and it was unlikely that the victors would allow it any additional control. Worse still, many of the German people were indifferent to it, and it was not even known to what extent they knew of the government's existence. To some of the German leaders, a dignified abdication seemed to be the answer. On the other hand, there was the obvious importance of having some type of government to guarantee the preservation of order. Doenitz and his advisers also believed that the Western powers might be willing to accept the continuance of the government not only because they counted on it to keep order and take some of the responsibility for coming events, but also because it might occur to them that a situation might develop in which a strong

---

[2] Operation ECLIPSE Appreciation and Outline Plan, 10 Nov 44, and Amendments, 17 Apr 45, SHAEF SGS 381 ECLIPSE (Case 2), I, and ECLIPSE (envelope).

[3] SHAEF to ANCXF, 21 A Gp *et al.*, FWD 20638, 5 May 45, SHAEF SGS 387/1 Germany, Policy and Incidents of Local Surrenders, I. The same file contains copies of all documents and orders presented to the enemy representatives at Reims.

[4] Notes on conf, 1000 hours, 7 May 45, at SHAEF, SHAEF SGS 322.01/28 OKW Liaison Detachment to SHAEF, I.

Germany would be desirable. After much discussion, the German leaders decided that while abdication was inevitable it should not be made too early.[5]

In his address to the German people on 8 May, Admiral Doenitz declared that the foundation on which the German Empire had been built was a thing of the past, and that unity of state and party no longer existed. All power in Germany had now passed into the hands of the occupying powers, who would decide whether he and his government were to continue.[6] Events of the next few weeks were to show conclusively that Doenitz' government had no real standing and that SHAEF was interested in dealing with the admiral only as head of the armed forces.

Disarming the German Forces

Controlling OKW

Four days after the surrender at Reims, General Eisenhower ordered General Rooks, a deputy G–3 of SHAEF, to establish a control party at Flensburg for the purpose of imposing the will of the Supreme Commander on OKW in the areas of Germany occupied by the Western Allies. To carry out his mission, General Rooks was to issue the necessary orders, supervise their transmission through German command channels, and compile information about the German command system through the collection and safeguarding of all OKW documents at Flensburg. The Soviets were informed of this order and invited to send a party to Doenitz' headquarters. The German commander in chief was ordered, in turn, to send liaison parties to Reims and to Soviet headquarters in Berlin. Headed by General der Infanterie Friedrich Fangohr, the party that was assigned to SHAEF had little to do inasmuch as General Rooks's mission was used as the chief channel of communication.[7]

General Rooks acted quickly to assert SHAEF's authority. In his first interview with Doenitz on 13 May, he ordered the arrest of Field Marshal Keitel and his replacement by General Jodl. He explained that all subsequent instructions to the German forces would be in the name of the Supreme Commander and that complete access to the offices and files of OKW for the control party was required. SHAEF, he said, would leave to its army group commanders the control of affairs in their zones and would deal with OKW only on matters common to all three armed services and to all Allied zones. General Jodl assured the Allied general that he would undertake to carry out SHAEF directives in the interests of maintaining order and saving the German people from catastrophe. Doenitz declared that the German armed forces had taken an oath to him personally and would obey his orders. He grasped the opportunity to mention severe problems such as food, currency, and fuel which beset the German people, and emphasized the need of a central German authority to keep order. General Rooks brushed aside this suggestion, making clear that the Western powers

---

[5] Conf, 8 May 45, Doenitz, Jodl, and other members of stf at Flensburg, German White Book 1945.

[6] German White Book 1945.

[7] Order, SHAEF to Gen Rooks, 11 May 45, SHAEF G–3 387–7 SHAEF Control Mission (OKW); Memo, G–3 SHAEF, 13 May 45, sub: Liaison Detachment From OKW; SHAEF to EXFOR, FWD 21656, 16 May 45; SCOFOR Main to SHAEF, DAF, 19 May 45; SHAEF to SHAEF Control Party, AEF 510, 13 May 45. All in SHAEF SGS 322.01/29 SHAEF Liaison Detachment to OKW, I.

intended to function through Allied military government.[8]

At General Rooks's request, Doenitz drew up a statement to the German armed forces which the SHAEF representative approved with minor changes on 17 May. This statement removed any doubt that the enemy had surrendered in the face of superior force and included the following: "The German Reich has had to capitulate because it was at the end of its power of resistance. The first consequence that we have to draw is the most loyal fulfillment of the demands made on us. There must be no officer and no soldier, who would try by illegal means to evade the consequences which have arisen out of the last war and an unconditional surrender." All records were to be shown the Allies. In the event that burdens imposed by the Allies proved too heavy, the Germans might emphasize the possible serious consequences of the orders, but were to make no other protest. Doenitz required every soldier and officer to behave correctly toward the occupying forces.[9]

Despite these evidences of co-operation, there were several incidents which led to demands in the United States and Great Britain for the termination of the Doenitz regime and the taking of stricter measures against enemy commanders. Angry questions were asked in the House of Commons as the result of a broadcast from Flensburg on 11 May by Field Marshal Busch, Commander in Chief Northwest. Busch declared that with the agreement of the British he had taken command of Schleswig-Holstein and the area occupied by the 21 Army Group and that all German military and civil authorities in the sphere had been subordinated to him. He was referring to an arrangement made on 5 May by which the 21 Army Group established a

German chain of command through which it could carry out the initial steps of disbanding the enemy forces, but the broadcast gave offense because it was sent from a transmitter in the OKW enclave at Flensburg which British troops were not able to enter. General Eisenhower promptly ordered firm control over the Flensburg radio and censorship of all future transmissions. The British closed the station, and General Rooks forbade the Germans to reopen it. Other criticism arose when senior Allied officers were photographed in friendly poses with high-level German commanders and when reports were printed that enemy leaders were receiving special treatment. The Supreme Commander condemned such actions and directed that steps be taken to stop their recurrence.[10]

The outcry over these incidents stemmed from a fear in some quarters that the Allies were not going to be firm enough with the

[8] Ewart, EXFOR TAC (21 A Gp), to SHAEF Fwd for Strong, 1/103, 9 May 45; Intervs, Gen Rooks and Brig Foord with Jodl, 13 May 45; Interv, Rooks and Foord with Doenitz, 13 May 45. All in SHAEF SGS 322 OKW, Organization and Personnel OKW–OKM–OKH.

[9] Instructions [Jodl for Doenitz] Regarding Conduct Toward the Occupying Powers, 17 May 45, SHAEF G–3 387–11 Clearance of OKW Messages. A notation of 22 May 1945 indicates that these were cleared by the SHAEF control party with the exception of a final sentence in which Doenitz said that he hoped that the demands of the Allies would not exceed the limits of international law which the Wehrmacht had respected throughout the war save in individual instances which might occur in any war and in any force.

[10] Morgan to Whiteley, 13 May 45; de Guingand to SHAEF for Whiteley, COS 116, 13 May 45; SAC to SHAEF control party, FWD 21475, 14 May 45; Rooks to SHAEF Fwd, 29, 15 May 45. All in SHAEF G–3 387–9 OKW Misc. New York Times, May 12–14, 1945; Eisenhower to U.S. comdrs, FWD 21421, 14 May 45, SHAEF G–3 387–8 Ops (C) OKW Mission to SHAEF. For investigation of treatment of OKW liaison detachment at SHAEF see SHAEF SGS 322.01/38 OKW Liaison Detachment to SHAEF, I.

enemy commanders and that some members of the old regime might be perpetuated in power. The Supreme Commander's statement of his aims at this time indicated that his main desire was to disband the German Army quickly in order to alleviate the growing problem of feeding enemy forces. He hoped that Doenitz' headquarters would be useful in controlling the enemy forces and in speeding up the disarmament process.

Members of the SHAEF control party at Flensburg and the SHAEF Political Officers had already come to a different conclusion. On 17 May, they agreed to recommend that General Eisenhower immediately abolish the "so-called government" of Doenitz and arrest the grand admiral and the members of his staff. SHAEF on the following day pointed out that this action would have to be cleared with the Russians, but ordered all steps short of arrest to assure that Doenitz and his staff ceased their executive functions. On 19 May, the Supreme Commander directed the 21 Army Group to consult with the SHAEF control party at Flensburg and then to arrest the members of Doenitz' "so-called government" and of OKW. The archives were to be seized and secured. Members of the high-level Navy headquarters were for the moment exempted from the order.[11]

On the morning of 23 May, General Rooks summoned Doenitz, Jodl, and Friedeburg to his office and informed them of the Supreme Commander's order. The officers were then put under guard, but, despite all precautions, Admiral Friedeburg killed himself by taking poison. The other two leaders were flown from Flensburg to a German prison camp that afternoon. In a statement approving the arrests, the Department of State said it could not understand why Doenitz and his group had been permitted to continue their pretense of action as a German government for so long, and asked that all German General Staff officers of whatever rank be arrested on the ground that their training and experience would be useful in reviving German militarism.[12]

With the arrest of Doenitz and members of his staff, the main work of the SHAEF Control Party at Flensburg was ended. General Rooks indicated his intention of leaving the area about 27 May and handed over local control to a small joint U.S.-British Ministerial Control Party. However, he retained general policy control of the southern branch of OKW which was still in existence and made attempts to disband German forces in that sector.

SHAEF's effort to work through the southern section of OKW was complicated by the confusion in command which followed the arrest on 10 May of Field Marshal Kesselring, who was commanding all forces in the southern area when the war ended. Since the two next senior commanders, Schoerner and Loehr, were somewhere on the Eastern Front and not available to take control, the command devolved on the next in line, Generaloberst Otto Dessloch, an airman. Busy with his own affairs, he appointed General der Kavallerie Siegfried Westphal, formerly Kesselring's chief of staff, as his representative at *OB WEST*. This arrange-

[11] SHAEF control party (OKW) to SHAEF Fwd, 37, 17 May 45; SHAEF Fwd to SHAEF Control Party, 21847, 18 May 45; Eisenhower to CCS, SCAF 398, 19 May 45; SCAEF to EXFOR Fwd, 21924, 19 May 45. All in SHAEF G–3 387–9 OKW Misc.

[12] Memo, Gen Nevins for G–3 SHAEF, 23 May 45, sub: Telephone Call From Gen Rooks, SHAEF G–3 387–9 OKW Misc; Murphy to Smith, 25 May 45, SHAEF G–3 387–7 SHAEF Control Mission (OKW).

ment was satisfactory to the 6th Army Group and the Seventh Army, which were dealing at that time with *OB WEST* in the disbandment of enemy forces, but it was displeasing to General Winter, the commander of the southern section of OKW. Winter felt that his headquarters was the proper channel through which orders should be passed on to subordinate units. The matter was clarified on 19 May when the 6th Army Group named General Westphal Commander in Chief South and subordinated to him virtually all Army and Air Force headquarters in General Devers' area, including the southern section of OKW. While the action represented a victory for Westphal, it made no basic difference since, as General Jodl wired so prophetically shortly before his own arrest, "All of us are expected to lay some eggs and then be put into the chicken soup." [13]

While this argument was in progress, SHAEF on 18 May directed Maj. Gen. Robert W. Harper to establish a SHAEF control party at the high-level air headquarters (OKL) in Berchtesgaden. He was to get as much intelligence information as possible, impose the will of SHAEF on the high command of the air forces, and close down OKL as an operating force as soon as he could do so without prejudicing Allied interests. Soviet forces were invited to accompany the SHAEF party. Discovering that the air headquarters was a policy staff only and of no value for SHAEF's purposes, General Harper promptly dissolved it. General Dessloch, commander of the *Sixth Air Force* and the senior airman in the area, was appointed to work with the Ninth Air Force in the disarmament and disbandment of the German Air Force, thus paralleling work being done by General Stumpff and his

air headquarters in the north. Toward the end of May the task had been nearly enough completed for General Harper's party to be replaced by a group interested mainly in exploiting the files of the air headquarters.[14]

Disbanding the German Navy

The high command headquarters of the German Navy (OKM) was retained longer by the Allies than either the OKW or OKL headquarters because of the difficulties faced in disbanding the enemy's naval forces.[15] Many of the ships were still at sea when the war ended and had to be brought back to home ports. In addition, the German naval forces had the task of locating and helping to remove mines which had been sowed in European waters.

The task of dealing with the German Navy was handed over by General Eisenhower to the Allied Naval Commander, Admiral Burrough, at the time of the German surrender. The extremely detailed orders for the disarmament and disbandment of the enemy fleet given to Admiral Friedeburg by Admiral Burrough at Reims required the Germans to submit, within forty-eight hours after they received the orders, charts of all minefields in western European waters, information as to German minesweeping activities, and lists

---

[13] Tel, Dessloch to *Army Group G* and others, 15 May 45; Tel, Winter to Jodl, *Nr. 047/45, 20 May 45.* Both in *OKW, Demob. Abt. 10.V.–15.V.45.* Rad, Winter to Jodl, *Nr. 010/45,* 15 May 45; Tel, Winter to *OB WEST, Nr. 09/45,* 15 May 45. Both in *OKW, Sued-Fuehrungsabt. 28.IV.–23.V.45.* Rad, Jodl to *OB SUED,* 20 May 45. *OKW, Nach der Kapitulation, Chef OKW, WFSt., Grossadm. Doenitz 4.–23.V.45.*

[14] Dir, SHAEF to Gen Harper, 19 May 45, SHAEF G-3 387–10 OKW South; SHAEF Fwd to Comds, FWD 22735, 30 May 45, SHAEF SGS 322 OKW, Organization and Personnel OKW–OKM–OKH.

[15] OKH had disappeared before the war's end.

of minesweeping vessels available. Within fourteen days, the enemy was to furnish the location of all ships and craft, locations of all naval establishments, the approximate number and the location of naval personnel, lists of stocks of fuel and locations of the principal naval depots, full details of all German minefields in the northern waters, full details of the enemy minesweeping organization, and copies of all coding and ciphering systems.[16]

While the Navy was compiling these various lists, Doenitz was instructed to order all enemy ships and craft at sea to report their positions to the nearest Allied wireless telegraph station and to proceed to the nearest German, Allied, or other port selected by the Allies. He was also to forbid the scuttling or damaging of any naval ship or naval aircraft and the damaging of any harbor works or port facilities. Minesweeping and salvaging vessels were to be prepared to begin work at once. Doenitz and OKM promptly began to comply with these demands.[17]

To see that his orders were carried out, Admiral Burrough appointed Rear Adm. H. T. Baillie-Grohman as commander of the naval forces east of the Elbe to the Soviet zone, and Rear Adm. G. C. Muirhead-Gould as commander of the forces west of the Elbe and in Hamburg. On 16 May, the Allied Naval Commander appointed Capt. G. O. Maund, RN, as his representative in charge of the naval element at OKW and OKM. Maund was later succeeded by Capt. E. Hale, RN.[18]

The Allied naval parties moved rapidly to collect intelligence from German records which might have a vital bearing on the war against Japan, and pressed activities to open the sea routes to the north German ports. In gathering information, the Allied Naval Commander relied heavily on British and U.S. intelligence and technical parties which had been exploiting records uncovered during the past several months as the enemy had been forced back. As for clearance of the sea routes, the minesweeping that had begun in the North Sea before surrender was steadily increased. Urgent traffic was first admitted to Hamburg on 9 May, and by mid-May Bremerhaven, Emden, and Kiel (via the canal) were open to urgent traffic. Normal traffic began to flow to Hamburg and Kiel (via the canal) on 1 June and to Bremerhaven by the middle of that month.[19]

The Allied Naval Commander, while anxious to use OKM as long as it could be of aid, arranged in late May to start closing it out. By the end of June it was possible to make plans for its termination. Orders were issued on 12 July to dissolve it and to form a new organization, known as the German Minesweeping Administration, which was to supervise the clearance of sea lanes. Under the control of the British Naval Commander in Chief, Germany, the new organization came into existence on 21 July 1945.[20]

---

[16] Photostat, Instr, Burrough to Friedeburg, at Reims, 8 May 45, SHAEF SGS 387/1 Germany, Policy and Incidents of Local German Surrenders, I.

[17] Instr, Burrough to Friedeburg, 7 May 45; ANCXF Main to Admiralty and C-in-C East Indies, 12 May 45. Both in SHAEF SGS 387.4–4 SHAEF 21542/2 Surrender Orders GCT.

[18] Rpt, Admiral Burrough to SAC, The Final Stages of the Naval War in North-West Europe, 13 Jul 45, OCMH files. Muirhead-Gould was in charge of the party which landed at Helgoland on 11 May and took its surrender.

[19] Rpt, Admiral Burrough to SAC, 13 Jul 45, OCMH.

[20] ANCXF to Capt Maund, OKM, 29 May 45, SHAEF SGS 322 OKW, OKW–OKM–OKH. Admiral Burrough in his report says that this message was handed to Maund on 6 June. ANCXF Main to SHAEF Main, 12 Jul 45, SHAEF SGS 322 OKW, Organization and Personnel OKW–OKM–OKH.

The Final German Surrenders

While the main headquarters were being dissolved and naval ships and craft were being brought into port for surrender, the Allied army groups and tactical air forces were busy completing the disarmament of the enemy air and ground forces. Their task, as opposed to the Navy's, was greatly simplified because most of the air and land personnel and the bulk of the equipment had been surrendered or overrun before the signing at Reims. The SHAEF control parties in the north and south attempted to get lists of personnel and commanders and locations of units from the German high command, but they frequently found that the Allied commanders were much better informed about the enemy order of battle than the Germans.

The chief German units which had not been overwhelmed in battle in the zone of the Supreme Commander by 7 May were those in the Channel Islands, Dunkerque, the western Netherlands, the fortresses of the French Atlantic coast, and those in Denmark, Norway, and Czechoslovakia. Except in Norway, the tasks of disarming these units were completed by the time SHAEF was dissolved.

Early Capitulations in Western Europe

In compliance with Allied demands presented to General Jodl at Reims, German garrisons in the Channel Islands and the ports along the French coast held themselves in readiness to capitulate to Allied representatives. Enemy forces in the Bordeaux area and along the coast directly to the north had been in the process of surrendering to French units since mid-April. Royan had surrendered on 18 April,

Ile d'Oléron on 1 May, and La Rochelle, which had virtually been taken on 4 May, made its formal capitulation on 9 May. German forces still held Lorient, St. Nazaire, the Channel Islands, and Dunkerque.

Negotiations for the surrender of the Lorient and St. Nazaire area began shortly after the surrender at Reims. Representatives of the commanders of these two garrisons signed surrender terms on 7 and 8 May. General der Artillerie Wilhelm Fahrmbacker formally surrendered the Lorient fortress, the Quiberon peninsula, Ile de Groix and Belle Isle to Maj. Gen. Herman F. Kramer of the 66th U.S. Division on 10 May, and Generalleutnant Hans Junck handed over St. Nazaire the following day.[21]

The Channel Islands, which the Allies had expected to collapse or surrender during 1944–45, still held out at the war's end. Far from surrendering, the garrison of the islands had staged a raid against Granville in early March 1945, startling the U.S. rear echelons and prompting them to ask for infantry protection. Plans for a greater raid scheduled for 7 May were canceled by Jodl and Keitel during the negotiations for the surrender at Reims. On 4 May, SHAEF rescinded arrangements which had been in effect since the previous September for the occupation of the Channel Islands in case of German collapse or surrender (Operation NEST EGG) and gave the task of taking the capitulation to the commander in chief of the British Southern Command. Arrangements were made on 8 May and the for-

---

[21] Copies of the surrender documents may be found in SHAEF SGS 387.4–4 SHAEF 21542/2 Surrender Orders GCT. Details of the surrender may be found in *History of the Fifteenth Army*, p. 39, and Siinto S. Wessman, *66th Division in World War II* (Baton Rouge, La., 1946), pp. 109–40.

mal surrender was signed on board HMS *Bulldog* the following morning by General-major Siegfried Heine. Brigadier A. E. Snow accepted the capitulation on behalf of the Supreme Commander.[22]

Shortly afterward on the same morning, another long-held prize of the Germans—Dunkerque—had given up. The garrison, sealed off by the British advance in early September, had been invested for months by the Czech Independent Armored Brigade Group, which was attached to the 21 Army Group. The one-hundred-square-mile area held by the enemy was reduced in the course of the year and a number of Germans were killed and wounded, but Allied strength was not sufficient to capture the city. Negotiations were opened on the subject of capitulation on 7 May shortly after the signing at Reims. Viceadmiral Friedrich Frisius, commander of the Dunkerque garrison, surrendered formally on the morning of the 9th to Maj. Gen. A. Liska, commander of the Dunkerque forces.[23]

In the western Netherlands, the problem was less one of arranging a formal surrender, which was technically covered by the capitulation of the Germans to Field Marshal Montgomery at Lueneburg Heath on 4 May, than of carrying out the final disarmament and evacuation of the enemy. As a result of the truce that had been in effect in the western Netherlands since 1 May in order to allow the dropping of food supplies for relief of the Dutch population, the enemy forces, unlike those withdrawing across central Germany, were still in prepared defensive positions and were capable of further resistance. To arrange for the orderly disarmament and withdrawal of these elements, Lt. Gen. C. Foulkes of the 1st Canadian Corps met on the afternoon of 5 May with General Blaskowitz, commander of the enemy forces in the Netherlands. Terms of local surrender were signed that day; two days later, elements of the Canadian corps began to occupy the area west of the Grebbe line. Inasmuch as the members of the German army in the Netherlands, the *Twenty-fifth,* had the status of capitulated troops, they were not given the status of prisoners of war nor were their units broken up. Instead the army was kept intact and was made responsible for the maintenance of its move and the building of its own staging camps during the operation. The movement began on 25 May under Canadian supervision and was virtually completed by 12 June 1945.[24]

Czechoslovakia

The chief problem faced in Czechoslovakia was not simply to persuade the Germans there to surrender. It was rather to get them to lay down their arms to the Soviets instead of fighting their way across Bohemia in an attempt to capitulate to the armies of the Western powers. The problem was complicated further by the question of what to do about Prague. Various persons wanted General Eisenhower to enter the city ahead of the Russians, but, although it would have been relatively easy for U.S. forces to move into the

---

[22] General H. Adeline, *La Libération du Sud-ouest* (Algiers, 1948); Msgs by Jodl, 5 May 45, and Keitel, 6 May 45, *Fuehrer Directives,* pp. 230–31; Eisenhower to Southern Comd, CinC Plymouth, and 11 Gp RAF, FWD 20609, 4 May 45, Eisenhower personal file; Rpt, Brig A. E. Snow to C-in-C Southern Comd, with copy of surrender instrument, 11 May 45, SHAEF SGS 387.4-4 SHAEF 21542/2 Surrender Orders GCT.

[23] Hq Line of Communications Periodical Intel Review 1, Dunkerque, 22 May 45, OCMH files.

[24] Brief Historical Outline of the Occupation of N. W. Holland by 1 Canadian Corps, pars. 1–30, OCMH files.

Czech capital, the Red Army wanted this task for itself.

The Supreme Commander's attention was directed to Prague on 5 May when optimistic reports were received at SHAEF saying that Partisan forces had risen against the Germans in that city and that the Czechoslovak flag was flying over the capital. A few hours later, however, German armor converged on the city, and on the following day the Czechoslovaks asked for help. In London a Czechoslovak representative, Minister Hubert Ripka, asked Allied diplomatic representatives and officials of SHAEF for the promptest aid by ground and air forces to stop an enemy advance which was reported to be about twenty miles southwest of the city. In order to be able to give instructions to leaders inside Prague, Ripka asked whether the Third Army, then in Czechoslovakia, had been ordered to advance to the capital. He also asked that forces of his country then operating with the Allied forces be sent to the aid of their beleaguered city. Gen. Stanislav Bosy, recently appointed chief of the Czechoslovak Military Mission, appealed directly to General Patton in an effort to get aid.

By the time a number of Czech appeals were transmitted to Col. Anthony J. D. Biddle of the European Allied Contact Section of SHAEF, the surrender terms at Reims had already been signed. His natural reply was that since hostilities had ceased no action on the matter was required. Later in the day, however, Prime Minister Churchill expressed to General Eisenhower the hope that the Supreme Commander's statements on Allied intentions would not prevent an advance to Prague if forces were available and if they did not meet the Russians before reaching the Czechoslovak capital.[25]

Throughout 7 and 8 May, other urgent requests came from various Czechoslovak representatives, who said that the Germans were committing atrocities in Prague. Minister Ripka appealed personally to Mr. Churchill on 8 May. On being informed of this action, SHAEF representatives, taking the view that the matter was one for the Combined Chiefs of Staff to decide, informed General Bosy that the Czechoslovaks had been correct in approaching Churchill inasmuch as the British Prime Minister had facilities for obtaining U.S. agreement to any changes in current military plans. "I think you can rest assured that if Mr. Churchill feels that something can be done to relieve the tragic situation in Prague, he will already have taken action, and that no good purpose would be served by a direct approach to SHAEF." [26]

SHAEF's policy concerning an advance to Prague was based on the Soviet request of 5 May that the Western forces not move east of the Budějovice–Pilzen–Karlsbad line into Czechoslovakia. Holding fast to this boundary, the Supreme Commander nonetheless kept Moscow informed of reports from Prague in case the Soviet leaders wanted the U.S. forces to continue their advance. Thus on 8 May, when the Czechoslovaks appealed for dive bombers to be sent to the Prague area to stop an

---

[25] Maj V. Pan to Col Biddle, 6 May 45; Memo, Maj Phillips, EACS, for SHAEF, 6 May 45, sub: Request for Help by Prague; Ripka to J. Nicolls, Br Ambassador to Czechoslovakia, 6 May 45; Ripka to Rudolf Schoenfeld, U.S. Minister to Czechoslovakia, 6 May 45. All in SHAEF EACS SH/9 Czechoslovak. Churchill to Eisenhower, 2920, 7 May 45, Eisenhower personal file.

[26] Maj Pan to Biddle, 8 May 45; Ltr to Gen Bosy, 9 May 45 (unsigned but apparently from Colonel McFie to EACS); Note, Nevins to liaison officer, 10 May 45, on transmittal slip of request from Czechoslovak Military Mission of 9 May 1945. All in SHAEF EACS SH/9 Czechoslovak.

enemy attack, SHAEF forwarded the message to the Soviets with the comment that SHAEF was taking no action. Members of the Czechoslovak Military Mission were informed that SHAEF forces, including attached Czech units, had stopped their advance at the request of the USSR and that all appeals for help had been passed on to Moscow.[27]

Meanwhile, the Combined Chiefs of Staff, SHAEF, and the Doenitz government were endeavoring to stop the fighting in Czechoslovakia. The Combined Chiefs, possibly in the desire to remove any Soviet suspicions that the Western powers were permitting the Germans to continue fighting on the Eastern Front, notified the USSR as early as 8 May that Germany had surrendered jointly to the Red Army and the forces under SHAEF and that continuation of hostilities for even an hour after the time set for the cease-fire would be considered an offense against all the Allied forces. If any sizable bodies of troops continued to fight, they would cease to have the status of soldiers. "We do not accept," the Combined Chiefs continued, "that any German forces may continue to fight the Red Army without, in effect, fighting our forces also."[28] To make certain that there was no misunderstanding of his position, General Eisenhower on 10 May ordered Doenitz to take immediate steps "to insure prompt compliance of these commanders to cease fire." To reinforce his action, Eisenhower directed all troops under his command to imprison German soldiers coming from the fighting area and hand them over to the Russians as violators of the Act of Capitulation. U.S. forces were to set up road blocks and to direct retreating Germans into areas forward of the U.S. lines to await capture by the Red Army. The Supreme Commander

stipulated that, in case certain officers— Field Marshal Schoerner for one—were taken, they were to be handed over to the Soviets.[29]

Doenitz' efforts to stop the fighting in Czechoslovakia were complicated by the fact that, before the surrender at Reims, he had ordered his commanders to do everything possible short of violating truce terms to reach the lines of the Western powers. They were to take advantage of every second left them between the signing of terms of surrender and the time the capitulation was to go into effect. Now that it was clear that his scheme could no longer work, Doenitz had to convince his commanders that they should lay down their arms. His task was made the more difficult because the first news of the surrender had reached the German forces in Czechoslovakia from the Prague radio station, which had been captured by the Partisans shortly before the capitulation at Reims. Many of the commanders either tended to believe that the announcement was propaganda or, at least, thought that such an assumption could excuse their failure to surrender. In order to make certain that Field Marshal Schoerner was informed of the capitulation, Doenitz on the evening of 7 May sent a member of his staff, accompanied by a U.S. escort, to

---

[27] Czechoslovak Military Mission to SHAEF, RR–17731, 6 May 45; 12th A Gp to SHAEF, QX–31923, 7 May 45; SHAEF to Mil Mission Moscow, FWD 21001, 8 May 45. All in SHAEF SGS 370.64 Czechoslovakian Resistance Groups. Eisenhower to Mil Mission Moscow, 8 May 45, Eisenhower personal file.

[28] CCS to Mil Mission Moscow, FACS 216, 8 May 45, Eisenhower personal file.

[29] Eisenhower to OKW, 10 May 45; Eisenhower to Mil Mission Moscow, 10 May 45. Both in Eisenhower personal file. *V Corps Operations in the ETO*, p. 458, gives details of the road blocks and the handling of the disarming of the enemy. Field Marshal Schoerner was captured on 18 May and handed over four days later to the Red Army.

find the German commander and instruct him to surrender. Schoerner, who was located near the Silesian border in northeast Czechoslovakia, indicated that he had already attempted to reach his troops with the surrender order, but that he would now go to western Czechoslovakia to seek out his commanders personally and see to it that the capitulation terms were carried out. At this time, there still remained a short period of grace before fighting had to stop and there appeared to be every disposition to continue the withdrawal until the surrender formally went into effect. Schoerner warned that virtually no order would make his troops leave their comrades behind or voluntarily surrender to the Red forces and that it would also be difficult to control them if they were attacked by Czechoslovak Partisans.[30]

By 12 May, Czechoslovak and Soviet troops had entered Prague and the Red Army was pressing westward to link up with the SHAEF forces. General Eisenhower's next consideration was how to move the Czech forces under Western command back to their own country. Czechoslovak units had been organized in the United Kingdom after the fall of France and in 1943 had been placed under British control with the understanding that they would be used against the Germans and ultimately concentrated in Czechoslovakia. In discussing these agreements with officers of SHAEF in February 1944, the Czechoslovak representatives had stressed that it was important for these troops to participate in the liberation of their country. The Czechoslovak brigade that had been given the task of investing Dunkerque in September 1944 was still engaged in that mission when the Allied forces neared the Czechoslovakian border in April 1945. As a result, the Supreme Commander had to postpone shifting it to the 12th Army Group front until after the surrender of Dunkerque on 9 May. He then moved the brigade to the Czechoslovak border, but held up its advance at the Pilzen–Karlsbad line.

When the Czechoslovaks in London pressed for permission to move east of the line, SHAEF proposed that they settle the matter by direct negotiation with the Soviet Government and directed General Bradley to permit the Czechoslovak brigade to move when he was satisfied that the USSR had given its authorization. Units were allowed to go to Prague on 28 May for a liberation parade, but three days later they were returned to the U.S. zone. As late as the first week in July, the Soviets had not yet given their approval. The Czechoslovak Government in Prague thereupon took the position that such assent was not necessary. Air Chief Marshal Tedder, then acting Supreme Commander, indicated that SHAEF had no objections to the move but considered it wise for the government to "formalize their arrangements with the Russians before entry is made." He noted that the shift might be simplified by arrangements which would leave Czechoslovak forces on their own soil when the U.S. forces withdrew from the section west of Pilzen. The shift had still not been made four days

---

[30] German White Book 1945; Copy of Rad, Schoerner to *OKW/WFSt*–Doenitz, 8 May 45, in Msg, Jodl to Friedel for Eisenhower, 8 May 45. *OKW, Kapitulationsverhandlungen 2.V.–11.V.45*; Report of Col Wilhelm Meyer-Detring, OKW officer who was sent by Doenitz to Schoerner, 10 May 45. *OKW, Einsatzabteilung Heer 2.V.–22.V.45*. The broad details of the report are confirmed by *V Corps Operations in the ETO*, p. 454, which is based on the report of Lt. Col. Robert H. Pratt, the V Corps officer who led the escort that accompanied Meyer-Detring during the trip from Pilzen to Prague and Velichovky and back.

later, the last day of SHAEF's existence, although one of the messages sent from that headquarters on 13 July indicated that the Supreme Commander had no objection when the Czechoslovaks requested that their brigade be released from its attachment to the Third Army.[31]

SHAEF's insistence that the officials in Prague come to an agreement with the Soviets may have been prompted to a degree by recent manifestations of a pro-Moscow orientation by the Czechoslovak Government. Nearly a month before the war's end, for example, the U.S. and British Ambassadors to Czechoslovakia, preparing to join that government at Košice, where it was located temporarily, were told that because of inadequate accommodations they could not be received. When it became clear that President Eduard Beneš had held several meetings with the Soviet Ambassador, the Allied diplomats protested to Vice-Premier Jan Masaryk, who promised to look into the situation but left for San Francisco for the United Nations meeting before doing anything to clarify the situation. The month of April also saw the resignation of many of the chief Czechoslovak officials in London, leading SHAEF officials to conclude that a housecleaning aimed at individuals who had been close to the Western Allies was in progress. The chief SHAEF liaison officer with the Czechoslovaks also concluded that SHAEF would meet a number of delays in the future when it tried to deal with the new government. His prediction proved accurate in the case of a SHAEF proposal to arm two Czechoslovak battalions to be used in the U.S. zone. This project, once acceptable to the Czechoslovaks, was allowed to die when SHAEF found that no reply on the subject would be received from the govern-

ment in Košice.[32] There was thus a lack of close liaison with the government at Kosice when the war ended.

By mid-June, however, there was evidence that the Beneš government, which by then was established in Prague, was somewhat worried about the continued presence of Soviet troops on Czechoslovak soil. Beneš was reported to want both U.S. and Soviet forces to leave the country. He was said, however, to desire that U.S. forces remain for the moment and that they synchronize their eventual withdrawal with that of the Soviets. The War Department, faced with problems of redeployment, the occupation of Germany, and an offensive against the Japanese, wanted to withdraw as quickly as possible regardless of Soviet action, but the State Department was reported to favor holding the current line until the Red Army forces began to pull out. In response to the War Department's request for his opinion, General Eisenhower declared in mid-June that "if Czechoslovak independence is to be maintained it seems undesirable that Russia be left in sole occupation. Moreover, our withdrawal now might hamper Czechoslovak efforts to secure early Russian withdrawal." On 4 July, the U.S. Chiefs of Staff decided to withdraw their forces simultaneously with and in propor-

---

[31] Brief for mtg with Czechoslovak military authorities, 16 Feb 44; Memo, Col McFie for Gen Morgan, 16 Feb 44; SHAEF to EACS for Czechoslovak Military Mission and 12th A Gp, FWD 21298, 12 May 45; SHAEF to 12th A Gp, FWD 22079, 21 May 45; SHAEF to Air Ministry, FWD 22587, 29 May 45; Air Ministry to SHAEF, AX–741, 7 Jul 45; SHAEF to U.S. Military Attaché, Czechoslovakia, for United States Ambassador, S–96228, 9 Jul 45; SHAEF (sgd Tedder) to Air Ministry, S–96640, 11 Jul 45. All in SHAEF SGS 091 Czechoslovakia Misc, I; Eisenhower to Military Attaché, U.S. Embassy, Prague, S–97316, 13 Jul 45, SHAEF G–3 370–62 Czechoslovakia.
[32] Memo, Biddle for Bull, 4 May 45, SHAEF EACS SH/9 Czechoslovak.

tion to the forces taken out by the Red Army. On the basis of an estimate that the initial Soviet contingents had been reduced two-thirds, General Eisenhower was told to withdraw a similar percentage of his forces.[33]

Disarming the Enemy in Denmark and Norway

The disbandment of enemy forces in Denmark and Norway differed in several particulars from similar efforts in other countries occupied by the Germans. For one thing, the forces had not been defeated in the field and were inclined to demand special treatment. For another, the large number of German wounded and refugees and non-German displaced persons threw a heavy burden on the occupied countries and the Allied units responsible for evacuating them. Moreover, the enemy forces in the two countries greatly outnumbered the Allied contingents sent to those areas. In both Denmark and Norway, the SHAEF representatives had difficulties with Soviet authorities. The task of disarming the Germans in the two countries was entrusted by the Supreme Commander to SHAEF missions which had been established in 1944 and to which forces had been attached in case of German collapse or surrender. The mission to Denmark had virtually completed its job at the time of the dissolution of SHAEF, but the mission to Norway did not wind up its affairs until the fall of 1945.

SHAEF Mission Denmark

Maj. Gen. Richard H. Dewing, head of the SHAEF mission to Denmark,[34] accompanied by his staff and a parachute company, flew to Copenhagen on 5 May

1945, shortly after the German surrender at Lueneburg, and issued orders to govern the evacuation of enemy forces from that country. He informed a representative of General Lindemann, commander in chief of German armed forces in Denmark, that he was to march his units back to the Reich under their own officers and with their usual weapons. Hungarian and Soviet troops who had served with the Germans were to march out with them. Hospitals, their patients, and staffs were to be allowed to remain for a time. General Lindemann was directed to arrest SD and Gestapo members in Denmark and send lists of them to the British.[35] Dewing forbade ships lying off Copenhagen with German soldiers and refugees to land and denied the use of Danish ports to ships that were in the process of evacuating troops from Kurland and East Prussia, but he promised to seek further orders on the matter.[36]

To handle German effectives, estimated at some 206,000, plus 80,000 sick and wounded and 48,000 soldiers and refugees in Danish ports or off Copenhagen, General Dewing had his original parachute company plus the 1 Royal Dragoons and a parachute battalion. These were aug-

---

[33] Murphy to Smith, 17 May 45; AGWAR to SHAEF Fwd, W–16162, 13 Jun 45; Memo, Bull for CofS, 16 Jun 45; Eisenhower to Marshall, S–91011, 16 Jun 45; JCS to Eisenhower, W–26489, 4 Jul 45; Memo, Bull for CofS, 6 Jul 45. All in SHAEF G–3 370–62 Czechoslovakia.

[34] Col. Ford Trimble was deputy head of the mission.

[35] SD—*Sicherheitsdienst des Reichsfuehrers SS,* the Party Security Service; Gestapo–*Geheime Staatspolizei,* the Secret State Police.

[36] Rpt 15, Dewing to SHAEF, 14 May 45, SHAEF Mission (Denmark) file; Report of Generalmajor Hellmuth Reinhardt on talk with Gen Fewing [Dewing], 5 May 45. *OKW, Befehle 13.IV.–20.V.45,* 6 May 45. For Montgomery's earlier orders concerning Denmark, see Msg, Kinzel to OKW, 5 May 45. *OKW, Kapitulationsverhandlungen 2.V.–11.V.45.*

mented by 6,000–9,000 Danish police. The number of Germans was increased shortly after the surrender at Reims when General Dewing ruled that wounded aboard the ships that had come from Kurland to Copenhagen could be unloaded there.[37]

A problem that concerned General Dewing indirectly was the disarming of Germans on the Danish island of Bornholm. Although the island was well east of the general line to be occupied by the Soviets, it was surrendered with other Danish territory to Field Marshal Montgomery on 4 May. Aware of this, OKW on 8 May ordered its forces on the island to oppose a Soviet landing before the formal surrender went into effect. The 21 Army Group proposed sending an Allied detachment to the island, but before this step could be taken the Red forces had acted. SHAEF ruled that, while the island was clearly included in the surrender to the 21 Army Group, it was also covered by the over-all capitulations at Reims and Berlin.[38] The Danes complained later in the year when the Soviet troops lingered after the Germans were evacuated from the island, but the Red Army forces did not finally withdraw until the spring of 1946.

The main difficulties in evacuating the enemy forces from Denmark arose when Danish resistance forces attempted to disarm the Germans. Already touchy on the subject of being disarmed though they had not been defeated in the field, the enemy commanders protested frequently that they had not surrendered to the Danes. In spite of British assurance that these incidents would not be repeated, enemy representatives concluded that it would probably be impossible to prevent the Danes from playing cowboys and Indians (*"Indianerspieler"*).[39] These troubles notwithstanding, the withdrawal of German forces proceeded rapidly. Some 43,000 had left the country by the end of the first week of liberation, and the number had nearly doubled at the end of the second week. By the close of the first week of June, General Dewing concluded that he could dispense with the services of General Lindemann and ordered his arrest. Fewer than 50,000 Germans remained in Denmark when SHAEF was dissolved. Since the task of the SHAEF mission was not finally completed, it was divided into its British and U.S. components with the troops in the country remaining under the British commander.[40]

The SHAEF Mission in Norway

Disarming German forces in Norway required much more elaborate planning and more extensive activities than in Denmark because of the extent of the country, the difficulty of access to parts of it, and the size of the forces involved. Spread out through Norway was a force of some 400,000 Germans, including Organization

---

[37] Rpt 15, Dewing to SHAEF, 14 May 45, SHAEF Mission (Denmark) file. German estimates made to OKW on 5 May 1945 show 230,000 armed forces, police, Organization Todt personnel (60,000 wounded), and 207,000 refugees. *OKW, Befehle 13.IV.–20.V.45.* The number of refugees, increased by the arrival of ships after the surrender, was finally estimated at 300,000.

[38] Tel, *OKW/WFSt/Op (M)* to OKM and others, 8 May 45; Rad, *OKW/WFSt/Op (M)* to Commander of Bornholm, 10 May 45; Note on Bornholm incident, *Vorfaelle Bornholm,* 10 May 45; Rad, Jodl to Commander of Bornholm, 11 May 45. All in *OKW, Befehle 13.IV.–20.V.45.*

[39] Note for the record in *WFSt/Op (H)* files (report by Lt Col Konrad Benze), 9 May 45. *OKW, Befehle 13.IV.–20.V.45.*

[40] Rpt 18, Dewing to SHAEF, SHAEF Mission (Denmark) file.

Todt workers, plus 90,000 Russian prisoners and displaced persons as well as some 30,000 displaced persons of other nationalities. These forces under General der Gebirgstruppen Franz Boehme, commander of the *Twentieth Mountain Army* and of the German armed forces in Norway, like those in Denmark, had not been defeated and were disinclined to surrender unless proper deference was paid to their dignity.[41]

The task of clearing the Germans from Norway was undertaken at General Eisenhower's direction by the SHAEF Mission (Norway) headed by Gen. Sir Andrew Thorne.[42] This officer, who had held the Scottish Command at Edinburgh since 1941 and who had been named commander of the Allied Land Forces (Norway) in 1944, was also asked to serve as head of the SHAEF mission late in 1944. Since the fall of 1943, he had been engaged in detailed planning for a return to Norway in case of German collapse or surrender. When the Germans surrendered at Reims, they were instructed to send Army representatives to Edinburgh to sign final surrender papers pertaining to their forces in Norway and were also told to expect the arrival of General Thorne's representatives shortly in Oslo.[43]

Representatives of General Thorne flew to Norway on 8 May to deliver his orders to General Boehme. During the next three days, airborne forces were flown in to aid the mission in its task of evacuating the Germans. British destroyers then entered all of the ports of entry, bringing naval and military disarmament parties, and pushed into northern waters when the Soviets seemed unduly interested there. The Allied forces were augmented at the beginning of June by a reinforced U.S. regiment. At most, fewer than 40,000

Allied troops were brought in to deal with some 400,000 Germans.[44]

During his stay in Norway, General Thorne found that some of his chief problems included persuading the Soviets to accept back into their occupation zone Germans from that area, handling Yugoslav displaced persons, and evacuating Russian displaced persons. The Norwegians, furthermore, resented the destruction of armaments in their country, an understandable reaction, but General Thorne felt that he was permitted no discretion by the Combined Chiefs of Staff directive on the subject. In the case of both Yugoslav and Russian displaced persons, trouble arose when some of them expressed unwillingness to return home and the SHAEF representatives refused to force them to do so. Relations with the Soviets were worsened when General Thorne commuted the death sentence of

---

[41] These forces were variously estimated. General Boehme spoke at one time of 500,000 Germans who would have no more rights when they were disarmed. Tel, Boehme to *OKW/WFSt*, 10 May 45. *OKW, Befehle 13.IV.–20.V.45.* General Thorne at one time spoke of 415,000 Germans including the Todt workers and at another time of nearly 400,000. Text of farewell press conf, 30 Oct 45; Hq Allied Land Forces (Norway) AAR, 1944–45. Both from Gen Thorne's file, now in OCMH files.

[42] Col. Charles H. Wilson was deputy head of the mission.

[43] For plans, see documents in SHAEF G–3 files under the code names RANKIN Case C (Norway), APOSTLE I, APOSTLE II, and ALADDIN. On the appointment of General Thorne as head of the SHAEF Mission, see Morgan to Thorne, 3 Nov 44; Thorne to Morgan, 11 Nov 44; Dir, SAC to Gen Thorne, 31 Dec 44. All in SHAEF SGS 322.01.10 SHAEF Mission (Norway). For orders to German commanders, see Keitel to General Boehme, commander of *Twentieth Mountain Army*, 7 May 45. *OKW, Befehle 13.IV.–20.V.45;* SCOFOR to G–3 SHAEF Fwd, DA 5, 12 May 45, SHAEF SGS 387.1 Germany, II.

[44] Fortnightly Rpt 8, SHAEF Mission (Norway), for fortnight ending 26 May 45, SHAEF Mission (Norway) file; SHAEF Mission (Norway) AAR, OCMH files.

a German officer who had killed a citizen of the USSR.[45]

Initial emphasis was placed by the SHAEF mission on evacuating Allied prisoners of war and Soviet displaced persons. In agreement with the Swedish Government, this movement was carried on through Sweden to Soviet ports on the Baltic. Before SHAEF was dissolved, some 42,000 Russians had been moved from the country while a similar number still remained. The task of taking enemy forces out of the country had scarcely been begun in mid-July when SHAEF's control came to an end and the SHAEF mission was split into separate U.S. and British components, with General Thorne continuing as commander in chief of Allied Land Forces (Norway).[46]

Closing Out Supreme Headquarters

It will be recalled that the Combined Chiefs of Staff had not accepted General Eisenhower's proposal of 1944 for retaining a combined headquarters for the occupation of western Germany. It was clear by the time of the German surrender, therefore, that Supreme Headquarters would soon cease to exist. General Eisenhower proposed, however, on 10 May, that his headquarters remain in existence until all organized resistance had ceased in Europe, the Allied forces were established in their zones of occupation, and the machinery was established to assume the functions of the separate national units in western Germany.[47] Meanwhile he ordered his staff to make plans for the termination of SHAEF and defined the duties of the occupying forces so as to reduce the amount of time needed to fulfill the conditions noted on 10 May.

He reminded the army group commanders on 11 May that they were not to assume the responsibilities of government but rather to establish control over the remaining German authority in order to insure that the government would be carried on according to the Allied will and that Nazis would be excluded from power. He directed the commanders to activate military government regional teams at once. These teams were to re-establish the German administrative machinery at a regional level to handle such immediate problems as the distribution of food, the effective use of available transport, and the reconstitution of enough industrial facilities to meet military needs and provide minimum essential civil requirements in Germany. The German administrative machinery, said the Supreme Commander, was so to be arranged that it could be separated when the armies withdrew to their various spheres of occupation. The army group commanders were to make their military boundaries conform as fully as possible to the regional administrative boundaries for military government. Insofar as military security permitted, restrictions on interarea travel and communications were to be removed.[48]

In a series of moves, whose story belongs to the opening chapter of military government in Germany rather than to the con-

---

[45] Hq Allied Land Forces (Norway) AAR, OCMH; Interv with Gen Thorne, 28 Jan 47.

[46] Rpt 11, SHAEF Mission (Norway), SHAEF Mission (Norway) file. Hq Allied Land Forces (Norway) AAR; Text of farewell press conf, 30 Oct 45; Rpts 7–16, Gen Thorne to Field Marshal Brooke. All in OCMH files.

[47] Eisenhower to CCS, SCAF 382, 10 May 45, SHAEF G–3 Ops C GCT 387–21 Termination of Combined Command.

[48] See SHAEF G–3 Ops C GCT 387–21 Termination of Combined Command.

VICTORY SPEECH *being delivered by General Eisenhower at the conclusion of hostilities. Air Chief Marshal Tedder is shown at right.*

cluding phase of SHAEF,[49] the Allied commanders started the governmental machinery functioning again in their various areas. Following a pattern which had been laid down when the first Allied forces reached German soil west of the Rhine in the fall of 1944, they installed under military control and supervision the administrative organization necessary to keep order, start the flow of foodstuffs to the civilian population, reopen means of communications, and provide military security. At the same time they suspended Nazi executive, legislative, and judicial machinery, and seized influential Nazi leaders and their records. These actions were intended merely as groundwork for the Allied military government activities that were to go into effect on the dissolution of SHAEF. With matters left largely to the separate armies, some of which would be likely to remain in occupation as the enforcement agencies of military govern-

ment, there was some assurance that no important change-over would have to be made.

General Eisenhower was relieved of his responsibilities for disbanding and disarming enemy forces in western Europe on 5 June when the commanders of the U.S., British, Soviet, and French forces in Europe, meeting in Berlin as the Allied Control Council, assumed control of Germany in the names of their governments. Thereafter, the SHAEF staff concentrated on the task of shifting to unilateral control those functions which had been conducted at Supreme Headquarters on a combined basis. These included activities of dozens of combined committees and commissions dealing with such matters as fuel, transportation, equipment of troops in liberated countries, civil affairs, displaced

---

[49] See the volumes on civil affairs and military government in preparation for the UNITED STATES ARMY IN WORLD WAR II series.

I. G. FARBENINDUSTRIE BUILDING *in Frankfurt-am-Main, Germany.*

persons, war criminals, psychological warfare, censorship, intelligence, communications, and prisoners of war. Further, the staff had the tasks of separating the U.S. and British components of the SHAEF missions in France, Belgium, the Netherlands, Denmark, and Norway without interfering with their work, and of making certain that combined agreements with the liberated countries would still apply after the change to national control.

While the Supreme Commander and many members of his staff were preparing to dissolve the combined headquarters, outlining the work of occupation authorities, and putting in appearances at victory celebrations, Supreme Headquarters moved from Reims and Versailles to the I. G. Farbenindustrie building in Frankfurt am Main, Germany. Shortly afterward, numerous new international organizations founded to deal with postwar problems began to pour their representatives into

Frankfurt and near-by cities, and the U.S. contingent of SHAEF was augmented in preparation for the day when it would become Headquarters, U.S. Forces in the European Theater (USFET). The Allied compound in Frankfurt took on a boomtown appearance as the number of personnel assigned or attached to SHAEF passed the 16,000 mark, and the addition of air, naval, UNRRA, special missions, military government, and other agencies swelled the total to 30,000 military or civilian personnel associated with Supreme Headquarters.[50]

Throughout western Europe, the redeployment of U.S. and Allied forces was under way, and units only recently in the line were made ready to return home for discharge or shipment to the Far Eastern theater of the war. Elsewhere, special Allied security parties were rounding up

---

[50] See below, Appendix B, on size of headquarters.

members of the German General Staff, German commanders, Nazi leaders, suspected war criminals, scientists with special knowledge of German weapons, and the like and bringing them to western Europe for interrogation. Along the Elbe, the Western powers prepared to move back into their own zones as soon as final arrangements could be reached with the USSR. Civil affairs agencies were restoring the local committees to order, stamping out potential sources of trouble, completing disarmament of troops, caring for displaced persons, and starting up the economic and administrative machinery of Germany.

Amidst all this bustle, there was also a certain festive air as passes for soldiers became more plentiful and as recreational and educational centers were set up for soldiers confronted with months of waiting before their return home. From the United States, the United Kingdom, and many other parts of the world, a steadily increasing number of notables and experts flocked to Paris and Frankfurt to have a look at the wreckage of Hitler's Reich and to suggest measures for the future. For the moment, past dreads were forgotten and some hope was entertained for an era of peace, although there were indications that the Soviets would be difficult to deal with. The reserved attitude which the USSR had maintained toward the Western powers in such matters as liaison and the drawing of lines of demarcation had become tinged with suspicion during the surrender negotiations.

On 29 June, the Combined Chiefs of Staff took steps leading directly to the termination of Supreme Headquarters as they ordered the Supreme Commander to begin withdrawing U.S. and British troops from the Soviet zone on 1 July. They also

directed him to send British and U.S. garrisons and a French token force to Berlin. Air Chief Marshal Tedder, now acting Supreme Commander, was also asked to outline steps to terminate SHAEF on 1 July or as soon thereafter as practicable. In preparation for the dissolution of the combined command, the U.S. Chiefs of Staff named General Eisenhower commanding general of U.S. Forces in the European Theater, commander in chief of U.S. Forces of Occupation in Germany, and representative of the United States on the Allied Control Council of Germany. The British named Field Marshal Montgomery as their representative on the council, and his army group became the British Army of the Rhine. General Koenig was appointed chief of the French occupation forces and representative of France in Berlin, while Marshal Zhukov filled a similar post for the Soviets.[51]

Plans for separating British and U.S. elements of Supreme Headquarters were announced on 6 July. Air Chief Marshal Tedder at that time transferred all U.S. units under SHAEF and the U.S. elements of ANCXF and the SHAEF missions to the Commanding General, USFET, the 21 Army Group and its naval and air elements to the control of the War Office, Admiralty, or Air Ministry, and the First French Army to the direct control of the French high command. U.S. members of SHAEF became the staff of the new Headquarters, USFET, and remained in the I. G. Farbenindustrie building in Frankfurt. The British elements were transferred to Headquarters, British Army of the Rhine. The various national

---

[51] CCS to SHAEF, FACS 253, 29 Jun 45, SHAEF G–3 Ops A GCT 322–2 Dissolution and Disbandment of SHAEF and SHAEF Divs.

missions accredited to SHAEF were instructed to terminate their relationship with Supreme Headquarters and to make separate accreditations to the British, U.S. and French commands. To speed the dissolution of any joint or combined machinery which could not be transferred to British and U.S. agencies, a Combined Administrative Liquidating Agency under General Gale was established. Its Documents Section, established at Headquarters, USFET, was given the special task of collecting, cataloguing, screening, and microfilming all documents belonging to Supreme Headquarters.[52]

Final disbandment of the headquarters was delayed at the request of General Eisenhower until he could return from the United States to bid farewell to the members of his staff. On 13 July, shortly after his return, he asked them to assemble in the Kasino of the I. G. Farbenindustrie building where he expressed his appreciation for their work. The headquarters was formally dissolved at 0001, 14 July.[53]

In recognition of the work of the Allied Expeditionary Force, the Supreme Commander issued this final Order of the Day:[54]

On this occasion, the termination of Combined Command, I welcome the opportunity to express my gratitude and admiration to the people of the Allied Nations in Europe whose fiighting forces and nationals have contributed so effectively to victory.

United in a common cause, the men and women of Belgium, Czechoslovakia, Denmark, France, Luxembourg, Netherlands and Norway joined with the British Commonwealth of Nations and the United States of America to form a truly Allied team, which in conjunction with the mighty Red Army smashed and obliterated the Nazi aggressors. I pay tribute to every individual who gave so freely and unselfishly to the limit of his or her ability. Their achievements in the cause for which they fought will be indelibly inscribed in the pages of history and cherished in the hearts of all freedom-loving people.

It is my fervent hope and prayer that the unparalleled unity which has been achieved among the Allied Nations in war will be a source of inspiration for, and point the way to, a permanent and lasting peace.

DWIGHT D. EISENHOWER.

---

[52] SHAEF to all comds, SCAF 474, 6 Jul 45, SHAEF G–3 Ops A GCT 322–3 Dissolution and Disbandment of SHAEF and SHAEF Divs. SHAEF SGS 320.3 War Establishment CALA.

[53] Eisenhower to all comds, SCAF 478, SHAEF G–3 Ops A GCT 322–3 Dissolution and Disbandment of SHAEF and SHAEF Divs.

[54] General Eisenhower's Orders of the Day are reproduced below, Appendix F.

Shoulder Sleeve Insignia
Supreme Headquarters
Allied Expeditionary Force

Upon a field of heraldic sable (BLACK), representing the darkness of Nazi oppression, is shown the sword of liberation in the form of a crusader's sword, the flames arising from the hilt and leaping up the blade. This represents avenging justice by which the enemy power will be broken in Nazi-dominated Europe. Above the sword is a rainbow emblematic of hope containing all the colors of which the National Flags of the Allies are composed.

The heraldic chief of azure (BLUE) above the rainbow is emblematic of a state of peace and tranquillity the restoration of which to the enslaved people is the objective of the United Nations.

Appendix A

SHAEF and the Press, June 1944–May 1945

The story of public relations in the European Theater of Operations, 1944–45, is that of an attempt by SHAEF and its subordinate headquarters to keep the public informed of operational developments without compromising the security of operations. A brief summary of SHAEF's efforts in that direction makes clear the difficulties confronting any agency which tries to reconcile these opposing interests.

To inform the Allied peoples of the D-Day landing, SHAEF began preparations weeks in advance to facilitate maximum coverage of the story. Col. Joseph B. Phillips and Col. (later Brig. Gen.) David Sarnoff installed special communications for the rapid transmission of news from northern France. In addition, the Press Signal Center was established at the Ministry of Information in London with direct teleprinter circuits to SHAEF (Main) and the air, ground, and naval advance headquarters. Teletype and radio links from London to Washington permitted quick transmission to the War Department. Before D Day, correspondents were permitted to file "color" stories which were censored and ready for transmission when the assault began. Early on 6 June, newsmen met at Macmillan Hall, University of London, where they were locked in the Press Room and furnished maps and background material on the attack. At 0830 Col. R. Ernest Dupuy, an American member of the SHAEF Public Relations Division (PRD), read the brief official communiqué which had been written several days previously and carefully censored to prevent the enemy from learning anything of the Allies' future plans. The correspondents then wrote their stories, had them censored, and were ready to send their copy when G–3 flashed the code word TOPFLIGHT which was the signal for release of information. Teams of censors at the Ministry of Information, at the beachhead, and on naval assault craft passed more than 700,000 words on D Day.[1]

Naturally, in the initial period of the invasion, the press coverage of D Day could not be maintained. Like everything else in the beachhead, press communications were limited and many newsmen were unable to file all their copy for transmission to the United States and the United Kingdom. The opening of new transmitters in late June and early July improved the situation, but the breakthrough and rapid pursuit which followed

[1] SHAEF PRD, Communications Section History; SHAEF PRD Press Censorship History; SHAEF Signals Division History.

put additional burdens on SHAEF, the army groups, and the armies, with the result that not until the Allies reached Paris were sufficient facilities available to meet the need of correspondents in the field.

Besides attempting to equalize opportunities for transmitting copy dealing with the various armies in Normandy, SHAEF also took steps during the first week of the invasion to avoid invidious comparisons between national armies. On 13 June, the authors of SHAEF communiqués were informed that the Supreme Commander desired "that in the future references to American and British troops, as such, be held to the very minimum and the term 'Allied troops' be used instead." As an example, they were told that a previous reference to "American" troops liberating Carentan should have read "Allied." Thus, in August, on the eve of the drive to Paris, Colonel Dupuy warned General Smith that unless the approaching American breakout was summarized and depicted as part of an integrated assault, "the importance of the British-Canadian offensive in its zone may be minimized, with resultant embarrassment to Anglo-American relations, as well as distortion of the over-all picture." He urged the chief of staff to give an interview which would put the contributions of the various armies into the proper perspective.[2]

Holding the view that democratic peoples must be told as much as possible concerning the accomplishments of their armies, the Supreme Commander went as far as he could, consistent with security, toward announcing full details of his forces' activities. He attempted to maintain the same policy for both British and U.S. armies, but found that the War Office was more conservative than the War Department in releasing names of units and com-

manding officers. In mid-July, he notified Montgomery that so far as U.S. units were concerned SHAEF would follow War Department practice.[3] He acceded, however, to a British request that senior British officers be reminded that they were not adhering to a directive of 7 February 1944 regarding interviews. This forbade statements on policy and future conduct of the war without approval of the British Government, and required senior officers to get approval of the service department concerned before granting interviews.[4]

Despite curbs on interviews by senior officers, the way was left open for frank comments in the form of "off-the-record" statements which were not attributable to the commander concerned. These were used, in particular, for guidance to correspondents on matters which had to be kept secret but on which they wished to be able to comment intelligently once the ban of secrecy was removed. The device was also exceedingly valuable in dealing with questions of military policy which might otherwise be misunderstood. In the latter case, an interesting example was shown in the handling of reports on the reception given Allied troops in Normandy by the French. After the enthusiasm of the first week of the invasion had passed, correspondents began to report stories of French unfriendliness. Evidence of well-filled shops in Bayeux was interpreted as meaning that the French had prospered under German rule. French citizens were

---

[2] Memo, SGS (for Gen Eisenhower) for G–3, 13 Jun 44; Col Dupuy to CofS SHAEF, 13 Aug 44. Both in SHAEF SGS 000.7, Policy re Release of Info to the Press, II.
[3] Eisenhower to Montgomery, 17 Jul 44, Eisenhower personal file.
[4] British COS to Eisenhower, COS(44) 237, 15 Jul 44, SHAEF SGS 000.7, Policy re Release of Info to the Press, I.

charged with sniping at Allied troops and giving aid to German troops. General Eisenhower found it necessary in late June to issue a special press release declaring that investigation had shown "no authenticated use of French civilian snipers." He emphasized on the contrary that French Resistance had been "a great contribution in support of Allied operations."

General Koenig, aroused at what he considered a campaign in the British press to underline unfriendly gestures on the part of the French, wrote to ask the Supreme Commander for information of such incidents. Before the letter arrived, General Smith had called a meeting of the Public Relations Council of SHAEF, which included representatives of SHAEF, ETOUSA, the Department of State, the Foreign Office, and the British and U.S. information agencies, to consider press trends regarding the French. This meeting led to other conferences with the newsmen in which they were given detailed information on the situation in Normandy and fuller details on the constructive contributions of the French to the Allied advance. By the beginning of July, General McClure of the Psychological Warfare Division was able to report a changed tone in newspaper accounts of the situation in France.[5]

Unfavorable reactions from the Allied governments to certain types of stories were responsible for changes in SHAEF censorship rules during the early weeks of invasion. The public relations director was reminded officially of Mr. Churchill's earlier reaction to reports of the chivalrous treatment by Germans of U.S. wounded. The Prime Minister had felt that, since for one good deed they committed four hundred bad ones, there was no need of singling out the unique experience for

publicity. Foreign Secretary Anthony Eden, equally certain of the need of curbing statements which might invite reprisals, pleaded for a stop to statements such as the one in which a U.S. officer was quoted as saying that Allied paratroopers did not take prisoners.

A strong official protest was made by the Soviet Embassy to the State Department in mid-July concerning a statement, attributed to SHAEF, which reflected on the fighting qualities of Russian troops in the German Army in Normandy. The Russian chargé described the remark as one "defaming the Soviet people and casting a shade on Soviet citizens in military service who found themselves in German captivity." After extensive correspondence between the War and State Departments and SHAEF, General Eisenhower denied that SHAEF officials had made any remarks on the subject to the Allied press. He agreed that statements similar to the ones mentioned had been included in dispatches filed by reputable correspondents, and that these had been passed by the SHAEF censors since no security question was involved. The War Department passed on this answer to the State Department, expressing its willingness to look further into the matter if such action was desired. One of the chief effects of this exchange of correspondence seems to have been the issuance of a memorandum by Headquarters, USSTAF, warning U.S. Strategic Air Forces in Europe of the danger of statements offensive to the Soviets which might be made to correspondents by airmen returning from Soviet

---

[5] Public Relations Council Mtg, at WIDEWING, 21 Jun 44; SHAEF Press Release 46, 26 Jun 44; Koenig to Smith, 30 Jun 44; Smith to Koenig, 7 Jul 44. All in SHAEF SGS 000.7, Policy re Release of Info to the Press, I.

bases, and directing that all officers and men be impressed with the fact "that they are to say nothing critical of the Russians which might endanger our present relations with them." While the War Department apparently took no similar action, Lt. Gen. Joseph T. McNarney, Deputy Chief of Staff, regretted that Allied press representatives had not seen fit "voluntarily to limit their news dispatches, so as to avoid causing resentment on the part of the Government of a nation that is contributing so greatly to the defeat of the common enemy." [6]

With the liberation of Paris, the SHAEF Public Relations Division entered a new phase. Until that time, the number of correspondents permitted on the Continent had been limited, and a rotation system had been imposed on all correspondents except those from news agencies and major independent newspapers. Correspondents were subject to recall to the United Kingdom after thirty days in the combat zone. The main offices of the PRD remained in London during this period with the result that it was somewhat out of touch with the situation on the Continent. In late August the division was able to get General Smith to withdraw his usual opposition to placing SHAEF agencies in Paris and approve the establishment of PRD in the French capital, where it was possible to receive a greater number of newsmen. The Hotel Scribe, near the Opera, was reserved for billets, messing, and accommodations for Allied correspondents in addition to SHAEF censorship, briefing, and information services.

The number of correspondents accredited to SHAEF for the European Theater of Operations grew steadily after the invasion. From 530 on 7 June the number rose to 924 on 1 January 1945 and to 996 shortly before the war's end. [7] Although the vast majority of this group was attached to units in the field, the task of furnishing censorship guidance, providing communications for copy filed at SHAEF, the accreditation of all correspondents for the ETO, and the outlining of broad policy for public relations throughout the theater imposed a heavy burden on SHAEF PRD.

The growing responsibilities of the division threw a heavy strain on its chief, General Davis, who had been ill for a number of weeks. He had asked in the summer to be relieved of his duties, but at the urging of General Eisenhower remained at his task while a search was made for a satisfactory replacement. One was finally found in September in the person of Brig. Gen. Frank A. Allen, Jr., then chief of intelligence of 6th Army Group. [8] He assumed his post on 28 September. General Davis later improved in health and returned to the less strenuous position of adjutant general of SHAEF which he had held earlier in the year. [9]

---

[6] Chief Military Adviser (Br) to Press Censorship (Br) to PRD, 28 Jul 44; Dupuy to CofS SHAEF, 27 Jul 44; Eden to Smith, 5 Aug 44; Smith to Eden, 6 Aug 44; Ltr, Hull to Actg Secy Robert P. Patterson, 18 Jul 44, with Incl, Ltr, Russian Chargé A. Kapustin to Hull; Ltr, McNarney to Eisenhower, 22 Jul 44; Ltr, Eisenhower to McNarney, 27 Jul 44; Dupuy to Eisenhower, 27 Jul 44; USSTAF Memo, 2 Aug 44, sub: Intervs regarding Russia; Ltr, Stimson to Hull, 2 Aug 44; Ltr, McNarney to Eisenhower, 2 Aug 44. All in SHAEF SGS 000.7, Policy re Release of Info to the Press, I and II.

[7] Of the 996, 362 were Americans, 349 British, 126 French, 61 Canadian, 38 Dominion, and 60 from other Allied newspapers. See lists of war correspondents accredited to SHAEF, 1 January 1945 and 25 April 1945, SHAEF SGS 000.74, Press Correspondents, II.

[8] In the period during General Davis' illness, Colonel Dupuy acted as chief of PRD. On General Allen, see 1st Lt. John J. Briscoe, The Kennedy Affair (unpublished thesis, 1949, University of Missouri), and Ltr, Gen Allen to author, 23 Jun 50.

[9] Surles to Smith, W–80405, 14 Aug 44; SHAEF GO 20, 24 Sep 44. Both in SHAEF SGS 322.01 PRD, Org and Personnel PRD. Butcher, *My Three Years With Eisenhower*, pp. 614, 640, 650.

The shift of the Public Relations Division from London to Paris was made gradually, and it was not until 10 October that the first briefing conference was held in Paris. By this time three commercial transmitters, Radio France, Press Wireless, and MacKay Radio, were in operation between Paris and the United States. One commercial and two Army links were open to the United Kingdom. These facilities were augmented and improved to the extent that by the end of the month an average of nearly 60,000 words per day was being handled by the radio transmitters. In addition, air courier service took a daily average of 3,729 words to the United States and 8,120 words to the United Kingdom (part of these also went to the United States). An Army broadcasting line which connected Paris with the British Broadcasting Corporation was replaced by a BBC transmitter in the Hotel Scribe. By the end of November the daily average of copy sent from Paris to the United States and United Kingdom had risen to about 108,000 words. More facilities were added in December with the laying of a BBC submarine cable, initiation of voicecasts from the city of Luxembourg, and the installation of an additional teleprinter line to the United Kingdom. The Public Relations Division, besides sending copy to the United States by mail, also provided means for making records of interviews to be sent to broadcasting stations in the United States.[10]

Censorship problems arose for the Public Relations Division even before its movement to the Continent. An advance party of SHAEF censors, going into Paris shortly after the first Allied forces had entered the city, reported that six American and British correspondents had broadcast details of the liberation of the French capital without submitting their copy to Allied censors. SHAEF suspended for sixty days the right of the correspondents to remain on the Continent, but permitted them to carry out their normal duties in the United Kingdom.[11]

A particularly difficult assignment for PRD was that of providing censorship for the French press. France, unlike Belgium, the Netherlands, and Norway, had not adopted the voluntary system of censorship. Instead, it had signed an agreement permitting the Supreme Commander to exercise strict military censorship of press, radio, cinema, and, in general, all publications in the forward zone. In the zone of interior the French authorities were required to consult SHAEF censors on all news pertaining to military operations and to carry out auxiliary censorship instructions communicated by SHAEF. French publicity services were to facilitate the task of the Supreme Commander. Forty-five SHAEF censors were allocated as liaison officers with censors in liberated countries. Of these, twenty-four were assigned to cover the French press. The first four of the group had come to France at the beginning of July, and the group steadily increased after the liberation of Paris.[12]

Press activities declined slightly during the period of the German counteroffensive in the Ardennes as security blackouts were imposed. For the first time since D Day the

---

[10] SHAEF Public Relations Division War Diary, Oct, Nov, Dec 44.

[11] Dupuy to Hq Comd SHAEF, FWD S–59828, 15 Sep 44; Dupuy to CofS SHAEF, 4 Sep 44; SHAEF to WD, S–59223, 6 Sep 44. All in SHAEF SGS 000.74, Press Correspondents, I.

[12] Press Censorship Detachment, SHAEF, History of United States and Supreme Headquarters, AEF, Press Censorship in the European Theater of Operations, 1942–1945 (hereafter cited as History of U.S. and SHAEF Press Censorship), July 1945, pp. 147–75. For French agreement see Memo 4 in CCS Directive for Civil Affairs Administration in Continental France, 26 Aug 44, SHAEF SGS 014 France, Civil Affairs Dir for France, I.

number of words sent in a given month dropped below that of the previous month. After mid-January the volume of words began to rise and continued to increase until the end of the war. The Public Relations Division expanded its censorship services and telecommunication facilities to take care of new demands. The army groups had their own teleprinter connections to Paris and London, and by the beginning of February the Ninth Air Force and army press camps had set up five commercial mobile transmitters. The BBC had its own mobile transmitters with the British and Canadian armies, and regular Army sets with the American armies. A special short-wave transmitter was opened at Luxembourg on Christmas Day for press voicecasting and direct broadcasting to the United States. To provide for a sudden news development, such as the entry into Berlin, the Public Relations Division built flying radio stations into two flying fortresses for use to the United States and the United Kingdom.

Through the Communications Zone SHAEF also had the use of the world's largest mobile radio station, housed in seventeen vans. Under construction by a French firm for the Luftwaffe, the apparatus had been seized by American forces and completed by them. The 60-kilowatt transmitter was capable of communicating with Washington over three teletype channels, which could be used simultaneously with a fourth channel that provided voice or picture transmission. General Eisenhower's train was also fitted up with radio equipment in case it should be needed for surrender negotiations. Near the end of the war it was estimated that the facilities in Paris could send an average of 250,000 words per day. An average of nearly one million words were sent weekly by tele-

graph, plus an uncounted amount by courier, and an average of 150 broadcasts a week by Paris studios. During the last week of the war, two million words were telegraphed, and 200 broadcasts made from Paris.[13]

SHAEF continued also to send an impressive amount of material from London. Some concept of the Public Relations Division's task may be seen in a breakdown of the words censored in the two cities during the last four months of the war.

Words of Copy Submitted for Censorship

Month	Paris	London
January 1945....	2,917,435	2,307,750
February	3,445,676	2,639,250
March	4,948,042	2,894,500
April...........	4,281,475	2,138,000

Photographs Submitted for Censorship

Month	Paris	London
January 1945....	16,133	224,103
February	22,886	226,765
March	36,691	339,537
April...........	27,861	148,599

These statistics do not tell the entire story, since censors were also on duty at army groups and armies, while others dealt with copy in liberated newspapers, and with amateur photographers' film. An example may be found in a busy, but not a peak, month such as February 1945 in which copy handled by censors at SHAEF and the three army groups totaled 13,075,600 words, public relations officer copy to be mailed home 9,529,345 words, scrutiny of domestic press 44,221,377 words, still pictures 208,965 feet, and amateur film 1,128,155 feet (still pictures 1,089,155 and movie 39,000 feet).[14]

SHAEF's Public Relations Division had the task not only of censoring stories to

---

[13] SHAEF Public Relations Division War Diary, Oct, Nov, Dec 44.
[14] PRD diary.

prevent breaches of security and the disturbance of good relations between Allies, but also of publicizing the exploits of various units to aid morale. This became difficult when commanders like General Patton by their personal color and their slashing advances overshadowed the hard work of other commanders and armies. SHAEF was concerned less by the disparity in coverage than by the possible harm done to the morale of units whose efforts had not been adequately recognized. General Smith reminded the Public Relations Division of this problem in early September and asked that briefing officers call especial attention to the work of General Hodges' First Army. "In other words," he said, "try to attract a little more attention to Hodges and Bradley as against Patton's colorful appeal to the press. This without detriment to Patton." [15] These efforts did not succeed in gaining additional recognition for the First Army, although they may have been responsible for growing Third Army suspicion of SHAEF.

In February 1945, the director of the Public Relations Division, General Allen, suggested that the morale of armies and corps could be developed better if there was more equitable coverage of their activities. To achieve this, he proposed that briefing officers no longer refer to armies by the names of their commanders, but merely call them by their official names. After a month of experiment, the Public Relations Division admitted that the plan did not work and that the colorful commanders were still getting most of the space. The less well known commanders, now that they were not being specifically identified, were no longer being written about. Colonel Dupuy, deputy director of PRD, proposed that the old method of referring to the commander and his army be

restored.[16] A similar problem existed in the First French Army because the press tended to play up the exploits of the French Forces of the Interior. So strong did feeling on the subject become in late September 1944 that SHAEF had to order that communiqués and press briefings emphasize the contributions of the First French Army and "soft pedal FFI." "Emphasis placed on FFI by French press and radio to the exclusion of the French Army is producing serious situation, political and otherwise." [17]

From time to time the Allied correspondents protested to SHAEF because of news blackouts, delays in passing stories, failure of censors at various headquarters to follow a consistent pattern, release of information at SHAEF which army headquarters were not allowed to release, use of censorship for political rather than security purposes, and refusals to release "horrifics" and stories of reverses. Of this group of complaints, the one most frequently voiced was the lack of consistency in clearing stories. Most correspondents agreed that the news blackouts during major attacks were necessary. The complaints concerned the way in which the lifting of these blackouts was timed. Frequently, by accident, an army censor would release part of the story. As soon as this was known, the correspondents at other headquarters would demand that they be allowed to use the same material. The other censors were still bound by their

---

[15] Smith to SHAEF Main, FWD 14009, 6 Sep 44, SHAEF SGS 000.7, Policy re Release of Info to the Press, II.

[16] Director PRD to CofS SHAEF, 6 Feb 45; Allen to A Gps et al., S–78199, 7 Feb 45; Dupuy to CofS SHAEF, 9 Mar 45; SHAEF to A Gps et al., S–81730, 12 Mar 45, SHAEF cbl log.

[17] SHAEF Fwd to SHAEF Main, FWD 1556, 23 Sep 44, SHAEF SGS 000.7, Policy re Release of Info to the Press, II.

instructions to continue the blackout until official clearance was given. Thus, sometimes a correspondent covering an action at one of the armies would find himself "scooped" by a correspondent at SHAEF and still be told by the army censor that he could not release the story. The censors struggled constantly to find a standard which all of them could use in passing copy. Considerable use of BBC broadcasts was made, since it was found that they normally contained all news released at the various headquarters. So far as delays in clearing copy were concerned, the censors were supposed to explain reasons for delays to the correspondents and to advise them of any changes in copy so that they could discuss the matter with the chief censor or carry the matter higher.[18]

On the question of "horrifics" and reverses, the censors acted in accord with the policy followed by both the War Department and Supreme Headquarters of passing any story which did not give information to the enemy. Statistics on casualties were issued rather regularly, although a time lag was maintained to prevent the enemy from determining the effectiveness of any current defense the Allies might be making. SHAEF applied a temporary stop to the report of more than 8,600 casualties in the 106th Division at the outset of the German counteroffensive in the Ardennes, but after a protest from the War Department agreed that the action of the censor was a mistake.[19]

SHAEF censors discovered that radio broadcasting, in particular, created a number of special censorship problems. Especially serious were premature releases of information on coming attacks. In several cases the chief difficulty came not so much from actual broadcasts as from preliminary statements made by the radio reporter to his home office before his censored broadcast began. The enemy could monitor the information thus sent and be forewarned. In other cases the British Broadcasting Corporation used uncensored information in its news announcements. On the eve of a First Army attack in early January 1945, Mr. Cyril Ray of BBC announced from the Third Army headquarters that an action was shortly to take place. His accreditation was withdrawn. Shortly afterward General Devers protested strongly a BBC announcement that a number of divisions were being withdrawn from the Allied right flank, leaving the Seventh Army with an extended front. This gave information to the Germans of the attack, and alarmed the French population of the area. General Devers suggested that, if the directors of BBC could not be controlled on the basis of military security, they should be warned that they were endangering Allied relations. The censors were particularly upset because they found themselves attacked in the first instance by correspondents at the First Army headquarters who had been "scooped." The SHAEF censors finally released as much of the story as had been announced by BBC.[20]

Because of the speed with which information from a BBC broadcast could be picked up, breaches of security by it were more helpful to the enemy than similar statements in the press. It was charged that enemy fire fell on Allied troops in seventeen minutes after a casual newscast indicated that they were entering the factory district of Aachen. As a result of this type

---

[18] History of U.S. and SHAEF Press Censorship, Ch. 19.

[19] Smith to Marshall, 12 Jan 45, SHAEF cbl log.

[20] Statement by PRD SHAEF, 11 Jan 45, SHAEF SGS 000.73, Policy and Infractions of Press Censorship, I; Devers to SHAEF, 7 Jan 45, SHAEF cbl log.

of incident, field commanders and troops sometimes overlooked the very great services which the British Broadcasting Corporation was rendering the Allied cause in its services to American and British radio programs, its propaganda work, its key contribution to Resistance activities, and the tremendous achievements in the field of morale building in liberated and occupied countries.

Partly because of their mistrust of BBC, there seems to have been a readiness on the part of many American troops and correspondents to accept as genuine a fake German broadcast which purported to be a BBC attack on General Eisenhower during the battle of the Ardennes. The reaction was sufficiently strong that Mr. Brendan Bracken, British Minister of Information, felt it necessary to disavow the program and affirm the complete confidence of the British people and the BBC in General Eisenhower and the American forces.

A particularly embarrassing episode for SHAEF came in late April when the BBC made a premature announcement of the link-up of the Russians and Americans near Torgau despite elaborate precautions to have the announcement made simultaneously in Moscow, Washington, and London. In this instance, a French news agency had sent out by radio the announcement to be held for a release date. The information was monitored by BBC, which interrupted a scheduled program to announce the news. SHAEF officials submitted sharp protests to the governors of BBC as a result of this action.[21]

The most widely publicized breach of censorship involved an American newsman who prematurely announced the signing of the instrument of surrender at Reims. One of the seventeen correspondents to witness the signature, Mr. Edward Kennedy, chief of the Associated Press bureau in Paris, made use of an open wire from the Hotel Scribe to give the story of the surrender to the Associated Press bureau in London. Unaware that the story had not been released, the London bureau flashed it to the United States. Kennedy, who had been in difficulties with SHAEF as recently as February 1945 over a story that President Roosevelt was coming to Paris to investigate scandals in the Army's handling of the relief program for French civilians, held that the story had been broken by the German radio which was broadcasting Admiral Doenitz' orders to his forces to cease fighting.[22] Since the German high command was supposedly acting under the orders of SHAEF, he felt that this action absolved him from his promise not to release the story until it had been released by SHAEF. Such an interpretation was not followed by the other sixteen correspondents at Reims nor by the other newspapermen in Europe, all of whom were aware of the surrender story. The story was branded as unofficial, and the Associated Press and its representatives in London and Paris were suspended until an investigation could be held. The Associated Press protested the suspension of its entire organization, and the War Department ruled that, since all agreements relative to censorship were made between correspondents and SHAEF, responsibility had to be placed on the individual newsman. The ban against the Associated Press was lifted despite the bitter protests

---

[21] History of U.S. and SHAEF Press Censorship, Ch. 20. Brendan Bracken to Gen Smith, RR–15103, 10 Jan 45; SHAEF to PRD, S–74607, 11 Jan 45. Both in SHAEF cbl log.

[22] Reichsminister Graf Schwerin von Krosigk announced the capitulation to the German people on 7 May.

of more than fifty correspondents at an indignation meeting in Paris on 8 May in which they attacked General Allen and the Public Relations Division of Supreme Headquarters. The G–1, SHAEF, and the Judge Advocate, ETOUSA, appointed to investigate the incident, announced on 12 May that there were no grounds for court martial proceedings but recommended that the credentials of Mr. Kennedy and his assistant, Mr. Morton Gudebrod, be withdrawn and that the two correspondents be returned to the United States. This action was carried out on 14 May, the Associated Press expressed its regrets, and on the following day SHAEF, in a statement praising the other correspondents for not releasing the story, declared the incident closed.[23]

---

[23] For full details of the incident see folder on Kennedy case in SHAEF PRD files. See also 1st Lt. John J. Briscoe, The Kennedy Affair (unpublished thesis, 1949, University of Missouri). Mr. Kennedy's side of the story is given in his article, "I'd Do It Again," *Atlantic Monthly*, CLXXXII (August, 1948), 36–41. In 1948, through the aid of Senator Sheridan Downey, Mr. Kennedy's case was presented to General Eisenhower, then U.S. Army Chief of Staff, who restored the newsman's credentials as war correspondent.

Appendix B

SHAEF Personnel

In the early organization of COSSAC, its British members were supplied by the Home Forces Command, while its U.S. members were provided under a plan by which the War Department allotted additional grades and ratings to Headquarters, ETOUSA, which in turn supplied officers and men to COSSAC. On 8 December 1943, the U.S. contingent at COSSAC consisted of 215 officers and 204 enlisted men and the British group consisted of 274 officers and 410 other ranks.[1]

The first Tables of Organization and War Establishments planned for SHAEF proper were set up in mid-January 1944 in accordance with the COSSAC form of organization and did not include personnel for G–1 or Headquarters Command. The U.S. portion was to consist of 291 officers and 459 men, and the British portion was to consist of 277 officers and 470 men for a total of 1,497.

With the formal appointment of a Supreme Commander in February 1944, steps were taken to get new allotments for his headquarters. Efforts were made to maintain a fairly equal proportion between U.S. and British personnel, although it differed sharply in the various divisions. The proportion depended in most cases on the nationality of the chief of division and the nature of the work to be performed. Thus, in G–2, headed by a British officer, the personnel was almost two to one British, whereas in the Adjutant General Division, organized completely along U.S. lines, there was only one British officer and the enlisted personnel was two to one American.

In March 1944, the British amended their existing War Establishments for COSSAC to provide more personnel for SHAEF (eight amended War Establishments were issued between the organization of COSSAC and the end of the war), and the War Department announced a Table of Organization for SHAEF (only one other U.S. Table of Organization was issued for Supreme Headquarters during the war).

The divisions of Supreme Headquarters grew rapidly as plans were pushed for the invasion, but Headquarters Command and special detachments made the chief demands for personnel. Americans constituted the greater part of the security forces, while the British provided a large

---

[1] This appendix was written by the author in 1946 as a part of a short History of SHAEF. It was based on the following files: SHAEF SGS 320.3 T/O and WE for SHAEF; SHAEF SGS 322 Organization and Personnel (Fwd); SHAEF SGS 322 Organization and Personnel (Rear); and files for each general and special staff division of SHAEF under the title Organization and Personnel. Additional information was furnished the author in 1945 by Brig. Gen. Robert Q. Brown, Headquarters Commandant, and in 1946 by Lt. Col. H. J. Rothwell, his British assistant. This section was checked as to accuracy by the Office of the Headquarters Commandant in 1946.

percentage of signal troops. By 12 July 1944, Supreme Headquarters (less special detachments) numbered 1,185 officers, 101 warrant officers, and 3,628 enlisted personnel. *(Table 4)*[2] The non-T/O increments had been added, in the case of the British, by constant amendments to the War Establishments and, in the case of the Americans, by additions from the theater non-T/O allotment granted to Headquarters, ETOUSA.

In July 1944, the War Office announced that the existing manpower shortage in the British Army made it necessary to limit the number of British personnel in Supreme Headquarters. A proposal was made to set 7,000 as the maximum British allotment to SHAEF. This number was to be cut 10 percent initially and then built up as needed to the maximum. No effort was made to discuss a similar limitation on U.S. personnel, since the Allies recognized that no limits could be set until it was known how large a staff would be needed to advise General Eisenhower in his capacity of theater commander of U.S. forces.

In early March 1944, the War Department, in issuing a non-T/O allotment for SHAEF, warned of the lack of U.S. personnel and said that the non-T/O overhead requirement then issued would be final for the theater unless additional functions were assigned by the War Department. Any increase requested for a unit, installation, or activity in the theater would have to be compensated for by decreases elsewhere. Mindful of this fact, and aware of the activities of the British to limit personnel in SHAEF, General Smith in October 1944 asked the G–1 to see if the U.S. staff of Supreme Headquarters could be reduced.

Instead of finding ways to reduce the U.S. contingent of SHAEF, the G–1 discovered a need for more men. Pointing to the inadequacy of the March 1944 allotment, General Barker indicated that whereas the British had issued several War Establishments the Americans had merely authorized overstrength. The result was a lack of ratings for many divisions. Americans remained for several months in grade, while their British opposites were being promoted one or more times. In sending this report to the War Department, the SHAEF chief of staff explained that initial personnel estimates for Supreme Headquarters failed to anticipate the growth of SHAEF and its activities. Part of the increase had become necessary when the G–6 Division was divided into the Psychological Warfare and Public Relations Divisions. A second increase had followed the formation of non-T/O operational field units which were required to aid field units. These included psychological warfare groups and units that handled Allied prisoners of war. Since these SHAEF-sponsored activities could not be transferred elsewhere, they had to remain a charge on Supreme Headquarters.

General Smith pointed out that SHAEF had been unable to solve the problem by reductions in staff and by reorganization. Instead of improving, the situation was growing worse as new demands were made for the U.S. Group Control Council, missions to liberated countries, and staffs for the control, disarmament, and demobilization of German ground forces.

SHAEF's requests for more personnel were granted in December 1944 although fewer high grades were made available than had been requested. Meanwhile, the British were attempting to cut their allot-

---

[2] See below, p. 533.

ment to Supreme Headquarters. In September 1944 the ceiling of 7,000 British personnel for SHAEF had been reduced to 5,245 after more than a thousand air troops had been transferred to the 21 Army Group. On 15 December British officers at SHAEF were told that any requests for an increase of personnel in one section would be granted only if it was clear that a corresponding reduction could be made elsewhere.

When the German counteroffensive in the Ardennes threatened to prolong the war and thus impose additional strains on Allied manpower, the War Office asked that the British contingent of SHAEF consider further reductions of personnel "irrespective of present approved establishments and with recognition of the fact that standards of performance may fall." The possibility of making increased use of local sources of manpower and of reducing security units on duty in nonoperational areas was suggested. In passing this information on to British officers in late December, General Morgan indicated that a minimum reduction of 5 percent should be kept in mind in making the survey.

After studying the situation, General Whiteley, deputy G–3 of SHAEF, concluded that there was little chance of reducing the British contingent. In reviewing the numbers of special troops at Supreme Headquarters, he showed that in the groups included under Headquarters Command the British furnished only seventeen officers and 268 other ranks in contrast to the 150 officers and 2,000 enlisted men provided by the Americans. The British security group at the headquarters, he continued, consisted of thirty-six men as opposed to 3,000 U.S. military police and a U.S. defense battalion of 1,000. Furthermore, in SHAEF

proper a 5 percent reduction would result in a saving of only twenty-two officers and fifty-seven other ranks. He noted that it was not feasible to reduce the personnel in SHAEF by substituting liberated or co-operationist manpower since in the Car Company, one of the few places where such personnel could be used on a wide scale, there was already a dilution of up to 60 percent.

General Whiteley made clear that the initial intention of the SHAEF planners to preserve a balance between British and U.S. personnel had been changed and that any further reduction in the British contingent would upset the balance even more. He added that this was not considered to be a material factor.

General Morgan in mid-January indicated that two problems were involved in the matter of staff reduction: (1) reducing personnel on the basis that the headquarters was overstaffed; and (2) releasing high-category young men who could give better service in more active employment. He asked, therefore, for further review of the possibilities of reducing the British staff and suggested a survey of U.S. personnel with the same end in mind. On 1 February, he pressed the point still further and asked that an effort be made to cut the staff by 10 percent and that young officers and men be replaced by limited service and ATS personnel. Under this directive, the divisions made reductions in their British members, with the result that General Whiteley on 26 April was able to report an 8.4 percent cut.

U.S. efforts to cut the number of military personnel in the headquarters were prompted by General Eisenhower's order of 31 December 1944 that drastic reductions be made to release every available man for combat or purely military duty.

On 7 January 1945, in a report to the Combined Chiefs of Staff, he announced that a reserve was to be created for use against further German counterattacks, by means of an order: "(1) to comb out personnel from the Communications Zone, Line of Communications units, and Army Air Forces and to train these personnel as replacements for combat units; (2) to convert units which are the least essential to our requirements; (3) to make the maximum use of liberated manpower both for combat and rear area duties."

Under this policy, headquarters and service troops were screened for men who could be replaced or who were fitted for combat duty. When suitable limited service or female replacements were found, changes were made in the existing organization. The U.S. policy established for officers during this period was to avoid if possible the use in headquarters of officers under thirty-five years of age who were in Medical Category A. Headquarters, SHAEF, was reduced by approximately 2,300 overall in the period between 1 February and 1 April. *(Tables 5 and 6)*[3] The reductions came, however, in special troops, since there was actually an increase of about 100 in the general and special staff sections.

After 1 April, there were no more great efforts to cut personnel. As the war reached its climax and the fall of Germany grew near, dozens of agencies had to be activated to deal with censorship, psychological warfare, prisoner of war exchange, civil affairs activities, and signal communications. The result was a mushrooming of units attached to or located near Supreme Headquarters. As early as 5 January 1945, the chief of staff had attempted to separate these agencies from the general and special staff divisions. On 19 April 1945, this goal was achieved with

the announcement that SHAEF would consist of three principal components: (1) Supreme Headquarters staff—Office of the Supreme Commander, Office of the Chief of Staff, general and special staff sections, EAC Section, and political advisers; (2) special troops—Headquarters Command, British Local Administrative Appointments, and operational agencies functioning under Supreme Headquarters control; (3) liaison agencies—SHAEF missions to France, Belgium, the Netherlands, Denmark, and Norway.

The pyramiding of special units assigned, attached, or located near SHAEF went on so rapidly that it is difficult to make any accurate estimate of the U.S. contingent at the end of the war. As additional officers and men were added in preparation for the activation of USFET at Frankfurt, the total number of American troops passed the 18,000 mark. The addition of air, naval, UNRRA, special missions, military government, and British personnel gave an estimated force of more than 30,000 military or Allied civilian personnel associated with Supreme Headquarters. This number in turn was swelled by displaced persons, German civilians, and prisoners of war who were used by the thousands in construction work and as drivers, clerks, housekeepers, cooks, waitresses, and janitors (six months after the dissolution of SHAEF this group employed by Headquarters Command, USFET, numbered 23,000, of whom 14,000 were civilians).

On the following pages are tables showing the size of SHAEF in July 1944 shortly before SHAEF elements moved to the Continent, in February 1945 when efforts were made to reduce the size of headquarters, and again in April 1945 when

---

[3] See below, pp. 534–35.

SHAEF was preparing the last great offensive. In interpreting these statistics it is essential to remember that many of the agencies and detachments carried on SHAEF rolls were never located at Supreme Headquarters but were attached to lower units. Press censorship detachments, psychological warfare consolidation teams, wireless sections, technical maintenance sections, and cipher sections are examples of these groups. The SHAEF missions to France, Belgium, the Netherlands, Denmark, and Norway were also located elsewhere.

Housekeeping and security detachments were considerably augmented because of the number of agencies located at or near SHAEF which had to be furnished communications and protection.

While it is almost impossible to arrive at the exact number of personnel at SHAEF at a given time, because of constant shifts in agencies and the separation of the headquarters into advance, forward, and rear echelons, one can approach an accurate figure by counting the officers and men assigned to the general and special staff sections and the Headquarters Command.

TABLE 4—AUTHORIZED STRENGTH OF SUPREME HEADQUARTERS ALLIED EXPEDITIONARY FORCE, 12 JULY 1944

ORGANIZATION	TOTAL			OFFICERS		WARRANT OFFICERS		ENLISTED	
	TOTAL	U.S.	BRITISH	U.S.	BRITISH	U.S.	BRITISH	U.S.	BRITISH
Total	4,914	3,476	1,438	764	421	52	49	2,660	968
Supreme Commander, Chief of Staff, Deputy Chief of Staff, Secretary General Staff	193	156	37	27	13	7	2	122	22
General Eisenhower's Personal Staff	24	24	0	11	0	1	0	12	0
European Allied Contact Section	19	10	9	4	4	0	0	6	5
Adjutant General Division	115	92	23	14	1	10	2	68	20
Assistant Chief of Staff, G–1	143	63	80	24	28	1	3	38	49
Assistant Chief of Staff, G–2	563	336	227	128	83	4	6	204	138
Assistant Chief of Staff, G–3	282	156	126	61	53	2	3	93	70
Assistant Chief of Staff, G–4	439	266	173	97	64	7	10	162	99
Assistant Chief of Staff, G–5	351	189	162	69	59	5	8	115	95
Psychological Warfare Division	428	361	67	118	25	2	1	241	41
Public Relations Division	116	67	49	28	25	1	2	38	22
Air Defense Division	48	26	22	6	6	0	1	20	15
Engineer Division	97	51	46	20	18	1	2	30	26
Signal Division	167	99	68	40	32	3	3	56	33
Medical Division	13	6	7	3	3	0	1	3	3
Local Administrative Appointments	342	0	342	0	7	0	5	0	330
Headquarters Command	1,574	1,574	0	114	0	8	0	1,452	0

Source: SHAEF SGS 320.3 T/O and WE for SHAEF.

Table 5—Authorized Strength of Supreme Headquarters Allied Expeditionary Force, 1 February 1945

Organization	Total			Officers		Warrant Officers		Enlisted	
	Total	U.S.	British	U.S.	British	U.S.	British	U.S.	British
Total	16,312	9,992	6,320	1,581	1,229	67	88	8,344	5,003
General Staff—Total	2,004	1,163	841	404	311	29	35	730	495
Supreme Commander, Chief of Staff, Deputy Chiefs of Staff, Secretary General Staff	216	157	59	27	14	7	3	123	42
European Allied Contact Section	14	5	9	3	4	0	0	2	5
Political Advisors	4	2	2	1	1	0	0	1	1
Assistant Chief of Staff, G–1	142	71	71	26	26	1	4	44	41
Assistant Chief of Staff, G–2	494	287	207	112	77	4	5	171	125
Assistant Chief of Staff, G–3	284	156	128	60	54	3	3	93	71
Assistant Chief of Staff, G–4	500	297	203	106	76	9	12	182	115
Assistant Chief of Staff, G–5	350	188	162	69	59	5	8	114	95
Special Staff—Total	722	464	258	144	107	20	12	300	139
Hq Commandant (U.S.) Camp Commandant (Br.)	2	1	1	1	1	0	0	0	0
Adjutant General Division	125	102	23	18	1	10	2	74	20
Engineer Division	87	41	46	16	18	1	2	24	26
Signal Division	167	99	68	40	32	3	3	56	33
Medical Division	13	6	7	3	3	0	1	3	3
Psychological Warfare Division	90	53	37	16	18	1	1	36	18
Public Relations Division	180	134	46	42	23	5	2	87	21
Air Defense Division	58	28	30	8	11	0	1	20	18
Special Troops—Total	13,100	8,170	4,930	973	719	17	39	7,180	4,172
Local Administrative Appointments	763	0	763	0	17	0	6	0	740
Headquarters Command (U.S.)	4,635	4,635	0	215	0	8	0	4,412	0
G–1 Agencies	500	293	207	97	65	5	1	191	141
G–2 Agencies	939	49	890	16	226	0	17	33	647
G–3 Agencies	229	0	229	0	12	0	0	0	217
G–4 Agencies	285	156	129	58	49	1	2	97	78
G–5 Agencies	532	236	296	79	80	2	3	155	213
Psychological Warfare Division	1,128	878	250	219	81	1	1	658	168
Public Relations Division	456	346	110	164	40	0	0	182	70
Signal Agencies	2,692	1,577	1,115	125	69	0	0	1,452	1,046
Air Defense Division	941	0	941	0	80	0	9	0	852
European Allied Contact Section	0	0	0	0	0	0	0	0	0
Liaison Agencies—Total	486	195	291	60	92	1	2	134	197
French Mission	199	129	70	39	23	1	0	89	47
Belgian Mission	85	26	59	8	30	0	0	18	29
Netherlands Mission	168	26	142	8	28	0	2	18	112
Danish Mission	34	14	20	5	11	0	0	9	9

Source: SHAEF SGS 320.3 T/O and WE for SHAEF.

TABLE 6—AUTHORIZED STRENGTH OF SUPREME HEADQUARTERS ALLIED EXPEDITIONARY FORCE, 1 APRIL 1945

ORGANIZATION	TOTAL			OFFICERS		WARRANT OFFICERS		ENLISTED	
	TOTAL	U.S.	BRITISH	U.S.	BRITISH	U.S.	BRITISH	U.S.	BRITISH
Total	14,028	8,374	5,654	1,495	1,077	61	99	6,818	4,478
General Staff—Total	1,952	1,102	850	378	314	29	35	695	501
Supreme Commander, Chief of Staff, Deputy Chiefs of Staff, Secretary General Staff	204	148	56	24	13	7	3	117	40
European Allied Contact Section	15	5	10	3	4	0	0	2	6
Political Advisors	4	2	2	1	1	0	0	1	1
Assistant Chief of Staff, G-1	150	52	98	22	40	1	4	29	54
Assistant Chief of Staff, G-2	495	296	199	112	75	4	5	180	119
Assistant Chief of Staff, G-3	261	141	120	51	46	3	3	87	71
Assistant Chief of Staff, G-4	472	269	203	96	76	9	12	164	115
Assistant Chief of Staff, G-5	351	189	162	69	59	5	8	115	95
Special Staff—Total	877	580	297	201	115	20	13	359	169
Hq Commandant (U.S.) Camp Commandant (Br.)	2	1	1	1	1	0	0	0	0
Adjutant General Division	125	102	23	18	1	10	2	74	20
Engineer Division	82	36	46	15	18	0	2	21	26
Signal Division	162	94	68	38	32	3	3	53	33
Medical Division	13	6	7	3	3	0	1	3	3
Psychological Warfare Division	171	104	67	41	25	2	1	61	41
Public Relations Division	266	211	55	77	24	5	3	129	28
Air Defense Division	56	26	30	8	11	0	1	18	18
Special Troops—Total	10,339	6,378	3,961	777	473	10	36	5,591	3,452
Local Administrative Appointments	765	0	765	0	20	0	7	0	738
Headquarters Command (U.S.)	3,239	3,239	0	190	0	2	0	3,047	0
G-1 Agencies	543	295	248	90	83	5	0	200	165
G-2 Agencies	545	98	447	18	91	2	17	78	339
G-3 Agencies	103	0	103	0	4	0	0	0	99
G-4 Agencies	269	140	129	52	49	1	2	87	78
G-5 Agencies	15	7	8	2	2	0	0	5	6
Psychological Warfare Division	986	767	219	171	74	0	1	596	144
Public Relations Division	357	269	88	129	30	0	0	140	58
Signal Agencies	2,627	1,556	1,071	122	71	0	0	1,434	1,000
Air Defense Division	883	0	883	0	49	0	9	0	825
European Allied Contact Section	7	7	0	3	0	0	0	4	0
Liaison Agencies—Total	860	314	546	139	175	2	15	173	356
French Mission	292	204	88	74	53	2	1	128	34
Belgian Mission	208	50	158	32	42	0	6	18	110
Netherlands Mission	197	27	170	8	48	0	4	19	118
Danish Mission	163	33	130	25	32	0	4	8	94

Source: SHAEF SGS 320.3 T/O and WE for SHEAF.

Appendix C

Roster of Key Officers, SHAEF

Supreme Commander

General of the Army Dwight D. Eisenhower (U.S.)

Deputy Supreme Commander

Air Chief Marshal Sir Arthur W. Tedder (Br.)

Chief of Staff

Lt. Gen. Walter Bedell Smith (U.S.)

Deputies Chief of Staff

Lt. Gen. Sir Frederick E. Morgan (Br.)

Lt. Gen. Humfrey M. Gale (Br.), Chief Administrative Officer

Air Marshal James M. Robb (Br.), Deputy Chief of Staff (Air)

Air Vice Marshal C. R. Carr (Br.), Deputy Chief of Staff (Air)

Allied Naval Commander

Admiral Sir Bertram H. Ramsay (Br.)

Vice Adm. Alan G. Kirk (U.S.)

Admiral Harold M. Burrough (Br.)

Rear Adm. George E. Creasy (Br.), Chief of Staff

Commodore H. W. Faulkner (Br.), Chief of Staff

Capt. L. A. Thackrey (U.S.), Assistant Chief of Staff in Charge of U.S. Forces

Air Commander-in-Chief

Air Chief Marshal Sir Trafford Leigh-Mallory (Br.), Commander, AEAF

Maj. Gen. Hoyt S. Vandenberg (U.S.), Deputy Air Commander-in-Chief

Air Chief Marshal James M. Robb (Br.), Air Chief of Staff

Air Vice Marshal C. R. Carr (Br.), Air Chief of Staff

Maj. Gen. William O. Butler (U.S.), Deputy Air Commander-inChief

Secretary, General Staff

Col. Dan Gilmer (U.S.)

Col. Ford Trimble (U.S.)

Col. Carter Burgess (U.S.)

Col. J. B. Moore, III (U.S.)

G-1 Division

Maj. Gen. Ray W. Barker (U.S.)

Brigadier R. F. R. Brecher (Br.), Deputy

Brigadier T. J. B. Bosvile (Br.), Deputy

G-2 Division

Maj. Gen. J. F. M. Whiteley (Br.), G-2

Maj. Gen. Kenneth W. D. Strong (Br.), G-2

Brig. Gen. Thomas J. Betts (U.S.), Deputy

G-3 Division

Maj. Gen. Harold R. Bull (U.S.), G-3

Maj. Gen. Charles A. West (Br.), Deputy

Maj. Gen. J. F. M. Whiteley (Br.), Deputy

Maj. Gen. Lowell W. Rooks (U.S.), Deputy

G-4 Division

Maj. Gen. Robert W. Crawford (U.S.), G-4

Maj. Gen. N. C. D. Brownjohn (Br.), Deputy

Maj. Gen. C. M. Smith (Br.), Deputy

Maj. Gen. Charles S. Napier (Br.), Deputy, Movements and Transportation

Brigadier Douglas H. Bond (Br.), Deputy, Petroleum and Fuel

Col. Howard A. Malin (U.S.), Deputy, Movement and Transportation

Col. Wilbur S. Elliott (U.S.), Deputy, Movement and Transportation

Col. Walter C. Pew (U.S.), Deputy, Petroleum and Fuel

Brig. Gen. John A. Appleton (U.S.), Director General, Military Railways

Col. E. K. Clark (U.S.), Deputy

Brig. Gen. Theron D. Weaver (U.S.), Deputy, Chief of Petroleum Branch

G–5 Division

Maj. Gen. Sir Roger Lumley (Br.), G–5

Lt. Gen. A. E. Grasett (Br.), G–5

Brig. Gen. Julius C. Holmes (U.S.), Deputy

Brig. Gen. Frank J. McSherry (U.S.), Deputy

Brig. Gen. Clarence L. Adcock (U.S.), Deputy

Adjutant Division

Brig. Gen. Thomas J. Davis (U.S.), Adjutant General

Col. Emil C. Boehnke (U.S.), Adjutant General

Signal Division

Maj. Gen. C. H. H. Vulliamy (Br.), Chief Signal Officer

Maj. Gen. Francis H. Lanahan, Jr. (U.S.), Deputy; Chief Signal Officer

Maj. Gen. L. B. Nicholls (Br.), Deputy

Engineer Division

Maj. Gen. H. B. W. Hughes (Br.), Chief Engineer

Brig. Gen. Beverly C. Dunn (U.S.), Deputy; Chief Engineer

Brigadier R. Briggs (Br.), Deputy

Medical Division

Maj. Gen. Albert W. Kenner (U.S.)

Brigadier E. A. Sutton (Br.), Deputy

Brigadier R. W. Galloway (Br.), Deputy

Brigadier H. L. Garson (Br.), Deputy

Public Relations Division

Brig. Gen. Thomas J. Davis (U.S.)

Brig. Gen. Frank A. Allen, Jr. (U.S.)

Psychological Warfare Division

Brig. Gen. Robert A. McClure (U.S.)

Air Defense Division

Maj. Gen. A. M. Cameron (Br.), Chief

Brig. Gen. Samuel L. McCroskey (U.S.), Deputy

Headquarters Command

Brig. Gen. Robert Q. Brown (U.S.)

Lt. Col. H. J. Rothwell (Br.), Camp Commandant in Charge of British Personnel

Col. Alan B. Jacobs (U.S.), Assistant Commandant in Charge of U.S. Personnel

European Allied Contact Section

Lt. Gen. A. E. Grasett (Br.), Chief

Brig. Gen. Cornelius W. Wickersham (U.S.), Deputy

British Control Commission Military Section

Maj. Gen. S. W. Kirby, Deputy Commissioner Military Section

United States Group Control Council

Lt. Gen. Lucius D. Clay, Head Deputy

Brig. Gen. Cornelius W. Wickersham, Assistant Deputy

Political Officers

Ambassador William Phillips (U.S.)

Mr. Charles B. P. Peake (Br.)

Mr. Christopher Steel (Br.)

Mr. Samuel Reber (U.S.)

Ambassador Robert Murphy (U.S.)

SHAEF Mission (France)

Maj. Gen. John T. Lewis (U.S.), Head

Maj. Gen. Harold Redman (Br.), Deputy

SHAEF Mission (Netherlands)

Maj. Gen. J. K. Edwards (Br.), Head

Maj. Gen. J. G. W. Clark (Br.), Head

Brig. Gen. George P. Howell (U.S.), Deputy

SHAEF Mission (Belgium and Luxembourg)

Maj. Gen. G. W. E. J. Erskine (Br.), Head

Col. John B. Sherman (U.S.), Deputy for Belgium

Col. F. E. Fraser (U.S.), Deputy for Luxembourg

SHAEF Mission (Denmark)

Maj. Gen. R. H. Dewing (Br.), Head

Col. Ford Trimble (U.S.), Deputy

SHAEF Mission (Norway)

Gen. Sir Andrew Thorne (Br.), Head

Col. Charles H. Wilson (U.S.), Deputy

Appendix D

Forces Under SHAEF, 1944–45

21 Army Group	Field Marshal Sir Bernard Law Montgomery
Second Army	Gen. Sir Miles C. Dempsey
1 Corps	Lt. Gen. Sir J. T. Crocker
8 Corps	Lt. Gen. Sir Richard N. O'Connor
	Lt. Gen. E. H. Barker
12 Corps	Lt. Gen. N. M. Ritchie
30 Corps	Lt. Gen. Gerard C. Bucknall
	Lt. Gen. B. G. Horrocks
1 Airborne Corps	Maj. Gen. R. N. Gale
Bomber Command	Air Chief Marshal Sir Arthur Harris
2d Tactical Air Force	Air Chief Marshal Sir Arthur Coningham
Eastern Task Force [1]	Rear Adm. Philip L. Vian

Divisions: 3d Infantry, 5th Infantry, 15th Infantry, 43d Infantry, 49th Infantry, 51st Infantry, 52d Infantry, 53d Infantry, 1st Polish Armored, 7th Armored, 11th Armored, 79th Armored, Guards Armored, 1st Airborne, 6th Airborne

Canadian

First Army	Gen. Henry D. G. Crerar
1st Corps	Lt. Gen. C. Foulkes
2d Corps	Lt. Gen. G. G. Simonds

Divisions: 1st Infantry, 2d Infantry, 3d Infantry, 4th Armored, 5th Armored

French

First Army	Gen. Jean de Lattre de Tassigny
I Corps	Lt. Gen. Emile Béthouart
II Corps	Lt. Gen. de Goislard de Monsabert
Detachment of the Army of the Alps	Lt. Gen. Paul Doyen
Detachment of the Army of the Atlantic	Lt. Gen. Edgar de Larminat

---

[1] This Allied unit is included in the British list because its commander was a British officer.

Divisions activated under North African rearmament program: 1st DMI (1re Division de Marche d'Infanterie), 2d DIM (2e Division de l'Infanterie Marocaine), 3d DIA (3e Division de l'Infanterie Algérienne), 4th DMM (4e Division Marocaine de Montagne), 9th DIC (9e Division d'Infanterie Coloniale), 1st DB (1re Division Blindée), 2d DB (2e Division Blindée), 5th DB (5e Division Blindée)

Divisions activated under Metropolitan program and assigned to First French Army: 10th DI (10e Division),[2] 27th DIA (27e Division d'Infanterie Alpine), 14th DI (14e Division d'Infanterie), 1st DI (1re Division d'Infanterie)[3]

	United States
12th Army Group	Gen. Omar N. Bradley
6th Army Group	Gen. Jacob L. Devers
First Army	Lt. Gen. Omar N. Bradley
	Lt. Gen. Courtney H. Hodges
Third Army	Gen. George S. Patton, Jr.
Seventh Army	Lt. Gen. Alexander M. Patch
Ninth Army	Lt. Gen. William H. Simpson
Fifteenth Army	Lt. Gen. Leonard T. Gerow
First Allied Airborne Army[4]	Lt. Gen. Lewis H. Brereton
III Corps	Maj. Gen. John Millikin
	Maj. Gen. James A. Van Fleet
V Corps	Maj. Gen. Leonard T. Gerow
	Maj. Gen. Clarence R. Huebner
VI Corps	Maj. Gen. Lucian K. Truscott
	Maj. Gen. Edward H. Brooks
VII Corps	Maj. Gen. J. Lawton Collins
VIII Corps	Maj. Gen. Troy H. Middleton
XII Corps	Maj. Gen. Manton S. Eddy
	Maj. Gen. Stafford LeR. Irwin
XIII Corps	Maj. Gen. Alvan C. Gillem, Jr.
XV Corps	Maj. Gen. Wade H. Haislip
XVI Corps	Maj. Gen. John B. Anderson
XIX Corps	Maj. Gen. Charles H. Corlett
	Maj. Gen. Raymond S. McLain
XX Corps	Maj. Gen. Walton H. Walker
XXI Corps	Maj. Gen. Frank W. Milburn
XXII Corps	Maj. Gen. Ernest N. Harmon
XXIII Corps	Maj. Gen. James A. Van Fleet
	Maj. Gen. Hugh J. Gaffey
XVIII Corps (Airborne)	Maj. Gen. Matthew B. Ridgway

---

[2] The 10th DI, initially equipped with old French equipment, had been withdrawn at the close of the war to be re-equipped with U.S. armament.

[3] The 1st DI was activated in February 1945, but had not become operational at the war's end.

[4] This Allied unit is included in the U.S. list because its commander was an American.

U.S. Strategic Air Forces in Europe	Gen. Carl Spaatz
Eighth Air Force	Lt. Gen. James H. Doolittle
Ninth Air Force	Lt. Gen. Lewis H. Brereton
	Lt. Gen. Hoyt S. Vandenberg
IX Tactical Air Command	Maj. Gen. Elwood R. Quesada
XIX Tactical Air Command	Maj. Gen. Otto P. Weyland
XXIX Tactical Air Command	Brig. Gen. Richard E. Nugent
Western Task Force [5]	Rear Adm. Alan G. Kirk

Infantry Divisions: 1st, 2d, 3d, 4th, 5th, 8th, 9th, 26th, 28th, 29th, 30th, 35th, 36th, 42d, 44th, 45th, 63d, 65th, 66th, 69th, 70th, 71st, 75th, 76th, 78th, 79th, 80th, 83d, 84th, 86th, 87th, 89th, 90th, 94th, 95th, 97th, 99th, 100th, 102d, 103d, 104th, 106th

Armored Divisions: 2d, 3d, 4th, 5th, 6th, 7th, 8th, 9th, 10th, 11th, 12th, 13th, 14th, 16th, 20th

Airborne Divisions: 13th, 17th, 82d, 101st

---

[5] This Allied unit is included in the U.S. list because its commander was an American.

Appendix E

Strength and Casualty Figures

TABLE 7—ASSIGNED STRENGTH OF U.S. ARMY FORCES IN EUROPEAN THEATER OF OPERATIONS, JULY 1944–JUNE 1945[a]

End of Month	Total Strength	Location		Type			
		On Continent	United Kingdom	Air	Ground	Service	Other [b]
1944							
July	1,770,614	790,519	980,095	365,429	749,476	355,805	299,904
August	1,904,709	1,017,817	886,892	377,325	838,108	374,054	315,222
September	2,053,417	1,353,079	700,338	429,671	928,042	402,192	293,512
October	2,203,583	1,401,165	802,418	426,266	1,095,682	419,156	262,479
November	2,588,983	1,921,481	667,502	435,692	1,337,981	506,889	308,421
December	2,699,467	2,048,421	651,046	438,428	1,410,514	522,142	328,383
1945							
January	2,829,039	2,184,184	644,855	432,304	1,484,330	534,700	377,705
February	2,934,924	2,329,042	605,882	429,822	1,585,242	551,466	368,394
March	3,029,579	2,539,334	490,245	438,051	1,644,986	565,221	381,321
April	3,065,505	2,623,086	442,419	447,482	1,671,008	572,478	374,537
May	3,021,483	2,639,377	382,106	442,155	1,703,613	580,497	295,218
June	2,811,820	2,488,406	323,414	368,064	1,682,593	568,876	192,287

[a] Excludes strength in Italy for July 1944 through June 1945 and in Southern France for August 1944 through November 1944 assigned to Mediterranean Theater of Operations.

[b] Theater overhead, replacements, patients in hospitals and personnel in process of transfer out of the theater.

Sources: Location, AGO, Machine Records Branch, "Strength of the Army, STM–30"; Type, Office, Chief of Staff USA, SARO report, "Strength of the Army"; respective months.

TABLE 8—BATTLE CASUALTIES OF U.S. ARMY IN EUROPEAN THEATER OF OPERATIONS, JUNE 1944–MAY 1945

Month	Total	Killed in Action	Wounded in Action		Captured or Interned		Missing in Action [a]	
			Returned to Duty	Died of Wounds	Returned to Duty	Died prior to Release	Returned to Duty	Died
Total _____	552,117	104,812	360,661	16,012	56,646	855	12,056	1,075
1944								
Jun _____	39,367	9,379	24,210	1,318	3,384	39	902	135
Jul _____	51,424	10,891	34,771	1,876	3,041	27	763	55
Aug _____	42,535	9,111	27,733	1,558	2,782	21	1,264	66
Sep _____	42,183	8,830	25,934	1,495	4,743	37	1,011	133
Oct _____	31,617	6,119	20,436	983	3,203	25	760	91
Nov _____	62,437	11,260	43,957	1,569	4,235	48	1,231	137
Dec _____	77,726	12,795	40,407	1,834	19,339	495	2,647	209
1945								
Jan _____	69,119	10,391	47,849	1,566	8,215	129	865	104
Feb _____	39,414	7,202	28,628	1,010	1,928	17	592	37
Mar _____	53,209	10,483	36,821	1,512	3,274	10	1,053	56
Apr _____	41,058	7,994	28,469	1,224	2,425	4	891	51
May _____	2,028	357	1,446	67	77	3	77	1

[a] Excludes those initially reported as missing in action but subsequently determined to have been killed in action, wounded in action, captured or interned. Such determinations were deleted from *Missing* and added to the appropriate category.

Source: AGO, Statistical and Accounting Branch, "Army Battle Casualties and Nonbattle Deaths in WW II, Final Report," 1953.

TABLE 9—BRITISH AND CANADIAN STRENGTHS, NORTHWEST EUROPE, 1944–45

Date	Total Strength [a]	British	Canadian
31 October 1944 _____	895,912	[b] 771,267	124,645
8 November 1944 _____	925,664	807,028	118,636
31 May 1945 _____	1,095,744	907,553	188,191
16 June 1945 _____	[c] 1,072,717	890,285	182,432

[a] Includes RAF and Royal Navy personnel. The totals under this column, broken down only in the 31 October 1944 report and the 16 June 1945 report, show for the former 82,902 RAF and 8,142 RN personnel; for the 1944 date they show 93,013 RAF and 20,856 RN personnel. The RAF figure of 93,013 is quite near the figure of 96,078 (plus 1,308 WAAF) for 1 May 1945 given in a statement furnished to OCMH by the Air Ministry, London.

[b] Because the strength reports for the other three dates do not include personnel in hospitals, this figure does not include the 13,893 listed in hospitals in the report of 31 October 1944. It does include 2,815 women.

[c] Does not include women.

Source: Cabinet Office, Historical Section, London.

Note. These statistics must be used with the warning that they cannot be the basis of comparison between the U.S. and British air efforts. U.S. air strengths listed in Table 7 include the air forces both in the United Kingdom and on the Continent. The British forces in this table include only those on the Continent. Total British air force strength (including WAAF) amounted to 819,578 on 1 May 1945. Needless to say a considerable part of this force was used in the preinvasion period and during the campaigns in northwest Europe in support of the Allied campaigns.

TABLE 10—BATTLE CASUALTIES OF THE BRITISH 21 ARMY GROUP, D DAY TO V-E DAY[a]

Formation	Total casualties	Killed	Wounded	Missing
21 Army Group	191, 219	41, 044	131, 386	18, 789
British	141, 291	b	b	b
Canadian	43, 249	b	b	b
Polish	5, 598	b	b	b
Dutch	127	b	b	b
Belgian	364	b	b	b
Czech	590	b	b	b

[a] Including firm figures to 0600 hours, 1 April 1945.
[b] Breakdown not furnished.

Source: 21 Army Group "A" SITREP No. 337, compiled by Q(AE) STATS (Quartermaster [Army Equipment] Statistics), 14 May 1945.

Note. The figures in this table, supplied by British authorities, are presented in the absence of any more definitive report and must be used with the understanding that they are subject to considerable error. They do not include air casualties, and they were compiled too soon to have the *Missing* total corrected. A revised British figure would probably show a sizable *Captured* total as well as a higher *Killed* total and smaller *Missing* total than the ones above. A comparison of the *Missing* figure above with the corrected figure given for U.S. forces in Table 8 will give some idea of the difference. The British figures are likely to be less accurate than the U.S. casualty figures of Table 8, inasmuch as the latter tabulation was prepared in 1953 on the basis of later data. The statistics of this table are useful for purposes of indicating the size of the British and Canadian casualties but not for purposes of exact comparison with U.S. statistics. As an example of variations in casualty figures one may note that a different casualty report (known as AG Hot Spot Casualties—Northwest Europe), which summarizes British, Canadian, and Royal Marine losses from D Day to 30 April 1945, shows a casualty total of 196,980 as compared to the 14 May 1945 cumulative figure above of 191,219.

TABLE 11—BATTLE CASUALTIES OF FRENCH ARMY, 8 NOVEMBER 1942–8 MAY 1945

Area and Dates	Total	Killed in Action	Wounded in Action	Captured	Missing in Action
Total	115, 600	24, 029	80, 355	6, 081	5, 135
North Africa, 1942–1943	18, 023	5, 187	7, 342	2, 088	3, 406
Italy, 1943–1945	30, 751	6, 255	23, 500	117	879
Northern Europe, 1944–1945	66, 826	12, 587	49, 513	3, 876	850

Source: Office, Chief of Staff, Ministry of National Defense, France.

Appendix F

The Supreme Commander's Orders of the Day*

I

Soldiers, Sailors and Airmen of the Allied Expeditionary Force:

You are about to embark upon the Great Crusade, toward which we have striven these many months. The eyes of the world are upon you. The hopes and prayers of liberty-loving people everywhere march with you. In company with our brave Allies and brothers-in-arms on other Fronts you will bring about the destruction of the German war machine, the elimination of Nazi tyranny over oppressed peoples of Europe, and security for ourselves in a free world.

Your task will not be an easy one. Your enemy is well trained, well equipped and battle-hardened. He will fight savagely.

But this is the year 1944! Much has happened since the Nazi triumphs of 1940–41. The United Nations have inflicted upon the Germans great defeats, in open battle, man-to-man. Our air offensive has seriously reduced their strength in the air and their capacity to wage war on the ground. Our Home Fronts have given us an overwhelming superiority in weapons and munitions of war, and placed at our disposal great reserves of trained fighting men. The tide has turned! The free men of the world are marching together to Victory!

I have full confidence in your courage, devotion to duty and skill in battle. We will accept nothing less than full victory!

Good luck! And let us all beseech the blessing of Almighty God upon this great and noble undertaking.

DWIGHT D. EISENHOWER

6 June 1944

II

This message was distributed to the troops with the D-Day statement.

You are soon to be engaged in a great undertaking—the invasion of Europe. Our purpose is to bring about, in company with our Allies, and our comrades on other fronts, the total defeat of Germany. Only by such a complete victory can we free ourselves and our homelands from the fear and threat of the Nazi tyranny.

A further element of our mission is the liberation of those people of Western Europe now suffering under German oppression.

* The term, *Order of the Day,* is used far more frequently by foreign armies than in the United States. Since SHAEF was a coalition command, the name was applied to certain documents of more than ordinary significance. An arbitrary numbering system has been used in this appendix.

Before embarking on this operation, I have a personal message for you as to your own individual responsibility, in relation to the inhabitants of our Allied countries.

As a representative of your country, you will be welcomed with deep gratitude by the liberated peoples, who for years have longed for this deliverance. It is of the utmost importance that this feeling of friendliness and goodwill be in no way impaired by careless or indifferent behavior on your part. By a courteous and considerate demeanor, you can on the other hand do much to strengthen that feeling.

The inhabitants of Nazi-occupied Europe have suffered great privations, and you will find that many of them lack even the barest necessities. You, on the other hand, have been, and will continue to be, provided adequate food, clothes and other necessities. You must not deplete the already meager local stocks of food and other supplies by indiscriminate buying, thereby fostering the "Black Market", which can only increase the hardship of the inhabitants.

The rights of individuals, as to their persons and property, must be scrupulously respected, as though in your own country. You must remember, always, that these people are our friends and Allies.

I urge each of you to bear constantly in mind that by your actions not only you as an individual, but your country as well, will be judged. By establishing a relationship with the liberated peoples, based on mutual understanding and respect, we shall enlist their wholehearted assistance in the defeat of our common enemy. Thus shall we lay the foundation for a lasting peace, without which our great effort will have been in vain.

Dwight D. Eisenhower

III

This message was not included in the SGS file of Supreme Commander's Messages to AEF, but it was broadcast by the Supreme Commander. It was issued to Communications Zone troops in mimeographed form by their commanding general, who indicated that he received a personal copy of the message at the Supreme Commander's field headquarters. This is included in the AG file 335.18, "Messages to the Troops of the A.E.F.," with the notation, "This is the only copy furnished AG." The writer personally received one of these copies in Normandy.

Allied Soldiers, Sailors and Airmen:

Through your combined skill, valor and fortitude you have created in France a fleeting but definite opportunity for a major Allied victory, one whose realization will mean notable progress toward the final downfall of our enemy. In the past, I have, in moments of unusual significance, made special appeals to the Allied Forces it has been my honor to command. Without exception the response has been unstinted and the results beyond my expectations.

Because the victory we can now achieve is infinitely greater than any it has so far been possible to accomplish in the west, and because the opportunity may be grasped only through the utmost in zeal, determination and speedy action, I make my present appeal to you more urgent than ever before.

I request every airman to make it his direct responsibility that the enemy is blasted unceasingly by day and by night, and is denied safety either in fight or flight.

I request every sailor to make sure that no part of the hostile forces can either escape or be reinforced by sea, and that our comrades on the land want for nothing that guns and ships and ships' companies can bring to them.

I request every soldier to go forward to his assigned objective with the determination that the enemy can survive only through surrender; let no foot of ground once gained be relinquished nor a single German escape through a line once established.

With all of us resolutely performing our special tasks we can make this week a momentous one in the history of this war—a brilliant and fruitful week for us, a fateful one for the ambitions of the Nazi tyrants.

DWIGHT D. EISENHOWER
14 August 1944

IV

To Every Member of the A.E.F.:

The enemy is making his supreme effort to break out of the desperate plight into which you forced him by your brilliant victories of the summer and fall. He is fighting savagely to take back all that you have won and is using every treacherous trick to deceive and kill you. He is gambling everything, but already, in this battle, your gallantry has done much to foil his plans. In the face of your proven bravery and fortitude, he will completely fail.

But we cannot be content with his mere repulse.

By rushing out from his fixed defenses the enemy may give us the chance to turn his great gamble into his worst defeat. So I call upon every man, of all the Allies, to rise now to new heights of courage, of resolution and of effort. Let everyone hold before him a single thought—to destroy the enemy on the ground, in the air, every-

where—destroy him! United in this determination and with unshakable faith in the cause for which we fight, we will, with God's help, go forward to our greatest victory.

DWIGHT D. EISENHOWER
22 December 1944

V

To Every Member of the A.E.F.:

The encirclement of the Ruhr by a wide pincer movement has cut off the whole of Army Group B and parts of Army Group H, thus forming a large pocket of enemy troops whose fate is sealed and who are ripe for annihilation. The most vital industrial area is denied to the German war potential. This magnificent feat of arms will bring the war more rapidly to a close. It will long be remembered in history as an outstanding battle—the Battle of the Ruhr.

DWIGHT D. EISENHOWER
3 April 1945

VI

To Every Member of the A.E.F.:

The battle of the Ruhr has ended with complete success. Following hard upon the final destruction of the German forces west of the Rhine, the 21st Army Group thrust powerfully across that river with the U.S. Ninth Army under command. Simultaneously, rapid drives across the Rhine and from the Remagen bridgehead by 12th and 6th Army Groups provided the southern arm of a great double envelopment which completely encircled the entire German Army Group "B" and two Corps of Army Group "H", whose mobility was rendered almost zero by our magnificent and tireless air forces. Thereafter, in the pocket thus created the 12th Army Group eliminated 21 enemy divisions, including 3 panzer, 1 panzer grenadier and 3 parachute divisions. Over 317,000 prisoners of war were captured including 24 generals and 1 admiral. Many tanks and more than 750 guns were destroyed or taken. Booty is immense and still being counted. The enemy's total losses in killed and wounded will never be accurately known.

The rapidity and determination with which this brilliant action was executed tore asunder the divisions of Field Marshal Model, and enabled all Army Groups without pause to continue their drive eastwards into the heart of Germany.

This victory of Allied armies is a fitting prelude to the final battles to crush the ragged remnants of Hitler's armies of the west, now tottering on the threshold of defeat.

DWIGHT D. EISENHOWER

20 April 1945

VII

The whole Allied expeditionary force congratulates the Seventh Army on the seizure of Munich, the cradle of the Nazi beast.

DWIGHT D. EISENHOWER

30 April 1945

VIII

VICTORY ORDER OF THE DAY
Men and women of the Allied Expeditionary Forces:

The crusade on which we embarked in the early summer of 1944 has reached its glorious conclusion. It is my special privilege, in the name of all Nations represented in this Theater of War, to commend each of you for valiant performance of duty. Though these words are feeble they come from the bottom of a heart overflowing with pride in your loyal service and admiration for you as warriors.

Your accomplishments at sea, in the air, on the ground and in the field of supply, have astonished the world. Even before the final week of the conflict, you had put 5,000,000 of the enemy permanently out of the war. You have taken in stride military tasks so difficult as to be classed by many doubters as impossible. You have confused, defeated and destroyed your savagely fighting foe. On the road to victory you have endured every discomfort and privation and have surmounted every obstacle ingenuity and desperation could throw in your path. You did not pause until our front was firmly joined up with the great Red Army coming from the East, and other Allied Forces, coming from the South.

Full victory in Europe has been attained.

Working and fighting together in a single and indestructible partnership you have achieved a perfection in unification of air, ground and naval power that will stand as a model in our time.

The route you have travelled through hundreds of miles is marked by the graves of former comrades. From them has been exacted the ultimate sacrifice; blood of many nations—American, British, Canadian, French, Polish and others—has helped to gain the victory. Each of the fallen died as a member of the team to which you belong, bound together by a common love of liberty and a refusal to submit to enslavement. No monument of stone, no memorial of whatever magnitude could so well express our respect and ven-

eration for their sacrifice as would per-
petuation of the spirit of comradeship in
which they died. As we celebrate Victory
in Europe let us remind ourselves that
our common problems of the immediate
and distant future can best be solved in
the same conception of cooperation and
devotion to the cause of human freedom
as have made this Expeditionary Force
such a mighty engine of righteous destruction.

Let us have no part in the profitless
quarrels in which other men will inevitably engage as to what country, what
service, won the European War. Every
man, every woman, of every nation here
represented, has served according to his or
her ability, and the efforts of each have
contributed to the outcome. This we shall
remember—and in doing so we shall be
revering each honored grave, and be sending comfort to the loved ones of comrades
who could not live to see this day.

Dwight D. Eisenhower

8 May 1945

IX

To All Members of the Allied Expeditionary Force:

The task which we set ourselves is finished, and the time has come for me to relinquish Combined Command.

In the name of the United States and
the British Commonwealth, from whom
my authority is derived, I should like to
convey to you the gratitude and admiration of our two nations for the manner in
which you have responded to every demand that has been made upon you. At
times, conditions have been hard and the
tasks to be performed arduous. No praise
is too high for the manner in which you
have surmounted every obstacle.

I should like, also, to add my own personal word of thanks to each one of you for
the part you have played, and the contribution you have made to our joint victory.

Now that you are about to pass into
other spheres of activity, I say Good-bye
to you and wish you Good Luck and God-
Speed.

Dwight D. Eisenhower

13 July 1945

X

On this occasion, the termination of
Combined Command, I welcome the opportunity to express my gratitude and admiration to the people of the Allied
Nations in Europe whose fighting forces
and nationals have contributed so effectively to victory.

United in a common cause, the men
and women of Belgium, Czechoslovakia,
Denmark, France, Luxembourg, Netherlands and Norway joined with the British
Commonwealth of Nations and the United
States of America to form a truly Allied
team, which in conjunction with the
mighty Red Army smashed and obliterated the Nazi aggressors. I pay tribute to
every individual who gave so freely and
unselfishly to the limit of his or her ability.
Their achievements in the cause for which
they fought will be indelibly inscribed in
the pages of history and cherished in the
hearts of all freedom-loving people.

It is my fervent hope and prayer that
the unparalleled unity which has been
achieved among the Allied Nations in war
will be a source of inspiration for, and
point the way to, a permanent and lasting
peace.

Dwight D. Eisenhower

14 July 1945

Appendix G
Table of Equivalent Ranks

U.S. Army	German Army and Air Force	German Waffen-SS
None	Reichsmarschall	None
General of the Army	Generalfeldmarschall	Reichsfuehrer-SS
General	Generaloberst	Oberstgruppenfuehrer
Lieutenant General	General der Infanterie	Obergruppenfuehrer
	Artillerie	
	Gebirgstruppen	
	Kavallerie	
	Nachrichtentruppen	
	Panzertruppen	
	Pioniere	
	Luftwaffe	
	Flieger	
	Fallschirmtruppen	
	Flakartillerie	
	Luftnachrichtentruppen	
Major General	Generalleutnant	Gruppenfuehrer
Brigadier General	Generalmajor	Brigadefuehrer
None	None	Oberfuehrer
Colonel	Oberst	Standartenfuehrer
Lieutenant Colonel	Oberstleutnant	Obersturmbannfuehrer
Major	Major	Sturmbannfuehrer
Captain	Hauptmann	Hauptsturmfuehrer
Captain (Cavalry)	Rittmeister	
First Lieutenant	Oberleutnant	Obersturmfuehrer
Second Lieutenant	Leutnant	Untersturmfuehrer

Glossary

AAR	After action report
Abn	Airborne
AEAF	Allied Expeditionary Air Force
AEF	Allied Expeditionary Force
AFHQ	Allied Force Headquarters
A Gp	Army group
AIS	Allied Information Service
ANCXF	Allied Naval Commander, Expeditionary Force
Anlage	Appendix or annex
ASW	Assistant Secretary of War
ATS	(Women's) Auxiliary Territorial Service
Br	British
Br COS	British Chiefs of Staff Committee
CAD	Civil Affairs Division
CCAC	Combined Civil Affairs Committee
CinC	Commander in Chief
CNO	Chief of Naval Operations
Comdr	Commander
COMZ	Communications Zone
Conf	Conference
COSSAC	Chief of Staff to the Supreme Allied Commander (Designate)
Dir	Directive, director
EACS	European Allied Contact Section
ETOUSA	European Theater of Operations, U.S. Army
Exec	Executive
FAAA	First Allied Airborne Army
FFI	*Forces Françaises de l'Intérieur* (French Forces of the Interior)
FO	Field order
Fuehrungsgruppe	Operations group
Fuehrungsstab	Operations staff
FUSA	First U.S. Army
FUSAG	First U.S. Army Group
G–1	Personnel section of divisional or higher staff
G–2	Intelligence section
G–3	Operations section
G–4	Supply section

G–5	Civil Affairs Division of SHAEF
G–6	Short-lived division of SHAEF which dealt with public relations and psychological warfare
Gen. St. d. H.	*Generalstab des Heeres* (General Staff of the Army)
Gp	Group
GO	General order
Heeresgruppe	Army group
Hq	Headquarters
Intel	Intelligence
JCS	Joint Chiefs of Staff
JIC	Joint Intelligence Committee
JPS	Joint Staff Planners
JSM	Joint Staff Mission (British mission to Washington)
Kampfgruppe	German combat group of variable size
Kanalkueste	Portion of the French coast generally coinciding with the *Fifteenth Army* sector. It included the Pas-de-Calais area and the Somme–Seine coast.
KTB	*Kriegstagebuch* (war diary)
LCT	Landing craft, tank
LST	Landing ship, tank
Ltr of Instr	Letter of instructions
Luftwaffe	German Air Force
Mil Mission Moscow	U.S. Military Mission to Moscow
MOI	Ministry of Information (British)
NATOUSA	North African Theater of Operations
NUSA	Ninth U.S. Army
Ob. d. H.	*Oberbefehlshaber des Heeres* (Commander in Chief of the Army)
OB NORDWEST	*Oberbefehlshaber Nordwest* (Headquarters, Commander in in Chief Northwest [northwest Germany, Denmark, and the Netherlands])
OB SUED	*Oberbefehlshaber Sued* (Headquarters, Commander in Chief South [southern Germany and several army groups on the Eastern front])
OB SUEDOST	*Oberbefehlshaber Suedost* (Headquarters, Commander in Chief Southeast [the Balkans])
OB SUEDWEST	*Oberbefehlshaber Suedwest* (Headquarters, Commander in Chief Southwest [Italy])
OB WEST	*Oberbefehlshaber West* (Headquarters, Commander in Chief West [France, Belgium, and the Netherlands]), highest German ground headquarters of the Western Front until May 1945
Oberkommando	Headquarters of an army or higher military organization
OCMH	Office, Chief of Military History

OKH	*Oberkommando des Heeres* (Army High Command)
OKL	*Oberkommando der Luftwaffe* (Luftwaffe High Command)
OKM	*Oberkommando der Kriegsmarine* (Navy High Command)
Op. (H)	*Operations Abteilung (H)* (Operations Branch [Army])
Org. Abt.	*Organisations Abteilung* (staff section in charge of organization)
Organization Todt	Paramilitary construction organization of the Nazi party, auxiliary to the Wehrmacht. Named after its founder, Dr. Todt.
OSS	Office of Strategic Services
Ost battalions	Non-German volunteer troops from east-European countries
OWI	Office of War Information
POL	Petrol (gasoline), oil, and lubricants
PRD	Public Relations Division, SHAEF
PWE	Political Warfare Executive
RAF	Royal Air Force
Rec	Records
Reichskanzlei	Reich Chancellory
SAC	Supreme Allied Commander
SACMED	Supreme Allied Commander, Mediterranean Theater
SCAEF	Supreme Commander, Allied Expeditionary Force
SFHQ	Special Force Headquarters
SGS	Secretary, General Staff
SHAEF	Supreme Headquarters, Allied Expeditionary Force
Sitrep	Situation report
SO	Special Operations
SOE	Special Operations Executive
SOP	Standing operating procedure
SS	*Schutzstaffel* (Elite Guard)
Tel	Telegram, teletype
TIS	Theater Intelligence Section
UNRRA	United Nations Relief and Rehabilitation Administration
USAFBI	U.S. Army Forces in the British Isles
USFET	U.S. Forces in the European Theater
USSBS	U.S. Strategic Bombing Survey
USSTAF	U.S. Strategic Air Forces
Volkssturm	A people's militia, partially organized in one of the last steps of German mobilization for total war
WD	War Department
Wehrmacht	German Armed Forces
Wehrmachtbefehlshaber	Armed Forces Commander
WFSt	*Wehrmachtfuehrungsstab* (Armed Forces Operations Staff)
WO	War Office

Code Names

ANVIL   The planned 1944 Allied invasion of southern France in the Toulon–Marseille area

ARCADIA   U.S.-British staff conference at Washington, December 1941–January 1942

BIGOT   Special security procedure for OVERLORD

ARGONAUT   Yalta Conference, February 1945

BENEFICIARY   Plan for breaking out of the Normandy lodgment by means of a combined airborne-amphibious attack on St. Malo

BOLERO   Build-up of troops and supplies in the United Kingdom in preparation for a cross-Channel attack

BRADDOCK II   Dropping of small fuze incendiaries to European workers for use in sabotage operations

COBRA   Operation launched by First U.S. Army on 25 July 1944, designed to break out of the Normandy lodgment

COCKADE   Diversionary operations in 1943 to pin down German forces in the west

COMET   British plan, not carried out, for an air drop on 7 September 1944 in the Arnhem–Nijmegen area

CROSSBOW   A general term used by the Allies to refer to the German long-range weapons program and to Allied countermeasures against it

ECLIPSE   Name given in November 1944 to posthostilities plans for Germany

EUREKA   Tehran Conference, November–December 1943

GARDEN   See MARKET-GARDEN

GOODWOOD   British attack to break out of the Normandy lodgment, late July 1944, coinciding with U.S. Operation COBRA

GREIF   German deception operation in support of the Ardennes counteroffensive

GRENADE   Ninth Army supporting attack for Operation VERITABLE

GYMNAST   1941 plan for invasion of North Africa

HANDS UP   Plan for breaking out of the Normandy lodgment by means of a combined airborne-amphibious attack on Quiberon Bay

HUSKY   Allied invasion of Sicily in July 1943

INDEPENDENCE	Plan for First French Army attack against German garrisons on French coasts, December 1944
LINNET I	Planned airborne drop at Tournai, Belgium, September 1944
LINNET II	Planned airborne drop at Aachen–Maastricht Gap, September 1944
LUCKY STRIKE	21 Army Group plan calling for an eastward drive and the capture of the Seine ports as an alternative to plans for the earlier capture of Brittany, considered in May and June 1944
MARKET-GARDEN	Airborne operation intended to establish a bridgehead across the Rhine in the Netherlands, September 1944. Operation MARKET involved seizure of bridges in the Nijmegen–Arnhem area, and Operation GARDEN was to open a corridor from Eindhoven northward toward Germany.
NEST EGG	Plan for occupation of Channel Islands in case of German collapse or surrender
NOBALL	Term used by the air forces in referring to target sites in their attacks on long-range weapons
NORDWIND	German counterattack in Alsace, January 1945
OCTAGON	Second Quebec Conference, September 1944
OVERLORD	Plan for the invasion of northwest Europe, spring 1944
PLUNDER	Montgomery's northern crossing of the Rhine, March 1945
POINTBLANK	The Combined Bomber Offensive from the United Kingdom against Germany
QUADRANT	First Quebec Conference, August 1943
RANKIN I, II, III	Plans for return to the Continent in the event of deterioration of the German position
REDLINE	Radio circuits set up in September 1944 for messages to and from the Supreme Commander
ROUNDUP	Various 1941–43 plans for a cross-Channel attack in the final phases of the war
SEXTANT	Cairo Conference, 22–26 November 1943
SHARPENER	Supreme Commander's advance command post at Portsmouth, May 1944
SHELLBURST	SHAEF advance headquarters at Tournières, France, near Bayeux, established August 1944
SHIPMATE	Enlarged SHAEF forward headquarters near Portsmouth, replacing SHARPENER
SLEDGEHAMMER	Plan for a limited-objective attack across the Channel in 1942 designed either to take advantage of a crack in German morale or as a "sacrifice" operation to aid the Russians

SPRING	Canadian attack, July 1944, coinciding with Operation COBRA
STARKEY	Threat directed in 1943 against the Pas-de-Calais
SWORDHILT	Plan for a combined airborne-amphibious operation to seize the area east of Brest, August 1944
SYMBOL	Casablanca Conference, January 1943
TALISMAN	Early name for posthostilities plans for Germany
TERMINAL	Potsdam Conference, July 1945
TINDALL	Threat directed against Norway in 1943
TOPFLIGHT	Signal for release of press information on D-Day assault
TORCH	Allied invasion of North and Northwest Africa, 1942
TOTALIZE	Post-COBRA attack in France
TRACTABLE	Post-COBRA attack in France
TRANSFIGURE	Plan for airborne operation to capture and control important road nets in Paris–Orléans area, 16–17 August 1944
TRIDENT	Washington Conference, May 1943
UNDERTONE	Seventh Army operation to breach West Wall and establish bridgehead over Rhine in Worms area, March–April 1945
VARSITY	FAAA operation in support of Operation PLUNDER
VERITABLE	21 Army Group plan for a Canadian attack between the Maas and the Rhine, January–February 1945
WADHAM	Threat directed against the Cotentin in 1943
WIDEWING	SHAEF headquarters at Bushy Park, near London

Bibliographical Note

The Supreme Command is based in large part on Allied and German documents in the possession of the Department of the Army, on Allied documents made available by French and British sources, and on private papers of General Eisenhower and key members of his staff. These sources have been supplemented by numerous interviews with various Allied leaders, by published memoirs and histories, and by detailed comments on the manuscript by persons mentioned in the volume.

Primary Sources

I

The most important single collection of documents used in this volume is that of Supreme Headquarters, Allied Expeditionary Force. In addition to letters, cables, memorandums, reports, records of conferences, plans, drafts of plans and messages, interoffice communications, and other papers normally kept in the files of any military headquarters, the SHAEF collection includes the records of its predecessors—Combined Commanders and COSSAC. The SHAEF file also contains a number of memorandums by the British Chiefs of Staff as well as extracts from the minutes of their meetings in which the campaigns in northwest Europe were discussed.

The SHAEF records have been supplemented by minutes of the meetings of the Combined Chiefs of Staff and the U.S. Joint Chiefs of Staff, including minutes of the great conferences attended by Mr. Churchill and President Roosevelt and their advisers. War Department records contain message files of cables and letters between the President and the Prime Minister (these include information copies, paraphrases which were sent by the War Department to General Eisenhower, and drafts of cables prepared by the War Department for the President's signature). They contain similar records of communications between the Combined and Joint Chiefs of Staff and the Supreme Commander, paraphrases of messages sent by the British Chiefs of Staff to the Joint Staff Mission for delivery to the U.S. Chiefs of Staff, and the correspondence between Allied commanders and Allied planners. Supplementing these are private letter files of the Supreme Commander and private papers furnished the author by Lt. Gen. Sir Frederick E. Morgan, Air Chief Marshal Sir James M. Robb, Brig. Gen. Robert A. McClure, Maj. Gen. Ray W. Barker, Marshal of the Royal Air Force Lord Tedder, Lt. Gen. Walter B. Smith, and Gen. Sir Andrew Thorne.

Details of the operations have come mainly from such secondary sources as after action reports, dispatches, and semi-official army group and army histories. A number of these accounts have been checked against primary sources found in the army group and army files. The book has also drawn on combat interviews conducted during the war by War Department historians.

In some cases photostatic or typewritten copies of British and Canadian documents have been furnished the author by the Historical Section, Cabinet Office, and by the Canadian Historical Section.

The sources have been supplemented by interviews conducted by the author with nearly 100 British, French, and U.S. officers and civilians in the period 1946–51 (see list at end of bibliographical note).

II

The collections of German primary sources vary greatly in completeness. For periods of disaster, such as the envelopments in the Falaise Gap and in the Ruhr Pocket, many papers of the field headquarters were destroyed. Many records were also destroyed at OKW. For high-level material, the author has drawn on *OKW/WFSt KTB Ausarbeitung, "Der Westen" 1.IV.–16.XII.44.* This draft War Diary (KTB) is based on the detailed daily working notes of Major Percy Schramm in his capacity as historian at the headquarters of OKW. Until the end of 1943 the diary consisted of a chronological listing of events supplemented by information from participants in operations. After 1943 the diary was arranged according to subject matter and fronts and was supplemented by a *Merkbuch* kept by Schramm, with notes of discussions at the situation meetings he attended and notes obtained from special interviews with the deputy chief of WFSt, General Warlimont. From 1 January 1945 the chronological order was reintroduced. In view of the subsequent destruction of OKW records, the copies of the *Ausarbeitungen* for 1944 and the personal notes of Schramm present a unique and valuable source. The original diary, as well as a copy designated as MS # B–034 (Schramm), is in OCMH files.

For information on battles, I have also relied on manuscript histories prepared after the war by more than two hundred German generals working under the direction of Col. Harold A. Potter and later under Col. Wilbur S. Nye. I was aided in assessing the general value of this material by Capt. Frank C. Mahin, Jr., and Capt. James F. Scoggin, who worked with the German generals for more than two years (1946–48). While the German accounts are weakened at times by a subjective approach and by lack of source material, they are of value in filling in the broad outlines of the German story of the war. An important source for the last chapters of the book is the file *OKW Politische Angelegenheiten*, which contains a draft for a German White Book. Intended as a defense of Admiral Doenitz' interim government in May 1945 the unsigned paper is accompanied by numerous documents which are of great value. The collection of German documents available to the Office of the Chief of Military History also contains a large file of OKW papers received or sent out by Field Marshal Keitel and General Jodl.

III

The following notes are intended as a convenient guide to the primary sources used in this volume.

AAF files. Army Air Force files containing records of Eighth and Ninth Air Forces, which were formerly in the Pentagon, are now located at the Air University, Maxwell Field, Montgomery, Ala.

ABC files. A collection kept by the Strategy and Policy Group of OPD (q.v.).

Barker files. Personal papers of Maj. Gen.

Ray W. Barker (ret.), deputy chief of COSSAC and G–1 of SHAEF. Located in OCMH files.

CAD. Civil affairs papers collected by the Civil Affairs Division of the War Department. They include papers of the Combined Civil Affairs Committee. Now in Departmental Records Branch, AGO.

COS. British Chiefs of Staff papers and minutes of conferences. Extracts pertinent to SHAEF operations were forwarded to the Supreme Commander for information. These are filed with the SHAEF SGS papers, and bound separately by year under the titles "Papers" and "Minutes."

CCS. Combined Chiefs of Staff papers and minutes of meetings. All of these may be found in the OPD collection (q.v.). The papers include reports, reprints of cables and letters, and memorandums prepared by the British or U.S. Chiefs of Staff or their planners. No stenographic notes of the meetings were kept, but British and U.S. secretaries kept a general statement of the main points advanced and the conclusions reached. These records in final form were specifically and individually approved by each of the Combined Chiefs. *Note.* The reader is reminded that quotations from CCS minutes are taken from the printed summaries and are not necessarily the exact words of the conferees. It should also be noted that, because no exact copy of a highly classified cable can be made because of security regulations, the language in War Department cables concerning classified matters may differ slightly from the minutes and from the cable which is on file in the SHAEF cable log. The paraphrases reflect the exact intent of the author, but vary in paragraph arrangement and wording. This reminder applies to every quotation from a highly classified cable used in this volume.

C/S file. Contains documents from wartime files of the Office of the Chief of Staff, War Department. Now a separate collection in the Departmental Records Branch, AGO. On these records see bibliographical note in Mark S. Watson, *Chief of Staff: Prewar Plans and Preparations* (Washington, 1951), UNITED STATES ARMY IN WORLD WAR II, pp. 520–23.

COSSAC. Papers of the COSSAC (Chief of Staff to the Supreme Allied Commander) headquarters and minutes of COSSAC staff meetings. These are separately bound and contained in the SHAEF SGS files.

Diary Office CinC. Diary kept in General Eisenhower's office for him by his naval aide, Capt. Harry C. Butcher. It was started in July 1942 and continued until the end of the war. It is less complete on General Eisenhower's activities after August 1944 when Butcher took up a job in the Public Relations Division of SHAEF. He was still a frequent visitor to General Eisenhower's office, but did not continue to have daily contact with the Supreme Commander. The collection includes daily entries dictated by Captain Butcher, summaries of conversations, reactions by the Supreme Commander or Butcher to events of the day, and items of human interest concerning the Supreme Commander and many of his staff. The diary was kept as a journal and not as a historical narrative and therefore tends to set down uncritically snatches of conversation as the narrator heard them. On the documentary side, Captain Butcher attempted to keep copies of all the high-level cables and letters sent or received by the Supreme Commander. Other important papers, such as intelligence estimates, situation summaries, and special reports, were also included. Of great value are the memorandums which Captain Butcher at irregular intervals persuaded General Eisenhower to write concerning major decisions and problems. Captain Butcher in *My Three Years With Eisenhower* (New York, 1946) printed edited excerpts from the diary. Many are printed as originally written, while others are edited slightly. These changes were usually made to eliminate information later found to be incorrect. It should be noted that Captain Butcher was careful to repeat his guesses that had been proved incorrect by later events. Several of the entries were edited for security reasons, and others in order to remove comments by Captain Butcher which might be deemed offensive by living persons. In quite a few cases the original entry has been summarized.

The diary varies in value to the historian because Captain Butcher, often unable to dictate his entries daily, would sometimes write an entry covering several days at one sitting. In such an entry the dates of events are occasionally confused. Unfortunately, no daily list of appointments was included. Captain Butcher, in his book, has failed in some cases to differentiate sufficiently between items based on conversations with General Eisenhower and those which are merely summaries of official documents. For example, an entry, "Ike says," published under 10 August, may have come from a table conversation that day or it may have been a summary of a paper signed by General Eisenhower several days earlier which happened to be included in the loose-leaf notebook along with the 10 August entry. These differences are apparent in the original. On a few occasions when the typist misdated a letter (an error perhaps corrected later in the SGS file copy, but not in the one preserved in the diary), the letter has appeared under the incorrect date in Captain Butcher's published book. At least one notable mix-up occurred as a result. A letter of 14 September, incorrectly dated 14 August, appears under the August date in the diary. Captain Butcher in writing of the letter, which actually refers to the Arnhem operation, assumed that it meant the landing in southern France and so interpreted it. As a result the book represents General Eisenhower as having discussed General Montgomery's plan for crossing the Rhine before the plan was actually presented to the Supreme Commander. For the most part, the diary—especially in the manuscript state—is extremely valuable for a study of the Supreme Commander and his headquarters.

At the time the author used this diary (1946), it was in the personal possession of General Eisenhower and kept in his office at the Pentagon.

Eisenhower personal file. For purposes of convenience and security several collections of letters and cables were kept in General Eisenhower's personal file. These included the following: personal letters between General Eisenhower and General Marshall (a collection of considerable value since the Supreme Commander was in the habit of outlining his future plans in these informal messages); a special file of letters between Generals Eisenhower and Montgomery; a file of cables and letters between the Supreme Commander and important political and military figures such as the Prime Minister, General de Gaulle, General Juin, Air Marshal Tedder, and General Bradley; and a file of "Eyes Only" cables which were delivered only to the Supreme Commander and his chief of staff. The Diary, Office Commander in Chief, described above, was also in this collection. The SHAEF

Cable Log (q.v.), which was physically kept in the Secretary of the General Staff files, might well be included with this collection. With the exception of the Cable Log, these papers at the time they were consulted by the author (1946–47) were in the personal possession of General Eisenhower.

Inasmuch as the file may well be consolidated when finally indexed, the author has referred to the entire collection under the general title of Eisenhower personal file. It is the richest single file for the purposes of this volume. Because the papers were selected for their importance and because each item was seen personally by the Supreme Commander, the file simplified the author's task of searching through the voluminous SHAEF records for the most important pieces of correspondence.

ETO file. Files of Headquarters, European Theater of Operations, U.S. Army (ETOUSA). Now held by Organizational Records Branch, Records Administration Center, AGO.

Fifteenth Army file. Official journals and papers of the Fifteenth Army. This file also contained some of the 12th Army Group papers at the time the author used it. In Departmental Records Branch, AGO.

FUSA file. Official journals and papers of the First U.S. Army. In Departmental Records Branch, AGO.

JCS. U.S. Joint Chiefs of Staff papers and minutes of their conferences. Located in G–3 Records, Department of the Army.

NUSA file. Official journals and papers of the Ninth U.S. Army. In Departmental Records Branch, AGO.

OCMH files. Documents containing material prepared by or collected by the author or members of the Office of the Chief of Military History staff. Much of the material so cited in this volume consists of answers by former members of the SHAEF staff to the author's questionnaires, British and French documents, and special studies collected by the author.

OPD files. Collection of cables and papers of the Operations Division, War Department. The division was known at various times in the period 1941–51 as the War Plans Division, Operations Division, and Plans and Operations Division. It is at present a part of the G–3 Division. A detailed bibliographical note on these papers may be found in Ray S. Cline, *Washington Command Post: The Operations Division,* UNITED STATES ARMY IN WORLD WAR II (Washington, 1951), pp. 382–85.

SHAEF files. Records of Supreme Headquarters, Allied Expeditionary Force. These are, naturally, the basic source for this volume. It consists of separate files for each of the general and special staff divisions, the SHAEF missions, and the Secretary of the General Staff (SGS), SHAEF. They will be designated in footnotes as SHAEF G–1, SHAEF PWD, SHAEF Mission (France), SHAEF SGS, and so on. The originals of these SHAEF papers are in the Departmental Records Branch, AGO, and microfilmed copies may be found in the British Historical Records.

The richest file of the SHAEF collection, apart from the Eisenhower personal file described elsewhere, is that of the SHAEF secretary of the general staff, which was kept for the personal use of the Supreme Commander and the Chief of Staff, SHAEF. It contains nearly all papers brought to the immediate attention of General Smith and/or General Eisenhower and all those which it was thought that they might wish to consult. The result has been a process of selection which puts before the historian the most important papers of the entire SHAEF collection. To copies of plans and final letters are usually attached the penciled notes and early drafts together with the final approval or disapproval of the Supreme Commander and the chief of staff. It is often possible to follow a paper from the stage of its first draft to a copy of the message which was dispatched. These copies are usually those containing changes made by Generals Eisenhower and Smith. Often, in order to make all pertinent papers available for examination, the secretary of the general staff had extracts or copies made from papers in other files. This not only provides a useful check on the completeness of other files but also makes it possible for the historian to see what information was laid before the Supreme Commander when he made his decision. A careful cross-reference system indicates the location of pertinent papers.

This collection formerly included the SHAEF Cable Log, which was brought up to date daily by the secretary of the general staff. It contained typewritten paraphrases of all cables (except those marked Eyes Only) addressed to the Supreme Commander or sent in his name which his subordinates felt that he should see. Copies of Eyes Only cables were sometimes included in this collection but were usually kept in a special Eyes Only file. The messages in the Cable Log were usually examined daily and initialed by the Supreme Commander. Occasionally one finds his notes asking for comments or suggesting possible answers. The Cable Log when used by the author (1945 and 1946) was in a group of files belonging to General Smith. This file was initially in the CALA collection at Headquarters, USFET, Frankfurt, Germany, and later in the Department of the Army Library at the Pentagon.

Smith papers. Collection of documents and books belonging to Lt. Gen. Walter B. Smith. These were deposited in the War Department library in 1946 and were consulted by special permission of General Smith. With these papers were the SHAEF Cable Log and some Eyes Only files which could not be as readily found in the SHAEF collection.

SUSA file. Contains journals and papers of the Seventh Army. In the Departmental Records Branch, AGO.

TUSA file. Official journals and papers of the Third U.S. Army. Held by Departmental Records Branch, AGO.

12th A Gp file. Operational files of the 12th Army Group. Now in the Departmental Records Branch, AGO.

Secondary Sources

Many unpublished preliminary historical studies by Army, Navy, and Air Force historians are available to the official historian. Studies used to a considerable degree by the author include some of the eleven volumes of a series called the Administrative and Logistical History of the European Theater of Operations prepared in 1945–46 under the direction of Maj. Roland G. Ruppenthal, Assistant Theater Historian, USFET. The 1500-page history of the French Forces of the Interior, prepared by Capt. Lucien Galimand, Capt. Marcel Vigneras, and Maj. R. A. Bourne-Patterson is based on basic documents of the French Resistance and the Allied agencies dealing with these forces.

The author's attention was directed to some of the sources for this volume by a 104-page typewritten History of SHAEF written by Maj. Duncan Emrich and Maj. F. D. Price, the SHAEF historians in 1944–45. Since they were mainly occupied until the end of the war with the preparation of a History of COSSAC (unpublished) and the Supreme Commander's report to the Combined Chiefs of Staff, they had not carried their story beyond the D-Day period at the time they left Supreme Headquarters. Many of the important papers of the Supreme Commander were not available to them at the time the manuscript was prepared. In 1945 the author of the present volume was employed to rewrite and complete this earlier study. This assignment was finished in 1946 before the present volume was begun. Virtually nothing of the original draft has been used in these pages except several useful charts. The short (forty-three-page) History of COSSAC mentioned above was valuable for its story of the administrative organization of SHAEF's predecessor.

Among the published sources, the author has made considerable use of official dispatches and reports, official histories, and memoirs. Three particularly important official reports are: *Report by the Supreme Commander to the Combined Chiefs of Staff on the Operations in Europe of the Allied Expeditionary Force, 6 June 1944 to 8 May 1945* (Washington, 1945); Air Chief Marshal Sir Trafford Leigh-Mallory, Despatch to the Supreme Commander, AEF, November 1944, *Supplement to The London Gazette,* December 31, 1946; and *Report by Allied Naval Commander-in-Chief Expeditionary Force on Operation NEPTUNE* (London, 1944), 3 vols.

The author has profited greatly from the use of the volumes written by his colleagues in the European Section of the Office of the Chief of Military History. Two of the published volumes—Hugh M. Cole, *The Lorraine Campaign* (Washington, 1950) and Gordon A. Harrison, *Cross-Channel Attack*

(Washington, 1951)—were especially helpful on German forces and tactical details concerning the U.S. forces. Other manuscripts now in preparation were made available. Volumes II and III of Wesley Frank Craven and James Lea Cate, eds., *The Army Air Forces in World War II* (Chicago, 1949 and 1951), were used for details relating to air operations in Europe in 1942–45. For Canadian Army activities in Europe, the author depended on Col. C. P. Stacey, *The Canadian Army, 1939–1945: An Official Historical Summary* (Ottawa, 1948), which is a preliminary study of Canadian operations.

Because of the impossibility of checking unit journals for all of the operational details needed for this volume, it has been necessary to rely on the semiofficial histories of the army groups and armies. While subject to error in details, the volumes are of considerable value for giving the broad outlines of campaigns. All of them have drawn heavily on the daily operational reports and intelligence summaries of their headquarters. Even where incorrect they are valuable for giving the operational picture as it was seen at the time by the field commanders and the Supreme Commander. These volumes include: 12th Army Group, *Report of Operations (Final After Action Report)* (printed in Europe, 1945), 14 vols.; 6th Army Group Operations Report (mimeographed report, by months); First U.S. Army, *Report of Operations* (printed in Europe, 1946), consisting of seven volumes on the period 20 October 1943–1 August 1944, four volumes on the period 1 August 1944–22 February 1945, and three volumes on the period 22 February 1945–8 May 1945; *After Action Report, Third U.S. Army, 1 August 1944–9 May 1945* (printed in Europe, 1945), 2 vols.; *The Seventh United*

States Army in France and Germany 1944–1945: Report of Operations (Heidelberg, 1946), 3 vols.; *Conquer: The Story of Ninth Army, 1944–45* (Washington, 1947); *History of the Fifteenth United States Army, 21 August 1944 to 11 July 1945* (apparently printed in Germany, 1946). Most of these volumes have only a limited distribution, but are available in the OCMH or the Department of the Army Library.

Field Marshal Montgomery, *Normandy to the Baltic* (New York, 1948) has been consulted. This volume, which was prepared in part by members of the 21 Army Group staff from official files and personal papers of Field Marshal Montgomery, was circulated in printed form to U.S. and British military headquarters shortly after the war, before its public appearance in Great Britain in 1947 and in the United States in 1948. In form it is an official dispatch rather than personal memoirs, in many cases being little more than a paraphrase of letters of instruction and situation reports. It is nonetheless a valuable summary of British operations. The author made use of the volume for an outline of Montgomery's operations and then submitted his narrative for the correction of operational details to the British Historical Section, Cabinet Office, and the Canadian Historical Section. In addition to checking the accuracy of the account, these sections have also made available documents, charts, casualty data, and other information from their files.

Special mention must be made of the memoirs of key figures in the SHAEF story. In addition to the Montgomery volume, which can be included in this category only with qualification, Gen. Dwight D. Eisenhower, *Crusade in Europe* (New York, 1948), and Gen. Omar N. Bradley, *A Soldier's Story* (New York, 1951), have

been used. General Eisenhower's volume was dictated by him over a period of months and then checked against his personal papers and official documents. Since all documents and papers cited in his volume were made available to the author of *The Supreme Command,* the general's book has been used mostly for judgments of men and events which are not available in his papers. General Bradley's volume was based on dictated material and on recordings of discussions of various phases of the book between himself and his aide. The statements were checked against private papers, official documents, and the memories of many participants. Some of the papers were not available to the author of *The Supreme Command.* Most valuable have been some of the frank appraisals of Allied commanders contained in General Bradley's book. The author was allowed to see both of these volumes in manuscript form.

An important volume for the study of the Supreme Commander and SHAEF is Capt. Harry C. Butcher, *My Three Years With Eisenhower* (New York, 1946). As noted earlier, I was given free access to the Diary, Office of the Commander in Chief, which is the basis for Captain Butcher's book.

Lt. Gen. Sir Frederick E. Morgan, *Overture to Overlord* (New York, 1950), which the author was allowed to see in manuscript, is valuable for showing the problems of the planner of OVERLORD and for his personal recollections. The COSSAC documents and many of General Morgan's private papers were made available to the author.

Other memoirs which were used include: Gen. George S. Patton, Jr., *War as I Knew It* (Boston, 1947); Maj. Gen. Sir Francis de Guingand, *Operation Victory*

(New York, 1947); and Gen. Henry H. Arnold, *Global Mission* (New York, 1949). Lt. Gen. Lewis H. Brereton's *The Brereton Diaries* (New York, 1946) supplied some details on airborne command and operations. Lt. Gen. Walter Bedell Smith's articles on "Eisenhower's Six Great Decisions," *The Saturday Evening Post*, Vols. 218–19, issues for June 8, 15, 22, 29, and July 6 and 13, 1946, were of value.

On high-level policy relating to operations in Europe, books of great value to the author were: Robert E. Sherwood, *Roosevelt and Hopkins: An Intimate History* (New York, 1948); Henry L. Stimson and McGeorge Bundy, *On Active Service in Peace and War* (New York, 1948); Cordell Hull, *The Memoirs of Cordell Hull* (New York, 1948), 2 vols.; Winston S. Churchill, *The Hinge of Fate* (Boston, 1950); Edward R. Stettinius, Jr., *Roosevelt and the Russians: The Yalta Conference* (Garden City, N. Y., 1949); and Admiral William D. Leahy, *I Was There* (New York, 1950). The author was permitted to examine the Leahy volume in manuscript form.

Two secondary sources on enemy actions and command organization should be noted. These are The War in the West, prepared by Dr. Wilhelm Scheidt, principal assistant to Generalmajor Walther Scherff, chief of the military history section of OKW. Dr. Scheidt indicates that a great part of his study was based on his own notes, but a comparison with the *KTB Ausarbeitung*, *"Der Westen,"* (see above) shows that he has relied heavily on Schramm's work. Another work is *Geschichte des Oberbefehlshaber West*, edited by Generalleutnant Bodo Zimmermann, formerly Ia (G–3) of *OB WEST*. The manuscript was prepared under the auspices of the Historical Division of the Department of the Army between 1946 and 1948 and includes contributions by a number of general and general staff officers of the Wehrmacht. All information of this nature must be used with the caution that the authors had to rely in many cases entirely on their memories. Many of them have a tendency to overemphasize the superiority of Allied manpower and equipment and their own disadvantages. Most of them also develop the thesis that all would have gone well had the views of the General Staff, rather than those of Hitler, prevailed.

For the last days of the Reich, two books are of considerable importance: Count Folke Bernadotte's *The Curtain Falls: Last Days of the Reich* (New York, 1945), which tells of Bernadotte's role in the surrender negotiations, and H. R. Trevor-Roper, *The Last Days of Hitler* (New York, 1947), which is an account by a British intelligence officer of his investigations into the details of the Fuehrer's final hours.

Interviews

The author is greatly indebted to nearly a hundred Allied military and political leaders for interviews granted to him in the period 1945–51. The number of interviews with the individuals named varies from one to ten. Nearly all of them spoke freely, although a few asked that they not be quoted. Several of them read to the author from private diaries or papers, but were unwilling to have the material cited. For that reason some controversial matters have been left without footnotes or with only a general reference to information supplied by Allied leaders. In the case of some thirty or forty persons named, the original interview material was supplemented by later detailed comments on the author's manuscript.

References in the list are to positions held by individuals in the 1943–45 period. Their titles and ranks are those they had when interviewed.

Alanbrooke, Field Marshal Viscount, Chief of the Imperial General Staff

Allen, Brig. Gen. Frank A., Chief of Public Relations Division, SHAEF

Barker, Maj. Gen. Ray W., Deputy Chief of COSSAC and G–1, SHAEF

(Bechtolsheim. See Mauchenheim.)

Belchem, Brigadier R. F. K., Chief of Operations, 21 Army Group

Betts, Brig. Gen. Thomas J., Deputy G–2 of SHAEF

Biddle, Col. Anthony J. D., Deputy Head of EACS

Bingham, Barry, Public Information Officer

Bonesteel, Col. Charles H., III, Member of G–3 Division, 12th Army Group

Bradley, Gen. Omar N., Commander of FUSA and later of 12th Army Group

Briggs, Maj. Ruth, Secretary to Gen. W. B. Smith

Broad, Wing Commander H. P., Member of Planning Staff of SHAEF

(Brooke, Field Marshal Sir Alan. See above, Alanbrooke.)

Brown, Brig. Gen. Robert Q., Headquarters Commandant, SHAEF

Brownjohn, Maj. Gen. N. C. D., G–4 of COSSAC and Assistant G–4 of SHAEF

Bull, Lt. Gen. Harold R., G–3 SHAEF

Butler, Maj. Gordon, Member of SHAEF SGS Staff

Caffery, Ambassador Jefferson, Ambassador to France

Cameron, Maj. Gen. A. M., Chief of the Air Defense Division of SHAEF

Carter, Col. Henry, Chief of Planning Coordination Section, Office of the Political Officer, SHAEF

Coningham, Air Chief Marshal Sir Arthur, Commander of Second Tactical Air Force

Crawford, Maj. Gen. Robert W., G–4 of SHAEF

Creasy, Rear Adm. George E., Chief of Staff of the Allied Naval Expeditionary Force

Cunningham of Hyndhope, Admiral of the Fleet Viscount, First Sea Lord

Curtis, Col. J. O., Member of SHAEF G–2 Division

Davis, Brig. Gen. Thomas J., Adjutant General and Public Relations Chief at SHAEF

Dempsey, Gen. Sir Miles C., Commander of Second British Army

Dickson, Col. B. A., G–2 of First Army

Eisenhower, Gen Dwight D., Supreme Allied Commander

Gale, Lt. Gen. Sir Humfrey M., Deputy Chief of Staff, SHAEF, Chief Administrative Officer

Gaulle, Gen. Charles de, Head of the French Committee of National Liberation and later of the French Provisional Government

Gault, Col. James, Personal Assistant to General Eisenhower

Gleave, Group Captain T. P., Air Member of SHAEF Planning Staff

Grasett, Lt. Gen. Sir A. E., G–5 of SHAEF

Helfers, Lt. Col. M. C., Special Intelligence Officer, Third Army

Hesketh, Lt. Col. R. F., Member of SHAEF G–3 Staff

Hickman, Maj. R. E., Member of SHAEF AG Staff and Officer in Charge of CALA Records

Hodges, Gen. Courtney H., Commander of First U.S. Army

Holmes, Brig. Gen. Julius C., Deputy G–5 of SHAEF

Huebner, Lt. Gen. Clarence R., Commander of 1st Division and V Corps

Hughes, Maj. Gen. H. B. W., Chief of Engineers of SHAEF

Hughes-Hallett, Capt. John, Naval Chief of Staff, COSSAC

Ismay, Gen. Sir Hastings L., Chief of Staff, Ministry of Defence

Jackson, W. D., Member of 12th Army Group Intelligence Staff

Johnson, Alan Campbell, Personal Assistant to Lord Mountbatten

Juin, Gen. Alphonse-Pierre, Chief of the French Bureau of National Defense

Keating, Maj. Gen. F. A., Commander of 102d Division

Kenner, Maj. Gen. Albert W., Chief Medical Officer, SHAEF

King, Fleet Admiral Ernest J., Chief of Operations, U.S. Navy

Kirk, Admiral Alan G., Commander of U.S. Naval Forces in the Invasion of Northwest Europe, Later Head of U.S. Naval Mission, SHAEF

Lambe, Rear Adm. C. E., Naval Member of Joint Planning Staff (British)

Laux, Lt. Col. Ray J., Executive Officer of War Department Civil Affairs Division

Leahy, Fleet Admiral William D., Chief of Staff to the Commander in Chief

Lear, Lt. Gen. Ben, Deputy Theater Commander, ETOUSA

Lee, Lt. Gen. John C. H., Commander of Headquarters, Communications Zone

Lewis, Maj. Gen. John T., Head of SHAEF Mission (France)

Lockhart, Sir Robert Bruce, Head of the British Political Committee

Lodge, Senator Henry Cabot, Chief of the Liaison Section of 6th Army Group

McClure, Brig. Gen. Robert A., Chief of Psychological Warfare Division, SHAEF

McLean, Maj. Gen. Kenneth G., Head of SHAEF Planning Staff

McSherry, Brig. Gen. Frank J., Deputy Chief of G–5, SHAEF

Mauchenheim genannt Bechtolsheim, General der Artillerie Anton Freiherr von, Representative of General Boehme in surrender in Norway

Moorehead, Alan, Newspaper Correspondent; Author of *Montgomery, a Biography* (London, 1946)

Morgan, Lt. Gen. Sir Frederick E., Head of COSSAC and Deputy Chief of Staff, SHAEF

Morgan, Gen. Sir W. D., Chief of Staff of 21 Army Group under General Paget

Mountbatten of Burma, Rear Adm. Viscount, Chief of Combined Operations Headquarters

Nevins, Brig. Gen. Arthur S., Head of Operations Section, G–3 Division, SHAEF

Nugent, Maj. Gen. R. E., Deputy Chief of Operations, Ninth Air Force, and Commanding General, XXIX Tactical Air Corps

Paget, Gen. Sir Bernard, Commander of 21 Army Group before Montgomery

Peterson, Col. L. O., Member of AEAF Staff

Pinette, Miss Mattie, Member of General Eisenhower's Personal Staff

Portal of Hungerford, Marshal of the Royal Air Force Viscount, Chief of the Air Staff, RAF

Reinhardt, Fred, Member of Staff of Political Officer, SHAEF

Robb, Air Chief Marshal Sir James M., Chief of the Air Staff, SHAEF

Rosengarten, Adolph G., Jr., Formerly a Member of G–2 Section, First U.S. Army

Rothwell, Lt. Col. H. J., Deputy Headquarters Commandant, SHAEF

Scarman, Wing Commander Leslie, Personal Assistant to Lord Tedder

Schlatter, Maj. Gen. David, Deputy Senior Air Staff Officer and Chief of Operations Headquarters, U.S. Component,

AEAF, and, later, Deputy Chief of Air Staff, SHAEF

Schultes, Col. Ernst, Chief of Staff of *15th SS Mountain Corps*

Sibert, Brig. Gen. E. L., G–2 of 12th Army Group

Simonds, Lt. Gen. G. G., Commander of 2d Canadian Corps

Simpson, Lt. Gen. William H., Commander of Ninth U.S. Army

Sinclair, Maj. Gen. J. A., One of the Combined Commanders' Planners

Smith, Maj. Gen. Frederic H., Jr., Deputy Chief of Operations, AEAF

Smith, Lt. Gen. Walter B., Chief of Staff of SHAEF

Strong, Maj. Gen. Kenneth W. D., G–2 of SHAEF

Tedder, Marshal of the Royal Air Force Lord, Deputy Supreme Commander

Thorne, Gen. Sir Andrew M., Chief of SHAEF Mission (Norway)

Trimble, Col. Ford, Onetime Secretary of the General Staff, SHAEF, and Deputy Chief of SHAEF Mission (Denmark)

Vulliamy, Maj. Gen. C. H. H., Chief of Signal Division, SHAEF

West, Maj. Gen. Charles A., G–3 of COSSAC

Whiteley, Maj. Gen. J. F. M., Deputy Chief of Staff, SHAEF

Wigglesworth, Air Marshal Sir Philip, Senior Air Staff Officer, AEAF

Williams, Brig. E. T., Chief of Intelligence, 21 Army Group

In addition to the interviews obtained by the author in person, information was obtained by him in telephone conversations with former Secretary of State Cordell Hull and Lt. Col. R. H. Merrick, Censorship Section, SHAEF Public Relations Division. Other information was obtained from answers to questions submitted by the author through other individuals who conducted interviews with Maj. Gen. Sir Francis de Guingand, Chief of Staff, 21 Army Group (Dr. Gordon A. Harrison), and with Brig. Gen. Cornelius W. Wickersham (Mr. Richard Welling).

Specific questionnaires of the author were answered by the following:

Bare, Maj. George S., Member of Headquarters Commandant Staff, SHAEF

Burrough, Admiral Harold M., Commander in Chief, Allied Naval Expeditionary Force

Erskine, Maj. Gen. G. W. E. J., Chief of SHAEF Mission (Belgium)

Lincoln, Col. George A., Member of OPD Staff

Murphy, Ambassador Robert D., Political Officer of SHAEF

Phillips, Ambassador William, Political Officer of SHAEF

Reber, Mr. Samuel, Political Officer of SHAEF

The following individuals, in addition to a number already listed in the interview group, submitted comments or new material after reading the manuscript of this volume: Maj. Gen. A. Franklin Kibler, G–3 of 12th Army Group; Capt. Tracy B. Kittredge, USNR, aide of Admiral Stark who was present at many of the important meetings between U.S. representatives and important French leaders.

UNITED STATES ARMY IN WORLD WAR II

The multivolume series, UNITED STATES ARMY IN WORLD WAR II, consists of a number of subseries which are tentatively planned as follows: The War Department, The Army Air Forces, The Army Ground Forces, The Army Service Forces, The Defense of the Western Hemisphere, The War in the Pacific, The European Theater of Operations, The War in the Mediterranean, The Middle East Theater, The China-Burma-India Theater, Civil Affairs, The Technical Services, Special Studies, and Pictorial Record.

The following volumes have been published or are in press:*

The War Department
> *Chief of Staff: Prewar Plans and Preparations*
> *Washington Command Post: The Operations Division*
> *Strategic Planning for Coalition Warfare: 1941–1942*

The Army Ground Forces
> *The Organization of Ground Combat Troops*
> *The Procurement and Training of Ground Combat Troops*

The Army Service Forces
> *The Organization and Role of the Army Service Forces*

The War in the Pacific
> *Okinawa: The Last Battle*
> *Guadalcanal: The First Offensive*
> *The Approach to the Philippines*
> *The Fall of the Philippines*
> *Leyte: The Return to the Philippines*

The European Theater of Operations
> *The Lorraine Campaign*
> *Cross-Channel Attack*
> *Logistical Support of the Armies (Volume I)*
> *The Supreme Command*

The Middle East Theater
> *The Persian Corridor and Aid to Russia*

The China-Burma-India Theater
> *Stilwell's Mission to China*

The Technical Services
> *Transportation Corps: Responsibilities, Organization, and Operations*
> *The Quartermaster Corps: Organization, Supply, and Services, Volume I*
> *The Ordnance Department: Organization and Research and Development*

Special Studies
> *Three Battles: Arnaville, Altuzzo, and Schmidt*
> *The Women's Army Corps*

Pictorial Record
> *The War Against Germany and Italy: Mediterranean and Adjacent Areas*
> *The War Against Germany: Europe and Adjacent Areas*
> *The War Against Japan*

---

* The volumes on the Army Air Forces published by the University of Chicago Press are not included in this list.

Index